# SELLING IN THE SPORT INDUSTRY

**Kendall Hunt**
publishing company

DAVID A. PIERCE

NELS K. POPP

CHAD D. MCEVOY

**Kendall Hunt**
publishing company

www.kendallhunt.com
*Send all inquiries to:*
4050 Westmark Drive
Dubuque, IA 52004-1840

ISBN 978-1-7924-2030-6

Published in the United States of America

# BRIEF CONTENTS

# CONTENTS

# PREFACE

Within the sport industry, sales positions offer great opportunity and upward mobility. The greatest number of positions available in professional sport franchises resides in sales. While sport management programs have slowly begun to add sport sales courses to their curricula, a textbook dedicated to teaching the key knowledge and competencies has heretofore not existed. This has resulted in challenges for faculty teaching classes, unprepared students applying for jobs in sport sales, and challenges for sales managers in hiring. In 2015 we embarked upon filling this need in the sport management landscape by creating a book devoted to teaching students how to sell.

The unique contribution of this book is the detailed analysis of each of the steps of the sales process. The content in each of the sales process chapters is a unique blend of industry and academic expertise culled from a wide variety of textbooks, sales books, conferences, online articles, interviews, newsletters, sales workshops, and personal experience. The combined sport sales teaching experience of the authors spans over 20 years, which includes nearly 40 different sections and hundreds of students. We have watched the professional growth of many students who have learned sales from our classes and have succeeded professionally upon graduation. In addition to faculty expertise, over 25 sport sales industry experts contributed to the text to provide the real-world perspective and examples throughout the text. Most chapters conclude with a competency assessment rubric that can be used by instructors and sales managers to evaluate sales performance. The competency assessment rubrics can be used by instructors to assess student learning outcomes and by sales managers to identify strengths and weaknesses of salespeople that can assist with developing training materials and evaluate progress in ways that extend beyond revenue generated. We also recognize that in many areas of sales, there are strongly differing opinions on how people should sell. In these instances, we tried to present a balanced viewpoint of the different approaches that exist in sales training. In these instances, there is also value in students and trainees being able to articulate the advantages and disadvantages of competing approaches.

The text was written with many different audiences in mind. First, this book was written for sport management majors taking a sport sales course. The skills taught in the book can give students a competitive advantage on sales projects in class and when looking for a job after graduation. We attempted to include examples from as many different types of sales contexts as possible so that students can see how sales skills can be used in many different types of jobs and sectors of the industry. While many students will pursue inside ticket sales positions to launch their career, we recognize there are many sport sales jobs selling technology, equipment, events, and memberships. The book is also written for students who may not be majors in sport management, but are looking to acquire sales skills that can be applied in many different types of industries. All students can benefit personally from acquiring sales and persuasion skills regardless of the job they hold in the future. Second, this book was written for college professors who have long searched for a textbook to use in a sport sales class. We have taught sales for the past decade and eventually became tired of not having a true textbook to use for the class. We also know that some faculty can be intimated by the topic of sales, so hopefully having an academic textbook that helps them teach students how to sell will alleviate their fears. Third, the book is written for salespeople launching their career in the sport sales industry, but who perhaps have not been trained at a high level before starting the job. The skills and concepts introduced in the text can be a primer for someone starting or transitioning into sales with little formal training. Finally, the text can be a resource used by sales managers and trainers looking for advice and ideas on how to lead their sales staff to better performance.

The order of the chapters in this book was established based on how we and others teaching sport sales sequentially teach such a course. However, if for a client-based sales project, the assignment will need to take precedence over the order of the chapters in the book. For example, if a class needs to make sales calls starting the fifth or sixth week of the semester, instructors may want to jump immediately into the sales process chapters and then cover other content later in the semester. For instructors not doing a hands-on project where students are selling, it may make sense to cover the chapters on communication and prospecting before opening the sale. Our intent was to create the chapters in such a way that instructors would have flexibility in the order in which the chapters are delivered based on the uniqueness of projects students might be completing in class.

In our experience in sport management education, we have seen the professional success that our students can have pursuing a career in sales in the sport industry. We are passionate about introducing sales as an appealing career choice for students and believe this textbook will help provide groundwork to be successful in the sport sales profession. We are also hopeful that more sport management programs consider adopting a sales course into their plans of study now that a sport sales textbook is available on the market. Because this is the first edition of a book that didn't previously exist in the marketplace, we welcome all feedback from users. There are bound to be issues we've missed or concerns users might have that we overlooked. Please reach out to any of us to discuss your observations. We are always happy to discuss the teaching of sport sales. Best wishes and happy selling!

# FEATURES OF THE TEXT

## PEDAGOGY

The following features are included to facilitate student learning and aid instructors in measuring learning outcomes:

- **Learning objectives** focus students on the key concepts and skills presented in each chapter.
- **Glossary of key terms** defines all the terms in the text; key terms are identified at the beginning and throughout each chapter.
- **Competencies** students must demonstrate to be successful at each stage of the sales process are identified at the beginning of most chapters.
- **Competency assessments rubrics** are included at the end of the sales process chapters to aid instructors and sales managers in creating assessment rubrics to measure student and salesperson performance in key competency areas.
- **Chapter activities** are provided to help stimulate discussion, increase understanding of chapter concepts, and create hands-on assessment opportunities.

## INDUSTRY EXPERTISE

Each chapter contains **industry perspectives** written by experts in the sport sales industry to help students and sales trainees put key sales concepts into action. The following sport sales experts made contributions to the book:

- Austin Allen—Fort Wayne TinCaps
- Jeff Berryhill—Major League Soccer
- Kyle Brant—San Jose Sharks
- J. W. Canon—UPS
- Jason Cohen—Washington Nationals
- Taylor Deckard—St. Louis Rams
- Buffy Filippell—Teamwork Online
- Scott Gordon—PGA Tour
- Bill Guertin—Stadium Gorilla
- Bob Hamer—Sports Business Solutions
- Carl Manteau—Milwaukee Bucks

- ▶ Jonathan Rossing—Gonzaga University
- ▶ Brian Schackow—Fort Wayne TinCaps
- ▶ Charlie Slonaker—Philadelphia Union
- ▶ Bryan Stine—Indiana Pacers
- ▶ Will Syring—Chicago Bulls

## INSTRUCTOR RESOURCES

The following resources were developed by the authors to aid instructors. These resources are available upon adoption of the book:

- ▶ The **test bank** offers several different types of questions to assess student understanding of key concepts.
- ▶ **PowerPoint slides** are provided for each chapter. Instructors may choose to use the presentations as they are provided or add their own content and features.
- ▶ **Instructor Resources** provide instructors and sales managers with links to additional articles and video content, additional assignments, classroom activities to help students demonstrate sales skills, and answers to selected chapter activities.

# ACKNOWLEDGMENTS

## DAVID PIERCE

I have many people to thank for helping me bring this book to fruition. First, I must thank my family. My wife Sara supported me through the arduous process of writing a textbook. Her support of me despite her hectic schedule as an OB/GYN physician has truly been a blessing. My children, Charlie and Kaitlyn, offer inspiration to be the best father and educator I can be.

My coauthors provided great insight and feedback throughout the entire process in addition to creating great content for the book. I also want to thank the many contributors and reviewers from the sport industry and academia who offered their time and expertise to help faculty, students, and sales managers better understand how to sell.

I want to acknowledge the seminal work of professors Bill Sutton, Dick Irwin, and Jim Kadlecek in laying the foundation for sport sales to be an integral part to sport management curricula. I am also grateful to Jeff Berryhill and Melanie Seiser at the Major League Soccer National Sales Center for opening their doors to me for three days to get an inside look at the best sales training operation in sports.

At IUPUI, I must thank my Dean, Jay Gladden, who encouraged me to pursue this ambitious project. He offered moral support along the way in addition to expertise in marketing and consumer behavior. Colleague Larry Jinkins' insights were invaluable from his 20+ years of sales experience in many different industries. Graduate student Mellissa Korobkin provided great organizational support.

Thank you to my current and former students who allowed me to experiment and take risks in the pedagogies I used to teach sales over the years. I am also grateful to Brian Shackow (Fort Wayne Tin-Caps), Bryan Stine (Indiana Pacers), Garrett Rosh (Indianapolis Indians), Adam Tschuor (University of Dayton), and Blake Boldon (Monumental Marathon) for supporting the student sales centers at Ball State and IUPUI respectively. And finally, thank you to Jeffrey Petersen for hiring me at Ball State and giving me the intimidating and challenging task to create and then teach sport sales.

The staff at Kendall Hunt Publishing has been great to work with. Thank you for giving me the chance to write this book. My hope is that students, faculty, sales managers, and salespeople can use this book to enhance their sales skills and performance.

To God be the glory.

## NELS POPP

I am grateful to have met so many amazing sport sales experts over the years who have been teachers and mentors to me. The generosity and enthusiasm displayed by these individuals has inspired my passion for the field of sport sales and my excitement in writing this text. I would like to thank all of them. In particular, faculty members like Jim Kadlecek at Mount Union, Bill Sutton at South Florida, and Dick Irwin at Memphis have been tremendous mentors and guides in helping me learn how to teach sport sales.

From the industry side of the ledger, I owe much of my sport sales knowledge to the numerous sport sales professionals who have taken time to teach me about the field and continue to be amazing resources. I would like to acknowledge in particular a few individuals who have been most influential including Matt DiFebo, Jake Vernon at the Timberwolves, Todd Fischer at GMR Marketing, Chris Zaber at the Mets, Tom Sheridan at the White Sox, Jason Martin at Arkansas State University, Adam Tschuor at the University of Dayton, Dennis Fryer at the Hurricanes, and Melanie Seiser at Major League Soccer.

In addition, I want to thank all my sales students over the years who have helped me become a better professor and who have been so receptive to learning the sales process. In particular, I want to thank those students who have started their sport industry career in sales and who continue to teach me and inspire their classmates.

I have certainly been blessed with outstanding colleagues and collaborators. Without my co-authors David and Chad, there would be no "Selling in the Sport Industry" and I truly appreciate their hard work to make this book a reality. It was great to work with both of them. I also appreciate the fantastic colleagues with whom I work at the University of North Carolina.

Most importantly, I would like to thank my family for their support and all the joy they bring me. My wife Stephanie is always my biggest advocate, which means the world to me. Gavin and Arden are simply the best kids ever.

## CHAD MCEVOY

I would like to thank all those involved in publishing this book, including those involved at Kendall Hunt. Thanks as well to the many reviewers who provided excellent advice on how to improve the text.

Thank you to all of my students and colleagues, both past and present. Because of you, coming to work each morning is a pleasure. Helping our students grow, learn, and chase after their dreams of working in the sport industry is an incredibly rewarding profession. I hope this book assists many students in finding that sales is a worthy path toward pursuing their career goals in sports.

Thanks also to my family—to my wife Kerry for being so supportive and for being such a terrific partner and mother, and to our children, Andy, Luke, and Abby, who bring a smile to my face each and every day. I look forward to continuing to share my love of sport with you in the years to come.

Finally, thank you to David and Nels for your collaboration on this project. I appreciate your shared passion for creating a resource to assist in teaching sport sales to students.

Together, we gratefully acknowledge the constructive comments of our reviewers who provided great feedback on the book:

- Melanie Seiser—Major League Soccer
- Brendan Long—The Madison Square Garden Company
- Mitch Ried—Cleveland Cavaliers
- Drew Ribarchak—Columbus Blue Jackets
- Drew Praster—Charlotte Hornets
- Paul Bee—Detroit Red Wings
- Chris Zaber—New York Mets
- Dennis Fryer—Carolina Hurricanes
- Garrett Rosh—Indianapolis Indians
- Clint Warren—Illinois State University
- James Weiner—University of Louisville
- Laura Miller—University of California Pennsylvania
- Larry Jinkins—Indiana University-Purdue University Indianapolis
- Larry DeGaris—University of Indianapolis

# ABOUT THE AUTHORS AND CONTRIBUTORS

## DAVID PIERCE

Dr. David A. Pierce is an Associate Professor of Sport Management in the School of Physical Education and Tourism Management at Indiana University-Purdue University Indianapolis. He has authored/coauthored over 50 peer-reviewed publications and given over 60 presentations at academic conferences. He has taught sport sales for over 10 years and pioneered the use of client-based sales centers in sport sales courses, as recognized by his Pedagogical Innovations paper in *Sport Management Education Journal*. Students in his classes have generated over $150,000 for seven sport organizations including the Indianapolis Indians, Fort Wayne TinCaps, Indianapolis Ice, Indy Eleven, Indiana Pacers, Ball State Athletics, and the Monumental Marathon.

The Sport Marketing Association has recognized his sales research with the Best Professional Paper Award in 2012 and the Bill Sutton research grant award in 2013. In 2014 he was awarded the Janet B. Parks research grant by the North American Society for Sport Management. He has been recognized as the sport management educator and young professional of the year by the Indiana Association for Health, Physical Education, Recreation and Dance. At IUPUI, he has been recognized as the researcher of the year in the Department of Kinesiology in 2015 and the Department of Tourism, Conventions, and Event Management in 2016.

Prior to his arrival at IUPUI, Dr. Pierce served six years at Ball State University as sport management program coordinator, associate chair in the Department of Kinesiology, and President's Fellow for Immersive Learning. He earned his doctorate in Sport Management from Indiana University Bloomington in 2007 under the mentoring of Dr. Lawrence W. Fielding.

## NELS POPP

Dr. Nels Popp is an Assistant Professor of Sport Administration in the Department of Exercise and Sport Science at the University of North Carolina. Prior to that, he spent five and a half years as an assistant professor and graduate program coordinator for the sport management program at Illinois State University. Popp earned his doctorate in Sport Administration from the University of Louisville.

Popp researches sport ticket sales and revenue generation for college athletics departments and professional sports teams. His work and expertise has been referenced in local and national media outlets such as *ESPN.com*, the *SportsBusiness Journal*, the *Milwaukee Journal Sentinel*, and the *Chronicle of Higher Education*. His research has been published in a variety of academic journals such as *Sport Marketing Quarterly* and *Sport Management Review*, while he has presented his work at numerous conferences, including the annual conferences of the *National Association of Collegiate Marketing Administrators*, *North American Society for Sport Management*, and the *Sport Marketing Association*. In 2016, Popp was given the Award of Excellence for Undergraduate Teaching at UNC's Department of Exercise and Sport Science and he was recently elected President of the Sport Marketing Association.

Prior to working in academia, Popp spent eight years working in small college athletics media relations. In addition, he spent three years working in the front office for basketball clubs in Queensland, Australia, including a stint with the Cairns Taipans of the National Basketball League. Popp has also done market research contract work with a variety of sport organizations such as the Atlantic Coast Conference, the Missouri Valley Conference, the Durham Bulls, and the Bloomington PrairieThunder. He has also worked or volunteered at numerous events including Super Bowl XLVI, the AVP Beach Volleyball Tour, and the National Senior Games.

## CHAD MCEVOY

Dr. Chad McEvoy is a professor and chair of the Department of Kinesiology and Physical Education at Northern Illinois University. Previously McEvoy served for three years as professor and graduate program director at Syracuse University's David B. Falk College of Sport and Human Dynamics in the sport management area. McEvoy also served in a similar capacity at Illinois State University from 2002–2012.

McEvoy has co-authored two other textbooks in the sport management discipline, *Financial Management in the Sport Industry*, and *Research Methods and Design in Sport Management*, and his research has been featured in more than 100 media outlets, such as *The New York Times*, *The Wall Street Journal*, *The Chronicle of Higher Education*, *PBS Newshour with Jim Lehrer*, *New York Daily News*, and *USA Today*. In June 2008, he served as a panelist before the prestigious Knight Commission on Intercollegiate Athletics in a discussion on the effectiveness of NCAA penalties for rules violations. McEvoy's research has also been published in leading sport management academic journals such as the *Journal of Sport Management*, *Sport Management Review*, and *Sport Marketing Quarterly*. McEvoy also recently completed his term as President of the Sport Marketing Association, now serving as Past-President of that organization, and McEvoy has also previously served as editor of *Case Studies* in Sport Management and co-editor of the *Journal of Issues and Intercollegiate Athletics*.

McEvoy's professional industry experience is in intercollegiate athletics marketing and he is an active consultant in sports revenue generation practices. His educational background includes earning a doctorate in sport administration at the University of Northern Colorado with a doctoral minor in applied statistics and research methods, a master's degree in sport management at University of Massachusetts, Amherst, and a bachelor's degree in sport management at Iowa State University.

## LIZ WANLESS

Dr. Liz Wanless serves as Assistant Professor/Undergraduate Coordinator of the Sport Administration program at Ball State University. Dr. Wanless researches sport business revenue generation; specifically, sport organization revenue generation strategy assessment and intercollegiate athletics finance investigation. Active consultation projects include sport fan experience surveys and analysis for football and men's/women's basketball, donor prioritization and retention tactics, and customer relationship management strategies for university athletic programs, sport event management companies, and community non-profit organizations. She received her undergraduate degree from Bates College, master's degree in Sport Administration from Ball State University, her doctorate in Higher Education from Ball State's Department of Education, and is currently pursuing a master's degree in Business Analytics from Penn State. Since Dr. Wanless accepted the program coordinator role in spring 2012, she has secured $35,916 in grant funding, $59,500 in fundraising projects, and $11,560 in revenue from contractual sport industry partnerships. As a scholar she has authored and co-authored 44 peer-reviewed publications and has presented in numerous conferences such as the North American Society for Sport Management Conference, Sport Marketing Association Conference, and the Scholarly Conference on Collegiate Sport. Prior to her academic career, Dr. Wanless competed for Nike, Asics, the New York Athletic Club, and Team USA as a professional track and field shot putter.

## BILL GUERTIN

Bill Guertin is CEO (Chief Enthusiasm Officer) of *Stadium Gorilla*, a sales training and consulting company whose focus is on improving the ticket sales skills of professional sport teams and collegiate athletic departments. Bill has been contracted by over 80 different pro and collegiate athletic teams throughout North America to improve ticket sales and cash flow, including the Boston Red Sox (MLB), Houston Texans (NFL), Golden State Warriors (NBA), Calgary Flames (NHL), FC Dallas (MLS), and the University of Kentucky (NCAA-I), as well as the 19 teams of LIGA MX, the first-division Mexican soccer league. He is the author of two books, including *The 800-Pound Gorilla of Sales: How to Dominate Your Market*, and answers e-mail inquiries personally at Bill@The800PoundGorilla.com.

## CARL MANTEAU

Originally from Waukesha, WI, Carl Manteau currently serves as the Senior Director of Group Sales for the Milwaukee Bucks (NBA). Prior to the Bucks, Carl spent time as the Group Sales Director with the Columbus Blue Jackets (NHL) and elevated through a multitude of sales and managerial roles in ten seasons with the Cavaliers Operating Company (Cleveland Cavaliers-NBA, Cleveland Monsters-AHL, Cleveland Gladiators-AFL, Canton Charge-NBA D-League). Carl received his undergraduate degree in kinesiology and his master's degree in education from the University of Minnesota Twin Cities. While in college, he held roles as a group intern for the Minnesota Timberwolves (NBA) and Lynx (WNBA) and as a student athletic trainer for the University of Minnesota Men's Athletic Department. Carl resides in Milwaukee, WI with his wife Nikita.

## JEFF BERRYHILL

Jeff Berryhill is the Director for the Major League Soccer, National Sales Center (NSC). He is responsible for all day-to-day aspects of running the program with a specific focus on leadership of recruitment and talent development. Before the NSC, he spent time with the Chicago Fire, Jacksonville Jaguars, and Minnesota Timberwolves. Jeff is a graduate of the University of Minnesota. Jeff's wife Samantha is a middle school teacher. Jeff and Sam and have a daughter named Emma Jean.

# CHAPTER 1

## INTRODUCTION TO SPORT SALES

### LEARNING OBJECTIVES

After completing this chapter, you should be able to:

- ▶ Discuss the importance of sales to sport organizations.
- ▶ Trace the growth of sales positions in sport organizations in relation to technological advancements over the past 20 years.
- ▶ Contrast the misconceptions about sport sales with the real nature of sport sales.
- ▶ Identify key characteristics of successful sport sales professionals.
- ▶ Describe the key job responsibilities in sport sales.
- ▶ Explain why sales jobs require a competitive nature.
- ▶ Discuss how the principles of selling are beneficial even to those who are not working in sales.
- ▶ Discuss the role a positive attitude plays in success.

### KEY TERMS

Boiler room approach              Outbound call
Cold call                         Prospecting
Customer Relationship Management  Sales force management
Inside sales                      Warm call

## CHAPTER OVERVIEW

Sales offers many job seekers and college graduates with a means to launch a career in the sport industry. However, sales jobs can be unattractive or even intimidating without understanding the nature of sales jobs or a solid foundation in how to sell. Negative stereotypes often create negative perceptions about the nature of sales jobs, yet the sport industry at all levels is full of leaders who began their career on the revenue generating side of the business. With an ample supply of jobs compared to nearly every other type of job in the sport industry, students completing a course using this textbook will understand why it is important to have a solid foundation in sales. This chapter sets the foundation for why sales are important to the financial viability of any sport organization and the critical need for competent salespeople in all organizations. In attempting to allay some of the misconceptions that can lead people away from pursuing a career in sport sales, the chapter also makes the case that anyone who is willing to learn and be coached can develop into a competent salesperson. Nearly all of the characteristics that successful salespeople possess can be taught or transferred through experiences.

Bob Hamer, Founder and President of Sports Business Solutions, is one of many sport sales success stories. After graduating with a Business degree from the University of Arizona, Bob launched his career in the sport industry on the Inside Sales team for the Phoenix Suns. Seven promotions and eight years later, Bob was the Vice President of Ticket Sales and Service for the Suns. One of the many benefits of a sales career is the upward mobility and career growth opportunities available. Bob's story is not uncommon from many others who have experienced success in sport sales.

If you told me 15 years ago that I would've become a sport salesperson, I would've said, "no way." That was the year 2000 and I was a junior in high school. At the time I was thinking about college, studying business, and then getting into real estate or human resources.

Fast-forward 15 years, I got my business degree and began a career selling tickets and hospitality for the Phoenix Suns. Even when I started as a seller in 2006, I didn't expect to be in sales long-term. However, I knew sales was a valuable skill, and I wanted to learn how to do it. I told myself I'd commit to a year and see how it went. I ended up loving it, performing well, and eventually became the VP of Sales at the Phoenix Suns over an eight-year tenure.

The reality is, you could be like me, a sport salesperson and not even know it. Think about your strengths and weaknesses. Ask yourself what you want most in your job each day and be open-minded to all professions, sales included. For me, I waited tables for years and loved meeting new people. I was always outgoing at social functions and trying to make new friends. I played sports through high school and was competitive and coachable. I had the traits to succeed. I just needed to give it a shot. I did, and it turned out to be the best decision I ever made. For those who pursue it, I hope it turns out the same for you!

Adapted from https://www.linkedin.com/pulse/traits-successful-sports-salesperson-bob-hamer

## WHY SALES ARE IMPORTANT TO SPORT ORGANIZATIONS

Sales are the lifeblood of any sport organization.[1] Tickets, premium seats, sponsorships, memberships, registrations, media rights, donations, licensing, concessions, and parking are all critical to the financial viability of contemporary sport organizations. Ticket sales are particularly foundational because attendance provides the fuel to drive the other revenue streams. For example, the value of a sponsorship package is determined in part on impressions, or the number of people reached with the sponsor's message. Attendance also determines concessions and parking revenue. These revenues are critical to generating the revenue to field a competitive team that people want to watch.

One common misconception about the sport industry is that because sports have such fervent fans, fandom is all that it takes in order to get people to buy—particularly when a team or sport organization is successful. The reality could not be more different. While there is generally a positive relationship between winning and attendance, there are always high performing teams that don't sell out and poor performing teams that still sell well. For example, the Atlanta Hawks earned the 4-seed in the Eastern Conference playoffs in 2016, but ranked 23rd in NBA attendance with only 89% of capacity filled, while the Chicago Bulls failed to make the playoffs and led the league in average attendance and seating capacity.[2] Similarly, the Montreal Canadiens missed the playoffs in 2016 but ranked second in the NHL in attendance, while the Florida Panthers finished with the fifth best regular season record yet ranked 24th in attendance with 90% of capacity filled.[3] Beyond this, the relationship

1. Mullin, B., Hardy, S., & Sutton, W. (2014). *Sport marketing*, 4th ed. Champaign, IL: Human Kinetics.
2. http://espn.go.com/nba/attendance
3. http://espn.go.com/nhl/attendance

between winning and attendance differs by sport and level of competition. For example, research has shown that Major League Baseball attendance is more sensitive to fluctuations in winning than the National Football League,[4] and fans attend minor league baseball games more for the experience and entertainment than team records.[5]

Consider the following scenarios that require teams to cultivate selling interactions between the team and its fans:

- ▶ Winning team that focuses on service quality to cultivate long-term fan loyalty to maintain high attendance levels when team performance declines.
- ▶ Mid-quality or improving team that places strong group sales effort on games against non-marquee teams that are unlikely to sell out.
- ▶ Losing team that can't rely on winning to sell tickets and must emphasize long-term relationships and experiences.

Most other departments within a sport organization are typically cost centers (i.e., marketing, community relations, media relations, management, and operations). These are able to exist and function only because of the revenue generated through sales. These revenue streams all play a different role in terms of relative importance. To illustrate, ticket sales account for roughly one-third of total revenue for Major League Baseball and National Basketball Association teams.[6] In high-profile Division I athletic departments, ticket sales on average account for nearly one fourth of generated revenues and as much as 40% for a few athletic departments.[7] Meanwhile, NASCAR teams rely heavily on corporate partnerships with three fourths of race team revenues generated from sponsorship.[8] The International Olympic Committee (IOC) generates about 5% of its revenue from ticket sales at Olympic Games, but about 45% from corporate sponsorship sales.[9]

---

4. http://www.businessinsider.com/nfl-standings-attendance-2011-1. http://www.fangraphs.com/blogs/what-do-we-really-know-about-attendance/

5. http://www.coastal.edu/business/publications/cbj/archives/pdfs/articles/spring2009/paul_toma_weinbach.pdf

6. Wakefield, K. (2015). *Team sports marketing*. Retrieved from teamsportsmarketing.com

7. Fulks, D. (2015). *Revenues and expenses, 2004–2014: NCAA Division I intercollegiate athletics programs report*. Retrieved from http://www.ncaa.org/sites/default/files/2015%20Division%20I%20RE%20report.pdf

8. Smith, M. (2009). Race teams combine to survive. *Street & Smith's SportsBusiness Journal*, *11*(36), 1.

9. Olympic.org. *Revenue Sources and Distribution*. Retrieved from http://www.olympic.org/ioc-financing-revenue-sources-distribution?tab=sources

## HISTORY OF SPORT SALES

The sport industry has historically been guilty of marketing myopia, or a lack of foresight into marketing issues.[10] Many sport franchises have operated with the attitude that spectators should feel privileged to attend their games, particularly when demand for the product was high.[11] This led to few innovations in customer service or the fan experience. Teams have also relied heavily on winning as their primary marketing strategy. Not only does winning not guarantee an increase in attendance, but teams must also have a plan for how to succeed when the team is not performing well. After all, by definition, whenever there is a winner, there is also a loser, and only one team can win a championship every year.

At the outset of the twenty-first century, sport sales expert Mark Washo summarized the state of the industry:

> I don't think many general managers, team presidents, or owners really know what is happening in the marketplace. I believe many of them are out of touch with what is happening on the front lines of trying to attract new customers. Too many of them are simply focused on the team and the product on the field. They are surrounded by people who love their teams. . . . Meanwhile, while they are surrounded by the bubble of everything that goes on with the team, their teams are losing fans every day and if attitudes don't change in sports, I am afraid professional sports are in jeopardy of losing many more fans for years to come.[12]

As a result, sport organizations saw little need to hire a sales staff to proactively secure new business because the assumption was simply opening the doors would cause people to show up. However, technological advancements, increasing competition for the entertainment dollar, and rapidly escalating player salaries over the past 15–20 years have forced sport organizations to invest in a sales infrastructure and view the role of sales differently.

Technology has created significantly more and higher quality entertainment options for consumers. The sport industry has always competed for consumers' time and discretionary income against a wide variety of other entertainment and leisure activities such as cultural attractions, participating

10. Mullin, B., Hardy, S., & Sutton, W. (2014). *Sport marketing*, 4th ed. Champaign, IL: Human Kinetics.

11. Washo, M. (2004). *Break into sports through ticket sales*. Kindle edition.

12. Ibid., p. 119.

in recreational sports, attending other sporting events or supporting other teams, watching television, going out to dinner, and the like. But the Internet and subsequent growth of online content (e.g., Netflix, video gaming) and devices to consume this content (smartphones, tablets, laptops) have exploded in recent years. The rapid improvement in quality of flat-screen and plasma televisions has become a significant competitor for the live sporting event industry.[13] Simply stated, the number of entertainment options has proliferated as a result of technological advancements. In addition to the increasing number of options, customer review websites, secondary ticket market sites, and the opinions of others on social media have given consumers more information prior to purchase, thus increasing the need for price and quality integrity among sport organizations.

Technology has also improved the ability of sport organizations to collect and analyze important information about customers. Organizations invest in a variety of different customer relationship management (CRM) or point of sale (POS) technologies allowing them to collect important data about their customers, such as demographic information, beliefs, and preferences. As a result, the ability to collect hundreds of thousands of names, e-mail addresses, and phone numbers is significantly easier today than 20 years ago. Technology has also bolstered other direct marketing strategies through e-mail, direct mail, and mobile technology.

© Monkey Business Images/Shutterstock.com

As a result of increasing competition in the entertainment and leisure landscape and the ability to generate targeted and qualified leads from a customer database, sport organizations have adopted more proactive outbound sales approaches over the past 20 years by increasing staff devoted to generating new business through outbound sales calls. An **outbound call** is a call initiated by a seller to a customer for the purpose of cultivating a relationship, disseminating information, providing customer service, while asking for the prospects to purchase tickets.

**OUTBOUND CALL**
call initiated by a seller with a sport organization to a customer

---

13.  Fain, I. (2013). Displaced fans remain connected and valuable to teams. *Street & Smith's SportsBusiness Journal, 15*(40), 13.

A philosophy that developed early in the growth of outbound sales was the **boiler room approach**. In this approach, teams would hire a large number of entry-level sellers, provide them with minimal sales training, give them a short window to sell as much as they could, and then retain only the top few producers, while dismissing the remaining employees or interns. The combination of low pay, lack of training, cutthroat environment, and expectation to hit aggressive sales targets led to high turnover in these positions. In fact, it is estimated that five out of every six entry-level ticket salespeople in major league sports either chose to leave sales or were let go from their position,[14] a rate much higher than the 18% to 23% annual turnover in other businesses.[15] The underlying philosophy in this model is to hire a large number of sellers on the Inside Sales Staff in order to find a couple of good ones. The size of an inside sales team varies greatly. Many NBA and NHL teams hire 6–15 new reps each year, but there is a growing trend in the NBA for lower-demand teams to have 30 or more inside sales reps. On the extreme end, one NFL team has had as many as 75 inside sales reps.[16] Inside Sales is where most sales reps spend their first year.

The **Inside Sales** staff who utilizes the telephone to contact targeted leads, essentially serves as a try-out for six months to one year to determine which salespeople can reach sales goals.[17] For many sport organizations, the boiler room approach is a poor management model because it focuses on outcome instead of process, and it abdicates management from investing in a quality training program. The strategy for these organizations is focused on short-term sales as opposed to building long-term relationships that have lifetime value for the organization. High turnover means account holders interact with new sales reps every year, negating the benefits of fostering a relationship. In addition, it results in poor outcomes because high turnover leads to sales departments stocked with entry-level employees compared to more experienced salespeople who typically generate more revenue.[18] The good news is that over the past 10 years, organizations have started to invest more strategically in a structured sales management philosophy, as outlined in Chapter 13, but vestiges of the boiler room model still exist in the industry today.

**BOILER ROOM APPROACH**
teams would hire a large number of entry-level sellers, provide them with minimal sales training, give them a short window to sell as much as they could, and then retain only the top few producers, while dismissing the remaining employees or interns

**INSIDE SALES**
utilizes the telephone to contact targeted leads generated from the data-based marketing process

---

14. King, B. (2010). Combine puts sales skills to true test. *Street & Smith's SportsBusiness Journal, 12*(45), 24–27.

15. American Society for Training and Development (ASTD). (2008). *Selling with competence: How sales teams succeed.* Retrieved from http://webcastsastdorg/uploads/assets/707/document/SellingwithCompetence.pdf.

16. http://www.workinsports.com/blog/a-sports-sales-directors-advice-on-surviving-your-first-year-as-an-inside-sales-rep/

17. Ibid.

18. Mickle, T. (2010). MLS will be first league to run extensive ticket sales training. *Street & Smith's SportsBusiness Journal, 13*(6), 5.

# THE NEED FOR SALESPEOPLE

In today's age of buying tickets online and communicating via social media and text message, it may appear to some that there isn't a need to employ salespeople anymore. Won't consumers simply buy online or through Facebook if salespeople didn't exist? Aren't there laws that prevent teams from making telemarketing calls? Wouldn't people rather text than make a phone call or meet face-to-face? What value do salespeople provide an organization?

A professional outbound sales approach is needed in sport organizations because it is the best forum to develop relationships with the rapport and trust required to close the season ticket sales and corporate sales necessary for the survival of sport organizations. Phone sales are a key component of the sales effort when used in conjunction with e-mail, texting, direct mail, social selling, and face-to-face appointments. While it may be true that over two thirds of single-game ticket purchases occur online, it is important to recognize that larger sales to corporations (group tickets, sponsorship, premium seats) and season ticket sales to consumers and corporations predominantly occur after multiple interactions on social media, over the telephone, and in person through appointments with prospective buyers. Effective salespeople leverage the power of social media to instigate and facilitate relationships, then use personal interactions with prospects to generate long-term relationships.

Social media tools at the organization level do not drive ticket sales. In fact, a recent study of NCAA Division college athletics programs found growth in social media metrics such as Twitter "Followers" and Facebook "Likes" had no correlation to increases in ticket sales or attendance.[19] The same can be said of data analytics. While data analytics allows sport organizations to identify trends and important relationships within very large data sets of consumer information, salespeople are needed to turn that knowledge into revenue. Finally, salespeople are valuable assets to any organization because they produce revenue and gather insightful feedback from customers, making them strong candidates for future management positions.

---

**Bill Guertin,** *The 800-Pound Gorilla*

### WHY A GOOD MENU ISN'T ENOUGH

The historic Gaslamp Quarter in downtown San Diego is a lively entertainment district of several city blocks, with dozens of unique nightclubs and restaurants. Most of these restaurants post their menus outside for passersby to review. The menus aren't enough to bring in the customers, however; each

---

19. Popp, N., McEvoy, C., & Watanabe, N. (in press). Do college athletics marketers convert social media growth into ticket sales? *International Journal of Sports Marketing & Sponsorship.*

restaurant has a hostess stand right next to where their menu is displayed, with a charming host or hostess whose job it is to engage menu readers in conversation.

Julia is one of those hostesses. She works at Fred's Mexican Café, a restaurant on Seventh Street in the heart of the district. "The menu doesn't work all by itself," she told me with a smile. "We're trained to engage with people who come up to read it—ask them questions, ask where they're from, what they like to eat, and make suggestions (from the menu)."

When the hostesses are tied up with other duties and they're not up front to do the engaging, Julia notices that tables don't fill up as fast. "It makes a big difference back there if I'm not talking to people up here," she said.

Posting a menu is one way to attract business. It's only with the addition of a friendly, engaging hostess—**a salesperson**—that business is increased exponentially.

**In the sport ticket sales world, that job is YOURS.**

The marketing department can generate all sorts of awareness for a sport team, but it's a lot like building a restaurant and putting up a menu board outside. You also need a salesperson—someone inviting that prospect in—to generate the maximum number of sales and exponentially grow your business.

## MISCONCEPTIONS ABOUT SPORT SALES

What words come to mind when you think of a salesperson? Typically, some are: aggressive, pushy, manipulative, insincere, and dishonest. These negative feelings might come from personal experiences of being pressured or manipulated into purchasing something you did not actually want. Nearly everyone can recall a trip to the car lot or an unwanted telemarketing call at dinner when a salesperson used high-pressure sales tactics. It is not uncommon for students to have a negative perception of sales prior to taking a professional selling course.[20] Public perception of salespeople is negative as well. Gallup annually tracks how Americans view the honesty and ethical standards of certain professions and found car salespeople rank higher only than lobbyists and members of Congress.[21] Hollywood feeds the negative stereotypes of the sales profession with movies like *Boiler Room,* where a brokerage firm deceives customers by running a "pump and dump" scheme artificially creating demand in stock of expired and fake companies; *The Wolf of Wall Street,*

20. Bristow, D., Gulati, R., Amyx, D., & Slack, J. (2006). An empirical look at professional selling from a student perspective. *Journal of Education for Business, 81*(5), 242–249.

21. Gallup. *Honesty/Ethics in professions.* Retrieved from http://www.gallup.com/poll/1654/honesty-ethics-professions.aspx

© holbox/Shutterstock.com

where the unethical sales of stocks created a lavish lifestyle for those getting rich off investors; sitcoms like *The Office*, where sales employees mindlessly sell paper in a digital age; or with classic films like *Glengarry Glen Ross*, where real estate salesmen glorified the use of deceptive and underhanded sales tactics to close land deals. The negative image of salespeople fuels several misconceptions about sport salespeople.

## MISCONCEPTION 1—TICKET SALESPEOPLE ONLY MAKE COLD CALLS TO PEOPLE WHO DON'T WANT TO TALK WITH THEM.

**COLD CALL**
a technique whereby a salesperson contacts individuals who have not previously expressed an interest in the product that is being sold. Door-to-door canvassing, calling names from a purchased lead list, or picking out names from a phone book or directory are common sources of unsolicited buyers

**WARM CALL**
sales calls made to prospects who have had some sort of prior contact with the organization

A **cold call** is a technique whereby a salesperson contacts individuals who have not previously expressed an interest in the product that is being sold. Door-to-door canvassing, calling names from a purchased lead list, or picking out names from a phone book or directory are common sources of unsolicited buyers. In reality, sport organizations make **warm calls**, which are sales calls made to prospects who have had some sort of prior contact with the organization. Prospects are cultivated from the organization's customer relationship management system. These are customers who may have attended games in the past, visited the website, purchased merchandise, entered a contest, or interfaced with the organization through social media. As a result, account executives predominantly call people who have an interest in the team or sport based on their past purchase or media usage history. While they may not be expecting a call, most customers have experienced a sporting event in the past, so no call is truly cold. Sellers can take advantage of the fact they are selling fun, entertainment, and sports.

## MISCONCEPTION 2—SALESPEOPLE ARE DECEPTIVE AND USE HIGH-PRESSURE TACTICS TO CONVINCE PROSPECTS TO BUY A PRODUCT THEY DON'T WANT.

> My big piece of advice is to have fun. We are selling experiences that will leave a lasting memory for each individual. Have fun knowing you are the one who can provide those lifelong memories.
>
> — Eric Cole,
> *Philadelphia 76ers*

Good sport organizations would prefer to develop fans for life and see the lifetime value in their customer relationships. Using manipulative selling tactics to make an initial sale rarely leads to the long-term, mutually beneficial relationships sought by sport organizations. Rather than persuading customers to buy, the use of consultative sales techniques, outlined in Chapter 4, help the salesperson lead the customer through a discovery process of why the product helps solve a problem or satisfies a need.

## MISCONCEPTION 3—SALES IS MERELY A WAY TO GET A FOOT IN THE DOOR IN SPORTS, WITH LITTLE LONG-TERM CAREER PROSPECTS.

Many entry-level sellers view a ticket sales position as the stepping stone to landing a more coveted position somewhere else in the organization, such as in public relations or marketing. This misconception is inaccurate for two reasons. First, sales can be a very rewarding career path, with plenty of room for advancement, promotion, and greater income. Unlike many other jobs in sports, sellers are typically compensated by how productive they are, and the results can be financially rewarding for the employee. Second, most sales managers are not interested in hiring entry-level sellers who are anxious to move into other areas of the organizations. Instead, managers are looking for employees who want to learn the art of sales and will work hard to become great revenue producers and potential sales managers within the organization. Can sales employees eventually make a transition to another area of a sport organization? Of course. In fact, the sport industry is studded with executives and administrators who got their start in the business selling tickets. However, aspiring sport managers should not view a position in sport sales as a job to occupy only for a minimum amount of time until another more "attractive" position opens up elsewhere. Managers are not interested in hiring sales representatives who have this attitude.

## MISCONCEPTION 4—SALES POSITIONS ARE AMONG THE LEAST ATTRACTIVE WITHIN SPORT ORGANIZATIONS.

This misconception stems from the fact that salespeople face constant rejection as part of their job. While it is true that all salespeople face rejection, it is important for sellers to not take rejection personally. When prospects tell a seller "no," it does not necessarily mean the seller has done a poor job or is an ineffective employee. Instead, the prospect may not have a strong enough need for the product, may not be ready to buy, or may not quite understand how the product may benefit him or her. The reality in sport ticket sales is that sellers will only close on a tiny fraction of their prospects; most major league teams average a close rate of between 2% to 5%. Salespeople who can move quickly to the next prospect after being told no are more productive.

## MISCONCEPTION 5—LEARNING ABOUT SALES IS A WASTE OF TIME FOR ASPIRING SPORT MANAGERS WHO WANT TO WORK IN OTHER AREAS.

Understanding the sales culture within any sport organization is important for sport managers working a variety of functions. As stated at the beginning of this chapter, sales is the lifeblood of nearly all sport organizations, which means every employee within the organization should understand the sales process, regardless of their day-to-day job duties. After all, putting "butts in seats" is not strictly the responsibility of the sales team; those working within media relations, event operations, facility management—even athletic directors and coaches—play a role in selling tickets. As such, it is important for any staff member of a sport organization to know the basic concepts of selling and have an appreciation for the members of the organization whose primary role is to sell.

## BENEFITS TO LEARNING SALES PRINCIPLES

Having a working knowledge of sales principles is important due to its prevalence in the industry. For example, there are approximately 6,000 jobs posted to the sports job search site workinsports.com, and over 53% of these positions require some form of sales. These positions range from jobs in analytics, customer service, sales, marketing, and research.[22] A recent study of job announcements on Teamwork Online revealed that half of the sales positions posted on the site were for jobs beyond the sale of tickets, sponsorship, and premium seats for sport organizations; these other positions are in areas like media advertising, box office management, sporting goods, customer service, retail, membership sales, and booking events.[23]

There are many benefits to acquiring sales skills. To begin, young professionals can use basic sales skills to "sell" themselves to future employers. The communication skills outlined in this book can help up-and-coming professionals put their best foot forward as they apply for future jobs through the use of cover letters, interviews, elevator pitches, and the like. For example, writing a unique, tailored cover letter is similar to the customized sales pitch that results from conducting a needs analysis during a sales call. While conducting such an analysis, salespeople call people they don't know in order to persuade them to do something, as well as send professional business communications, diagnose problems, and propose relevant solutions, all the while thinking creatively out of the box. All of these activities can be honed and refined through learning sales principles.

For those who pursue careers in the sport industry, a knowledge of sales skills will be beneficial for two reasons. First, some organizations dedicate time during the workweek where all employees are on the phone making sales calls. This is particularly popular in smaller organizations where an

---

22. Clapp, B. (2016). *53% of jobs in the sports industry require this skill.* Retrieved from http://www.workinsports.com/blog/53-of-jobs-in-the-sports-industry-require-this-skill/

23. Pierce, D., Petersen, J., Clavio, G., & Meadows, B. (2012). Content analysis of sport ticket sales job announcements. *Sport, Business and Management: An International Journal, 2*(2), 137–155. doi:10.1108/20426781211244015

all-hands-on-deck philosophy exists, bolstering the belief that everyone is in sales, regardless of their actual job title. As the general manager of a minor league hockey team once said, "Even our team bus driver makes sales calls for us." Second, some organizations have sales goals for employees who do not work in sales. This may not require a dedicated time where everyone is making calls, but an expectation that employees will proactively sell to those in their personal sphere of influence.[24]

Finally, for those who ultimately land sport sales positions, it is important to realize sales is perhaps the most cross-functional area of the front office. Sales interfaces with community relations, service, ticket operations, marketing, and public relations on a regular basis. As a result, those who are successful in sales and who build a positive reputation within the organization are visible to a broad spectrum of functional areas and managers. When a salesperson has been successful in sales, the ability to move from sales to another department within the organization may exist.

For those not pursuing a career in sales, nearly all employees are selling their vision, mission, ideas, methodologies, and value to an organization. Think about college coaches. They must recruit the best talent to be competitive. What is involved in the process of recruiting the best players? Effective coaches need to sell the university, a particular playing style, their personal coaching style, and the prospects of the team's success. Persuasion of young athletes is fundamental to the success of college coaches. Sport fundraisers and development officers need to sell the vision and positive attributes of an athletic department or non-profit organization to procure donations. Golf club managers need to sell members and guests on the benefits of taking additional lessons, joining a league, or buying the latest merchandise. Media relations directors need to sell editors and journalists on stories and angles that might be appealing to their media consumers. People in all of these positions can use the fundamentals of selling to become more effective in their jobs.

24. Sutton, W. (2011). How teams can tap sales power of their employee networks. *Street & Smith's SportsBusiness Journal, 14*(9), 16.

# THE NATURE OF JOBS IN SPORT SALES

## *Five Key Job Responsibilities*

Salespeople within sport organizations execute a variety of job responsibilities. Five stand out as being the most universal and important.

1.  *Selling* (Chapters 5 to 10)

    **Selling** includes making outbound warm calls, setting appointments, making face-to-face sales presentations, giving arena tours, receiving inbound sales calls, and using electronic communications to communicate with prospects. In addition to the traditional 9–5 workday, salespeople also work on game days. For example, sales reps interact with fans on the concourse of a stadium or arena, visit key accounts in their seats prior to the game starting, and organize ancillary sales events that occur in and around the game. These activities are focused on developing new business or renewing accounts for the next season. Each step of the sales process is covered in Chapters 5–10, and the competencies needed to be successful at each step are identified.

2.  *Prospecting* (Chapter 12)

    **PROSPECTING**
    the continual process of identifying and contacting businesses and individuals to create a pool of qualified buyers

    **Prospecting** is the continual process of identifying and contacting businesses and individuals to create a pool of qualified buyers. Salespeople are responsible for developing new business by finding new customers. Salespeople leverage technology, social media, personal connections, and sales calls to identify potential buyers. For example, sales reps follow social media conversations and attend community events to develop new prospects.

3.  *Customer Relationship Management* (Chapter 14)

    **CUTOMER RELATIONSHIP MANAGEMENT**
    a holistic process that includes identifying, attracting, differentiating, and retaining customers with the assistance of technology

    **Customer Relationship Management** (CRM) is a holistic process that includes identifying, attracting, differentiating, and retaining customers with the assistance of technology. The purpose of CRM is to establish individual relationships with customers and to treat them differently based upon their preferences and spending patterns that have been gathered and stored via technology. For salespeople, this means managing the customer database by maintaining accurate records. Leveraging the team's CRM system is one means of prospecting, but the system is only as good as the information fed into it by salespeople. Nearly all of the work completed in a day by a salesperson has a digital footprint inside the CRM system.

4.  *Product Knowledge* (Chapters 2 and 3)

Salespeople must have a solid understanding of the product. Salespeople must understand the benefits of purchasing, pricing structures, the details of specific product features, how different options compare to each other, and the post-sale logistics of delivering a high level of service after the sale. For example, a salesperson needs to know the pricing of different ticket packages to ensure he or she quotes an accurate price to the customer.

5.  *Sales Force Management* (Chapter 13)

Salespeople who have been promoted into **sales force management** are also responsible for planning, staffing, training, directing, and evaluating salespeople. Sales managers supervise salespeople, recruit future salespeople, motivate salespeople, and attempt to build a positive sales culture. Management positions are more likely to identify developing sales strategies, supervising accounting executives, developing sales goals, motivating account executives, financial management, and negotiating contracts than non-director level positions.[25]

**SALES FORCE MANAGMENT**
planning, staffing, training, directing, and evaluating salespeople

## *Transferrable Skills of Successful Sellers*

The characteristics needed by salespeople are skills that almost anyone can possess or improve upon, which means many different types of people can be successful in sales-oriented positions. There is no "sales gene," and sales skills are teachable for those who want to learn. When looking at job announcements, pay attention to transferrable skills as well as specific job responsibilities. Some transferrable skills include the following:

1.  *Communication Skills* (Chapter 11)

Communication skills are the most commonly identified transferrable skill for ticket sales, premium sales, and sponsorship sales position announcements.[26] The ability to demonstrate strong verbal and non-verbal communication skills in person and in writing is essential to any type of sales position and any stage of the sales process.

25.  Pierce, D., Petersen, J., Clavio, G., & Meadows, B. (2012). Content analysis of sport ticket sales job announcements. *Sport, Business and Management: An International Journal, 2*(2), 137–155. doi:10.1108/20426781211244015

26.  Diamond, K., Pierce, D., Johnson, J., & Ridley, M. (2014). Content analysis of sponsorship sales job postings in the United States. *Graduate Journal of Sport, Exercise & Physical Education Research, 2*, 19–36. Pierce, D., Lawrence, H., Johnson, J., & Ridley, M. (2013). Selling the best seats in the house: Content analysis of premium sales positions announcements. *Journal of Venue and Event Management, 4*(2), 1–14.

2. *Computer Skills*

Computer skills are the second most identified transferrable skill noted in the ticket sales, premium sales, and sponsorship sales position announcements.[27] The ability to execute the five key job responsibilities listed previously is highly dependent on a salesperson's computer skills. Salespeople need to be competent with the suite of Microsoft Office products, business e-mail, social media applications, and be adaptable enough to learn the company's specific CRM system.

3. *Creativity*

Creativity is the trait of having imagination and inventiveness and using it to come up with new solutions and ideas.[28] Sales requires improvisation, quick thinking, and creativity during customer interactions. One way to improve your creativity is to practice improv comedy techniques. Research has shown that students who completed a course that included improv sales training outperformed a control group of students who did not receive the training.[29] Improv helps sellers learn to listen to the customer and think on their feet to form your next response.

4. *Organizational Skills*

Organizational skills are critical for salespeople in order to manage their schedules, handle customer information, and gain knowledge of the product. Salespeople with strong time management and organizational skills can efficiently utilize their time to take advantage of prime time selling opportunities, travel and appointments, and face-time with customers at events.

5. *Professional Development*

Professional development is the means by which people maintain and improve their knowledge and skills related to their profession. In sales, professional development consists of activities like reading books and articles on sales technique and attending sales training

---

27. Ibid.

28. Weitz, B., Castleberry, S., & Tanner, J. (2007). *Selling: Building partnerships*, 7th ed. New York: McGraw-Hill Irwin.

29. Rocco, R., & Whalen, D. (2014). Teaching yes, and . . . Improv in sales classes: Enhancing student adaptive selling skills, sales performance, and teaching evaluations. *Journal of Marketing Education, 36*(2), 197–208.

workshops. Past research has shown that sport sales managers highly value the time salespeople spend in professional development, but salespeople do not rate it as highly with respect to its impact on their overall success.[30] For high performers, it is an indicator of commitment to the sales profession.

## The Competitive Nature of Sales

Successful sellers are competitive by nature. Sales is a numbers game that lends itself to quantitative comparisons between salespeople. These comparisons are often used to make promotion decisions. Leaderboards and other sales metrics are frequently utilized by sales managers to publicly show job performance and justify the awarding of incentives or prizes. Competitive individuals often do well in sales.

> My advice to any new ticket sales rep is to stay positive, work hard and be consistent. Sales is a numbers game, the more dials you make the more conversations you have, the more appointments you book, the more pitches you make, the more sales you get and the more money you make. Block everything else out, control what you can control and work hard.
>
> — Bob Hamer,
> Owner, *Sports Business Solutions*

While there is always an element of sales success that depends on the quantity of calls made, it is also important to recognize that improving competence at each stage of the sales process and the quality of the leads can dramatically impact sales productivity. To illustrate, let's say a seller wants to earn $25,000 in commission this year. There are four factors that will determine how many people the seller needs to contact to reach the goal.

- ▶ # of Dials Made—the number of total phone calls made
- ▶ Appointment Ratio—ratio of calls to total appointments or interested prospects
- ▶ Closing Ratio—ratio of appointments to closes
- ▶ Dollars to Total Sales—ratio of revenue generated to number of sales made

**Good salespeople are competitive**

© ESB Essentials/Shutterstock.com

---

30. Pierce, D., & Irwin, R. (2016). Competency assessment for entry-level sport ticket sales professionals. *Journal of Applied Sport Management, 8*(2), 54–77.

## Table 1.1

**Calculating Calls per Day From Commission Goal**

|  | Scenario 1 | Scenario 2 | Math |
|---|---|---|---|
| Revenue Generation Goal | $250,000 | $250,000 | Given |
| **Dollars to Total Sales** | $1,500 | $1,500 | Given |
| Commission Rate | 10% | 10% | Given |
| Average Commission per Sale | $150 | $150 | 1,500 * 10% |
| Income From Commissions | $25,000 | $25,000 | 1,500 * 150 |
| Number of Sales Needed | 167 | 167 | 25,000 / 150 |
| **Appointment Ratio** | 15 | 12 | Given |
| **Closing Ratio** | 5 | 4 | Given |
| Appointments Needed | 2,500 | 2,000 | 15 * 167 |
| Total Dials Needed | 12,500 | 8,000 | 2,500 * 5 |
| Working Days | 250 | 250 | Given |
| **Average Number of Dials per Day** | 50 | 32 | 12,500 / 250 |

Table 1.1 shows the number of calls needed can be determined from a sales goal. In Scenario 1, the following assumptions are made:

- ▶ Commission Rate—10%
- ▶ Appointment Ratio—15:1
- ▶ Closing Ratio—5:1
- ▶ Dollars to Total Sales—$1,500:1

Given these assumptions, the seller needs to make 12,500 total calls, or 50 calls per day to reach the goal. However, in scenario 2, through a combination of better leads and improved sales competence, the appointment ratio drops to 12:1 and the closing ratio drops to 4:1. Assuming dollars to total sales ratio stayed the same, the number of calls needed each day to reach the goal drops from 50 calls per day to 32 calls per day. Of course, the other way to conceptualize the process is that making the same number of calls per day will result in exceeding the goal.

## *Characteristics of Successful Salespeople*

In addition to being competitive, successful salespeople are characterized by being coachable, confident, emotionally intelligent, passionate, positive, self-motivated, and trustworthy.

Sales managers universally recognize the importance of *self-motivation* to a salesperson's success. While compensation and incentive plans can be effective tools used by sales managers to improve performance, motivation to succeed over the long-term in sales must come from within. It is the job of sales managers to find self-motivated people rather than teach people how to motivate themselves once they arrive on the job. Sales managers want to spend their time coaching new salespeople on getting better at each stage of the sales process, not motivating them to succeed. Nearly all new hires for a sport sales position are working in sales for the first time, so the salesperson has to be coachable and take the advice of more experienced managers.

One of the major challenges faced by a new seller is being rejected by customers. *Confidence* and high self-esteem are critical in overcoming rejection. Salespeople who can weather the storm by maintaining a *positive attitude* can survive the down times and thrive in the good times. Mark Washo advises, "Sales is a tough profession where you will be tested throughout your career. You must always remain confident in yourself and what your abilities can bring to the table."[31] In the face of rejection from customers, salespeople must be passionate about their job and the experience they provide. Successful sellers are *passionate* about watching families spend time together and businesses network with their clients. Passion manifests itself in strong work ethic, willingness to work the hours required in the sport industry, and dedication to the sales profession. Passion cannot be taught, but can be caught by those working around you.

Sellers also need to possess *emotional intelligence*, which is defined as the "ability to effectively understand and use one's own emotions and the emotions of people with whom one interacts."[32] Emotional intelligence is comprised of knowing one's own feelings and emotions, controlling those emotions to avoid acting impulsively, recognizing customers' emotions, and using emotions to interact effectively with customers. *Empathy* is the ability to put oneself in the shoes of the customer. For example, a retention specialist might need to put him or herself in the shoes of a recently retired season ticket holder who now lives on a more fixed income in order to better understand their renewal decision.

Finally, sales managers are looking for people who are *trustworthy* in relationships with co-workers and customers. Those who are stealing leads, sales, and commissions from other salespeople won't be around very long in the industry. Similarly, a customer will not develop a long-term relationship with a salesperson who puts on a false front or doesn't follow through on

31. Washo, M. (2004). *Break into sports through ticket sales*. Kindle edition, p. 37.
32. Weitz, B., Castleberry, S., & Tanner, J. (2007). *Selling: Building partnerships*, 7th ed. New York: McGraw-Hill Irwin.

promises made. Austin Allen and Brian Schackow with the Fort Wayne Tin-Caps offer their perspective on trustworthiness in salespeople in the article below.

---

**Austin Allen, Senior Ticket Account Manager, Fort Wayne TinCaps**
**Brian Schackow, Vice President, Finance, Fort Wayne TinCaps**

### THE IMPORTANCE OF TRUSTWORTHINESS IN SALES

The attitude of a salesperson genuinely seeking to help people and look out for their best interest is embodied in the concept of consultative sales. You will face many different types of situations as a ticket sales representative that require you to be trustworthy. Being a trustworthy salesperson is about being honest. You need to be honest with your client, as well as honest with your place of employment and the people that you work with. You need to put your client in the best position to have a successful outing, and you need to put your organization in the best position to succeed as well. You have to be honest about your product from the start. For example, if you are trying to sell season tickets to a prospective client, and that type of seat is only available by signing a multi-year contract, you need to let them know about that from the start. You won't want to get their hopes up, and then send them a contract without telling them how long they are locked in for. They may not be ready for a multi-year commitment, and might also start wondering what other things you are leaving out. By being honest from the start, it will help you build a better relationship with your prospective client. Don't avoid your client's question if you don't think they would like the answer. Answer the question, even if they may not like the answer. Your client will appreciate your honesty, and they will learn that they can trust you. Once you build a relationship with a client, and earn their trust, it becomes much easier to sell to them in the future.

You will also face issues when working with other salespeople. For example, issues can arise when working with sales territories. If you take an incoming call and help the client book an area or season tickets, then find out that they are not in your territory, you are then faced with an ethical dilemma. You can either take the sale, add the numbers toward your goal, and take the commission; or you can pass along the sale to the sales rep in that territory. By doing the right thing and passing that client along, you are not only earning the trust of your coworkers, but you are also making your workplace a better place to work, and your coworker will be more likely to do the same thing in the future.

---

**Bob Hamer, Owner, Sports Business Solutions**

## TRAITS OF A SUCCESSFUL SALESPERSON

In my time, I've seen some fantastic sport sales professionals and seen many people struggle with sales. Some job candidates looked great on paper but couldn't do the job and some had no sales experience and a disheveled resume and they became sales superstars. So what does it take to succeed in sport sales?

I believe there are some common characteristics of great sport salespeople and many of them are intangible. You can learn sales techniques and the product but you have to have the right DNA if you want to succeed selling in sports.

Here are the traits that I think are important to succeeding in sport sales:

1. **Strong work ethic**—Sport sales is a contact sport, the more conversations, the more appointments, the more pitches, the more you sell. It is heavy outbound calling, and usually the deals are smaller and more transactional. It's a volume play. Early on you build your account base through lots of cold calls, events, and appointments. If the thought of calling on strangers scares you, you won't enjoy selling in sports.

2. **Tough**—Sport sales is tough. You deal with rejection on a continual basis. There are hang-ups, and lots of no's. It's hard to keep getting knocked down. However, just like a prize fighter you have to pick yourself up off the mat and keep going. It's not for the faint of heart and if you're looking for a worry-free 9–5, sport sales isn't for you.

3. **Outgoing**—If you wait by the phone for people to call in and buy, you're not going to succeed. The reality of sport sales jobs (and most sales jobs), is that you have to be outgoing and go out and find business. You need to be that person at the game in front of the sales table, smiling and talking to strangers, approaching people and getting to know them, putting yourself out there. If you thrive in that environment, love meeting new people and helping others, you could be a great salesperson.

4. **Competitive**—The very nature of sales is competitive. You're either winning business for your team or you aren't. It's results oriented and it's public. Everyone knows your numbers each day you step into the office. If you want to be great you have to embrace the pressure of competition. You have to hate to lose and be eager to get to that next prospect. If the thought of closing a deal doesn't get your heart pumping, sales might not be for you.

5. **Genuine**—The best sellers I know care deeply about their customers. They see the value in making sure they have a good buying experience. If you put someone in a product you know they can't afford, or offer them more games than you know they're going to attend you run the risk of losing them in the future. Build relationships through great service and a great experience for your customers and they'll reward you multiple times over with referrals and more buying. If you care about people and making them happy, you could be great at sport sales.

6. **Coachable**—Whether you're in entry level sales or you've been selling for years, you can always get better. Learn from people who have done it before you, pick up new skills, and work on your craft. Sales isn't something you ever perfect, and there is always room to grow. The minute you get comfortable and think you have it figured out, you get complacent, and your results suffer. Keep getting better each day. If you like challenges and always learning, sales could be a great fit for you.

Source: https://www.linkedin.com/pulse/traits-successful-sports-salesperson-bob-hamer
Reprinted by permission of Bob Hamer.

## *Five Key Characteristics of Sales Careers*

Sales offers people the opportunity to launch their career in the sport industry, differentiate themselves from other people based on observable performance metrics, advance quickly up the organizational chart, and be upwardly mobile. Jobs in sales have five characteristics that distinguish them from other jobs in the industry.

1. *Job Security*

   There are more available positions in sales than any other department in professional sport organizations, and college athletics has followed suit in recent years.[33] Opportunities abound for those seeking to launch a career in the sport industry. In addition to job opportunities, salespeople produce revenue and thus enjoy relatively good job security compared with other occupational groups.[34] Those who produce revenue are generally the last to be affected by cutbacks in personnel. In addition, competent salespeople have job security based on the universal nature of their sales skill set. Because of their largely transferrable sales skills, they can move to another sport organization or even to an employer outside of sport.

---

33. Teamwork Online Industry hiring reports. (2011).

34. Ingram, T., LaForge, R., Avila, R., Schwepker, C., & Williams, M. (2006). *Professional selling: A trust-based approach*, 3rd ed. Mason, OH: Thomson Southwestern.

2. *Advancement Opportunities*

A quick examination of any major league team staff directory will show far more sales related positions than any other job function. Sales departments also see considerable movement of employees due to promotions, other opportunities, or turnover. As a result, salespeople who are successful and stick with the job have opportunities to advance within the organization that are often not available in community relations, public relations, and marketing. Beyond this, those in upper management positions such as athletic directors, chief revenue officers, and chief executive officers must have an understanding of sales. As a result, those who have generated revenue in the past have a pathway to upper management positions. For example, the ability to fundraise is an important characteristic for athletic directors, so it is no surprise that development (fundraising) is the most common background of recently hired athletic directors.[35]

3. *Compensation*

Salespeople typically have a better opportunity to quickly improve their pay than other entry-level jobs in sport. Successful salespeople can earn more than their non-sales counterparts in the sport industry. The structure of compensation packages varies wildly across different types of sport organizations, but the commission-based structure of sales positions can drive successful salespeople to higher salaries. For those who want to work in a job that rewards performance, sales is an attractive profession.

4. *Immediate Feedback*

Good sales managers provide salespeople with constant and timely feedback on their performance through coaching, a sales leaderboard, and analysis of call volume metrics. A salesperson almost always knows where he or she stands in comparison to coworkers. In addition, salespeople receive immediate feedback from their customers on the product. Such feedback can be challenging in that it requires salespersons to adapt and think on their feet to respond to customer concerns, but it is also rewarding in that they really get a feeling for the customers' feelings toward the team and product offering.

---

35. Wong, G. (2014). The path to the athletic director's office. *Street & Smith's SportsBusiness Journal, 17*(9), 32.

5. *Job Variety*

While many people think of a sales job as being a monotonous job of picking up the phone and calling people all day, it is important to recognize that each customer is different and the product being sold is consistently in a state of flux. Sport salespeople talk to and work with many different types of customers. Building relationships and consistently interacting with these people and helping them really enjoy their experiences as a fan (or helping them improve their business) is something that is not really found in other areas of sports. Sales reps also have opportunities to interact with powerful, influential, and wealthy ticket buyers and decision-makers. Building relationships with such people is rarely possible in other entry-level sport industry positions. On the team side, in the blink of an eye the team's star player could get hurt, a key player could get traded, the team could go on an unexpected winning streak, or the coach could be fired. With parity such a prevalent feature in professional sports, the worst team can be the best team within just one season. Finally, there are also some sales positions, particularly in the sporting goods industry and business-to-business (B2B) sales for team, where salespeople are traveling or working from home and not within a highly structured corporate office environment.

## Typical Workweek

A recent study examined the typical workweek of a diverse sample of over 450 sport sales professionals.[36] The respondents of the survey responded that they worked an average of 53 hours per week. The greatest amount of time was spent making sales calls over the phone (14.6 hours per week), followed by servicing, organizational tasks, and prospecting. The complete list of hours spent on sales tasks is presented in Table 1.2. A few differences were identified between business-to-consumer (B2C) salespeople and business-to-business salespeople. B2B salespeople reported spending significantly more time prospecting, planning, presenting, preparing bids, and traveling than B2C salespeople. Not surprisingly then, B2C salespeople spent significantly more time selling on the phone than B2B salespeople.

---

36. Pierce, D., Petersen, J., & Lee, D. (2013). Time allocation of sales activities in professional sport organizations. *The Journal of SPORT, 2*(1), 1–20.

## Table 1.2

**Hours per Week Spent on Sales Tasks**

| Task | M | Pct |
|------|-----|------|
| Selling on the Phone | 14.6 | 27.3 |
| Servicing | 8.6 | 16.1 |
| Organizational Tasks | 7.3 | 13.7 |
| Prospecting | 5.5 | 10.3 |
| Sales Force Management | 4.1 | 7.7 |
| Presenting | 3.5 | 6.5 |
| Planning | 3.1 | 5.8 |
| Preparing Bids | 2.4 | 4.5 |
| Traveling | 2.2 | 4.1 |
| Professional Development | 2.1 | 3.9 |
| Total | 53.4 | 100 |

## YOUR BELIEFS DETERMINE YOUR SUCCESS

Many students think about a career in sport sales with a certain amount of fear and skepticism. If you believe that you would never be successful making sales calls, then more than likely you won't be successful making sales calls. However, if you keep an open mind and change your belief about your potential in sales, the training material in this book and the coaching you receive from your professor or sales manager will become part of a formula for success in sales. Changing what you believe can change what you think you can achieve. The reality is many aspiring sport managers can be successful in sales with the right attitude and approach to the profession, as well as a willingness to work on the right skills and put in the right effort.

Several beliefs can be barriers to success in sales:

- ► I shouldn't talk about other people's money
- ► I shouldn't bother people when they are home
- ► It's not appropriate to talk with people I don't know
- ► I need to be liked by people
- ► Rejection means people don't like me
- ► Others will think less of me if I fail

For example, refraining from talking about other people's money, bothering people when they are at home, or talking to people you don't know are rules likely acquired sometime during childhood. These principles could be seen as incompatible with a job that requires asking for a financial commitment, or that involves making cold calls to people while they are at home or at work. Additionally, the need to be liked, avoid rejection, and avoid failure to save face in front of friends and colleagues might not be seen as compatible with a profession in which the majority of interactions end with prospects not purchasing.

Job seekers who hold these beliefs need to change them in order to change their behavior and ultimately their results in sales. For example, consider the need to be liked by people. In reality, no sales representative needs to be liked by every prospect. Instead, sellers should seek respect first and likeability second. Salespeople who are liked but not respected become professional visitors who have engaging and likeable conversations, but never close the sale. Some sales managers call this phenomenon being a prisoner of hope. Thus, the belief "I need to be liked by people" should change to "I need to be respected by people."

The fear of rejection is triggered by the "possibility of rudeness, disapproval, or criticism toward the salesperson by the prospect."[37] Sellers must realize a rejection to a sales proposal does not mean a prospect does not like the seller personally, but rather the customer is rejecting the product or prices. Moreover, many sport sales executives can experience rejection the vast majority of the time and still be a top-producing salesperson, with high levels of job satisfaction. In this case, the belief changes from "rejection means people don't like me" to "rejection means the customer didn't want to purchase the product."

Because the sales profession has such publicly-visible results, many entry level sellers worry others will think less of them when they fail to make a sale, close a big deal, or if they hit a sales slump. It is important to realize nearly everyone who is successful in sales has struggled at some point in their career. Nobody started their career as the top salesperson in the office. Consider all the influential companies that didn't reach their greatness until after their leader had failed in other business ventures: Bill Gates failed with his first company Traf-O-Data before Microsoft was a success; George Steinbrenner bankrupted the Cleveland Pipers before leading the New York Yankees to greatness; Walt Disney was once fired by a newspaper for lacking creativity before building the Disney empire; Steve Jobs was booted from his own company before being brought back and taking Apple to new heights; and Milton Hershey failed with three candy ventures before finding the right recipe with the Hershey Company. A summary of changed beliefs is presented in Table 1.3.

---

37. Tracy, B. (2004). *The psychology of selling.* Nashville, TN: Thomas Nelson.

## Table 1.3

### Old and New Beliefs

| Old Belief | New Belief |
| --- | --- |
| I shouldn't talk about other people's money | I need to talk with people who can spend money |
| I shouldn't bother people when they are home | I need to take advantage of prime-selling times when people are at home |
| It's not appropriate to talk with people I don't know | If I don't talk to new people I will run out of prospects |
| I need to be liked by people | I need to be respected by people |
| Rejection means people don't like me | Rejection means people don't like the team or product |
| Others will think less of me if I fail | Others will think less of me if I don't try to improve |

---

**Carl Manteau, Senior Director of Group Sales, Milwaukee Bucks**

### A SPORTS SALES DIRECTOR'S ADVICE ON SURVIVING YOUR FIRST YEAR AS AN INSIDE SALES REP

## WHAT YOU CAN EXPECT IN YOUR FIRST YEAR

### Fun (Seriously)

First and foremost, sports is and should be fun. We get paid to watch the greatest athletes in the world. People love watching, talking about, and playing sports. No matter how stressful the job may feel, it's important to keep your perspective and understand that we are in the business of fun.

Don't take that for granted! Enjoy the sights, sounds, and opportunities that this industry provides.

### Competition

As an inside sales rep, you are competing for a position on the full-time staff. The people sitting on either side of you are competing for that same spot. This may sound cutthroat, but it really isn't (hopefully). Teams put parameters in place to make the competition as healthy as possible.

You should always support your teammates, but don't ever take your sights off your own goals.

### Friendships

Look at the wedding party pictures of almost any tenured sales rep/executive and you will probably see someone from their inside sales class standing alongside them. Your inside sales teammates become family. You train together, work alongside each other (often in an isolated area), work events together, and you hang out together outside of the office.

It's almost impossible to spend that much time with people and not develop deep bonds that turn into lifelong friendships. This is why the competition is usually healthy—you want your friends to succeed and they want the same for you.

**Long Hours**

The role of sports is to entertain people when they are not at their jobs. This means we work nights, weekends, and holidays. A typical game day in the NBA is 12–14 hours. If you work in baseball, you can expect to go weeks without a day off during the season. This is the same for everyone.

Beyond this, inside sales reps are often required to work additional hours, making night calls, setting up information tables at games and community events, assisting with the setup and cleanup of prospecting and stakeholder events, plus performing a variety of tasks that fall outside normal work hours.

If you aren't passionate about selling and don't love what you are doing then the long hours will probably be intolerable.

**Phone Calls**

Inside sales reps can expect to make over 25,000 phone calls in their first year.

Sales reps make (lots of) phone calls. It's that simple. Inside sales reps are required to make more phone calls than other sales teams in the organization (usually 80–100 calls a day). This is for a few reasons:

1.  The leads provided to inside sales reps are typically not the warmest so more calls are needed to reach qualified prospects.

2.  Older reps already have an established book of business to draw on, whereas inside sales reps are starting with a clean slate. Given this, inside sales reps need to make more calls to build up their book of business.

3.  Making more calls helps young reps develop and refine their skills, which increases confidence and the ability to close more sales.

4.  Inside sales reps are also asked to make more calls than others simply to prove if they can. Managers need to know if the reps can be relied on to meet and surpass expectations should they be promoted into a more senior role.

I've never met anyone that's enjoyed making 100 calls a day. I know I never did. As your skill set develops and you get better at prospecting, you won't have to make as many calls. In this era of social selling, reps are getting much better at using LinkedIn and other tools to circumvent the cold call.

No matter what resources you use, at some point you will still need to pick up the phone and talk to people . . . lots and lots of people. Inside sales reps will be asked to make more than 25,000 calls in their first year. If you aren't willing to make the calls the person sitting next to you is, and that person will probably get promoted ahead of you.

### Micromanaging

As an inside sales rep you are going to get micromanaged.

It is the job of the inside sales manager to make sure you know as much as possible about selling techniques, products, the team, the organization, the resources, etc. To accomplish this, the manager needs to be near you, watch you, listen to you, and study you. Your manager will be your shadow, but he/she is doing it to help you be the best you can be.

The faster you can show that you are confident and competent in all areas of the business the more freedom your manager will give you.

### Accountability

Whether you are a first-year rep or in your 20th season, you are going to be held accountable to metrics.

Sales is a numbers game and there are certain numbers that management will require you to hit. Your #1 priority is to generate revenue. You will be given a sales goal and will most certainly be held accountable to hitting it. You will also be held accountable to other metrics—like the number of phone calls and appointments you complete each day. (I wasn't kidding about the micro-managing. Your stats are monitored constantly.)

### Dwindling Numbers

Inside sales is a lot like *Survivor*, *America's Got Talent*, *American Idol,* or any other elimination show. As the year goes on, the number of reps will continually dwindle and only the strongest will be left standing at the end. People leave for a variety of reasons:

▶ A handful of reps will probably quit after a couple of weeks/months because they realize that the job is not for them, which is fine; this job isn't for everyone.

▶ Some reps may be asked to leave because of low productivity or they violate a company policy.

▶ Others may leave because they get a job somewhere else.

▶ Some reps leave because they are so good they get promoted early. I love when I get to promote someone!

### Not a Lot of Money

It can be a financial struggle to make it through the first year.

Like any sales position, reps earn most of their money from commission earned on sales. To earn big commissions you need to put up big sales; however, it usually takes time for new reps to put up big sales. It also takes time to get trained, to grow confidence, to prospect new leads, to improve skills, and to get people to the closing stage.

Additionally, inside sales reps are not given a base of accounts so all sales need to be self-generated (this is another part of the proving process). It's not all bad—inside sales reps usually earn a decent base salary and many teams offer benefits.

When I started with the Cavaliers (many, many years ago), inside sales reps only received a base salary of $13k with no benefits.

My first year was brutal—I had to defer my student loans, I went without car and health insurance, I could barely pay my rent, and eating out was a luxury. On top of this the Cavs were awful (this was pre-LeBron) and sales were not easy to come by.

This sounds unbearable but I loved it!

The desperation to succeed made me work harder and we still found ways to have fun. It was difficult, but I learned so much and I wouldn't trade the experience for anything.

## NOW FOR SOME ADVICE

Now that you know what to expect, let's talk about ways to put yourself at the head of your inside sales class. Here are the essentials:

### Revenue

Money talks. Closing deals and hitting revenue goals is how you will be measured in sport sales.

When managers look to promote someone from inside sales to a full-time position the first thing they look at is revenue. You could be the nicest, friendliest, most-respected person in the company but if you can't close deals then you won't be promoted.

Knowing this, don't settle for mediocrity. Don't allow yourself to be at the bottom of the sales board. Fight, claw, and scratch for every sale. Always make sure your sales funnel is full. Always make time each day to prospect new business.

### Hustle

Revenue is the most important thing, but it's not the only thing. Hiring managers also look at hustle to determine if you have the traits to be successful. Never let yourself be out-hustled. If you consistently do the little things that your colleagues aren't, you will definitely stand out to your manager and likely be standing at the top of the revenue board.

### Hustle Tips

1. Don't just hit your daily call goal—blow it out of the water. Your goal should be to make more calls than everyone else in your inside sales class every day.

2. After everyone else has gone home for the night, force yourself to make three more calls.

3. Making extra calls is relatively easy when you are just getting started. Doing it consistently every week is what truly separates good from great. Don't get lazy!

4. Spend more time studying than everyone else. Your products and your team are your life so it's on you to learn as much about them as you can. Likewise, to be good at selling you should study the habits and teachings of the best sellers.

5. Do more prospecting than everyone else. In order to close more business you need to have more in your funnel than your counterparts. To fill your funnel you need to carve out time to prospect every day. Most IS reps are given leads to help get them started, which is great, but to excel you also need to find your own prospects. Managers need to know that, if promoted, you will not depend on someone else to provide leads to you.

**Attitude**

A positive attitude is everything.

You can't work the hours we work and bring a negative attitude or it will spread like cancer. I have personally refused to promote some high-revenue generators because their attitudes were poor. You are part of a team and if your team can't rely on you, or if your attitude brings the team down, then you're better off not being a part of it.

My advice: always be a positive, motivating force. If you are having a bad day then take a walk outside to reduce your stress, DO NOT complain to the people sitting around you. If someone makes a big sale, be the first to congratulate them. If someone is struggling, be the first to offer words of encouragement. Support your teammates but don't distract them either. Be respectful. Remember, your time in inside sales is limited. You can either make the most of every minute or you can squander it. You may not always be able to control what happens to you, but you can control how you react to it. Choose the high road.

**Knowledge**

Invest in making yourself better. I'm 12+ years into this business and I still read books, attend seminars, listen to podcasts, and network with people around the industry in an attempt to be better at what I do.

I recommend you do the same.

Training never ends. Learning never ends. As a new sales rep, you should soak up as much knowledge as you can. Don't just rely on your manager to do all of the educating. Set aside some time each week on your personal development.

**OTHER WAYS TO STAND OUT (FOR GOOD REASONS)**

**Network Internally**

You've only got 6–12 months to make an impact. You should do this by putting up big numbers, but you can also get a boost by networking with those around you. Take the time to get to know the senior reps and managers. Ask them for advice. Ask if you can go on appointments to see them in action.

If your goal is to get promoted to a full-time sales team (and it should be), then take the time to get to know the people on those teams.

I am the Director of Group Sales, which means I am in a position to promote people out of inside sales. Sadly, most inside sales reps wait until the end of their term before attempting to get to know me or any of my reps.

It's difficult to promote someone I don't know! Don't wait! Get to know the team leaders and senior reps early. Ask them out to lunch or to get a coffee every couple months. Stay on their radar and give them updates on your progress.

### Arrive Early/Stay Late

Inside sales is a short-term commitment, so make the most of it! Be the first to arrive in the morning. Be the last to leave at night. Use that extra time to prospect and get organized.

Trust me, you aren't missing out on anything if you meet your friends at the bar 30 minutes later than you expected. Remember, you are competing for a full-time position and hiring managers definitely notice the people that put in extra effort.

### Be Professional

If you want to be a professional then dress like one.

Come to work every day looking the part. Make sure your shirts are clean and ironed. Make sure your belt matches your shoes. Make sure your outfit is appropriate (if you would wear it to the club, then don't wear it to work). Wear dress socks, not black athletic socks—there's a difference. Wear dress shoes and keep them polished.

Guys—shave!

Trust me, all eyes are on you. Your hygiene habits and wardrobe make an impression. You are an ambassador for the team. Take that responsibility seriously and always put yourself and your team in the best light. This applies to social media as well. Never say anything negative about any of the players on your team, in your league, or in your sport. If you ever have to question whether or not to hit send—don't send it!

### Stay Active

It's easy to disregard your health in inside sales because you are working so many hours. DON'T! I've seen people put on 30 pounds in a year (I put on 20 pounds in my first year)! Added weight kills your energy and impacts your confidence, which affects your ability to sell. If you don't sell, you won't get promoted. It's an unhealthy downward spiral that can be avoided. Schedule time to be active and hold yourself accountable to it.

### Volunteer

Always be the first to volunteer for opportunities—even if it is for a task you aren't thrilled to do (like mascot duty). Show your manager that you are a team player and willing to do whatever it takes to make the team better. I know the last thing you want to do is give up a Saturday to work at some community festival, but that experience will help your skill development and give you an opportunity to close more business than your counterparts.

---

Reprinted by permission of the author and WorkinSports.com.

## CHAPTER SUMMARY

A career in sales can be rewarding with a significant amount of upward mobility for individuals who are coachable, competitive, passionate, self-motivated, and positive. Sales is a critical function for all sport organizations, and there is always a need in the marketplace for those who can generate revenue. Even for those who don't have sales in their job title or primary job responsibility, an understanding of the sales process and what salespeople do is important because it is the end product for those who work in analytics, research, marketing, service, business development, and other areas in sport organizations.

Chapters 2 and 3 offer a peak behind the curtain at the structure and strategy of the sales department in sport organizations. Chapter 4 sets a theoretical and conceptual foundation for using a consultative sales approach throughout each of the steps of the sales process, which are described in detail in Chapters 5–10. Chapter 11 addresses the key communication skills that are needed throughout the sales process. Chapter 12 offers an in-depth look at prospecting, which is the process of cultivating customers. Chapter 13 examines sales force management from the perspective of sales managers, and Chapter 14 considers the efforts taken by the sales department to retain customers in future sales cycles. Finally, Chapter 15 applies the sales principles already addressed in the textbook to the sale of corporate sponsorship.

## CHAPTER ACTIVITIES

1. Contrast your opinion of sales prior to reading this chapter to your opinion after completing this chapter. Describe how your opinion may have changed.

2. Discuss your motivation for taking this class and your current attitude toward sales in relation to what you want to achieve through this class by the end of the semester. Then make a self-assessment about whether you think you have what it takes to be successful in sport ticket sales.

3. Go to LinkedIn and find five profiles of people who work in sport sales positions. Identify trends, themes, and other observations from examining the five profiles.

4. Find five sport sales job announcements on Teamwork Online or Work in Sports. Based on these job descriptions, identify and describe three skills that you have that are a good fit for sales positions. Then, identify and describe three skills you will need to improve on to be successful in sales.

# CHAPTER 2

## SALES IN THE SPORT ORGANIZATION

**LEARNING OBJECTIVES**

After completing this chapter, you should be able to:

▶ Understand the role and importance of sales within sport organizations.

▶ Describe the structure of a typical sales staff.

▶ Appreciate the differences in sales structure across different sectors of the sport industry.

▶ Understand career opportunities in sport sales.

**KEY TERMS**

| | |
|---|---|
| Account Executive (AE) | Inside sales |
| Analytics | Operations side |
| Business side | Outbound sales |
| Corporate sales | Outsourcing |
| Customer Relationship Management (CRM) | Premium sales |
| | Retention |
| Customer service | Season ticket sales |
| Group sales | Ticket operations |
| Inbound sales | Ticket Sales Representative (TSR) |

## CHAPTER OVERVIEW

Sales is a crucial part of nearly any business organization, including the sport industry. This chapter focuses on the role and importance of sales within a sport organization. Without sales and revenue, funding doesn't exist to field a team, pay administrative salaries, or even play a single game. In Major League Baseball (MLB), a sales staff might be responsible for selling four million game tickets over the 81-game home season. That revenue is essential in order to support a team payroll of $100 million or more annually. Across the industry, it is estimated that approximately $15 billion is spent on sport sponsorships. Salespeople are needed to sell that type of inventory. The chapter will explore the composition of sport organizations and how sales staffs fit into that structure. In addition, the makeup of sales staffs and the different types of sales positions will be examined. Finally, sport sales career opportunities will be discussed.

## MAJOR LEAGUE TEAM SPORTS

Among the most high-profile North American sport organizations are the major leagues in team sports, including MLB, Major League Soccer (MLS), the National Basketball Association (NBA), the National Football League (NFL), and the National Hockey League (NHL), as well as the franchises contained within those leagues. These leagues attract vast media coverage, generate large television ratings, draw strong crowds, and pay athletes millions of dollars in salaries. Unsurprisingly, many aspiring sport industry candidates desire careers with major league sport franchises. They often dream of being the next general manager of a team and one day receiving a championship ring alongside the athletes they admire. While these dreams are attainable (someone must hold those general manager positions after all), probabilities suggest they are extremely difficult to obtain. There are three times as many Fortune 500 CEO positions than there are general manager positions in the five major leagues listed above. Accordingly, let's examine the role of sales within major league sport franchises and where the multitudes of jobs do exist.

### *Organization Structure*

Major league sport franchises typically are structured with two distinct sides of the organization, as shown in Figure 2.1. Like most businesses, a pro sport franchise has an owner or group of owners that serve as the operator and

## Figure 2.1

**Standard Major League Sport Franchise Structure**

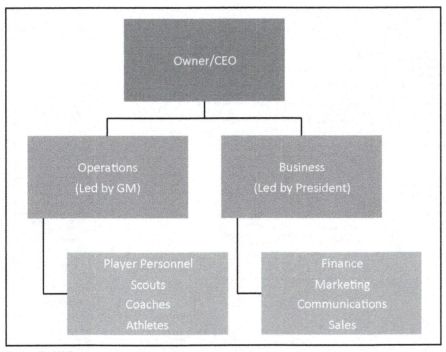

Courtesy Chad McEvoy

ultimate decision-maker for the organization. In many organizations, the leader of the organization may carry the role of chief executive officer or CEO. Beneath the owner/CEO role are the two sides of the franchise: the operations side and the business side. The **operations side** of the professional sport team is the sports aspects of the franchise, including the players, coaches, scouts, and oftentimes the medical staff. The general manager is most commonly the leader of this operations side of the organization. Conversely, the **business side** of the sport franchise is typically led by the team president, although these titles do vary from organization to organization. Similar to a standard corporation or company in other industries, professional sport franchises employ staff across a variety of function areas such as communications, finance, human resources, marketing, and sales. These standard function areas comprise the business side of the professional sport team.

Figure 2.2 shows an organizational chart from the Boston Celtics of the NBA. Note that the far left column represents the operations side of the Celtics, while the rest of the chart represents the business side. This disparity in the size of the two sides of the Celtics is not unusual among major league franchises. In many of these organizations, the vast majority of employees work on the business side, compared to relatively few in operations. The

**OPERATIONS SIDE**
the sports aspects of the franchise, including the players, coaches, scouts, and oftentimes the medical staff

**BUSINESS SIDE**
typically led by the team president, although these titles do vary from organization to organization

## Figure 2.2

**Boston Celtics Organizational Chart**

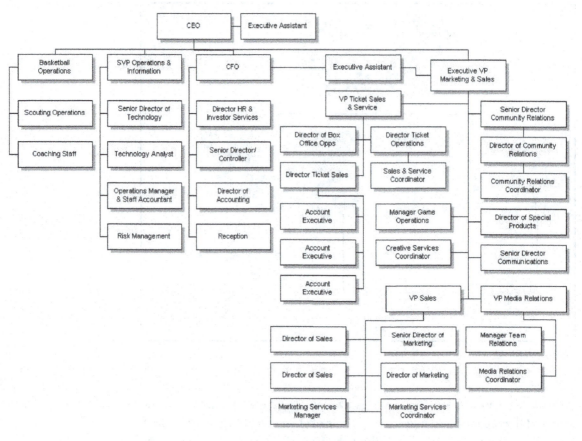

Wong, G. M., *The Comprehensive Guide to Careers in Sports,* © 2013: Jones & Bartlett Learning, Burlington, MA. www.jblearning.com. Reprinted with permission.

operations side of the organization is often no more than 10% of the number of staff positions within the franchise. For those with aspirations of becoming the general manager of a team, this presents an extremely difficult challenge. Not only are there thousands of competitors with the same career goals, but operations staffs are quite small, meaning that there are a very limited supply of positions available along the career path that could lead toward a general manager position.

In contrast to the operations side, the business side of the professional sport organization is considerably larger, presenting more employment opportunities for aspiring sport industry employees. In particular, the highest percentage of jobs on the business side of the professional sport franchise is in the sales area. From a probability perspective, you have a much greater chance of securing full-time employment with a professional sport team in sales than you do in operations, marketing, communications, or other functional areas.

## Sales Staff Structure

Many major league professional sport franchises employ 50 or more salespeople, with some teams having sales staffs as large as 100. The Philadelphia 76ers possess the largest sales staff in the industry, with 180 sales personnel in 2015.[1] With staffs this large, teams often subdivide their salespeople into smaller groups, or teams, which specialize in specific aspects of sales. As the Boston Celtics example in Figure 2.2 typifies, most sales organizations are structured under the leadership of a vice president (or similar) of sales, with directors of different sales function groups reporting to that vice president. Let's examine each of these aspects, or function groups, of the sales operation.

### INSIDE SALES

**Inside sales** is the most common starting point for new salespeople beginning their careers in sport sales. The traditional definition of the term "inside sales" refers to sales personnel who utilize the telephone and/or online means to sell rather than traveling outside the organization's facility to sell face-to-face. Note that while telephone and online sales are the most common mediums used by inside sales representatives in professional sports, many teams do utilize inside sales staff in face-to-face sales as at least a small part of their responsibilities.

Major league franchises commonly use their inside sales team as a training and proving ground for potential advancement opportunities into the organization's other sales teams. Inside sales employees, often referred to as "**ticket sales representatives**," or "TSRs," are full-time employees, although the term of employment is typically for a length of approximately one year. During that time, TSRs receive extensive training about all aspects of the sales process, and then begin to sell under the direction and mentorship of the inside sales director. As their term progresses, TSRs who show promise and initial success as salespeople will have opportunities for promotion to sales functions such as group sales and season ticket sales. Those that are promoted often earn the new title of "**account executive**," or "AE," and receive an increase in compensation and job security. TSRs who struggle or who don't show the same level of work ethic and future promise will not receive those

**INSIDE SALES** sales personnel who utilize the telephone and/or online means to sell rather than traveling outside the organization's facility to sell face-to-face

**TICKET SALES REPRESENTATIVE (TSR)** also known as inside sales employees, these employees are tasked with selling tickets to customers

**ACCOUNT EXECUTIVE (AE)** TSRs who show promise and initial success as salespeople will have opportunities for promotion to account executives

1. Shelly, J. (2015, June 18). Sixers rely on army of 22-year-olds for marketing. *Philadelphia Magazine*. Retrieved from www.phillymag.com.

same opportunities. Quality franchises will help those less successful TSRs find employment elsewhere.

## GROUP SALES

**GROUP SALES**
focused on selling tickets
to groups of customers

As implied by the term, the **group sales team** is focused on selling tickets to groups of customers. Professional sport teams often define a group as a ticket purchase of 15 to 20 or more tickets to a game. In return for buying this sizeable block of tickets, the group usually receives a price discount, and the tickets may be combined with additional benefits such as hospitality options. Groups traditionally include a variety of community and business organizations, such as a Boy Scout troop, employees from a local insurance company, or a youth sport team. As will be discussed in the next chapter on ticket packaging and pricing, an important aspect of group sales is the cultivation of relationships with group leaders. If the account executive can identify and connect with a key person within an organization, that person can be vitally helpful in convincing peers to buy tickets with the group and even in collecting the ticket money.

## SEASON TICKET SALES

**SEASON TICKET SALES**
focused on the sale of
season tickets

Another area within the sales force that is often a landing spot for new AEs after being promoted from inside sales is the **season ticket sales team**. This team is focused on the sale of season tickets. An indication of the importance of season ticket sales to the success of a pro team is demonstrated by the fact that a specific sales team is charged with focusing solely on season tickets. Consider a team such as the New York Yankees, which plays in the 49,642-seat Yankee Stadium. As Major League Baseball teams play 81 home games, the Yankees sales staff is responsible for trying to sell more than four million total tickets per season. If the Yankees sell 25,000 season tickets, the number of remaining tickets is cut by one half to two million. With demand for individual game tickets subject to factors such as weather, success of the two teams, day of the week, and so on, securing a strong number of season ticket sales prior to the start of the season dramatically reduces the strain on the sales force to sell individual game tickets and other types of ticket inventory during the season.

**RETENTION**
retaining existing
customers

In line with this same notion, a recent trend in major league professional sports is an increased focus on season ticket sales **retention**—the effort to retain and renew season ticket holders from one year to the next. If a team can successfully renew 80% of its season ticket holders from one year to the next, it has far fewer tickets left to sell that next season. Accordingly, some franchises have relabeled this sales group as "season ticket sales and retention" to signify an increased emphasis on retaining and renewing these key customers, while others have gone even further to create a separate sales team focused solely on servicing and retaining season ticket holders. As examples, the Miami Heat have a sales team called the "season ticket services department," while the Yankees' "season ticket sales and service department" has several staff members carrying the titles of "retention sales specialist."

## PREMIUM SALES

One of the most prestigious sales teams is the **premium sales team**. Sales professionals on premium sales teams have generally been promoted multiple times and have established their credentials as strong sellers. This team is tasked with selling the franchise's premium inventory. This includes the luxury suites, club seats, and any other unique, high-priced inventory. A

**PREMIUM SALES**
sales of the franchise's premium inventory

premium sales professional may commonly sit down with a senior executive from a Fortune 500 corporation proposing a five-year contract for a luxury suite valued at well over $100,000 per year. Accordingly, this is not a common starting place for a young, new sales representative still learning the craft. As discussed above with season ticket sales, many franchises have placed an increased emphasis on the retention and renewal aspects of premium sales in recent years.

©Ken Durden/Shutterstock.com

## CUSTOMER SERVICE AND RETENTION

Consistent with the previous discussion, professional sport franchises have learned that it is generally much easier to serve and retain existing customers, particularly key customers like season ticket holders and premium buyers, than it is to replace those customers. As a result, franchises have increased their emphasis on successfully serving and retaining their existing customers and have, correspondingly, hired more staff specifically focused on these key functions.

In two 2013 *Sports Business Journal* columns,[2] expert Bill Sutton discussed the sales staffing hunter/farmer model, and how this model can be

---

2. Sutton, B. (2013, January 7). On realignment, big screen distractions and sales cultures. *Sports Business Journal*. Sutton, B. (2013, February 11). More on managing hunters and farmers in your organization. *Sports Business Journal*. Retrieved from www.sportsbusinessdaily. com.

utilized by sport organizations. In this model, a "hunter" is a salesperson with strengths in hunting for new customers by actively prospecting for new potential customers and generating sales from those prospects. In contrast, a "farmer" is skilled at building and cultivating relationships with customers, typically existing ones, and can leverage those relationships into retention and renewal success. Organizations utilizing the hunter/farmer model strive to employ a balanced mix of hunters and farmers and to identify which of these roles each sales employee best fits. The organization places its hunters in areas like season ticket sales and premium sales to capitalize on hunters' skills in generating new business, and places its farmers in areas such as customer service/retention to utilize their skills in taking care of existing customers and increasing the likelihood those customers renew the following year.

## CORPORATE SALES

**CORPORATE SALES**
team focused on the sale and service of corporate sponsorships

While many of the sales teams within a professional sport franchise are focused on the sale and service of tickets, the **corporate sales** team is instead focused on the sale and service of corporate sponsorships. This sponsorship inventory can include a wide variety of opportunities customized to meet the needs of sponsors, such as naming rights, signage, advertising, and hospitality. Similar to premium sales, a salesperson usually must be promoted multiple times in order to reach this function team as it takes experience and skill to meet with a senior executive from a corporation and close a sponsorship sale that may be valued in the millions of dollars.

## TICKET OPERATIONS

**TICKET OPERATIONS**
sometimes called box office management, is a support function to the sales force of a professional sport franchise

In contrast to the sales function areas, **ticket operations**, sometimes called box office management, is a support function to the sales force of a professional sport franchise. The ticket operations area, sometimes referred to as the box office area, is responsible for the processing and fulfillment of ticket purchase orders, the invoicing and charging of payments for those orders, and other issues related to seating and ticketing within the franchise's arena or stadium. The ticket operations managers work closely with the sales staff in performing the functions listed above, and often also work

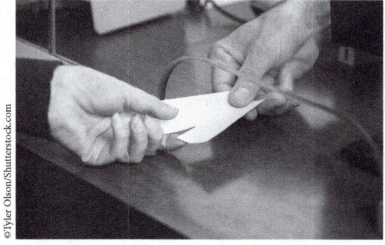
©Tyler Olson/Shutterstock.com

closely with the financial operations of the organization as it relates to the handling of cash and debit/credit card orders, managing the ticket inventory, and financial record keeping. The ticket operations area can be one where farmers instead of hunters are stationed in the organization's staffing strategy.

## CRM AND ANALYTICS

Another sales support area is CRM and analytics. **CRM** stands for customer relationship management. Professional sport franchises have hundreds of thousands of tickets to sell over the course of a season, and those tickets are sold to thousands of separate customers. In previous decades, the extensive record keeping needed for this great number of customers was attempted through paper-based filing systems, but through technological advances, this is now conducted through computerized CRM and ticketing systems. With a few clicks of a computer keyboard or mouse, a sales professional can now instantly identify a specific customer or a desired type of customer profile. In this same vein, professional sports have witnessed a dramatic increase in the use of **analytics** in the business and sales aspects of franchise operations. Ten or more years ago, few if any teams employed specialists in the area of CRM and analytics, but some teams now possess several such staff members. These employees are responsible for using statistical and technological expertise to assist the sales staff in identifying prospects with higher likelihood of purchasing tickets. Consider that if a franchise makes a thousand or more phone calls per day in trying to sell tickets, increasing the closing percentage of those calls by just a couple of percentage points increases the organization's sales revenue by a significant amount. The CRM and analytics teams work to help sales representatives be more efficient in their efforts along these lines.

**CUSTOMER RELATIONSHIP MANAGEMENT (CRM)** allows employees to merge all information collected from any touchpoint with a customer into a single, easily accessible database, providing a 360-degree picture of that fan or prospect

**ANALYTICS** the systematic analysis of data in order to provide information and/or insight

©Rawpixel.com/Shutterstock.com

## MINOR LEAGUE SPORTS

In contrast to their major league counterparts, minor league sport franchises have much smaller staffs, both in sales as well as the entire organizations. Major league franchises may employ hundreds of full-time staff, whereas minor league teams often employ two dozen or fewer on a full-time basis. The level of minor league sport is related to staff size; AAA-level (sometimes called Triple-A level) franchises typically have 30–50 employees on the business side of the organization, but A-level or independent franchises may have just a few full-time staff. At the AAA-level in baseball, or the comparable American Hockey League in hockey, these moderately-sized organizations are sometimes large enough to allow for specialized employee roles. If so, the organizational chart might resemble a smaller version of the major league teams described previously. A Triple-A baseball team might have a group sales function, for example, but it might consist of just one or two full-time staff and interns instead of a group of 8–10 full-time staff as on a major league team. Below this AAA level, organizations are much smaller and this reduced size makes it difficult to have specialized employee roles. In a lower-level minor league team, with perhaps 10 or so full-time employees, those employees often perform several different functions within the organization. An employee might help make outbound sales calls in the morning, prepare the facility for a game in the afternoon, and then work in the box office as game time approaches. That same employee might pitch in to serve hot dogs when the concessions lines get backed up or pull the tarp on the infield during a rain delay when the need arises. The potential downside to this limited staffing is that it becomes difficult to specialize and focus on a single function such as ticket sales, but the trade-off is that the variety of functions performed can keep the job from becoming mundane. Finally, while minor league baseball and hockey are among the best-known minor league team sport organizations, sales opportunities exist in professional sports such as lacrosse, softball, arena football, and other sport leagues as well.

## OTHER PROFESSIONAL SPORT ORGANIZATIONS AND INNOVATIVE SALES MODELS

Ticket sales opportunities extend beyond just major and minor league team sports. In auto racing, both individual tracks and governing bodies employ sales staff. One of the more interesting sales models has been implemented by the Professional Golfers Association (PGA) Tour in recent years. Most PGA Tour tournaments are operated locally by the individual event organizers, with small full-time staffs and rely heavily on volunteer assistance. The PGA Tour, housed in Ponte Vedra Beach, Florida, has created an inside sales team at its Florida headquarters patterned after the model used in major league team sports. Instead of selling tickets for a single PGA Tour event, this centralized team sells tickets for ten events managed by the PGA Tour itself. With this bundle of events, the total ticket inventory and corresponding ticket revenues are large enough to support the hiring of 12 full-time salespeople plus

2 executives to lead the team. Tickets are sold primarily over the phone and Internet out of the Tour's Florida headquarters even though the golf events take place across the country. Successful salespeople in the PGA Tour team may have the opportunity to be hired as sales managers for individual Tour events or elsewhere in the sport industry.

---

**Scott Gordon, Inside Sales Manager, PGA Tour**

### THE PGA TOUR INSIDE SALES PROGRAM

The PGA TOUR started an Inside Sales program in January 2014 that focuses on developing sales skills for entry level sales reps for senior level positions and driving new business revenue. With the major focus being on training, the team is provided with three hours per week of sessions involving anything from overcoming objections to appointment training. One way the TOUR's Inside Sales program is unique is how reps are coached on how to drive new business revenue throughout six different markets across the country. Reps are focused on selling corporate hospitality, expo space, advertising and Pro-Am opportunities to businesses who have never spent any money with the TOUR. With each lead that the Inside Sales rep mines, they get the opportunity to co-sell the package with a rep at the tournament. Reps will get the chance to learn from 14 different reps throughout the country and ultimately take what they learn to make it their own. This way, when they are promoted to one of the tournaments in a full-time sales role, they now have learned the fundamentals of what it takes to be successful.

© Kendall Hunt Publishing Company

---

Another innovative professional sport sales model is Major League Soccer's National Sales Center (NSC). Somewhat similar to the PGA Tour's inside sales team, the MLS NSC is a centralized model, but the focus of the MLS NSC is on training salespeople more than in generating sales revenue. Located in Blaine, Minnesota, outside of Minneapolis/St. Paul, the MLS NSC selects a group of trainees from its applicant pool and provides approximately four months of hands-on training during which trainees learn sales skills, receive feedback from expert trainers including the use of video and audio analysis, and even receive training in interpersonal skills through a partnership with a local improvisational comedy company. Successful trainees through the MLS NSC program are then interviewed and hired by MLS franchises across North America. To date, more than 160 MLS NSC graduates have been hired into full-time sales positions with MLS teams.

©George Rudy/Shutterstock.com

## COLLEGE ATHLETICS

While many professional sport teams have possessed extensive ticket sales operations for decades, operations at the college athletics level have been much slower to develop. Historically, college athletic departments have possessed box offices, or ticket offices, that were focused on **inbound sales**, but not outbound sales. In short, these box offices were order-takers, waiting for the phone to ring from an inbound call, an order form and check to arrive in the mail, or for someone to show up at the ticket window. In the 1990s and early 2000s, when professional sport teams were rapidly developing their outbound ticket sales teams, college athletics was slower to adapt and focused predominantly on inbound sales. This is not atypical in the sport industry, as college athletics can sometimes lag behind their professional counterparts in innovation. Other examples of the lag include the growth of sponsorship sales, developments in the public relations/communications area, and in the use of analytics and technology. One potential explanation for this could be that professional sport teams have an owner demanding success both on the playing field and in the financial aspects of the organization, whereas college athletic departments aren't owned but operate as a non-profit organization. Another explanation for slower innovation in college athletics is that athletic departments are a part of a larger university community that typically possesses considerable layers of management and bureaucracy, while professional sport teams are smaller, and thus nimbler business organizations.

**INBOUND SALES**
order-takers, waiting for the phone to ring from an inbound call, an order form and check to arrive in the mail, or for someone to show up at the ticket window

Regardless of these reasons for slower development in **outbound sales**, college athletic departments have begun to catch up over the last decade. The early leader in this area was the University of Central Florida (UCF), which hired Matt DiFebo in 2005 from the NBA's Seattle SuperSonics, to help increase its sales revenues. DiFebo's new sales team increased football season ticket sales at UCF by 12,000 tickets and increased annual football ticket revenue by more than $4.5 million in just three years.[3] Other university athletic programs took note and attempted to emulate UCF's ticket sales success. By the early 2010s, most Division I athletic departments had formed their own outbound ticket sales teams, although they typically remain much smaller in scope than their professional sport counterparts. For example, whereas many major league pro teams have 50 or more sales employees, college athletic departments generally have fewer than 10.

**OUTBOUND SALES**
sales personnel who make outbound calls to prospects

One interesting aspect to this development of ticket sales forces in college athletics has been the use of **outsourcing**. While some athletic departments utilize their own staff to sell tickets, others have outsourced their sales operations to an external third-party company (this is also common with the sale of sponsorships in college sports). External companies may provide an expertise in sales that an athletic department does not possess internally. Furthermore, external companies may compensate their sales employees with commission pay structures, which is often difficult for athletic departments to otherwise do internally because of its rarity in university systems. Two leading outsourcing companies in this area are IMG Learfield Ticket Solutions, originally led by Matt DiFebo after his departure from UCF, and The Aspire Group, which is overseen by longtime NBA executive and sport marketing pioneer Bernie Mullin.

**OUTSOURCING**
hiring third-party organizations to handle a portion of the business, such as selling tickets

## PURSUING A CAREER IN SPORT SALES

What does a career path in sport sales look like? The starting place for most new salespeople in sports is inside ticket sales. As mentioned earlier in the chapter, these positions are not intended to be long-term positions but, rather, typically last 9–12 months. Inside sales representatives who show success and promise have opportunities to move up in the organization into more permanent, and higher-paying, sales roles. Those who do not have success do not have such opportunities. For those considering whether to pursue the sales path and inside sales positions, this lack of permanency may be concerning, or perhaps even scary. One way to consider this is not only does the

---

3. DiFebo, S. (2008, September 8). *Season-ticket sales success often starts with staffing, training.* Retrieved from www.sportsbusinessdaily.com

organization have this time period to evaluate the sales representative, but the new sales representative also has the same time period to evaluate both the organization as well as the sales profession, to examine whether this path is right for them. Inside sales representatives who are not successfully promoted often find that this is as a result of effort and/or passion for the sales profession, rather than simply not selling enough tickets.

---

### TIPS FOR INTERVIEWING FOR YOUR FIRST SALES POSITION

You have secured an interview for an inside sales position with a professional sport team, or perhaps a college athletic department. You have likely spent years preparing for such an opportunity with hard work in college classrooms and gaining experience through volunteer opportunities and internships. Here is some advice for being successful in that sales interview:

1. Dress conservatively. While relatively casual attire is commonplace in some areas of the sport industry, sales departments typically dress more formally. Unless you have strong evidence that the sales department you are interviewing with has a much more relaxed dress code, wear a suit or comparable type of formal attire. For men, choose subdued, rather than bold, shirts and ties. For women, err on the side of simple and conservative with jewelry and other accessories.

2. Be ready to sell yourself. As you are interviewed for a position as a salesperson, hiring managers will be evaluating your ability to sell. In the interview, you are, first and foremost, selling yourself. Be prepared to confidently describe why you will be successful in this position. Do your homework on the organization and the people you will be interviewing with so that you can show how well prepared you are.

3. Don't be a fan. Your interest in working in sports likely stems from being a sport fan to some degree. That said, sales managers are not looking to hire fans. They are looking to hire employees who can help them reach their sales goals. If you are asked a question like "Why are you interested in this position?" consider discussing your passion for sales and revenue generation more so than your passion for that team or sport. Some hiring managers will go so far as to automatically eliminate any candidate whom answers such a question with a "super-fan" type of answer.

---

**CUSTOMER SERVICE**
the interactions a business has with a customer before, during, and after a customer purchases a product

Inside sales representatives who are successfully promoted often earn positions in group sales, season ticket sales, or **customer service** and retention. Sometimes the path to one of those options is based on how the organization's sales managers believe the representative's skill set fits those options, but the coincidental timing of openings in one area or another can be a factor as well. In terms of fit, the organization learns a lot about the sales representative's strengths and weaknesses as a seller during the inside sales period. Those with a strength as a "hunter" in the hunter/farmer model described earlier in this chapter may be best used in a season ticket sales department as they work hard to drive new business. Those with abilities to develop relationships with potential group leaders from area businesses and community organizations may fit best in a group sales capacity. Finally, those that may not be best suited at making 100 cold calls per day, but who have skills in working with clients, may fit well on a service and retention group.

After a couple of years of success in areas such as group sales, season ticket sales, or customer service/retention, opportunities for further career growth may present themselves. Those with continued success in generating new business may be a fit for the premium sales team, selling luxury seats, club seating, and other premium inventory. Another similarly prestigious area of the sales operation is in corporate sales and sponsorships. Both the premium and corporate areas often involve making single sales worth several hundred thousand dollars, or perhaps even more than a million dollars, so these advancement opportunities are typically reserved for elite sellers. Another path that might emerge is in sales management, such as being the director of the inside sales team, the group sales team, and so on. The skill set needed for success as a sales manager may be quite different than the skills needed to simply sell tickets or other inventory, as the managerial role focuses primarily on leading people rather than selling products. Organizations often struggle to identify and train these managers/leaders given the differences in skills and duties compared to the standard sales role. Sales managers found to have success in leadership capacities may eventually climb to positions like Vice President of Ticket Sales, or even Team President.

---

**Kyle Brant, Director of Group Sales, San Jose Sharks**

### SUCCEEDING IN SPORT SALES

So you want to be the next "Wolf of Wall Street"? But you also have a strong passion for the business of sports, knowing full well that you most likely won't be rubbing elbows with the likes of Steph Curry or Aaron Rogers, but rather playing an integral part in the creation of a memory that your soon-to-be clients will recall for the rest of their lives.

Well, everyone has to start somewhere. And when it comes to breaking into the Sport Sales Industry there are ways you can stand out from the pack.

### Internship Tips

Having been in the role of Inside Sales Manager for an NBA team and hiring rookie-sellers, I can attest to the important role internships play in standing out. Specifically, when it comes to breaking into sport sales, a general sport team internship where you're doing everything from being an usher to running on-field promotions is great. A more specific sport sales internship where you're cold calling and experiencing the ground floor of selling is better.

As for general sport internships, when you're rolling a tarp on a rainy July morning you probably won't learn much about what it's like to cold-call a single game buyer or how to overcome buyer objections. But you will build character and you will quickly find out during those long hours whether or not you are truly passionate about the *business* of sports. Most hiring managers, like myself, were involved in multiple sport internships before becoming full-time. The hustle does not go unnoticed and gets you one step closer to your dream.

Sport internships in which you are engaged in selling are better for both you and hiring managers. These internships provide you with hands-on, real-life experience of what your future could be like. Many look to sport sales as a way to break into the industry, but when they actually break in, they quickly realize what selling is all about and they typically find themselves out of sports shortly thereafter. This hands-on internship experience provides you the basic building blocks of sport sales: what it's like to cold-call, the importance of relationship-building, and of course, what it's like to be told no 99 times out of 100 . . . not to mention the sweet taste of victory on that 100th call. Experiencing this provides no "surprise" of job expectations on your first day because you know exactly what you're getting into.

For hiring managers, sport sales internships are more attractive for many of the same reasons. As a hiring manager, you want to ensure that there is no surprise of job duties when hiring. The goal is to always have your new employee comfortable with their surroundings and daily expectations before they accept the position. From my experience, very few hiring managers look toward these internships as a way to hire polished ticket sales experts. Being polished is not the expectation from these internships. The expectation is that you've experienced a taste of what sport sales is and that you've found passion in your time spent doing so. My belief has always been that I can teach you how to sell; I can teach you how to build relationships; I can teach you how to overcome objections; I can teach you when to be assertive; I can teach you how to close . . . but I can't teach you to be passionate about what you do; I can't teach "want"; and I can't teach work ethic.

### Seeking Employment Tips

As I'm sure you've learned by now, full-time positions within the sport industry don't grow on trees. There are certainly great portals online where you can easily view openings, learn about them, and apply to them online. The downside is that you're relying on just a resume and/or cover letter to get noticed while competing against a mass amount of other applicants with similar background and education as you.

Fortunately, there is another avenue for those seeking employment within the sport sales industry where you not only receive training from some of the best in the industry, but you also have the ability to network and interview with hiring sales managers from both collegiate and professional sport franchises. These are called "Sport Sales Workshops" and they're growing in both popularity and in number; a favorite is the annual "Mount Union Sport Sales Workshop" in Cleveland, Ohio. This is the workshop where I was hired out of, and most teams see it as a must-attend. However, there are other workshops growing in popularity around the country and teams are starting to host their own as a way of attracting local talent.

It is not enough to just attend one of these workshops. Although these workshops provide you a great opportunity to network and build relationships with employers, you still need to stand out amongst the hundreds of other candidates who are attending by taking advantage of that opportunity.

Here are four tips on how to stand out at your next workshop:

1. Come Prepared:
   - Have copies of your resume, printed on quality paper, as well as any other applicable documents. Have experience selling? Include your stats!
   - Research the teams attending and who is representing each team.
   - Create a solid LinkedIn profile with a professional looking headshot.
   - Meeting with a team? Do your research on LinkedIn, have a general idea of that person's background. This will create talking points for you as you find common ground, and you will stand out since most attendees will not take the time to do this.

2. Be Professional:
   - Business professional—there is no such thing as being overdressed.
   - Firm handshake, good eye contact, speak well.

3. Get Comfortable Being Uncomfortable:
   - During the training sessions, volunteer when asked.
   - If you're nervous or frightened about saying or doing something wrong, then you're on the right track. Just remember, be professional and do your best.
   - Don't hide—network, build relationships, be confident.

4. Put Your Passion on Display:
   - When it comes to networking and interviewing, tell your story. Everyone has a story, make yours stick out. Many call this an "elevator speech," where you have 30–45 seconds to sell YOU. If you can't sell yourself first, then teams won't trust you to sell for them.

Sport Sales is an industry that generously rewards those willing to step outside their comfort zones and those willing to go the extra mile. Breaking into Sport Sales requires these same abilities.

It should be noted that career paths are often not linear. An examination of a professional team's staff directory generally reveals a majority of employees in their 20s and 30s. It is not uncommon for a salesperson in professional or collegiate sport to get hired away by one of their own clients in another line of business, particularly as many other industries pay higher wages or have less demanding hours. Transitioning out of sport is fairly frequent along these lines. Even within sport, sales representatives may move elsewhere within the organization or to another peer organization commonly.

Finally, compensation increases as salespeople move from inside sales to account executive and beyond. Even more encouraging, job and career satisfaction also generally increase as sellers move up the organizational chart.[4] In comparison to non-sport sales positions, Kirk Wakefield notes that "teams are able to attract able-bodied candidates with compensation levels markedly below starting salaries of sales and marketing graduates working in other industries ($51,900). That said, once promoted to an account executive position, prospects begin looking up." Table 2.1 shows the average total compensation, job satisfaction, and career satisfaction for salespeople in various sales positions in professional sports.

## Table 2.1

**Compensation and Satisfaction**

| Title | Average Total Compensation | Job Satisfaction | Career Satisfaction |
|---|---|---|---|
| Vice President | $226,820 | 93 | 94 |
| Senior Director | $168,820 | 80 | 81 |
| Director | $109,430 | 91 | 92 |
| Manager | $ 74,560 | 77 | 81 |
| Senior Account Executive | $ 84,360 | 80 | 79 |
| Account Executive | $ 48,700 | 82 | 84 |
| Inside Sales | $ 26,670 | 77 | 73 |

Note: N = 633*

*Baylor S3 Report. Retrieved from http://baylors3.com/top-5-things-we-learned-about-compensation-salespeople-and-their-managers/.

4. *Baylor S3 Report.* Retrieved from http://baylors3.com/top-5-things-we-learned-about-compensation-salespeople-and-their-managers/.

**Buffy Filippell, Owner, Teamwork Online**

## HOW TO MAKE YOUR APPLICATION STAND OUT

TeamWork Online is a mobile platform for anyone aspiring to land a career in sports and live events, particularly sales executives. We host a mobile recruiting and networking platform, network events, and career fairs. We also conduct executive searches on behalf of employers in the sports and live event industry. Over 100,000 people have been matched to their dream jobs through TeamWork Online's products and services.

Here are four stories of TeamWork Online hires and how they augmented their applications and landed a position in sales.

**Casey Katz, 2015 Mount Union Sport Sales Workshop Attendee, now Account Manager, Miami Heat**

One of the more popular events on the calendar for aspiring young ticket sales professionals is the Mount Union Sport Sales Workshop held in February. TeamWork Online is a promoter of this event. Over 50 Inside Sales Managers from the NBA, NFL, MLS, MLB, and other leagues trek to Cleveland, Ohio, to be able to meet up with the next up-and-comers in the sport industry who think they want to start their careers in sales. There have been wonderful connections made and a number of outstanding executives hired.

Casey Katz offered these suggestions on how to interview and land a job after her successful event:

- ▶ Don't be afraid to talk to anyone, and have a value proposition—what can you provide the employer?

- ▶ When you meet a sales hiring manager, keep the conversation going by asking a lot of questions, about his/her background, how he/she landed the position, what he/she likes most about his/her job, etc.

- ▶ Ask for feedback. Sales hiring managers really like "coachable" employees. Show you are willing to learn.

- ▶ Line up meetings in advance of events. If you can find out who will be attending an event ahead of time, you will beat out the competition; reach out to the sales hiring managers early. Ask for e-mail addresses from the event organizer, or use the team's home page to figure out someone's e-mail address and write them. Most sport executives use e-mail to communicate.

- ▶ Keep introducing yourself to people and remind them of your value proposition.

- ▶ After a conference, job fair, or networking event—almost immediately—send an e-mail to each person you met, remind them of your value proposition, and if you can remember anything about your conversation, add that to your e-mail.

Sales is all about how much money have you raised.

Many individuals have raised money for their fraternity or charities of their choice. Whether you've raised $500 or $10,000, any amount is a meaningful and significant accomplishment that can catch the eye of a sales manager in the sport industry.

### Matt Ritchie, Manager of Inside Sales, Cincinnati Reds

Matt landed his management position online. How he stood out was through his online 140-character headline, "In my last 4 years of selling I hit my sales goal for selling by over $100,000 in my last 3 out of the 4 years selling." If you can put metrics to what you have to offer, you get attention.

### Melanie Seiser, Manager of Major League Soccer's National Sales Center

Melanie was one of the first class of hires for Major League Soccer's National Sales Center. All applicants were asked to send in a video. Melanie's video became one of the most watched elevator pitch videos of all sport and of course landed her in the first class of executives trained to become sales executives. It's pleasing to see she is training the next generation: https://www.youtube.com/embed/hoKztt13WEg

Melanie, a journalism major from Ohio University, is often asked why she chose sales as a profession. She believes that sales is all about relationship building and providing the best possible fan experience. "If you are looking for the opportunity to connect with the fan and create lifelong memories for them, then I would highly recommend getting into ticket sales and particularly the MLS National Sales Center."

Senior executives interested in moving into sales roles need to have a track record of sales as well as good references.

### Michael DeMartino, Vice President Corporate Partnerships, Jacksonville Jaguars

Michael DeMartino, was living in New Jersey working for the New Jersey Jets as a suite sales executive and wanted to move from premium seating sales to corporate sponsorship sales. He had sold some sponsorships earlier in his career. His resume said his title was Director of Premium Sales. Michael decided to use a social media platform to tell his story. He crafted an about.me page and made a headline that said: "Sold millions of dollars in corporate sponsorships." He applied for the job online then sent a link to that page to the hiring manager for the Jacksonville Jaguars, who read the headline, called a friend of his in New Jersey, received a good reference, and hired Michael for a sponsorship sales job.

---

## CHAPTER SUMMARY

Sales is a vital part of nearly any sport organization. The revenues are the backbone of successful organizations. Professional sport teams and, more recently, intercollegiate athletic departments utilize sales personnel to generate revenue. A career in sport sales can provide an opportunity for employment in the industry and room to grow in this regard.

## CHAPTER ACTIVITIES

1. Find a current job posting online for one group sales, inside sales, and premium sales position in professional sports. Based on these descriptions, describe the similarities and differences between these three types of sales positions.

2. Create a graphic or image that illustrates the typical career progression in sport sales, beginning at the entry-level and moving toward senior management levels.

3. Explain the hunter/farmer model of sales staffing. What is meant by the terms "hunters" and "farmers"?

4. What function does the CRM personnel serve within a sales team?

5. How does the sales staff differ between a major league professional sport franchise and a minor league franchise?

6. Explain why college athletics programs have been slower to adopt significant sales structures compared to their professional sport team peers.

# CHAPTER 3

## PRODUCTS AND PRICING

**LEARNING OBJECTIVES**

After completing this chapter, you should be able to:

▶ Understand the types of ticket packages offered by spectator sport organizations.

▶ Comprehend the connection between product usage and ticket packaging through the frequency escalator model.

▶ Appreciate the importance of pricing strategy to an organization's revenue generation efforts.

▶ Understand the internal and external factors typically influencing price setting.

▶ Comprehend common strategies used in the setting of ticket prices.

▶ Understand recent trends in pricing within the sport industry.

**KEY TERMS**

| | | |
|---|---|---|
| Branding | Elasticity | Premium pricing |
| Bundle pricing | Flex-book plan | Primary ticket market |
| Business-to-business (B2B) sales | Frequency escalator | Product line pricing |
| | Group tickets | Season ticket |
| Business-to-consumer (B2C) sales | Luxury suite | Secondary ticket market |
| | Membership club | Single game ticket |
| Club seat | Partial plan | Skim pricing |
| Consumer demand | Penetration pricing | Ticket package |
| Customary pricing | Personal seat license (PSL) | Value |
| Dynamic pricing | | Variable ticket pricing |

## CHAPTER OVERVIEW

Before beginning to sell, it is imperative that any new salesperson first understand exactly what it is they are selling. New sales representatives hired by a major league professional sport team often spend hours touring the stadium or arena of the team they work for to get a feel for the layout of seating sections and may take written exams after memorizing the facility map and price guide for the team. This chapter will discuss sport products and packages commonly sold in the industry, as well as pricing strategies and trends. These topics will focus on the ticket sales context, with a secondary discussion of sport sponsorships also included.

## THE SPORT PRODUCT

A ticket to a sporting event is unlike many other products we purchase. When a consumer goes to the grocery store to buy a bag of tortilla chips, they know what they are getting. The product is tangible, predicable, and consistent. Those chips look, feel, and taste the same as the last time the consumer bought a bag, and they will the next time of purchase as well. In fact, if that wasn't the case, the consumer would likely be displeased to the point where they wouldn't buy that brand of chips again in the future. The spectator sport product is very different in nature. The home baseball team may win today's game 9–6, but lose tomorrow's game 3–0, despite both teams playing on the same field with the same players. The inconsistent and unpredictable nature of the sport product is one of its essential elements. If every sporting event was a repeat of the same plays and ended with the same results, the suspense factor would be taken away and fans would quickly lose interest. Again, this is quite opposite of many products we buy, such as tortilla chips or other goods.

Another key difference between the spectator sport product and other products is its intangible nature. When buying a piece of clothing, a laptop computer, or other goods, they are tangible in that the consumer can touch them, hold them, and use them for a length of time into the future. That also is not the case with attending a sporting event. The fan cannot touch and hold the soccer match in their hands as they can a laptop computer. Additionally, that sporting event is being produced and consumed simultaneously, and when it is over, it is over. It cannot be used for years into the future as a laptop can.

At its core, selling tickets to a sporting event involves selling an experience and memory rather than a tangible product like a tortilla chip or laptop computer. Many years later, a spectator might vividly remember attending a game with their parent, and then subsequently having the same experience with their own children someday. This experiential, intangible, unpredictable, and inconsistent nature makes sports the original reality show and truly a unique product to sell.

## TICKET PACKAGES

When visiting the website for professional sport teams, as well as many college athletic programs, the ticket offering page of the website likely reveals numerous types of **ticket packages** for sale. Such a menu might include season tickets, half-season tickets, a variety of other smaller packages, or bundles, of tickets such as 10-game packs of tickets, 5-game packs, weekend or weeknight packages, single game tickets, group tickets, club seats, luxury seating, and so on. This menu of offerings is so vast for some organizations that it can even be a little overwhelming to certain potential customers. As such, this raises the question of why do teams offer so many choices. In short, sport organizations offer a variety of different packages in order to meet the variety of different needs and wants possessed by consumers. For example, some fans only want to attend every home game. The season ticket was, of course, designed for this type of fan. Other fans, however, are only interested in attending one or two games a season. Purchasing season tickets for thousands of dollars does not make sense in this case, but rather, a single game ticket is likely a better fit.

An essential framework for understanding the needs of different consumers in purchase frequency is the **frequency escalator** model, which is more thoroughly discussed in the series of sport marketing textbooks by authors Bernie Mullin, Steve Hardy, and Bill Sutton.[1] In their discussion of market segmentation and target marketing, Mullin, Hardy, and Sutton put forth the frequency escalator as a framework for understanding how different types of consumers can be viewed based upon their level of using or purchasing the product. As seen in Figure 3.1, the escalator portrays an increasing purchasing pattern from non-consumers to light users to medium users to heavy users. Mullin, Hardy, and Sutton explain that the goal of sport marketing and sales personnel is to help move customers up the escalator, from a medium user to a heavy user, for example. As discussed previously, sport organizations provide different types of ticket packages in order to meet the various needs and wants of different types of consumers.

**TICKET PACKAGE**
a variety of different packages in order to meet the variety of different needs and wants possessed by consumers

**FREQUENCY ESCALATOR**
a framework for understanding how different types of consumers can be viewed based upon their level of using or purchasing the product

---

1. Mullin, B., Hardy, S., & Sutton, W. (2014). *Sport marketing,* 4th ed. Champaign, IL: Human Kinetics, 303.

## Figure 3.1

**Frequency Escalator**

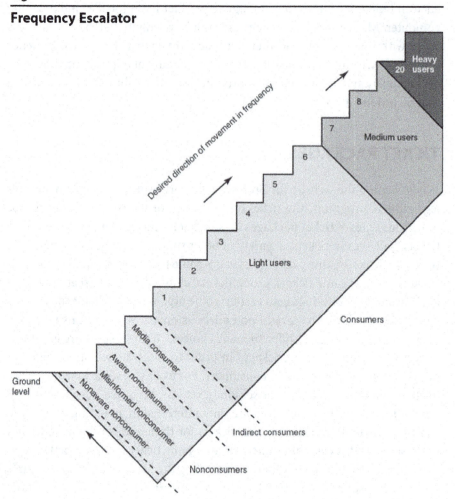

Reprinted with permission from B. J. Mullin, S. Hardy, and W. A. Sutton, 2014, *Sport Marketing*, 4th ed. (Champaign, IL: Human Kinetics), 303.

## *Season Tickets*

**SEASON TICKET**
provides access to every home game for the organization

A common ticket packaging type offered by virtually all spectator sport organizations is the **season ticket**, which provides access to every home game for the organization. In college or professional football, this might represent just 6–8 games, whereas in Major League Baseball, season tickets include 81 home games. Related to the frequency escalator framework, season tickets are, of course, targeted for heavy users. As the largest bundle of tickets, season tickets to major league professional sport teams or high level collegiate athletic programs can be quite expensive. A pair of season tickets to one of these teams could cost $10,000 or more. Accordingly, a salesperson would qualify prospective buyers to examine whether they possessed both the financial ability and desire to attend so many games. Selling season tickets is, of course, a top priority for spectator sport organizations. Not only are they lucrative as a revenue stream, but it provides the organization's sales staff with the security that those seats are sold for the entire season, no matter how well or poorly the team may perform. No further effort will be required from the sales staff to continue to sell those same seats throughout the season to game after game.

Because of the high cost and high volume of tickets, particularly in sports like baseball, basketball, and hockey, season tickets are often sold in a **business-to-business (B2B)** manner, as businesses are more likely to have the financial means to afford such an expensive ticket package. Businesses can then use the tickets for a variety of purposes, such as entertaining clients and rewarding employees. When sold to personal consumers rather than business, what is known as **B2C (business-to-consumer) sales**, these individuals will often sell some of the tickets on the secondary market through outlets such as StubHub. For example, an individual that buys a pair of season tickets from a Major League Baseball team may end up attending 50 or 60 of the games themselves, which is still quite a few of course, but selling the remaining tickets to recoup part of the cost of their season ticket investment for games they cannot or will not attend. Another common way that B2C buyers sometimes utilize the large volume of events that come with a season ticket package is to split them with friends, family, or other acquaintances. For example, four couples may split a pair of season tickets to a National League Hockey franchise where each couple gets the pair of tickets to 10 home games. The movie "Fever Pitch" showed a group of friends selecting Boston Red Sox games they would attend through a draft-style format.

**BUSINESS-TO-BUSINESS (B2B) SALES**
selling to businesses

**BUSINESS-TO-CONSUMER (B2C) SALES**
selling to consumers

As sport organizations rely on a strong season ticket base as the backbone of their ticket sales revenues, teams emphasize strong customer service and often provide a variety of perks in order to entice medium users to increase their purchase level up to the season ticket, and, in particular, to retain their season ticket holders from one year to the next. Season ticket retention rate is a commonly used metric in sport sales to track how successful the organization is in getting their season ticket holders to renew their tickets for the next season. While this may vary from sport to sport or organization to organization, a season ticket retention rate in the 80–85% range is generally considered good with 90% or more considered very strong. As it is far easier to keep an existing customer satisfied and renewing their tickets than it is to identify and cultivate a brand new buyer into becoming a season ticket holder, service and retention is a top priority for ticket sales departments.

## *Partial Plans*

Professional sport franchises, particularly those in sports with high numbers of home games, typically offer a number of different types of ticket bundles below the size of the full season ticket but larger than just a game or two. These are referred to in the sport industry as partial plans, meaning that they are a partial segment of the full season ticket. One common form of a **partial plan** is bundles like a half season ticket or a quarter season ticket. In MLB, for example, these would represent 40-game and 20-game options, respectively. Similar to the full season ticket, these options still represent a significant investment in both cost and frequency of attendance, and thus target the medium-to-heavy user on the escalator model. Organizations will also often offer some smaller partial plan bundles in the 5–10 game range. A three-game or four-game bundle is likely the smallest partial plan teams will provide. These represent and attempt to entice the light user who might otherwise buy a single game ticket to consider upgrading toward becoming a moderate user. As discussed with the frequency escalator framework, the marketing and sales strategy with this type of bundling is aimed toward meeting the needs of different types of users as well as to encourage consumers to move a step up the escalator toward heavier usage, and therefore increased revenue for the organization.

**PARTIAL PLAN**
different types of ticket bundles below the size of the full season ticket but larger than just a game or two

One factor the sport organization must account for in designing its partial plan strategy is whether the team or the customer chooses which games are part of the package. With a 10-game plan, for example, does the customer get to pick which 10 games or are the games pre-chosen by the team? There are advantages and disadvantages to both formats. Many fans prefer the flexibility to customize their package, providing them with the opportunity to select the opponents or dates they desire. Some fans, however, prefer the simplicity of the games being pre-selected by the organization, and the organization thus maintains control over its inventory in this model. A common format is a tiered menu of choices, where the customer might, for example, have the ability to select a certain number of games from a top, elite tier of match-ups, another number from a secondary tier of somewhat desirable matchups, and then some games from a lesser tier. Another common format is what is known as a coupon book of tickets, where purchasers receive a specific number of tickets to use however they choose throughout the season. A 20-ticket coupon book could be redeemed as 4 tickets to each of 5 different games, 2 tickets to 10 games each, or any other combination. This again provides flexibility and customization opportunities for the consumer. Some organizations call this option a **flex-book plan** based on its flexible nature.

**FLEX-BOOK PLAN**
buyers receive a specific number of tickets to use however they choose throughout the season

In order to motivate potential buyers to consider purchasing a partial plan instead of simply buying single game tickets instead, organizations offer various incentives in this regard. A simple incentive is a financial discount. Buying tickets to five games for the regular price of four games is a common example. Other financial incentives could include discounts on concessions, merchandise, or parking with the purchase of the partial plan. Another type of incentive used is exclusivity. A partial plan might include tickets to games that are otherwise difficult to obtain, such as those against an elite opposing team or player, or events like homecoming in college football or opening day in professional baseball.

## *Group Tickets*

Another ticket type offered in many spectator sport settings is **group tickets**. Whereas season tickets and partial plans are focused on having the same customers attending a higher quantity of games, group tickets are instead focused on having a higher quantity of customers as a group attending a single game. While season tickets and partial plans target heavy and medium users on the frequency escalator, group tickets are often an effective tool for introducing the product to a non-consumer. Some non-consumers may follow the team, but for reasons such as cost or access are not in the practice of buying tickets and attending. These non-consumers may simply need some sort of catalyst to get them to the game. The organization's hope then is that they will enjoy their experience and attend more frequently in the future. Group tickets can serve as this sort of catalyst where the potential consumer chooses to buy tickets and attend a game with a group.

**GROUP TICKETS** focused on having a higher quantity of customers as a group attending a single game

Sport organizations, particularly those that are effective with group sales, target a wide variety of different types of groups in their sales efforts. Common group types include employees from a business and civic groups such as schools, organizations like Boy Scouts and Girl Scouts, and youth sport teams or leagues. Many teams get creative in their group sales efforts. The next time you attend a sporting event, you might be surprised to learn that the choral group singing the national anthem was not chosen because they were the best choral group in the area, but rather because they committed to buying a block of tickets to the game (hopefully also possessing strong singing voices). Similarly, band, cheer, and dance group sales are often cultivated in a similar manner. A team might invite a group of 100 youth cheerleaders to perform on the field with the team's own cheer squad, and even provide free admission for those 100 youths, if they can sell a few hundred tickets to the group's parents, grandparents, and siblings who want to watch their young family member cheer on the field.

Buying a group block of tickets often carries the incentive of a discounted price, although those discounts can be moderate in nature, typically between

10% and 20%. Sport organizations specify their definition of a group by stating a minimum number of tickets necessary to receive the discounted price. This ticket minimum varies by team, but standard minimums are often 15 or 20.

A key aspect to successful group sales is identifying and cultivating strong group leaders. For salespeople, finding the right person within an organization is extremely valuable, often doing a lot of the sales work in a sense, in that the group leader can take the initiative to organize the group and promote the event to their peers. For example, if the salesperson connects with a particular member of a local youth sport organization, that member could persuade dozens of their peers within the organization to buy tickets as part of the group activity. The key for the salesperson in this regard is finding the right group member that is willing to be the leader, organize the event as a group activity, and to promote it within the group. Once an effective group leader is found, the sales organization is wise to work hard to serve and incentivize that group leader, as they may be helpful in bringing their group back to games in the future. This might include providing free tickets to another contest to that group leader or providing them with some team merchandise from existing inventory.

## Single Game Tickets

Selling individual tickets to games is a common practice for almost nearly every spectator sport organization. Thousands of spectators, typically light users on the frequency escalator, buy tickets to just one or two games per year on a game-by-game basis. These consumers may be attending with family, friends, business associates, or some combination thereof. The challenge for the sport organization is in how to strategically to sell individual game tickets. Tasking the inside sales team to make hundreds of calls in hopes of selling **single game tickets** in batches of perhaps two-to-four is not a strong return on investment of the sales personnel's time and effort. Likewise, it doesn't make sense to arrange face-to-face sales appointments in an attempt to sell a pair of $20 tickets. That is not an effective use of the time and energy of sales personnel. Instead, sport organizations may advertise that individual game tickets are on sale through both traditional media and digital media, and then hope sales are made in an inbound manner, through buyers calling the ticket office phone number or purchasing online through the organization's website. Special events and giveaway promotions are sometimes used in an effort to increase the sale of single game tickets. Prospective buyers might be enticed to purchase in order to receive a collectable bobblehead or to celebrate the reunion of the team's championship winning squad from years ago.

**SINGLE GAME TICKET**
individual tickets to games

## Premium Seating

As discussed in Chapter 2, premium seating areas in a stadium or arena carry amenities beyond most seats in the facility. The two primary types of premium seating are luxury suites and club seats. **Luxury suites** are private boxes that allow the customer to have a high-end living room of sorts within the stadium or arena. Suites vary in size, but commonly hold between 10 and 25 people, with larger ones typically priced higher of course. One common amenity with luxury suites is the option to purchase catered food and beverage. This adds to both the exclusivity and cost of purchasing a suite. Suites are commonly purchased on a multi-year basis, with 5- or even 10-year purchases normal. **Club seats**, in contrast, are more analogous to a first-class ticket on an airplane flight. Just as first-class seating on a plane may include larger and more comfortable seats, wait staff service, and higher end food and drink options, club seats at a stadium or arena share similar attributes.

**LUXURY SUITE**
private boxes that allow the customer to have a high-end living room of sorts within the stadium or arena

In line with the elite benefits possessed by both luxury suites and club seats, these are very expensive purchases compared to other seating options at a sporting event. Luxury suites at a major professional sport franchise can cost hundreds of thousands of dollars per year, or even greater than one million dollars per year in some cases. Accordingly, the cost is often far beyond the budget of individual consumers and prospective buyers are almost always businesses. Cultivating and closing on the sale of a multi-year luxury suite sale is a long and difficult sales process, but one that, if successful, can be very lucrative financially for the sport organization and the salesperson who earns the corresponding commission for that sale.

**CLUB SEAT**
more expensive seating that may include larger and more comfortable seats, wait staff service and higher end food and drink options

## Sponsorship

One last sport product type sold by sport organizations is corporate sponsorship. Just as sport organizations offer a menu with a variety of ticket products to meet the different wants and needs of spectators, the same is true with sponsorships as well. As will be discussed further in Chapter 15, businesses approach sponsorships as an opportunity to meet certain business objectives, and those vary from company to company. Examples include increasing brand awareness, shaping public image, reaching a certain target market, or entertaining clients. Sport organizations offer a menu of different types of sponsorship products in order to meet these diverse business objectives. Common sponsorship inventory offered by sport organizations includes:

- ► Naming rights for a facility or event
- ► In-venue signage

- ▶ Advertising on organization controlled or partnered television, radio, Internet, or print media
- ▶ Logo placement on team products such as schedule posters and cards, ticket backs, and promotional items
- ▶ Event hospitality

## PRICING

In addition to understanding the types of products to be sold, it is also imperative that sales personnel comprehend the pricing of those products. In many industries, an organization's marketing and sales staff has considerable control of nearly all aspects of the product. Take a piece of apparel for example. Marketing and sales personnel will likely have input into the color, pattern design, cut, packaging, and price of the apparel item. This is not the case with a professional sporting event or other spectator event. The pro team's marketing and sales personnel cannot dictate to the general manager which players they want to draft or sign as most marketable. Likewise, if the marketing and sales staff tried to tell a football coach to run certain plays in order to make the team's offense more exciting, one could only imagine how the coach might react. Pricing is one area, however, that marketing and sales personnel can typically control.

In considering an organization's pricing strategy, a key focal point must be what the organization's goals are in their pricing. For most sport organizations, as is true throughout so many industries, maximizing revenue generation is the primary pricing goal. In ticket sales, organizations seek to find price points where they can make the most revenue. This is not always the case, however. In college athletics, for example, most athletic departments provide their university's students with discounts far below what the general public pays. At many of these universities, the athletic department could instead choose to maximize revenue by converting those student tickets to general public ones and charging a much higher price. The rationale for charging students a lower price is aligned with the goal of providing students with affordable entertainment and connecting them with the university in a positive manner. While revenue maximization is a standard pricing goal, this example shows that this is not always the case and that multiple pricing goals might exist for particular sport organizations.

Pricing is an important aspect of the organization's sales and marketing efforts, and not something to be taken lightly. While organizations aspire to set their prices at an optimal price point where tickets sold multiplied by the price yields the maximum revenue generation, pricing is an inexact science where that optimal price point is unknown at the time in advance of an event when prices are established. Let's assume hypothetically that we happen to know that for a particular professional basketball game, the optimal price point for the 20,000-seat arena is $50, thus yielding $1 million in ticket revenue for a sellout game in multiplying those two figures together. Again, sales and marketing professionals do not know what an optimal price point will be in advance, but rather are attempting to identify it through examining past ticket sales data and other analytics. If the team sets prices at an average of $35 per ticket, what is the likely outcome? Tickets will sell well and the facility will be full, but the organization will fall far short of maximizing ticket revenue. Selling 20,000 tickets at $35 each would yield $700,000 in revenue, far short of the $1 million shown above. If the organization were to set prices at $70 per ticket for this game, well above the optimal price point, what will happen? The likelihood is that many seats will go unsold as prospective buyers will not pay the high prices. Let's assume that the team sells just 10,000 tickets at this $70 price point, generating $700,000 in ticket revenue. As this hypothetical example shows, selecting price points close to the optimal figure can help the sport organization generate considerably more revenue than if the prices are not set well. Sales and marketing professionals do not have the luxury of knowing what the optimal price point is in advance, however, as was the case in this example. As mentioned, pricing is a complex and challenging task that is best accomplished through strong analytical decision-making and an understanding of sound pricing principles, as will be explained throughout this chapter.

---

### UNDERPRICING VERSUS OVERPRICING

Considering the hypothetical basketball game pricing example used in the preceding section, if the team was unable to price at the optimal point to maximize revenue generation, is it better to price above or below the optimal level? Of course both scenarios would result in less than optimal revenue generation—in our hypothetical example, both the underpricing and overpricing scenarios yielded $700,000 in ticket revenue, well short of the optimal $1 million figure. Consider two factors here. First, ticket revenue is not the only source of revenue connected to attendance. Increased attendance should lead to additional revenue in areas such as parking, concessions, and merchandise sales. Second, think about the optics for a moment. The underpriced game with all 20,000 seats sold represents a full building with a higher energy level and feel than the half-full building with 10,000 seats sold. In addition to that energy and feeling, all sales and marketing personnel report to bosses and team ownership, and is perhaps more likely to receive a compliment from their supervisors when the game is sold out compared to when it is half full. Accordingly, there is a conservatism and risk aversion tendency where underpricing is somewhat preferable to overpricing. A consequence of underpricing is that ticket brokers may profit from buying underpriced tickets and reselling them through the secondary market.

---

## *Pricing Theory*

Whether conscious or subconscious, consumers make a decision whether or not to purchase something based on their assessment of its value. Marketing and sales experts have long defined value as follows:

**VALUE**
perceived benefits in relationship to the cost

$$\text{Value} = \frac{\text{Perceived benefits}}{\text{Price}}$$

In other words, potential buyers make their purchasing decision in comparing what they perceive the benefits of the product or service to be with the price. If benefits are greater than price, the consumer will purchase, but if price is higher than benefits, the consumer will not make the purchase.

It is important to note that perceived benefits vary greatly from consumer to consumer. There are diehard football fans that couldn't care less about baseball, and conversely, there are diehard baseball fans that couldn't care less about football. The football fan may be willing to pay hundreds of dollars to attend an NFL game, but near zero for an MLB game. The opposite could be true for the baseball fan. Note also that a variety of other factors may affect this perception of benefits, such as financial conditions, geographical limitations, and time constraints.

## *Factors Influencing Pricing*

When determining what price to set for sport products such as tickets or sponsorships, organizations may evaluate a variety of different factors. For this brief discussion of such factors, they are organized into internal and external factors. Internal factors are those that are organization specific and under the control of the organization. External factors, in contrast, are outside of the organization's control.

## INTERNAL FACTORS

A number of factors within the organization's control may factor into their price setting strategy. These include:

*Organizational objectives.* As discussed already in this chapter, the sport organization must examine what their primary goals are as they analyze their pricing options. Revenue generation is a common objective, but others may be in play. As mentioned, many college athletic departments provide ticket discounts to students, consistent with their role in the university's mission. Another potential objective is a competitive one. Walmart has long been known to utilize this strategy to put pressure on its competition.

*Branding.* From a marketing perspective, organizations brand themselves in different ways. **Branding** refers to the process of creating a unique name and image for a product in the minds of consumers. Some organizations' brand images indicate prestige or luxury. Examples include Mercedes-Benz in the automobile industry or Apple in technology. Consistent with these luxury brands, the corporations consistently price their products higher than competitors. The New York Yankees are a sports example, where the Yankees attempt to project a brand image of luxury and first class. In line with their brand, the Yankees have among the highest price tickets, premium seating, and sponsorship prices in the sport industry.

**BRANDING**
the process of creating a unique name and image for a product in the minds of consumers

*Promotion.* An organization's promotional strategy can connect with its pricing strategy. Some businesses, for example, offer many various price promotions, while others do not. Outside of sport, Kohl's department store is a company that positions itself as being friendly to value shoppers. As such, Kohl's discounts its apparel and goods extensively. Sport organizations must evaluate their strategy in this regard. Many consumers are bargain-seekers, and thus attracted to price promotions, but there are risks involved in discounting. First, the organization should consider price integrity. Utilizing price promotions frequently may condition buyers to expect discounts in the future. For example, if a team frequently discounts its single game tickets midseason each year, fans may get used to this and start refusing to pay full price earlier in the season, knowing that discounts are likely forthcoming later. Second, the sport organization must be attentive to how it treats its key customers. If loyal heavy users, the team's season ticket holders, pay $50 per ticket per game and a team later discounts similar seats to $40 in order to attract single game buyers, there is a risk of upsetting the season ticket holders where they may not renew their purchase in future years. Given the importance of cultivating a strong season ticket base, such discounts are likely not worth the risk.

*Cost*. While organizations generally focus their price setting on attempting to identify the optimal price point for revenue generation, organizations often examine their costs alongside their revenues. Costs in this regard include personnel, production, promotion, and distribution. If it costs Under Armour $20 to make and sell a particular type of shirt, they likely want to avoid selling it in the $20 range, but instead desire to make a considerably larger profit margin on that product.

## EXTERNAL FACTORS

Many factors outside of the organization's control can impact price setting strategy. These external factors include:

**CONSUMER DEMAND**
the quantity which consumers are willing to buy at a particular price, varies widely from product to product

*Consumer demand*. One of the most critical factors influencing pricing is the demand for the product among potential buyers. **Consumer demand**, defined as the quantity which consumers are willing to buy at a particular price, varies widely from product to product. Football is more popular than cricket in the United States, and thus more consumers will pay $50 to see a football game than a cricket match. There are additional issues involved however. In India, for example, cricket is extremely popular and American football is not. As such, the example above regarding willingness to pay for football versus cricket is likely false, and, in fact, the opposite is probably true. Another issue here is the level of play. While football is the most popular spectator sport in the United States, most consumers would not pay $50 per ticket for a high school junior varsity game, but a great many would pay much more than $50 to see an NFL game. Even within a particular sport and league setting, aspects such as opponent, day of the week, and time of year can significantly influence the level of demand, and therefore should be factored into a sport organization's pricing strategy.

In addition to demand affecting price, price also affects demand. If an NHL team prices their single game tickets at $5 each, demand for tickets will likely be quite high; however, if the NHL team charges $500 for the same tickets instead, demand will certainly be much lower. The discipline of economics offers elasticity as a construct for understanding how sensitive demand is to price change. A detailed examination of **elasticity** is beyond the scope of this text, but it is important to understand that some products are considered elastic, where small changes in price can cause larger changes in corresponding demand, and other products are inelastic, where changes in price cause relatively smaller changes in demand. Economics and marketing texts can provide a fuller discussion of the important concept of elasticity.

**ELASTICITY**
small changes in price can cause larger changes in corresponding demand

*Competitors' prices*. Organizations are wise to account for their competition's prices when establishing their own price points. For ticket sales in professional sports, a team should be aware of how their prices compare to the other professional teams in the same market. Competition should be interpreted broadly, however, as a spectator sport organization is not only competing with other sport organizations, but rather is a part of the competitive marketplace for consumers' entertainment dollars. In this regard, competition could include concerts, theater, movies, festivals, and other entertainment options.

*Economy*. Another factor that may potentially impact a sport organization's pricing strategy is economic trends. If economic conditions in the nation or local market are strong, consumers should have more money to spend on sports and entertainment. Similarly, businesses may have larger marketing budgets to spend on sport sponsorship opportunities. On the other hand, if the economy is struggling, such budgets for sport tickets and sponsorships may be tighter. These trends could impact whether a sport organization chooses to price its products more aggressively or conservatively.

## Pricing Strategies

A number of different pricing strategies have been developed across all industries. Based on the internal and external pricing factors an organization possesses, as discussed in the previous section of this chapter, a sport organization may choose to utilize some of the following strategies.

## PENETRATION PRICING

These first two strategies refer to the elasticity discussion earlier in this chapter. With a product possessing elastic demand, meaning that changes in price

**PENETRATION PRICING**
prices are kept relatively low in order to sell a greater quantity with consumers finding the product to be a good value for the money

**SKIM PRICING**
keep prices high in order to generate higher revenues

cause even larger changes in demand, organizations may consider penetration pricing. With **penetration pricing**, prices are kept relatively low in order to sell a greater quantity with consumers finding the product to be a good value for the money.

## SKIM PRICING

In contrast to penetration pricing, **skim pricing** is used in conjunction with inelastic pricing, which is the condition where changes in price cause relatively smaller changes in consumer demand. Skim pricing refers to keeping prices high in order to generate higher revenues.

## PREMIUM PRICING

**PREMIUM PRICING**
also known as prestige pricing and involves charging high prices, those above other competitors, as it is consistent with a brand image of luxury and high quality

**CUSTOMARY PRICING**
when a product is priced at a particular level for an extensive time period, perhaps even developing a known association with that certain price level

Similar to skim pricing, **premium pricing** (also known as prestige pricing) involves charging high prices, those above other competitors, as it is consistent with a brand image of luxury and high quality. Companies such as Bose and Nike utilize premium pricing strategies.

## CUSTOMARY PRICING

**Customary**, or traditional, **pricing** occurs when a product is priced at a particular level for an extensive time period, perhaps even developing a known association with that certain price level. For a number of years, Redbox DVD rentals were priced at just $1 and had become known for that price point during the early successful growth period of the company's existence. In 2011, Redbox elected to raise prices and faced some negative publicity for doing so. The same is often true with ticket prices in professional sports and collegiate athletics, where local media may write negative stories when the team announces new ticket prices that are higher than the previous year's.

## PRODUCT LINE PRICING

**PRODUCT LINE PRICING**
an organization not just setting prices for a single product, but rather establishing a systematic range of prices across a group of related products

**Product line pricing** refers to an organization not just setting prices for a single product, but rather establishing a systematic range of prices across a group of related products. Golf ball manufacturers like Titleist and Callaway offer not just one golf ball as a single product, but rather offer several different types of balls in a cohesive line, where price increases along with quality. A pack of 12 Titleist golf balls may range from $20 to $50 depending on quality. Spectator sport organizations often utilize this strategy in stratifying seating sections in their facility where seats closest to the action may cost several times more than those in the upper level far from the playing surface.

# BUNDLE PRICING

**Bundle pricing** involves packaging a group of separate products together into a single bundle at one price. A noteworthy example of bundle pricing is an all-inclusive resort as a vacation destination. While many resorts charge customers separately for lodging, meals, drinks, and activities used, an all-inclusive resort charges a single price that includes each of those amenities. A sport example of bundle pricing is tickets that include unlimited concession items in addition to game admission.

**BUNDLE PRICING**
packaging a group of separate products together into a single bundle at one price

## *Pricing Trends*

As sport organizations have become more sophisticated business operations over the past two decades, a number of trends and strategies have emerged related to pricing. These include personal seat licenses, the secondary ticket market, variable and dynamic pricing, and membership clubs.

# PERSONAL SEAT LICENSES

A **personal seat license,** or PSL, is a purchase that provides the PSL holder with the right to buy season tickets in a particular seat within a stadium or arena. If a consumer buys PSLs for two seats in a new stadium, that does not provide them with any tickets, but rather the right (and often an obligation) to buy season tickets in those two seats. PSLs typically cost between a couple thousand dollars to as much as tens of thousands of dollars, depending on the facility and the quality of seats involved. PSLs are often sold in advance of the opening of a new stadium or arena, as they can provide a sport organization with a means by which to generate millions of dollars in revenue to use toward funding stadium/arena construction. The San Francisco 49ers sold PSLs during the construction process for Levi's Stadium and generated more than $300 million toward the construction cost by selling PSLs. The Dallas Cowboys and New York Giants/Jets each generated more than $600 million toward the construction financing of AT&T Stadium and MetLife Stadium, respectively. From a sales perspective, PSLs can provide a method for generating significant capital funding, but also take a considerable sales effort requiring the organization to add to their sales staff.

**PERSONAL SEAT LICENSE (PSL)**
a purchase that provides the PSL holder with the right to buy season tickets in a particular seat within a stadium or arena

# SECONDARY TICKET MARKET

When tickets are sold by the organization hosting the event, this is referred to as the **primary ticket market**. Millions of consumers buy their tickets directly from the organization or from companies authorized to sell on their behalf,

**PRIMARY TICKET MARKET**
when tickets are sold by the organization hosting the event

**SECONDARY TICKET MARKET**
the subsequent reselling of tickets

such as Ticketmaster. The subsequent reselling of those tickets is known as the **secondary ticket market**. The secondary ticket market has existed for perhaps as long as tickets have been sold, although this model has evolved in recent years. For decades, the secondary ticket market was more commonly known as ticket scalping. Scalpers were individuals either working alone or perhaps in the employ of a ticket brokerage company, and these individuals could be found outside of the facility selling tickets before the event. While this practice still occurs, much of the secondary market has migrated to the Internet since the late 1990s and early 2000s. Today, consumers utilize online platforms such as StubHub and eBay to buy and sell tickets.

In both the traditional ticket scalping model and the more recent online version, ticket resellers on the secondary market include a mix of typical fans trying to sell extra tickets and professional ticket brokers attempting to profit. Reflecting back on the sidebar column earlier in this chapter, sport organizations are frequently inclined to underprice tickets in a risk averse manner, making sure the facility is as full as possible. As stated, the consequence of underpricing is that the secondary market will capitalize by reselling tickets closer to their actual value. Assume that someone is willing to pay $100 per seat in a particular area of the arena for an NBA game, but the team sold those seats for $35 each originally. Someone, whether a professional ticket broker or an opportunistic ticket holding fan, is likely to sell those tickets on the secondary market and reap the rewards of the $65 gap between the original price on the primary market and what someone will pay on the secondary market.

©DW labs Incorporated/Shutterstock.com

---

### I'VE GOT A GOLDEN TICKET

Sport organizations offer a variety of creative price promotions to generate ticket sales. Examples include tickets that include all-you-can-eat concessions and a Priceline-style name your price promotion implemented by the NHL's Florida Panthers a few years ago. One noteworthy price promotion was the Golden Ticket, sold by the University of Minnesota's men's basketball team in 2012–2013. The Golden Ticket was a pass that provided access, potentially, to the ticket holder for all nine Big Ten Conference games for just $75. This was a considerable value at just $8.33 per game, compared to the regular price of all nine games for $315. The unique hook to this promotion was that if the ticket holder used their ticket at a game lost by the Golden Gophers team, the ticket would become void and unusable for the remainder of the season. In this regard, ticket holders faced a decision or gamble each game as to how likely it was that the home team would win, or otherwise the tickets would be unusable after a loss they attended. The team, somewhat unexpectedly, won seven of their nine home Big Ten games, including two wins over nationally-ranked opponents.

---

## VARIABLE PRICING

For decades, spectator sport organizations charged the same price every game for a particular seating section. For example, the Chicago Cubs would sell a particular group of seats for $30 regardless of the time of year, day of week, opponent, or any other factor. Consider this momentarily: is a Tuesday afternoon game in April versus the Oakland Athletics equivalent to a Saturday evening game in July against the St. Louis Cardinals, the Cubs' primary rival? Are tickets to these two games of equal value? Will consumer demand be equal for these two games? In all likelihood, the answer is no. There are a variety of factors that influence demand for tickets to different sporting events, even if the seat locations are the same. Factors such as quality of opponent and day of the week are such common factors that influence the level of demand.

After decades of charging the same ticket prices for all games, beginning in the late 1990s it became common for sport organizations to vary their prices from game to game, trying to anticipate in advance what the likely demand might be for particular games. This notion of varying prices based on anticipated demand is called **variable ticket pricing**. Demand can vary widely from one game to another based on certain factors, so it is logical the price should vary accordingly in order to optimize attendance and sales revenue. Researchers Rascher, McEvoy, Nagel, and Brown (2007)[2] found that

**VARIABLE TICKET PRICING**
prices vary based on anticipated demand

---

2. Rascher, D., McEvoy, C., Nagel, M., & Brown, M. (2007). Variable ticket pricing in Major League Baseball. *Journal of Sport Management, 21*(3), 407–437.

MLB teams not using variable ticket pricing were potentially losing hundreds of thousands of dollars per year in unrealized revenue by not varying their ticket prices based on anticipated demand.

## DYNAMIC PRICING

**DYNAMIC PRICING**
when organizations have the ability to change prices on a daily basis, or even more frequently, as demand changes

One limitation to variable ticket pricing is that decisions about how to price tickets to each game based on anticipated demand are typically made before the season begins. The challenge in this regard is that anticipated demand is not always accurate. Demand for tickets to a particular game can change over time. For example, an opponent that is expected to have a strong season may instead have a weak one, or vice versa. In response, the strategy of variable pricing has evolved to **dynamic pricing**, where organizations have the ability to change prices on a daily basis, or even more frequently, as demand changes. The San Francisco Giants became the first franchise to utilize dynamic ticket pricing in collaboration with the firm Qcue, which is based in Austin, Texas. Based on the revenue generation success of this collaboration, a number of major league professional sport franchises now utilize dynamic pricing.

## MEMBERSHIP CLUBS

**MEMBERSHIP CLUB**
fans join a club as members rather than purchasing tickets as season ticket holders with the purpose of fostering a sense of belonging and connection

A recent trend in ticket pricing is the use of **membership clubs** to increase engagement and retention among full and partial season ticket holders. The membership model is in some ways a different type of packaging as much as it is a different type of pricing. The main thrust of the membership model is that consumers are joining a club as members rather than purchasing tickets as buyers. In practice this may just appear to be a difference in semantics, as the product and price may not be dramatically different. Instead of buying a 10-game partial plan ticket to an NBA franchise, you are joining that team's membership club at the 10-game level. Again, the price may be the same and the core product, the tickets to 10 basketball games, may be the same as well. So what is the difference? A primary difference is the organization wants to give consumers a sense of belonging. Buying tickets is a commercial transaction. The membership model provides an opportunity for consumers to feel a sense of belonging and connection, which is quite different than the transactional nature of simply buying a product. Organizations hope the sense of belonging and connection of a membership club leads to increased loyalty and retention of customers from year-to-year. Many teams utilizing this membership club model have increased their level of special perks and amenities provided to club members in order to enhance the feelings of belonging and connection.

---

**BUYING TICKETS NETFLIX-STYLE**

In a twist on the membership club ticket model, the Atlanta Braves in 2016 launched a subscription based ticket program patterned after examples such as Netflix for movies or Spotify for music. With the Braves Monthly Pass, subscribers have the option to attend every home game for an automatically-renewed $39 per month. Each game day, subscribers receive a text message asking whether they plan on attending that day's game. Those that reply affirmatively are sent an electronic ticket with a seat assignment that varies by game. With the low price point, the Braves targeted younger consumers who tend to be well-connected via their smartphones, hoping to build an audience in this demographic group, which is typically difficult for teams to reach.

---

## CHAPTER SUMMARY

Understanding how tickets are packaged and priced is essential knowledge for sales personnel in the sport industry. Sport organizations utilize a variety of ticket packages to meet the differing needs and wants of many different consumers. Optimal pricing optimally is another key piece of a sport organization's revenue generation strategies.

## CHAPTER ACTIVITIES

1. What differences exist between the spectator sport product and most products sold in other industries?

2. Which type of ticket package could be used to target each of the following levels of users related to the frequency escalator:

   a. Heavy users?

   b. Medium users?

   c. Light users?

   d. Nonconsumers?

3. Using the Internet, explore the ticket packages offered by a specific professional sport team. List three different partial plans offered by that team.

4. Describe the internal and external factors affecting an organization's price setting strategy.

5. List three common pricing strategies. Provide an example of how each could be used by a professional sport team in establishing ticket prices.

6. Research the ticket pricing of a particular spectator sport organization using the Internet. Which of the recent pricing trends discussed in this chapter, such as variable pricing, dynamic pricing, and membership clubs, does this organization utilize?

# CHAPTER 4

## SPORT SALES FOUNDATIONS

**LEARNING OBJECTIVES**

After completing this chapter, you should be able to:

▶ Differentiate between product-focused selling and customer-focused selling.

▶ Analyze why a consultative sales philosophy is preferred to a product-focused sales philosophy in the sport industry.

▶ Recognize and define the dominant buying motives for fans, spectators, participants, and corporate buyers.

▶ Differentiate features from benefits.

▶ Translate features and benefits into value propositions and selling points.

▶ Outline the steps of the sales process.

▶ Explain how the unique nature of the sport product impacts sales professionals.

**KEY TERMS**

| | |
|---|---|
| Authority | Need |
| Benefit | Pain |
| Consultative selling | Product-focused selling |
| Customer-focused selling | Scarcity |
| Desire | Selling point |
| Dominant buying motive | Social Proof |
| Drive State | Spectators |
| Fans | Tension |
| Feature | Value |
| Incentives | Value proposition |
| Motivation | Want Pathway |

## CHAPTER OVERVIEW

Sport ticket sales executives seemingly all sell the same product—a ticket. Yet, fans and businesses make purchase decisions for many different reasons, and they experience the event in many different ways. People don't buy a ticket; they buy an experience, but people experience the product differently. As a result, sellers don't use the same sales pitch to each customer. The pitch has to be customized in a way that speaks to the unique needs and situation of the customer. Some people attend for family entertainment while others go because they passionately follow the team. Some businesses purchase season tickets in club seats to reward their hard-working employees, while others focus on developing new business. In order to meet the needs of diverse groups of customers and businesses, sellers must first understand what motivates and compels people to attend their games or events. This happens by asking questions and learning about the customers and their needs, wants, desires, pain, and problems. Without identifying what motivates a customer to purchase the product, sellers can't effectively leverage product features in a way that is relevant to the customer. Trying to push the same features on all customers results in a sales approach that is focused more on the product than the customer. The sales process introduced in this chapter is based upon the key concept that salespeople first diagnose the needs and motives of the customer before transitioning the conversation to product knowledge. This philosophy forms the heart of consultative selling.

## CONSULTATIVE SALES PHILOSOPHY

Why do many people have a negative perception of salespeople? In most cases, it is probably because of a bad experience in which they felt pressured, misled, or tricked into buying a product they did not want or need. The fast-talking real estate agent or manipulative car salesman might gloss over important details or rush buyers into making decisions before they are ready. When these sort of tactics are employed in the sales process, all the emphasis is on the product and making a quick sale. Unfortunately, many inexperienced salespeople will make the rookie mistake of immediately talking about all the great features of the product without having any idea whether the information they are sharing matters to the prospect. While the new sales representative may not intentionally be trying to pressure the prospect into a quick, uninformed decision, the result is the same: the potential buyer does not feel comfortable making a decision or feels like the sales representative does not have his or her best interest in mind. Sometimes this sort of approach can generate short-term sales, but it rarely turns into a long-term relationship.

When poorly trained sellers immediately discuss things like team quality, seat location, discounts, and price without asking any questions to understand the customer's needs or concerns, they are making a critical error. These sellers have unknowingly adopted the ineffective "spray and pray" strategy, where they spray product knowledge on the customer and then pray the customer will say *yes* at the end of the call. This approach is frequently rejected by the prospect because it fails to uncover the needs that drive the purchase decision. Sellers using this technique are missing the chance to solve a problem or improve the customer's condition. A good rule of thumb is to imagine a customer is thinking "so what" every time a seller talks about a product feature.

This type of sales approach is called **product-focused selling**. In product-focused selling the salesperson focuses exclusively on the benefits, features, quality, and reputation of the product when trying to persuade a customer to buy. It is primarily a one-way presentation in which the salesperson does 95% of the talking. In the product-focused sales approach, the salesperson utilizes features in the sales presentation without asking questions to determine which benefits might be relevant to the customer. In the context of sport season tickets sales, a product-focused sales conversation emphasizes the following types of features:

- Team performance or quality
- Price
- Added-value items
- Stadium features
- Seat locations
- Access to VIP areas and events
- Discounts on ancillary products and other events
- Loyalty points
- Entry into sweepstakes or contests
- Electronic ticket transfer systems
- Renewal rights

**PRODUCT-FOCUSED SELLING**
the salesperson exclusively focuses on the benefits, features, quality, and reputation of the product when trying to convince a customer to buy

---

### COLLEGE FOOTBALL SEASON TICKET FEATURES

- ▶ Team quality and tradition
- ▶ Per game price discount compared to buying each game individually
- ▶ Added value items (framed pictures, bumper stickers, autographed memorabilia)
- ▶ Entry into sweepstakes for a prized item (entertainment, electronics)
- ▶ Stadium features (renovations, sight lines, technology, history)
- ▶ Guaranteed/best seat locations
- ▶ Access to special events (banquets, luncheons, speeches)
- ▶ Electronic ticket transfers and exchanges
- ▶ Access to "members only" areas
- ▶ Renewal rights
- ▶ Parking (spaces, passes, discounts)
- ▶ Mobile or smart tickets
- ▶ Ancillary product discounts (merchandise, concessions)
- ▶ Access to a personal sales rep
- ▶ Loyalty points (tied to donations)
- ▶ VIP experiences (meet players and coaches, social outings)
- ▶ Discounts at other events (golf course, Olympic sports)

---

**CUSTOMER-FOCUSED SELLING**
the salesperson talks about the product or service in terms of what the customer wants, not in terms of what they are selling

**CONSULTATIVE SELLING**
a customer-focused sales method where the sales consultant asks questions in order to learn more about the customer before presenting a customized solution that will specifically address the needs or desires of the customer

Sharing features is a normal part of the sales conversation. However, good sellers know they should only share the benefits of their product after understanding a potential customer's needs. Thus effective salespeople should adopt a customer-focused selling approach. In **customer-focused selling**, the salesperson talks about the product or service in terms of what the customer wants, not in terms of what they are selling. Personalizing the product recommendation helps the salesperson to satisfy needs, solve a problem, or quantify improvement for the customer. The focus of the entire conversation is on the customer. Table 4.1 identifies the core differences between these approaches.

The predominant customer-focused sales methodology adopted by sport organizations and many other industries is called consultative selling. **Consultative selling** is a customer-focused sales method in which the sales consultant asks questions in order to learn more about the customer before presenting a customized solution that will specifically address the needs or desires of the customer. Successful salespeople accurately identify needs by asking questions and building a relationship. Key elements of a consultative sales approach include "diagnosing and determining customer needs, facilitating sound decision making by purchasers, and rejecting the use of

## Table 4.1

**Core Differences Between Product-Focused and Customer-Focused Selling**

| Product-Focused Selling | Customer-Focused Selling |
| --- | --- |
| Customers are the same | Every customer is unique |
| Presentations are the same | Personalize your presentation to the audience |
| Persuade the customer to buy | Help lead the customer to a solution |
| One-way conversation with salesperson doing most of the talking | Two-way conversation with customer doing most of the talking |
| Focus on the product | Focus on the right solution |
| Offer opinions | Ask relevant questions |
| You won't see the customer again | You will be judged by what happens after the sale |

manipulative, unethical sales techniques."[1] According to sales expert and author Brian Tracy, "The very best salespeople today see themselves more as consultants and advisors to their customers than as salespeople. As a consultant, your job is to help the customer solve his problems with what you are selling."[2]

Effective consultative sellers ask good questions, actively and empathetically listen to the customer's responses, uncover needs, build high trust relationships through conversations, and ultimately present the product as a customized solution for that customer. In taking this approach, the salesperson is partnering with the customer to find a solution, not trying to convince the customer to purchase something he or she doesn't need or want. Salespeople adopting a consultative sales philosophy utilize their influence with integrity and do not utilize manipulative or deceptive closing tactics.

Demonstrating credibility as an expert consultant leverages the rule of **authority**, which states people tend to follow the lead of credible and knowledgeable experts.[3] Think of a college student attending the first day of college and meeting a professor for the first time, or someone being pulled over for speeding as a uniformed officer with sirens on pulls up to the car. In these instances, individuals are often eager to comply with the requests of the person

**AUTHORITY**
rule stating that people tend to follow the lead of credible and knowledgeable experts

1. Lassk, F., Ingram, T., Kraus, F., & Mascio, R. (2012). The future of sales training: Challenges and related research questions. *Journal of Personal Selling and Sales Management*, 33(1), 141–154. doi:10.2753/PSS0885-3134320112

2. Tracy, B. (2004). *The psychology of selling*. Nashville, TN: Thomas Nelson. p. 73.

3. Cialdini, R. (1993). *Influence: The psychology of persuasion*, 2nd ed. New York: William Morrow.

in authority. In a sales setting, it is critical for a salesperson to establish his or her role as an expert consultant prior to making a product recommendation. This can be accomplished through knowledge of the product, use of titles such as Account Executive, professional attire, use of technology in presentations, and strong personal social media presence on platforms such as LinkedIn.

A consultative sales approach works best when salespeople are selling from a full menu of options. For example, an account executive with the ability to sell individual game tickets, group packages, partial season plans, full season plans, and premium seats can offer a tailored ticket solution to fit the needs of the customer more effectively than an account executive restricted to selling only full season tickets or only group tickets. However, teams organize their sales staffs differently, and some teams prefer to have salespeople specialize in one type of ticket product. Even if a salesperson specializes in one type of product, many teams have now introduced new ticket products, which allow salespeople to offer an even greater customized product to potential customers. These new products might include a ticket plan in which the customer chooses which games she wants to see or the ability to exchange or resell unused tickets.

In the article below, Ben Milsom, Chief Ticketing Officer with the Tampa Bay Buccaneers, explains the difference between telling the prospect about the product and selling the product.

---

**Ben Milsom, Chief Ticketing Officer, Tampa Bay Buccaneers**

### SELLING VS. TELLING

Recently I attended a recruiting meeting with a local college football coach where the goal was to get the high school senior to commit to attend his school. I agreed to attend the meeting after I was sure that I wasn't breaking any rules and also because I knew I was going to learn something. I met the coach before the meeting and we discussed the goal and the best practices when it came to this type of meeting. The college had a great history of success as well as a fine reputation of placing students into great jobs once they graduated. Needless to say the coach really had a great product to sell.

#### Info Dumping

Most new salespeople come into sport sales really excited about many things: a new city, an exciting player, a winning record, or just the fact that they are working in professional sports. This leads many times to what is called "info dumping." The excitement leads the salesperson to do more telling than consultative selling. Many times in meetings the salesperson has done most of the talking without gaining information from their prospect. This is exactly how this meeting went. The coach introduced us and began discussing team record, school history, alumni, and the city where the school was located. The whole time the student was eating his lunch with a somewhat glazed look on this face. I kept thinking about how many times this occurs in sport sales. This "pitch" only really works when your product is winning. There was still so much information to be learned from the student. What are some of the questions that could have been asked?

- ► What is important to you in your college selection?
- ► How important is education vs. football?
- ► How comfortable are you with the location of the school?
- ► Tell me about what you would like to study? Why?
- ► MOST IMPORTANTLY after all the information is gathered: What is it going to take for you to commit to X college?

**Pitching in sales works in the same way it works in baseball. It's one direction and irreversible. To be an effective sales professional you need to engage in strategic listening to understand your customers' preferences, priorities, level of interest and more before you propose, pitch, tell, and sell.**

**—Gregg Baron, President, Success Sciences**

### Selling Not Telling

Matt Smith, Regional Manager, IMG Learfield, shares, "When I think of this mindset of selling not telling, I think of a doctor and a pharmacist. Old-school salespeople were pharmacists, while we must be doctors. A good doctor must know everything about the problems of the patient, and everything about the possible treatments, then they must have an idea of how to tie the problem to the right solution . . . and they must do it all with the right heart and mindset. Pharmacists simply must know about drugs and prescriptions." As a salesperson, offering a solution before learning all you can about the customer is like a doctor prescribing treatment without first knowing the ailment.

### Conclusion

So many times we miss the opportunity to let our prospects tell us what they want and how they want it. This also misses a chance for us to ask for referrals, build a stronger relationship, and ultimately upsell our product. The difference between a good and great salesperson in my mind is the ability to ask effective and productive questions and use those questions to make a consultative and productive sale. The telling approach usually leads to buyer remorse and ultimately money left on the table.

———

Source: http://baylors3.com/milsom-selling-vs-telling/. Reprinted by permission of Ben Milsom.

## CONSUMER MOTIVATION

The purpose of asking questions in the consultative sales process is to diagnose why the customer wants to purchase the product. For instance, people buy cars for many different reasons. Some buyers want a vehicle that provides good gas mileage for the work commute. Others need a way to transport their family to soccer practice or piano lessons. Still others are looking for a car that makes a statement, for example, a vintage red convertible with all-leather interior. While all of these buyers are all interested in purchasing an automobile, a seller needs to understand each of their motivations and desires in order to find the right fit for the customer.

Selling live sport events is no different. People attend games, matches, and tournaments for a variety of reasons. Effective sport sales professionals know the unique features of the product they are selling and can match the product's attributes to the desires of potential buyers. Sport fans may not really consider their favorite team, athlete, or event as a product, but they are. And while the decision-making process might be made subconsciously, anyone who buys a product must determine if it offers enough value to warrant an exchange of resources (financial and time). Thus, it is important to understand why people attend sporting events in order to set the stage for the sales strategies and techniques presented in later chapters.

So why do people buy products? There are many different reasons why people buy products. To effectively sell a product such as sport tickets, professional sellers need to understand each of these reasons and learn how to uncover which ones are most at play within different sales interactions.

Basically, consumers are motivated by what they need or perceive they want. Someone who is hungry buys food. An individual who needs protection against potential financial loss purchases insurance. The golfer who needs to put more drives in the fairway procures a new driver. The sport fan who wants to support his or her favorite team goes to the big game. People buy in an attempt to satisfy a need. During a sales call, the job of the salesperson is to uncover the customer's needs because needs are what motivate people to buy. **Motivation** is the driving force within individuals that impels them to action.[4] Thus, needs can be motives.

**MOTIVATION**
the driving force within individuals that impels them to action

The motivation process described below illustrates why consumers make the decisions they do regarding the products that sport organizations are selling. The process outlined below is based on the assumption that people consume sport because such consumption has attractive outcomes. People

---

4. Schiffman, L., & Kanuk, L. (2004). *Consumer behavior*, 8th ed. Upper Saddle River, NJ: Pearson Prentice Hall.

seek to satisfy internal needs and receive benefits through a five-stage process: needs, tension, drive, want, and goal.[5]

## Stage 1: Need Recognition

The motivation process begins with an individual recognizing he or she has a need. A **need** is created when there is a gap between an individual's present state and an ideal state. As a result, the recognition of a need stems from an individual's processing information relevant to his or her actual state and comparing it to an ideal state. A needs gap exists when there is a difference between these two states. The needs gap activates the motivation or drive to fill the gap and reach the desired state. If a gap doesn't exist, then there is no need and no active motive to buy.

**NEED** is created when there is a gap between an individual's present state and an ideal state

Needs originate from pain and desire.[6] **Pain** stems from problems that evoke emotions like frustration, discontentment, confusion, boredom, embarrassment, anger, incompetence, stress, lack of knowledge, and the like. For instance, parents may have kids with a short attention span, resulting in the need to seek activities that are high energy and that can be engaging for a long period of time. Or perhaps a group of friends getting together over summer break need a new place to hang out and catch up with each other. In the sale of sport technology, a golf course manager may be angry that a golf cart was stolen, creating the need for security that is solved in the form of GPS technology installed on all golf carts. To alleviate pain, prospects will seek immediate relief to prevent the pain from occurring in the future.

**PAIN** stems from problems that evoke emotions like frustration, discontentment, confusion, boredom, embarrassment, anger, incompetence, stress, lack of knowledge, and the like

Needs are also created by **desire**. Without recognizing the role of desire, it is impossible to explain why someone would pay $500 for courtside seats when that individual could see the same game with $15 balcony seats. Or, why someone would pay $5,000 per year for a membership at a private country club when s/he could play for $15 per round at the public course a mile down the road. Desire stems from wanting to experience power, prestige, luxury, or instant gratification. It may arise from craving improvement in self-esteem, social status, or personal growth. To satisfy a desire, individuals attempt to improve their existing condition.

**DESIRE** stems from wanting to experience power, prestige, luxury, self-esteem, social status, instant gratification, significance, growth, and the like

> "Needs are formed when people who are dissatisfied with the status quo (*what is*) recognize that they would be better off if their situation was improved (*by what could be*)."[7]

---

5. Funk, D. (2008). *Consumer behavior in sport and events.* Oxford, UK: Butterworth-Heinemann.

6. Freese, T. (2013). *Secrets of question based selling.* Naperville, IL: Sourcebooks.

7. Ibid., p. 31.

## *Stage 2: Tension Reduction (Unpleasant Feeling)*

**TENSION**
the unpleasant feeling when there is a need that remains unfulfilled

The needs gap creates a sense of tension in people. **Tension** is the unpleasant feeling that occurs when there is a need that remains unfulfilled. The prospect realizes the gap between their desired state and their status quo or current state.

## *Stage 3: Drive State (Strength of Motivation)*

**DRIVE STATE**
exists when an individual is aroused to reduce or eliminate the unpleasant tension, thus restoring balance

The **drive state** exists when an individual is aroused to reduce or eliminate the unpleasant tension, thus restoring balance. The degree of pressure exerted on someone to restore balance reflects the strength of the motivation. The pressure a person feels creates a "push" toward doing something to alleviate the tension.

## *Stage 4: Want Pathway (Sport Consumption Motives)*

**WANT PATHWAY**
the pathway toward a specific consumption decision chosen by a person to reduce tension

The **want pathway** stage is the pathway toward a specific consumption decision chosen by a person to reduce tension. There is a "pull" that draws an individual toward a product, service, or experience that can offer a way to restore balance with a positive outcome. Sports create a want pathway that reduces tension, fulfills needs, improves one's condition, and achieves desirable outcomes.

## *Stage 5: Goal Behavior (Decision)*

The final stage is the attainment of a goal through a specific consumption decision that fulfills a need, reduces a tension, and improves the customer's condition. The fact that people buy to improve their condition is a fundamental principle in sales. Simply put, people buy products, services, and experiences because they believe the purchase will satisfy their physical, emotional, or spiritual needs.

As a result, the job of a sport salesperson is to uncover or create the need and communicate the positive features and benefits of attending that can "pull" the consumer to a specific pathway that satisfies the need. Salespeople persuade customers they will be better off buying from them than if they bought a different product or service, or if they did not buy anything at all. The customer must be substantially better off with your product than without it. The improvement gained must be great enough to justify the cost, plus the investment of time and emotional energy, called psychic costs. People want to get as much satisfaction as possible from their purchases, so it is important that the salesperson can articulate all of the ways in which a purchase will satisfy the customer.

---

## HOW THE MOTIVATION PROCESS WORKS

### Need Recognition

Andre just accepted his first job out of college. Andre realizes that he needs to find ways to cultivate friendships with his coworkers because he is new in the organization (present state) and he desires to fit in with his coworkers and organization (ideal state). His need as he is transitioning into his new job is related to belonging and ego.

### Tension Reduction

Andre feels tension while he is transitioning into his new job because he has not yet made connections with his coworkers.

### Drive State

Andre's strength of motivation reflects how unpleasant having no relationships at work makes him feel and whether he believes the positive outcomes from doing something about it can reduce the tension. The strength of motivation will push Andre toward considering ways of restoring balance. Thus, Andre might look to purchase tickets to a sporting event as a means to escape the pressures at his new job, or he might seek to use a sporting event as a means to get to know his coworkers better and develop a friendship.

### Want Pathway

Andre decides that inviting three coworkers to an NBA game can reduce his tension about fitting in with his colleagues at work by socializing with them at the game.

### Goal Behavior

Andre reduced the tension of not fitting in at work and improved his condition by inviting his coworkers to a sporting event for which he had purchased tickets. Based upon the unique nature of the sport product and certain features of an NBA game, Andre determined that a sporting event provided the best pathway to attain his goal of restoring balance.

In another example, Maria and Tim feel an unpleasant state created by a desire to spend quality time with their two children. Maria and Tim both want to get out of the house and spend Saturday with the family. After creating a list of five activities they could pursue (zoo, museum, sporting event, park, pool), they decided to attend a baseball game. The desire to spend time with the family provided a "push" while the "pull" directed them to a sporting event.

# DIAGNOSING DOMINANT BUYING MOTIVES

Attending sporting events "creates numerous pathways for individuals to seek opportunities to receive benefits and satisfy needs through goal-directed behavior. These pathways motivate an internal desire to seek out and experience sport or sport events to fulfill physical, social, and personal needs."[8] Sport marketing researchers have identified over 40 motives that help explain why people seek out sport experiences to satisfy their needs. Various authors have published different lists and taxonomies of motives, but for the purpose of this book we focus on the 19 motives identified by leading sport marketing researchers Dr. Galen Trail and Dr. Jeffrey James.[9] Their model distinguishes motives for fans and spectators. **Fans** are highly attached to the team, organization, coach, or players, while **spectators** typically do not have a strong social-psychological commitment to one of these groups.[10]

The motives listed in Table 4.2–4.4 are not mutually exclusive and sometimes a customer is driven by several different motives. The primary goal of the seller during the needs analysis phase of the call is to determine the customer's **dominant buying motive** that has the greatest influence on the decision to buy. The dominant buying motive then becomes the focus of the transition into product knowledge and a solution tailored to the customer.

**FANS**
highly attached to the team, organization, coach, or players

**SPECTATORS**
typically do not have a strong social-psychological commitment to the team, organization, coach, or players

**DOMINANT BUYING MOTIVE**
buying motive that has the greatest influence on the customer's decision to buy

## Table 4.2

### Motives for Both Fan and Spectator

| Motive | Definition | How the Customer Benefits |
|---|---|---|
| Acquisition of knowledge | Need for gaining knowledge (i.e., learning) about a sport, team, or players through media consumption or attendance | Teach your kids the rules of the game. Learn techniques you can use to improve your own skills. |
| Escape | Sport viewing is a means to relieve the tedium (i.e., boredom or fatigue) associated with everyday life | Stress reliever from your busy schedule at the office. Offers fun for your family on your vacation or staycation. |

---

8. Funk, D. (2008). *Consumer behavior in sport and events*. Oxford, UK: Butterworth-Heinemann. p. 23.

9. Trail, G., & James, J. (2015). *Sport consumer behavior*. Sport Consumer Research Consultants LLC.

10. Ibid.

| Motive | Definition | How the Customer Benefits |
|---|---|---|
| Interest in specific sport | Attachment to a specific sport (i.e., being a fan of the sport) | Our league/team has top quality talent. Baseball fans love coming out to our ball-park. |
| Interest in the level of the sport | Attachment to a specific level of sport (i.e., fan of college basketball) | Save money without sacrificing the experience at Minor League Baseball games. |
| Nostalgia | Extent to which an individual is drawn to sports because of fond or idealized memories associated with sport events that took place in the past | You'll be able to create so many great memories with your son just like you had with your dad. Bring back great memories. |
| Physical attractive-ness of participants | Interest in watching a sport event because of the sex appeal of an athlete or a group of athletes | You may not get that many chances to watch [insert attractive athlete] in person. |
| Physical skill of the athletes | Appreciation that an individual may have of the physical skills of an athlete during the performance of that athlete's sport or event | This tournament is the only chance you get each year to watch Jordan Spieth's golf swing in person. |
| Social interaction | Opportunity to interact with other people (includes spending quality time with friends, family, and coworkers) | Getting out to the ballpark is a great way for your family to spend time together. This is a great way for the kids in your youth group to get to know each other better in a fun environment. |
| Style of play | Watching a game or being a fan of a particular team because of a preference for a particular style of play | With our new coach, you'll get to see a hard-nosed defensive style that takes no prisoners. You will be entertained by our fast-paced exciting brand of ball. |
| Supporting a cause | Supporting a team, league, or sport because the individual believes that the support will further a cause beyond the financial or competitive success of the entity | You can play a key role in pushing soccer forward in this community. Give to your community through proceeds from the game that support a local non-profit charity. |

Trail, G., & James, J. (2015). *Sport consumer behavior.* Sport Consumer Research Consultants LLC. Benefit examples: Courtesy of David Pierce.

## Table 4.3

**Motives Unique to Being a Fan**

| Motive | Definition | How the Fan Benefits |
|---|---|---|
| Interest in players | Attachment to a specific player or players | You can cheer on your favorite player.<br><br>Purchase an all-access grounds pass for a better chance to get player autographs. |
| Interest in team | Attachment to a specific team | Root your team onto a championship this season.<br><br>Be a part of something special this year.<br><br>Support your team through thick and thin. |
| National or community pride | Showing support for one's own country or community | Be proud of how your team represents your community.<br><br>Support your country. |
| Players as role models | Players serving as role models for young children | Introduce your children to positive role models in the community. |
| Vicarious achievement | Extent to which fans are attracted to watching sports because of their need to enhance self-esteem vicariously through the success of an athlete or sport team | Feel the thrill of winning.<br><br>Be a part of the action.<br><br>Experience the ups and downs of the season. |

Trail, G., & James, J. (2015). *Sport consumer behavior*. Sport Consumer Research Consultants LLC. Benefit examples: Courtesy of David Pierce.

## Table 4.4

**Motives Unique to Being a Spectator**

| Motive | Definition | How the Spectator Benefits |
|---|---|---|
| Aesthetic qualities of the event | Beauty and artistry exhibited in competitive sport | Seeing Steph Curry's jump shot up close is much different than watching it on TV.<br><br>You can appreciate the speed at which the game is played by sitting down close. |
| Aggression displayed by the participants | Enjoyment of aggressive plays in sport | Seats down by the Plexiglas puts you right down by the fights on the ice.<br><br>Sitting in the lower level puts you right in the middle of the action and you'll hear the pop of the shoulder pads. |
| Economics | The potential for economic gains through wagering on sport and participation in fantasy leagues | Seeing the horses up close at the event helps you place better bets than being off-site. |
| Dramatic aspects of the event | Need to experience pleasurable stress or stimulation associated with watching a sport competition | Most of our games go down to the wire.<br><br>You can feel the energy in the crowd late in the fourth quarter in the big games. |

Trail, G., & James, J. (2015). *Sport consumer behavior*. Sport Consumer Research Consultants LLC. Benefit examples: Courtesy of David Pierce.

## Participant Motives

There are also unique motives for participant sport (see Table 4.5). The examples below are not intended to be comprehensive, and it is important to keep in mind that each sport has its own unique set of motives that have been identified by researchers. For example, the motives to participate in golf are different from the motives to participate in a triathlon. The broader point is that a salesperson must know how to uncover what motivates customers to participate in order to sell the product, service, or experience.

## Corporate Purchases

In addition to the motives of individuals and families to purchase tickets to sporting events, sport salespeople need to understand the reasons why businesses purchase items like season tickets, premium seats, and corporate partnerships (see Table 4.6).[11]

### Table 4.5

**Participant Motives**

| Motive | Definition | How the Participant Benefits |
|---|---|---|
| Performance | Desire for aesthetic and physical pleasure that can result from opportunities to enjoy the grace, skill, and artistry of physical activity | Enjoy the feeling you get after spending time in physical activity. |
| Achievement | Desire for a sense of achievement that can result from opportunities to engage in physical activity that produce an intrinsic (personal best) or extrinsic (trophy, medal, peer recognition) reward or incentive system | Beat your friend. Reach your personal best. Earn a medal. |
| Craft | Desire to develop or observe physical skill that can result from opportunities to engage in physical activity (lessons, training) | Improve your game. Learn new skills. |
| Health and Fitness | Desire to derive physical and mental health benefits that can result from physical activity such as self-esteem, self-actualization, and value development | Feel better about yourself. Reach your fitness goals. |
| Affiliation | Desire to be associated or identify with a recognized group. Being a participant can become a part of a person's social identity. Affiliation with sport enhances one's self-concept. | Spend time with other cyclists. Find other people who are also passionate about running. |

Irwin, R., Sutton, W., & McCarthy, L. (2008). *Sport promotion and sales management,* 2nd ed. Champaign, IL: Human Kinetics. Benefit examples: Courtesy of David Pierce.

11. Titlebaum, P., & Lawrence, H. (2010). Perceived motivations for corporate suite ownership in the "big four" leagues. *Sport Marketing Quarterly, 18,* 87–95. Titlebaum, P., & Lawrence, H. (2011). The reinvention of the luxury suite in North America. *Journal of Sponsorship,* 4, 124–136.

## Table 4.6

**Corporate Purchase Motivation**

| Motive | Description |
|---|---|
| Exclusivity | Desire to be linked to the team. |
| | Businesses are attracted to the use of suites on non-game days; going behind the scenes at the game; personal use of suites; exclusive VIP events for B2B opportunities; and the value of attending premium events. |
| Market Driven | Desire to achieve business building objectives such as driving retail traffic, increasing marketing share, increasing awareness of the product, enhancing company image, increasing brand loyalty, and obtaining target market data. |
| Trade Networking | Desire to incentivize retailers, suppliers, and distributors with pieces of the sponsorship inventory that enhance trade relations and goodwill. |
| Hospitality | Desire to entertain clients to achieve sales objectives and to entertain employees for human resources objectives. |
| Product Demonstration | Desire to demonstrate the ways in which the company and its associated products can perform within the production of the event itself. |
| Cause-Related | Desire to demonstrate corporate philanthropy and social responsibility by affiliating sponsorship with a popular cause in the community. |

## Incentives

**INCENTIVES**
items of perceived value added to an offer that encourage a purchase decision

While the motives identified above refer to an *internal desire* to fulfill needs, it is important to recognize that customers will also respond to *external stimuli* prompted by sport marketers, such as incentives. **Incentives** are items of perceived value added to an offer that encourage a purchase decision.[12] Incentives are used to change the perceived price of an offer in an effort to reach customers who have shown indifference or apathy toward the offer. This may include price deals, premium offers, contests, free samples, and a variety of other benefits that will encourage the customer to buy. Promotional incentives are used to alter a consumer's perception of the other three P's of marketing:

- price (e.g., discounts, coupons, free trials, contests, and sweepstakes) and value-added items (e.g., giveaways, entertainment, concessions, attractions)
- product (e.g., rule changes, star players, rivalries)
- place (e.g., virtual tours, stadium features, atmospherics)

12. Irwin, R., Sutton, W., & McCarthy, L. (2008). *Sport promotion and sales management*, 2nd ed. Champaign, IL: Human Kinetics.

The implication for sport sales professionals is these incentives are offered in the hopes of triggering or activating one of the internal behavioral motives identified above. For example, a college night promotion offering reduced ticket prices to college students wearing their school colors leverages the motivation of college students to hang out with friends (socialization) and show pride in their school (identification). The increasing amount of promotional incentives created by the marketing and promotions staff create complex product offerings and packages that requires the salesperson to possess a significant level of product knowledge in order to effectively leverage the right incentive at the right time with the right customer. Incentives like sweepstakes are also a great opportunity to learn more about the prospect by capturing their information.

## SELL BENEFITS, NOT TICKETS

Once the customer's dominant buying motive has been identified, the seller needs to tell the customer how they will benefit from making a purchase. Think about this. Do people buy cars because they want to possess a machine made up of metal, rubber, and glass sitting in their driveway? No, people buy cars because they want the freedom to quickly travel to places. They need transportation to work, school, or home. Perhaps they need a way to transport materials, groceries, or other human beings from one destination to another. An automobile's value comes in the benefits it provides the owner, not the raw materials of which the product consists.

The same is true of sport tickets. Fans do not simply buy sport tickets because they wish to sit in an arena chair or stadium bleacher to watch skilled athletes compete against one another. They buy tickets to satisfy a need or desire to be entertained, mesmerized, or escape from their everyday activities. Companies purchase tickets to create an entertainment experience that rewards employees and customers. The motives discussed earlier in this chapter are the critical link between the features of the product and the perceived benefit for the customer. Sellers ask questions to determine if the customer's emotional need can be fulfilled by the product because people buy ways to satisfy their needs.

Returning to the example from the sidebar, Andre bought a seat at the arena not so he can watch two teams play basketball, but so he would have an opportunity to socialize with coworkers and reach a desired state of developing relationships at his new workplace. Thus, Andre is buying the benefit of a socializing experience with coworkers, not a ticket or seat.

A major challenge for nascent ticket salespeople is getting out of the mindset that they are selling a ticket. Instead ticket sellers should focus on

> I have never sold a ticket. That's what the Internet is for. That's what box office windows are for. I don't sell tickets. I create and build relationships. I recommend based on needs. I create memories. I offer experiences. I propose a win–win partnership. I present opportunities. I suggest ways to bring new business onboard for companies. Sometimes, their need and our product is not a fit, so there are times I don't recommend our product. But I don't sell tickets.[13]
>
> — Kathy Burrows, Owner, *Sold Out Seating*

selling the benefits of attending a live sporting event. The key to selling sport tickets is to help the prospect better understand how the product can satisfy a need or desire. To do this, effective sellers think in terms of benefits as opposed to features or attributes. Sellers build value in the sales conversation by articulating features of the product in terms of the benefit received by the customer.

**FEATURE**
an attribute, quality, or characteristics of a product or service

A **feature** is an attribute, quality, or characteristics of a product or service. Features describe what the product is. Common features of season ticket packages might include access to hospitality areas, parking privileges, early options to purchase playoff tickets, or the ability to exchange tickets for other games. While these features may seem like benefits, the seller's job is to ensure the prospect sees the true benefit rather than just the feature.

**BENEFIT**
answers the question "what's in it for me" and is linked directly to their motivation for buying. It is important to remember that your prospect does not care what your product is, but only what your customer can do with the product

A **benefit** answers the question "what's in it for me" and is linked directly to the motivation for buying. It is important to remember that your prospect does not care what your product *is*, but only what they can do with the product. If you can't articulate what the ticket or package can *do* for the customer and what the customer *gets* out of a purchase, you will find a closed door when it's time to ask for the sale.

**VALUE PROPOSITION**
benefits the customer has confirmed are relevant

Prior to doing a needs analysis, there are many potential benefits that a customer could receive as a result of purchasing the product. Once the customer acknowledges the importance of a benefit to his or her situation, it becomes a confirmed benefit. Confirmed benefits, also called the **value proposition**, represent customer value that is provided by the proposed solution. Confirming benefits and articulating the value proposition is crucial because *customers do not purchase products and features; they buy value through relevant benefits*. Good salespeople focus on building value because prospects only buy when they feel the value of the purchase exceeds the cost.

---

13. Burrows, K. (2015, November 16). Why do people buy our sports entertainment options? (Secret: Don't sell tickets). *LinkedIn.* Retrieved from https://www.linkedin.com/pulse/why-do-people-buy-our-sports-entertainment-options-secret-burrows

As a result, the benefits presented to the salesperson presents to the customer must be tailored to the needs and problems uncovered in the needs analysis phase. Making generic statements about benefits is not as effective as benefit statements that build on the salesperson's understanding of the customer's situation. Simply emphasizing product features and potential benefits leaves the customer unpersuaded. However, selling confirmed benefits is persuasive because it creates value for the customer. The combination of relevant product features and their corresponding benefit is called a **selling point**.

Once the seller has identified relevant selling points to the customer, the seller should spend time on that selling point by highlighting the benefit, and then ask a trial close question to solicit feedback from the customer. In each of the examples below, the product feature is followed by the benefit:

**SELLING POINT**
combination of relevant product features and their corresponding benefit

- ▶ Our season ticket packages include a reserved parking pass. The pass gives you a guaranteed spot close to the stadium. The benefit for you is that you don't have to hunt for a place to park and it cuts down on the distance you have to walk to your entry gate. How would that impact your game day experience?
- ▶ Season tickets guarantee you the same seat for each game, right where you want to sit. Since you want to have easy access to the restrooms and concessions, we can get you set up with aisle seats near the top of the seating bowl.
- ▶ Our corporate season ticket packages include a reserved tailgating spot in Lot 9. The great thing about this pass is that it will give you a prime spot to tailgate with all of those important clients.
- ▶ All of our season ticket packages allow you to participate in the electronic ticket exchange program. This allows you to send tickets to friends, family, and coworkers electronically. I know you have a very busy schedule, so what this means for you is that you can reduce your unused tickets and get the most out of your season ticket purchase. How would this be beneficial for you?
- ▶ The purchase of club seat season tickets includes access to the Founders' Club. The benefit to you will be the opportunity to wine and dine your top clients in a very exclusive area.
- ▶ The Picnic Pavilion provides a large shade structure in the outfield. A lot of other group leaders like it because it provides a comfortable dining experience on muggy summer days. The great thing for you is that it can keep your clients more comfortable than roasting in the bleacher seats in the hot sun. From what you've told me I think that will be important to you. Am I right?
- ▶ The RX 490 driver is made with a new blend of titanium metals that increase power at impact. The benefit for you is increased power for longer driving distances. How will that impact your game?

You can even use the same approach when selling yourself in a job interview:

> ▶ I served as a group leader on three major class projects where we had to work with industry partners to solve real world problems. What I can bring to the table in this job is the ability to lead others and collaborate with team members.

Another effective way for sellers to introduce a benefit is by telling the customer what they do:

> ▶ What I do is work with families just like yours to have a great time at the ballpark.
> ▶ I work with other companies like yours to help generate new business.

Effective sellers are able to leverage the selling points by painting a picture in the prospect's mind. For example, to illustrate the true benefit of the early playoff ticket buying feature, the seller might explain to a business owner that when the team qualifies for the playoffs, the community's support for the team reaches a fever pitch. Tickets are quickly snapped up and many fans are left out or paying exorbitant prices for tickets on websites like StubHub and eBay. When one of the business owner's key clients calls to say she will be in town during the playoffs and would love to go to a play-off game, the business owner can calmly assure her that company tickets are in hand and are in a great location to watch one of the most exciting and sought after games of the year.

## INTRODUCTION TO THE STEPS OF THE SALES PROCESS

The heart of the consultative sales process is asking questions to diagnose the customer's dominant buying motive and making a customized, tailored recommendation that fits the customer's situation by explaining how the product will benefit them. This section introduces some of the key tenants at each stage of the sales process that comprise the next section of the book. The sales process can be defined many different ways, but the steps below are consistent in each type of approach. The sales process is outlined in Figure 4.1.

### *Prospecting*

Prospecting is the continual process of identifying and contacting businesses and individuals to create a pool or list of qualified buyers. In recent years,

# Figure 4.1

**Sales Process Overview**

**Sales Process Overview**

| Prospecting | Opening | Needs Analysis | Present Solution | Overcome Objections | Close | Maximize Sale | Service |
|---|---|---|---|---|---|---|---|
| ▶ Use CRM and social media to find qualified leads<br>▶ Get to know customer before first call or meeting<br>▶ Work smarter, not harder | ▶ B2C<br>  • Build rapport<br>  • Set agenda<br>  • Obtain permission<br>▶ B2B<br>  • Break the customer's pre-occupation<br>  • Set appointment<br>  • Connect with social selling | ▶ Get the customer talking by asking questions<br>▶ Diagnose dominant buying motive<br>▶ Uncover facts, feelings, needs, and concerns<br>▶ Build value in customer's mind | ▶ Synthesize information learned in needs analysis to present tailored solution that fulfills the customer's need<br>▶ Position relevant benefits as solutions | ▶ Move the conversation forward<br>▶ Explain the benefits of purchasing<br>▶ Continue to build value | ▶ Bring the sales process to a logical, natural conclusion by asking for the customer's business<br>▶ Establish next steps for the relationship or conversation | ▶ Offer additional products to compliment the package the customer wants to buy<br>▶ Investigate all of the ways in which the customer can use tickets<br>▶ Justify purchase of more or better tickets | ▶ Deliver high quality experience<br>▶ Fulfill all features and benefits<br>▶ Focus on long-term value of the relationship<br>▶ Renew packages or membership for next year |

technology has allowed salespeople to work smarter when it comes to prospecting. Before the development of customer relationship management systems and social media, sellers relied exclusively on lists of names and calling them on the phone. Now, customer relationship management systems allow salespeople and managers to develop targeted lists of prospects that meet desired criteria. Social selling has created new venues for sellers to make initial "soft" contacts with prospects even before making the first call or setting the first meeting. Once prospects have been identified, sellers can begin doing research on the prospect that paints broad strokes of the prospect's needs and situation.

## Opening

In a business-to-consumer (B2C) setting, it is important to establish rapport early in the conversation in order to build credibility and hold the prospect's attention. Rapport can be built by using an energetic and professional voice, using the prospect's first name, and revealing information about yourself. Sales managers disagree on whether sellers should attempt to close the sale on the phone or pursue an appointment for an arena tour, but they do agree that a strong opening sets the stage for a successful sales call. In a business-to-business (B2B) setting, sellers use a mix of social selling and phone calls to set appointments with decision-makers. LinkedIn is the typical platform used by corporate salespeople to engage prospects with a soft contact. Over the phone, sellers have to get past the gatekeeper in order to reach the decision-maker and set the appointment.

## Needs Analysis

**VALUE**
total benefit provided to the customer

In order to understand what motivates and compels people to purchase, sellers ask questions to learn about the customer and their needs, wants, desires, pain, concerns, and problems. Identifying the customer's dominant buying motive allows sellers to effectively leverage product features and benefits in a way that is relevant to the customer. Contrary to what most people think about sales, the customer should be doing approximately 80% of the talking during the sales conversation, with the seller mostly focused on asking high-yield, open-ended questions that keep the conversation natural and free-flowing. Asking the right questions at the right time allows the seller to help the customer discover how the offering can satisfy their needs. Value is built as needs are uncovered. **Value** is the total benefit that the seller's product or service provides to the customer. Good salespeople allow customers to discover the value of the product by talking about it rather than telling the customer about it. As the seller builds value with open-ended questions, picture the information gleaned from the customer as coins in a piggy bank. Once the customer articulates the value they see in making a purchase, the seller can cash in those coins and make a recommendation.

## Presenting Solutions

This is the first point in the conversation where the seller should confidently present packages, prices, tickets, or other product knowledge. The goal of this stage is to apply relevant product knowledge in a way that fulfills the customer's need. The challenge for salespeople is to synthesize all of the information learned in the needs analysis to present a customized solution for the customer. Sales trainers and managers have different approaches and philosophies on presenting solutions, but a common bridge between the needs analysis and the product recommendation is for sellers to use the phrase "Based on what you've told me." Then sellers position the relevant benefits of buying as solutions for the customer's situation. The first product recommendation serves as a trial close. If the customer agrees with the recommendation, the salesperson can move to close the sale. Or, the customer may have a concern, which will bring up some sort of objection they have with the package. The seller is the expert on the product and should display confidence when presenting the package.

## *Overcoming Objections*

Objections are any concern or question raised by the customer at any point during the sales process. Objections should be welcomed by the seller because they present an opportunity to explain the benefits of purchasing in ways that continue to build value in the customer's mind. Objections come in many different forms and can be responded to in many different ways, but all good responses to an objection require the seller to listen to what the customer is saying, empathize with their perspective, ask questions to clarify the objection, educate the customer with product knowledge and important benefits, and close on the objection before returning to the sales cycle. Successful salespeople demonstrate persistence at overcoming objections and don't give up when customers begin to have objections. In fact, most product features and benefits are designed to overcome specific objections.

## *Closing/Next Steps*

Closing is the process of asking for the customer's business. Closing brings the sales process to a logical and natural conclusion. Assuming the seller has developed rapport, uncovered needs, articulated a relevant and customized value proposition, overcome objections, and communicated the sales message effectively, the next logical step is to close. The seller has earned the right to ask for the sale if they have uncovered and presented value to the customer. Unfortunately, closing is often perceived as a special skill and detached from the rest of the sales process and contributes to the negative image of salespeople.

## *Maximizing the Sale*

Maximizing the sale has been reported by sport salespeople and managers as the primary driver of success.[14] The three primary strategies for maximizing each sale are cross-selling, upselling, and generating referrals. Cross-selling involves offering additional products to support or complement the product or package the customer has already decided to purchase. Upselling involves persuading a customer to purchase an upgraded version of the same type of product they are intending to buy. Referrals are the name of a person or company given to the salesperson by other customers.

---

14. Pierce, D., Lee, D., & Petersen, J. (2014). Sport sales personnel perceptions of factors impacting job performance: A factor analysis of sport sales activities. *International Journal of Sport Management, 15*(1), 71–90.

### Servicing

The final step of the consultative sales process is to deliver the high quality experience that was promised. The focus of this stage should be the long-term value the customer relationship can bring to the organization. The end result is renewing or upgrading the customer's purchase for the next season. The organizational structure of the sport organization will determine whether the salesperson has continued interaction with the customer or plays a role in fulfilling on the product features and benefits. This is a troubling issue within sales because entry-level sales reps are rarely incentivized to develop long-term relationships. Instead, they are promoted on their ability to produce immediate results. The end result is limited ability for the entry-level sales force to cultivate long-term value with the customer because they have either been promoted to a new position or fired.

## UNIQUE NATURE OF THE SPORT PRODUCT

The sales process and competencies needed to be successful are similar to other industries, but selling sport experiences is different from selling other goods or services, such as computer software, farm machinery, or tax return preparations. Few brands elicit the consumer fandom of sport teams, few products have the short shelf life of a live sporting event, and nearly all other consumer product manufactures have far greater control over the final product. For instance, someone selling a Harley Davidson motorcycle or Disney vacation may sell to a highly identified consumer (a big fan of the product), but a motorcycle does not disappear after a certain date and Disney maintains great control over the quality of their rides and resorts. Southwest airlines, meanwhile, may not be able to sell a January 17th flight on January 18th, but the airline has great control over flight schedules, in-flight experiences, and the quality of the planes they fly. By contrast, the Chicago Bulls have many highly identified fans, cannot sell tickets to a game against the Lakers after that game has been played, and cannot control whether their team wins on a given night, or even if all of their team members will be able to compete injury-free.

> The challenge for sport marketers is to market the experiences and manage the expectations of an emotionally laden, inconsistent, unscripted, unpredictable, and uncontrollable momentary social product that will be desired and experienced differently from person to person and place to place.[15]

---

15. Armstrong, K. (2014). Sport marketing. In P. Pedersen & L. Thibault (Eds.), *Contemporary Sport Management*, 5th ed. (p. 296). Champaign, IL: Human Kinetics.

It is differences such as these that can provide a challenge to the sport event ticket seller. Further thoughts on some of the aspects which make selling the sport product different than selling other goods or services include:

1. **Sport possesses a subjective nature**. People assign their own meaning to sport based on the construction of their own reality. Sport means different things to different people, and it can even mean different things to the same person depending on the time in the season, team performance expectations, or the people with whom they attend the game. Sport is an experience and the value of that experience changes from person to person. The feelings each consumer has toward the sport product is highly subjective. The implication for the sport sales professional is that each customer brings a unique set of needs, desires, motives, and beliefs about the team or event. This is why it is important to ask questions that uncover customer motives and needs before recommending a product or experience. Recommending the same product to every customer regardless of their situation is ineffective.

2. **Sport is intangible**. Many live sport attendees are attracted to an event because of the emotions it elicits, the social opportunities it presents, and the overall experience it provides. Much of this appeal is intangible, which can be difficult for a seller to adequately describe to a potential buyer. While everyone knows exactly what they are getting when purchasing a cup of coffee at Starbucks, selling the experience of a sporting event can be more challenging, particularly in today's environment of high-definition television and a sports bar on every block. Successful sport salespeople are able to paint a picture for the customer that gets them to feel the emotion of being in the arena, an experience that cannot be replicated elsewhere. Sellers need to be well versed in storytelling to bring the intangible experience to life.

3. **Sport creates an ephemeral experience**. Sport marketers and salespeople are in the business of selling experiences that are transient and short-lived. The game is the prop for entertainment or any engagement of a customer in a personal, memorable way. Viewed in this light, organizations are not putting on an athletic competition, but instead athletic competitions are organized to deliver a personal, memorable experience for fans. This reality places significant importance on the product extensions (such as mascots, autograph sessions, and photo opportunities) that are offered to supplement the core product (the game itself). Sport salespeople need to know the in-venue experience inside and out, particularly what other customers and clients appreciate about attending a game.

4. **Sport evokes strong emotional attachment and fandom**. Sports have the ability to create fans instead of just customers.[16] Fans are people who are ardently devoted enthusiasts of their team, not simply a person who buys goods and services (customer). Sports teams develop a devoted fanatical following due to high levels of identification. Highly identified fans describe themselves in terms of being a fan, even to the point that the fan feels as if they are part of the team. The more identified fans are, the more they will engage in purchasing tickets, buying licensed merchandise, and consuming media related to the team.[17] Sport salespeople can leverage this strong team identification into greater revenue for their organization. Asking questions in the needs analysis that determine the customer's level of identification helps to diagnose the customer's needs and pitch the right package. For example, some sales managers recommend asking the question *what is your favorite memory* at the start of the needs analysis to evoke a customer's strong emotional attachment to the team or experience.

When people are deciding whether or not to buy, typically the strongest emotion operating at that moment will determine what decision is made. People decide based on their emotions, and then justify the decision to others (e.g., parents, friends, spouse, partner) based on logic or reason.[18] As a result, salespeople must sell to both the logic and emotion of the customer. This should be natural for salespeople in sport in light of the emotional investment that fans place in their favorite teams, athletes, and sports. To illustrate, Sandy purchases a 25-person suite for her husband's retirement party because she loves her husband, wants to celebrate the accomplishment in style, create an environment for their closest friends to socialize, and for nostalgia since their first date was at a baseball game. The decision to purchase for Sandy is an emotional one, but when justifying spending the amount of money she did on the event to other people, Sandy will emphasize how a suite compares to renting a space at local restaurants or taking a vacation, the great view they will have of the game, and the ease of having the team set up, organize, and clean up after the event is over.

5. **Sporting events are perishable products that are simultaneously produced and consumed**. Sporting events are produced and consumed at the same time. Not only does this allow for the fans to

---

16. Wakefield, K. (2015). *Team sports marketing*. Retrieved from teamsportsmarketing.com
17. Ibid.
18. Tracy, B. (2004). *The psychology of selling*. Nashville, TN: Thomas Nelson. p. 73.

help create the atmosphere of the game, but fans must purchase a ticket prior to the game because that specific game only occurs once. Possessing a ticket to a live event that has occurred in the past is worthless, except for the possible sentimental value of the physical ticket. As a result, registration deadlines and game dates provide sport salespeople the opportunity to create a sense of urgency when selling items like season ticket packages or yearly memberships. Because tickets must be purchased prior to the start of the event, scarcity is inherent in the sport product. The **scarcity** principle suggests people often want what they can't have.[19] If something is rare or becoming rare, it becomes more valuable.

**SCARCITY**
principle stating people want what they can't have

In addition, arenas and specific seating sections have capacities, premium seating areas only have so many suites, and participant events have registration capacities. All of these facts can be utilized by effective sellers to create a sense of scarcity or urgency with the product. As a result, there are many ethical ways to leverage the scarcity principle to create a sense of urgency with the customer. Being honest about seating capacities and important deadlines creates a sense of urgency. Good sellers want to let the customer know that 50% of the games sold out last year, and they don't want the customer to end up at the box office and not be able to secure tickets to the game. The use of scarcity, done in an ethical manner, is a strategic tool in the salesperson's tool kit that can benefit the salesperson and the customer.

6.  **Enjoyment of sport occurs in social settings**. People attend live sporting events with other people. They rarely attend by themselves. As a result, sport salespeople must consider how their event can create socialization opportunities for their customers. They also may find ways to include others in the buying process. Sales managers recommend asking questions like *who is the biggest baseball fan in your office* to get the customer talking about other fans in their personal network. Understanding the scope of a customer's network is important in selling group packages and upselling customers to the appropriate amount of tickets.

Sport fans also turn to and accept the actions of others as correct. The principle of **social proof** states people use information about how others have behaved to help determine their own course of action.[20] People view a particular behavior as more correct in a situation to the

**SOCIAL PROOF**
states that people use information about how others have behaved to help determine their own proper conduct

19.  Cialdini, R. (1993). *Influence: The psychology of persuasion*, 2nd ed. New York: William Morrow.

20.  Ibid.

degree that they see other people performing it. This is based on the assumption that the greater the number of people who find an idea correct, the more correct the idea will be. Social proof can explain the bandwagon effect in sports, where the increase in the popularity and interest in a team increases as the belief in the team is taken up by others. Salespeople use social proof to their advantage in the following ways:

- Telling customers that tickets are going fast conveys the message other people are buying.
- Starting the conversation with a referral from a customer that has recently purchased tells the customer "your friend just bought with me."
- When responding to objections, salespeople often tell customers what other customers have done (some of my best customers have found that . . .).
- Telling prospects that "we help other businesses just like yourself achieve their business goals."

7. **The sport product is unpredictable and inconsistent**. One of the major attractions to sport is not knowing who is going to win the game, which athletes are going to compete, and how well athletes will perform. If people knew these outcomes in advance, sport would lose its allure. Beyond this, situational factors like climate, weather, time of year, team records, and momentum can impact the outcome of the event. As a result, sport salespeople are selling the ultimate reality show full of unpredictable human drama.

8. **Sport marketers often lack control over the core product**. Sport marketers are required to sell a core product (the game or competition) over which they have very limited control. Winning and losing, injuries, referees' decisions, weather, and strength of opponents are just some of the factors which are out of a team's control when they sell their core product. As a result, sport salespeople often rely on product extensions not directly related to the core product (e.g., entertainment, promotions, and activities). Product extensions create the atmosphere surrounding the event and are used to complement attraction to the unpredictable nature of the game. Sport sales professionals must be well versed on the benefits provided by the product extensions, particularly when the team is not performing well.

# CHAPTER SUMMARY

Every customer is unique. People and businesses attend sporting events for many different reasons. People experience sport in subjective and different ways. Fans passionately care about their team. For these reasons and many others outlined in this chapter, the fundamental role of the salesperson is to get to know the customer by asking questions and understand what motivates him or her to purchase. Once you've determined what makes a customer tick (found their dominant buying motive), you can position the benefits of your product/team/package/event to meet his or her needs and desires. Recognizing that each customer is unique prevents the salesperson from talking about product features the customer does not value.

# CHAPTER ACTIVITIES

1. Explain why a consultative sales approach puts the seller in a better position to close the sale than the "info dumping" strategy.

2. Describe a time when you made a sport-related purchase for pain reasons and for desire reasons. How did your thought process differ when making these two purchases?

3. Consider these five sporting events: high school football game, gymnastics at the Olympic trials, NFL playoff game, minor league hockey game, and Iron Man competition. For each event, identify what you believe are the top three motives for people to attend or participate in these events. Analyze the differences you notice in motives for these events, and explain how your presentation of benefits might change depending on the dominant buying motives.

4. Identify five product features that appear on professional sports teams' season ticket sales webpages. Describe the benefit for each feature.

5. Select one of the **sport consumption motives** that you believe are the most relevant for consumers attending a sporting event of your choosing. Think of one person in your circle of influence that would attend the game for the motive you selected. Then develop a story about that person that articulates how the game can solve a problem, fulfill a need, reduce tension, or eliminate a gap for that person. Be specific about the situation and provide enough detail that the motive you selected makes sense within the context of the story. End your story with how attending the game BENEFITS that person. Use this format:

    a. **Motive**: _____(phrase)

    b. **Person**: _____(name)

    c. **Need/Problem/Tension**: _____(phrase)

    d. **Story**: this should be approximately three sentences in length

    e. **Customer Benefit**: this can be one sentence

# CHAPTERS 1–4 COMPETENCY ASSESSMENT[21]

## COMPETENCY DOMAIN: KNOWLEDGE AND SKILL DEVELOPMENT

*Exemplary:* Consistently does all or almost all of the following:

- Demonstrates expert knowledge of the sales process
- Rarely makes mistakes about product knowledge with customers
- Viewed by others as a go-to resource by others on the sales staff when questions arise
- Relentlessly pursues acquisition of knowledge in order to improve sales performance
- Independently seeks out professional development and training opportunities
- Cultivates new business and is never content with past performance

*Skilled:* Does most of the following:

- Demonstrates above average knowledge of the sales process and the product
- Occasionally makes mistakes about product knowledge with customers
- Only on occasion requires intervention and additional training to master a competency
- At times could do a better job seeking out independent professional development opportunities or taking advantage of internal sales training
- Seller may have been exemplary at one point, but has become complacent due to a large book of business

*Adequate:* Does most of the following:

- Fails to reliably demonstrate knowledge of the sales process
- Fails to reliably demonstrate knowledge of the product
- Makes product knowledge mistakes at inopportune times
- May be beginning to show improvement during sales training and coaching sessions, but still needs close supervision

*Novice:* Consistently does all or almost all of the following:

- Demonstrates very little knowledge of the product
- Fails to reliably demonstrate knowledge of sales process making fundamental mistakes
- Does not have a handle on sales process or product where management is comfortable putting the Seller in front of customers
- Fails to improve after sales training and other interventions have been provided
- Does not recognize in what areas they need to improve

---

21. From "Competency Assessment for Entry-Level Sport Ticket Sales Professionals" by David Pierce and Richard Irwin, *Journal of Applied Sport Management*, Volume 8 (2), Summer 2016. Reprinted by permission of Sagamore Publishing. www.sagamorepub.com

# CHAPTER 5

## OPENING THE BUSINESS-TO-CONSUMER RELATIONSHIP

### LEARNING OBJECTIVES

After completing this chapter, you should be able to:

- ▶ Discuss the antecedents and consequences of sales call anxiety.
- ▶ Identify ways to build rapport at the beginning of a consumer sales call.
- ▶ Contrast the agenda setting philosophy with the direct-to-question philosophy when opening a consumer sales call.
- ▶ Perform an opening dialogue for how to open a consumer sales call.
- ▶ Create a script for delivering voice mails.

### KEY TERMS

| | |
|---|---|
| Agenda | Referral |
| Business-to-consumer sales | Sales call anxiety |
| I/My statement | Scripted outline |
| Mismatching | |

### COMPENTENCIES

- ▶ Ability to pique the customer's interest in the opening of the conversation/presentation.
- ▶ Ability to create a customized game plan for the sales call or meeting (agenda).

## CHAPTER OVERVIEW

Sport ticket sellers approach individual consumers who buy tickets for their own personal use and business owners/managers who buy tickets for business purposes. Sellers often use different approaches to open the call for these two groups. This chapter covers opening the sales call in a **business-to-consumer** (B2C) environment, where the salesperson is calling individuals who are probably interested in using sport tickets for their own personal use. A solid opening is integral to every sales call. This chapter provides a framework for establishing a strong foundation to start each call that can be rehearsed until it becomes second nature. This chapter investigates the components to a successful opening that builds rapport, gains trust, and piques the customer's interest.

**BUSINESS-TO-CONSUMER SALES** salesperson calls individuals who are probably interested in using the sport tickets for personal use

## PURPOSE OF THE OPENING

In sales, the purpose of the opening is to engage potential buyers in the hopes of ultimately selling them a product offering. The reality in sport sales is that successful sellers typically initiate dozens of conversations before finding a prospect who is interested in buying. Along those same lines, sellers must understand very few sales occur on the initial call. One ticket sales manager for an NBA team shared that sales made over the phone are typically completed between the fifth and sixth call with the prospect. Another ticket sales manager from an NHL club suggested the purpose of the initial sales call is rarely to close, but rather to start a conversation that may lead to a sale at another time. Such information might suggest to a seller that initiating sales conversations are not important. Nothing could be further from the truth. Sellers must go into every call with the mindset of starting a relationship with the person on the other end of the phone, even if this rarely happens. A seller who does not take this approach will likely miss opportunities when the right prospect is on the line.

> You will never make a sale solely off a great introduction, but you can lose a sale with a bad one.
>
> —Jeff Berryhill,
> *Major League Soccer*

## PRE-CALL PREPARATION

Before making any sales calls, sellers need to have a firm grasp on all elements of the organization's sales training, including mastery over the scripted

Courtesy David Pierce.

outline, knowledge of the customer, the right mindset, and an objective for the call.

## Scripted Outline

A **scripted outline** details the prescribed language used by sellers at certain points in the conversation, while providing a road map for other parts of the call. The most likely stage of the call with prescribed language is the opening. Sellers should never pick up the phone without knowing the precise strategy, language, and tone they will employ on the call. Effective sellers, particularly early in their career, never just "wing it." Rehearsing and perfecting the opening of a sales call is vital because it is the only time the seller controls the direction of the call. Some teams suggest having two or three "go to" opening statements, which can be interchanged from call to call. This strategy helps sellers stay fresh in their approach, particularly if the seller's job entails making dozens of calls a day. Organizations will often have new sales representatives rehearse reading the script verbatim until the new seller knows the script by heart, including which words to emphasize and where to pause while reading. In general, sellers have no more than seven seconds to convince prospects that "investing" in a conversation will be worth their while. Because of this, it is critical for the seller to get the opening message just right, eliminating useless or irrelevant communication. A script allows the seller to know exactly what should be said during the outset of the conversation. Sellers may only get one chance with the prospect and don't want to blow it by "winging it" with a poorly delivered opening.

**SCRIPTED OUTLINE** details the prescribed language used by sellers at certain points in the conversation, while providing a road map for other parts of the call

However, once the seller starts asking questions the call can go in any number of directions, making the scripting of every single word difficult and less effective. As a result, many sales managers also create an outline or call tree for stages of the call like the needs analysis due to the many different directions the call could go. The outline provides a roadmap for the sales call, but does not designate the specific words used by the seller. Outlines provide a way to think through the various answers and paths a customer might direct the conversation. Outlines place the focus on the prospect's responses instead of the words the seller uses. Call outlines emphasize creativity and improvisation during the call and eliminate the notion that the prospect is being given a canned presentation or being read to.

## Customer Information

Sellers should find out as much information as they can about a prospect before picking up the phone. While it is not necessary to perform an FBI background search, sellers can learn some things about their prospect relatively easily and quickly before calling. For starters, what information does the team already know about the customer? How was the prospect's name acquired? Has he or she purchased tickets before? What can be uncovered about the prospect after a quick look on social media? In addition, the seller should have tools handy to be ready to answer any questions the prospect might pose. Game schedules, pricing, ticket packages, and upcoming promotions or opponents are all important items that should easily be accessible on the seller's desk or be just a click away on the seller's computer screen. After learning a little about the prospect, the seller should think about what sort of objections might be brought up and what sort of benefits might be suggested. While a seller should never propose benefits or inventory without first learning about the prospect's wants and needs, it is still good to have an idea about the direction the conversation might go. This is particularly important for new sellers who cannot rely as much on past experience. Access to a calculator and the CRM system is also a necessity.

## The Right Mindset

If all of the seller's "tools" are handy and the seller knows how the conversation will start, it is nearly time to make the call. One challenge for sellers who engage in high-volume calling is to treat each call as an individual selling opportunity. If a seller has encountered a streak of rejection, hang-ups, or non-answers, it can be easy to fall into the trap of treating all calls the same way or not being prepared for a live conversation. Sellers never know when someone will answer the sales call, so they must always be ready to strike up a conversation. To help make sure the seller is in the right frame of mind, it is advisable to take a deep breath and relax between each call. Some sales managers suggest "smiling before dialing" to ensure the seller is in the right frame of mind.

## *Objective for the Call*

Finally, the seller needs to set an objective for each call. The objective depends on how many times the seller has spoken with the customer. Common objectives for the first call are to complete a needs analysis and set an appointment to talk to the prospect in the future. Some sport organizations use the first call as the opportunity to set an appointment to meet the prospect at the sport venue for a tour, while other organizations recommend closing the sale on the phone. If the seller has already had positive conversations or meetings with the customer in the past, the goal may be to close the sale.

## SALES CALL ANXIETY

This is the moment of truth. You're sitting at your desk, preparing to make your first phone call to someone you don't know. Your heart is pounding, you feel anxious and nervous, not sure what to expect. Several questions are racing through your mind like *will this person be mean to me*, *what if I forget what to say*, and *how will I be able to remember everything about sales that I've learned*? For many new sellers, the start of the sales conversation can be intimidating for a variety of reasons. Seller may feel unsure of their abilities. The seller may also feel intimidated about the prospect of trying to sell a product, particularly if the seller has never sold before. In fact, sales researchers have developed a typography known as **Sales Call Anxiety (SCA)**.[1] SCA is a fear of being negatively perceived or rejected by potential customers, involving both negative self-evaluations ("I don't know what I'm doing"; "Customers won't like me") and physiological symptoms (sweaty hands, quavering voice, talking too fast, avoiding eye contact). While these reactions are normal and part of human nature, they are not productive in a sales environment. Some of the best ways to overcome SCA are to rehearse and role-play sales conversations, observe other successful sellers, and analyze fears by writing down or articulating

**SALES CALL ANXIETY**
fear of being negatively perceived or rejected by potential customers

---

1. Anderson, R., Dubinsky, A., & Mehta, R. (2007). *Personal selling: Building customer relationships and partnerships*. Houghton Mifflin.

©VGstockstudio/Shutterstock.com

specific concerns and discussing them with managers. The next section establishes guidelines for starting a sales conversation to help new sellers get past some of these barriers.

---

### SALESPEOPLE REMEMBER THEIR FIRST SALES CALLS

**Eric Cole—Philadelphia 76ers[1]**

My first call I ever made was very stressful. I had just come off of a week and a half of training and it was "go time." I felt very nervous, palms were sweating, and my heart was racing. I wanted to make sure that everything went perfect and hoped it would have followed the way every role-play went. But in all actuality, the role-plays were different and not everyone wanted to speak with a Sales Rep from the Pacers. When I had my first person answer, I can remember talking extremely fast and using the word "Um" all the time. What got me through the phone call and my advice to all rookie sales reps is to follow the sales process you were taught. The individual on the other line didn't know it was my first day on the phones. Follow the process to a T because it works. That is what got me through that first call.

**Bob Hamer—Sport Business Solutions**

The first sales call I made was one of the scariest moments of my professional life. We had trained for two plus weeks as a class of new inside sales reps and we all hit the phones at the same time. All of us looked around wondering who'd be the first to make a call. Once we got going it was a ton of fun and we all fed off of each other but I'll never forget picking up that phone for the first time. What helped me was understanding that rejection is a part of the process. Not everyone is going to want to talk to us; all we can control is our attitude and energy on our side of the phone. We can't control what they're going to say or if they'll even answer.

**Charlie Slonaker—Philadelphia Revolution[2]**

When my boss, John Davis (now VP of Ticket Sales with the Cleveland Browns), told me I was able to start making calls, I was incredibly pumped. I knew I wanted to get a full-time job with the team and I figured proving my worth by making sales was the best way to do it. My boss was really helpful and provided training, so I went in with a decent understanding of what I was trying to achieve.

During my internship with Dayton Dragons I was calling Former Group Buyers. I had a lady from the City of Vandalia who picked up and said she was looking for a summer outing for their employees. She ended up buying 100 group seats. Pretty basic stuff. The cool/memorable part was when she called me back about six months later. Apparently two people in the group met, started dating, and ended up getting married on the Dragons plaza! Her call was to let me know that their wedding was that weekend and they wanted to thank me for cold-calling her.

**Hillary Anderson—Golden State Warriors[2]**

I remember being extremely eager to hit the phones after two weeks of training with our management staff. I could not wait to speak to a real prospect instead of role-playing with my coworkers and boss. I took my time and did my best to listen to the client instead of rule the conversation by talking. Within my first couple of days I began to feel really comfortable and started making some sales! I'd advise any rookie rep to take it slow. Act like you're on the phone with someone that you're comfortable with. Listen to what the prospect is saying. Let them lead the conversation. Start with some banter and build that rapport. Make the prospect feel like they're talking to a friend.

---

1. Reprinted by permission of Eric Cole.
2. © Kendall Hunt Publishing Company

## SALESPEOPLE RECALL AWKWARD PHONE CALLS

**Bob Hamer—Sport Business Solutions**

One of the funniest/terrifying moments I ever had was a prospect calling me out for reading off of my **sales script**. I'm a big believer in phone scripting and it was early on in my career and I still sounded a little robotic. He asked if I was reading off of a script, I sheepishly said "no" then he barked a couple more things and hung up. I was really shaken after I got off the phone but I picked it back up and had a great call right after that. You just have to keep moving. But my friends and I definitely got a kick out of that one!

**Charlie Slonaker—Philadelphia Revolution[1]**

My most memorable moment on the phones was when I was working at the Cincinnati Bengals. Carson Palmer was in the process of demanding a trade, otherwise he planned to retire. I was battling with a big fan about buying a full season ticket package for the coming season. He was really getting on me about Carson holding out and how that said a lot about our organization. I tried everything I could to play up the rest of the team and bring up other positives, but he wasn't having it. I guess I pushed him to his breaking point because all of the sudden he screamed out, "This is ridiculous . . . you know what . . . YOU CAN JUST GO TO HELL!!!" I was a little taken aback by that and asked him if he was serious. He immediately felt really bad and apologized and quickly rushed off the phone out of embarrassment. I'll never forget that one.

1. © Kendall Hunt Publishing Company

**SALES SCRIPT**
prescribed language used by sellers when speaking to prospects

## ESTABLISHING RAPPORT EARLY IN THE CONVERSATION

The opening of the sales call is the first chance for the salesperson to establish rapport with the prospect. It is important to establish rapport because customers prefer to buy from people they like.[2] The first 30 seconds of a sales call is important because it allows the seller to make a positive impression, establish credibility, and set the direction for the call. The old adage "You never get a second chance to make a first impression" is particularly relevant when opening the sales call.

Nearly all prospects will be caught somewhat off guard on the first phone call. When calling an individual buyer outside of working hours, the seller might be interrupting personal time; the prospect may be cooking dinner, doing yard work, or watching television. When calling during working hours, the seller may be interrupting a business meeting, calling while the prospect is travelling for business, or catching prospects preparing their own sales presentations. At other times, sellers catch prospects at awkward times like at a funeral, at the doctor's office, feeding an infant, in the shower, or when they are sick. Or even the most dreaded scenario—speaking with the widow of a former customer who just recently passed away. Regardless of their mental and physical state, the customer will not be anticipating your phone call.

Customers will be thinking *should I cut this person off*, and *do I want to talk to this person?* The prospect may experience anxiety because they don't know what to expect from the call, they might be asked to spend money, or they might be misled, not to mention they are speaking with a stranger. Oftentimes, the natural reaction to being caught off guard by a sales call is to immediately say *no*. As a result, it is important for sellers to quickly build rapport, establish credibility, and earn the right to begin asking the customer questions. Four quick ways to help establish rapport in the opening of the call

2. Cialdini, R. (1993). *Influence: The psychology of persuasion*, 2nd ed. New York: William Morrow.

are to smile, use an energetic and professional voice, use the prospect's first name, and reveal information about yourself.

## Smile

Customers can tell the difference when someone is smiling and when someone is dreading the next call, even on the phone. Sales managers recommend that sellers think about someone or something you like before making the call. This is something that can be practiced by looking at yourself in the mirror while calling. Smiling conveys warmth and friendliness in your voice.

## Use an Energetic and Professional Voice

A salesperson can demonstrate professionalism in a face-to-face meeting by wearing a suit. On the phone, however, the only tool the salesperson has is his or her voice. Voice projection is critical to show energy, enthusiasm, and professionalism. It's also important to speak clearly and not too quickly. It is recommended that the seller underline or highlight specific words on the script to emphasize to ensure voice inflection and enthusiasm.

## Use the Prospect's First Name

Using the prospect's first name sends a message of familiarity and helps to establish rapport. People pay attention when they hear their first name. Some sales managers recommend using the prospect's first name at least every other sentence in the opening stage of the call.

## Reveal Information About Yourself

**I/My statements** are a great way for salespeople to reveal personal information, which is the cornerstone to starting a relationship with the customer. An I/My story describes a personal experience or the experience of someone else. Salespeople can reveal information about themselves by relating to the customer's experience. The first couple of questions asked by a salesperson should be followed with a short response about yourself. Sellers typically should have several I/My statements prepared to use at the appropriate time. For example,

**I/MY STATEMENT**
Story that describes a personal experience or the experience of someone else

- ▶ Salesperson: What is your favorite part about coming out to X Stadium?
- ▶ Prospect: I love getting a chance to come out with my sons.

▶ Salesperson: I love it when fans say that. I remember when I used to go to games with my dad when I was little. Those are some of my favorite memories with him.

Other examples include:

▶ I remember coming to games with my dad when I was little. I always remember the smell of popcorn when we walked in the stadium and then coming through the entry-way seeing the field for the first time. I'll never forget going to those games. It was such a great experience growing up.

▶ My neighbors bought their first season ticket package last year, and they were telling me about how they were surprised how many games they ended up coming to.

▶ My parents would always take me to the July 4th game because there were fireworks at the end of the game. It was always a special experience because we would eat downtown before the game and then stay late to watch the fireworks. I'm thinking about doing the same thing with my kids when they get a little bit older.

▶ I remember seeing Rickie Fowler play in person for the first time. We followed him for the entire 18 holes of the tournament and I've been a fan of his ever since. He wore pink pants and I went out and bought the same pants the next week.

## STEP 1: INTRODUCTION

While prospects are never anticipating a sport sales call, they are often familiar with the sport organization making the call. This is because most teams provide their sellers with leads cultivated from lists of past ticket buyers, people who have entered team contests and raffles, referrals from other ticket holders, or parents whose children may have attended team sport camps. Calling on prospects who have a prior "relationship" with the team makes it much easier for a seller to begin a conversation.

While the opening lines and order will vary by sport organization, the introduction to a sales conversation generally starts with the following six components:

1. Ask for the prospect

2. Greeting

3. Title/Role

4. Team

5. Your Name

6. Pause

### 1. ASK FOR THE PROSPECT

*Hello, may I please speak with Megan?*

### 2. GREETING

Begin with a simple two-word greeting—*Hi, Megan* or *Hello, Megan.*

### 3. TITLE/ROLE

Identify your title or role within the organization. Sales managers should select titles that help salespeople establish credibility and relevance with the customer. For example, teams commonly use titles such as personal account manager, account representative, and account executive.—*I'm your personal account manager* or *I'm your account representative*

### 4. TEAM

Identify the name of the team or organization for which you work—*with the XYZ City Tigers*

### 5. YOUR NAME

State your name. *My name is Kevin.*

### 6. PAUSE

After stating your name, allow the prospect a second to respond to what you have just said. They may respond favorably since you are calling from a sport team, which could provide a forum for you to build rapport. If they do nothing more than say "Hi," then move on to the next step of setting the agenda.

#### PUTTING IT TOGETHER

*Hello, may I please speak with Megan . . . Hi, Megan, I'm your personal account representative with the XYZ City Tigers. My name is Kevin.* [pause]

The rationale for leading with a title prior to the seller's name is that the customer is not expecting to receive a sales call. In the first few seconds of the call, they are relatively inattentive and just trying to orient themselves to who is calling. The quicker they can be given an important sounding title and the name of the team, the quicker the prospect can orient themselves to the call. Once prospects become more attentive to the call, they are more likely to remember the seller's name.

In contrast to the scripting provided above, Paul Neuberger, The Cold Call Coach, recommends not using the phrase "My name is" instead opting for the following introduction:[3]

*Hello Megan! Kevin Johnson; how are you?*

The purpose of this introduction is to offer a level of familiarity with the prospect and get them thinking about how they know the seller instead of how they are going to get the seller off the phone.

## STEP 2: BEGIN THE SALES CONVERSATION

After the introduction, sales managers differ on how to proceed with the sales call. There are two general philosophies. The first philosophy is to set an

---

3. Ticket Galaxy. *Three worst words you can say during a cold call.* Retrieved from http://sportssalesbootcamp.com/wp/2016/03/04/three-worst-words-you-can-say-during-a-cold-call/

**agenda** for the call and then seek the customer's permission to continue with the call. The second philosophy is to advance immediately into asking questions that can aid in building rapport with the customer. Both philosophies are outlined below.

**AGENDA**
customized game plan for the sales call or meeting

## Philosophy 1: Set the Agenda and Ask for Permission

After completing the introduction, some sales managers recommend setting an agenda for the call and confirming the prospect is willing to engage in a conversation. The philosophy for setting the agenda is that sales reps should not be ashamed of their profession, nor hide the fact they are calling to talk about getting the customer out to more games in the future.

## 1. AGENDA

Typically sellers are calling to talk about the customer's past experience and what opportunities they have to purchase tickets in the future.

> *The reason for my call is to learn about your experience at the ballpark last season and follow up with you on the e-mail/letter that we sent you last week about opportunities for this upcoming season.*

Notice this statement does not refer to the lead list that contained the prospect's phone number. Many salespeople lead with *I saw that you came to a game last year . . .* or *Our records indicate that . . .* which leaves the customer wondering how much of their information and data you are tracking.

Some sales reps position the call as a customer satisfaction survey in the agenda. ("We're calling to discuss your experience at the ballpark last year.") The problem with this agenda is two-fold. First, it is not entirely honest since that is only part of the reason the seller is calling. Second, customers are surprised about three minutes into the call when all of a sudden the sellers start talking about plans that will fit them for next year. If they haven't agreed to talk about tickets for next year, they may become upset at the change in the nature of the call. On the other hand, other organizations teach sales reps to not ask for the sale on the first call, instead preferring to spend the first call doing a needs assessment regarding the customer's experience and preparing for the second call or in-person meeting at the arena or stadium.

> The opening agenda statement for a sales call must be concise and articulately communicate to the client why you are calling. Having an agenda statement that is too long and vague is the most common mistake I see with new sales reps. When you go over the top with 'buzz' words and dance around the real reason you're calling them (to sell them something), it turns the client off. The client appreciates honesty. Being upfront from the beginning of a sales call will go a long way in taking the next steps toward closing the client.
>
> —Jeff Berryhill, *Major League Soccer*

## 2. SEEK PERMISSION

The simplest way to seek permission to enter a sales conversation with the prospect is to ask them a question like:

> *How does that sound? Does that make sense? How do you feel about that?*

## PUTTING IT TOGETHER

> *Hi, Megan, I'm your personal account representative with the XYZ City Tigers. My name is Kevin. Megan, the reason for my call is to learn about your experience at the ballpark last season and follow-up with you on the e-mail/letter that we sent you last week about opportunities for this upcoming season. How does that sound?*

This approach gives the customer the opportunity to opt out of the conversation, thus generating rapport with the customer. The criticism against this approach is that the customer has a way to get out of the conversation. The counterargument is that customers who are unwilling to engage even in a brief conversation are unlikely to buy anyway. Later in the conversation, asking for permission may yield benefits because the customer won't be surprised when the seller transitions into discussing product options. However, since the goal of sales is to have as many conversations with as many likely buyers as possible, getting to a "no" earlier in a conversation opens up more time in your schedule to talk with more qualified prospects.

### *Philosophy 2: Move Directly to Questions*

Other sales managers recommend a brief introduction followed by asking the first question. Sport organizations will have their own preference on whether or not to seek permission on the call. Below are examples of openings where the salesperson moves into asking the customer questions:

> ▶ Hi, Name, this is (your name) with the front offices of X team. It's great to speak with you today because I'm calling as your personal account executive for this season. I wanted to reach out and personally thank you for your support in the past, Name. As your personal

account executive, the easiest way for me to get to know you is to find out [insert question].

▶ Name, it's great to meet you because I'm going to be your personal contact with the X team this season and I'd like to get to know you. So, Name, the best place for us to start our conversation is by asking [insert question].

Questions like *what is your favorite memory?* and *what is your favorite part about coming to a game?* are good conversation starters because the customer will give an answer to which the seller can provide personal information about him or herself. Finally, asking *when did you fall in love with the team?* is also a good conversation starter because fans experience an intense, personal relationship with their favorite team. It is important for sport salespeople to connect these positive experiences and emotions to the value of purchasing tickets and other experiences. These questions help the prospect tie positive emotions to the purchase of tickets. These questions are also avenues for sellers to reveal information about themselves, which breaks down the barrier of distrust between seller and customer.

## *Other Strategies for Starting the Call*

### LEVERAGE REFERENCES

A **referral** is a name of a person or company given to the salesperson as a lead by a customer. If you have a referral, utilize it in your introduction to pique the prospect's curiosity, form a sense of familiarity with the prospect, and build credibility. Referrals show prospects that other clients have already been satisfied with purchasing (social proof), which increases the chances that they will want to know more what the seller has to offer. For example:

**REFERRAL**
a name of a person or company given to the salesperson as a lead by a customer

**Salesperson:** Hi, Megan, I'm your personal account representative with the XYZ City Tigers. My name is Kevin. Did Michelle Johnson from your daughter's softball team let you know I would be calling?

**Customer:** Yes, I think she told me that.

**Salesperson:** Great, Michelle has been a loyal customer with us for several years now and she mentioned that you would be a great person for me to get to know.

## ENGAGE IN SMALL TALK

Sales books and sales managers differ on whether or not sales representatives should initially engage in small talk with the customer. Asking questions like *How are you today?* at the outset of a call has advantages and disadvantages. On the positive side, engaging in small talk helps the seller identify social anchors that can be used to connect with the prospect. For example, sellers could talk about the weather, an upcoming sporting event, or big news in the city. These topics can be used as ice breakers to get the customer to open up and begin a conversation. Perhaps most importantly, it is important to remember that you are selling SPORTS. People love to talk about sports in any setting, so it is important to leverage the fact that people can always talk sports, particularly the sport that you are selling. Follow the lead of the customer in talking about sports. Once the customer hears that the seller works for their favorite team or sport, they may want to talk about the recent headlines related to the team. Ultimately, every decision to buy from you depends to some extent on what the prospect thinks of the team. Talking about the team is a great way to make the conversation interactive, build rapport, find common ground, pique the customer's interest in the call, and segue into the needs analysis phase of the call. Starting a conversation with this sort of statement feels very natural in day-to-day conversations.

However, many sales managers and trainers recommend avoiding small talk questions during an *initial sales call* for several reasons. One, prospects who receive an unsolicited sales call often determine whether to allow the conversation to take place within the first few seconds of answering the phone. The precious initial seconds of the conversation cannot be wasted on small talk that does not give the prospect a good reason to continue the conversation. Second, small talk questions do not provide the seller with valuable information. These sorts of questions almost always generate a reflexive answer like *"fine"* or *"good"* which does not move the sales conversation forward. Third, it is possible the prospect might give an unexpected or negative response, which can quickly derail the conversation. If the prospect says she is having a lousy day or that things are kind of crazy today, it becomes difficult for the seller to follow up with a response that sounds empathetic, but also gets the conversation shifted back toward selling.

One way to reconcile the advantages and disadvantages is to consider the context of the call. On first calls, sellers are better served by using their well-rehearsed opening and keeping the call on track. Once rapport has been established through previous conversations, sellers can benefit from small talk by using past conversations as ways to build rapport. Finally, using the pause at the end of the introduction allows the customer to opt into friendly small talk, which can quickly help build rapport. This pause provides the best of both worlds—the possibility of small talk without asking a question that intentionally generates small talk. Finally, the personality of the prospect may dictate the extent to which engaging in small talk will aid in your ability to generate rapport with the prospect. Perhaps the best strategy as it relates to using small talk is to find your own personal style and determine what works and what doesn't work in certain various situations.

The example below examines the thorny issue of asking *"Did I catch you at a good/bad time?"* for sales managers when teaching how to open the sale.

**MISMATCHING**
the notion that people have an instinctive tendency to resist, push back, or respond to things you say in a contrarian manner

---

### DID I CATCH YOU AT A GOOD/BAD TIME?

"Did I catch you at a bad time?"

Sport sales trainers and managers disagree on the use of this particular question during the opening of a sales conversation. Some suggest using this sort of question provides a way out of the conversation for the prospect. Others, however, believe asking such a question allows the seller to save time by not trying to develop a conversation with a distracted prospect who is not going to be engaged with the conversation.

Asking the question *Did I catch you at a bad time?* at the outset of the call leverages the notion that people have an instinctive tendency to resist, push back, or respond to things you say in a contrarian manner (**mismatching**).[1] Classic mismatching responses come in the form of the contradiction, unnecessary clarification, one-upmanship, and "I know."[2]

1. Contradiction—Reflexive response that directly opposes a comment or statement.

2. Unnecessary clarification—Clarifying or restating something that has already been said but in a way that doesn't add value to the conversation.

3. One-Upmanship—Sends the message that *I'm better than you.*

4. I know—Occurs when the need to acquire additional information is superseded by one's own feelings of inadequacy or self-esteem.

You can minimize the risk of mismatching during a sales call by asking questions with a negative disposition. Thus, when someone takes the opposite position they will actually be agreeing with you. There is a decent probability that the customer will respond to the *Did I catch you at a bad time* question with the mismatched statement *No, now is fine.*

Leveraging the negative actually invites people to offer you an invitation to engage in conversation. In the event this isn't really a good time to talk, you avoid the situation of bulldozing your way into a conversation that really isn't coming at a good time for the prospect. You can then simply ask, *When*

---

1. Freese, T. (2013). *Secrets of question based selling.* Naperville, IL: Sourcebooks.

2. Ibid.

*can I call you back?* It is important to realize, however, this is <u>not</u> a manipulation strategy used to close the sale (i.e., *you wouldn't want to buy these tickets anyway, would you?*).

**Putting It Together**

> *Hi, Megan, I'm your personal account representative with the XYZ City Tigers. My name is Kevin. Did I catch you at a bad time?*

## VOICE MAILS

Many professional sport teams and college athletic departments ask their outbound sales representatives to make upward of 100 calls a day. The reality is that very few of these calls will reach a live person on the other end. In fact, sport ticket sales trainer Bill Guertin suggests roughly 70% of all sales calls go directly to voice mail.[4] What should a seller do in those cases? The correct answer: it depends.

Some sport organizations believe leaving a voice mail from a sales representative is ineffective or even counter-productive. Other organizations believe messages should always be left. Others recommend leaving a voice mail only after two or three previous calls have gone unanswered. The majority fall somewhere in the middle, suggesting the context surrounding the call makes a big difference. For example, a cold call during the off-season to a business that has never purchased a ticket package before might not be responsive to a voice mail. However, an in-season call to a prospect from a strong referral in which the seller is offering an exclusive promotion might warrant a better response rate from voice mail. In any case, it is strongly recommended the seller at least listen to the prospect's voice mail greeting, which might offer some information about the person such as when they might be available ("I will be out of the office until Tuesday") or who else lives in the household ("You've reached the Smiths. Alex, Mindy, Stephen, and Lily are not home right now, so please leave a message.").

If a seller does leave a voice mail, it should be for one purpose and one purpose only: to earn a call back. The voice mail is never the place to deliver a sales pitch, or talk about features, benefits, and needs. Think about what is going through your mind when you are checking a voice mail. You want

---

4. Guertin, B. *Get out of a sports ticket sales slump.* Retrieved from
http://www.sportsnetworker.com/2010/02/11/get-out-of-a-sports-ticket-sales-slump/

information that is short, concise, and not going to take too much of your time. In fact, voice mails tend to be returned in inverse proportion to the amount of information left in the message. Effective voice mails are generally around 15 seconds.

So, what sort of voice mail messages produces the most callbacks?

First and foremost, if sellers want a callback, they need to leave a contact number. Any voice mail should be spoken at a clear and steady pace and include the seller's phone number. Second, the seller needs to leave the prospect a compelling reason for returning the call. These reasons might be related to an exclusive or limited-time offer. They may also be related to something unique or important to the prospect. Whatever it is, it should be something other than a generic voice mail that any person might receive. Effective voice mails force the recipient to think *I should probably call that person back to learn more.* One way to accomplish this is to create some element of suspense or mystery with the call. For example, a seller may leave a voice mail suggesting she has something important to give the prospect, but needs more information from them. Table 5.1 on the following page introduces nine strategies for leaving effective voice mails.

---

### THE MEMPHIS GRIZZLIES TRAIN THEIR SALES STAFF ON THE GUTSY, MYSTERY, AND EXCLUSIVE APPROACHES

- ▶ Gutsy: I've got an offer I want to run past you. It may not be for everyone, but it could be for you. Give me a call in the next day.
- ▶ Mystery: We've sold out in certain seating areas, and I'm calling to guarantee you a seat next season.
- ▶ Exclusive news: I've got some exclusive news I wanted to share with you, so give me a call as soon as you get this.

---

Ticket sales trainer Bill Guertin suggests some sellers may be willing to get even more daring with the voice mail strategy. He would never advocate being dishonest, but consider the potential effectiveness of the following approaches:

> *"Hi Jim, this is Marty with the XYZ City Tigers. I'm holding a copy of a receipt of yours from last year and I had a question. If you would, please call me back at 987-654-3210."*

*"Jim, this is Marty with XYZ City Tigers. My number is 987-654-3210. I had a question about your seats from last year, and wh. . . (message gets cut off)"*

Regardless of which approach is chosen, sellers should always have a voice mail plan before they call a prospect. It is important for the sales representative

## Table 5.1

**Voice Mail Strategies**

| Approach | Definition | Example |
|---|---|---|
| Ask a question | When calling a prospect with whom you already have a relationship, position the voice mail as you needing to ask them a question | I was hoping to reach you today because I have a question that only you can answer. If you could please call me back, I should be in my office until 5 p.m.<br><br>In the follow-up call, ask the person their opinion or feelings about an X topic. |
| Thinking of you | When calling a prospect with whom you already have a relationship, position the voice mail as you having thought of them | I am calling you this morning because something happened at the game last night that made me think of you. If you get a chance, call me back. |
| Preferred Customer | Make the prospect feel unique or special | I am reaching out to you today because we have a unique opportunity for your family. |
| Indirect | Leading into a direct mail campaign, you can ethically be indirect with the purpose of your call by seeking to confirm the prospect's address. | I was going to mail you important information about this upcoming season, and I wanted to confirm your address. |
| Fun | Leverage your access to complimentary tickets | I have two extra tickets to the game to-night and I thought you might be interested. Give me a call to let me know. |
| Social Proof | Leverage the momentum of what others are doing to pique the customer's interest | We wanted to let you know that many other fans are purchasing the mini-game package to see the top teams in the league. |
| Urgency | Create urgency by including a specific deadline for action | Use phrases like "by the end of business day today" or "only a few packages/tickets are remaining." |
| Benefit | Entice the prospect with a valuable benefit | If our marketing program could increase your company's sales by 20%, would you want to learn more? |
| Associative Reference | Use the name of someone else that you've spoken to in the organization to legitimize the reason for your call | I just got off the phone with Nancy in Human Resources and I've got a question for you. |

to note when the voice mail was left and what approach was used. Mixing up approaches and tone can make voice mails sound more personal. Calling at different times of the day or different days of the week can also be more effective in landing a call. No matter what voice mail strategy is adopted, the reality is many calls will go unreturned. If multiple voice mails are left, they should generally be spaced about three days apart. It can also be helpful to use other mediums such as postal mail, e-mail, or even Twitter or LinkedIn in conjunction with a voice mail. Utilizing these platforms to share something of value such as a free copy of a team newsletter or a recent story about the prospect's business success can also incentivize prospects to return a call.

## CHAPTER SUMMARY

Even though sales are never closed based on a good opening, a bad opening can cost a sale right off the bat. Sellers have a short window to convince a prospect that it is worthwhile to engage in a conversation. The opening of the sales call is the one time in the sales process where the seller is in complete control of the conversation. The opening of the sales call sets the foundation for a successful sales call by establishing rapport with the customer and piquing their interest in the call. While sales managers may differ on specific tactical details of how to execute the opening of the call and leave voice mails, successful sellers always exude an energetic and professional voice, use the customer's first name, and reveal information about themselves. More than any other stage of the sales call, a script is recommended during the opening of the call. Scripted outlines help rookie sellers overcome sales call anxiety and become more comfortable engaging with customers over the phone.

## CHAPTER ACTIVITIES

1. On a scale from 1 to 10, rate your level of sales call anxiety and explain your rating. What strategies can you utilize to overcome sales call anxiety?

2. Create three I/My Statements that you could use on the phone with a customer.

3. Describe the circumstances in which engaging in small talk with the customer would be an effective strategy to opening the call.

4. Analyze the difference between the two main philosophies presented in this chapter on how to open a call in a B2C environment.

5. Assume that your class is selling season tickets for your university's athletic department. Craft an opening to the call that you would use when calling a prospect who attended one game last year. Then create a script for the opening using the following approaches:

   a. Agenda setting with permission

    b.   Direct to questions

    c.   Referrals

    d.   Voice mail

6.  Using this script created in question 5, partner with a classmate and role-play the opening of the call.

# CHAPTER 6

# OPENING THE BUSINESS-TO-BUSINESS RELATIONSHIP

## LEARNING OBJECTIVES

After completing this chapter, you should be able to:

▶ Contrast the differences between the opening of a consumer sales call and a business-to-business call.

▶ Analyze the three steps to becoming an effective social seller.

▶ Create an opening dialogue for a corporate sales call with a gatekeeper and a sales call with a decision-maker.

▶ Apply strategies for overcoming stalls by the decision-maker.

▶ Identify strategies that can be used to schedule an appointment.

▶ Contrast the bottom-up and top-down approaches to reaching the right decision-maker.

## KEY TERMS

| | | |
|---|---|---|
| Anti-champion | Indifferent | Social selling |
| Bottom-up approach | Influencer | Sport hospitality |
| Business-to-business sales | Informant | Stalls |
| Decision-maker | Internal champion | Top-down approach |
| Gatekeeper | References | Valid business reason |

## COMPENTENCIES

▶ Ability to navigate the gatekeeper and set an appointment with the decision-maker.

## CHAPTER OVERVIEW

Many sport sellers spend significant time selling to businesses and corporations, known as **business-to-business sales** (B2B). In B2B sales, sport tickets are purchased for business purposes, such as entertaining clients, rewarding employees, or networking with other businesses. Nearly all premium seating and the majority of season tickets for major league sport teams in North America are purchased by businesses and used for client entertainment.[1] For some sport organizations, B2B sales can represent as much as 70% of season ticket sales. The goal in making an initial contact to a corporate account is to set an appointment, preferably face-to-face, with a decision-maker so that a more detailed sales presentation can be given. The **decision-maker** is the individual who can both approve the purchase of the product and has the authority to pay for the product. This bears repeating, so we will state it again: in B2B sales calls, the first objective is to determine who the decision-maker is and to make an appointment with that individual. The purpose of the initial sales call is NOT to give a sales presentation. This is different than B2C calls in which the seller may be able to close a sale on the first call. This chapter addresses how to initiate contact with a corporate decision-maker through traditional telephone methods and also through social selling. The chapter concludes with an overview of the key players involved in B2B buying decisions.

**BUSINESS-TO-BUSINESS SALES**
selling sport products to businesses for the primary purposes of entertaining clients and employees

**DECISION-MAKER**
the person who has the final authority to accept or reject a proposal and is held accountable for that decision

**SPORT HOSPITALITY**
food, beverage, and entertainment assets that accompany premium tickets in suites and club seating areas

## SPORT HOSPITALITY PROVIDES RETURN ON INVESTMENT

Businesses invest in sport hospitality because they can achieve a return on investment (ROI). **Sport hospitality** is the food, beverage, and entertainment assets that accompany premium tickets in suites and club seating areas to any type of sporting event. Tickets to sporting events are assets for salespeople in building relationships and trust with prospects and clients. Over 75% of all sport hospitality tickets are used by businesses to attract and retain key prospects and clients.[2] The objective of any corporate sales pitch is to demonstrate to the decision-maker how his or her company can achieve a return on their investment through sport hospitality assets. Effective B2B sellers are able to ask questions that quantify how a business can realize ROI from sport

---

1. DeGaris, L. (2015). *Sports marketing: A practical approach*. New York: Routledge.
2. Ticket Manager. *Corporate ticket consumer case study*. Retrieved from https://ticketmanager.com/education/whitepapers/

hospitality through increased sales. Three key questions that need to be asked by the salesperson are:

1. What percentage of customers do you think will close a deal with your salespeople after attending a game?
2. How many transactions will be made by those customers?
3. What is the average size of each sale?

Table 6.1 shows how the answers to these questions help calculate the ROI from increased sales.

## Table 6.1

**Return on Investment Calculation From Increased Sales**

| Key Facts | Values | Question | Math/Notes |
|---|---|---|---|
| Number of Games in the Ticket Package | 16 | | |
| Number of Guests | 3 | How many prospects do you want attending the game with your salesperson? | A minimum 1:1 ratio is preferred |
| Number of Prospect Tickets Needed | 48 | | 16 * 3 = 48 |
| Conversion Rate | 25% | What percentage of customers do you think will close a deal with you after coming to a game? | These assumptions will vary, but in general 20% should be the minimum number assumed. |
| Customers | 12 | | 48 * 25% = 12 |
| Transactions per customer | 2 | How many deals with each customer transact with you? | These assumptions will vary, but in general 1 should be the minimum number assumed. |
| Average Sale | $1,000 | What is the average size of those sales? | |
| Revenue Generated | $24,000 | | 12 * 2 * 1,000 = 24,000 |
| Cost of the Package | 6,000 | | Note: This includes the cost of 1 ticket for the salesperson, so the price for each ticket is $93.75. |
| Return on Investment | 4.0 | 4 to 1 Return on Investment using these assumptions | 24,000 / 6,000 = 4.0 |

A more detailed ROI calculator can be retrieved from https://ticketmanager.com/education/full-featured-business-impact-roi-calculator/

## Table 6.2

**Return on Investment at Each Stage of Sales Process**

| Stage | Average Account | Number of Accounts | Conversion Rate | Expected Total | Improved Conversion | Improved Total |
|---|---|---|---|---|---|---|
| Repeat Business | $25,000 | 20 | 80% | $400,000 | 90% | $450,000 |
| Under Negotiation | $25,000 | 5 | 70% | $87,500 | 80% | $100,000 |
| Contact Established | $25,000 | 10 | 50% | $125,000 | 60% | $150,000 |
| Cold Prospect | $25,000 | 10 | 10% | $25,000 | 20% | $50,000 |
| | | | | $637,500 | | $750,000 |

Adapted from DeGaris, L. (2015). *Sports marketing: A practical approach*. New York: Routledge, p. 120.

A second way to conceptualize ROI from increased sales is to show how sport hospitality can improve the conversation rate of prospects at each stage of the firm's sales pipeline. Table 6.2 demonstrates a simplified example of how using sport hospitality to improve the conversion rate at each stage of the sales process increased a company's sales total by $112,500. If the proposed package cost $25,000, the ROI would be 4.5.

A third way to calculate return on investment for a decision-maker is to quantify the loss of the organization's best salesperson. Instead of quantifying new revenue generated, the focus is on revenue that would be lost through the defection of the best salesperson. In the example below, the salesperson walks the prospect through the value of having the top salesperson, Joe, stay with the organization and use sport tickets as a weapon in his sales arsenal. Four key questions that need to be asked by the salesperson are:

1. How much revenue does your best salesperson generate?
2. What percentage of the revenue generated by your best salesperson would be lost if that person left?
3. How much would it cost to retrain a new salesperson?
4. If your best salesperson had a shot to close your top prospects with tickets, how much revenue would that salesperson generate?

Table 6.3 shows how the answers to these questions can help calculate the return on investment from employee retention.

## Table 6.3

**Return on Investment Calculation Using Employee Retention**

| Key Facts | Values | Question | Math/Notes |
|---|---|---|---|
| Revenue Generated by Joe | $500,000 | How much revenue does your best salesperson generate? | |
| Loss Rate | 20% | What percentage of the revenue generated by Joe would you lose if he left? | |
| Revenue Lost with Joe's Departure | $100,000 | | 500,000 * 20% = 100,000 |
| Training and Replacement Cost | $20,000 | How much would it cost you to retrain a new salesperson? | |
| Opportunity Cost | $80,000 | If Joe had a chance to use these tickets and close your top prospect, how much would you generate? | |
| Total Cost of Losing Joe | $200,000 | | 100,000 + 20,000 + 80,000 = 200,000 |
| Cost of Package | 50,000 | | |
| Return on Investment | 4.0 | | 200,000 / 50,000 = 4.0 |

## COMPARING B2B TO B2C SELLING

B2B selling offers salespeople a great opportunity to sell full season ticket packages, particularly in sports where there are a large number of home games and there is seating capacity to fill on a regular basis. B2B sales offer some advantages over B2C sales. First, corporations have a stronger likelihood of being able to use all of the tickets. One of the most common objections when selling to an individual consumer is that there are too many games in a season ticket package. However, businesses have a value chain full of salespeople, employees, prospects, vendors, suppliers, and customers who can use the inventory of tickets. Second, corporations can afford the price of full season tickets more realistically than individual fans. The average face value of a company ticket in 2014 was $154, and when companies buy tickets from the secondary market they pay $366 per ticket on average. Businesses average 4.7 tickets per event attended.[3] These statistics illustrate the spending

3. Ticket Manager. *Corporate ticket consumer case study.* Retrieved from https://ticketmanager.com/education/whitepapers/

power of a company is greater than an individual fan. Beyond this, businesses can allocate money toward the purchase of sport hospitality from a variety of different budget areas and line items, while fans are typically pulling money from their discretionary income, which can be volatile in times of economic downturn or uncertainty. When companies budget for an expense, it tends to stay budgeted for the next year, while families are more likely to closely reevaluate their expenditures on an annual basis. Third, because the main selling point to businesses is how sport hospitality can benefit their business, team performance becomes much less important to a business than a fan. Fans are more sensitive to swings in team performance and may ditch tickets until the team shows signs of improving.

While there are distinct advantages of selling season tickets B2B, there are also some drawbacks compared to selling B2C. First, the sales cycle is longer when selling to corporations because it includes additional steps that are not a part of the consumer sales cycle. There are additional steps at the start of the sales cycle that occur when selling to businesses before conducting a needs analysis or making a sales presentation. Not only does the seller have to get past the gatekeeper to speak with the decision-maker, but they must also set an appointment to meet with the decision-maker before having an in-person meeting outside the office where a sales conversation takes place. After an initial meeting, there may be committees or other groups of people within the company that have a say in how the decision is made. The sales cycle for selling to fans is much shorter and can be completed over the telephone. Second, when calling on people who have never expressed an interest in your team, decision-makers may be unaware of how sport hospitality can benefit their business, unlike most fans inherently understand what attending a game is like and why they want to go.

---

### GUIDELINES FOR TARGETING BUSINESSES FOR SEASON TICKETS

1. Target businesses with at least 10 employees and $500,000 in annual sales.

2. Target businesses in the professional services, energy and utilities, financial services, media, and leisure industries (these industries account for over 50% of all sport ticket purchases by businesses). In general, don't prioritize retail businesses, government agencies, or schools.

3. Businesses should purchase at least four tickets.

4. Recommend that salespeople for businesses should receive tickets to one game per month to meet with prospects.

> 5. Recommend that 75% of tickets go directly to salespeople and customers for business development and retention.
>
> 6. Recommend that approximately 25% of the tickets be used for employees or other uses.
>
> _____
>
> Ticket Manager. *Corporate ticket consumer case study.* Retrieved from https://ticketmanager.com/education/whitepapers/. Reprinted by permission of InviteManager.

## INITIATING NEW B2B RELATIONSHIPS

New B2B relationships can be started by reaching out to a business using the telephone or by engaging a business decision-maker through social media. The goal of both approaches is to set an appointment where the sales conversation can continue. It is important to note that both approaches should be used in tandem by salespeople to reach decision-makers; in other words, social selling and using the telephone are not mutually exclusive approaches.

### Initiating Relationships Through Social Selling

**Social selling** is the process of leveraging the seller's personal brand on social media to build relationships with clients that lead to appointments. Social selling is used by sellers to identify, connect, and engage with decision-makers. It involves sales reps using social media to develop the reputation of a venue and their own individual personas. A socially present employee identifies new opportunities and opens new lines of communication with prospective customers.[4] A study of business-to-business salespeople found that nearly three out of every four millennials frequently use social media in their selling efforts to build awareness, prospect, obtain leads, connect with customers, maintain good business relationships, obtain referrals, and communicate thoroughly.[5]

Business decision-makers are more sophisticated today than twenty years ago due to the proliferation of information available on the Internet about products and packages, such as the secondary ticket market, virtual seat tours, and online reviews. The ability to research a potential purchase

**SOCIAL SELLING**
process of leveraging the seller's personal brand on social media to build relationships with clients that lead to appointments

_____

4. Troupe, K. *How social selling leads to increased ticket sales on LinkedIn.* Retrieved from http://ticketingtoday.com/how-social-selling-leads-to-increased-tickets-sales-on-linkedin/

5. Schulz, R., Schwepker, C., & Good, D. (2012). An exploratory study of social media in B2B selling: Salesperson characteristics, activities, and performance. *Marketing Management Journal, 22*(2), 76–89.

before discussing it with a salesperson puts the decision-maker in a position of power with information. A recent study of more than 1,400 B2B customers across industries revealed that 57% of a typical purchase decision is now made before potential customers even talk to a seller.[6] Decision-makers can do their own research prior to developing a relationship with the seller. As a result, decision-makers are becoming less likely to respond to cold calls and e-mails, so jumping into a conversation "cold" has become less effective. Some sellers believe that reaching out to clients via social media is less intrusive and more genuine than a cold call. Leveraging connections and existing relationships to get introduced to decision-makers has become increasingly important in recent years.

With over 360 million members and 5.7 billion people searches in 2014, LinkedIn is seen by most sales professionals as the premier business-to-business sales platform due to its professional networking environment. While many think of LinkedIn as an online resume and job search tool, it is also a networking site for businesses where professionals flock to grow their business connections. LinkedIn gives sellers an opportunity to identify, connect, and engage with decision-makers in their target market while providing a way to develop a relationship and create dialogue before ever meeting in person for a sales presentation. Social activities are important at the outset of

©ArthurStock/Shutterstock.com

the sales cycle to establish a relationship that may lead to a future sale. Connecting with buyers on social media is all about building trust in the relationship. A sale is rarely finalized on LinkedIn, but LinkedIn provides a platform to find the right person to connect with, build a relationship, and establish trust.[7] Sellers who add value to their social networks by educating them on the industry and trends will be the successful sellers of the future.[8] The next section focuses on connecting and engaging with prospects to

---

6. CEB Global. *Sales: Content (marketing) is king.* Retrieved from https://www.cebglobal.com/blogs/dummy-proof-your-social-selling-strategy/

7. Hyer, G. *Social selling is about opening, not closing.* Retrieved from https://www.linkedin.com/pulse/20140709143615-17163783-social-selling-is-about-opening-not-closing

8. Kirby, T. *Rise of the Rock Star Ticket Rep.* Retrieved from http://sportstao.com/rise-of-the-rock-star-ticket-rep/

open the sales relationship, and Chapter 12 discusses how LinkedIn Sales Navigator can be utilized to identify prospects.

## *Three Steps to Engaging Decision-Makers on Social Media*

### 1.  CREATE A PROFESSIONAL BRAND ONLINE

The first step in establishing social selling relationships is to create a professional brand on social media sites like Twitter, Facebook, LinkedIn, Google+, and others. Developing a professional brand identity on social media helps to generate business demand at a micro-marketing level. On a LinkedIn profile, sellers can establish this identity in their headline, summary section, and from recommendations. To establish a useful headline, sellers need to reverse engineer what the prospect might search for if they were looking to find sport hospitality assets. Relevant search engine-optimized (SEO) terms for the headline include keywords such as business networking, client entertainment, or hospitality.[9] A good headline also provides potential prospects with a cursory overview of what the seller does.

The summary section provides a more detailed description of what you can do for clients. Give potential clients a clear idea of who you are and what you can offer. Include information like why you love working in sales and how you can help clients. Let your personality shine through in this section so the potential client gets to know you better. Consider using SEO keywords that could show up in search results, and list your contact information.[10]

Finally, recommendations from satisfied clients leverages social proof and testifies to the fact that the seller is an expert and delivers on what is promised. Other elements of a professional LinkedIn profile should be present as well, including a professional photograph, accurate information presented on the profile, and avoidance of bragging about accomplishments.[11] Also, LinkedIn should cater to business-related information and avoid personal information that would be more appropriate for Facebook. All photos visible on Facebook should be appropriate for a business audience. The following example shows Tyler Bayly's LinkedIn profile, which follows the best practices described in this section.

---

9. Troupe, K. *How social selling leads to increased ticket sales on LinkedIn.* Retrieved from http://ticketingtoday.com/how-social-selling-leads-to-increased-tickets-sales-on-linkedin/

10. Ibid.

11. Hughes, T. *Top 10 flagrant social selling mistakes reaching pandemic proportions.* Retrieved from https://www.linkedin.com/pulse/top-10-flagrant-social-selling-mistakes-reaching-pandemic-hughes

---

**Tyler Bayly, Premium Account Executive, Denver Nuggets**

**BEST PRACTICE LINKEDIN PROFILE**

**Headline**

Premium account executive with the Nuggets. Helping businesses provide unprecedented experiences to clients and employees

**Summary**

In my role as a Premium Account Executive, I focus on helping companies grow their business by utilizing the Denver Nuggets platform to build relationships with their clients and employees.

My goal is to help you get face-time with clients, host thank you events for returning business, and reward your employees in an exciting environment with a sport that gets you closer to the action than any other.

I have successfully grown market share and sales revenues through relationship building, analyzing sales data, identifying trends in the marketplace and capitalizing on uncovered opportunities.

To talk about ways the Denver Nuggets can benefit your business, please contact me at any of the platforms below. I look forward to working with you!

*I also have access to Colorado Rapids and Colorado Avalanche amenities as well for your company.

Office: (303)-615-xxxx
Professional Cell: (303)-956-xxxx
e-mail: Tyler.Bayly@TeamKSE.com

---

Reprinted by permission of Tyler Bayly.

---

## 2. BUILD CREDIBILITY IN YOUR NETWORK

The second step is to build credibility within your social network. Social sellers build credibility within social networks by being viewed as a subject matter expert. This is achieved by contributing valuable and relevant insights in social networks via participating in online discussions, writing and sharing content relevant to customers, and engaging in social conversations with industry experts, clients, and potential clients. Sellers should join sport sales industry groups (e.g., Ticket Sales Best Practices, Association of Luxury Suite Directors, Use Sport Tickets to Grow Your Business) and groups that are relevant to the seller's target market. The key is to join communities where your customers reside and create an online presence that is likeable, authentic, and trustworthy. Presence is built by commenting on posts, retweeting people, answering questions, and sharing content. Contributing to online discussions can add value to that particular network. The goal is to make it natural for your clients to follow you and for you to follow them.

The creation of content is an important issue for teams to address as social media channels become more integral to the sales process. Brett Zalaski, Founder of Get After It Sales, believes that professional sport teams will create new positions in the area of Ticketing Content in order to streamline and organize the sharing of content on social media.[12] Content marketing is an important source of leads for B2B marketers in many industries. Sport organizations can be leaders in promoting the value of client entertainment and generating best practices for leveraging sport hospitality. Larry DeGaris argues that sport properties should become thought leaders in the field of client entertainment and corporate hospitality.[13] The example below was contributed to LinkedIn by Tyler Bayly, Premium Account Executive for the Denver Nuggets.

---

**Tyler Bayly, Premium Account Executive, Denver Nuggets**

### THE IMPORTANCE OF SPORTS:
### FROM BUSINESS TO FAMILY THE IMPACT WE PROVIDE IN TICKET SALES

My life, like many of you, has taken its fair share of twists and turns, ups and downs, and moments I both want to forget and on the other hand, will never forget. Through all of the changes in my life, there has always been one constant . . . sports.

I guess it's true what I was always taught. You have to work for something you want. Have to grind. Have to hustle. Have to outwork the other thousands of people with the same exact dreams and goals as you. If I couldn't play a professional sport someday, I was bound to at least make a career working in them.

When I was just a young boy my family would attend Indiana Pacers games. I remember corner 3's from Reggie Miller. I remember hearing the sound of Jeff Foster blocking Gary Payton's shot in the post. More importantly, I remember being there with family and friends. That was time spent with my family that I would have never gotten without sports, yes. But more than that, it was memories made with family that I will never forget. And now, I am in the business of creating those same memories for young kids like Tyler sitting in the stands with his family rooting on his favorite team.

---

12. Zalaski, B. https://www.youtube.com/watch?v=PAKilh30kHk
13. DeGaris, L. (2015). *Sports marketing: A practical approach.* New York: Routledge.

Family is everything. More than work, more than money, more than anything you can ever acquire in life, at least to me. I am a pretty darn passionate guy. But REALLY, how hard is it to be passionate about sports?! Tens of thousands of fans screaming at the top of their lungs, families sharing the biggest slice of pizza known to man, high-5's with your brother you just had an argument with last night but have now forgotten, smiles, and "I Love You's" that extend far beyond the four corners of any stadium in America. We, as ticket salesmen and women, are in the business to create those memories.

Businesses get great use out of tickets and amenities that we can provide too. No, not because the CEO is the biggest die-hard fan you've ever met. Not because it always is easy financially. Not because it's "been on the agenda" for years. Businesses buy from people. People like us, in ticket sales. Positive, enthusiastic, hard-working, hustling ticket-salesmen and women. Businesses have a wide array of objectives and needs for any given fiscal period. I've worked with several and can absolutely say no two businesses have the same idea for how to utilize the NBA or any other given sport's platforms for their business. In ticket sales, we are thought leaders, solution finders, and problem solvers. We help businesses solve their problems, whether or not they have ever considered a ticket package. Whether it's improving ROI, retaining employees, entertaining clients, or rewarding top performers, businesses can and will benefit from us, us in ticket sales.

I write this because I am passionate. I am passionate about feeling like our industry, ticket sales, is important and that what we do every day is very entrepreneurial. I write this not because I have answers, surely not that, but because I am passionate about the impact we make on everybody. Businesses, family, friends, daughters, sons, nephews, nieces . . . sports is not bias. Its sole purpose is to provide you with entertainment and memories. To me, that is important.

Source: https://www.linkedin.com/pulse/importance-sports-from-business-family-impact-we-provide-tyler-bayly. Reprinted by permission of Tyler Bayly.

---

Sellers can then begin to gather real-time insights about the customer by examining all of the information available on social media channels, which should lead to a cursory understanding of their needs. Sellers can also learn important information about the prospect like where they went to college, career path, personal interests and hobbies, and professional accomplishments.

In short, good relationships develop into good leads.[14] Sellers gather information on prospects by finding shared interests and relationships, identifying common buying signals, following prospects on social channels, following and commenting on blogs and articles, joining a LinkedIn group the prospect

---

14. Smith, J. *How to use social media to make sales.* Retrieved from http://www.forbes.com/sites/jacquelynsmith/2014/01/10/how-to-use-social-media-to-make-sales-2014

participates in, retweeting something the prospect has posted, reading their LinkedIn profile, and watching podcasts/videos they have produced.[15]

## 3.  ENGAGE WITH DECISION-MAKER

Once credibility has been established, the third step is to privately message the decision-maker. Some sellers make the mistake of jumping directly to the third step of engaging with the decision-maker. Simply connecting with them on LinkedIn and following up with an InMail message asking for a 15-minute meeting is unlikely to yield long-term successful results. Decision-makers are safeguarding their network since they have been spammed by sales professionals looking to sell to them on social media.[16] Blasting the prospect an InMail message as a form letter template is essentially spam. In other words, the InMail message is not a quick pitch with a link to buy tickets. Instead, the seller should capitalize on all of the insights gained in the previous step to craft an InMail message that will yield a response. InMail should be used to make personalized introductions and connections with clients in your network. Good social sellers do the following in a genuine and personal InMail message: [17]

- ► Create a unique subject line
- ► Customize and personalize the message
- ► Reference a referral
- ► Establish common ground
- ► Offer a brief overview of how the seller can help
- ► Mention why you want to engage
- ► Provide a call to action—request an appointment

Table 6.4 on the following page identifies InMail best practices.

---

15.  Stone, A. *The sales pro's semi-colossal guide to social selling.* Retrieved from http://blog. pipelinersales.com/crm-sales-software/the-sales-pros-semi-colossal-guide-to-social-selling/

16.  Kosakowski, J. *7 ways a social selling ninja always connects on LinkedIn.* Retrieved from https://www.linkedin.com/pulse/20141114150300-161366190-7-ways-a-social-selling-ninja-always-connects-on-linkedin

17.  Hughes, T. *Top 10 flagrant social selling mistakes reaching pandemic proportions.* Retrieved from https://www.linkedin.com/pulse/top-10-flagrant-social-selling-mistakes-reaching-pandemic-hughes; and Viveka von Rosen. *Social selling on LinkedIn—A distinctive recipe.* Retrieved from https://business.linkedin.com/content/dam/business/sales-solutions/global/en_US/c/pdfs/n/the-guide-to-social-selling-success.pdf

## Table 6.4

**LinkedIn InMail Best Practices**

| | |
|---|---|
| Be brief | Be polite, brief, and to the point. Shorter is better. |
| Start a conversation | More "salesy" InMails get lower response rates. Instead, start a conversation. |
| Personalize your messages | Customize your messages and make them highly personalized. Avoid spam and canned messages. Consider some of the following tips:<br><br>▶ Mention a common contact<br><br>▶ Refer to a common LinkedIn group<br><br>▶ Comment on a LinkedIn group posting (theirs or someone else's)<br><br>▶ Discuss a common company, experience, or personal interest based on reading their profile<br><br>▶ Ask for an opinion |
| Make it about them | What's in it for me? Make it about their needs, interests, and goals, not your product or service. Avoid product and service descriptions. |
| Develop a clear call to action | Make the next steps clear. Assuming that the InMail is forwarded, as InMails frequently can be from CXOs, will it be clear what the recipient should do? |
| Combine InMail with other contact methods | By itself InMail can generate response rates substantially higher than e-mails or cold calls. Some industry consultants have increased contact to meeting ratios with InMail as much as 8% using a multi-contact approach. Mix it up and find the pattern and approach that generates the best response rates for you. |
| Select recipients carefully | Who you choose to InMail matters as much as what you say. Recipient response rates are likely to be higher for active LinkedIn users (high number of connections, member of many LinkedIn groups, frequent updates, and complete profile). |
| Remember the option to get introduced | InMail may not always be the most direct path. Where appropriate, take advantage of the LinkedIn option to get introduced. The two most successful ways to gain access to a senior executive are through an internal referral (someone in their company) and an external referral (someone outside their company that they know and trust). |
| Build your sales profile | The first thing an InMail recipient will do is review your profile. Poor profiles reduce InMail response rates. |

LinkedIn. *Social selling with LinkedIn sales navigator: A step-by-step guide to social selling best practices with LinkedIn sales navigator.* Retrieved from https://business.linkedin.com/content/dam/business/sales-solutions/global/en_US/site/pdf/ti/sn-step-by-step-guide-01282014.pdf

Finally, a request to connect should be followed with a personalized InMail message when:[18]

- ► An appointment is set
- ► Someone views your LinkedIn profile
- ► Someone adds you on Twitter
- ► The seller reads a published LinkedIn article posted by a potential decision-maker
- ► Someone reads an article the seller published on LinkedIn
- ► A referral is earned
- ► The seller meets people at professional networking events

Finally, it is important to note that social selling does not occur only in B2B contexts. It can certainly be used in a similar fashion for consumer sales as the millennial generation continues to gather more purchasing power. For the millennial generation, the smartphone is a device for texting and connecting via social media, and less for actually talking on the phone than older generations. This means that young sales reps are adept at communicating through social media, and it means the next generation of ticket purchasers are also looking to connect with their favorite teams and products through personalized connections on social media. The article below discusses the success of the Sacramento Kings in adopting LinkedIn for social selling.

---

### SACRAMENTO KINGS LEVERAGE SALES NAVIGATOR TO GROW SALE

Since the team's move to Sacramento in 1985, the Kings have become the pride of the region. In recent years, city leaders, the Kings passionate local fans, and a new ownership group led by Chairman Vivek Ranadivé all stepped in as a major force against the team's potential relocation away from the capital city. That dedication has been matched by the franchise's growing sales force, which is now in a key position at the center of a revitalization effort for both the team and the city. With building underway on the Kings new downtown arena, the Golden 1 Center, the sales team is charged with selling season tickets and experiences for a sport complex that is still under construction while maintaining excellent sales results for the existing arena.

#### Who is the Target Customer?

The Kings play in the country's 20th largest media market, in a metropolitan area of 2.2 million. The team's target corporate audience is primarily small- and medium-sized businesses looking to buy

---

18.  Kosakowski, J. *7 ways a social selling ninja always connects on LinkedIn.* Retrieved from https://www.linkedin.com/pulse/20141114150300-161366190-7-ways-a-social-selling-ninja-always-connects-on-linkedin

tickets to engage prospects, clients, and vendors, as well as an entertainment reward for employees. The solid support of the Kings fan base, along with renewed excitement around the new arena, has provided fresh opportunities to target even more new customers, from commercial businesses to law firms to non-profits.

### What was the Sales Challenge?

With the opening of the new arena just two years away, the Kings Ticket Sales Team needed a capacity strategy in both the current and future facilities. But with a large portion of the sales team made up of new, less experienced reps, the franchise's sales leadership needed to invest in their training to ensure they could keep up with the more senior reps. And the franchise's traditional cold-calling tactics weren't a great fit for the tech-savvy millennials that made up a significant portion of the sales team. After providing the sales team with Sales Navigator licenses, sales leadership saw a major shift in confidence, especially among its newer reps.

"All of a sudden they have the power and the same skill set as anybody else to reach out to C-level contacts or business owners and engage with them," says Phil Horn, Vice President of Ticket Sales and Service. "One new rep was able to get in touch with a decision-maker at a powerful law firm in town using Sales Navigator on her first try. The deal came together about 10 times faster than it would have using a cold calling approach. There's also an excitement for the team around having access to the newest, best-in-class tools, and when the sales team knows that you're investing in them, you start to get a whole other level of effort."

### What did the Kings do to achieve success?

Vital to the sales team's success with social selling and Sales Navigator was the solid support and buy-in from the franchise ownership, sales team leaders, and the sales reps themselves. The team's LinkedIn account manager first provided Horn with initial training on LinkedIn fundamentals, such as building a solid profile before moving on to Sales Navigator training. Horn then ensured the team's social selling efforts got off on the right foot by leading LinkedIn training for a core group of tech-savvy reps. From there, the rest of the sales team received training both for LinkedIn and Sales Navigator.

With the sales team's proactive leadership at the helm and several highly enthusiastic reps, the Kings sales force has hit the ground running, following a philosophy they call "Sales 3.0": a three-pronged approach that matches social selling with team collaboration and accelerated technology. The addition of Sales Navigator fit in perfectly. During daily sales huddles, the team shares their Sales Navigator success stories with one another along with tips for how best to leverage the tool. "Somebody will share, 'Hey, I found this person through LinkedIn,' and we'll dig in—tell us more, how did you find them? What insight did you use to start the conversation?" Horn says. "That's great learning for the rest of the team, too."

### What about the Results?

Horn collaborated closely with the sales team to provide LinkedIn and Sales Navigator trainings and to generate enthusiasm for social selling across the sales force. That investment has yielded major results. Since implementing Sales Navigator, the team's ticket sales have soared—particularly those where face-to-face appointments were the result of initial contact—the Kings beat their own goal for in-game ticket sales by 50%, more than tripling the team's previous high and ranking them among the top teams in the NBA. These engagement efforts with fans and local businesses have led to more than a 20% increase in attendance since new ownership took over.

In recent months, the sales team has seen roughly 6% of its overall new business come from deals sourced from LinkedIn or Sales Navigator. Using information from Sales Navigator and reaching out with InMail, the sales team has also connected with more existing leads that were already in their CRM system. Sales Navigator proved to be similarly valuable in supporting stronger relationships with existing customers, helping the team bring in a higher-than-usual rate of season ticket membership renewals. "We found that by sending our customers an InMail we got a higher rate of response, when we weren't getting a response through other methods," Horn said.

▶ Starting with just 18 seats across the sales team in 2014, the Kings have since rolled out more than 40 Sales Navigator licenses.

▶ The team's new reps using Sales Navigator have increased the size of their deals by 42% compared to the previous class of reps, who were not using the tool.

▶ The Kings' deals sourced through LinkedIn are 3.2 times larger than others.

▶ Reps who use Sales Navigator have higher Social Selling Index (SSI) scores than those who don't.

Source: http://www.slideshare.net/JillSida/sacramento-kings-leverage-sales-navigator-to-grow-sales. Reprinted by permission of Phil Horn.

## Initiating Relationships Over the Phone

The second approach to reaching decision-makers is to reach them on the telephone. Getting past the gatekeeper is the first major step in the sales process when selling over the phone. Many decision-makers in the business world employ a person that sales professionals refer to as the **gatekeeper**. The role of the gatekeeper is to keep the decision-makers' work life organized by answering incoming calls, keeping his/her schedule, setting meetings, and generally protecting the decision-maker from time wasters. Gatekeepers are more commonly known as administrative assistants or executive assistants. Gatekeepers typically stand between a seller and an appointment with a decision-maker. Getting past the gatekeeper in order to set an appointment is critical to one's success in B2B sales.

**GATEKEEPER**
a person who keeps the decision-maker's work life organized by answering incoming calls, keeping his/her schedule, setting meetings, and generally protecting the decision-maker from time wasters

Just like interacting with any other person in a business setting, the best way to approach gatekeepers is to treat them with respect. People generally respond positively to being treated with respect and negatively to being treated with arrogance or rudeness. Doing simple things like learning and

"She has a 2:42 and a 2:43 appointment. I can try to fit you in."

©Cartoonresource/Shutterstock.com

calling gatekeepers by their first names, asking and thanking them for their help, using a confident and relaxed tone of voice, and demonstrating knowledge about the business are all ways to gain the cooperation of gatekeepers. Using simple phrases like *It's nice to meet you* and *I was hoping you could help me* also help you enlist the support of the gatekeeper.

In some instances, the gatekeeper can provide valuable information for the seller. For example, if the seller does not know who the decision-maker might be within the business, the seller might ask the gatekeeper who makes decisions regarding new customer acquisitions or new business development. In fact, research suggests 60–80% of gatekeepers have "significant influence" over purchases.[19] Professional sport teams such as the San Antonio Spurs have gone so far as to invite gatekeepers to their sales training sessions to help sellers understand the mindset of the gatekeeper and how best to utilize them in a sales conversation. In some cases, sellers might call a gatekeeper simply to extract key information, with little intention to speak with the decision-maker on the first call. Armed with knowledge about the decision-maker's schedule, title, or previous buying habits, the seller will call back a week later better prepared for making an appointment.

---

### BILL GUERTIN OFFERS SOME OFFBEAT QUESTIONS TO GET PAST THE GATEKEEPER

**Suggestions include:**

I have a strange question. If sales are down at your company, who's the one person that usually gets the MADDEST? That's who I need to talk to.

I have the weirdest question you've had all day. Who's the biggest _____ fan in your office? (once you speak to the fan, ask "If you wanted season tickets for the company, who would you have to convince?")

© Kendall Hunt Publishing Company

---

On the first interaction with the gatekeeper, good sellers will ask for the decision-maker by first name. Use of first name creates a level of familiarity

19. Lill, D. (1999). *Selling: The profession.* Antioch, TN: DM Bass Publications.

and reduces the sense that the seller is an outsider trying to sell something the decision-maker would not want. If the decision-maker is not available, sellers should ask when the decision-maker might return, then call back at that time. If the gatekeeper asks for more information regarding the nature of a call, it is critical to provide a **valid business reason** (VBR) for calling. A VBR is a statement that justifies asking for the appointment with a decision-maker.

> ▶ Valid—you are worth making time to hear about how you can help solve a problem
> ▶ Business—you demonstrate that you understand their business challenges
> ▶ Reason—you tell the customer what you want to meet about and why you think it could be of value

The two primary ways to justify asking for the appointment are to utilize a benefit statement and a reference. The benefit statement is a brief statement about how your offering can deliver a tangible and specific benefit for the client. Beyond the benefit statement, there is no need to go into any more specific detail with the gatekeeper. A few common examples within sport sales are listed below:

> ▶ We have a marketing program that helps you reach key target markets with your message
> ▶ We can help your company retain employees and boost morale
> ▶ We have a business program that can help you bring in new clients and retain existing ones

The second strategy is to use a **reference**. References can be geographic, industry, personal, or associative.

> ▶ Geographic—reference to other companies you have successfully worked with in the same geographic market (i.e., city, state, region)
> ▶ Industry—reference to other companies you have successfully worked with in the same industry (i.e., healthcare, manufacturing)
> ▶ Personal—reference to another person that recommended you call the decision-maker (referral)
> ▶ Associative—reference to another person within the organization that you've spoken with prior to calling the decision-maker

For example, if a gatekeeper asks a seller what is the purpose of the call, the seller might respond with *Michael's business associate Javier suggested I give him a call* or *We have had a lot of success helping other insurance companies*

**VALID BUSINESS REASON**
a statement which justifies asking for the appointment with a decision-maker

**REFERENCES**
can be geographic, industry, personal, or associative

*improve their profile and generate new customers, and would like to discuss some of our business-improvement strategies with Janet.* When responding to the gatekeeper's question about the nature of the call, sellers need to focus on the benefit statement and refrain from giving a sales presentation to the gatekeeper.

When gatekeepers handle a sales call, they can respond in a variety of ways. Good sales representatives have a rehearsed response to each. Here are some possibilities:

**Gatekeeper:** "Mr. Decision-Maker is unavailable, try again later."
**Sales Advice:** Obtain more information about the decision-maker and/or the business, including when the decision-maker might be in the office again.

**Gatekeeper:** "Our organization would not be interested in what you are offering."
**Sales Advice:** Good sellers understand the gatekeeper is not the decision-maker so is not qualified to determine if sport tickets would represent a business advantage. In a polite manner, sellers should stress to the gatekeeper their product is proven at improving similar businesses and that just a short window of time with the decision-maker would allow them to show all the advantages of the product.

**Gatekeeper:** "Please put a proposal together in writing and send it to us via e-mail."
**Sales Advice:** Sending a written proposal will likely not get adequate attention and may never get to the decision-maker's desk. Sellers should emphasize that they develop successful programs that help businesses meet their objectives, but are highly customized and need to be presented face-to-face so that questions can be answered and details can be explained in greater detail. Sales representatives should follow-up by asking again for an appointment.

**Gatekeeper:** "Mr. Decision-Maker is not available, but you should talk to Mr. Lower-Rung who handles our marketing."
**Sales Advice:** There is a very good chance Mr. Lower-Rung is not a decision-maker, and therefore will only slow down or impede the sales process. This is typically an effort by the gatekeeper to pawn off a sales representative to someone who does not really have the authority to make a decision on buying. If a seller is confident in who has been identified as the decision-maker, the seller should politely insist on meeting with that person.

**Gatekeeper:** "Mr. Decision-Maker is not available, but I can put you through to voice mail."

**Sales Advice:** While organizations take different approaches regarding voice mail, sales managers would advise at least listening to the voice mail to see if any additional information can be gleaned about the decision-maker. In some cases, executives will leave details on when they plan to return to the office. In other cases, the tone of the voice mail message may give an indication of the decision-maker's personality. If a seller does leave a message, it should be strategic and well-rehearsed.

## INCENTIVIZING GATEKEEPERS

In the 2010 film *Love & Other Drugs*, actor Jake Gyllenhaal plays a pharmaceutical sales representative who struggles to land appointments with the medical doctors who might prescribe the drugs he is selling. Eventually to get past the female gatekeepers (receptionists) in the hospitals and clinics to meet with the doctors, Gyllenhaal's character uses a combination of charm, gifts (food or flowers), and flirtation. While the movie might show a bit of an extreme approach, it does raise an interesting point. In sales, is it appropriate to offer a gatekeeper gifts in order to get an appointment with a decision-maker? Some sport organizations and sales managers say no. Others will say it depends. For example, Bill Larsen, former General Manager of the Kane County Cougars independent league baseball team, used to send sales representatives out to local businesses armed with bags of ballpark peanuts, with the sole objective of landing appointments with decision-makers.[20]

Being in sales for a professional team allows you to be very creative in trying to gain a prospect's attention. Most teams will give you some access to team merchandise, complimentary tickets for games, or invitations to private team events. All of these things make it easier for you to get your foot in the door with a prospect. How many people would not like receiving a free t-shirt in the mail, or a free invite to a sporting event or a complimentary invitation to attend a team luncheon or dinner? Most teams have a ton of events that you can invite prospects to. I even heard one sport sales story where the sales rep sent one autographed basketball sneaker in the mail to a prospect, and told the prospect he'd have to take a meeting with him to get the second one.

—Mark Washo

Washo, M. (2004). *How to break into sports through ticket sales*. Kindle edition.

20. Miller, L. (1999). *Sales success in sports marketing*. Events Unlimited.

Using incentives to secure a meeting with a decision-maker depends on several factors. First, how does the sport organization feel about the practice? Sellers should know they have permission from their supervisors before offering any sort of gift. Second, is the decision-maker a strong lead? Is the prospect likely to buy a significant ticket package, or is the seller wasting time by distributing gifts to everyone? Third, is the offer of a gift likely to improve the chances of landing an appointment? If the seller knows the gatekeeper is a big fan of the team, there is a much better chance of the incentive being seen as a reward.

## WHAT IF I'M REALLY STRUGGLING TO GET PAST THE GATEKEEPER?

It can be quite challenging at times to get past the gatekeeper. Professional sellers employ a few tools that can be effective in bypassing the gatekeeper. Most gatekeepers work standard business hours while many decision-makers come in early or stay late. As a result, the decision-maker may be accessible if sellers are willing to call early or late. While most decision-makers do not answer their own phones during regular business hours, they are likely to answer their phones when the gatekeeper is not at their desk. Many sales professionals consider the early morning (7 a.m. to 8 a.m.), lunch time (12 p.m. to 1 p.m.), and after the close of business (5 p.m. to 6 p.m.) as great times to call decision-makers because the gatekeeper is gone. Consider prioritizing these times to make prospecting calls and then spend the remainder of the day on appointments.[21]

## ON THE PHONE WITH THE DECISION-MAKER

What happens when a seller does manage to get past the gatekeeper and through to the decision-maker? The key at this stage of the conversation is to focus on landing an appointment. Because the decision-maker is likely in the midst of a hectic schedule and is wondering if taking a call is worth the time, the best approach is to get straight to the point. This is not the time to pitch the product, or even spend time on needs assessment. Instead, good sellers present a benefit statement and then ask for a face-to-face appointment. In some cases, the call might be used to gather a little extra data on the prospect, but if the decision-maker starts asking too many questions of the seller, it is best to save the conversation for the face-to-face meeting.

---

21. Spoelstra, J., & Delay, S. (2013). *The ultimate toolkit: Getting the appointment handbook.* Retrieved from www.theultimatetoolkit.com

## Step 1: Introduce Yourself

The steps here are the same as described in Chapter 5.

> *Hi, Katie, I'm the corporate marketing executive with the XYZ City Tigers. My name is Kevin.*

## Step 2: Generate Interest

The next step is to use a benefit statement to generate interest. The benefit statement focuses on the benefit the prospect will receive from the offer, but does not refer to seats or ticket packages. There are two reasons to confidently lead a B2B call with a benefit statement. First, the decision-maker is likely preoccupied with whatever they were doing before receiving the call. Keep in mind that nearly all B2B calls are to someone busy thinking about other things. The appointment call needs to break the preoccupation of the decision-maker. Second, starting the call with idle small talk is not recommended since no rapport has been made with the decision-maker in the past. The goal of the benefit statement should be to get the decision-maker to hear the statement and wonder "*How do you do that?*" "*What is it?*" or "*What's your idea?*"

Below are sample benefit statements that can be used to generate interest with the decision-maker:

▶ Our organization has a proven track record of improving employee morale with organizations like yours.
▶ For many companies in your industry, we have been able to increase their client retention.
▶ We've developed a method to increase your sales by 10% over the next three months.
▶ I have an idea that I think will help you attract top-notch employees to the area.

Notice none of the statements emphasize buying or selling tickets. The goal of the benefit statement is to deliver the benefit to the prospect but keep the nature of the product offering somewhat vague. This is not to be deceptive. Instead, the reason for being vague is that selling face-to-face is far more effective than over the phone. Landing an appointment allows the seller to do more research on the prospect, spend more time assessing the prospect's needs in person, and better prepare to handle questions and objections the decision-maker may raise. Sharing too many details over the phone may give the decision-maker the impression she has all the information needed to make a decision, which at this stage is typically *no*. Saying no is certainly easier to do over the phone rather than in-person.

### Step 3: Ask for the Appointment

Following the benefit statement, sellers should request the decision-maker invest a small amount of time hearing about the idea presented in the benefit statement.

▶ It will just take me 10 minutes to explain. Do you have 10 minutes at some point next week?

▶ If possible, I'd like to talk with you about this opportunity on Tuesday morning or afternoon next week. Which is more convenient for you?

Ideally, the decision-maker will respond with a question like *What's your idea?* or *How do you do that*?, in which case the seller might reiterate the importance of meeting for a short period of time. Brendan Long, Director of New Business Development for The Madison Square Garden Company, suggests downplaying it a bit with indifference. *I'm not sure this will work for you, but others have seen success with it, so it makes sense to meet and see if you can benefit.* Other examples include:

▶ I just need 10 minutes of your time to show you how this works, and you can decide where we go from there, how does that sound?

▶ I'd really love to tell you more over the phone, but I've got something I have to show you.

▶ It will just take me 10 minutes to explain how this works.

It is important to note, however, if the meeting will actually take longer than 10 minutes, then the seller should provide the prospect with a reasonable estimate for the time commitment to demonstrate honesty from the outset of the relationship.

### Tips for Scheduling an Appointment

There are four approaches to scheduling a time to meet with the decision-maker. It is important to note that these are not mutually exclusive approaches. The first approach is to provide the decision-maker a choice between two times. For example, *Would Wednesday morning or Friday afternoon work best for you?* This approach forces the decision-maker to look at their calendar and think about their upcoming schedule, but it also provides them with a choice for what works best for them. It is specific enough to prevent them from giving the blanket *I'm too busy* stall, but general enough that the seller is not forcing her way into the schedule.

TThe second approach is for the seller to mention he or she will be in the area at another business. For example, *I'm going to be on that side of town at another meeting Friday at 2. I can stop by right before or right after that.* This approach leverages social proof because there is evidence that other people are also interested. It also eliminates the objection that the decision-maker doesn't want the seller to waste a lot of time driving all the way to the business.

The third approach uses language that softens the perception of time the decision-maker will need to invest. Using phrases like *let's pencil in 10 minutes, if I could get on your calendar for 10 minutes,* and *if I could stop by your office for just a few minutes* reduces the decision-maker's perceived investment of time. It is important to remember the word "meeting" might be associated with requiring a longer time than the seller is actually seeking from the decision-maker. (To emphasize the succinctness of his appointments, sport sales trainer Steve DeLay has told decision-makers, "I only need 600 seconds of your time. And to prove it, I will bring a stop watch and a shotgun.")

> I only need 600 seconds of your time. And to prove it, I will bring a stop watch and a shotgun.
>
> —Steve DeLay, *The Migala Report*

In some cases, offering to bring the decision-maker a cup of coffee might help establish a reasonable time frame for the appointment as it connotes brevity.

## Step 4:  Confirm Time and Place

The conversation should end with confirmation details of the meeting. Planting a strong suggestion in the mind of the decision-maker to mark the appointment in his or her calendar helps the seller reduce no-shows. For example, *So we're confirmed for 1:00 on Tuesday, March 15 at the city market, is that correct? I'm going to go ahead and note that on my calendar.* Many sellers recommend actually sending the outlook calendar invite so it shows up on the client's calendar because cancellation rates increase when the appointment is not on their calendar.

Salespeople disagree on whether calling the day or two before an appointment is a good idea. On the positive side, calling ahead to confirm is courteous, professional, and may save a seller the time going to a meeting that is not going to occur. On the negative side, calling ahead to confirm opens the door for the decision-maker to back out of the meeting. In general, if the travel distance to the meeting location is great, it probably makes sense to call ahead. However, if a seller is already going to be in the area or has a full schedule for that day, there may not be a need to confirm the day before. Even if a decision-maker forgets about an appointment, showing up at an office may elicit some sympathy from the decision-maker for forgetting the meeting, giving the seller a greater opportunity.

## OVERCOMING COMMON STALLS OR PUT-OFFS

While it would be great if every decision-maker simply agreed to every appointment, unfortunately the sales world doesn't work this way. However, effective sellers are prepared for the most common **stalls**, delays, or put-offs to establishing a sales appointment. It is important to distinguish objections, which are related more to the product, from stalls, which are related to investing time in an appointment. Eight common appointment stalls include:

**STALLS**
delay to establishing an appointment

- ▶ Save yourself a drive to our office and tell me over the phone
- ▶ Send it in writing first
- ▶ You should talk to our Chief Marketing Officer (or any other department head)
- ▶ We don't have any sport fans in our company
- ▶ I don't have the time to meet with you
- ▶ I'm not interested
- ▶ Call me next week and I'll see if my calendar clears up
- ▶ We're cutting back right now and don't have money to spend

Response to stalls should include social proof, a restatement of the benefit, or an emphasis on the small time investment. These three strategies can be used to respond to any of the stalls identified above. After implementing these strategies, ask again for the appointment.

- ▶ **Social proof**—Provide an example of another client that was in the same situation, but that you were able to help:
  - — I want to show you what several other major companies in your industry are doing to achieve [the benefit].
  - — I want to show you what a number of other influential executives have been doing for their company to achieve [the benefit].
  - — This has been successful for other companies in the city.
  - — Do you know John Smith over at ABC Corporation? He loved our concept and is using it right now.

- ▶ **Restate the benefit**—Re-state the benefit that you used to open the call in step 2:
  - — We can help you reach your key demographics in a unique way.
  - — We can help you reward your top employees and keep them satisfied.

- ▶ **Emphasize the small time investment**—Remind the decision-maker you are only seeking 10 minutes of their time by softening their perception of the time commitment:
  - — It's only going to cost you 10 minutes.
  - — I promise our meeting will last only 10 minutes.
  - — Our meeting will last only 10 minutes and then you can decide where to go from there.

- ▶ Ask for the appointment again
  - — See Step 3 above

Each stall has a unique element that can be included in the response in addition to utilizing the four strategies listed above. For example:

- ▶ Save yourself a drive to our office and tell me over the phone
  - — I could tell you over the phone, but there is something I need to show you.

- ▶ Send it in writing first (they won't read it)
  - — I could send it in writing, but there is something I need to show you.

- ▶ You should talk to our Chief Marketing Officer (or any other department head)
  - — I plan to speak to this person at some point, but other presidents have said they appreciate seeing me first.

- ▶ We don't have any soccer fans in our company
  - — The good news is you don't have to be a soccer fan to get excited about achieving [benefit].

- ▶ We're cutting back right now and don't have money to spend
  - — I understand what you mean. Another one of my clients was in a similar situation and we helped them [benefit].

- ▶ I'm not interested
  - — That's why I'm reaching out to you. Many of my satisfied customers also weren't interested to begin with, but we were able to help them reach [benefit].
  - — John Smith at ABC Industries wasn't interested either, but he found that we could help them [benefit].

> ▶ I don't have the time to meet with you
>   — I understand your schedule is busy. I often meet with clients before 8 or after 5. Would that work for you?

> ▶ Call me next week and I'll see if my calendar clears up (it won't)
>   — I have my schedule right in front of me, do you have access to yours? Let's go ahead and set a time right now.

Decision-makers respect professional persistence if the seller demonstrates a willingness to help and offers a legitimate benefit. However, after three attempts to secure a meeting, it is likely time to move on to the next prospect. If decision-makers have been given multiple reasons for a meeting with no avail, it is likely they are not ready to buy at that time. Good sellers, however, keep in mind a "No" today does not mean a "No" next season.

## TARGETING THE RIGHT PERSON

A major challenge in B2B sales is finding the decision-maker. For a small business, the decision-maker might be the owner. For a large corporation, the decision-maker might be a CEO, marketing director, financial officer, director of client acquisition, human relations supervisor, or accounts payable employee. In some cases, the decision-maker might be a group of people all of whom need to approve a spending decision.

Disagreement exists among sales trainers and managers on whom to target within a company to initiate the sales process. Every sale is unique and the people involved in the decision-making process vary from company to company based on corporate culture, decision-making structure, personality and leadership style of the decision-maker, and geographic region of the country. In some companies, senior executives want to be heavily involved in the decision-making process and be involved in many aspects of the decision. In other organizations, senior executives will delegate decision-making to lower levels of authority. In other cases, there are multiple decision-makers, some of whom are detached from actually using the end product. This means the people actually making the decision are not the one's utilizing the tickets. There are two basic approaches to reaching the right person—the top-down approach and the bottom-up approach.

**TOP-DOWN APPROACH**
based on the idea that a company's top officer has the greatest amount of decision-making power

### *Top-Down Approach*

The **top-down approach** is based on the idea that a company's top officer has the greatest amount of decision-making power. In cases where this is true, calling the top of the organizational chart provides the seller with the person who has the power to call meetings, gather the right people around the table, and ultimately sign off on the purchase. If the seller starts high and is then referred to someone lower in the organization, they generated an important associate reference because the lower-level employee will want to talk with the seller as instructed by the boss. However, there are risks of starting high in the organization with the initial call. Perhaps most obviously, a top-level executive can kill the sale before it ever gets started by giving a quick "no." Top-level executives are also extremely busy, which means they are more difficult to reach at their desk and they employ more stringent gatekeepers than lower-level employees. Sellers also encounter top-level decision-makers that are so far up the organizational chart they are distant from the problem that the benefit statement is trying to address. With their focus more on strategic issues and the benefit focused more on operational issues, the benefit statement may not connect with them as something relevant. Finally, there might be political consequences for bypassing lower-level employees and going straight to the top of the organization.

## *Bottom-Up Approach*

The **bottom-up approach** takes the opposite approach and begins the sales process by reaching out to lower-level executives, and then works its way up the organizational ladder as the sale progresses to a final decision. The primary advantage of starting low is that these employees tend to be more accessible than upper-level executives. While they are still busy, they tend to be more likely to pick up the phone when called or have time in their schedule for an appointment. Garnering the support of a lower-level employee helps to potentially identify someone who will champion the idea of buying hospitality assets and move the proposal forward in the organization. It also provides a strong associative reference. However, working a bottom-up approach is also fraught with risks. Arguably the biggest disadvantage is the employee will block the ability to continue the sale, even though the employee does not have real decision-making authority. The sale might be blocked with a firm "no," or by the employee instructing the seller not to contact anyone else within the organization. Another potential risk is the seller offending the employee by exposing or assuming a weakness in their job performance. For example, an employee in the human resources department might be offended if you recommend a group outing that can improve employee morale or retention because it indirectly implies the human resource department is not doing enough to satisfy and retain employees. Finally, this approach is time-consuming because it ultimately includes having to sell to more people. Table 6.5 summarizes the pros and cons of using the top-down and bottom-up approaches to finding the decision-maker.

**BOTTOM-UP APPROACH** begins the sales process by reaching out to lower-level executives and then work your way up the organization ladder as the sale progresses to a final decision

## Table 6.5

**Advantages and Disadvantages to the Top-Down and Bottom-Up Approaches**

| Approach | Advantages | Disadvantages |
|---|---|---|
| Top-Down | Power to call meetings<br><br>Power to gather the right people<br><br>Power to purchase<br><br>Create associative references | Difficult to reach<br><br>More stringent gatekeepers<br><br>Far removed from the problems you are trying to help them solve<br><br>Can kill the sale right off the bat<br><br>Circumventing lower-level employees (politics) |
| Bottom-Up | More accessible<br><br>Closer to problems that need to be solved<br><br>Create internal champions<br><br>Create associative references | Blocked by someone without decision-making authority<br><br>May not see forest through the trees<br><br>May expose a weakness in their job performance<br><br>Time-consuming |

## KEY PLAYERS IN THE DECISION-MAKING PROCESS

**INFLUENCER**
the individual(s) who have access to the decision-maker and provides input that can sway the decision

**INTERNAL CHAMPION**
Individual(s) supportive of ideas who will support a proposal within the organization to help secure a positive decision, essentially becoming a pseudo-salesperson within the organization

In many instances, the decision to purchase group or season tickets, premium seats, and corporate sponsorship involves more than just one decision-maker. As the investment becomes more expensive, more individuals are likely to get involved. Many different people can halt the sales process even though not everyone actually makes the final decision. Below is a list of some of the key players sellers may encounter in a corporate sales environment.[22]

▸ **Decision-maker**—The person who has the final authority to accept or reject a proposal and is held accountable for that decision.
▸ **Influencer**—The individual(s) who have access to the decision-maker and provides input that can sway the decision.
▸ **Internal champion**—Individual(s) supportive of ideas who will support a proposal within the organization to help secure a positive decision, essentially becoming a pseudo-salesperson within the organization.

22. Freese, T. (2013). *Secrets of question based selling.* Naperville, IL: Sourcebooks.

▶ **Informants**—Individual(s) without a say in the final decision but who can provide critical information that will help the seller plan the next step in the sales process. Gatekeepers can make great informants by providing key information about other offers, the budget, the content of a meeting agenda, etc.

▶ **Indifferent**—Individual(s) who don't care about the outcome of the sale.

▶ **Anti-champion**—Individual(s) who proactively speak out against the proposal because they prefer a proposal from a different organization or they prefer the status quo.

**INFORMANT**
individual(s) without a say in the final decision but who can provide critical information that will help the seller plan the next step in the sales process

**INDIFFERENT**
individual(s) who don't care about the outcome of the sale

**ANTI-CHAMPION**
individual(s) who proactively speak out against the proposal because they prefer a proposal from a different organization or they prefer the status quo

In order to determine who the key players will be in the decision-making process, sellers need to ask specific questions, such as:

▶ Are you the right person to speak with about company outings?
▶ Who else needs to be involved in the discussion about client entertainment?
▶ At the end of the day, who will sign off on the purchase?
▶ Can you think of anyone who might not support this proposal?
▶ How do you feel about the proposal we just discussed?

## CHAPTER SUMMARY

B2B sport salespeople focus on the sale of season tickets, premium seats, group outings, and sponsorships to businesses and non-profit organizations who purchase these sport hospitality assets to realize a return on investment from generating new business and retaining their best employees. B2B relationships are initiated through social selling and phone calls. Social selling allows sellers to identify, connect, and engage potential decision-makers on social media and serves to warm up what would otherwise be a cold call to set an appointment. Social selling allows the seller to remove the gatekeeper from the equation and develop a relationship directly with the decision-maker. However, in many instances, picking up the phone and navigating through the gatekeeper is preferable. Once the seller is able to get past the gatekeeper, the goal is to set an appointment for the near future where more information can be learned about the prospect.

## INDUSTRY ADVICE

**Bill Guertin,** *The 800-Pound Gorilla*

### GETTING PAST THE GATEKEEPER: THE SALE *BEFORE* THE SALE

Imagine you've been given the job of protecting a valuable, rare automobile. You've got specific instructions not to let anybody drive it, touch it, or even look at it. During your first day on the job, however, you get a phone call from someone you've never met, asking if they can take the car for a spin.

What would someone have to say to you to convince you to hand over the keys?

Welcome to the world of the gatekeeper.

Regardless of what you sell, whether it's sport tickets or jumbo jets, your skill in navigating past (or with!) the gatekeepers you encounter will be an enormous factor in your eventual success. Whether their title is executive assistant, secretary, or receptionist, these gatekeepers will all have different agendas, based on their job description, their skill level, and their set of instructions.

If you find it tough to get through the gatekeeper, it's usually because he or she is actually doing their job. They're making sure their bosses aren't disturbed unnecessarily, just as when you were protecting the valuable car, you wouldn't toss the keys to just anyone.

But what if there were circumstances that made sense for someone to get into the car and drive it? What if the call was from the fire department, saying that the building next door was on fire, and the car should be moved to avoid it from being destroyed? What if it was from the car owner's spouse, saying that he or she needed to use it?

In those situations, you would have to use "professional judgment." And in a gatekeeper situation in sales, this is where your skills must be at their peak.

Gatekeepers are evaluating who you are and what you want from their boss, and making a judgment call based on your presentation. You must create a situation that causes the gatekeeper to suspend a negative judgment of you, and think of you as an exception to the rule, rather than just another waste of the boss's time.

Some sales reps believe that gatekeepers have little or no value to them; they are simply nameless, faceless people to be eliminated on their way to the front office. I have found the opposite to be true: the most successful sales reps in sports have found ways to *include* gatekeepers in their sales process, rather than treating them as someone to get rid of or avoid.

Gatekeepers are often a trusted part of the boss' success team, and their opinions are highly valued by their supervisors.

Here are some of my keys to a successful navigation of the gatekeepers of the world as a sport sales professional:

- **Consider the gatekeeper to be your FIRST sale.** Get to know them, and ask questions that would be asked in a sport sales situation, like *"When was the last game of ours that you attended?"* or *"Do you have kids that enjoy sports?"* Some salespeople may feel that this is a waste of time, but several executive assistants wind up being the "administrators" of the sport tickets for the company, and they will control the destiny of the company's renewal decision more than anyone. Long-term, you will WANT an awesome relationship with this person!

- **Respect what's important to them.** Some salespeople consider the gatekeeper as a necessary evil, and collateral damage inflicted on them is of no consequence. Yelling, threats, or sneaky tactics (faking that you're someone else) will come back to bite you AND your team. Gatekeepers are people too; treat them with respect, and make sure you ask if there's something you can do to help THEM along the way.

- **Be prepared to answer the question, "What's this regarding?"** Nine times out of 10, you're going to get this question. Gatekeepers have their radar on, and if you fumble for an answer, they'll instantly write you off. Have a response ready, such as *"It's about our new program here at the (team). It'll just take a moment; I appreciate your help."*

- **Consider asking if the gatekeeper would like to be in on the idea.** Many executive assistants are looking for ways to make a splash in their company, and if he or she finds your objective to be a good one, they might agree to help you in presenting it to the boss. It could be that they may want to present it jointly with you, or even present it themselves without you in the room. If the gatekeeper isn't going to let you through anyway, this may be your best shot at the deal. Your "ask" might go something like this: *"Hey… are YOU ever involved in presenting new ideas? If I were to tell you what I had in mind, and you thought it was a good idea, would you be in a position to bring it to your boss?"*

Despite what you may have heard about the position, gatekeepers hold a great deal of influence in the company. Respect them, treat them professionally and with courtesy, and more often than not, you will win the day.

---

## CHAPTER ACTIVITIES

1. Assume that a prospect is interested in purchasing 4 tickets in a 20-game season ticket package. The prospect estimated that the sales force can close 20% of the deals after attending a game with an average of 1.5 transactions per customer. On average, those sales will be approximately $1,500. Assuming the cost of the package is $10,000, calculate the return on investment for the business.

2. Assume that a prospect is interested in purchasing a club seat season ticket package valued at $50,000. The prospect estimated that the company would lose nearly 75% of the revenue generated by Brittany, the company's best salesperson, who generates 250,000 in sales each year. It costs the company $10,000 to train and replace each salesperson. Assuming the cost of the package is $15,000, calculate the return on investment for the business.

3. Assume you are a corporate ticket sales executive for an NBA team. Draft a 500-word article that you would post on LinkedIn to reach corporate decision-makers about the value of purchasing hospitality assets with professional sport teams.

4. Identify and examine five LinkedIn profiles of sport salespeople in your local market. Assess the strengths and weaknesses of their profiles from a social selling perspective.

5. Draft a warm LinkedIn InMail introduction to a corporate decision-maker you've previously engaged with online.

6. Assume your class is selling tickets for your university's athletic department. Develop a benefit statement that you would use during the first call to a decision-maker when attempting to schedule an appointment to meet in person.

7. Using a sales situation given to you by your professor, partner with a classmate to complete the following role-playing situations:

    a. Get past the gatekeeper at a local business.

    b. Open the call with a decision-maker at a local non-profit organization that provides health services to low-income residents in the community.

    c. Develop a response to a decision-maker who says "Send me your proposal in writing first, then we can talk."

    d. Schedule an appointment with an interested decision-maker.

# CHAPTERS 5 AND 6 COMPETENCY ASSESSMENT[23]

## COMPETENCY DOMAIN: OPENING THE CALL

*Exemplary:* Consistently does all or almost all of the following:

- ► Clearly states purpose for the call
- ► Sets an agenda
- ► Asks for permission to engage in conversation
- ► Piques the customer's interest at the start of the conversation or presentation
- ► Transitions smoothly into conducting a needs analysis
- ► Achieves a high appointment ratio with decision-makers by getting past the gatekeeper
- ► Engages in a significant number of calls that last longer than five minutes

*Skilled:* Does most of the following:

- ► Clearly states purpose for the call
- ► Sets an agenda
- ► Asks for permission to engage in a conversation
- ► Piques the customer's interest at the start of the conversation or presentation
- ► Transitions smoothly into conducting a needs analysis
- ► Achieves above average appointment ratio with decision-makers by getting past gatekeeper
- ► Engages in an above average number of calls that last longer than five minutes

*Adequate:* Does most of the following:

- ► Starts the call with a professional introduction and establishment of an agenda, but too often is unable to engage the customer in conversation or set clear direction for the call
- ► Show improvement in establishing common ground, interest, or an agenda for the call, but too often misses one of these key ingredients
- ► Needs to improve appointment ratio when attempting to secure meetings
- ► Too many calls last less than three minutes

*Novice:* Consistently does all or almost all of the following:

- ► Customers do not take Seller seriously due to poor communication skills in the first twenty seconds of the call
- ► Fails to clearly state the purpose of the call
- ► Fails to set an agenda at the start of the conversation
- ► Achieves low appointment ratio and struggles to get past the gatekeeper to have meaningful conversations with decision-makers
- ► Most calls last less than three minutes

---

23. From "Competency Assessment for Entry-Level Sport Ticket Sales Professionals" by David Pierce and Richard Irwin, *Journal of Applied Sport Management*, Volume 8 (2), Summer 2016. Reprinted by permission of Sagamore Publishing. www.sagamorepub.com

# CHAPTER 7

## NEEDS ANALYSIS

**LEARNING OBJECTIVES**

After completing this chapter, you should be able to:

▶ Identify, recognize, and define the different types of sales questions.

▶ Explain the purpose of the needs analysis in the sales process.

▶ Identify and define the four types of questions in the SPIN questioning system.

▶ Create a sales conversation using the SPIN questioning system.

▶ Apply the SPIN questioning system to a sales call.

▶ Understand how to manage the flow of a conversation through the use of questions.

**KEY TERMS**

| | | |
|---|---|---|
| Clarification question | Global question | Needs analysis |
| Close-ended question | Humble disclaimer | Open-ended question |
| Commitment question | Hypothetical question | Problem question |
| Comparison question | Implication question | Redirect question |
| Confirmation question | Issue-based question | Situation question |
| Double-barreled question | Lock-on question | SPIN questioning system |
| Expansion question | Need-payoff question | |

**COMPENTENCIES**

▶ Ability to ask the right questions to uncover the needs of the customer.

▶ Ability to ask the right questions to qualify the customer.

▶ Ability to think on your feet and adapt quickly to new information.

## CHAPTER OVERVIEW

Think about the last time you were sick and went to the doctor's office. Consider the steps the doctor took to determine what course of action you should take to get well. Did the doctor walk into the exam room and immediately prescribe medicine? Hopefully not! Prescribing a medicine before diagnosing the illness is medical malpractice. Instead, a competent doctor likely asked a series of questions, listened intently to the answers, and developed a plan of action to help you recover. Just as a doctor asks questions to determine the right prescription, a salesperson should diagnose the customer's needs before telling them what they should buy. The more accurately the seller can diagnose the needs of the customer, the more appropriately the seller can recommend the right product or service, the right package, and the right prices for that customer. If the seller is able to diagnose their needs, he or she will be in the right position to recommend the right product to meet those needs. The best salespeople never try to sell a feature without reason to believe it will be perceived as valuable to a prospect. Stated differently, it is impossible for the seller to identify the right product unless he or she first asks questions to understand the problem or need faced by the customer.

## PURPOSE OF THE NEEDS ANALYSIS

**NEEDS ANALYSIS**
process of asking questions to identify customer needs, desires, motives, and problems

The process of asking questions to identify customer needs, desires, motives, and problems is called **needs analysis**. Needs analysis is a crucial part of the sales process because it sets the stage for the seller to make an appropriate, customized product recommendation and close the sale. It allows sellers to uncover the facts, feelings, needs, and motives used to pitch the appropriate product or package for that customer's specific situation. The seller will experience more success in sales by asking questions and listening than by talking at the customer. Inexperienced salespeople believe they must take control of the conversation by doing most of the talking (what some in sport sales call "show up and throw up"), but this results in distrust and frustration for the customer. If sellers jump into their sales pitch too early, the result can be confusion, resistance, and damaged rapport. Beginning a presentation before the customer understands his or her needs will result in more objections than starting with a needs analysis.

Let's take an example. Imagine two different prospective ticket buyers. Both attended five games last year. Prospect A is a die-hard hockey fan. He played hockey growing up and coaches youth hockey now. He watches as many games as he can on TV and follows the team closely through the media. He owns jerseys of his favorite players and has several autographed pucks on his desk at work. Once a season, he and his buddies plan a trip to a road game. Prospect B is a grandfather who loves taking his grandkids to games when they are in town visiting. He follows the team in the newspaper but is not a hard-core fan. Most of his friends are not really into hockey, but his grandkids are all on youth teams. He and his wife may go to one or two games a year without the grandkids, typically on Sunday afternoons, followed by a night out for dinner and the casino. Selling to these prospects would take two very different approaches. A sales representative who doesn't conduct a good needs analysis and just jumps into a sales pitch will likely strike out on upselling one or both prospects. Prospect A is likely not going to be interested in the team's new kids club, while Prospect B probably does not care about the team's promising draft picks this off-season. However, if the sales representative asks the right questions and gains beneficial information, the conversation could easily be steered toward the appropriate package.

In a recent survey conducted by the RAIN Group, the top reasons customers become annoyed during the sales process is because salespeople don't listen, don't understand the customer's needs, and talk too much.[1] In reality, the salesperson should only talk approximately 25% of the conversation and control the conversation by asking questions. Remember: *the one who asks the questions controls the conversation.*

The purpose in asking questions during the needs analysis is to build value in the customer's mind. Asking the right questions at the right time allows the seller to help customers discover how the offering can satisfy their needs. As the seller uncovers the customer's needs, he or she begins to build value. Value is the total benefit that the seller's product or service provides to the customer. The best way for customers to discover value is to have the customer talk about it, not listen to the seller tell them about it. As the seller builds value with questions, picture the information gleaned from the customer as coins in a piggy bank. Once the customer articulates the value they see in making a purchase, the seller can cash in those coins and ask for the sale. Or, picture value as weights on the scales of justice. At some point during the call, the customer will discover enough value to tip the scales in favor of making a purchase. It is important for sellers to make product recommendations after the needs assessment is complete.

There are many benefits to uncovering needs through asking questions. First, asking questions helps to create dialogue with the customer. It prevents the seller from dumping potentially irrelevant product information on the

---

1. Tabita, J. *Understanding the sales cycle: Uncovering needs.* Retrieved from http://www.sitepoint.com/understanding-the-sales-cycle-uncovering-needs/

Let the customer do most of the talking. Patience and listening are traits that successful sales reps must possess. Take your time with the process. Ask the question you want to ask, then listen intently to the answer. Let me say that again, *listen* to the answer instead of thinking about what your next question should be. Stay in the moment and focus on the prospect. Their answer will usually guide you to your next question and may uncover opportunities you didn't even know existed.

—Carl Manteau, *Milwaukee Bucks*

customer by keeping him or her involved in the conversation. It also helps the seller build rapport because most people like to hear themselves talk. Second, in listening to the customer's answers and using those to form the next relevant question, the seller shows the customer that he or she is interested in what the customer has to say. It allows the seller to demonstrate that he or she is placing the customer's needs above the seller's own needs. This allows the seller to build rapport and trust with the customer. Third, asking questions lays the groundwork for demonstrating that the seller is the expert on the product and makes him or her appear professional. The seller's recommendation will be taken more seriously by the prospect if the customer believes the seller is knowledgeable. Fourth, questions provoke the customer to think about how to answer the seller's questions, thus engaging him or her in the conversation. Thoughtful and accurate answers from the customer allow the seller to gather information and gain clarification on the thoughts, feelings, and attitudes of the customer. Finally, asking questions allows the seller to test agreement throughout the sales process and advance the sale to the next step, giving the seller control over the direction of the conversation.

Every organization is different and there are many approaches to needs assessment. Below we will examine many of these techniques and styles. However, not every sales conversation will follow the same pattern or use the same types of questions. While each sport organization is different, some of the different approaches teams may use are presented below.

## KEY PRINCIPLES FOR PHRASING QUESTIONS

There are a variety of different ways to categorize questions that the seller can ask during the needs analysis. The seller can also utilize different questioning techniques. It is important to keep in mind there are different terms used by sales trainers, sales managers, and sales books to describe nearly all of the following question types. However, nearly all sales managers agree on four key principles to follow when asking questions to customers:

1. Ask open-ended questions and limit the use of close-ended questions.
2. Phrase questions in a positive manner to elicit a favorable answer.
3. Ask questions one idea at a time, avoiding the use of double-barreled questions.
4. Diversify the question style to provoke in-depth answers from the customer.

## Ask Open-Ended Questions

One way to categorize the types of questions that the seller can ask a customer is based on the type of answer that the seller is trying to elicit. **Open-ended questions** allow customers to answer with varied responses and respond freely and spontaneously. Open-ended questions usually begin with who, what, when, where, or how, but there are many different ways to ask open-ended questions. For example, the section below discusses the use of issue, expansion, comparison, status, and clarification questions. Nearly all of the seller's questions should be open-ended. Common open-ended questions are shown in Table 7.1.

**OPEN-ENDED QUESTION** allow customers to answer with varied responses and respond freely and spontaneously

In order to reach the point in the sales process where you feel confident enough to make a strong recommendation and ask for the sale, you must first learn some very important details about your prospect and how they (or their company) may use your product or services. Asking open-ended questions greatly increases the likelihood that the prospect will engage in deep conversation. Conversely, the more yes/no questions you ask, the greater the risk of getting short answers that either don't steer you towards the best value proposition, or worse, that cut off the dialogue all together.

—Carl Manteau, *Milwaukee Bucks*

## Table 7.1

**Common Open-Ended Questions**

| Who | What | When | Where | How |
|-----|------|------|-------|-----|
| Who will be making the final decision? | What are your plans for entertaining clients this year? | When do you think the key players will be able to get together for a meeting? | Where do you like to sit? | How many games did you attend last season? |
| Who do you normally come to games with? | What does your budget look like for the upcoming year? | When was your first ever soccer game? | Where did you purchase your tickets? | How was your experience at the game last year? |
| Who else do you know that is a huge hockey fan? | What has been your experience with mini-season ticket plans in the past? | When does your family like to come to games? | Where did your clients decide to eat before the game? | How familiar are you with our arena? |

**CLOSE-ENDED QUESTION**
questions that trigger a limited response, often yes or no answers

On a limited basis, the seller can utilize **close-ended questions** that trigger a limited, brief response focused on a specific point. Answers to close-ended questions tend to be a single word or answer like *Yes* or *No*. Choice questions are like close-ended questions in that they trigger a short response to the choices the seller provided.

- ► Do you prefer to attend games early in the season?
- ► Are you the decision-maker?
- ► Do you like to sit behind the goal?
- ► Could we get the contract signed by May 30?

Asking too many close-ended questions, or asking them too early in the conversation, can interrupt or stall the flow of the conversation. Most close-end~~ed~~ questions can be rephrased in an open-ended manner (see Table 7.2). W~~ith~~ the MLSNSC training facility, the sales coaches ring a bell every time ~~a~~ necessary close-ended question to condition the trainees to ~~open~~-ended questions.

> ~~A~~ proper needs analysis is asking a large volume of open-~~ended questions~~. The goal is to learn as much about the client and how ~~they will~~ utilize tickets. If the conversation is choppy and includes a ~~lot of "yes" a~~nd "no" answers, the client will most likely get impatient and ~~t~~he s~~eller w~~ill not reach the goal of meeting their needs. We believe a good sales cal~~l~~ should include over 20 total questions, with over 80% of them being open-ended.
>
> —Jeff Berryhill, *Major League Soccer*

## Table 7.2

**Rephrasing Close-Ended Questions**

| Close-Ended | Open-Ended |
|---|---|
| Do you have a favorite part of the stadium? | Tell me about your favorite part of the stadium. |
| Did you play sports growing up? | How involved were you in sports growing up? |
| Do you reward employees? | What does your company do to reward employees? |
| Did you have a good time? | On a scale of 1–10, how would you rate your game day experience? |
| Did you come to a game last season? | How many games did you attend? |

## *Phrase Questions Positively to Evoke Emotion*

Sellers should phrase open-ended questions in a positive manner to reduce the possibility of a negative response by the prospect. Consider the difference between these two questions:

1. How was your experience at the ballpark last season?

2. Tell me about your favorite memory last year.

Both questions ask customers to reflect on their experiences, but the first question opens up the possibility of a negative answer, while the second question focuses the customer's thinking on their favorite memory, which brings a favorable response.

Basic fact-finding questions can also be phrased in a way that increases the customer's emotional attachment to the experience. Consider the difference between these two questions:

1. Where did you sit?

2. Where is your favorite place to sit?

Both questions uncover where the fan has sat in the arena, but the first question will evoke a short response based on a specific recent visit, while the second question focuses the customer's thinking on positive feelings behind their favorite memories. It also tells the seller the preferred seat location of the fan, not just where they sat on the last visit.

> There are almost no reasons to be negative when selling sports. After all, we are selling fun, excitement and entertainment! Sports are engrained in our society and people love talking about them on a daily basis. Sure, there may be some 'negative' things to overcome (like poor team performance, price increases, etc.), but the best reps are masters of not injecting these into conversations and pivoting as quickly as possible if they are raised by a prospect.
>
> —Carl Manteau, *Milwaukee Bucks*

## Ask Questions One Idea at a Time

**DOUBLE-BARRELED QUESTION**
two questions at once

Ask questions that focus on one idea at a time. Some salespeople get into the bad habit of asking **double-barreled questions,** or two questions at once. The danger is that the customer will only respond to one half of the question. For example, the question *"Do you think you would enjoy the atmosphere and prices in the pavilion section?"* asks two different questions, but will likely only garner a response to one. The first question is whether the customer will enjoy the atmosphere, and the second question is whether the customer would enjoy the prices. The seller takes the risk of the customer answering only one of the questions. Beyond this, prematurely asking about price potentially moves the conversation off track because the question is really designed to focus on atmosphere.

## Diversify the Question Style to Provoke In-Depth Answers

The seller can utilize expansion and comparison questions to get more detailed information from the customer than a typical open-ended question. These questions diversify the way in which the seller asks questions to provoke deeper thought and responses on the part of the customer. They also give the seller alternative ways to phrase questions to avoid using "why" to start the question, which makes prospects feel like they are being interrogated. However, expansion questions should be used sparingly in the conversation so as not to become repetitive.

### EXPANSION QUESTIONS

Expansion questions seek to acquire the same information as the open-ended questions identified above, but in a way that elicits more detailed information from the prospect (see Table 7.3).

**EXPANSION QUESTION**
seek to acquire the same information as the open-ended questions identified above, but in a way that elicits more detailed information from the prospect

**Expansion questions** are phrased as a statement beginning with phrases such as:

- ▶ Describe for me . . .
- ▶ Share with me . . .
- ▶ Explain . . .
- ▶ Walk me through . . .
- ▶ Tell me . . .

## Table 7.3

**Expansion Questions**

|  | Question | Response |
|---|---|---|
| **Open-Ended** | When will you make a decision? | Hopefully by Friday |
| **Expansion** | Walk me through your department's decision-making process. | I will need to speak with my boss, who will present it to the Employee Affairs committee by the end of next week. If there is enough support from the committee, I'm pretty sure my boss will sign off on it. |
| **Analysis** | By asking an expansion question, the seller is able to elicit significantly more information than with the open-ended question. Such questions also allow the seller to follow up on different components of the answer, such as who is on the Employee Affairs committee, and what elements of the proposal the boss might like or dislike. | |

|  | Question | Response |
|---|---|---|
| **Open-Ended** | Where did you sit? | We sat in the upper level. |
| **Expansion** | Share with me the factors you consider when deciding where to sit. | Well, it depends on whether I am going with family or with a group of friends. If I go with family and my young kids, we prefer to sit behind home plate so we're protected by the screen. If I go with friends, we like the Outfield Cove since it's more like a bar atmosphere. |
| **Analysis** | By asking an expansion question, the seller learned that this customer attends with both family and friends and that his/her seating preference depends on which group is in attendance. Now the door is open to at least two different types of sales, referrals, and upselling opportunities. | |

**COMPARISON QUESTION**

use words like compare, contrast, differ, whether, and versus to yield more detailed information than the traditional open-ended question

## COMPARISON QUESTIONS

**Comparison questions** use words like *compare, contrast, differ, whether,* and *versus* to yield more detailed information than the traditional open-ended question. The comparison question engages the prospect to ensure that his/her answer yields usable information (see Table 7.4).

## Table 7.4

**Comparison Questions**

|  | Question | Response |
|---|---|---|
| **Open-Ended** | What are your goals this year? | We want to improve our market position and brand loyalty. |
| **Comparison** | Share with me what you hope to accomplish in the next year compared to where you are today. | Right now we are third in market share for our product category, but we've implemented a new production process and marketing campaign that we believe can get us past X Corporation and into second place within the next year or two. |
| **Analysis** | By asking a comparison question, the seller was able to get the prospect to think about where they are now and where they want to be, which elicited information about their market share position, new initiatives within the company, and key competitors. | |

|  | **Question** | **Response** |
|---|---|---|
| **Open-Ended** | What do you like about attending Tigers games? | We really like coming for fireworks nights on the weekends during the summer. |
| **Comparison** | Tell me what you like about attending Tigers games versus what you do not like. | We really liked coming to the fireworks nights on the weekends during the summer, but we really don't like how we have to fight downtown rush hour traffic after getting off work because we live about 25 miles away from the stadium. It's hard to get to a game by 7:00 p.m. |
| **Analysis** | By asking a comparison question, the seller was able to find out the positives and negatives of coming to a game in the mind of the customer. It could help the seller forecast and prepare for a potential objection later in the sales call. | |

## SPIN TECHNIQUE

In addition to applying these four principles, it is important for sellers to sequence questions in a way that builds value for the customer. As we discussed in Chapter 4, people buy to satisfy needs, and the role of the salesperson is to uncover a customer's needs, even when the customer may not initially recognize that one exists. If the seller is unable to uncover the true needs of the prospect, he or she will never be able to recommend the appropriate product, service, package, or experience. The process of uncovering a need requires the seller to ask predominantly open-ended questions that reveal facts about the prospect.

The **SPIN questioning system** sequences four types of questions designed to uncover a prospect's current situation and inherent problems, enhance the buyer's understanding of the consequences and implications of those problems, and lead to the proposed solution.[2] SPIN is an acronym for the four types of questions that comprise the sequence of questions: situation questions, problem questions, implication questions, and need-payoff questions. The purpose of using a technique like SPIN is to provide the seller with a framework for how to construct a logical series of questions based on answers given by customers. It is important to recognize that organizations will use different terminology to describe the types of questions below. The SPIN technique provides an overarching framework to illustrate how sales reps can build value through asking questions in any type of sales setting.

**SPIN QUESTIONING SYSTEM** sequences four types of questions designed to uncover a prospect's current situation and inherent problems, enhance the buyer's understanding of the consequences and implications of those problems, and lead to the proposed solution

## Situation Questions

**Situation questions** gather facts and background information about the prospect's existing situation. These investigative, fact-finding questions are analytical and set the foundation for the seller to ask emotional questions later in the conversation that reveal the impact of those needs in their life or business. Once the seller starts to uncover needs with well positioned open-ended questions, he or she earns the right to ask about the emotional implications of the issues that were uncovered. At this stage, the seller is trying to get inside the customer's mind to understand what drives their thought process to get information that enables the seller to help them.[3]

**SITUATION QUESTION** gather facts and background information about the prospect's existing situation

Situation questions are narrow in scope and diagnose the status of the prospect's buying habits, beliefs, business condition, purchase history, budget, and sphere of influence. They give the salesperson a foundational knowledge of the prospect's situation. The following questions are examples of open-ended situation questions in selling tickets for sporting events.

2. Rackham, N. (1988). *SPIN selling*. McGraw-Hill.
3. Stephens, N. (1996). *Customer-focused selling*. Holbrook, MA: Adams Media Corporation.

## Goal: Determine customer motives

- ► What brings you out to the ballpark?
- ► Tell me more about why you come out to our games.
- ► What is your favorite thing about coming to an X game?
- ► What is your best memory of X games?
- ► How was your experience at the ballpark last season?
- ► Share with me what makes one X game better than another game.

## Goal: Understand customer attendance patterns and preferences

- ► If I gave you the keys to X stadium and you could pick any seat, where would I find you sitting?
- ► How many games do you typically attend each year?
- ► How many games did you make it out to last season?
- ► Where do you like to sit when you come out to the ballpark?
- ► Which types of X games do you like the best?

## Goal: Understand the customer's sphere of influence and social networks

- ► Who do you typically come to games with?
- ► Where do you work?
- ► Who is the biggest [insert sport] fan you know?
- ► What other groups are you involved with?
- ► What charitable organizations are you involved with?

## Goal: Quantify passion for team or sport

- ► How big of an X fan are you?
- ► How long have you been a fan of the team/sport?
- ► When was it that you fell in love with the game of X?

## Goal: Understand how the prospect spends leisure time

- ► Besides coming to an X game, what else do you like to do in your free time?
- ► How often are you able to get out and spend time with _____?
- ► Walk me through how your family decides how to spend your free time.

## Goal: Understand the prospect's budget

- ► In a perfect world, how much could you spend?
- ► In a perfect world, how many games would you like to attend this year?

## Goal: Assess likelihood of buying

▶ On a scale of 1–10, how likely are you to buy?

Unfortunately, many rookie sales reps never progress beyond situation questions and immediately move into presenting the product. Sellers who prematurely stop the needs analysis after asking situation questions have not helped the prospect understand the benefits of purchasing the product. The prospect will not see the value in buying after answering six to eight situation questions and then being presented with a package. Effective sellers move beyond situation questions to asking problem questions.

---

**Carl Manteau, Senior Director of Group Sales, Milwaukee Bucks**

### SITUATION QUESTIONS FOR B2B SALES

Asking these questions of a prospective business group leader can help give you enough of a base to make a strong value proposition (these questions do not need to be asked in order. Let the flow of the conversation dictate when they get asked):

**Understand the organization**

- ▶ What does your company do?
- ▶ What is your company's mission? What are you doing to accomplish it?
  - — Probably the single greatest question and follow-up question you can ask! If you know their mission/goal/vision then it will be easier to recommend a ticket program that is in line with it.
- ▶ How many full-time employees do you have? How many part-time?
- ▶ How many local customers do you serve?
- ▶ How do you currently reward deserving employees?

**Understand their history**

- ▶ What past event sticks out as the most successful?
- ▶ What made it a success?
- ▶ How many people were a part of it?
- ▶ Was it just for employees or was it open to family and friends?
- ▶ Were customers invited?
- ▶ What would have made it an even better event?
- ▶ How did you communicate this event? (e.g., how did people find out about it? Word of mouth, intranet, e-mail, fliers, paycheck stuffers, etc.)

---

---

**NBA INSIDE SALES SITUATION QUESTIONS**

**Reasons for Buying**

- ▶ When did you first fall in love with the team?
- ▶ What's your favorite thing about the team?
- ▶ Who is your favorite player?
- ▶ Share with me why you decided to purchase last season.

**Number of Seats**

- ▶ Who do you normally come to games with?
- ▶ Who else do you know that is a big fan?
- ▶ How do you typically use your tickets?
- ▶ What is an average client worth to you?
- ▶ How many employees/salespeople do you have?
- ▶ How does your company generate new business?
- ▶ How does your company thank its employees?

**Seat Location**

- ▶ What did you think of your seats last season?
- ▶ If I gave you the keys to the arena, where would you sit?
- ▶ What is the most important thing to you in terms of seat location?
- ▶ What is your favorite angle to watch the game from?

**Package Type**

- ▶ How many games do you typically attend each season?
- ▶ What opponents do you want to see?
- ▶ How many games can you attend each month based on your schedule?
- ▶ Which promotional nights do you typically enjoy?

---

## *Problem Questions*

While situation questions are foundational to the process of qualifying a prospect, most situation questions are low in value for the prospect because they already know the answers to the questions being asked. Situation questions build a profile of the customer, but they do not reveal any information about the gap that may exist between where the customer is and where they want to be (see Chapter 4). Many rookie sales reps fail to move beyond situation questions and into problem, implication, and need-payoff questions.

**Problem questions** bring a customer's implied needs, problems, and motives to the surface, or make them explicit. Problem questions are used to focus the customer's thinking on a particular point of interest related to a need that the seller thinks has been identified while asking situation questions. These questions are useful questions to get the prospect talking about their needs, problems, or motives in a way that actively helps the buyer better understand the need. The more explicit needs the seller can discover, the more vividly he or she can relate the product features and benefits to what the prospect actually cares about. There are three types of problem questions that can be effective in generating explicit needs: issue-based, clarification, and lock-on.

**PROBLEM QUESTION**
bring a customer's implied needs, problems, and motives to the surface, or making them explicit

## ISSUE-BASED QUESTIONS

**Issue-based questions** get prospects talking gaps between their present state and an ideal state. These questions are broad in scope and get to the heart of any needs that may exist, but do so in a way by having the prospect do most of the talking. Issue-based questions also identify anything that is preventing a prospect from experiencing the positive outcomes they are seeking. For example:

**ISSUE-BASED QUESTION**
get prospects talking gaps between their present state and an ideal state

- ▶ Share with me the biggest challenges that _____ is facing right now in reaching its most important goals.
- ▶ What are the results you're most interested in achieving as a result of _____?
- ▶ What do you envision being different about your _____ a year from now?
- ▶ Share with me three things that make it difficult for your family/business to _____?
- ▶ Are there times when you need to _____?
- ▶ What kinds of problems have you experienced with _____?
- ▶ Has ____ ever complained about _____?
- ▶ What are the three things you want to get out of _____?
- ▶ To what extent is _____ important?

## CLARIFICATION QUESTION

The **clarification question** is used to gather specific insight into a general word, phrase, or statement made by a prospect so as to eliminate confusion over its meaning. There are phrases repeatedly used by customers that hold entirely different meanings for different people. These phrases represent good information to glean during a needs analysis, but they don't necessarily tell

**CLARIFICATION QUESTION**
used to gather specific insight into a general word, phrase, or statement made by a prospect so as to eliminate confusion over its meaning

the seller anything about the prospect's needs, preferences, or motives. For example, take a look at these common statements made by customers:

- ▶ We like to have a good time.
- ▶ This is one of our favorite teams.
- ▶ We want to have good seats.
- ▶ We want the process of getting to the game to be convenient.

Typical Customer Statement: *We just want to get out of the office and have a good time.*

Clarification Question: *You just said that you want to have a good time. What exactly does a good time mean to you?*

The meaning of "have a good time" could mean any number of things. If the seller makes an assumption on what it means for the group to "have a good time," he or she could propose a solution or highlight benefits that are irrelevant to the prospect. Having a "good time" for one group may be the ability to socialize while paying minimal attention to the game, while another group may want the best seats possible for the most important games of the season because of their interest in the team. By asking the clarification question, the seller has a much better understanding of what the group is really seeking from its experience at the event.

## LOCK-ON QUESTIONS

**LOCK-ON QUESTION**
get the customer to elaborate on a feeling or emotion that the seller believes is important to confirming the needs he/she might have

**Lock-on questions** get the customer to elaborate on a feeling or emotion that the seller believes is important to confirming the needs the customer might have. Proper use of the lock-on question maintains the natural flow of a conversation while offering a way to steer the conversation in a particular direction. Most importantly, lock-on questions give the seller the opportunity to hear customers go into more detail about their needs. Certain keywords that indicate a customer has a need, desire, or problem to be solved should trigger the seller to ask a lock-on question. Examples of these words or phrases include: include trying to, dealing with, problems, concerns, hopeful, stressful, seeking, needs, struggling, challenges, afraid, frustrated, search, and goals.[4]

### Example 1:

> **Prospect**: We have been trying to find activities that the whole family can enjoy.

---

4. Cherry, P. (2006). *Questions that sell*. New York: American Management Association.

**Lock-on question**: I noticed that you said the word "trying." What has worked so far and what has not?

**Prospect**: We have been experiencing problems with our service rep with the Panthers recently.

## Example 2:

**Lock-on question**: Can you give me an example of the problems you have been experiencing?

**Prospect**: It's really tough to find a place to hang out after work in X city.

**Lock-on question**: When you say it's tough, what exactly do you mean?

**Lock-on question**: I understand what you mean about it being tough. What other activities have you tried in the past?

The key to using lock-on questions is to listen carefully to what the customer says, and then ask questions using their own words.[5] Customers will point the seller toward the need that exists, and it is the seller's job to probe deeper into the need to confirm the need and have the customer reflect on it so the seller can begin to help them understand the impact of the need.

## *Implication Questions*

**Implication questions** help the customer think about the impact of the problem and understand the urgency of satisfying the need or resolving the problem. The purpose of an implication question is to motivate prospects to seek a solution based upon the impact the need or problem has on their life, family, business, group, etc. Implication questions get the customer thinking about the size of the problem.

A mistake inexperienced salespeople make is to jump quickly into a solution based on product features and benefits at the first hint that a problem exists. However, just because a customer admits that a need or motive exists does not guarantee they will see any reason to change or make a purchase. The role of the implication questions is to let the customer expand on why or how the problem affects their life or business. If the seller takes the customer through the process of analyzing how the problem or need affects them, they will see how important it is to fix the problem or satisfy the need.

Implication questions follow the logical flow of the conversation and should not be asked until a need or motive has been identified through problem questions. If the customer answers impact questions in a way that leads the seller to believe the customer does not see the impact of the problem,

**IMPLICATION QUESTION**
help the customer think about the potential consequences or impact of the problem and understand the urgency of satisfying the need or resolving the problem

---

5. Ibid., p. 85.

then the seller will need to go back and ask additional problem and situation questions. There is a back-and-forth that occurs with problem and implication questions. However, the seller shouldn't move forward to the final step, the need-payoff question, until the seller is confident the customer sees that there are relevant ramifications if the needs are not met or the problem is not solved.

The questions that best capture the spirit of an implication question are:

▶ How does [insert problem or need] affect your [family, business, organization]?
▶ What impact does [insert problem or need] have on [something important to the prospect]?
▶ What happens when [problem occurs or need goes unsatisfied]?
▶ What would happen if [problem occurs or need goes unsatisfied]?
▶ If you don't [satisfy the need or fix the problem], then what is the impact?

Sample implication questions:

▶ How does this problem affect your family?
▶ How does this concern impact your group of friends?
▶ How does this difficulty impact your social time?
▶ What happens when your schedules get hectic and you don't have time to spend together?
▶ What do you think these problems are costing you?
▶ How much is this problem impacting the bottom line?
▶ How many employees have to worry about this problem?
▶ Have you lost customers or employees because of this problem? How much were these worth to you?
▶ How is this problem affecting other areas of your business?
▶ If you don't fix this problem, what is the impact on your business?
▶ Has company morale been affected by this problem?
▶ How much does it cost you to recruit a new employee?
▶ How much is that client worth if they walk out the door?

**NEED-PAYOFF QUESTION**
focuses the customer's attention on the benefit derived from solving the problem or satisfying a need

## *Need-Payoff Questions*

After the prospect has identified the need and assessed its impact, it is time to ask a **need-payoff question** that focuses the customer's attention on the benefit derived from solving the problem or satisfying a need. Need-payoff questions ask about the usefulness of solving a problem and get the customer talking about the benefits. It is the final step in taking an implicit, unstated need into an explicit need recognized by the customer.

Common need-payoff questions commonly take the form of the following:

- ► How would that help you?
- ► Why is that important?
- ► Is there any other way this could help you?
- ► Would it be useful if you could [benefit]?
- ► If I could show you a way to [benefit], would you be interested?
- ► Would you like to see/experience [benefit]?
- ► Would [benefit] help you [meet need]?

Specific examples in selling sport assets include:

- ► Would it be useful to you if I could recommend a way for your family to have a night of entertainment for less than $75?
- ► Why is it important for you to find a way for members of your community association to spend time together?
- ► Would childcare at our gym help you find time to work out more?
- ► Why is it important for you to play golf at least twice a week?
- ► Would you like to find a way to get employees excited about spending time together outside of normal work hours?
- ► If I could show you a way that your top salespeople could entertain key prospects in a unique and exclusive environment, would you be interested?
- ► Would a uniquely themed integrated marketing approach help you reach key customers in this area?
- ► Would a tennis racket that produces a reliable hit help you be more consistent?
- ► Would you like to find an activity that everyone in the family can enjoy?
- ► If I can show you a way that we can help you improve client retention by at least 10%, would it make sense for us to schedule a time to discuss this further?

As can be seen from these questions, the value of asking need-payoff questions is that the customer is telling the seller about the benefits, instead of the seller telling the customer about the benefits. Once the customer confirms the benefit they are seeking, they will be more receptive when the seller positions the product as a way to receive that benefit.

Finally, it is important to note that product information (packages, prices, seat locations, etc.) is not emphasized in the SPIN approach. This allows the seller to develop the prospect's need first without revealing exactly what is being sold. If the seller was to enter into the conversation with *I want to talk to you about season tickets today,* then the possibility of a negative response increases because the prospect does not yet perceive there is a need for the product.[6]

## PUTTING IT ALL TOGETHER

### MINOR LEAGUE BASEBALL NEEDS ANALYSIS SCRIPTED OUTLINE

**Opening and Building Rapport**

1. Hello, may I please speak with _____? Hi _____, this is _____ with the [insert team]. [Pause]

2. [Insert name], the reason for my call is to learn about your experience at [insert stadium] last season and take a look at some of our ticket options for the upcoming season. How does that sound?

3. [Insert name], the best place to start our conversation is by asking, of all the [insert team] games you've attended, what is your best/favorite memory?

   ▶ *I/My statement* (baseball/sports memory)—Favorite memory, when was the first moment you loved baseball?

4. Name, when you come out to games, who is it that you come with?

**Needs Analysis**
*Situation Questions*

1. Team passion

   ▶ How big of an [insert team] fan are you?
   ▶ How long have you been an [insert team] fan?
   ▶ When was it that you fell in love with the game of baseball?

2. Attendance Patterns

   ▶ If I gave you the keys to the stadium and you could pick any seat, where would I find you sitting?
   ▶ How many games do you typically attend each year?
   ▶ How many games did you make it out to last season?
   ▶ Where do you like to sit when you come out to the ballpark?
   ▶ Which types of [insert team] games do you like the best?

---

6. Futrell, C. (2006). *Fundamentals of selling*, 9th ed. New York: McGraw-Hill/Irwin. p. 323.

3. Sphere of Influence

   ▶ Who do you typically come to games with?
   ▶ Where do you work?
   ▶ Who is the biggest baseball fan you know?
   ▶ What other groups are you involved with?
   ▶ What charitable organizations are you involved with?

4. Motives

   ▶ What brings you out to the ballpark?
   ▶ What is your favorite thing about coming to a game?
   ▶ What is your best memory of [insert team] games?
   ▶ How was your experience at the ballpark last season?
   ▶ Share with me what makes one [insert team] game better than another game.

5. Leisure Time

   ▶ Besides coming to an [insert team] game, what else do you like to do in your free time?
   ▶ How often are you able to get out and spend time with _____?
   ▶ Walk me through how your family decides how to spend your free time.

6. Budget

   ▶ In a perfect world, how much could you spend?
   ▶ In a perfect world, how many games would you like to attend this year?
   ▶ On a scale of 1–10, how likely are you to buy?

**Problem Questions—Based on responses to situation questions. Look for needs, problem, and dominant buying motives**

   ▶ To what extent is _____ important to you?
   ▶ Share with me the one thing that makes it difficult for your family/group to _____.
   ▶ What is the number one thing you want to get out of bringing your family/group to a game?
   ▶ You just said that you want to _____. What exactly does ____ mean to you?
   ▶ When you say ____, what do you mean?
   ▶ I understand what you mean when you say _____. What does that mean for your group/family?

**Implication Questions—Follow up on the answer to the problem question above**

   ▶ How does _____ affect you?
   ▶ What impact does _____ have on _____?
   ▶ What would happen if _____?

**Need-Payoff Questions**

   ▶ Would it be useful if you could [insert benefit]?
   ▶ If I could show you how the [insert team] could [insert benefit], would you be interested?
   ▶ Would [insert benefit] help you to reach [need/goal]?

## QUESTIONS MANAGE THE FLOW OF THE CONVERSATION

Asking questions puts the seller in control of the conversation. The questions the seller chooses to ask can help control the pace, depth, and topic of conversation. Asking questions can help the seller move forward with the agenda without the prospect feeling dictated to. While it is true the seller wants customers to feel comfortable enough to ask questions throughout the sales process, the seller doesn't want the customer to take control of the sales process. The seller can use questions to manage the flow of the conversation by:

- ► Getting more information
- ► Confirming the customer's understanding
- ► Uncovering the ideal scenario
- ► Redirecting the conversation
- ► Soliciting accurate feedback
- ► Softening suggestions
- ► Gaining commitment

### Figure 7.1

**Manage the Flow of the Conversation**

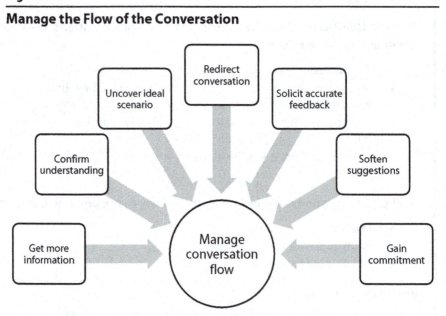

## *Ask Questions to Get More Information*

**Global questions** ask the customer to expand on a statement they just made in a way that invites them to *please continue.*[7] Global questions help probe further into what a customer is thinking by prompting with an easy-to-ask question. They essentially serve as an opening for the customer to expand on a statement he or she just made in the conversation. Global questions help build rapport because they indicate the seller is interested in what they are saying, and they serve as a balance to asking too many overly sophisticated questions.

**GLOBAL QUESTION**
ask the customer to expand on a statement they just made in a way that invites them to please continue

Examples of global questions include:

- ► Will you tell me more?
- ► How so?
- ► Like what?
- ► How does that work?
- ► What happened next?
- ► What else?

Finally, global questions can put the seller in control of the conversation by finding out why a customer is asking a question. By answering a customer's question with a question, the seller can more accurately determine why the customer really wants to know the answer to the question, which allows the seller to respond in the most appropriate manner.

## Example 1:

**Prospect**: How much are tickets?
**Salesperson**: Which tickets are you interested in?

## Example 2:

**Prospect**: What advantages would we get with buying a suite with you compared to another team?
**Salesperson**: How familiar are you with our suites?

By answering a question with a question, you are able to find out what the prospect already knows and why they want to know it, instead of launching into a long explanation of product features and benefits that may or may not be relevant to the prospect.

---

7. Freese, T. (2013). *Secrets of question based selling.* Naperville, IL: Sourcebooks.

## Ask Questions to Uncover the Ideal Scenario

**HYPOTHETICAL QUESTION**
asked out of interest when the answer has no real effect on the situation

**Hypothetical questions** are asked out of interest when the answer has no real effect on the situation. Hypothetical questions can help the seller see what the customer really thinks about the product if objections didn't exist in the customer's mind. For example,

- ▶ Taking your busy schedule out of the equation, how many games would you like to attend each year?
- ▶ In a perfect world, how much could you spend?
- ▶ If someone set tickets in your lap right now, how would you use them?
- ▶ If money wasn't an issue, where would you want to sit?
- ▶ All prices aside, if we gave you the keys to the stadium, where would you sit?

## Ask Questions to Confirm Your Understanding

**CONFIRMATION QUESTION**
used to confirm the seller's understanding of something the customer has just stated

**Confirmation questions** are used to confirm the seller's understanding of something the customer has just stated. Confirmation questions are usually asked within the context of paraphrasing something the customer has just said. The purpose of the question is to show that the seller is listening to the prospect, to build credibility and rapport, and to make sure the seller is following the prospect's line of thinking. Confirmation questions typically end with the question, *Is that correct?* after a paraphrased statement. For example,

- ▶ If I'm understanding you correctly, it sounds like your work schedule prevents you from coming to games on the weekend. Is that correct?
- ▶ What I'm hearing you say is that your company really believes in the quality of life for your employees. Am I hearing this correctly?
- ▶ Let me see, Bob, if I understand you correctly . . .
- ▶ It sounds like you are planning to make the decision this week. Is that correct?

## Ask Questions to Redirect the Conversation

**REDIRECT QUESTION**
channel the customer's thinking back to the agenda and the purpose of the conversation or meeting

**Redirect questions** are used to change the direction of the conversation and bring up a new subject when the discussion gets offtrack or when a line of questioning proves to be of little value. Redirect questions channel the customer's thinking back to the agenda and the purpose of the conversation or meeting. For example,

- ▶ **Earlier you mentioned that** your parents take your kids to a few games a year. Could you tell me more about why they like to attend?
- ▶ **Let's go back to something you said earlier** about your boss. Could you tell me more about her past experiences with suites?

Redirect questions can also be used to bring up a new subject and point the conversation toward the direction of closing the sale. This is not a closing question, but can serve as a bridge or segue to closing. For example,

- ▶ **With that in mind**, how can we begin to strategize a way to improve your brand loyalty with millennials in this demographic market area?
- ▶ **Based on what you just said** about your family's passion for tennis, do you think it would make sense to come out and look at the facilities we have on-site?

## Ask Questions to Solicit Accurate Feedback

The seller must have accurate information from the prospect throughout the sales cycle to effectively close a sale. It is imperative that the seller knows when things are not going well or when there is a problem on the horizon. Without accurate information, the seller won't be able to identify problems or issues when they arise. To obtain the accurate information that is needed, neutralize the disposition of the questions by offering the prospect a choice to respond either positively or negatively.[8]

Instead of asking, *Mr. Jones, does it still look like we'll have a deal by the end of this week*, a question with a neutral disposition sounds like this: *Mr. Jones, does it look like we'll have a deal by the end of this week, or do you think it might get delayed?* The neutralized question gives the customer the chance to agree that the deal is on track, or reveal that something might cause it to get delayed. By adding this phrase, the seller invites the customer to share good news and bad news, both of which work together to give the seller an accurate picture of the status of the sale. If the seller finds out that the sale might get delayed, he or she now has the accurate information needed to most appropriately approach the situation. The customer now has an open invitation to be truthful and share what is really going on behind the purchase decision. Questions can be neutralized by adding the phrase "or no" to the end of any question. For example, *Do you think we will have the support of the budgetary affairs committee, or no?*

---

8. Ibid.

## Ask Questions to Soften Suggestions

Part of controlling the conversation is realizing that the seller can't tell a prospect what to do. The seller can't tell the prospect to have a phone conversation, meet at the arena for a tour, meet in person for a meeting, and the seller certainly can't tell the prospect to buy tickets. While the seller can't tell prospects what to do, he or she can ask them to make a decision that moves the sales process forward. For example, the seller can't tell a prospect to meet him or her at the arena for an in-person tour, but he or she can ask them if it would make sense to follow up the conversation with a visit to the arena. These types of questions soften the suggestion and allow the seller to be more assertive without making prospects feel pressured.[9] The seller is controlling the sales process by making a relevant suggestion, but the customer can still make the final decision whether they want to move forward in the process.

**HUMBLE DISCLAIMER** injects humility into an assertion that precedes a statement or question with the purpose of getting prospects to openly share their opinions and lower their defenses

A second way to soften a suggestion is to use a **humble disclaimer**, which injects humility into an assertion that precedes a statement or question with the purpose of getting prospects to openly share their opinions and lower their defenses.[10] Examples of humble disclaimers include:

- ▶ I don't want to ask too many questions, but I would like to understand _____ a bit more.
- ▶ Do you mind if I ask you a couple of specific questions about _____?
- ▶ I'm not sure the best way to ask, but would you mind if . . .
- ▶ Without being too forward, can I ask you about _____?
- ▶ I don't want to ask the wrong thing, but could we revisit what you said about _____?
- ▶ I was hoping I could . . .
- ▶ I was wondering if I could . . .
- ▶ Do you think I might be able to . . .

> If you are respectful of someone else's right to not share with you, it's amazing how much information you can get. Humility is a very attractive human quality, and one that people are naturally drawn toward. Thus, you can significantly enhance the value of the responses you receive by strategically preceding your most sensitive questions with a humbling disclaimer. Simply put, causing people to 'want to' share more information with you gives you a strategic advantage over other sellers who are just out there probing for needs.[11]

---

9. Ibid., p. 196.

10. Ibid.

11. QBC Research Inc. *Try using humbling disclaimers.* Retrieved from http://qbsresearch.com/1671/use-humbling-disclaimers/

## *Ask Questions to Gain Commitment*

Obtaining commitment is not a one-time event that occurs when the seller closes the sale at the end of the sales cycle. It is important to secure commitments from the prospect throughout the sales process because it puts the prospect in the role of decision-maker, builds rapport with the prospect because it gives him or her a say in where the conversation is headed, foreshadows the positive response to be received when the seller asks for the sale, and advances the sales process to the next logical step.

**Commitment questions** are used to test agreement and pace the discussion toward a decision. A variety of terms are used for commitment questions in the industry, including *chasers*, *trial closes*, and *tie-downs*. They are typically short phrases that are added to a statement, or short stand-alone questions. These short phrases can be added to statements to turn them into questions that get the customer saying yes long before going in for the close.

**COMMITMENT QUESTION**
used to test agreement and pace the discussion toward a decision

Common commitment questions include:

- ► How does that sound?
- ► Do you agree with that?
- ► Would you agree?
- ► Does that answer your question?
- ► Will that work for you?
- ► Does that make sense?
- ► Does this help?
- ► How do you feel now?
- ► Is that correct?
- ► Are you following me?
- ► Do you see what I mean?
- ► Right?
- ► [statement], isn't it?
- ► [statement], doesn't it?
- ► [statement], shouldn't it?
- ► [statement], aren't they?

Commitment questions can be used in a variety of ways, including overcoming objections, setting a meeting agenda, summarizing what the seller heard, and closing the sale. Notice how the commitment questions below all move the conversation forward to a new issue or step in the sales cycle.

- ► If I understand you correctly, you want to have your tickets at least three weeks before the game so you can distribute them to friends. Is that correct?

▶ It's really tough in today's marketing climate to cut through all of the advertising clutter, isn't it?

▶ I think we're ready to set a meeting with your boss, wouldn't you agree?

▶ Your tickets can be e-mailed directly to one of your friends, family, or coworkers. Does that answer your question about giving tickets to other people?

▶ The reason for my call is to learn about your experience at the ballpark last season and follow up with you on the e-mail/letter that we sent you last week about opportunities for this upcoming season. How does that sound?

## Table 7.5

**Summary of Types of Sales Questions**

| Question | Definition | Example |
|---|---|---|
| Expansion | Seek to acquire the same information as the open-ended questions but in a way that elicits more detailed information from the prospect | Share with me . . . |
| Comparison | Use words like *compare, contrast, differ, whether,* and *versus* to yield more detailed information than the traditional open-ended question | Describe for me what you like about attending games versus what you do not like. |
| Situation | Gather facts and background information about the prospect's existing situation | Who do you go to the games with? |
| Problem | Bring a customer's implied needs, problems, and motives to the surface | Issue-based, clarification, and lock-on |
| Issue-based | Get prospects talking gaps between their present state and an ideal state | To what extent is _____ important? |
| Clarification | Gather specific insight into a general word, phrase, or statement made by a prospect so as to eliminate confusion over its meaning | What exactly does ___ mean to you? |
| Lock-on | Get the customer to elaborate on a feeling or emotion that you believe is important to confirming the needs s/he might have | Can you give me an example of the problems you've been experiencing? |
| Implication | Help the customer think about the potential consequences or impact of the problem and understand the urgency of satisfying the need o r resolving the problem | How does [insert problem or need] affect your [family, business, organization]? |
| Need-payoff | Focuses the customer's attention on the benefit derived from solving the problem or satisfying a need | How would that help you? |
| Global | Ask the customer to expand on a statement they just made in a way that invites them to *please continue* | How so? |

| Question | Definition | Example |
|---|---|---|
| **Hypothetical** | Used to see what the customer really thinks about the product if objections didn't exist in the customer's mind | Taking your busy schedule out of the equation, how many games would you like to attend each year? |
| **Confirmation** | Used to confirm your understanding of something the customer has just told you | Let me see if I understand you correctly |
| **Re-direct** | Used to change the direction of the conversation and bring up a new subject when the discussion gets offtrack or when a line of questioning proves to be of little value | Earlier you mentioned that _____. Could you tell me more about that? |
| **Accurate feedback** | Neutralize the disposition of your questions by offering the prospect a choice to respond either positively or negatively | Do you think we will meet by the end of this week, or no? |
| **Humble disclaimer** | Injects humility into an assertion that precedes a statement or question with the purpose of getting prospects to openly share their opinions and lower their defenses | I'm not sure the best way to ask, but would you mind if . . . |
| **Commitment** | Used to test agreement and pace the discussion toward a decision | How does that sound? |

## APPLYING THE SPIN QUESTIONING TECHNIQUE IN CONVERSATION

With an understanding of the different types of questions that the seller can ask during a sales conversation, let's turn our attention to how these questions can be used to help the customer build value. There are a few general principles that the seller should follow to effectively leverage the various question types identified in the previous section.

**Keys to Conversation**

1. Probe from general to specific

2. Don't interrupt

3. Form next question based on response

4. Be conversational

5. Focus on quality questions

6. Be prepared for questions

7. Keep an open mind

1.  Probe from general to specific

2.  Don't interrupt

3.  Form the next question based on the customer's response

4.  Be conversational and don't interrogate

5.  Focus on quality, not quantity of questions

6.  Be prepared for common questions

7.  Keep an open mind

## Probe From General to Specific

The flow of the seller's questions in the needs analysis should move from general to specific, or broad to narrow. Begin with broad questions and progress to more specific questions that follow up on a particular point made by the customer. Open-ended questions allow the seller to probe at a general level, and close-ended or directive questions obtain specific facts in a follow-up question. Asking questions in this manner helps the seller maintain a logical flow to the conversation and use close-ended questions at the right time to prevent the conversation from being stifled. For example,

> **Salesperson:** How was your experience at the game last season? [general]
> **Customer:** It was a beautiful day and our group had a great time. We were able to get some really good seats down by the dugout. Our VP said those were the best seats we've ever had for our group. Our only complaint was the parking situation.

> **Salesperson:** What problem did you have with parking? [specific]
> **Customer:** The Blue Parking lot was full and we had some older folks in our group that had a hard time walking all the way from the Red Lot.

## Don't Interrupt

Allow the customer to give a complete response and finish their thoughts. Cutting off a customer prevents the seller from gathering all of the information needed to complete the needs analysis, but even more importantly it can destroy the seller's credibility and any rapport that had been developed previously in the conversation.

## Form the Next Question Based on the Customer's Response

The seller needs to listen to the customer's answers to form the next question. Failing to follow a customer's response with a question that maintains the logical flow of the conversation can frustrate the customer because it sends the message the seller does not care about the customer's answer. While needs analysis is a critically important element of a consultative sales philosophy, an inability to build on the buyer's previous responses when formulating the seller's next questions can be debilitating to the salesperson.

> One of the common mistakes young salespeople make is not asking enough questions. They will often have a small list of questions to ask. Once they get a client that allows them to ask all of them, the sales executive feels lost and will start "spewing" product information at them because they have nowhere else to take the conversation. With experience and practice, sales executive's questions will develop a flow and will change depending on the client's answers.
>
> —Jeff Berryhill, *Major League Soccer*

Finally, Jeff Berryhill recommends that salespeople always "keep their antennae up" because the seller never knows what direction the call might go. For example, the seller might be making a call to a single game buyer in an attempt to sell a season ticket package, but finds out through good questioning that the customer is the CEO of a major corporation. This is why it is important to not prejudge the prospect's situation and keep an open mind for where the call might go.

## Be Conversational and Don't Interrogate

Sales managers often urge salespeople to use their "bartending skills" when conducting a needs analysis to ensure that the conversation remains social and does not turn into an interrogation. Sellers face three potential challenges when conducting a needs analysis. First, customers can feel interrogated if questions are too confrontational. Questions that can become confrontational are those that start with "WHY." Sellers who ask too many "why" questions can come across like an interrogator in a police investigation, leaving the prospect feeling attacked. This technique fails to generate rapport and trust. Second, sellers are at risk of failing to develop a connection or relationship with the prospect because they are focused on asking too many questions without having any conversation. Too many narrow, fact-finding questions can become monotonous and boring to the prospect. This is why it is important for the seller to continue the rapport building process by making use of I/My statements that reveal personal information about the seller. Third, in a corporate sales setting, asking too many situation questions could make it appear that the seller is unprepared for the meeting since many of these answers could have been determined by doing research prior to the meeting. It is also advisable to save "high trust" questions until later in the conversation. For example, early in the needs assessment, sellers often avoid asking about how much money a business makes off a typical client or how much money a business has allocated for marketing efforts. Personal or financial subjects can be sensitive areas for many prospects. They may not be ready to open up regarding those topics until greater rapport has been established.

## *Focus on Quality, Not Quantity of Questions*

While there are certainly a minimal number of questions that the seller needs to ask in order to obtain the basic information about a prospect's situation, the focus should be on the quality of the questions and not the quantity of questions. Every question asked should add value in the conversation by uncovering additional information, or clarifying something that's already been said.

## *Be Prepared for Common Questions*

Sellers need to know the most common things they are going to hear from customers and be prepared to respond. While these questions and answers will vary depending on the product being sold, knowing the typical responses that will emerge from the customer during the needs analysis can help prepare the seller to respond. For example, a common question is "how will I use all of those tickets?" One technique to prepare for this question is to consider all of the different ways the customer might use the product. Most teams have a "100 ways to use tickets" list that can be used for this purpose.

---

### 100 WAYS TO USE TICKETS—TULSA DRILLERS

1. Donate a group of unused tickets to a local kids' organization (all unused tickets good for general admission tickets to most Sunday–Wednesday games).
2. Invite a customer who hasn't ordered/done business with you recently.
3. Thank volunteers for all they do!
4. Improve communications with key coworkers.
5. Help part-time workers feel more like part of the organization.
6. Reward suppliers and vendors who help you meet your deadline.
7. Take a loyal customer for his or her birthday.
8. Run a sales contest and reward the winner with tickets.
9. Boost your own career potential by networking.
10. Give tickets to your newspaper delivery guy with the accurate arm.
11. Offer them to someone who has given you helpful business advice.
12. Hold a drawing at work to surprise your employees.
13. Thank a neighbor who takes care of your pets, gets your mail, etc.
14. Give them to your child's teacher as a thank you.
15. Take your mother/father to rekindle that inner child your therapist has been talking about.
16. Enhance relationships with those in a position to recommend you or refer new business.
17. Take a potential customer and close a sale at ONEOK Field.
18. Offer them to your friends on Facebook.

---

19. Take one of your smaller accounts and try to enhance their business with you.
20. Reward a customer who gives you a referral.
21. Give to an employee who comes up with a cost savings suggestion.
22. Tweet that you're giving away your tickets to a fireworks show and see who responds.
23. Reward teams who have accident-free job sites.
24. Use as an attendance incentive at meetings.
25. Win back a customer for their business.
26. Thank a customer who praised your business.
27. Take someone who does business with a competitor.
28. Thank a vendor for delivering in a crunch.
29. Give tickets to your local fire department.
30. Give tickets to charity and use it as a tax write-off.
31. Say "thanks" to a retiring officer or employee.
32. Welcome a new employee to the company with tickets.
33. Offer your tickets to your accountant/lawyer who has done a great job.
34. Give tickets to your computer technician to boost productivity.
35. Give tickets to the bereaved at a funeral, because a 98 mph fastball can cheer anyone up.
36. Give tickets to your mail carrier who always brings your *Sports Illustrated* on time.
37. Give them to a manager whose department exceeds its goals.
38. Give tickets to the hairstylist who stopped you from growing a mullet.
39. Give them to a front-line person who appeased an angry customer.
40. Give them to an employee who's having a rough time to put a smile on their face.
41. Give to a business person, or persons whom you owe a favor.
42. Show your appreciation to a company intern.
43. Offer your tickets to a service person from another company who has "taken care of you."
44. Send your co-workers/subordinates to a game together, with a meeting over dinner.
45. Give to an employee who doesn't get commission to boost morale.
46. Give tickets to a representative on your local school board or union for goodwill.
47. Give tickets to the Youth Minister at your church.
48. Offer your tickets to someone who always gives you great service.
49. Reward an employee for making the most appointments out of the office.
50. Offer tickets to a customer for the holiday (Memorial Day, Father's Day, etc.)
51. Give tickets to your office cleaning crew as a thank you.
52. Use tickets as raffle gifts.
53. Give to potential vendors to enhance your business relationships.
54. Give to an employee who generates the most amount of new business.
55. Give tickets to your payroll department.
56. Give to an employee who has worked the most overtime.
57. Reward a department that hits their quota for the week or the month.
58. Give tickets to the Little League coach so he can bring his team to ONEOK Field.
59. Give tickets to the auto mechanic who hasn't attended a game in years.
60. Give tickets to your trainer for helping you fulfill that New Year's resolution.
61. Give tickets to a team you might sponsor.

62. Give to members of a club you might be in (Lions Club, Kiwanis, etc.)
63. Use as an auction item for your favorite charity.
64. Give tickets to an employee on his or her birthday.
65. Use tickets for trade opportunities.
66. Give to an employee or customer who has been sick as a "get well soon. "
67. Appease an angry customer with some tickets to a Drillers game.
68. Give them to your drivers for being on time.
69. Give them to your security guards.
70. Donate tickets to your church's youth group.
71. Give to restaurants that you frequent with clients or customers.
72. Offer to your secretary, or his or her family.
73. Give to a prospective employee who might be coming to town and looking for something to do.
74. Congratulate an employee who exceeded his or her duties.
75. Congratulate an employee for hitting their yearly goal.
76. Offer tickets to your babysitter as a thank you.
77. Give to a customer who makes timely payments or pays in full.
78. Give to an employee who is the most punctual.
79. Give tickets to your dry cleaner, landscaper, dentist, doctor, etc.
80. Give tickets to your brother/sister.
81. Use them as an excuse to meet a coworker whose name you can't remember.
82. Give tickets to an employee who makes the most sales calls in one day.
83. Give tickets to an employee who renews the most accounts.
84. Reward for service recognition by a customer.
85. Use tickets for a Christmas stocking stuffer.
86. Give tickets to your recreation league teammates (basketball, softball, etc. )
87. Give tickets to the dry cleaning attendant you don't speak to every morning.
88. Get to know your family again.
89. Give tickets to your daughter's boyfriend to keep him away from her house.
90. Surprise a stranger in your office building with a gift.
91. Take a date to the ballpark.
92. Give tickets as a thank you to the public service employees who worked tirelessly to restore your power after the ice storm.
93. Give tickets as a thank you to the city workers who are doing their best to remove the debris.
94. Give tickets to the homeless so they might enjoy a game.
95. Take your daughter because it's better than going to the ballet.
96. Take your wife; it's cheaper than buying a diamond.
97. Enjoy a fireworks show, even when it's not July 4th.
98. Include tickets in a thank you card.
99. Give tickets to the girl your son has a crush on so she'll spend some time with him!
100. Use them yourself.

---

Source: http://www.milb.com/content/page.jsp?sid=t260&ymd=20101011&content_id=15575122&vkey=tickets. Reprinted by permission of Tulsa Drillers.

## *Keep an Open Mind*

While it is important to be prepared for the most common answers you will receive from customers, it is equally important to keep an open mind heading into each sales conversation.

> One of the biggest challenges new sales executives have conducting needs analysis is freeing their minds of preconceived notions. They have to realize that each client is unique. On top of that, many clients will have needs and preferences that will go directly against what you would prefer. You must take the opinions of past clients and yourself out of the equation. Start each call with an open mind and only present a product by information gained by doing a thorough needs analysis.
>
> —Jeff Berryhill, *Major League Soccer*

## EFFECTIVE QUESTIONING EXAMPLES

The conversations below illustrate the utilization of the question types identified above in a variety of different sport sales settings. The conversations are designed to illustrate the SPIN selling technique.

### EFFECTIVE QUESTIONING EXAMPLE

**Inside Sales—Minor League Baseball**

{Enter conversation after opening}

Salesperson: How old are your kids? [Situation]

Prospect: We have 6- and 9-year-old boys and a 12-year-old girl.

Salesperson: What activities does your family do together? [Situation]

Prospect: We do a lot of different things together. The main thing we do each week is do dinner and a movie on the weekend. We also really like heading downtown to the museum, zoo, and park.

Salesperson: Wow that sounds like your family is really active. [confirmation]

Prospect: Well, we have to do a lot of different things because it's so difficult to find something that everyone in the family can enjoy at the same time.

Salesperson: I notice you said it was difficult. What makes it difficult? [Problem]

Prospect: It's amazing how different a 12-year-old girl is from a 6-year-old boy! They have almost nothing in common! No matter what we're doing as a family at least one of them is unhappy.

Salesperson: How does that affect your family? [Implication]

Prospect: It just takes the fun away from doing things together when the kids are complaining and whining.

Salesperson: Would finding an activity that everyone in the family would enjoy help you? [Need-payoff]

Prospect: That would be great, but we haven't found it yet!

Analysis: Through the effective use of questions, the salesperson helped the prospect uncover the need of *finding an activity that everyone in the family can enjoy*. Each question helped the prospect build value in his or her mind regarding how attending minor league baseball games can help fill this need.

**Inside Sales—Professional Hockey**

[enter conversation after opening]

Salesperson: You mentioned that you have kids. How old are they? [Situation]

Prospect: I have four kids under the age of 12. It gets pretty crazy around here.

Salesperson: I can only imagine. I grew up with three siblings as well. I know things can get pretty hectic. My parents never wanted to take us anywhere because it was such a pain to get around. [I/My statement]. So, what does your family do for entertainment? [Situation]

Prospect: We try to take one Saturday a month and do something together, but it just gets so expensive to do something that we really only do it once a month.

Salesperson: Are there times when you need to find entertainment for your family at a more affordable price? [Problem]

Prospect: Yeah, we'd love to do more things but our budget definitely gets in the way.

Salesperson: How much does this problem affect your family? [Implication]

Prospect: If we could be spending less than $200 every time we want to head out, we would definitely take the kids out more.

Salesperson: If I could help you find a way to entertain the whole family for less than $50, would you be interested? [Need-payoff]

Prospect: Definitely.

Analysis: Through the effective use of questions, the salesperson helped the prospect uncover the need of *finding affordable family-friendly entertainment*. Each question helped the prospect build value in his or her mind regarding how attending a professional hockey game can help fill this need.

**Corporate Sales—Group Tickets for Non-Profit Organization**

[enter conversation after opening]

Salesperson: How many volunteers do you have in your organization? [Situation]

Prospect: We have around 25 fairly regular volunteers, plus another 75 or so that volunteer once a year.

Salesperson: To what extent are good volunteers important to your organization? [Problem]

Prospect: They are everything. We couldn't operate without them.

Salesperson: How do you typically reward your volunteers? [Situation]

Prospect: We haven't done a really good job of that in the past. We've been talking about this issue with our Board because several of them believe that we could get some of those once-a-year volunteers to be regular volunteers if we could find more ways to engage them. But, all of that costs money that we need to be spending on the services we deliver.

Salesperson: I noticed you said you haven't done a good job with rewarding volunteers. Can you explain that? [Problem]

Prospect: We just get so busy with everything that needs to be done on a daily basis that we sometimes can forget to say thanks to our volunteers. It doesn't really fit in anybody's job description, so nobody ends up doing it.

Salesperson: I completely understand that. I work with a lot of other non-profit organizations and they have told me the same thing. [Empathy, social proof]

Prospect: Yeah, everybody has to work hard to keep their best volunteers.

Salesperson: Share with me some of the biggest challenges that you are facing right now in keeping your volunteers. [Problem]

Prospect: Volunteers are one of our most challenging issues. There are just so many things that take people's time and attention. We have about a 30% no-show rate at our events.

Salesperson: How does that affect your organization? [Implication]

Prospect: It creates a ton of stress on our site leaders. Plus, our service delivery can be hampered if we aren't staffed at an appropriate level for some events.

Salesperson: Would you be interested in a cost-effective volunteer reward program that doesn't create very much work for you? [Need-payoff]

Analysis: Through the effective use of questions, the salesperson helped the group leader uncover the need of *rewarding their top volunteers through a cost-effective, turnkey entertainment experience*. Each question helped the prospect build value in his or her mind regarding how attending an NBA game can help fill this need.

**Corporate Sales—Premium Suite**

[enter conversation after an initial meeting and opening]

Salesperson: What are your goals for the next year? [Situation]

Prospect: Our sales focus for the next year is definitely increasing sales to put us on solid financial footing for the future.

Salesperson: To what extent is generating new business important? [Problem]

Prospect: We are in growth mode right now, so it's everything to us.

Salesperson: What is the ballpark value of your biggest prospect? [Situation]

Prospect: Oh, probably $500,000.

Salesperson: If you don't mind me asking, how much revenue does your best salesperson generate? [Humble disclaimer, Situation]

Prospect: Easily over $1 million each year.

Salesperson: What would it mean to lose that salesperson? [Implication]

Prospect: That would be terrible. Our top guy has been with us from day one. We would lose a lot of knowledge and productivity.

Salesperson: If he stays with you and I could give him 41 attempts to close your top prospect, do you think they would be able to do it? [Need-payoff]

Prospect: Oh yeah, Jim is the man. He would close more than one!

Analysis: Through effective use of questions, the salesperson helped the decision-maker uncover the need of *closing new business and retaining top sales talent*. Each question helped the decision-maker build value in his or her mind regarding how a premium suite could help solve this problem.

**Fitness—Gym Membership**

[enter conversation after introductions]

Salesperson: How often do you currently exercise? [Situation]

Prospect: I usually work out three days each week for an hour.

Salesperson: Are you currently a member at another gym? [Situation]

Prospect: Yeah, I've had a membership at Purple Gym for the past two years.

Salesperson: What are the kinds of problems you have experienced over at Purple Gym? [Problem]

Prospect: I've enjoyed my time there, but I have a busy schedule and the times that I can go work out are peak times.

Salesperson: What is it like over there at peak times? [Problem]

Prospect: It just gets really busy and they limit you to 20 minutes on the cardio machines. I get really frustrated that it takes me longer to work out because of those time limits.

Salesperson: How do those time limits affect you? [Implication]

Prospect: It's just not an effective use of my limited free time. If I'm taking time out of my schedule to work out, I need to get the most out of it.

Salesperson: So it sounds like you're saying you need to find a club with more machines, less wait time, and no time restrictions. Does that sound right? [Need-payoff]

Analysis: Through effective use of questioning, the salesperson helped the prospect solve the problem of *waiting in line to use equipment*. Each question helped the prospect build value in his or her mind regarding how a membership at this gym could help solve this problem.

**Golf—Series of Golf Lessons**

Salesperson: What do you typically shoot? [Situation]

Prospect: I shoot in the mid-90s.

Salesperson: How often do you get to play?

Prospect: I play once a week in a men's club choose-up with other golfers about as good as me.

Salesperson: What results are you expecting to achieve as a result of taking four golf lessons? [Problem]

Prospect: I really want to beat the other guys I usually play with in the men's club. I just haven't been able to play well enough this year to win any of the choose-ups.

Salesperson: I understand what you mean. It used to drive me crazy to have my buddies beat me on those choose-up tournaments. [Empathy, I/My Statement]. When you say you want to win, what score do you think you need to shoot? [Problem]

Prospect: For the flight that I play in, you usually need to break 90 to win.

Salesperson: What is keeping you from breaking 90? [Problem]

Prospect: I've been really inconsistent off the tee this year. I've tried to tweak my swing on my own, but I think I need some professional help at this point.

Salesperson: What do you think this problem is costing you? [Implication]

Prospect: It's costing me several penalty strokes each round. I just can't keep the ball in play.

Salesperson: It sounds like you could benefit from a few drills you can run through before your choose-ups that will keep the ball in play to put you in a position to beat your buddies. Does that sound right? [Need-payoff]

Prospect: You got it.

Analysis: Through effective use of questioning, the golf pro helped the golfer uncover the need of *hitting the ball straighter, which stems from the motivation to win the weekly men's choose-up*. Each question helped the golfer build value in his mind regarding how a series of golf lessons could help solve this problem.

---

**INEFFECTIVE QUESTIONING EXAMPLE**

*Inside Sales—Single-Game Buyer*

[enter conversation after opening]

Salesperson: Did you attend a game last year? [Situation; Close-ended]

Prospect: Yes

Salesperson: Did you have a good time? [Situation; Close-ended]

Prospect: Yes

Salesperson: Where did you sit? [Situation]

Prospect: In the upper deck.

Salesperson: Are you interested in buying a mini-ticket plan for this year? [Close-ended; ineffective need-payoff question]

Prospect: Nope, not this year.

Analysis: The salesperson asked too many close-ended questions that resulted in one-word answer or short responses from the prospect. The conversation lacked a logical flow and clear direction. The salesperson did not build value with the questions that were asked and never uncovered a need or the motivation behind why this prospect attended games. Finally, the salesperson jumped too quickly into the need-payoff question by attempting to close the sale with a close-ended question, which abruptly ends any future conversation with this prospect.

---

## CHAPTER SUMMARY

Conducting a needs analysis is at the heart of consultative sales. Without a quality needs analysis, there is no way for the seller to know anything about a customer that could lead to an appropriate product recommendation. Asking effective questions builds value in the mind of the customer and moves them from wanting to purchase to realizing they have to purchase. It sets the stage for the tailored product recommendation that the seller will make to the customer. However, asking questions does not come without risks. Following the guidelines set forth in this chapter will help the seller avoid loss of rapport and trust with the customer as a result of poorly conceived and executed questions.

## INDUSTRY ADVICE

**Bill Guertin,** *The 800-Pound Gorilla*

### DON'T "SELL" TOO SOON: GETTING TO YES THROUGH GREAT QUESTIONS

In the movie, *The Wolf of Wall Street*, the main character, Jordan Belfort, is speaking to a group of salespeople in New Zealand in the final scene of the film. He takes a silver pen from his pocket and hands it to one of his sales reps.

"Sell me this pen," he commands.

The rep starts to describe the pen, detailing the features of the barrel, to which Jordan removes it from his hand and puts it in the hand of the person to his right. "Sell me this pen," he commands the second gentleman. He begins to describe the prestige of the design, and after only a few seconds, Jordan takes it from the second person.

He hands it to a third person in the front row. "Sell me this pen," after which the scene fades out and the film ends.

If the film were to go on for just a few moments more, here's what Jordan would have told the large crowd:

> "I'm afraid that you all have failed to sell me this pen. You started talking about its amazing features, its sleek design, but no one thought to ask anything about ME! What do I do for a living? How will I be using the pen? What attributes of a pen are important to me? How are you going to sell me unless you know something about why I even WANT or NEED a pen?"

It's a valuable lesson for anyone in sales, but especially important in sport sales. All too often, salespeople jump to talking about their team's success, the ticket prices, or the fancy benefits attached to their season tickets, without first understanding what someone wants or needs from a relationship with the team. They prescribe a product before diagnosing—and prescription without diagnosis in sales is malpractice.

Here are some guidelines for asking the right questions in sport sales:

- *Have a great list of open-ended questions memorized.* You don't have to ask them in order, but by committing some of the vital questions to memory, it frees you up to listen closely to their answers vs. concentrating on the next question you're going to ask. Some of the solid questions I include in my live training sessions are:

  — *Other than a win or loss, what's the most important thing to you when you come to a game?*
  — *How does your spouse feel about coming to games with you?*
  — *How often do you and your family take the time to get out to do something together? What are some of your favorite things that you like to do?*

- — *What's the #1 goal or initiative your company (or group) is focused on this year? What's being done to make that goal happen? How's it working out so far?*
- — *How has your customer base changed in the past 12 months? What do you think is causing that change, and how are you responding to that?*

▶ *Be curious about everyone and everything.* Gatekeepers, spouses, even the children of the person to whom you're selling can give you valuable information that can help you to determine what ticket plan would suit them best:

- — *What does _____ enjoy doing when he's not at work?*

- — *What kinds of company outings have you done in the past? How have they worked out?*

- — *Is she usually the one who makes the call on these things, or is there someone else that I should include?*

- — *If I was to schedule a 15-minute conversation with him, when do you think would be the best time to do that?*

▶ *Listen closely to your prospect's answers, and build on their answers with related comments and questions.* Many rookie reps don't fully pay attention to what their prospect is saying because they're so worried about what their next question is going to be. Good conversations are based on dialogue, not one-way question-fests. Ask something, listen, and respond to what they say with thoughts and add-ons of your own. It proves you're listening, and also shows courtesy.

▶ *Use "I/My" Statements to build rapport.* If someone should answer a question in a way that you can relate to, bring up your own experience as a part of your response:

- — *"We aren't here during the winter months; we have a home in Naples." "Oh, Naples is a beautiful area! My family has good friends that live there, and I've been there several times. The downtown area is gorgeous!"*

- — *"I'm originally from Grand Rapids, Michigan." "Grand Rapids! My college roommate is from there; do you happen to know the Peters family? I believe they own the Honda dealership there."*

▶ *Be listening for "gaps" that your team's product can help close.* For example, if a prospect says they have no time to go the games because they work too much, and they also enjoy spending time with their kids, the "gap" in their lives may be that they don't get to spend the kind of time they would like with their children. Purchasing a ticket plan in advance would be a benefit to their lives, because it would mean that they would prioritize the games and purposely carve out family time.

When you make things more about THEM (your customers) and less about YOU (the team, the price, the locations, etc.), everyone wins. Be more interested *in* others than interesting *to* others, and not only will you sell more "pens," you'll be helping them to get exactly what it is they want and need.

## CHAPTER ACTIVITIES

1. Explain why the needs analysis is a fundamental component to the consultative sales process.

2. Explain how asking questions puts the salesperson in control of the conversation even though the customer is doing most of the talking.

3. Turn the question "How many games did you attend last season?" into an expansion and comparison question.

4. Create a customer conversation in a consumer sales environment using the SPIN questioning method. Begin the conversation after the opening, and ask at least three situation questions, two problem questions, one implication question, and one need-payoff question.

5. Assume you are selling season ticket plans for a minor league baseball team in your market. Partner with another classmate and record your needs analysis. Write a brief summary answering the following questions:

    a. What did you do well?

    b. What do you need to improve on?

    c. What was the hardest part about doing a needs analysis?

    d. What surprised you about watching the footage of your call?

## CHAPTER COMPETENCY ASSESSMENT[12]

## COMPETENCY DOMAIN: NEEDS ANALYSIS

*Exemplary:* Consistently does all or almost all of the following:

- ▶ Utilizes diverse mix of open-ended questions to engage customer in meaningful conversation
- ▶ Asks open-ended questions that uncover relevant facts, needs, and motives of customer
- ▶ Integrates chasers or tie-down questions to move conversation forward and test agreement
- ▶ Actively listens to the customer and thinks on their feet to develop next question to maintain flow of conversation
- ▶ Talks 10–20% of the call; customer does the majority of talking
- ▶ Obtains appropriate information to qualify the customer through questions
- ▶ Makes seamless transition into discussing product

12. From "Competency Assessment for Entry-Level Sport Ticket Sales Professionals" by David Pierce and Richard Irwin, *Journal of Applied Sport Management*, Volume 8 (2), Summer 2016. Reprinted by permission of Sagamore Publishing. www.sagamorepub.com

*Skilled:* Does most of the following:

- Utilizes diverse mix of open-ended questions to engage customer in meaningful conversation
- Asks open-ended questions that uncover relevant facts, needs, and motives of customer
- Integrates chasers or tie-down questions to move conversation forward and test agreement
- Actively listens to the customer and thinks on their feet to develop next question to maintain flow of conversation
- Talks 20–30% of the call; customer does the majority of talking
- Obtains appropriate information to qualify the customer through questions
- Makes seamless transition into discussing product

*Adequate:* Does most of the following:

- Asks questions that are only sometimes open-ended and don't aid in qualifying the customer
- Asks too many close-ended questions, particularly at the beginning of the call
- Fails to identify critical information about the customer or leaves key questions unasked that could uncover the most important facts, needs, and motives about customer
- Engages in decent dialogue, but has difficult time transitioning into presenting product
- Transitions abruptly from asking questions to discussing product
- Recognizes that asking questions is important, but does not actively listen to develop the next most appropriate question, or always asks the same set of questions to each customer
- Talks 30–50% of the call

*Novice:* Consistently does all or almost all of the following:

- Emphasizes product information without understanding which product offering is appropriate for the customer with whom they are speaking
- Fails to recognize the fundamental importance of asking questions to understand the needs and motives of the customer
- Asks primarily close-ended questions
- Does not have a logical flow to conversation
- Talks in over 50% of the conversation
- Spends more time telling than selling

# CHAPTER 8

## PRESENTING SOLUTIONS

### LEARNING OBJECTIVES

After completing this chapter, you should be able to:

- ▶ Identify and describe each step of the SPET process.
- ▶ Apply the SPET process to making the appropriate product recommendation.
- ▶ Develop relevant selling points and describe them to the customer.
- ▶ Paint a picture for the prospect using storytelling principles.
- ▶ Describe the key principles in making a product recommendation.
- ▶ Contrast different types of sales presentations.
- ▶ Discuss the key characteristics of effective face-to-face sales presentations.
- ▶ Differentiate between types of approaches to opening a face-to-face sales presentation.

### KEY TERMS

| | | |
|---|---|---|
| Canned presentation | Halo effect | Sales event |
| Consistency | Impression management | Site tour |
| Eduselling | Sales collateral | Small talk |
| Formula presentation | | |

### COMPENTENCIES

- ▶ Ability to adapt each presentation (sales pitch) to the needs of each customer.
- ▶ Ability to use information learned in the needs analysis to tailor an appropriate recommendation to the customer.
- ▶ Ability to solve problems for customers.

## CHAPTER OVERVIEW

One of the most challenging parts of the sales process for young sales professionals is making the transition from asking questions in the needs analysis to making the appropriate product recommendation. Taking all of the information acquired in the needs analysis and leveraging it in a way that drives value in the customer's mind and emotion can be challenging.

Consultative selling provides solutions that solve the customer's problems and meet their needs. An expert salesperson stands as the critical link between what the organization offers and the needs of the customer. It is in this phase of the sales process that the seller presents a solution to the customer's needs, nurtures the perceived value of the experience as a unique solution, and confirms their interest in obtaining the benefits offered.[1]

The seller's goal is to get customers to realize they can satisfy their needs by purchasing the recommended product or experience. Through asking questions using the SPIN selling technique, the seller helps the prospects see problems, feel their impact, suffer their consequences, and experience the urgency of fulfilling the need by getting them to openly express their motives and concerns. Eventually the seller will uncover the prospect's needs or problems and then be in a position to determine which products or services will meet their needs. If the seller is able to get the prospect to open up and speak freely, he or she can be more assertive and persistent in presenting solutions and ultimately asking for the sale.

At the heart of making a tailored recommendation is synthesizing the information gleaned in the needs analysis and explaining to the customer why the recommendation is the right fit. This is done by connecting the benefits of the product to the needs, motives, and problems of the customer. By presenting benefits that are reinforced with information acquired in the needs analysis, the seller can ensure that the feature or benefit is perceived as such by the customer.

## MAKING THE RECOMMENDATION—THE TRIAL CLOSE

Just because a prospect has the ability to buy and has a need does not necessarily mean that he or she feels an obligation to buy. As a result, it is important at this stage of the sales process to articulate how a customer's needs will be met as a result of purchasing the product and how the product features translate into benefits for the customer. By this point in the sales process the seller

1.  Ingram, T., LaForge, R., Avila, R., Schwepker, C., & Williams, M. (2006). *Professional selling: A trust-based approach,* 3rd ed. Mason, OH: Thomson Southwestern.

## Figure 8.1

**Making the Tailored Recommendation**

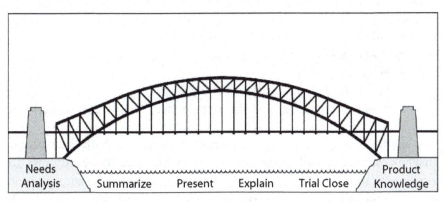

has already addressed key selling points and confirmed several benefits with the customer.

Now it's time to make a product recommendation. This should be one of the first times during the conversation that the salesperson integrates product knowledge into the conversation. Up to this point, the focus has been on building value through asking questions that identify needs, motives, and problems. If the seller has received positive confirmation from the customer on the need-payoff questions, then the seller has earned the right to confidently make a recommendation. It's time to cash in on those need-payoff questions that were asked during the needs analysis.

The simple four-step process (SPET) for making the recommendation is as follows:

1. **Summarize** the need, motive, or problem
2. **Present** the solution
3. **Explain** why
4. **Trial close**

## *Summarize*

The first step is to summarize the need, motive, or problem that has been developed during the needs analysis. The seller should refer back to the positive response received from the needs payoff questions generated through the SPIN questioning system and the customer's response to the trial close question when key selling points were addressed. The needs and benefits that were confirmed through this process form the foundation of the summary statement that begins the product recommendation. Introduce the need through the use of phrases like:

- ▶ Based on what you've told me . . .
- ▶ It sounds like you're saying . . .
- ▶ What I'm hearing you say . . .
- ▶ We've also had many other fans say . . .
- ▶ Based off the fact that . . . this is the perfect time for this conversation

The summary phrase allows the salesperson to confirm with the customer that he or she successfully pinpointed the need that exists. If the customer disagrees with the statement or question, the seller needs to ask more questions and continue in the needs analysis phase until the need has been successfully identified.

**CONSISTENCY** focuses on the desire to be and to appear consistent with what you have already said or done

The salesperson may also choose to add a commitment question to the end of these statements to leverage the principle of **consistency**, which suggests that people will respond in ways that justify an earlier decision or statement.[2] Once a person makes a commitment, they align their self-image with the commitment and adjust their image according to the way other people perceive them. By getting customers to speak to their values, priorities, and goals, effective sellers are able to leverage the principle of consistency when offering appropriate packages and services that align with their statements. Securing a commitment in words or actions from someone sets the stage to leverage this principle.

For example, Mitch Ried, Senior Director of New Business Development for the Cleveland Cavaliers, teaches sellers to "create a pattern of yes" throughout the conversation. When the seller learns that a customer attends games to spend time with his or her family, later in the conversation the seller can confirm this with a statement like *So it sounds like family time is really important to you.* Assuming the customer says "yes," the customer has made a commitment about his or her values and priorities. Later in the conversation when it's time to pitch the right package, the seller can leverage the commitment the customer has already made about the importance of family time.

> Creating a pattern of yes is very important because I want to reaffirm that we are listening to what the prospective client is telling us, and I want them getting into a pattern of YES thinking in a positive mindset so hopefully when the seller makes a strong recommendation the customer will say YES.
>
> —Mitch Ried, *Cleveland Cavaliers*

---

2. Cialdini, R. (1993). *Influence: The psychology of persuasion*, 2nd ed. New York: William Morrow.

Other examples:

- ▶ Based on what you've told me, it sounds like your group really needs to find a game on the weekends during the summer. Is that right?
- ▶ What I'm hearing you say is that you're looking for five or six different games to attend with your entire family. Do I have that right?
- ▶ It sounds to me like your company could really benefit from a unique environment to help close your biggest clients. Does that sound right?

## Present

Confidently present the appropriate product recommendation with phrases like:

- ▶ I would recommend . . .
- ▶ What could work for you . . .
- ▶ You should really consider . . .
- ▶ We can get you into this package . . .
- ▶ What I would love to do for you is . . .
- ▶ I have two options that will work for you . . .
- ▶ I've got a perfect plan for you . . .

For example:

- ▶ I would recommend the 10-game mini-plan.
- ▶ You should really consider the birthday package for your kids.
- ▶ I think we can get you into the half-season package.
- ▶ What I would love to be able to do for you is get you set up in the skybox suite for your boss's retirement party.

## Explain

The third step is to justify why the product is a good fit for the customer based on the features and benefits of the product. At this point the seller links his or her knowledge of the product to solutions that meet the customer's needs by delivering a strong statement about the product. This is the statement that makes the product relevant for the customer. A thorough understanding of the features, advantages, and benefits of the product will be useful in making this statement. Use conjunctions like *because*, *so*, and, *for* to introduce the statement.

For example:

- ▶ **because** these seats will be great for those close games in the fourth quarter . . .
- ▶ **so** we can create a really unique entertainment experience for your employees . . .
- ▶ **because** this package gives you a flexible and cost-effective way to get into a season ticket package . . .
- ▶ **because** our gold-level sponsorship platform gives you the most bang for your buck if you're trying to reach new customers in this market . . .

## Trial Close

Finally, finish your statement with a commitment question like:

- ▶ What do you think?
- ▶ How does that sound to you?
- ▶ Will that work for you?
- ▶ Would you agree?
- ▶ Does that make sense?

The seller might also choose to pause for a moment and allow the prospect to think about what has been said. Silence can be an effective tool in addition to a trial close. According to Melanie Seiser, Manager at the Major League Soccer National Sales Center, "Silence is powerful. Salespeople need to be comfortable in silence. He who speaks first will lose."

The customer will respond to the trial close with an objection or agreement. The customer's response at this point will dictate whether the salesperson needs to respond to an objection (Chapter 9), ask more questions (Chapter 7), or close the sale (Chapter 10).

## All Together

Table 8.1 helps visualize the four steps of the recommendation and how they fit together to form a strong, cohesive product recommendation in a variety of sport sales settings.

## Table 8.1

**The 4 Steps of the Product Recommendation Process in Various Sport Sales Settings**

| Setting | Summarize | Present | Explain | Trial Close |
|---|---|---|---|---|
| Season Ticket | Based on what you've told me, your group of friends is looking for cost-effective weekend entertainment. | I would recommend the Weekend Mini-Plan. | Because it gives you 12 weekend games for the price of 10 and your friends will be able to get together on the weekend. | How does that sound to you? |
| Group Package | What I'm hearing you say is that your group is looking for a way to get to know each other better. | What I would love to do for you is get you into one of our group packages. | We can give you a unique environment to socialize before, during, and after the game. | Does that make sense? |
| Premium Suite | We've had several other small businesses like yours express the need to reward top employees. | You should really consider what ABC company did last year with the half-season package. | Because it achieved all of their human resources objectives and kept costs reasonable. | In fact, I think they are looking for a sharing partner for this year. What do you think? |
| Sponsorship | What I'm hearing you say is that you really want to create a positive image of your company in our community. Is that right? | In that case, I think you would benefit from sponsoring select community relations initiatives. | Because it will attach your name to key philanthropic efforts we are doing in the community. | Would you agree? |
| Gym Membership | Based on what you've told me, you're looking for the expert help of a personal trainer. | I would recommend our Ultimate membership. | Because it will give you access to a personal trainer that will develop customized goals for you. | How does that sound? |
| Sports Equipment | After looking at the size of your foot and the type of surfaces you run on. | I think your best bet would be the Trail Runner shoe. | Because it will give you the most protection from roots and rocks. | Does that make sense? |
| Technology | Your situation is a lot like ABC Event in Cleveland. They were having a difficult time managing volunteers like you. | We were able to service them with our new Volunteer Manager software. | That saved them time by doing all of the volunteer management in a software system instead of papers and Excel files. | Do you think this would also work for you? |

## KEY PRINCIPLES

There are eight key principles to follow when using the four-step process to make an effective product recommendation:

1. Present benefits when they can be reinforced with information learned in the needs analysis.

2. Explain the value proposition.

3. Don't be afraid to tell a customer when a product is not in their best interest.

4. Start the presentation of realistic offers with the most expensive, then work down.

5. See the big picture.

6. Use social proof to bolster recommendation.

7. Be confident in product and expertise.

8. Educate the customer on the product.

### PRINCIPLE #1: PRESENT BENEFITS WHEN THEY CAN BE REINFORCED WITH INFORMATION LEARNED IN THE NEEDS ANALYSIS.

Sellers should make the product recommendation after a successful needs payoff question. Novice salespeople simply wait to hear one or two key facts and then make the pitch without knowing that the recommendation will have value for the customer. For example, the salesperson will hear within the first few questions that the customer came to five games last year, and then immediately jump into recommending a six-game mini-plan. But finding out that the customer attended five games is a fact, not a need. The salesperson still does not know what motivates the customer to attend and what needs are fulfilled through coming to games. In this case, the salesperson has collected factual information (who, what, when, where), but is missing the *why*, which is what provides value in the solution. This is why Jeff Berryhill suggests holding off on making a product recommendation as long as possible during the sales call. The goal is to have the customer uncover as much value as possible in the product before making a recommendation. Throughout the call, the seller can allude to the fact that they have options that are good for the customer, which gets the customer thinking, *what is she thinking for me?*

If the seller can't refer back to the needs that were uncovered during the needs analysis phase, then the process of asking questions is just an exercise in the art of conversation, and holds no bearing on the product being sold.

## PRINCIPLE #2: EXPLAIN THE VALUE PROPOSITION.

Uncovering customer needs and developing a customized recommendation is at the heart of the value proposition. It is the salesperson's job to explain why a product is the right fit for the customer. However, it's not enough to simply help the customer uncover the need, but the salesperson needs to take the next step of explaining why the product is a right fit for the customer (step 3 above). It is important to note that the process of explaining why the product is a good fit may require more than the one sentence that is provided in Table 8.1. Depending on what is being sold, the seller may need to spend several minutes focused on the explanation of product fit. The salesperson takes the features and benefits of the product and translates those into what matters for the customer. It is also important to consider word choice because the explanation of fit is a great opportunity to paint a picture or tell a story. Successful execution at this step helps create a powerful value proposition for the customer. Table 8.2 explains how motives can be translated into benefits that tell a story that the prospect can visualize.

## Table 8.2

**Translating Motives Into Benefits**

| Motive | Benefit |
|--------|---------|
| Escape from stress at work | Getting out to a hockey game will be a stress-reliever for you and get you out of the office. |
| Interest in sport, Interest in team | These lower-level tickets will put you right in the middle of the action. You'll be able to hear the quarterback call out the signals. |
| Supporting a cause | You can play a key role in pushing soccer forward in this community. We are fortunate to have supporters like you. |
| Nostalgia | You'll be able to create so many great memories with your son just like you had with your dad. |
| Social Interaction | You will be able to bond with your family and create unique lasting memories. |
| Style of Play | With our new coach, you'll get to see a hard-nosed defensive style that takes no prisoners. Just like back in the 90s when we were going to the championship game. |

Selling sports is about selling an idea, an experience, a memory. It's not about selling a tangible product that we can showcase or demonstrate. To do this effectively, sport sales reps have to sell with their words by painting a positive picture in our prospects' minds of how our services can be of value to them. A couple simple ways to form this vision is to use phrases like, "How cool would it be?", "Picture this," or "Imagine." For example:

▶ How cool would it be for your customers to sit on the team bench during halftime of a game?

▶ Picture this, an entire section in the arena filled with your employees and their families smiling, laughing, and having a great time.

▶ How cool would it be for your church group to high-five the players as they make their way out of the locker room?

▶ Imagine a suite filled with your top prospects networking with your best customers.

—Carl Manteau, *Milwaukee Bucks*

## PRINCIPLE #3: DON'T BE AFRAID TO TELL A CUSTOMER WHEN A PRODUCT IS NOT IN THEIR BEST INTEREST.

Sometimes it becomes apparent that a particular product or package is not the best fit for the customer. Perhaps the customer revealed new information after the initial recommendation, or the seller lacked the right information to make a recommendation. Regardless of the preceding circumstances, don't shy away from telling a customer that a particular product is not in their best interest. Instead, use it as a bridge to making the next suggestion. For example, *It sounds like this product might not really be the best fit for you, but in thinking about it more I think X package will be.*

This principle can be one of the hardest things for a new sales rep to do, but it is necessary if you truly want to show your customers the best value, the best experience and, hopefully, get them to come back again. For example, a customer may express interest in season tickets in a premium location, however, you know (based on a thorough needs analysis), that they would need to spend their entire marketing and entertainment budget to get the seats. When you factor in ancillary items like parking, food, and beverages, you are pretty confident that it would put a real strain on their business. No sales rep wants to give up a big sale, however, you shouldn't squeeze a customer for all they have just because you can. That customer will probably have a negative experience and not renew the following season. If you show the customer you were listening, however, and recommend a package that would be a better fit for their needs and their budget, then they will respect you more, be far more likely to get the full value out of their tickets, and be a better candidate to renew their seats and remain a loyal customer year after year.

Conversely, a rep should not be afraid to present an upgrade option if it will be the best fit. For example, a Sales Manager may tell you she is considering a half season ticket plan for her reps to entertain clients. Based on the number of sales reps she manages and the number of customers each one has, you know that a half season package wouldn't provide enough games/opportunities to entertain at their desired volume. Given this, you should make the strong recommendation for the full season plan.

—Carl Manteau, *Milwaukee Bucks*

## PRINCIPLE #4: START THE PRESENTATION OF REALISTIC OFFERS WITH THE MOST EXPENSIVE, THEN WORK DOWN.

Sellers can use the rule of reciprocity and the contrast principle to their advantage by starting the presentation of realistic offers with the most expensive, then retreating to smaller or cheaper packages. The rule of reciprocity suggests people generally try to repay what others have provided them, and the contrast principle states that when someone experiences two similar things in succession, their perception of the second is influenced by the first.[3] This sense of obligation makes people more likely to comply with the wishes of another person if they feel they owe them. Research has indicated the more personalized and unexpected the gift, the more effective the giver is in receiving.

One consequence of the rule of reciprocity is an obligation to make a concession when someone else has made a concession first. Cialdini calls this "rejection-then-retreat." Effective persuaders offer a concession in order to secure a concession, or agreement, from others. The rejection-then-retreat technique is effective because it leverages the contrast principle. This principle offers a compelling justification for starting the recommendation as high as reasonably possible, then retreating to a lower offer if the customer rejects the initial offer. Sellers should start their presentation of solutions with the most expensive realistic package. If the top offer is rejected, smaller offers will seem more suitable for the customer. However, this does not mean the seller should recommend an unacceptably large package with the intent of manipulating the customer into a smaller package, nor does this mean the seller always starts with the most expensive package, but it does mean that he or she should recommend the most expensive package that could potentially fit the customer.

---

3. Ibid.

Sellers should avoid offering the cheapest package available out of fear of asking people to spend more money, or because it is the package the salesperson feels most comfortable purchasing. A common mistake by young salespeople, who tend to be either in college or recent college graduates, is to forget that people have money and are willing to spend money. Because many young sellers are working hard to pay off student loan debt and have entry-level salaries, they are conditioned to purchase the least expensive product offerings in a variety of settings. They apply this same logic to the customers and corporations they sell to, but forget that decision-makers in businesses are spending someone else's money and that some consumers are not bound by price restrictions when considering what to buy.

When I was a first-year sales rep I booked an appointment with a small company (less than 10 employees) that expressed some interest in purchasing a suite. Being such a small company, I assumed that a suite would be out of their budget, that they wouldn't be able to get the full use out of it, and that I'd be lucky to sell them season tickets. I invited them to the arena for a needs analysis and asked my VP of Sales to sit in the appointment (because I had zero experience pitching suites). My VP did a great job of asking open-ended questions, learning about their business and exploring ways for them to get value out of a suite.

At the end of that meeting, he pitched them on doing a multi-year suite contract at an average investment over $180,000 each year. I was floored when he asked for that much—I couldn't fathom anyone being able to make such a large investment, let alone a company of that size. I honestly thought my VP had blown the sale, however, the prospect took about 10 seconds to think about it and said, "Ok, let's do it. How much do I need to put down today?" Without skipping a beat, my VP said, "Given the time of year, we will prorate the first season to $93,000. Do you just want to pay that in full right now and be done with it?" Again, I was shocked at how straightforward my VP was. He didn't mention our payment plan options, he just asked for the full amount. At that point in my career, I lacked the confidence to ask for $1,000 from an established client, let alone $93,000 from someone I had spent less than an hour with.

To my surprise, the prospect pulled out a checkbook and wrote a check for the full amount right there …the largest check I'd ever seen! I'm so appreciative that I was able to have this experience at such an early and formative stage in my sales career. It taught me to never make assumptions before talking with a prospect and that money is relative. If you make a proposition based on their wants and needs, then don't ever be afraid to ask for the investment that goes with it.

—Carl Manteau, *Milwaukee Bucks*

## PRINCIPLE #5: SEE THE BIG PICTURE.

Sales managers like to think of this principle as being able to "connect the dots." It's the ability to synthesize all of the information gleaned in the needs analysis and create a logical proposal to the customer. It requires the seller to put small bits of data together in a way that helps them see the bigger picture. Selling requires analytical abilities to think about what has been learned from the customer, identify the right offering, and then describe it in a way that helps the customer understand why it is the best fit. Any sales environment that includes a full menu of items to sell requires a salesperson to listen, think, synthesize, and create. It requires equal knowledge of the prospect's situation and knowledge of the product. Lack of knowledge in either area will prevent the seller from connecting the dots.

One strategy to help salespeople see the big picture is to avoid making assumptions about the prospect. For example, if the seller asks them how many games they went to last year, and the customer says they went to one game, don't assume they attend one game each year. There may have been unique circumstances that led them to only attend one game last year (e.g., health, family, change in schedule), when they actually averaged seven games per year in the five previous years. One way to avoid this error is to alter the wording of questions from *How many games did you attend last year"* to *"How many games would you ideally like to attend?* In other words, the bigger picture is that they would really like to attend seven games, but the smaller picture is that they only attended one game last year. According to Melanie Seiser, "The notion should always be that just because it's what they've done in the past doesn't mean it has to be what they do in the future. As true salespeople, we should take someone who usually does four games to eight games this year, and then season seats the following year."

## PRINCIPLE #6: USE SOCIAL PROOF TO BOLSTER RECOMMENDATION.

Recall from Chapter 4 that people use information about how others have behaved to help determine their own proper conduct. Social proof is a powerful tool at all stages of the sales process, and it can easily be woven into the recommendation to the customer. For example, sellers can use social proof to explain why certain seats are worth the extra money compared to other seats by describing the cheaper seats, and then telling the customer that most customers choose the better seats because they have a better view.

When you ask most group leaders where they would like to sit, they will often defer to the least expensive tickets. This makes sense because they are making a decision on behalf of many people and typically prefer to err on the side of caution to lessen the risk of outpricing some of the people in the group. This is where the experienced sales rep can step in and say, "I can appreciate that. Price sensitivity is important and I've heard that from a lot of my best group leaders. What they found is that most people are willing to pay a few extra dollars to have a better seat and a better experience. For a lot of people, this may be the only game they attend all season, as such, they want to make the most of their experience. This being the case, how would you feel about moving to (this) location?"

—Carl Manteau, *Milwaukee Bucks*

## PRINCIPLE #7: BE CONFIDENT IN PRODUCT AND EXPERTISE.

It is important for salespeople to be confident in the product they are selling and in their expertise as a sales consultant. Even though a decision-maker may be 40 years older than the seller, it is important for sellers to perceive themselves as the expert on the team and its ticket offerings. If a salesperson doesn't have a passionate conviction that the product he or she is recommending will truly help customers meet their needs, then it may be time to sell for a different organization or switch professions. It is important for salespeople to believe that their product or experience can deliver on the benefits that they are describing to the customer.

It's one thing to *act* confident, it's another to *be* confident. The best way to be confident is to thoroughly know your stuff. I can't over-emphasize the importance of studying. Study your products, your pricing, your players, your team's history, your venue, etc. You need to be an expert in all of it. If you need to pull out a chart to answer a customer's question about pricing then you've just lost some credibility. If a group leader wants to know the number of seats there are in each row and you say "I'm not sure, let me get back to you on that," then you've lost credibility. If a fan stops you on the concourse and asks where the nearest ATM is, you better know. The more knowledgeable you are, the more confident you will be. As a professional seller, you also need to study and continually refine your sales techniques. Read books, watch videos, role-play with coworkers, get in sales discussion groups. Do the things that will make you a better seller and you'll be able to walk into any situation with confidence. Learning never stops.

—Carl Manteau, *Milwaukee Bucks*

## PRINCIPLE #8: EDUCATE THE CUSTOMER ON THE PRODUCT.

**Eduselling** is the systematic and continuous dissemination of knowledge and assistance to the customer to enhance his or her knowledge about the product's benefits. While eduselling is typically applied to corporate sales with long sales cycles, eduselling can be applied in any setting to educate the customer on how to effectively utilize the product and activate all of the features and benefits that were purchased. Eduselling can occur during the sales presentation, but should also occur with customer support after the purchase. For example, if a customer is not educated on how to exchange tickets through an electronic ticket exchange system, he or she will not be able to activate this important benefit of their season ticket package.

**EDUSELLING**
the systematic and continuous dissemination of knowledge and assistance to the customer to enhance his or her knowledge about the product's benefits

## THE THREE BIG MISTAKES

Inexperienced salespeople make three common mistakes at this point in the sales process that create unreceptive customers and greatly diminish their chance at closing the sale. These are:

1. Presenting benefits that don't match the prospect's perception of their needs.

2. Presenting solutions with incomplete information.

3. Impatiently jumping into the recommendation assuming the customer sees the need.

### MISTAKE #1: PRESENTING BENEFITS THAT DON'T MATCH THE PROSPECT'S PERCEPTION OF THEIR NEEDS.

Salespeople present benefits that don't match the prospect's perception of needs either because (1) they attempt to sell the product instead of having customers sell themselves, or (2) because they fail to make logical connections between the needs analysis and the recommendation. First, salespeople who focus on the features and benefits of the product without regard to the unique characteristics of the customer have adopted a product-focused selling approach. As defined in Chapter 1, in product-focused selling, the salesperson exclusively focuses on the benefits, features, quality, and reputation of the product when trying to convince a customer to buy. It is primarily a one-way presentation with the salesperson talking the majority of the

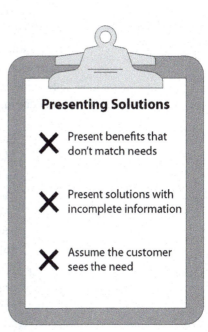

**Presenting Solutions**

✗ Present benefits that don't match needs

✗ Present solutions with incomplete information

✗ Assume the customer sees the need

conversation. Using a product-focused approach, the salesperson emphasizes what they believe to be the most powerful features when speaking with the customer. The fundamental problem with this approach is that a feature or benefit is not necessarily perceived as a benefit by the prospect unless it satisfies a definite need.

For example, Jeff Berryhill recalled one season when the Chicago Fire offered free parking as a product feature for full season ticket packages. Instead of following the proper line of questioning, the sales reps were leading the conversation with free parking as the biggest benefit of purchasing a full season ticket plan. This was an incredible deal in a city like Chicago where parking prices are extremely high and free parking is not found anywhere. However, this benefit was completely irrelevant to those who did not own a CAR. As a result, sellers were hurting their credibility with the customers because they were pitching benefits that did not meet the needs of the customers.

Product features are great assets and can help articulate benefits of buying a product, but they are meaningless until placed in the context of the customer's needs, motivations, and problems. Regardless of what is being sold, sellers should never place the emphasis of the conversation on reading benefits that are listed on a brochure. It is important to remember that if the prospect wanted the information on a brochure or website, they would seek that information on their own. Sellers can add the value of human interactions and relationship to the sale.

The second factor that leads to mismatching features and needs is the inability to make logical connections between information gleaned in the needs analysis and knowledge of the product. When selling in a full menu marketing environment for the first time, synthesizing all of the information learned in the needs analysis and then creating the right recommendation is challenging. Below are a few examples:

- ► Early in the conversation, the seller asked a customer, *Where do you like to sit?* and received the answer, *It doesn't really matter to me.* Later in the conversation, the seller must have forgotten about this information, because they proceeded to go on a long-winded explanation of the different views and prices in the various seating sections. This essentially ended the conversation because the customer was not engaged in the conversation.
- ► A seller was talking to an elderly couple who brought their grandchildren to two or three games a year, but the seller spent most of the conversation touting the benefits of a newly created seating section that

offered all-inclusive food, drink (alcohol), and entertainment options geared for millennials 21-and-over. The salesperson lost credibility with the prospect.

▶ A seller was speaking to a customer who did not own a smartphone about the benefits of mobile tickets and stadium Wi-Fi.

▶ A seller was talking to a youth pastor at a local church who wanted to find a social activity for the youth group. Instead of emphasizing the social atmosphere of a minor league baseball game and the Kids Zone area with games, the salesperson placed a heavy emphasis on how you can see tomorrow's major league players today in the minor leagues.

▶ A seller was talking to a customer who liked coming to games with his fiancée. The couple did not have any children, but the salesperson transitioned from needs analysis to product knowledge by talking about how kids can run the bases after the game on Sundays.

▶ A seller was talking to a customer who attended over 30 minor league baseball games the year before, taking at least one other person with them each time, and recommended a 10-game mini-ticket plan. Clearly, a half-season (35-game) plan would fit the customer better.

## MISTAKE #2: PRESENTING SOLUTIONS WITH INCOMPLETE INFORMATION.

As noted in Chapter 7, the SPIN questioning technique ends with the needs payoff question. Unfortunately, most young salespeople gather only factual information with situation questions and never uncover the real motive or need, which is what drives the value in the solution. Salespeople present solutions with incomplete information when they have failed to move beyond situation questions in the needs analysis. This leads to not understanding the customer's true need, which means the seller can only guess at what the relevant features and benefits might be. Ultimately, there are questions left unasked during the needs analysis that would have revealed information that could have led to a better product recommendation. Below are a few examples:

▶ A seller was talking to a customer who was the Executive Vice President of a large non-profit organization. Upon learning this in the needs analysis, the seller proceeded to ask questions only about the President's family and recommended a single-game ticket for the family on the Fourth of July. The seller failed to create a line of questioning about group outing possibilities.

▶ A seller was talking to a customer who had three kids who were very active in sports, which created busy schedules for the family. The seller accepted the rejection without asking any more questions, and missed the opportunity to learn more about all of the different teams for which the kids played. All of these teams were potential group sales opportunities that went untapped.

▶ A seller learned during a needs analysis that the customer was really excited about the upcoming summer because they were retiring at the end of July. The seller interpreted this to mean that the customer was still too busy to purchase season tickets and invited the prospect to attend a few single games. The seller missed the opportunity to ask the prospect what plans he had for a retirement party with his family, friends, and coworkers. This avenue was left unexplored and a potential group outing opportunity was missed.

## MISTAKE #3: IMPATIENTLY JUMPING INTO THE RECOMMENDATION ASSUMING THE CUSTOMER SEES THE NEED.

A bad habit to get into is asking the same four or five questions and then assuming the customer has uncovered a need. This is rarely the case. Put simply, asking questions does not in and of itself guarantee that the seller will know the customer's needs. Impatiently jumping into the recommendation by assuming the customer sees the need will create an unreceptive and resistant prospect. Here are some worst-case scenarios:

▶ In the absolute worst-case scenario in the classroom environment, students introduce themselves, tell the customer they are doing a sales project for class, then ask them if they want to buy tickets this year. This is neither telling nor selling. It's asking. The same thing could be accomplished through sending an e-mail or direct mail. Making a personal sales call added no value to the marketing process if this is the approach a salesperson takes.

▶ Sellers ask a few perfunctory questions like *How was your experience?* and then start telling the customer about the ticket packages available for the upcoming season. They conclude their spiel with poorly worded close-ended questions like *Are you interested in coming to some games this year?*, *Are you familiar with any of the ticket packages?*, or *Have you heard about our ticket packages?* These questions are conversation killers and devalue the value-building process that occurred during the needs analysis. Not only is the seller asking low-value questions, but he or she is also presenting solutions too early in the conversation.

# MAKING FACE-TO-FACE PRESENTATIONS

In a consumer sales or inside sales environment, sellers typically make the product recommendation over the phone. In a corporate sales environment, the telephone is typically utilized to set an appointment and sales presentations are made in-person. This section is devoted to situations where the salesperson is communicating the sales message in person.

## *Types of Face-to-Face Presentations*

There are three general types of sales presentations that range from limited customer interaction to full customer participation.

### CANNED

The **canned presentation** is a memorized presentation that exclusively focuses on the product. The needs analysis step does not exist in the canned presentation as the salesperson does almost all of the talking. While organizations can ensure consistent delivery and control over the sales message using a canned presentation approach, there are significant disadvantages because customer participation is limited and the salesperson cannot accurately match product information to customer needs. Canned presentations are utilized when the salesperson is speaking in front of a large group of people, such as a sales event (described below). Canned presentations are also used when there are limited product options from which customers can select, thus minimizing the need for a needs analysis that could reveal a customized solution.

**CANNED PRESENTATION** is memorized presentation that exclusively focuses on the product

© antoniodiaz/Shutterstock.com

## FORMULA

**FORMULA
PRESENTATION**
highly structured
presentations that
follow a prepared
outline that directs
the overall structure
of the presentation,
but includes time for
customer interaction and
needs analysis

**Formula presentations** are highly structured presentations that follow a prepared outline that directs the overall structure of the presentation, but includes time for customer interaction and needs analysis. Salespeople do approximately 70% of the talking in a formula presentation. Formula presentations are based on the acronym *AIDA*. The salesperson must get the customer's attention, create interest in the product, develop a strong desire for the product, and move the customer to action.[4] Formula presentations are best used when a relationship has already been established and the salesperson is already familiar with the needs and motives of the customer because the presentation is fairly inflexible and cannot handle complex customer interactions.

## NEED SATISFACTION

In contrast to the canned and formula presentations that put the emphasis of the presentation on the product, the need satisfaction presentation moves the focus to the customer. The salesperson does more listening than talking. This presentation style fits the best with a consultative sales philosophy and utilizes the needs analysis process to successfully determine the customer's needs.

## *Sales Settings Unique to Sport*

In addition to giving sales presentations over the phone, at the prospect's place of business, and neutral locations (e.g., restaurant, coffee shop), there are three sales settings unique to the sport industry that allow the seller to leverage the emotion and passion that people have for the sport industry: in-game, site tour, and sales event. According to Bob Hamer:

> For those of us selling sports and entertainment we have a true advantage. With all due respect to insurance salesmen, retail sellers, and financial services providers, in most cases they don't have the secret sauce that we do . . . The emotional connection to the team and product.[5]

---

4.  Johnston, M., & Marshall, G. (2013). *Salesforce management,* 11th ed. New York: Routledge.

5.  Hamer, B. *Selling sports at a sales event.* Retrieved from https://www.linkedin.com/pulse/selling-sports-sales-event-bob-hamer

## IN-GAME

The day of an event for the sport organization is an important sales opportunity. For example, the Indiana Pacers recently built a season ticket preview center at the entry of the main concourse to provide salespeople a chance to interact with fans in a quieter environment than the busy concourse. The space contains large flat-screen televisions and places for salespeople to have conversations with prospects.

Major League Soccer recommends their salespeople follow the following guidelines for maximizing sales opportunities on game day:

▶ Know where your customers are sitting and plan your route in advance.
▶ Get yourself mentally (positive attitude, energy) and physically (look and smell your best) prepared for the game. You are on stage!
▶ Have ample business cards and pocket schedules with you.
▶ Connect with all members of your group.
▶ Review your notes on your customers and groups so you are familiar with them when you meet.
▶ Takes notes on new information or updates immediately.
▶ Meet any guests that your customer brings to the game and get their business cards.
▶ Follow up with brief e-mails the day after the event.
▶ Have small gifts prepared for group leaders or key accounts.
▶ Prepare order forms and list of best available season tickets before the game.
▶ Be proactive—look for people who are lost or are in need of help.
▶ Don't travel in packs with other sales reps—spread out.

Fans will be experiencing all of the emotions of attending a sporting event and the service team will be delivering on everything that was promised. Salespeople spend time on game day balancing prospecting, fulfillment, and servicing.

Salespeople should also treat the servicing of the groups as a prospecting opportunity. Think of the potential that exists when a seller has 200 people attending as part of a group outing. If each of those people becomes the leader of a new group, the seller can significantly increase the pool of prospects. Because the salesperson has already worked with the group leader and (hopefully) has a strong reputation with the leader, he or she has a built-in reference when approaching the future group leaders. Developing relationships with these group members is a critical game day prospecting task.[6]

---

6. Kirby, T. *Are you maximizing your group sales efforts in-game?* Retrieved from http://sportstao.com/maximizing-group-sales-efforts-game/

Sellers can use the rule of reciprocity to their advantage by offering complimentary tickets to a key prospect. The rule of reciprocity suggests people generally try to repay what others have provided them (e.g., favors, gifts, invitations).[7] This sense of obligation makes people more likely to comply with the wishes of another person if they feel they owe them. Society has a general distaste for those who do not make an effort to give in return, so it is human nature to avoid being counted in this group. As discussed earlier in the chapter, research has indicated the more personalized and unexpected the gift, the more effective the giver is in receiving. Sellers who surprise prospects with complimentary tickets and access to other organizational assets (e.g., memorabilia, autographs, meeting players) hope to be repaid with a ticket purchase in the future.

## SITE TOUR

**SITE TOUR**
tour of the facility for the purpose of advancing the sale

The sales cycle can be extended by offering to bring prospects to the sports venue for a tour. Offering a **site tour** is useful when the seller has already had a positive conversation with a prospect. Offering to provide the prospect with an arena tour also helps the seller separate the serious buyers. The value in offering a facility tour is that the customer has the opportunity to see and experience the difference in seat locations, which creates an emotional connection to those locations. While technology on websites can create the seating environment virtually, there is no replacement for experiencing it in person. The key to successfully showing the prospect a seating location is to be quiet and let the customer talk. Paul Bee, Director of Ticket Sales for the Detroit Red Wings, teaches his salespeople to step back and let the customer have the entire view of the arena from the seat. This allows the customer to make the next move in the conversation and prevents the salesperson from ruining the moment.

In addition to providing the customer with an opportunity to experience and compare seat locations, site tours may also include behind-the-scenes areas like locker rooms, suites, and front offices that have an appeal to fans. These experiences can be used to close the deal by providing the prospect with a unique experience they can brag to their friends and family about. Site tours can occur on game days where salespeople invite prospects to the event as a guest, or on non-game days where the facility is empty and seat locations are easier to access. Site tours essentially serve as a product demonstration for the prospect.

---

7. Cialdini, R. (1993). *Influence: The psychology of persuasion*, 2nd ed. New York: William Morrow.

**Bryan Stine, Director of Group Sales, Indiana Pacers**

## GIVING SITE TOURS

We offer 100% All-Access Tours as a selling point. The tours are an added incentive to get a company to purchase season tickets. We create *Wow Moments* for their clientele to make the company look good. One of the perks for purchasing a season ticket package is a certain number of All-Access tours during certain games. Therefore, regardless of whomever is using their tickets on those games (key clients, prospects, or employees), our sales reps will take those people on a no-limits tour of Bankers Life Fieldhouse before or during the game (other than the Locker Rooms of course). The selling point is that they get a behind-the-scenes tour that not many other people get to experience in the NBA. We take them to the following areas:

- ▶ Practice Court—let them take some shots on the court
- ▶ Weight Room/Training Room if not in use
- ▶ Press Conference Room
- ▶ Player/Coaches Parking Area—get to see all the fancy cars
- ▶ Star Rooms where celebrities stay before/after concerts
- ▶ Media Room
- ▶ Media Truck—where all of the live TV broadcasts are televised
- ▶ Front Offices
- ▶ Meeting Spaces

The idea is to make them feel like VIPs and give them WOW moments. We feel that if we can help a company close some business by bringing their clients out and being "wowed," then they will continue to renew their season tickets with us because they can see the return on investment.

While on those tours, our reps become storytellers about the team, but more importantly the reps talk about ways other companies have used their tours to achieve various business objectives. This gets the client thinking about how their company could use them. We're not pushing anything too hard with these tours, but we do want to make sure that we show how our clients can drive value from their season ticket purchase. The key is creating good memories and good experiences.

We also give prospects tours of the building on non-game days with the purpose of selling a ticket package on the spot. The key is getting them out to the building so they can see the court from those seats. It's much more powerful that way. On these tours, the sales reps will push harder for the sale. The strategy we implement here is to wow them right from the start by starting with the best seats in the lower bowl and then working our way higher within the lower bowl. Once they start going up higher, they realize that their first option down lower and closer to the court was much better. To overcome stalls and delays, our sales reps can start offering to take them around the building on a tour if the prospect purchases. They can also throw in a pair of free tickets to an extra game if needed. Or they can bring a basketball and allow the prospect to shoot some hoops on the court if they purchase right there on the spot. Little things like that seem to go a long way if the prospect is teetering.

## ORGANIZED SALES EVENTS

**SALES EVENT**
uniquely themed events typically hosted at a sport venue that leverage organizational assets to create excitement and attract a large quantity of qualified prospects

**Sales events** are uniquely themed events that leverage organizational assets to create excitement and attract a large quantity of qualified prospects. In order to be effective, sales events need to leverage organizational assets to generate interest, deliver a strong sales message, and be executed flawlessly. Quality sales events have a compelling program that captures the interest and attention of the prospect. Events that are held at center court, in a suite, in the locker room, or have current or past star players and coaches generate excitement among fans. The inclusion of bands, mascots, television personalities, dance teams, and cheerleaders create the image of a special event that evokes strong emotional attachment. Take-home items like flags, bobbleheads, shirts, and collectible souvenirs allow the memory to stay with the customer long after they leave the event. In addition to the buzz generated by these organizational assets, it is also important that the event delivers a strong sales message. After listening to speeches from team presidents, coaches, players, and broadcasters, interest should be at its highest point. At this point, a brief canned sales pitch should be delivered that creates urgency and shows how the prospect can support the team. This speech is followed by an opportunity for the prospect to explore seating options, meet with sales reps, and make a purchase decision. There should be constant reminders that the prospect is expected to buy if they are interested at the time of the event. Finally, the events must be executed flawlessly. Long lines, running out of food, and insufficient staffing can kill the momentum of the event and leave a negative impression with the prospect.

---

**Deno Anagnost, Director of Sales, Tampa Bay Buccaneers**

### BLUEPRINT FOR EXECUTING SALES EVENTS

**Who:** We invited 150 of our top premium prospects interested in buying Stadium Club Season Passes or seats in our Legends Suite product. These potential customers were fairly far along in the sales process. Other departments involved were our:

- ▶ Events department in setting up and planning the event,
- ▶ Creative Services department for designing the e-mail invitation for the event, and our
- ▶ Database Marketing department to help us identify the best possible leads to target.

**What:** This was an exclusive cocktail party for prospects to meet one of our all-time greats and to get a behind the scenes look at our state of the art training facility. The idea is to offer an experience they can't buy and can't get anywhere else.

**When:** The Mike Alstott Cocktail Party was held Wednesday, March 13th, from 6 p.m.–8 p.m. Wednesday is the least scheduled night of the week for kids' sports, so we scheduled it for prospects to attend right after getting off work.

**Where:** The party was located in the main lobby of One Buccaneer Place, the training facility and headquarters of the Tampa Bay Buccaneers. The main issue is convenience, but also enough space for ease-of-movement to not feel crowded, but also not too big so guests could feel isolated. We also wanted to make it easy for our sales reps to get around to all the guests.

**Why:** The purpose for this event was to make it easier to get face-to-face with key decision-makers and show them the type of events they would be a part of in the future once becoming a Stadium Club or Legends Suite Member. Each event is designed to drive revenue, and create a one of a kind experience for our guests.

**How:** Invitations—Personalized attention by first inviting over the phone and then an e-mail invitation to the event so we could fill all of our available space for the event.

**Arrival:** Upon arrival guests were personally greeted and invited to enjoy appetizers, beer, wine, and soda.

**Entertainment:** An acoustic cover band helped transform our lobby into a high-end lounge.

**Opening:** Director of Sales Ben Milsom thanked the crowd for coming and provided a rundown of how the evening would go.

**The Main Event:** Mike Alstott took photos and signed autographs with our prospects.

**Selling:** During the event we had all hands on deck. Account Executives engaged their prospects further in a sales discussion which involved asking for, and receiving orders for seats face-to-face at the event.

**The Takeaway:** Each guest received a tour of our facility and left with a framed photo taken of them at the event and also received a Buccaneer flag.

**Results:** From this event we were able to close important sales in a great experiential setting. Guests were in the right frame of mind and our reps were able to listen and share the benefits of membership in the club.

———

Source: http://baylors3.com/a-blueprint-for-executing-sales-events/. Reprinted with permission from Deno Anagnost.

# CHARACTERISTICS OF EFFECTIVE SALES PRESENTATIONS

Much of the information below assumes that the seller has earned an appointment over the phone and is meeting a prospect in-person for the first time, but many of these principles apply in a variety of sales settings. The principles outlined below add to important concepts that we've already identified throughout the textbook. For example, it assumes that the seller will uncover needs, ask questions that drive value, and create a powerful value proposition for the prospect. The key principles are:

1. Make a good first impression.

2. Deliver an opening that grabs the prospect's attention.

3. Use storytelling to illustrate why people change.

4. Create and utilize powerful visuals.

## *Make a Good First Impression*

**IMPRESSION MANAGEMENT**
the process used by salespeople to manage the prospect's impression of them

It is often said that you only have one chance to make a good first impression. Successful salespeople become adept at **impression management**, which is the process used by salespeople to manage the prospect's impression of them. Based predominantly on appearance and attitude, first impressions are formed before the meeting, when greeting the customer, and at the beginning of a presentation.

Prior to the meeting, it is essential for the salesperson to be on time. The general rule is that the customer should never be left waiting on the salesperson. It is polite for the salesperson to call the gatekeeper or prospect from their phone if they are going to be late for a meeting for whatever reason. By not calling, the salesperson compounds a negative situation and potentially risks the opportunity to meet. Salespeople need to effectively utilize technology on mobile phones and electronic calendars to ensure arrival at least 10 minutes early, accounting for traffic, parking, and taking elevators.

Time management is an important skill for salespeople. Upon arrival, the seller should let the gatekeeper know that they have arrived for the meeting. It is acceptable to ask the gatekeeper when the meeting will start in case a late start at this meeting will cause the seller to be late to another meeting. If there is a significant delay, it may be time to schedule a new meeting time depending on the circumstances. Assuming the salesperson has arrived 10 to 15 minutes early for the meeting, he or she has time to be productive in advance of the meeting. This means not wasting time playing the trendiest game on the smartphone. This time should be used to review any last minutes notes for the presentation, check e-mail, update the presentation, research the company, or make small talk with the gatekeeper to learn more about the company or how to pronounce certain names of people that will be in the meeting. The prevalence of mobile devices makes it fairly easy to be time efficient with small windows of time. This time could also be used to freshen up and make sure appearance is professional as possible. Cell phones and other devices should be placed on silent or airplane mode so they don't interrupt the meeting with ringing or vibrating. Keep in mind that the gatekeeper is observing the salesperson's behavior. If the seller sends negative verbal or nonverbal cues, the word will get back to the decision-maker. Finally, there is a balance to be achieved with how early to arrive. Arriving too early sends the message that one's time is not valuable, but obviously cutting it too close risks being late for the meeting.

The prospect will be making judgments based on the salesperson's appearance. Keys for positive first impression based on appearance include:

- ► Wear business clothes that are suitable and fairly conservative
- ► Be neat in dress and grooming
- ► Refrain from smoking, chewing gum, or drinking when in your prospect's office (you are not a character in *Mad Men*!)
- ► Keep an erect posture to project confidence
- ► Leave all unnecessary materials outside the office
- ► Appear organized
- ► Smile
- ► Maintain eye contact

The greeting also includes a proper handshake and use of the prospect's name. The five tips shown below can help with remembering names. Then follow the prospect's lead on where to sit in the room.

---

**FIVE WAYS TO RECALL THE CUSTOMER'S NAME**

1. Use their name: "It's good to meet you, Mr. Manning"

2. Spell their name in your mind

3. Relate the name to something with which you are familiar, such as relate the name of Manning to Peyton Manning

4. Use the name in conversation

5. Repeat the name at the end of the conversation: "Take care, Mr. Manning"

**SMALL TALK**
conversation centered on current events, hobbies, mutual friends, shared backgrounds, and sports that is used to break the ice prior to the actual sales presentation

After the greeting, the seller needs to read the situation to determine whether small talk is appropriate. **Small talk** is conversation centered on current events, hobbies, mutual friends, shared backgrounds, and sports that is used to break the ice prior to the actual sales presentation. In general, when meeting a customer for the first time with a limited amount of time for the meeting, most sales trainers recommend not engaging in small talk but getting right down to business. For the first meeting, it is safer to avoid small talk unless there is an obvious point of connection between the seller and the prospect. Ultimately, the salesperson shouldn't waste three minutes of a 10-minute presentation engaged in small talk.

In other circumstances, once rapport has been established through several visits or when the customer is a repeat customer, it may be appropriate to engage in small talk to break the ice and help build rapport. Avoid controversial topics or hot-button issues like politics and religion. In addition to the level of familiarity with the prospect, also consider the prospect's personality style. For example, if the prospect is focused on getting straight to business, then avoid small talk and get to the presentation. However, if the prospect is more talkative and friendly, then small talk is a great way to engage the prospect. Salespeople can also choose to match and mirror intensity level and mood of the customer if needed.

**HALO EFFECT**
how and what one does in one thing changes a person's perception about other things the person does

The goal of first impressions is to be on the positive end of the **halo effect**, which states that how and what one does in one thing changes a person's perception about other things the person does. If the seller is perceived by the customer as competent and professional at the beginning of the presentation, he or she will be perceived the same way during the remainder of the meeting. Of course, the opposite is also true.

> **MAKING A GOOD FIRST IMPRESSION**
>
> ► Be confident
> ► Dress appropriately
> ► Make a personal connection
> ► Be on time
> ► Be prepared

### Select a Powerful Opening

The goal in the first 60 seconds of the meeting is to break the prospect's preoccupation with whatever they were doing before the salesperson arrived. Sellers often catch the prospect in the midst of a busy day, and the prospect's mind will be on anything and everything besides a sales presentation. It is imperative that sellers capture the customer's attention. Table 8.3 overviews

# Table 8.3

## Opening Approaches

| Opening Approach | Definition | Example | Considerations |
|---|---|---|---|
| **Introduction** | Professionally greet the prospect with your name and company. | Mr. Jackson, thank you for clearing time in your busy schedule to see me. My name is Jessica Smith, and I'm the marketing manager with the XYZ City Tigers. | Simple approach, but does not generate interest. Should be used in conjunction with other approaches. |
| **Referral** | Mention the name of a mutual contact who referred you to the prospect. | Mr. Jackson, thank you for seeing me. When I spoke with your former colleague Tonya Smith last week she suggested I give you a call. | Increases your credibility and creates a sense of familiarity, but some customers do not want to be used as referrals. Be sure you have permission to use someone as a referral. Don't stretch the truth. |
| **Compliment** | Offer a compliment to the prospect about the prospect or the company. | I've heard a lot about the great work you do here for underserved children in the community. | Compliment must be sincere, not just flattery. |
| **Reciprocity** | Give a novelty item, free tickets, complimentary passes, etc. | Mr. Jackson, here are a couple of the limited edition LeBron James bobbleheads. | Bring enough for the number of people who will be sitting in on your presentation. |
| **Prop** | Bring a sports-themed prop the customer can hold. | Good morning Mr. Jackson, would you mind holding this hockey puck that Jeff Johnson used to score the game winning goal against the Stars in the playoffs last year? | A sports-themed prop immediately grabs the attention of the prospect. Select a prop that is portable and not a distraction during the presentation. |
| **Question** | Start the conversation with a question. | How many employees do you have on staff? | Launches into the needs analysis. |
| **Benefit** | Start the conversation by revealing a benefit of the product. | Mr. Jackson, I'm here today to tell you about a way to increase your sales productivity by at least 10%. | Choose a benefit that is likely to apply to all situations. May risk talking about a benefit that is not relevant to the customer. |
| **Mutual Agenda** | Allows the prospect to have input into the direction of the presentation. | To prepare for today's presentation, I spoke with Jessica Thomas in Human Resources. But rather than assume I already know everything about your business, it might be better for me to ask: What would you like me to accomplish in this presentation today? | Gives prospect a say in the direction of the conversation. Lets prospects know that you plan to tailor your presentation to make good use of their time. Prospect may bring up a topic you are not prepared for. |

eight common approaches to opening a sales presentation. The selection of an opening approach depends on five key situational variables:[8]

- ▶ The type of product being sold;
- ▶ The amount of rapport developed through previous interactions;
- ▶ Degree of knowledge about the customer's needs;
- ▶ The amount of time you have available to give the presentation; and
- ▶ The extent to which the customer is aware of their needs or problem.

## Use Storytelling to Illustrate Why People Change

People make buying decisions when they decide they need to make a change—to move from where they are to where they want to be. Telling a story can help illustrate to customers why people make changes. There are five elements to every story.[9]

- ▶ **Setting**—communicates the time, location, context, and characters for the story. The setting answers important questions such as: When and where does the story take place? Who are the key characters? What background information is needed to provide context for the story?
- ▶ **Complication**—the internal or external obstacles and challenges that a character faces between the setting and turning point. Complications form the plot of the story.
- ▶ **Turning point**—the emotional peak of the story where the character experiences a change in direction. Turning points occur when a decision, event, or action changes the anticipated outcome of the story.
- ▶ **Resolution**—the final outcome of the story that illustrates the point.
- ▶ **Point of the story**—the key message the seller wants to communicate through the story. Without a point there is no story.

---

### TELLING STORIES

You are an account executive for the Philadelphia 76ers. You are on an inside sales call with Nancy, who is a mother of a 12-year-old boy who plays competitive basketball for the Valley Cats. Nancy is an

---

8. Futrell, C. (2006). *Fundamentals of selling,* 9th ed. New York: McGraw-Hill/Irwin. p. 313.

9. Bosworth, M., & Zoldan, B. (2012). *What great salespeople do: The science of selling through emotional connection and the power of story.* New York: McGraw Hill.

assistant coach for the Valley Cats youth basketball program. She is really interested in a Family Night group outing for the basketball program because the kids can high-five the team coming out onto the court, but there is a 35-kid minimum for this unique fan experience. She is disappointed because there are only 13 boys on the team.

## STORY DEVELOPMENT

- ▶ **Setting**—I worked with the head coach of an AAU basketball team over in Westville last year. John coached the Westville Stars who won the 11-year-old state championship last year. John realized he really wanted to reward the kids on his team for winning the state championship.

- ▶ **Complication**—He actually faced a very similar concern that you have because he only had 15 kids on the team and there weren't enough siblings that were the right age to reach the 35-kid minimum for the on court experience.

- ▶ **Turning Point**—After finding out that he lived in a neighborhood with many young families, I suggested he involve them to hit the minimum.

- ▶ **Resolution**—He lived in a neighborhood with lots of young families and we combined the basketball team and his neighborhood together to do the group outing.

- ▶ **Point of the story**—We can be creative to find enough people to reach group minimums. I am in your corner to help you reach your objectives.

By using this story, the seller can identify other groups with which John is associated to combine groups and reach the minimum. While the same objective could be accomplished by asking the question, *What other groups are you associated with?*, telling a story helps the seller illustrate to Nancy how to think creatively about how to use 76ers tickets to meet her needs.

## *Create Powerful Visuals*

Sales collateral supplements the story being told to the customer. **Sales collateral** is the collection of printed or electronic visual documents that are designed to generate sales, including items such as brochures, graphics, samples, photographs, illustrations, video, and testimonials. Depending on the size and organizational design of the sport organization, sales collateral could be developed in-house through the marketing department's creative services, or could be outsourced to a graphic design firm. In small business or entrepreneurial settings, the owner or salesperson could be responsible for developing sales collateral, which speaks to the importance of acquiring at least a minimal level of graphic design skills at some point during college.

**SALES COLLATERAL** the collection of printed or electronic visual documents that are designed to generate sales, including items such as brochures, graphics, samples, photographs, illustrations, video, and testimonials

People remember 10% of what they read, 20% of what they see, 30% of what they hear, and 50% of what they hear and see. This means sellers maximize the possibility of customers retaining information from a sales presentation if it includes visual elements. This section offers general guidelines for the use of visual aids and an overview of the types of sales collateral. However, not all types of sales collateral should be used for every sales presentation. An assessment of the situation and the customer will dictate which sales collateral elements should be utilized. It is important to recognize that selecting which pieces of sales collateral to utilize depends on audience size, stage of the sales process, information needed by the customer, past purchase history, location of the presentation, and the customer's communication style.

There are many benefits of using sales collateral to communicate the sales message during a presentation. Effective utilization of sales collateral helps to capture the customer's attention, reinforce the message being delivered, increase retention of information, make presentations more persuasive, increase the customer's involvement in the presentation, create a unique or lasting impression, and enhance the image of a professional salesperson who can be trusted.

## *General Principles*

When developing the content of sales collateral and visual aids, there are several important general guidelines to follow that will ensure the message is received by the customer. Visual aids should be simple, focused, accurate, and supplement the message.

1. Ensure that the visual accomplishes the single point it is intended to make.
2. Have one focus point on which the customer should place his or her attention.
3. Main point should be understood by the customer within seven seconds of looking at the visual.
4. Always say more than you show in the visual.
5. Keep the visual simple by not placing too much information or text on a visual.
6. Visuals should supplement, not overshadow your role as the expert on the product.
7. Don't use visuals as a crutch. Visuals help you make information clear and memorable, but they should not be used as notes for you to follow.
8. Be consistent in the use of stylistic elements such as fonts, logos, headers, etc., across all visual aids.

9. Check visuals for typographical errors, misspellings, and other errors.
10. Obtain copyright for use of images from the Internet.

When it is time to reference sales collateral during the presentation, follow a simple four-step process to help the customer understand the point being made with the visual aid.

▶ *Introduce*—Introduce the sales aid by stating its purpose. For example, *This handout of the stadium map demonstrates where season ticket holders sit compared to single-game ticket buyers.*

▶ *Present*—Present the sales aid. Give the customer a few moments to review the sales aid before saying anything.

▶ *Explain*—Explain the sales aid. Make sure the customer doesn't miss the point of the collateral by providing a brief explanation. Remember, it's the combination of what the customer sees and hears that leads to retention of information.

▶ *Summarize*—Summarize the contribution of the sales aid to the discussion and then remove it so it does not become a distraction.

### *Types of Sales Collateral*

#### PRINTED MATERIAL

Printed materials include items such as brochures, pamphlets, pocket schedules, catalogs, articles, reports, testimonial letters, and handouts. These documents can help salespeople effectively communicate information to the prospect. Printed materials can be used during the presentation to make a key point, be left with the prospect as a reminder of the information covered during the presentation, and then referred to in future conversations.

*Brochures and pamphlets* summarize key points and contain answers to frequently asked questions. These should be creatively designed and allow the salesperson to tell the story of the product or service being sold.

*Pocket schedules* contain all of the information about the games played including location, opponent, date, and promotions.

*Testimonial letters* are written by satisfied customers or partners. Testimonial letters should be solicited from respected companies or individuals who are genuinely satisfied with their experience. A salesperson should confirm with this person that the letter can be used as a testimonial. Testimonial letters should be used strategically in a sales presentation when the prospect is similar in nature or has similar needs as the person writing the testimonial. Not every testimonial letter needs to be presented in every sales presentation.

*Catalogs* are used more commonly in selling sporting goods and equipment. Catalogs provide detailed information about product specifications and product options.

*Handouts* are written documents provided to help customers remember what was discussed in the presentation. Handouts are used as a way to distribute more detailed and complex information than is presented in the other visual aids. Examples could include PowerPoint slides, complex diagrams or charts, and other reading that helps supplement what was said during the presentation.

## CHARTS AND GRAPHS

Charts and graphs help the salesperson communicate large amounts of information by illustrating relationships. In addition to the general principles listed above, the following guidelines should be followed when creating charts and graphs:

- ► Use no more than six columns and remove all unnecessary zeros
- ► Use bullets to differentiate issues and emphasize key points
- ► Clearly label with a title
- ► Label all columns and rows
- ► Use graphs instead of tables to display relationships
- ► Use consistent art styles and layouts

## MAPS

In many sport sales settings involving spectators, maps provide a valuable tool to help the prospect visualize where events will occur. For example, helping the customer orient themselves within the facility helps paint a picture of what the sightlines will look like, where to park the car, and how to find baby changing stations. For corporate partners, maps can help illustrate where sponsorship signage will be located and where the corporate hospitality area is compared to the main entrance to the facility.

## VIDEO AND PHOTOGRAPHS

The use of video and photographs is a powerful tool when selling many types of sport products because it is intangible. Because the prospect cannot touch and feel the product, the salesperson needs to re-create the game day experience through video and photographs in an attempt to have the prospect feel the emotions associated with the team, game, or sport. For corporate partners, video and photographs can help the business visualize what their sponsorship or corporate hospitality environment will look like based on what has occurred in the past. Video and photographs help make the intangible seem more tangible.

## PRODUCT DEMONSTRATION

Product demonstration can be used during a facility tour to show the customer a seat or suite location, but it is perhaps best leveraged by those selling sporting goods equipment or technology. For example, golf retail stores allow customers to hit golf clubs on a driving range or simulator to allow the customer to get a feel for the club and compare its performance to other clubs. Salespeople for golf club manufacturers often hold "demo days" where they demonstrate to groups of golfers the product features and benefits of new clubs before letting customers try them on their own. A salesperson selling event management software will log into the software and show the prospect how to perform key tasks while consistently relating to the customer how the functionality of the software helps solve his or her problems. A salesperson selling running shoes for a shoe manufacturer will utilize a shoe to demonstrate key characteristics of the shoe like durability, flexibility, and shock absorption to buyers at retail establishments.

## COMPUTER-BASED PRESENTATIONS

Rapid advances in technology have allowed salespeople to harness the power of laptops, tablets, and smartphones for use in sales presentations. The proliferation of presentation software has given salespeople the ability to create powerful multimedia presentations. Agencies like Sportsdigita help sport organizations create engaging multimedia presentations in business-to-business sales environments. For lower budget operations, one of the most popular presentation software programs is PowerPoint. Unfortunately, PowerPoint is too often used ineffectively and has led what people in business call *death by PowerPoint*, which occurs when a presenter is too reliant on the slides, uses PowerPoint as a script, and places too much text or data on slides.

Each slide should communicate one main point and place more emphasis on images than text. Two recent studies by Decker Communications and the Wharton Research Centre showed that the use of visual slides dramatically increases the likelihood that the receiver of the message will retain information for a longer period of time than the use of bullet points.[10] Communication

---

10. Association for Institutional Research. *Bulletproof presentations.* Retrieved from http://forum.airweb.org/2011/Documents/WebResources/Bulletproof_Presentations.pdf

experts advocate presenters follow the 6-6-6 rule, which states the presenter should use no more than six words per bullet point, use no more than six bullet points per slide, and not spend longer than six minutes on any slide. Simplicity is the key to communicating the key sales message contained on each slide. As a result, presenters should also limit the use of animation and sound effects, check slides for grammatical errors and typos, and choose a simple background that is branded with the organization's logo and style. When printing the slides for distribution as a handout, print them so that the prospect can easily read the content.

---

### TAKING YOUR SHOW ON THE ROAD

1. Be able to access digital presentation materials from multiple sources in the event one does not work (i.e., e-mail, cloud, thumb drive, hard drive).

2. Bring power cords and other charging devices to avoid losing power.

3. Bring extra cables to connect computer to project or technology system.

4. Determine in advance if Wi-Fi is available and the password to access it if Wi-Fi is protected.

5. Get to the room early to set up if possible.

6. Ask the gatekeeper for assistance with room setup, Wi-Fi, power outlets, etc., if needed.

7. Test video clips to ensure audience will be able to hear the sound.

8. Know how to recover your computer from a system crash.

9. Ensure all handouts are crisp, clean, and don't look worn or used.

10. Utilize a checklist to ensure that you have all sales collateral and equipment needed to deliver a high quality presentation.

---

## CHAPTER SUMMARY

The SPET process helps sellers transition from conducting the needs analysis to making a customized recommendation. The SPET process is the bridge that connects information gathering to the tailored sales pitch. At the heart of making a tailored recommendation is synthesizing the information gleaned in the needs analysis and explaining to the customer why the recommendation is the perfect solution. Effective sellers are able to explain the value proposition to the customer by using social proof, telling stories, grasping the big picture, educating the customer on the product, and making a confident recommendation. In face-to-face appointments, effective sellers make a good first impression, deliver an attention-grabbing opening, use stories to explain why people change, and use powerful visually pleasing sales collateral.

## INDUSTRY ADVICE

**Bill Guertin,** *The 800-Pound Gorilla*

### "WHAT COLOR WOULD SUIT YOU BEST?"
### SECRETS TO SUCCESSFUL HIGH-END FACE-TO-FACE SELLING IN SPORTS

In the early days of the automobile, Henry Ford was famously quoted as saying, "You can have any color of car you want—as long as it's black." At that time, competition in the auto industry was non-existent, and so Ford didn't have to offer anything else, but as competition increased, and choices became more varied, people became more interested in choosing a car based on their individual tastes and preferences.

Henry Ford's early color philosophy would be a failure with today's consumers. And in sport sales, for the modern B2B buyers of premium seats, sponsorships, and sports media, the "one-color-fits-all" approach is about as appealing as driving a black Model T on the interstate.

Companies measure success in hundreds of different ways—in increased consumer recognition of their brand, the successful introduction of new products, specific consumer engagement tactics, strategic competitive advantage, increased demand for product channel partners, loyalty from distributors and retailers, and many more. You may have a specific idea for a prospect that would fit perfectly with your team's assets, but until and unless you know that idea helps them achieve THEIR objectives, it's not a fit.

It's easy to assume that everyone wants increased sales, but it may not be your prospect's #1 objective. A sport sales executive may see a prospect's competitor and assume their biggest goal is to beat the competition, but may learn in a discussion with them that their #1 objective is to go deeper with the customers they currently have.

There is no such thing as a successful "one-size-fits-all" philosophy in today's successful sports entities, especially when it comes to the kind of discerning customer that buys our higher-end inventory. Here are the elements of a logically-crafted, professional proposal:

- ▶ **Cover Page**—These typically contain a medium-sized, high-quality logo of the prospect in the center of the page, along with your name, title, contact information, and a smaller logo of your team centered toward the bottom of the page.

- ▶ **Summary of Observations**—relevant bullet-point facts about the client, as gathered in your initial fact-finding session.

- ▶ **Objectives**—What are the goals of the proposal? What will the plan achieve for the prospect (relative to the observations made in our fact-finding)? Use language that you heard directly from your prospect in your fact-finding. If you heard them say "fire up the staff," then use that phrase in your verbiage.

- ▶ **Action Plan**—The specifics of what you're proposing, with time lines and actions that are required of both parties for each section of the plan. If possible, put in specific measurables you'll both be looking at during the course of the proposal time frame, such as monetary or percentage increases in sales, percentage of reduction in employee turnover, a boost in the number of retained customers, etc.

▶ **Investment Page**—Some salespersons leave this page out of the proposal, and keep it to present it at the end, when it's time. Often in a meeting, the people in attendance go right to the "back page" to find out how much it is, and the presenter is in a position of having to defend the price throughout the presentation. By waiting until the very end to hand out the Investment Page, the sales professional has the opportunity to build value in the mind of the prospect, so that when the final number is presented, it has the potential to be significantly less than what they had expected for the value you've demonstrated.

▶ **One-Page Review** (optional)—This is a confirmation of all the salesperson has talked about, including the objectives, what actions will take place to achieve those actions, and the time lines. It may also have a place for the signatures of the two parties, in lieu of an official Contract that may need to be drawn up after the deal and the terms have been agreed on.

Black is always in season, but not always in sales. You'll show your true professional colors as a sport sales rep by asking specific questions regarding their current situation and how they would view a successful partnership in your initial call, and then presenting a proposal that's a grand canvas of the prospect's most desired colors.

## CHAPTER ACTIVITIES

### Sales Scenario

You are an account executive for an AA-level minor league baseball team responsible for selling season tickets packages to individuals. Packages include mini-season plans of 12, 17, and 35 games, in addition to full season packages of 70 games. There are many promotional nights throughout the season, including Monday autograph days, Thirsty Tuesdays where certain beers are $1, Wednesday Dollar Nights where select concessions items are $1, Fireworks Nights on weekends during the summer months, and a variety of promotional acts throughout the season. The stadium was built in 2014 and contains all modern amenities, including inflatable games for kids, batting cages, lawn seating, and picnic areas.

## SITUATION 1

In your needs analysis, you find out that Tom is a married father of two boys who play little league baseball (8 and 10 years old). He and his wife, Mary, have a busy schedule based on the fact they both work and their kids are heavily involved in sports. Tom typically attends four or five games each year and usually buys at the box office on game day. The family lives five miles from the stadium, and both parents work within one mile of the stadium. Family time is important to Tom, but equally important is how well his two sons perform in baseball. He played college baseball growing up and is an avid baseball fan. Mary does not care for baseball, but attends to be a part of important family activities.

## SITUATION 2

Assume you find out the following information in your needs analysis: James is single and graduated three years ago from a Division I university 30 miles from the stadium. After college, James obtained a good job in the city near the ballpark. He works with quite a few young professionals his age who are always looking for things to do after work and on the weekends. James is 25 years old and lives one mile from the stadium. He attended seven games on Tuesdays last year. All purchases were made online at least two days in advance of the game. Use the SPET process to recommend a product to James.

### *Assignment*

1.  Assume you have sufficiently completed the needs analysis and you are ready to transition to discussing the product. Record your product recommendation using the SPET process and principles presented in this chapter. This is part of a real conversation you are having with the customer after the needs analysis is complete. You can "make up" product information that is not included in the synopsis described above, if it helps tell your story. The recording should be approximately 30 to 45 seconds. Use the SPET process, describe selling points in a compelling way, and use storytelling. While you may want to write out a script for what you want to say, be sure that when you are recording your video that you do not sound like you are reading a script.

2.  Assume you are selling volunteer registration software that helps event managers manage their volunteers more efficiently. Through the needs analysis, you learned that the customer would benefit from software that will help make changes to shifts and responsibilities that are communicated to the volunteers immediately through text and e-mail. Use this information to make a product recommendation using the SPET process.

3.  Paint a picture for the prospect by telling a story about how attending a professional sporting event can help close a big deal they have been working on for months.

4.  Assume you are opening a title sponsorship proposal for an event of your choosing. Select four of the "Opening" methods and describe how you would start the presentation using each method.

**CHAPTER COMPETENCY ASSESSMENT**[11]

## COMPETENCY DOMAIN: PRESENTING SOLUTIONS

*Exemplary:* Consistently does all or almost all of the following:

- Earns the right to make product recommendation after having acquired enough information about how the customer would benefit from the offer
- Tailors an appropriate, logical recommendation based on information gleaned in needs analysis
- Leverages product knowledge to articulate benefits and value proposition of recommendation
- Provides customer with accurate information on price and availability
- Adapts each sales call and recommendation to match the needs or concerns of the customer by placing the needs of the customer over their own

*Skilled:* Does most of the following:

- Earns the right to make product recommendation after having acquired enough information about how the customer would benefit from the offer
- Tailors an appropriate, logical recommendation based on information gleaned in needs analysis
- Leverages product knowledge to articulate benefits and value proposition of recommendation
- Provides customer with accurate information on price and availability
- Adapts each sales call and recommendation to match the needs or concerns of the customer by placing the needs of the customer over their own

*Adequate:* Does most of the following:

- Makes product recommendations before knowing enough information about customer
- Fails to connect the dots from the needs analysis into presenting the right solution
- Makes appropriate recommendations on occasion, but too often recommends the same product to each customer or the cheapest/easiest package to sell without considering information gleaned in the needs analysis
- May understand the product, but does not utilize product benefits and value propositions at the appropriate time

---

11.   From "Competency Assessment for Entry-Level Sport Ticket Sales Professionals" by David Pierce and Richard Irwin, *Journal of Applied Sport Management*, Volume 8 (2), Summer 2016. Reprinted by permission of Sagamore Publishing. www.sagamorepub.com

*Novice*: Consistently does all or almost all of the following:

- Fails to connect the dots from the needs analysis and presents irrelevant information
- Rarely earns the right to make a recommendation due to failure to build rapport or learn relevant information about the customer during the needs analysis
- Does not understand the product well enough to leverage information gained in needs analysis to make an appropriate recommendation
- Abruptly presents solutions that are disconnected from the rest of the conversation
- Spews product information without having a clear understanding for what might be a fit for the customer, or provides product information that is irrelevant for that customer

# CHAPTER 9

# OVERCOMING OBJECTIONS

## LEARNING OBJECTIVES

After completing this chapter, you should be able to:

► Describe the attitude successful salespeople have toward objections.

► Explain why it is important to anticipate and overcome objections.

► Understand why prospects raise objections.

► Describe the seven major types of sales objections.

► Apply the major approaches to overcoming objections to a specific situation.

► Construct responses to objections using the key approaches.

► Demonstrate the key characteristics to successfully overcoming objections.

## KEY TERMS

| | | |
|---|---|---|
| Boomerang method | Hidden objection | Product objection |
| Compensation method | Indirect denial | Sales objection |
| Direct denial | Logistics objection | Sport organization |
| Educational approach | No-Need objection |    objection |
| Feel-felt-found | Postponed objection | Stall objection |
| Forestalling | Price objection | Third-party approach |

## COMPENTENCIES

► Ability to anticipate and overcome objections.

## CHAPTER OVERVIEW

The ability to anticipate and overcome objections whenever they are raised by the customer is essential to success in any type of selling. While many veteran salespeople suggest selling really starts when the first objection is raised, objections are often the most frightening aspect of sales for many "rookie" sellers. The inability to resolve a prospect's objections quickly and accurately makes it more difficult to obtain commitment when the salesperson asks for the sale. Objections are an important part of the sales process because customers will possess some level of skepticism, confusion, hesitancy, or disagreement about their need, the product, the salesperson, the team, or the price. This chapter introduces 10 approaches that can be used to help salespeople overcome different types of objections that might be posed during the sales process. Beyond this, the salesperson needs to display empathy, understanding, a positive attitude, honesty, and persistence in the process of overcoming objections. This chapter introduces the major types of objections, approaches to overcoming objections, and the characteristics that successful salespeople demonstrate when overcoming objections.

## OBJECTIONS MOVE THE CONVERSATION FORWARD

Imagine purchasing any big ticket item; a new television, a car, or even a house. If the sales representative or real estate agent asked the potential buyer several questions, listened to the answers, then made a recommendation, would the potential buyer be ready to hand over a credit card or sign the loan papers? Most people would probably say no. With a big purchase, there might still be hesitancy by the buyer to really know the right decision is being made. Buyers want to feel confident they are making a good purchase, so they ask even more questions or raise concerns. A potential buyer may have the money to make a down payment on a car or house, but wants to know she is not being ripped off. So she might say she thinks the asking price is too much or suggest she needs to do more research online before signing the contract. Such comments don't necessarily mean she isn't ready to buy, but rather that she wants to know she is making the right buying decision. In the sales world, these concerns are called objections.

**SALES OBJECTION**
any concern or question raised by the customer at any point during the sales process

Objections are a normal part of the sales process and present an opportunity to learn more about the customer. A **sales objection** is any concern or question raised by the customer at any point during the sales process.

Objections can occur at any time during the sales cycle, from first call to renewal. Qualified customers raise objections for almost any reason, but objections are typically linked to customers not possessing enough information to make a decision, not recognizing a need to buy, being resistant to change, or not developing enough trust or rapport with the salesperson to feel comfortable making a decision. Receiving an objection during the sales process does not mean the seller has done anything wrong, but instead it is indicative of a customer who is invested enough in the dialogue to seek additional information, which creates an opportunity to sell and advance the sales process.

For sales representatives, it is essential to maintain a positive attitude when encountering objections. Objections should be received by the salesperson as an opportunity to advance the sale and not perceived as a road block or message that the customer will not buy. Objections provide feedback about what the customer is really thinking. Objections are simply a way for customers to ask for more information. In fact, the customer may actually be signaling they want to buy, but they need help before doing so. Objections show an investment of time and interest from the customer. Think of it this way—objections show that the customer cares enough about what the salesperson is saying to raise an objection. The worst type of objection is one that the customer never discloses because it can never be addressed by the salesperson. The quickest way to lose a sale is to never uncover a customer's objections.

Objections should be expected, accepted, invited, and never taken personally. The better job a seller does in building rapport and trust, the more comfortable the customer will be in raising objections. Despite how outlandish the objection might seem to the salesperson, it is logical in the mind of the customer, so it is critical that responses convey a tone of sincerity, empathy, and respect for the customer's position. It is recommended that salespeople show gratitude in their attitude when an objection is raised by using phrases like *I see what you mean, I understand where you're coming from,* and *I would want to know the same information.* Perhaps most importantly, never argue with the customer. Remember, the customer is not the enemy.

Sometimes the customer just needs reassurance in the purchase decision. What may seem like an objection is really a disguise for seeking "permission" to buy. Customers want to know they are making a good decision. Thus, it is the salesperson's job to provide

TURN 'NO' INTO 'YES'

☑ LISTEN & LEARN THE OBJECTION

☑ SHOW ALTERNATIVE SOLVES PROBLEM

☑ ASK IF SOLUTION IS THE BEST OUTCOME

©iQoncept/Shutterstock.com

timely and accurate information to the customer to help alleviate concerns and give them permission to buy. For example, if the objection is price, the seller can counter with a statement that shows how the tickets will actually help the business, followed by a statement like *Your clients are really going to be impressed*. A good response to an objection provides the seller with an avenue to sell the benefits of the product and pace the conversation toward asking for the sale. A seller's response to a customer's objection provides him or her with a platform to continue building value.

## TYPES OF OBJECTIONS

Objections come in many different shapes and sizes, but can be categorized into the following seven types of objections:

- ► No-Need
- ► Product or service
- ► Sport organization
- ► Price
- ► Logistics
- ► Hidden
- ► Stall

### *No-Need Objections*

**NO-NEED OBJECTION**
objections stemming
from a lack of need

Salespeople can avoid the **no-need objection** by qualifying the prospect. However, even when a prospect is qualified and a need should exist, the customer may not realize or admit that a need exists. Because the entire sales process is predicated on the assumption that the salesperson's job is to establish a need in the customer's mind, failure to do so results in this type of an objection. Failure to uncover the need may stem from poor questioning by the salesperson during the needs analysis or an unwillingness of the customer to change. The following objections occur when the customer is not convinced that a need exists:

- ► We have no use for this package
- ► I'm not interested in any seats
- ► I have all the ticketing software I can use right now
- ► We don't do any client entering
- ► I can't see this working for us

## Product or Service

**Product objections** are related to the product, service, or experience and focused on a particular characteristic the customer does not like or need. The specific objections related to the product will depend on what is being sold, but in general these objections will focus on the sport, facility, equipment, service, or experience. For example, common product-related objections in the sale of tickets include:

- I didn't like my seats
- There are too many games
- The arena is falling apart
- Parking is too hard
- The stadium is in a bad part of town
- I don't like hockey
- I only want single game tickets
- I won't be able to use my tickets

Common product related objections in the sale of sporting goods or technology include:

- I don't like the design
- The product doesn't perform well enough for me
- The product is poor quality
- I use a competitor's product

## Sport Organization

In the sale of tickets, objections related to the **sport organization** focus on issues like team performance, reputation, image, and stability. For example:

- The team is awful. Call me back when they are good again.
- The team doesn't have a chance of winning
- I don't support teams that have so many players in trouble with the law
- I heard the team is moving to a new city. Why would I support a team that is moving anyway?
- I've supported the team for years but they just keep losing

In the sale of sporting goods, equipment, and technology, the focus of these objections revolve around loyalty to another manufacturer, brand, or vendor. People can be unwilling to change what they've done in the past

**PRODUCT OBJECTION** are related to the product, service, or experience and focused on a particular characteristic the customer does not like or need

**SPORT ORGANIZATION OBJECTION** objection related to team performance or quality

because they are creatures of habit. The tendency of customers to remain loyal to another brand and resist trying something new lies behind many customer objections. The following objections occur when the customer is unwilling to consider or make a change:

> ▸ We've never purchased X before
> ▸ The X I am using right now is working really well
> ▸ We are satisfied with the way things are right now
> ▸ I've never heard of your company before

## *Price*

**PRICE OBJECTION**
when prospects claim that the price is too high, they can't afford the product, or that the product is not in their budget right now

**Price objections** are probably the most common form of customer resistance. Prospects often claim that the price is too high, they can't afford the product, or that the product is not in their budget right now. Customers raise price objections because they actually can't afford the product, they are covering up the real objection they have with the product, or because they are trying to negotiate a lower price with the salesperson. In order to overcome any price objection, the salesperson must demonstrate how the customer can afford the product by emphasizing how the benefits outweigh the cost. The good news for the salesperson is that the price objection signals that the customer is highly interested in buying. In many cases it implies the customer would purchase the product if he or she believes the value exceeds the price. Common price objections include:

> ▸ I can't afford it
> ▸ It is too expensive
> ▸ There is a better offer from your competitor
> ▸ We need something much cheaper
> ▸ Is there a discount?

Price is arguably the common objection a salesperson will encounter. Every organization has different policies regarding payment conditions, but common tactics to reduce the perceived cost of a product or package include offering payment plans, ticket sharing, money back guarantees, and trial offers. Charlie Slonaker, Vice President of Ticket Sales and Service for the Philadelphia Union offers his strategy for overcoming pricing objections on the following page.

**Charlie Slonaker, Vice President Ticket Sales and Service, Philadelphia Union**

## OVERCOMING THE PRICE OBJECTION

Price is one of the most common objections any team faces. Whether you are talking to a general fan or a company, almost everyone has a budget. The key is get your prospect to utilize as much of that budget as possible toward tickets for your team.

Everything will seemingly be going great. You have built rapport, asked some great open-ended qualifying questions, and made the perfect recommendation to your prospect. They come back telling you, "I'm sorry. That's too much money." What should you do next?

Don't panic. There are plenty of solutions for the price objection. Acknowledge what they have just told you and make sure this is an actual objection as opposed to just a simple statement that does not impact their buying decision. If it is a true objection, make sure price is the only objection you are facing and ask them to elaborate before offering solutions.

When talking about the price, you simply want to find out if it is the up-front cost (paying everything at once), or the total cost that is causing them to hesitate. The up-front cost objection is much easier to overcome because you can easily combat that with a payment plan. Most people are not open enough to tell you what their budget is, but that is also worth asking prior to offering solutions.

Whether they say up-front cost or total cost in your question above, you will still want to follow a simple step-by-step solution process.

First, talk to them about the value and explain why the package is worth their money. If for personal use, talk about how it will be invaluable to spend time with the prospect's son, or whoever they are going to games with. If for business, talk about the return on investment the company will see from entertaining clients and prospects.

The next step would be to offer them a payment plan. Most teams have payments plans available. If a team does not, they usually do not have much of a need for selling tickets. For example, a team may offer five installments of 20% per month or 10 installments of 10% per month based upon when they purchase. Some teams will occasionally allow custom payment plans if the set plans do not work for the prospect.

If that does not overcome the objection, or if the prospect says that will help but they still are not going to buy, there are more options. The next thing you should do is ask if they can find a partner. Give them a thought jogger by saying, "Who do you know, maybe family, a friend, or a coworker, that could go in on the tickets with you?"

Assuming that still is a no-go, you can try educating them on re-selling tickets. Most teams have a relationship with a ticket provider that allows season ticket holders the opportunity to quickly post tickets for re-sale on the secondary market. If a client can sell a few big games to make some money back and pay for a portion of their ticket package, it should be a viable solution.

If all else fails, the final, and I mean the absolute final step, is to offer a package or seating location that is at a lower price point. Less veteran salespeople have a tendency to jump to this option right from the start. Doing so will absolutely cost them and the team significant revenue.

## Logistics

Objections based on logistical issues revolve around how sports fit into the lifestyle of the customer. Season tickets, memberships, and other sport products that require planning and a time investment are susceptible to the **logistics objection**. The challenging part about the logistics objection is that these customers attend events and buy products, but they purchase through other mechanisms besides from the salesperson. Because spectator sports are a perishable product that must be presold, attending a sporting event requires advanced planning on the part of the customer.

**LOGISTICS OBJECTION** objection related to how the experience fits the customer's lifestyle

For example, the logistics objection arises from fans who don't purchase a season ticket plan, but decide on the day of the game to purchase single game tickets at the box office or through secondary ticket websites like StubHub. These fans will tell the salesperson that they don't know their schedule far enough in advance to plan for a game, or that they have a busy schedule and never know when they will be available to attend a game. Others may not like to plan anything in advance for some other reasons. Participant sports are less restricted by time and date, but still require a significant investment of time in order to reap the value of a membership or yearly package. For a golf course, the logistics objection may arise from golfers who purchase single rounds of golf at the pro shop or through online tee time booking sites like Golf Now, but who don't purchase a season membership. The logistics objection requires the salesperson to reposition the customer's sense of time investment. For sports equipment, the logistics objection arises when a customer wants to purchase a piece of sports equipment, but doesn't see the value in buying new equipment.

For example, the logistics objection may sound like:

- I don't know my schedule that far in advance
- I have a busy schedule
- We don't plan that far in advance
- We just buy the day of the game
- I'll buy my tickets on StubHub
- I'll buy used equipment

## Hidden

Finally, salespeople need to overcome a **hidden objection**, which is an objection that has never been stated by the customer. In some cases, the customer may not even know what the true objection is, but in other cases customers may intentionally hide the true objection because they don't want the salesperson to know the objection, they are afraid of offending the salesperson, or they don't believe the sales call merits their focus. It is quite possible to have a very positive conversation with a customer, but never uncover the objections, which makes it difficult to close the sale. An example of a hidden objection might be a prospect who wants to buy but knows his spouse will not approve. The buyer may not want to reveal that he cannot make a spending decision without his spouse's consent. Another example could be a prospect who has heard something negative about the seller from someone else, but does not want to share this information with the seller because it would create an awkward situation.

**HIDDEN OBJECTION**
an objection that has never been stated by the customer

## Stall

The **stall objection** is used by customers to put off the buying decision until a later time. It usually occurs when a prospect is not comfortable with the salesperson or product. Stall objections sound like this:

**STALL OBJECTION**
used by customers to put off the buying decision until a later time

- ▶ I need to talk to my wife before I decide
- ▶ Let me think about it and call you back
- ▶ Call me back in a month
- ▶ I haven't made up my mind
- ▶ Send me more information
- ▶ I will shop around
- ▶ I'm just looking

Inexperienced salespeople miss the underlying meaning in one of these statements by a prospect. In some cases, a relationship has been developed appropriately and the customer is genuinely taking more time to think about the decision or have to get approval from someone else before purchasing. But in most instances the customer is attempting to do one of two things:

1. Hide the true objection that the salesperson has yet to uncover.

2. Get rid of the salesperson without having to officially reject the offer.

In either case, it reveals that the salesperson has not built a strong enough relationship with the prospect so that the customer feels comfortable revealing their true thoughts and feelings. It is important for the salesperson to deepen the relationship with the prospect so he or she can probe deeper into the root of the stall tactic. Inexperienced sellers often interpret a stall objection as coming from a very interested prospect who is considering buying, when in fact the opposite is true. Nothing is more detrimental to efficient selling; good salespeople prefer hearing "no" rather than "maybe" because it means they can move on, rather than delay inevitable rejection.

The article below by Steve Delay offers advice on how to handle the "Let me think about it stall."

---

Steve Delay, *The Migala Report*

## 5 DEADLY WORDS

**This 5-word sentence can kill you if you let it.**

*"Let me think about it."*

Doesn't sound too painful, does it? It might sound reasonable, but that's the killer sentence a prospect can say toward the end of a sales call.

Young ticket salespeople love to hear that sentence. After all, if the prospect is thinking about buying, then there is at least a decent chance for a sale. Heck, thinking about it is almost a sale. It's not a sale, of course, but it's not a rejection! Hooray!

I would like to quantify the prospect's thinking, but that's for another column. For this column, let's say that the prospect sticks with the five-word killer sentence. What should the young salesperson do?

BEWARE OF THE SO-CALLED FOLLOW-UP PHONE CALL

The prospect might say to phone him in a couple of weeks. If I was sitting on your shoulder as an invisible little elf, I'd whisper in your ear, *"You just lost the sale, pal."* Never, ever, ever settle for a tentative follow-up phone call. The follow-up phone call is too easy for the prospect to avoid, not return, and ignore.

So, when the prospect suggests a follow-up phone call, you immediately try to get a second meeting. Yep, a second meeting. It could go like this: *"I'm going to be back in this area next Tuesday for another meeting,"* you say. *"Why don't I stop by for 10 minutes and answer any additional questions and get this wrapped up?"*

*"I'm gonna be out of town next week,"* the prospect may say. Then you ask for the follow-up meeting the following week. If the prospect says no to the follow-up meeting, then that prospect isn't buying. Sorry to tell you that. But, it's been proven time and time again over years of ticket sales calls. If they won't meet with you for the follow-up meeting, they aren't buying.

But wait, there is still a last-gasp chance.

To set the stage: The prospect uses the five deadly words: "Let me think about it." The prospect won't set up a follow-up meeting. So, the sales call didn't produce a sale, but it didn't get a rejection. Not getting a rejection doesn't hurt, but unfortunately, teams don't pay commissions on not getting rejections. Instead of accepting a non-decision, Jon Spoelstra, my partner in the *Ultimate Toolkit,* would do the following:

Jon would call the prospect a week later or so. This is the rare time that he'd leave a voice mail when setting up an appointment. His voice mail would be: *"I've been thinking about your situation and I have a new idea for you. I'd like to stop by for a quick cup of coffee next Tuesday at 10 a.m. and explain it. Just 10 minutes. If that doesn't work for you just let me know what time works better. If I don't hear from you, I'll see at 10 next Tuesday."*

You might wonder if it's that easy to get a cup of coffee meeting. Well, you're not having a cup of coffee with a stranger. After all, you've met with that prospect and it was probably amiable. A *"cup of coffee"* connotes that it will be a short meeting, that it wouldn't be a full bore long meeting. You'll be surprised how easy it is to get the cup of coffee meeting.

If the prospect calls and says that a cup of coffee meeting isn't possible, that's when I would give you the bad news, *"You ain't gonna make the sale."* Sorry I was so blunt. But, you can waste a lifetime trying to reach that prospect and not connect.

However, it's great news if you do indeed get the cup of coffee meeting. I've used that cup of coffee strategy hundreds of times since I learned it from Jon, and sure, I'd have a new idea when having a cup of coffee with the prospect. And, most likely, by the end of the cup of coffee I'd have a sale.

---

http://migalareport.com/fivedeadlywords. Reprinted by permission of Steve DeLay.

## TEN APPROACHES TO OVERCOMING OBJECTIONS

This section contains ten approaches to overcoming customer objections. These approaches are not mutually exclusive; many of them can be used together. The commonality in all of the approaches is the salesperson is educating the customer with information and selling the benefits of the product. In addition, sellers should always respond to objections with empathy and understanding. Objections should never spark an argument or confrontation with a prospect. Instead, sellers should reassure prospects that their objections are understandable and have been raised by others. Only after this should sellers start disarming the objection itself. While it is impossible to list every potential objection that might be encountered, the purpose of these methods is to show how sellers can respond to the customer with the information, facts, and relevant benefits.

## Forestall

**FORESTALLING**
addressing the objection before the prospect has a chance to

Salespeople know which features of the product or service are likely to raise concerns from prospects. **Forestalling** can address these common objections by addressing the objection before the prospect has a chance to utter it. An advantage of forestalling is the customer never feels like he or she has to defend their position about their stated objection. A disadvantage is that the seller alerts customers to an objection they may not have previously realized. For example, a salesperson might forestall a concern about a new method for ordering season tickets online:

> **Salesperson:** I know that you'll be concerned about this new process for ordering season tickets, but I think you will find the online system very easy to navigate and significantly more convenient than having to come to our office to select the seats that you want. How does that sound?

The salesperson below forestalled a concern about team quality.

> **Salesperson:** I know there are some offseason moves that might be concerning for you, but let's focus on how your tickets were able to benefit you last year first.

## Direct Denial

**DIRECT DENIAL**
relatively harsh responses that contain information and facts that indicate the prospect is incorrect

**Direct denials** should only be used when the customer makes a statement that is factually untrue. Direct denials are relatively harsh responses that contain information and facts that indicate the prospect is incorrect. This should be used sparingly and done with tact and caution to prevent the customer from becoming upset or angry. In this case, how the salesperson delivers the message is just as important as what is said. The salesperson in the example below uses a direct denial to overcome a customer's misunderstanding about how season ticket seat locations were assigned.

> **Customer:** I'm not very happy with you guys right now. I read that article in the *Tribune* about how all of the rich people are getting the best seats now and I'll get moved to the end zone because I only give $250 each year. You guys really need to rethink what you're doing to your loyal fans.
>
> **Salesperson:** I'm glad you brought this up. There has been a lot of misunderstanding about how we assign seats based on that article written in the *Tribune*. What we actually do is use a complex formula that takes into account how many years you have purchased season tickets, how

many years you have donated money, along with how much money you give. I would recommend going to our website and see exactly how the formula works. What do you think of that?

## *Indirect Denial*

Indirect denials are a less threatening approach than the direct denial. **Indirect denials** are used to correct a customer's misunderstanding, but in a gentle and tactful way that avoids directly telling the customer he is she is wrong. The first sentence is used to take the edge off the answer by empathizing with the prospect that the objection is important or understandable before explaining why their objection is untrue or misdirected. This approach avoids a direct confrontation with the prospect. The salesperson in the example below uses an indirect denial to overcome the prospect's misunderstanding about how sport marketing could benefit his or her business.

> **Customer:** All of these high-priced sport marketing deals are for large corporations with huge marketing budgets.
>
> **Salesperson:** I'm glad you brought that up. We've heard that from many small business owners over the years. But I've worked with many owners over the past 10 years who will attest to the fact that sport marketing is extremely successful for small, local businesses, just like yourself. Does that make sense?

## *Postpone the Objection*

On occasion customers will raise an objection early in the conversation. In these situations, it may be beneficial for the seller to ask permission to **postpone the objection**, or address the objection at a later time. It is important to then address the customer's objection at the appropriate point in time; otherwise it will appear the seller is simply ignoring the customer's concern. If the customer does not honor the request to postpone the objection, then the salesperson should respond to the objection immediately and not risk alienating the customer. If used appropriately, postponing the objection leaves the seller in control of the conversation or presentation. The most common objection to postpone revolves around price or cost, because it is preferable to avoid discussing price until the needs analysis has been completed. In the example below, the personal trainer postpones the question about price until he or she understands more about the client's goals.

> **Client:** I came in today to learn more about your personal training sessions.

> **Salesperson:** Great, I'm glad you stopped by.
>
> **Client:** So how much does it cost for three sessions a week?
>
> **Salesperson:** We have a variety of different pricing structures depending on your goals. Can you tell me what you're really looking to achieve in a personal training program?

### *Boomerang Method*

**BOOMERANG METHOD** turns the objection into the reason to buy

The **boomerang method** turns the objection into the reason to buy. By convincing the prospect that an objection is actually a benefit, the seller can turn the prospect in favor of the product. The danger of this method is that it can come across pushy or aggressive if not delivered with care. In the example below, the tennis professional turns the time investment into the reason to buy.

> **Customer:** I'm just really concerned about the amount of time that I will need to commit to this 10-lesson package.
>
> **Tennis pro:** I can appreciate your feelings on that. Maybe a different way to think about it is that the time investment is precisely what will help you improve your game and reach your goals.

> **Customer:** Our business just doesn't have the budget to buy four club seats this season.
>
> **Salesperson:** I certainly understand where you are coming from. However, what if you used those seats to entertain your business prospects and actually developed ten new clients this year through relationships you build at our games. The new revenue from those clients would more than triple what you invested for those seats.

---

**Carl Manteau, Senior Director of Group Sales, Milwaukee Bucks**

#### BOOMERANG METHOD

## EXAMPLE 1

**Customer:** We just went through a round of downsizing and it wouldn't look right to spend money on non-essentials like sports tickets.

**Sales Rep:** I can appreciate how you feel and I agree that perception is important. Whenever a company has to make the tough decision to downsize, it can take a big toll on the people that remain with the company. At times like this, it's important to let these people know how much you still value them. Something as simple as inviting everyone to a game and allowing them to invite their families could be a great step in showing your appreciation.

---

---

> **EXAMPLE 2**
>
> **Business Prospect:** Our sales haven't been the strongest this year, so I'm not sure if this would be the wisest investment for us right now.
>
> **Sales Rep:** As a fellow salesperson, I respect where you are coming from. When sales aren't the strongest you need to be strategic with where you invest your time and resources. This is why a lot of companies continue to hold onto their sports tickets through the good times and the bad, because they know the tickets and the in-arena experience can be used as a tool to close new business and also maintain strong relationships with their best customers.

## Compensation Method

Despite how great the product or service might be, no product is picture-perfect and possesses at least one weakness or disadvantage. The **compensation method** acknowledges the validity of the customer's objection and then attempts to highlight a product feature that counterbalances the objection with an offsetting relevant benefit. Typical tradeoffs involve price and features like seat location, time investment, quality, and level of service. In this example, the salesperson uses the compensation method to counterbalance an objection about price with the benefit of better sight lines.

**COMPENSATION METHOD** acknowledges the validity of the customer's objection and then attempts to highlight a product feature that counterbalances the objection with an offsetting relevant benefit

> **Decision-Maker:** The price of this package is a bit more than we wanted to pay.
>
> **Salesperson:** This is certainly one of our more expensive packages, and the benefit to you is the great seat location where you'll be right next to all of the action. Our past clients have told us that their customers love sitting courtside. In fact, ABC Company purchased this package for the first time last year and saw an increase in sales right off the bat.

## Third-Party Approach

In the **third-party approach**, the salesperson uses the facts and opinions of others to justify a position. There are two types of third-party approaches—the referral approach and the educational approach. In the referral approach, the salesperson relates that other customers have found their initial opinion to be unfounded or incorrect after they used or experienced the product or service. The referral method is rooted in the concept of social proof. One longstanding use of the referral method is a three-step process called *feel-felt-found*.

**THIRD-PARTY APPROACH** salesperson uses the facts and opinions of others to justify a position

**FEEL-FELT-FOUND** three-step process including acknowledge the customer's feelings, extend the same feelings to a larger audience, and counter with a legitimate argument

Step 1—Acknowledge the customer's feelings (I can see how you *feel*)

Step 2—Extend the same feelings to a larger audience (Other customers/members have *felt* the same way)

Step 3—Counter with a legitimate argument (Yet they have *found* that . . .)

The feel-felt-found method is particularly effective when objections are based on customer attitudes, opinions, and feelings as opposed to statements of fact. Statements like *In my opinion* and *I believe* can cue the salesperson into a feel-felt-found response. The downside to this approach is that it is a longstanding sales method and decision-makers in the business world may perceive the seller as disingenuous or prepackaged. In the example below, the salesperson uses the feel-felt-found method to overcome a price objection.

**Decision-Maker:** The season ticket packages are just too expensive.

**Salesperson:** I understand how you feel about the season ticket packages. Other businesses I've helped felt the exact same way at first. I know First American Corporation had the same concern, but they found that they could create an excitement level that far exceeded any other promotional event they were trying to use. Let's talk about how you could do the same.

The referral approach relies on using customer testimonials. Amanda Dennis, Senior Account Executive for the Colorado Rapids, uses the following testimonials from satisfied customers:[1]

---

▶ Bringing clients to games is a great icebreaker and opportunity to know them outside the office. We've been using Rapids tickets like this for a long time and will continue to do so.

▶ These tickets provide a gift for referrals. I gift tickets to other people who refer cases to me. They are always so appreciative of the tickets I get them. It keeps my name on their mind when they are looking to refer cases.

▶ I create contests on social media for our customers to win tickets. It's fun to post the contests and see their reaction when they win. It's a nice win-win since people see that we like to give back to our customers and community.

▶ I used tickets as a rewards program for employees and sub-contractors. Tickets motivate them to do more and have a better attitude which then leads to better job performance.

---

1. https://www.linkedin.com/pulse/season-ticket-member-testimonials-amanda-dennis-303-727-3591

In the **educational approach**, the salesperson uses research and facts to support their claims. In the example below, the salesperson uses an industry study to demonstrate the return on investment that can be earned on season tickets for a corporation.

**EDUCATIONAL APPROACH**
uses research and facts to support claims

> **Decision-Maker:** Let me stop you before you go any further. There's just no way I could justify a program like this if we can't show a return on investment.
>
> **Salesperson:** You're exactly right, and I wouldn't want you to. A recent study conducted by *Ticket Manager* found that when a business person invites a guest to a game, that guest represents on average $161,000 for the company. What value does a new client have to your business?

## Rephrase as a Question

In some instances, it can be easier to answer a question than to overcome an objection, so it may benefit the salesperson to rephrase an objection as a question. Rephrasing the objection as a question should be preceded by acknowledging the customer's viewpoint and followed by obtaining agreement that the rephrased question is what the customer is really asking. Once the seller obtains this agreement, the salesperson should focus on key selling points and the value proposition. In the example below, the salesperson uses this strategy to enter into a discussion about how the business can effectively utilize tickets even though nobody in the office likes soccer.

> **Customer:** Nobody in our office even likes soccer. I'm not sure that we would use these tickets.
>
> **Salesperson:** I can appreciate that. So you are really asking how you can effectively utilize soccer tickets. Is that correct?
>
> **Customer:** Yeah, I guess so.
>
> **Salesperson:** Well, we've actually had a lot of success with other companies in your industry with entertaining clients from around the world because soccer is such a popular game worldwide. In fact, General Corporation made a great impression on a group of distributors they had over from Germany because those folks were huge soccer fans. You mentioned earlier that you do a ton of business over in Spain and other Western European countries, so I believe this could be a good fit for you. What do you think?

## *Ask a Question*

At times the salesperson needs additional clarification or information about the objection raised by the customer. In this case, the salesperson should simply ask a question to solicit more information from the customer to better understand the nature of the objection. Global questions ask customers to expand on statements they just made in a way that invites them to continue with more information. Global questions serve as a prompt for the customer to expand on an objection so the salesperson can understand it better. Then the salesperson can respond using any of the other approaches outlined in this section. Global questions used in the context of an objection include:

- ► How do you mean?
- ► Can you tell me more?
- ► Can you tell me why?
- ► Could you clarify that?

The article below explains how the seller can use the phrase "how do you mean" to begin overcoming an objection.

---

**Steve Delay,** *The Migala Report*

### HOW DO YOU MEAN

**You can't solve an objection unless you really know what it is**

Ever get in an argument with your significant other?

We guys usually lose the argument. It's primarily because we're trying to win it, or change the mind of our significant other. Nobody likes to be told they are wrong. My experience is even if I did win the argument and proved they were wrong, I usually ended up losing.

The reason we usually lose the argument is because we didn't really understand why our significant other was unhappy in the first place. We never really clarified the objection.

**HOW DO YOU MEAN?**

My all-time favorite response to any objection or argument is *"How do you mean?"* It absolutely, positively forces the person on the other side of the table to tell you more. Instead of just jumping in (and many times even interrupting,) this gets the person to expand on their reasons why they don't like what you're saying. Then, you have more complete information and a better chance to respond and solve the problem. You know the true objection.

Try it out the next time you get in an argument with your partner. Ask, *"How do you mean?"* (and then duck the shoe flying at you). I can promise you your partner will tell you a lot more about why they are mad at you. I knew one sports executive who would ask his wife until she finally started shouting back, *"Don't give me that sales B.S. You know exactly what I mean!"*

I sat in on a community meeting last night in Las Vegas with a group of developers trying to build an MLS stadium in Las Vegas. The public threw all kinds of crazy objections at the idea but the city officials never asked, *"How do you mean?"* to clarify the public concerns and then be able to respond to them. When someone stated, *"Don't spend one nickel on a project that helps private industry,"* city officials would have been able to tell the attendees about all the other public/private projects the city had invested in that turned out spectacularly or even tell the public about how their investment in the stadium was going to turn into three times that amount in annual tax revenue back to the city.

The next time you're on a sales call and you get an objection like *"It's too expensive,"* ask *"How do you mean?"* before immediately defaulting to a cheaper ticket product. They may have an entirely different need. If someone says, *"I don't think this will help my business,"* don't argue with them, ask *"How do you mean?"* so you have a better understanding. Make it seem like you're listening. Then provide a calculated response that answers the question and solves their concern.

I used to write HDYM as an abbreviation on my hand when I first started in sales, just to remember to always ask. It's the best way to truly know an objection and be able to answer it to move the conversation forward.

------

Source: http://migalareport.com/knowyourobjection. Reprinted by permission of Steve DeLay.

---

**Carl Manteau, Senior Director of Group Sales, Milwaukee Bucks**

### USING QUESTIONS TO OVERCOME OBJECTIONS

Before attempting to overcome any objection, it's important to first clarify the objection and to make sure there aren't any others. Prospects will sometimes throw out an objection because they are trying to be nice or because they don't want to tell you the real reason they don't want to buy. By asking a couple clarifying questions, you can cut to the heart of the matter and focus your time on overcoming the real objection. Sometimes you need to clarify multiple times before you reach a buying decision. For example:

- ▶ Prospect: The price is too high.
- ▶ Sales Rep: When you say the price is too high, what do you mean by that?

    *(Don't say anything until the prospect responds. Let them define their own objection. Don't assume you know what they are thinking.)*

▶ Prospect: I don't think we have it in our budget.

▶ Sales Rep: Thank you for clarifying that for me. Investments are important. Just so we are on the same page, if we can overcome your reservations about the budget, are you saying you'd be in a position to move forward with a ticket plan today?

*(This answer to this question will tell you exactly where you stand. If there is only one objection then you can battle it and work to close the deal. If there are multiple objections, then you may need to re-assess where things are at and go back to asking more needs-analysis questions.)*

▶ Prospect: Yes

Rep: Ok, that's great. Let's talk about budget then. What is your budget process?/How much is in your budget/What is the size of a typical sale for you?/How much value do you place on keeping your current customers/employees happy? *(These are all examples of clarifying questions you can ask to get to the heart of the objection. Once you have it clearly defined you can work to resolve it.)*

▶ Prospect: No. I wouldn't be able to move forward today.

Rep: Ok. What else is holding you back?

## Use a Sequence of Questions

Sellers can also use a question sequence to identify the real objections that are preventing a prospect from buying.[2] Nonverbal cues or statements like "I want to think about it" demonstrate that the customer has an unstated or hidden objection that was not unveiled during the sales presentation. Table 9.1 shows how these questions can be used in sequence to find the real objection.

Another set of questions that can help salespeople uncover the true nature of a customer's objection is used by the Major League Soccer National Sales Center. To assess how likely it is the customer will buy, Jeff Berryhill recommends asking the question, *On a scale of 1 to 10, with 1 being I'm never buying and 10 being I want to buy right now, how interested are you in this product?* The question also helps the seller open the door to uncovering any unstated or hidden objections because he or she can follow this question up with, *What do we need to do to get you from a 7 to a 10?* At that point, the customer will open up with relevant information about what conditions need to be met for them to purchase.

2. Futrell, C. (2006). *Fundamentals of selling*, 9th ed. New York: McGraw-Hill/Irwin.

## Table 9.1

**Question Sequence**

| Step | Question | Result | Customer Answer |
|------|----------|--------|-----------------|
| 1 | What is holding you back from moving forward today? | Customer will give you an objection. Move to Step 2. | I have a busy schedule that time of year. |
| 2 | Is there anything else besides your busy schedule that would keep you from buying today? | Customer may give you another objection. Creates buying condition. Move to Step 3. | No, my schedule is the big issue. |
| 3 | Supposing we lived in a perfect world and you had a wide open schedule, would you buy tickets? | If **negative** response, move to Step 4. If **positive** response, discuss how you can help and return to the sales cycle. | Negative: No, I still wouldn't buy. Positive: Yep, I'd be on board 100%. |
| 4 | There must be some other reason. If you don't mind me asking, what is preventing you from buying today? | Return to Step 2 and follow cycle through Step 4 or move ahead to Step 5. | Actually I'm not sure my kids would enjoy going to the games. |
| 5 | What would it take to convince you? | | |

---

**Mike Brooks, Mr. Inside Sales**

### OVERCOMING "THE MOTHER OF ALL SMOKESCREEN" OBJECTIONS

**"I want to think about it"**

Out of all the possible objections you get when <u>selling</u> your product or service, the nebulous, "I want to think about it" is probably one of the hardest ones to overcome. I mean, the prospect isn't saying no, exactly, but he isn't giving us an objection that we can overcome either. So what do you do?

If you're like most sales reps, then you fumble around for some kind of response and end the call with a wimpy, "Well, when should I call you back?" The prospect is thinking, "How about the 12th of never?"

Any good closer knows that this <u>objection</u> is the mother of all smokescreens and can hide a number of real objections. The real skill in dealing with this is to get your prospect to reveal what the real reason he's not going with it is. And that's what the following responses to this objection provide you with.

OK, now this first response is to give your prospect some options so they can give you an idea of what they really mean—and their answer will give you the direction. YOU then need to go in to <u>close the sale</u>:

**Response #1:**

"_____, whenever I tell someone I need to think about it, it usually means one of three things: (1) I'm not going to be a deal for whatever reason, and I just want to get them off the phone, (2) I kind of like the idea but I'm going to have to find the money or talk to my partner, or something else is holding me back, or (3) I really like the idea, and I just have to move something around before I say yes.

Be honest with me; which one of those things is it for you right now?"

As always when asking questions, use your MUTE button and let your prospect get everything out. Use the "Oh?" technique to prod him/her on further . . .

This next response is one of my favorites because in going through each of these options, you're actually qualifying your prospect as well. Especially when you get to the last question about budget.

**Response #2:**

"Perfectly fine. Just to be sure, you do understand how this (your product or service) would work in your environment, right? And are you confident that if you moved forward with it you would get positive results? And finally, if you decide to give this a try, is the budget there to move forward with it?

Then just to clarify my thinking, what factors will you be considering in thinking about this?"

Again, listen carefully and give your prospect the time to finish his thoughts and give you all the info you need—in other words, use your MUTE button when he/she is speaking.

This tenth response is a little tongue in cheek, but it works! The important thing is not only what your prospect responds with, but HOW they say it . . .

**Response #3:**

"No problem, _____. When should I call you back on this? And what is going to happen between then and now that will convince you to move forward with this?"

So there you have it! Three proven ways to handle the bane of every salesperson's existence: the dreaded "I want to think about it" smokescreen. Use them today and put an end to the stalls you get when trying to close your sale.

**About the author:**

*Mike Brooks* "Mr. Inside Sales" is the recognized authority on inside sales. Voted one of the most Influential Inside Sales Professionals by The American Association of Inside Sales Professionals for the past five years in a row, Mike is the go-to inside sales trainer and phone script writer in the industry. Mike is the best-selling author of *The Ultimate Book of Phone Scripts* which Brian Tracy calls "One of the best books on inside sales phone scripts I've seen." Mike is hired by business owners to implement proven sales processes that help them immediately scale and grow Multi-Million Dollar Inside Sales Teams. For more information, you can visit his website: www.MrInsideSales.com.

---

Reprinted by permission of Mike Brooks.

**USING THE APPROACHES TO OVERCOME OBJECTIONS**

**Setting:** Season tickets for SEC football.

**Objection:** I'm not going to buy a package in a year when the team is going to be terrible.

**Direct Denial:** I don't think that will be the case. We have a strong senior class returning and a couple of our freshman are blue chip recruits.

**Indirect:** That's certainly a valid concern. But I think there is reason for optimism with seven returning starters on defense and a couple of blue chip recruits.

**Postpone:** We've heard that quite a bit this year. Before we get into how well the team will perform this year, I would like to talk about how we can drive value for your business this year.

**Boomerang:** I can see what you mean. But think of it this way—now is the time to get in because you'll end up with better seats in a few years when Coach Johnson has us competing for championships.

**Compensation:** I can understand your concern there. The good news is that your prospective clients will be enjoying your exclusive suite and awesome food up on Suite Level regardless of what is happening on the field.

**Feel-Felt-Found:** I completely understand how you feel. I've had several other customers tell me the same thing going into last season. But by the end of the season they found that they were still having a great time coming to campus with their kids on Saturdays during the fall.

**Educational:** That could be the case, but did you see where Steve Smith had us picked to finish third in the division in *College Football Weekly* last week?

**Rephrase:** That definitely remains to be seen! We'll see how the season plays out. So you're really wanting to know how you can enjoy your tickets even if we're losing. Is that correct?

**Questions:** Is there anything else besides the team's projected record that would keep you from buying today? Supposed we were going to go undefeated this year, would you get season tickets?

It is important to realize that these are not necessarily the best answers to the objection. The purpose here is to show how each approach *could* be used.

# NINE KEYS TO OVERCOMING OBJECTIONS

Regardless of the objection and the method used to overcome it with, there are key principles to successfully overcoming objections. The nine keys to overcoming objections are to:

- ▶ Be prepared for the objections you expect to encounter
- ▶ Anticipate objections during the call
- ▶ Listen to what the customer is really trying to tell you

- ▶ Empathize with the customer's situation
- ▶ Educate the customer
- ▶ Confirm that you have adequately addressed the customer's concern
- ▶ Be persistent in the face of objections
- ▶ Be honest in your responses
- ▶ Be positive

> Continued practice is the best way to master the art of handling objects. The tricky part, especially early in a career, (is that) sales executives might not get a lot of opportunities to practice handling objections on live calls. The key to improvement is getting as many reps as possible fine-tuning their objection handling skills.
>
> —Jeff Berryhill, *Major League Soccer*

## Be Prepared for the Objections You Expect to Encounter

Sales managers should help salespeople prepare for all of the possible objections they might face and develop a set of responses to each objection. While unpredictability exists because the seller can never know what objection a customer might have, the seller can control his or her preparation.

## Anticipate Objections During the Call

Within a sales conversation, anticipate what objections are likely to occur with that specific customer. Past experience, the customer's personality, and the customer's nonverbal signals can help the salesperson anticipate what objections the customer might bring forth. The forestall technique discussed earlier in this chapter is a specific strategy that can be used to discuss the objection with the customer before he or she has a chance to bring it up.

## Listen to What the Customer Is Really Trying to Tell You

While planning and anticipating are characteristics of successful salespeople, be careful not to jump to conclusions before the prospect has had a chance to finish his or her statement. Because salespeople become accustomed to routinely hearing the same objections, it can be tempting to cut the prospect off and hurriedly respond to the objection but miss the prospect's point. This will create resistance with the prospect. Instead, use the listening techniques addressed in Chapter 11 to listen to what the customer is saying.

"When an objection is provided or a customer is venting about team performance, it is crucial the rep listens instead of interrupting. If a rep cuts off or gets defensive, it will damage the relationship and sales process."

—Drew Ribarchak, Senior Director of Ticket Sales, *Columbus Blue Jackets.*

## Empathize With the Customer's Situation

Effective salespeople acknowledge a customer's point of view and demonstrate an understanding of their concern. This is called empathy. Using statements like *I see what you mean* or *I can understand your concern* give the salesperson a chance to compose their thoughts and mentally compose the proper response. It also sends the message that the customer's opinion is valued. Using empathy to start the response is like a pillow that cushions your response to the customer.

## Educate the Customer

After empathizing with the customer, the salesperson should respond to the objection by educating the customer on the product. Knowledge of the product features and benefits is critical to overcoming the customer's objection.

## Confirm That You Have Adequately Addressed the Customer's Concern

After responding to the customer's objection, it is important that the salesperson confirm with the customer that the objection has been adequately addressed before moving forward with the sales cycle. This can be done through the use of trial close questions. In some cases, if this question comes after a major objection has been resolved, it may be an appropriate time to ask for the sale. If the customer is still not comfortable or has further objections, a question like *Putting that objection aside, what else is holding you back?* can bring the real objection to the surface.

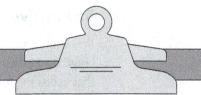

### Overcoming Objections

1. Be prepared for the objections you expect to encounter
2. Anticipate objections during the call
3. Listen to what the customer is really trying to tell you
4. Empathize with the customer's situation
5. Educate the customer
6. Confirm that you have adequately addressed the customer's concern
7. Be persistent in the face of objections
8. Be honest in your responses
9. Be positive

Other questions like *If you were convinced that we could meet your concerns, would you be willing to move forward?* help propel the seller forward in the conversation.

### Be Persistent in the Face of Objections

Salespeople should remain persistent when facing an objection or stall from the customer. Inexperienced and unsuccessful salespeople give up on the call after just the second or third objection. In contrast, successful salespeople expect objections to occur and view objections as an opportunity to sell, and they passionately advocate for the product.

### Be Honest in Your Responses

Honesty is important at all stages of the sales process, but it can be particularly tempting to fudge the facts to overcome objections, especially when customers dig their heels into a particular issue. However, it is not worth losing a sales relationship over white lies and half-truths.

### Be Positive

It is important to welcome the customer's objection through positive body language and empathetic verbal statements. The goal is to respond in a way that keeps the mood friendly and positive. Personal style will determine how this message is conveyed, but it needs to be clear to the customer that the salesperson does not take the objection personally.

**Figure 9.1**

**Process for Overcoming Objections**

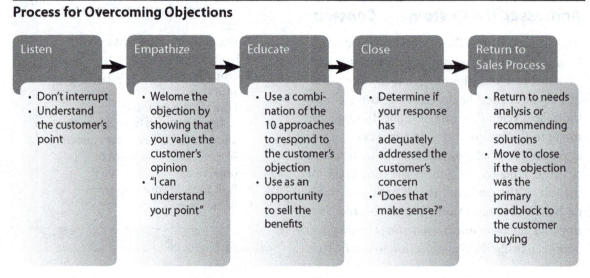

# RESPONDING TO COMMON OBJECTIONS

**I don't know my schedule**

▶ That is completely understandable. We all have full schedules with a busy life these days. The great thing about any of these ticket packages is that if you have a conflict with your schedule, and you know this more than two days in advance, you can trade the ticket in at the box office for a game later in the season. We designed these packages with your busy schedule in mind. Does that help?

**I'll just wait until the day of the game to buy tickets**

▶ That is certainly done by quite a few of our fans. But the last thing I would want to have happen is for you to come all the way out the ballpark and then not be able to buy a ticket. We sold out almost half of our games last year so it's 50/50 on whether you would be able to get a ticket on game day, especially if you want your family to sit together.

**I can't use that many tickets**

▶ We hear that a lot from companies buying tickets for the first time. But actually our research department found that companies on average use over 80% of their tickets each season. While we hate to see any tickets go to waste, 80% is still enough to generate a solid return on investment.

▶ I completely understand how you feel about the number of tickets. That is a common concern felt by many first-time season ticket buyers. But they have found that a great solution is to share their season tickets with another family in their neighborhood.

**My family doesn't like baseball**

▶ You would be surprised how many of my satisfied customers tell me the same thing. The great thing is that we have so many national entertainment acts, fireworks shows, on-field promotions, and kids' games around the stadium that your family will barely have time to watch the baseball game anyway!

**Nobody in our office even likes hockey**

▶ We hear that a lot. The great thing about leveraging tickets to increase sales is that we can create a unique environment for your salespeople to cultivate business relationships regardless of what sport they are a fan of. Johnson Brothers thought the exact same thing, but they realized they could schmooze new prospects in a unique way by sitting rink side.

**The economy is tight right now**

▶ We hear that a lot. Fortunately, most of the fans that I work with have been able to find a ticket plan that fits their situation without sacrificing too much of what they really enjoy. We pride ourselves on being affordable family entertainment. What is it you like about coming to the games?

> ► We totally understand that. That's why we've priced the tickets competitively with other entertainment options in town. You can get your family of four out to a game and sit in our best seats for 25% less than going to dinner and a movie, and we're 50% less than taking them to Kids Island theme park.

**We don't have the budget for tickets this year**

> ► We hear that a lot. Even though your budget is gone, do you still have a need for new business development?
>
> ► Budgets are definitely always challenging. What do you think is your biggest challenge this year?
>
> ► Let's say the budget wasn't an issue, how would you use these tickets to help build your business?
>
> ► Is your marketing budget already spent, or are these funds still available?

**I need to speak with my husband first**

> ► That is certainly understandable. When do you think you will find time to talk to him about this package? The earlier we can get you signed up, the better seats I can make sure you get.
>
> ► When you do speak with him, what do you think he will say?
>
> ► That's great, both of you should come on down and do the arena tour together.

**I need to speak with my friends before I can decide.**

> ► That's great. How many other friends are going to be involved in this decision?
>
> ► Would it help you if I help you coordinate the ticket package with your friends?

**We can save a lot of money by just buying the best games on StubHub.**

> ► I can understand why StubHub seems like a solution to getting tickets. But I don't want you to be left out of those sold out games that your customers would want to be at as well. Also, it may not even save you that much money. A recent industry report revealed that companies were paying twice as much for a ticket when buying from the secondary market compared to the price of a ticket in a season ticket package.
>
> ► I'm glad you brought up the issue of tickets on the secondary market. We had several firms do that last year, but they ended up finding that they missed out on all of the benefits of being a season ticket holder like [insert benefits here], and they renewed with us for this year.

## INDUSTRY ADVICE

**Bill Guertin, *The 800-Pound Gorilla***

### GIVE CUSTOMERS THE RIGHT OPTIONS TO TURN THEIR 'NO' INTO A 'YES'

Michael is new to inside sales. His personality is excellent for the kind of phone work he's doing. His call numbers are strong, his attitude is good, and his notes from each call couldn't be better.

There's only one problem, and it's a big one: Michael's sales results just don't match the effort he's putting forth. What's wrong?

We all know that selling isn't for everybody. In times like these, there are days where it can feel like selling isn't for anybody, including the sales staff.

When things become tight, the overwhelming number of negative responses become "I can't afford it," "The economy's bad," or "I just don't feel good about spending any money right now." And because we read the newspaper, listen to others around us, and know that things may not be rosy for us personally, many times we tend to agree.

And mentally, that's a dangerous place to be.

Every team I work with has a number of new account representatives like Michael who have a great work ethic, know their product, but may be caving too quickly after the prospect has said "no" one time. When we emphasize numbers of calls over call quality, account reps can simply pad their numbers by accepting a no, logging it in their computer or on their tally sheet, and move on. We see the number of activities on the record for each rep, but the production just isn't there, and we wonder why.

The answer isn't completely due to the economy. It's in the discipline of the account reps to continue to battle through the first "no" they receive.

### How customers think

Put yourself in the position of a customer. All of us are predisposed to a certain amount of risk avoidance. We don't want to get burned, and the word "no" is a safety device that protects us from making a decision we may regret later. We say "no" far more quickly than we say "yes"—and for good reason.

If you're a potential customer for a landscaper, for example, you may be saying "no" several times as the landscaper goes over the elements of the proposal he's drawn up for you. You may still eventually want the product, but as a customer, many of us have to feel like we have to say "no" enough times to feel like we have some control in the deal, and to feel good about the transaction.

So when we accept the first "no" we receive from a prospect, and decide that the conversation is over, we're doing many of our customers a disservice by not hanging in there.

Some people are "three-no" people. Others are "five-no" people, "10-no" people, and so on. You'll never know how many "no's" someone could be if you simply accept the first one and move on.

The objective is to maintain a continued conversation with the prospect in a slightly different direction.

**Keep the dialogue going**

If a prospect says, "Business is bad, and I just can't afford it," the account rep should anticipate that objection beforehand, and be prepared with several sound, confident answers to that objection, such as:

- ▶ "It sounds like you know how much they cost. Have you checked out how affordable we've made these seats recently?"

- ▶ "We hear that a lot, and that's why we've put together these very affordable programs with a lot of value attached. Can I share with you what kinds of plans we have available?"

- ▶ "I understand. But if you were to be interested, and knowing money is tight, what sort of price range would you be looking into? Maybe between $___ and $___?" (quoting two dollar figures in the blank spaces)

- ▶ "If it were affordable, would you have any other issues with becoming a season-ticket holder? Is it just the money part?"

- ▶ "We know how tight it is, and that's why we've made the (team name) one of the best sports values in all of (city). Let me share with you what I mean . . . "

These are the kinds of phrases that can continue to move a conversation forward without overly offending the person on the other end.

**It's the words, and how you use them**

The delivery of these phrases is just as important as the words you use.

People want to do business with those who exude confidence, but without sounding cocky or overbearing. If your best response to the "Business is bad" objection is, "What do you mean? Business is great down here," you won't get very far.

On the other hand, no one likes to deal with incompetence. Imagine you being the customer in line at the supermarket on the cashier's first day on the job. It's a slow, frustrating experience, and most of us would rather deal with the person who knows the ropes, who can deal with an item without a price tag, can get us the discounts we're entitled to, and get us in and out quickly.

It's no different in our world. People want someone who can show them the best available options for their needs and budget, and make them feel confident that the choice they're about to make is the best one available. If you sound tentative or unsure, people will use any excuse they can to exit the call—and the easiest excuse in the world today is, "The economy is bad; I can't afford it."

The bottom line is: Don't take the first "no" for an answer, and be ready for every common objection, especially the ones that are coming up most often. There's a sale waiting beyond that first roadblock; have the courage to break through, and your income will soar.

---

## CHAPTER SUMMARY

Objections are a welcomed part of the sales process that allow the seller to learn more about the customer's feelings toward the offer. Objections provide a pathway to educate the customer and sell the benefits of the product. Customers object to a variety of different things, from the team to the experience to the time it takes to engage with the product. Being prepared for the most common types of objections allows the seller to develop effective responses. The first step is to listen to the customer and truly understand what the customer is trying to say. Next, demonstrate empathy to show the customer his or her feelings are understood. The next step is to respond to the objection using one of the methods presented in this chapter. Regardless of the method chosen, be positive and non-confrontational with the customer. Finally, use a trial close or commitment question to confirm that the customer's concern was adequately addressed before returning to the sales process.

## CHAPTER ACTIVITIES

1.  Using the five-step process outlined in Figure 9.1, create a dialogue between you and the customer that:

    a.  overcomes the objection "I don't know my schedule" by rephrasing the objection as a question.

    b.  uses feel-felt-found to overcome the objection "I don't really like basketball all that much."

    c.  uses the compensation method to overcome the objection "This package is awfully expensive for a business our size."

2.  Explain how salespeople can turn an objection into an opportunity to sell the benefits of the product.

3.  Assume you are selling in a full menu marketing environment for a minor league baseball team. Craft a response for the "My Schedule is Busy" objection using six of the approaches to overcoming objections outlined in this chapter.

4.  Using a sales scenario given to you by your professor, create a video recording where you respond to the following objections:

    a.  We're a small company with only 10 employees, so we really don't have a need for season tickets.

    b.  There are too many home games in a half-season package. Our family is too busy to go to that many games, so we just buy on the day of the game.

# CHAPTER COMPETENCY ASSESSMENT[3]

## COMPETENCY DOMAIN: OVERCOMING OBJECTIONS

*Exemplary:* Consistently does all or almost all of the following:

- ► Welcomes customer objections as an opportunity to move the sale forward by displaying empathy and asking the right questions to clarify the objection
- ► Uses objections to gather additional information about the customer
- ► Is able to educate the customer or offer a solution that overcomes the objection after gathering the appropriate information
- ► Confirms with customer that all objections have been addressed before moving forward
- ► Remains persistent when facing an objection or stall from the customer
- ► Passionately advocates for the product facing objections with confidence

*Skilled:* Does most of the following:

- ► Welcomes customer objections as an opportunity to move the sale forward by displaying empathy and asking the right questions to clarify the objection
- ► Uses objections to gather additional information about the customer
- ► Is able to educate the customer or offer a solution that overcomes the objection after gathering the appropriate information
- ► Confirms with customer that all objections have been addressed before moving forward
- ► Remains persistent when facing an objection or stall from the customer
- ► Passionately advocates for the product facing objections with confidence

*Adequate:* Does most of the following:

- ► Gives up on the call after the second or third objection
- ► Becomes or sounds defensive when customers have an objection
- ► Misses cues in the conversation that the customer has an unstated objection
- ► Recognizes there is an objection, but is unable to identify the true nature of the objection
- ► Rushes to educate the customer without first asking questions to clarify the objection or utilize empathy or social proof to set up the solution

*Novice:* Consistently does all or almost all of the following:

- ► Gives up on the call at the first sign of resistance from the customer
- ► Becomes or sounds defensive when customer has an objection
- ► Fails to recognize objections when they occur
- ► Fails to show empathy or ask questions to further clarify objections
- ► Attempts to disprove the customer rather than focusing on a solution

---

3. From "Competency Assessment for Entry-Level Sport Ticket Sales Professionals" by David Pierce and Richard Irwin, *Journal of Applied Sport Management,* Volume 8 (2), Summer 2016. Reprinted by permission of Sagamore Publishing. www.sagamorepub.com

# CHAPTER 10

## OBTAINING COMMITMENT

**LEARNING OBJECTIVES**

After completing this chapter, you should be able to:

- ► Distinguish between manipulative and ethical closing methods.
- ► Recognize buying signals.
- ► Recognize when it is time to close during a sales call.
- ► Apply closing methods to obtain commitment.
- ► Illustrate how to create a sense of urgency in the sales call.
- ► Explain strategies for maximizing each sale.
- ► Discuss the keys to obtaining commitment from prospects.

**KEY TERMS**

| | | |
|---|---|---|
| Assumptive close | Continuous yes close | Negotiation close |
| Balance sheet close | Cross-selling | Purchase requirements |
| Benefit-in-waiting close | Direct request close | Standing-room only close |
| Benefit summary close | Fear close | Upselling |
| Buying signals | Legitimate alternative | |
| Closing | choice close | |

**COMPENTENCIES**

- ► Ability to confirm specific next steps with the customer (in the event there was not a sale).
- ► Ability to recognize customer buying signals.
- ► Ability to close the sale.
- ► Ability to maximize each sale by upselling.
- ► Ability to ask for and obtain referrals.

## CHAPTER OVERVIEW

Closing has often been shrouded in mystique, as evidenced by the hundreds of books, videos, seminars, and blog posts devoted to the topic of how to make a customer say *yes*. The image of pushy salespeople manipulating customers through sleight of hand techniques into decisions they don't want to make is probably the part of the sales process that people find most uncomfortable. Manipulation techniques are designed to reduce or eliminate choice because the salesperson is trying to sell a product or service the customer does not need.

In reality, if the client understands how the offering can fulfill a customer's needs, there is no need to engage in manipulative tactics that pressure and deceive the customer. These tactics are ineffective because persistent pressure does not help close a customer who has not uncovered a need or still has unresolved issues or objections. A customer not yet sold on the solution the seller has to offer is not going to be pushed or manipulated into buying. Manipulative tactics damage trust and risk losing the sale. The right mindset to have toward closing is that closing is a mutual experience that the seller has with the prospect, not something the seller does to the prospect.

Every sales call has three possible outcomes. First, the call can result in a "no" from the customer, with no follow-up, meaning the customer is definitely not going to purchase. Second, the call could result in an objection or a stall, where the customer is still considering the seller's proposal. In this case, it is important to establish the next steps that will guide the future of the conversation. Third, the call or meeting can result in a sale. This chapter will address when to close the sale, how to recognize positive buying signals from the customer, six common methods for closing the sale, how to successfully obtain commitment, what steps the seller should take if commitment is obtained from the customer, how to maximize the sale through upselling and referrals, and what to do if the customer decides to not purchase.

## CLOSING—ASKING FOR THE CUSTOMER'S BUSINESS

**CLOSING**
the process of asking for the customer's business

**Closing** is the process of asking for the customer's business. It should be viewed as a natural outcome of the value building process. Closing is not a unique event in and of itself, but rather a natural continuation of a well-orchestrated sales process. It is the logical, natural result of the sales process where the seller had helped someone make a decision that will benefit him or her. Assuming the seller has developed rapport, uncovered needs, articulated a relevant and customized value proposition, overcome objections, and communicated the sales message effectively, then the next logical step is to seek commitment from the customer. In sum, if the salesperson presented value to the customer, the right to ask for the sale has been earned.

Don't think of closing as a one-shot opportunity at the end of the sale. Obtaining commitment actually occurs throughout the entire sales process, such as when the seller sets an appointment, agrees on an agenda, confirms needs, and many other trial close questions. Closing occurs at all points during the sales cycle. Every time the seller asks for agreement, a commitment, or a decision, the seller is closing. These smaller commitments help the seller test agreement and pace the conversation toward the final close. Every time the prospect makes a commitment it brings the salesperson one step closer to closing the sale.

The likelihood of closing a sale depends on the extent to which the seller has developed rapport, helped the customer uncover needs, and confirmed the value proposition of the offering. The

## Figure 10.1

### Likelihood of Closing the Sale

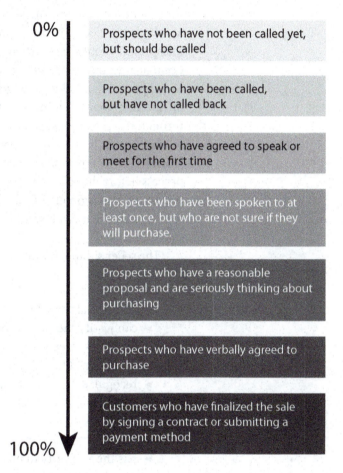

likelihood of closing the sale can be visualized along a continuum from prospects who have been contacted to those who have signed a contract or given their credit card information (see Figure 10.1). It may take multiple phone calls and in-person meetings to advance along this continuum, while in other instances it may take just one phone call to close a sale. In general, the more significant the investment of time and money by people or businesses, the longer it will take the seller to move along the continuum. While each sales interaction is unique and depends on a variety of factors, the goal throughout the sales interaction is to move the customer along the continuum toward a positive purchase decision. However, it is important to recognize that a quick decision not to purchase is just as important because it allows the salesperson to spend valuable time on other prospects who have a greater likelihood of buying.

# WHEN TO CLOSE

On occasion the salesperson will get lucky and the customer will approach the seller about closing the sale, but in most cases the salesperson will need to initiate the close with the customer. Ultimately, each sale is unique and the salesperson should close when the customer seems ready to buy, which can occur at any point in the sales conversation. The close doesn't necessarily have to happen at the end of a long sales process. The decision to close is based on the customer's readiness to buy, not the salesperson's ability to make it through the entire presentation. When the customer gives the seller positive buying signals and expresses value in buying, it's time to ask for the order. However, it is important to keep in mind that closing too early in the sales process before the seller has uncovered relevant needs and developed rapport will result in customer resistance. Equally important is not waiting too long to close because it can result in the customer talking him or herself out of the sale.

The seller should ask for the sale when the prospect

- ► agrees there is a need;
- ► agrees that the offering will meet their needs;
- ► can justify the value proposition;
- ► expresses interest;
- ► is comfortable with the decision;
- ► recognizes a sense of urgency;
- ► responds favorably after the seller has overcome an important objection;
- ► gives a strong buying signal; and
- ► has the authority to buy.

Missing any of the components above could yield another objection and result in not closing the sale. Think of these items as signposts that the customer is ready to buy.

Salespeople must pay attention to buying signals at all times during the sales process. **Buying signals** are nonverbal and verbal indications that the customer is ready to buy. The nonverbal signals are similar to the positive nonverbal cues presented in Chapter 11. For example, positive gestures and expressions from a relaxed and friendly customer indicate it may be time to close. In addition, what the customer says gives the seller a strong indication of whether or not they are ready to buy. Customers show strong verbal buying signals by asking questions, providing purchase requirements, giving positive

**BUYING SIGNALS**
nonverbal and verbal indications that the customer is ready to buy

feedback, and positively answering trial closes. When the seller spots strong buying signals, even if they occur early in the sale, the seller should ask for the sale.

▶ *Asking questions.* Not all questions signal a readiness to buy, but when customers become more engaged in the conversation, they have a tendency to ask more questions.
  — How does this process work again?
  — So we don't have to buy all the tickets we put on hold?
  — Can you explain how I can transfer my tickets to friends?
  — How soon would I be able to start?

▶ *Providing purchase requirements.* **Purchase requirements** are conditions that have to be satisfied before a purchase can take place. These statements demonstrate a readiness to buy because they are related to how the purchase will be finalized. In other words, the customer is concerned with how the seller is going to work out the details.
  — The only way this will work is if I can make monthly payments.
  — We're going to need to pick the tickets up at will call.
  — We can make this work, but only if we can start at the first of the year.

**PURCHASE REQUIREMENTS** conditions that have to be satisfied before a purchase can take place

▶ *Giving positive feedback.* Positive feedback about the product indicates strong feelings toward making a purchase.
  — I like the flexibility available in that package.
  — Having the 15% discount will really help out our group leader.
  — I think this is a better deal than the packages offered by the Tigers.

▶ *Answering trial closes positively.* As discussed in Chapter 7, the seller can use trial closes throughout the sales conversation to test the customer's agreement on opinions, gain agreement on minor points, and to assess the customer's readiness to buy.
  — Salesperson: How does that sound? Customer: That is really going to work for us.
  — Salesperson: What else do you need to know? Customer: That's about it—I think the proposal makes sense.

©iQoncept/Shutterstock.com

## CREATING A SENSE OF URGENCY

Sellers should always be looking for ways to use scarcity to create a sense of urgency. Recall from Chapter 4 that the scarcity principle suggests people often want what they can't have. If something is rare or becoming rare, it becomes more valuable. The sport product yields itself to the ethical use of urgency because every stadium and seating section has a seating capacity, and every game has a date on which it is played. Because the salesperson can't sell more tickets than capacity for the stadium or seating section, and a ticket to a game played yesterday is useless, urgency is an important closing tool that should be ethically and honestly employed when trying to close the sale. The use of scarcity, done in an ethical manner, is a strategy that helps the seller nudge indecisive customers toward making a decision. Making statements of fact that create urgency should be used throughout the call and not necessarily relegated to when it's time to close the sale.

Using urgency fits a consultative sales philosophy because it helps customers make an informed decision as to how to get the best possible seats to the games or packages they want. Viewed in this light, the seller has important information the customer needs to make an informed decision. Such information includes:

▶ The number of sellouts in recent seasons (we sold out 75% of our games in the summer last season, so I recommend getting signed up now to guarantee your seat).

▶ The number of seats left in specific seating sections (we only have a handful of tickets left in the lower bowl where you'll be closest to the action).

Duane Haring, Director of Ticket Sales and Service for the Cincinnati Bengals, trains his sales staff to say "*I can't get you a better seat tomorrow than I can today*" because it is always a true statement. The pricing strategies discussed in Chapter 3 are also important ways to create urgency for the sales staff. For example, creating exclusive events for people who buy tickets before a certain date gives them a reason to buy now rather than wait until later. Periodic price increases on certain dates also help sellers create a sense of urgency. For example:

▶ Registration deadlines to qualify for price discounts or access to certain benefits (you need to get signed up by October 1 to attend the season ticket holder party).

▶ Dates for price increases (the price goes up $20 starting next Tuesday).

Creating urgency also helps the salesperson leverage the power of social proof. Inherent in any discussion about sellouts and how many tickets have been sold is the message that other people are buying tickets too. Urgency can also help the seller build rapport and credibility because he or she is providing customers information they would not have otherwise obtained. Beyond this, urgency can help the seller paint a picture that the customer is special and the seller doesn't want him or her to be left out. Urgency statements are statements of fact that provide the customer with the information they need. But urgency statements are strengthened further when tied to the reason why the customer wants to attend the event. For example,

▶ Tickets in the reserved pavilion area sell faster than any other area, so I would recommend getting in those orders by the end of the week so we can get the best seats for your company to entertain clients.
▶ We had 20 sellouts last year. I would hate for you to come all the way out to the ballpark with your family and find out at the box office that we don't have any more tickets for the game.
▶ We're down to 16 days before Opening Day, so if you're going to be able to use the free Opening Day tickets that come with the 12-game mini-plan, we'll need to get confirmation of your order by next Thursday so you can start to enjoy all of the benefits of being a season ticket holder.
▶ We sold over 95% of the Concourse Suites last year, which is why I am giving you a call before the season starts so we can get our most valued clients the best games possible.
▶ Coming off last season's success, people are really excited about the team this year. Ticket sales are really strong this year, and I want to be sure we are able to get you in the seating section you want.

Finally, sellers can create urgency for buyers on the fence who want to delay making a decision using the "You/I can, but" technique, which allows sellers to explain why purchasing now is a better decision.[1] This technique is illustrated in Table 10.1.

1. Long, G. *Encourage urgency in your sales staff*. Retrieved from http://ticketingtoday.com/encourage-urgency-in-your-ticket-sales-staff/

## Table 10.1

**You Can, But...**

| Customer | Salesperson |
|---|---|
| I am going to wait until later in the season to get that mini-plan. | Sure, **you can** purchase this package anytime during the season, **but** what you won't be able to do is get these great seats we are talking about right now next week or next month. I'd be doing you a disservice if I didn't tell you that today. |
| Let me check with my husband and call back in a few days. | **You could, but** we may not be able to get you the seats you really want. If we can get your credit card now we can hold the seats for you. |
| The season is still over a month away, so I'll wait and get my tickets closer to Opening Day. | **You could, but** if you wait the price will increase on April 1 and you will miss our season ticket holder party. |

**STANDING-ROOM ONLY CLOSE**
manipulative closing technique that uses urgency in an unethical manner by making false claims about product availability, prices, and deadlines

Using scarcity to create a sense of urgency is an essential skill. Unfortunately, salespeople have historically used urgency in an unethical manner by making false claims about product availability, prices, and deadlines, called the standing-room only close. The most likely way the seller will come across as a pushy salesperson is through the unethical use of urgency, so urgency must be used with extreme care. Examples of the **standing-room only close** include:

- ▶ If you can't decide now, I'll have to offer this to another customer.
- ▶ These prices are only good until tomorrow.
- ▶ Once you leave this meeting, this offer won't be available.
- ▶ The price will increase if you don't buy today.

## CLOSING METHODS

Creating a sense of urgency is an important tool that can help the seller advance the sale toward a decision, but only if it is done in an honest manner. Sellers doesn't need to use manipulative closing techniques in order to be successful at closing sales. Unfortunately, the traditional, product-focused closing techniques have given closing a negative perception because these techniques are aimed at getting customers to make a purchase even if they don't want to. The good news is that there are non-manipulative ways to close the sale so the customer can benefit from the package or offering. The purpose of learning these methods is to nudge a qualified and willing prospect to a decision that will benefit him or her in a straightforward and honest manner. Within each method, manipulative or deceptive sales "tricks" are also addressed, just like the standing-room only close described above. Successful salespeople learn different approaches to closing the sale because the context of each sale will be different based on the attitude and personality of the customer, the product being sold, and the relationship that the seller has previously been able to develop with the customer. Mastering these closing techniques and knowing when to use them takes practice and improves over time.

## Direct Request

Ostensibly the simplest method of obtaining commitment is to ask the customer for the sale. This **direct request close** is particularly effective when the customer is communicating strong buying signals or when working with those who like to get down to business right away. Assuming the salesperson has confirmed the value proposition with the customer, the salesperson can be confident in asking for the sale. It should go without saying that if this approach is used before the seller has helped the customer uncover needs or problems, it will be met with resistance. Examples include:

**DIRECT REQUEST CLOSE**
asking the customer for the sale in a straightforward manner

- ▶ It sounds like you're ready to get signed up for this year. Let's go ahead and get your order in so you can get the best seats.
- ▶ If you don't have any more questions, I think it sounds like we're ready to get this deal started. What do you think?
- ▶ Tom, I'd really like to get the ball rolling today so we can get all of your signage printed before the first game.

## Benefit Summary

The **benefit summary close** focuses on the most relevant features and benefits the prospect agreed to earlier in the conversation. Effective salespeople keep track of these important points discussed in the call so they can be emphasized when it's time to close. The goal is to help the customer synthesize all of the key points already discussed in the conversation. The summary of benefits close is a closing method that can be used in nearly any situation. Examples include:

**BENEFIT SUMMARY CLOSE**
closing strategy summarizing the most relevant features and benefits that the prospect has agreed to earlier in the conversation

- ▶ Based on what we've talked about today, it has become clear that you are looking for a technology solution that will help you be more efficient in recruiting and managing volunteers for the 35 different events that you organize each year. We also discussed how you will need training and follow-up support to make sure that implementation goes smoothly. Is that right? (Decision-maker agrees.) Based on your timetable for the upcoming year, let's go ahead and get the order placed so we can begin training Nancy on how to use the software.

▶ Sarah, based on what you've told me, it sounds like you are looking to do something different and fun for Jackson's birthday this year. Is that right? (Parent agrees.) I would recommend that you get signed up for our birthday package because it will provide you with a really unique way to host a party with all of his friends. Plus, you'll receive a birthday cake and a significant discount on each ticket compared to buying them at the box office.

### Balance Sheet

**BALANCE SHEET CLOSE** closing strategy using a visual to compare the advantages and disadvantages of buying

Assuming the seller is in a face-to-face setting, another way to approach the summary close is to create a hand-drawn visual aid known as the **balance sheet** to help the customer visualize how the advantages of buying outweigh the disadvantages. In front of the customer, on the top of a sheet of paper draw a large "T" and then write the headings "Reasons for Buying" on the top left and "Reasons for not buying" on the top right (see Table 10.2). This visual aid allows the salesperson to summarize the benefits accepted in the left column and use the right column to uncover objections that may prevent the prospect from purchasing. Obviously this approach will not work if there are fewer reasons to buy than to not buy.

**FEAR CLOSE** unethical closing technique emphasizing that something negative might occur if the customer does not purchase

While it should go without saying, fear should never be listed in "reasons for buying" in the balance sheet. In the **fear close**, the salesperson emphasizes something negative that might occur if the customer does not purchase. For example, telling a cyclist they will risk serious injury if they don't purchase a certain type of bicycle is unethical and manipulative.

### Table 10.2

**Balance Sheet Close**

| Reasons for Buying | Reasons for Not Buying |
|---|---|
| ▶ Associate with respected organization in town | ▶ Significant increase in our marketing budget |
| ▶ Reach most important target markets as a captive audience | ▶ Not in the right budget cycle |
| ▶ Use of the team's logo in marketing materials | |
| ▶ Directly measurable results to assess return on investment | |

## Questions

After the seller has convinced the prospect that the product or service discussed can benefit them, sales guru Zig Ziglar recommends using the "three questions close" to close the sale.[2]

- ► Can you see where this would [insert benefit or value proposition]?
- ► Are you interested in [experiencing benefit or value proposition]?
- ► If you were ever going to start [experiencing benefit or value proposition], when do you think would be the best time to start?

Questions can also be used in the event that the first closing attempt is unsuccessful. It may be beneficial for the salesperson to ask additional questions to uncover what is causing the customer to hesitate. The approach here is similar to the series of questions approach presented in Chapter 9. Examples include:

- ► Jessica, do you mind if I ask why you are reluctant to move forward with this idea?
- ► Tom, there must be some reason why you are hesitant to meet with me. Do you mind if I ask what it is?
- ► Is there anything besides the price that is preventing you from getting signed up today?

Once the answers are received to these questions, the seller can return to the selling cycle. This examples illustrates the non-linear process that occurs within the sales cycle.

Another approach that uses questions is the **continuous yes close** where the salesperson asks questions that are logically answered "yes" by the customer. The hope is that because the customer is so conditioned to say yes, the natural response will be "yes" when the salesperson goes to ask for the sale. While it is based in Cialdini's concept of consistency and self-perception theory, salespeople should be careful with the continuous yes close because it may be perceived as manipulative by perceptive customers. However, it is important to keep in mind that asking questions to confirm benefits throughout the conversation is a helpful tool to build a solid value proposition for the customer. The key is to ensure the questions being asked are unique to that specific sales call, and not asked from a scripted set of questions designed to manipulate the customer.

**CONTINUOUS YES CLOSE**
the salesperson asks questions that are logically answered "yes" by the customer

---

2.  Ziglar, Z. (2006). *Secrets of closing the sale.* Grand Rapids, MI: Revell.

## Legitimate Alternative Choice

**LEGITIMATE ALTERNATIVE CHOICE CLOSE**
tests agreement by presenting the prospect with a choice between viable purchase options

The **legitimate alternative choice close** tests agreement by presenting the prospect with a choice between viable purchase options. For example, a salesperson selling mini-ticket plans might ask a qualified prospect, *Which works best for you? The 12- or 18-game mini-plan?* Or, a salesperson might ask, *Would you prefer your tickets on the East side or the West side?* The choice presented should be between two viable options, and not a choice between buying and not buying. There are two possible results from asking the question. First, the seller might receive a positive response and commitment. In this case, the seller can move to close the sale. The second possibility is that the customer shows some hesitation, which leads to a new objection that can be uncovered. Either way, the seller has learned important information about the prospect.

It is important to emphasize that the legitimate choice approach does not assume that the customer is going to make the purchase. Traditional sales approaches assume that the customer is going to make the purchase, and this is perceived by some as manipulative and not effective for building a strong long-term relationship. The **assumptive close** is phrased as a statement and matched by nonverbal cues such as starting to complete an order form or setting up paperwork. In contrast, the legitimate alternative close is phrased in the form of a question, which means customers have a range of ways in which they can answer without becoming defensive. While the assumptive close carries risk, it is worth noting that the seller's general attitude during the entire sales process should be positive and the seller should operate under the assumption that the prospect will ultimately purchase. Without this attitude, working in sales could become discouraging.

**ASSUMPTIVE CLOSE**
phrased as a statement and is matched by nonverbal cues such as starting to complete an order form or setting up paperwork

## Negotiation

**NEGOTIATION CLOSE**
attempts to find a fair deal with which the customer and salesperson can be content

There is some element of negotiation in every sales transaction. While price and value tend to be the most common issues of negotiation in which a customer will demand concessions from the salesperson, other issues may arise like service, time commitment, weather, and other situational factors. The **negotiation close** attempts to find a fair deal with which the customer and salesperson can be content. This approach shows concern for the customer's opinion and a genuine willingness to help the customer. Examples include:

- ▶ I'll tell you what, if there was a way that I could guarantee you that you won't sit behind the rowdy student section, would you be onboard for season tickets again this year?
- ▶ What about if we compromise on this a little bit. I don't have the flexibility to give you a discount on the six-pack of tennis lessons, but I can let you pay in three installments instead of paying for all of the lessons up-front.

▶ Unfortunately, you can't pick your own games in the 12-game mini-plan, but I can go ahead and get your tickets reserved to ensure the best seat location, and give you another three weeks to select the package you want.

It is important to note that the **benefit-in-waiting close,** or offering additional benefits or discounts, is not a part of the negotiation close. Offering new benefits or discounts is a manipulative strategy because it leaves the customer wondering if they would have overpaid had they bought earlier in the sales cycle. In addition, the customer may realize that by holding out even longer they might receive additional benefits.

**BENEFIT-IN-WAITING CLOSE**
unethical closing technique that offers the customer additional benefits or discounts after the initial offer has been presented.

## HOW TO SUCCESSFULLY OBTAIN COMMITMENT

There are key principles that the seller needs to follow regardless of the choice of closing method. These principles include:

▶ Make the right recommendation
▶ Be quiet
▶ Overcome the fear of closing
▶ Be positive
▶ Be persistent
▶ Be assertive without being aggressive

## Figure 10.2

**Obtaining Commitment**

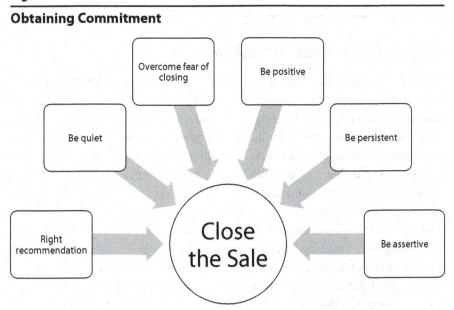

## *Make the Right Recommendation*

All of the legwork done up to this point in the sale should point the seller to an appropriate, customized recommendation for the prospect. However, failure to conduct enough research on the prospect, ask the right questions, uncover relevant needs, overcome objections, and sell the right solutions will likely lead to a "no" regardless of how well the seller executed one of the closing methods. Another mistake is making the wrong recommendation based on the information that has been gathered. For example, as we've noted in other places in the book, inexperienced salespeople have a tendency to sell the cheapest package because it is the package they could afford themselves, instead of considering what makes the most sense for the prospect to achieve their objectives. At the other end of the spectrum is the salesperson who always tries to sell the most expensive packages regardless of what information has been uncovered.

## *Be Quiet*

After using one of the closing methods described above, it can be tempting to continue talking, but it is important to allow the prospect the time to respond to the close. In other words, be quiet after attempting to close the sale. Silence helps the seller actively listen to the customer's answer and prevents talking oneself out of the sale. Silence can be golden.

> Silence is powerful. Salespeople need to be comfortable in silence. He who speaks first will lose.
>
> —Melanie Seiser, *Major League Soccer*

## *Overcome the Fear of Closing*

In order to overcome a fear of closing, the seller first needs to overcome the fear of rejection. It is important to remember that a "no" is not a personal rejection of the seller, but it's simply a decision not to buy today. The customer may say "yes" tomorrow. Second, the seller needs to be comfortable with asking customers to make a decision. The seller's job is to sell, and most people will understand that it's the seller's job to sell. Asking for the order will not alienate the prospect or ruin the seller's chances of getting the sale if the seller has given the prospect enough good reasons to buy and received agreement from them throughout the sale. Sellers can close with confidence and conviction when they are asking the customer to make a good decision. This conviction communicates an urgency and a sincerity that the customer should make a good decision. People tend to delay making purchase decisions if they can, so moving to close the sale simply moves the process along to a decision.

## Be Positive

Showing confidence and passion about the package can rub off on the prospect, just like a negative attitude about job or team can be felt by customers. People want to do business with salespeople who are confident in themselves, their product, and their organization. A positive approach to the seller's job and life in general will carry over into relationships with prospects. The worst thing a seller can do is assume that nobody wants to buy a product because that assumption will become a self-fulfilling prophecy.

## Be Persistent

While sales training methods and approaches differ on exactly how many times a seller should attempt to close the sale, there is universal agreement the seller needs to be persistent in asking for the sale. Walking away from the sale after hearing the first "no" from the prospect is an ineffective strategy. As a general rule in most sales contexts, it is recommended that the seller attempt to close the sale a minimum of three times during the sales call, provided the seller is with a qualified prospect who has a demonstrated need. If the seller is confident in the recommendation, customers are generally not offended by attempts to close the sale. Keep in mind that a "no" is typically accompanied with a reason why the prospect does not want to buy, which means that the seller has uncovered another objection. Assuming the seller can overcome this new objection, it is logical to attempt to close the sale again.

## Be Assertive Without Being Aggressive

While it is important to be persistent, the seller shouldn't be aggressive, but rather assertive. There is clear distinction between being assertive and aggressive. Assertive salespeople are able to convey their point in a nurturing manner and are motivated to satisfy the needs of the customer through the sale of the right package or product for that specific customer. Assertive salespeople build mutually beneficial relationships with customers, tell the truth, and make ethical decisions. In contrast, aggressive salespeople believe they know the customer's needs the best without asking, which leads to pushing the sales message regardless of the customer's actual needs. Aggressive salespeople approach the sales process with the belief that it is the salesperson's job to change the customer's mind as opposed to uncovering needs. Aggressive salespeople utilize manipulative closing approaches in an attempt to deceive the customer because their solution does not benefit the customer. In sum, people respond favorably to assertive, persistent closing, provided the seller has built high trust and rapport and has made recommendations that make sense.

# WHAT TO DO IF THERE IS COMMITMENT

Once the seller has obtained a commitment to purchase from the customer and investigated any referrals or upselling opportunities, the next steps are to confirm the details of the purchase, finalize the sale with a signature or form of payment, educate the customer on how to best leverage the benefits of the purchase, prepare the customer for the transition to the service team (if applicable), and review what will happen next. These steps set the stage for a long-term relationship built on trust and the ability of the organization to follow through on everything that was promised during the sales process. This process should be professional and efficient, because most customers or decision-makers don't want to linger for too long after they have decided to buy. Of course, each situation is different and the attitude and personality of the customer may impact how quickly the seller completes the post-commitment process.

## Figure 10.3

**Steps After the Close**

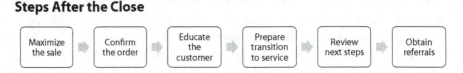

## *Maximize the Sale*

Recent research into sport sales competencies has revealed that leveraging opportunities to maximize sales is the most important competency for the success of ticket salespeople.[3] Upselling and cross-selling are the two ways to maximize the sale and get the customer to spend more money.

**CROSS-SELLING**
involves offering additional products to support or complement the product or package the customer has already decided to purchase

**Cross-selling** involves offering additional products to support or complement the product or package the customer has already decided to purchase. For example, if a customer has already committed to buying a ticket package, cross-selling opportunities include a parking pass, t-shirt, concessions vouchers, souvenirs, collectibles, or any other item that is not included as a benefit of purchasing the plan. An example of cross-selling occurs when you order a sandwich at a fast food restaurant and are asked, *Would you like fries with that?*

3.  Pierce, D., & Irwin, R. (2016). Competency assessment for entry-level sport ticket sales professionals. *Journal of Applied Sport Management, 8*(2), 54–77. Pierce, D., Lee, D., & Petersen, J. (2014). Sport sales personnel perceptions of factors impacting job performance: A factor analysis of sport sales activities. *International Journal of Sport Management, 15*(1), 71–90.

**Upselling** involves persuading a customer to purchase an upgraded version of the same type of product they are intending to buy. An example of upselling occurs when purchasing an electronics device with more storage, faster processing speed, higher quality, or larger size. Typical upselling opportunities in ticket packages include additional games and additional seats. When selling season tickets to corporations, the minimum number of tickets per package is typically four. Sellers utilize social proof and other testimonials to justify the four tickets. Additionally, keep in mind that sport is consumed in social settings, so it's always appropriate to ask if additional tickets are needed to maximize the socialization motive.

Four questions addressed in Chapter 7 help the seller identify the various ways in which a customer can utilize a larger investment of tickets.

▶ Where do you work?
▶ Who is the biggest X fan in your network?
▶ What other groups are you involved with?
▶ What charitable organizations are you involved with?

Being creative and familiar with all of the ways that a customer could utilize tickets is the key to maximizing the sale. Most organizations have lists of ways that customers can utilize their tickets besides attending the game themselves (see Chapter 7). Thus, it is important to understand the customer's need, budget, and decision-making process, just like any other part of the sales process.

The contrast principle can also help sellers maximize the sale. The contrast principle states that when someone experiences two similar things in succession, their perception of the second is influenced by the first.[4] For example, if someone picks up a heavy box prior to picking up a lighter box, the second box will feel lighter than it really is. In a sales setting, the contrast principle dictates it is in the best interest of the salesperson to sell the most expensive items first (e.g., season ticket package) because the add-on items will not seem as expensive in comparison (e.g., parking pass, collectibles, additional tickets). Add-ons should be brought up independently of one another, so that each small price will seem insignificant when compared to the much larger one.

One great opportunity to upsell occurs when the seller has a large number of people who are attending games together. Instead of selling individual game tickets to all of the people in the group, the seller should investigate the possibility of upselling the group into a season ticket package and having the people in the group split the tickets in the package. This allows the group

**UPSELLING**
involves persuading a customer to purchase an upgraded version of the same type of product they are intending to buy

---

4. Cialdini, R. (1993). *Influence: The psychology of persuasion*, 2nd ed. New York: William Morrow.

greater flexibility in how they use their season tickets, but it also provides them with all of the benefits associated with being a season ticket holder. Along the same lines, when the seller has a prospect who is attending individual games in a similar quantity to a season ticket option, the seller should investigate an upsell into a season ticket package because some people are willing to pay a little bit more to have all of the benefits that are included with a season ticket package.

Upselling does not necessarily have to occur after a commitment to purchase has been made. It is fundamentally a part of the needs analysis process, and the information learned from that process should be integrated into the recommendation that the seller makes to the prospect. The point of including cross-selling and upselling at this point is that the seller should not forget to investigate the complementary products and upgraded packages and seats once commitment is earned. This can be done through simple questions such as:

- ▶ Are you sure that two tickets are enough?
- ▶ Do you think you need the 20-game package, or is 12 enough?
- ▶ We talked about sitting in the 200 section. I just wanted to let you know that we still have availability for Section 102 if you want to get down in the lower level.
- ▶ I know your family is really going to love the birthday package. I was looking on our events calendar and saw the Disney on Ice is coming in September. Would that be something you would want to do as well?

---

### KEYS TO MAXIMIZING THE SALE

1. **Identify new ways to use the product**. Get customers thinking beyond the product they just purchased into new ways tickets and experiences can be used.

2. **Remember that people consume sport in social settings**. Would the experience be more entertaining with four friends instead of just two?

3. **Bundle**. Bundle game tickets with other ancillary purchases like parking, concessions, merchandise, and access to premium areas. Product features such as stored credit tickets and all-you-can-eat options can add to the total sale price.

4. **Know your product**. Be able to describe the difference in seating quality between price points. Provide benefits for improving seating quality.

In situations when the seller is renewing a customer or a group for the next year, resist the temptation to take the easy road and book them for the exact same package. Be sure to go through the needs analysis again to determine if anything about their situation has changed that would justify upselling them into more tickets. Jason Cohen, account manager for premium sales with the Washington Nationals, discusses the importance of upselling during the renewal cycle in the following example.

---

**Jason Cohen, Premium Sales Account Manager, Washington Nationals**

### GROUP RENEWAL UPSELL

I had a rep inherit a series of dance related groups that performed a routine on our court in exchange for buying 50 tickets. The previous rep often sold exactly 50 tickets. They never asked how the organizations were structured and asked additional questions about how they market as they had been trained. After we restructured our training, we often uncovered that the group leader not only could market to the parents of the dancers but also other parents that might want to enjoy the routine/game entertainment while saving money, plus they often had other groups within the same business such as gymnastics. When we would suggest would they want to open it up to these other audiences, every time their answer would be, "sure why not?" We would then ask if they wanted to turn it into a fundraiser. Often they would say yes and then be motivated to aggressively market. The end result was many of these 50 ticket sales turned into 100–200 ticket sales.

© Kendall Hunt Publishing Company

---

## Confirm the Order

The last step before accepting payment or getting a signature is to confirm the details of the order with the customer. First, congratulate the customer on their purchase on reassure them they will benefit from the product to reduce any insecurity or buyer's remorse. Second, get confirmation on the exact purchase details, such as how many games, which games, and how many tickets. This step ensures the customer receives exactly what they purchased. For example: *Your employees are really going to love the Treetop Suites. I'll get you booked for 25 tickets on July 15.*

Once the order has been confirmed with the customer, secure the customer's signature or form of payment (i.e., cash, check, credit card). Order forms should be accessible so the customer can complete any necessary paperwork. At this point the seller will reveal the final price to be paid and discuss any terms and conditions of collecting and processing the payment.

### Educate the Customer

The extent to which customers are satisfied with the product is partially dependent on whether they enjoyed the benefits of their purchase. Previously, we discussed the importance of eduselling to help customers become aware of, utilize, and then fully maximize the benefits of their purchase. The moment after a sale has been completed is an optimal time to educate the customer on the important information they need to know to leverage benefits of the purchase. For example, if a customer just purchased a season golf pass, then the salesperson should remind the customer how to make tee times, how to negotiate any restrictions that might exist on when they can play, how to access discounts on equipment and food/beverage, how to book golf lessons, etc. In the sale of premium seats to corporations, it is important that the seller begins to lay out the steps the company should take to order food for their suite, or the details of any pre-season suite holder parties prior to the start of the season. In sum, the benefits discussed at this stage relate directly to those features and benefits that were relevant in the preceding sales discussion.

### Prepare for Transition to Service

It is important for the salesperson to prepare the customer for the transition to the service team by informing the customer who their service rep will be for the upcoming season. The customer needs to know what to expect from the service rep, the service rep's role for the upcoming season, and how to contact that person. The season ticket holder will also need to know where and how to access any important season ticket holder service information online.

### Review Next Steps

The salesperson needs to review what will happen next with the customer. Information such as delivery dates and distribution method are important for customers to be aware of so they can access the product. For example, if a customer purchases a season ticket package three days before the first game of the season, the salesperson should inform the customer they can pick up the tickets to their first game at will call or explain that all tickets can be accessed online through a mobile device. In this case, the salesperson needs to explain to the customer how to access the tickets in this manner to prevent the customer from becoming frustrated when they are unable to access the benefits of their purchase.

### *Obtain Referrals*

Another way to maximize the sale is to obtain referrals from a customer who just purchased. Instead of looking to the CRM system or hoping for a better leads list, think of the hottest lead as the customer with whom a high trust relationship has just been developed. According to Duane Haring, relationship building is the foundation of maximizing the sale: "You won't get any referrals or upsell many clients if they don't relate to and trust you. Building a strong relationship for the long haul with a client will yield many more referral and upselling opportunities over the life of that customer." However, some salespeople fail to seize the opportunity even though asking for referrals is a simple process. According to Jason Cohen, "Some salespeople don't prioritize asking for referrals and upselling and prefer to choose the path of least resistance."[5] Another sales manager has commented, "Referrals would seemingly be a pretty easy thing to train, but it never seems to sink in no matter what team I'm at."[6]

> You won't get any referrals or upsell many clients if they don't relate to and trust you. Building a strong relationship for the long haul with a client will yield many more referral and upselling opportunities over the life of that customer.
>
> —Duane Haring,
> *Cincinnati Bengals*

Use the answers to the cross-selling questions and other information gleaned in the needs analysis to ask specific questions that focus the customer's thinking to specific people who might also benefit from purchasing. Avoid asking generic questions like, *Who else might be interested?* A better question would be, *Who else do you know in your office that could benefit as well?* Other common areas that customers will provide the seller with information include youth sports teams, coworkers, neighborhood, nonprofit organizations, religious organizations, and affinity groups. Sellers ask more relevant referral questions when they can put themselves into the customer's shoes. Another strategy is to use social media to identify who else might be a part of a customer's personal or social network.

## WHAT TO DO IF COMMITMENT IS NOT OBTAINED

Of course, the possibility exists that the seller's hard work does not result in a sale. If the seller is unable to close the deal, the following actions should be taken:

- ▶ Establish next steps
- ▶ Deal well with rejection

5.  Pierce, D. (2014). *Who's your hottest lead? How to leverage post-sale opportunities.* Retrieved from http://baylors3.com/leveraging-post-sale-opportunities/

6.  Pierce, D., & Irwin, R. (2016). Competency assessment for entry-level sport ticket sales professionals. *Journal of Applied Sport Management, 8*(2), 54–77.

- ▶ Never take it personal
- ▶ Realize that a no today may not be a no tomorrow
- ▶ Leave things on a positive note
- ▶ Remember that sales is a numbers game
- ▶ Obtain referrals

### Establish Next Steps

In some cases, the customer is not ready to buy, but is still considering the proposal. In this case, establish the next steps that will occur in the sales cycle. The key to establishing next steps is to be specific with what actions the customer should take before the next call or meeting. Take the initiative to make the phone call to the customer using the guidelines in Chapter 6 for setting the day, time, and location for the next call or meeting. Even for products with a fairly simple sales cycle, like Inside Sales calls to consumers for ticket packages, it may take three or four calls to finalize the sale.

### Deal With Rejection

However, in other cases, despite the seller's best efforts, there are times when the customer will decide to not buy, signaling the end of the sales process for the present time. When this happens on the first prospecting call, it is a good thing because it opens valuable time on more qualified prospects. However, there are times when the seller has had several meetings or calls with qualified prospects who still decide to not buy. Dealing with rejection is an important skill in sales because it will occur often, even for the best salespeople. Without the ability to deal with rejection, sales can become a defeating job.

### Don't Take It Personally

Remember, there is a difference between self-worth and performance. A prospect's decision to not buy is not an attack or an indictment on the seller as a person. Even when the seller has done everything right in the sales process, the prospect might not be able to close the deal due to budget constraints, bad timing, or other people or committees that had a say in the final decision. There are many factors outside of the seller's control when it comes to the decision made by the customer. Thus, the seller should not take the decision personally. A sense of self-worth should not be determined by what a customer does or fails to do. Nobody should make sellers feel inferior without their permission.[7] The goal at the end of every sales call should

---

7. Johnston, M., & Marshall, G. (2013). *Salesforce management,* 11th ed. New York: Routledge.

be to walk away thinking everything possible was done to make the sale. Salespeople should focus on what can be controlled instead of what can't be controlled.

## No May Not Mean No Forever

The "no" received today can still result in a "yes" at some point in the future. Just because a prospect declines the initial proposal doesn't mean there isn't an opportunity to sell to them in the future. The rejection may be temporary. Circumstances may change in the future that alter the prospect's situation and needs. Use the CRM system or an organized filing system to keep all notes on the prospect so it's easy to recall the important information from the previous sales cycle when the sales conversation is reinstated in the future.

## Leave on a Positive Note

Because there is always a possibility for a sale in the future, leave the conversation on a positive note. Thank the prospect for their time and for considering the decision. Offer to keep open lines of communication at the conclusion of the sales process. This can be done by offering a business card, connecting through social media, or confirming that the prospect would be willing to be contacted six months to a year down the road.

## Obtain Referrals

Earlier in the chapter we discussed the importance of obtaining referrals from customers who just purchased. Referrals can also be solicited from customers who did not buy, especially when the seller was able to generate rapport through the sales cycle. Inexperienced salespeople tend to find asking for referrals from a customer who didn't purchase to be uncomfortable, but they are missing an opportunity to find qualified leads and begin that conversation with a warm introduction.

---

**Thomas P. Reilly,** *Selling Power Magazine*

### HANDLING REJECTION

How well do you handle the feelings of rejection that accompany failure? If your answer is "not well," all is not lost. You can develop strategies that enable you to cope more effectively with the emotional trauma you experience when your objectives are not realized.

Rejection has been defined as accepting someone else's opinion that you are worthless. Eleanor Roosevelt once said that no one can harm you without your permission. There are a handful of professions that offer unlimited opportunities to get rejected. Selling is one.

After muddling through the initial job-hunt rejection, the salesperson gets rejected in a number of ways. Weary prospects are reluctant to meet with unknown salespeople and use a variety of excuses to avoid them. Overprotective secretaries and receptionists are often so skilled at evasion tactics that they dissuade even the most persistent salespeople.

Assuming we penetrate these first two lines of resistance, there are still many ways in which the salesperson gets rejected: "Your price is too high!" "I want to think about it!" "I'm happy the way things are!" "I don't see any need to change!"

All of the above represent potential rejection situations for the salesperson. When these are coupled with feelings of alienation from his or her company and peers because the salesperson is not meeting the sales quota, the potential for emotional crisis exists. How these potential crisis situations are met determines the likelihood of one's sales success.

Proactive salespeople understand rejection and handle it well. They have a greater chance at a longer and more productive sales career. Proactive salespeople have developed a healthy personal philosophy about rejection. They know that they will enjoy making a sale.

Conversely, they accept that they will feel an appropriate amount of disappointment when they do not sell. They do not accept that "phony macho image" that it does not hurt. Proactive salespeople are realistic. It is this focus on reality that permits them to persevere in the face of disappointment.

Proactive salespeople have a variety of methods for dealing with rejection. They are able to divorce their egos from the sale. They understand the difference between performance failure and self-worth. The self-esteem comes from healthy self-respect as worthwhile people.

Consequently, they do not engage in distorted self-talk such as "I'm no good because I missed that sale!" or "I'm really worthless today—I haven't sold a thing!" A proactive salesperson will skip this step and perform a situation analysis to determine what went wrong.

Another strategy is a "leveling technique" in which the salesperson examines the rejection situation and might use more positive self-talk like "How can they be rejecting me as an individual—they don't even know me!" Someone once said, "If we could read the secret history of another person, we would find enough pain, sorrow and hurt on the pages of that diary to disarm all hostility toward that person."

Proactive salespeople believe this and perceive the other person accordingly. Proactive salespeople allow an appropriate amount of disappointment if it is due. If you have worked hard on a proposal and lose the business, you are going to feel disappointment. Try to moderate the emotion by asking yourself how much misery it really deserves.

Another proactive strategy for dealing with rejection is to plant a lot of seeds. Salespeople who generate a lot of activity have very little time to mourn over one piece of business that is lost.

Because proactive salespeople positively anticipate rejection, they are never overwhelmed by it. They know they will get rejected because it is part of the game. They expect it, but do not create it.

Positively anticipating rejection means giving thought in advance to how one should handle it or which response method to use.

Proactive salespeople do not rationalize. However, they recognize that there may be other variables to consider which may prevent the salesperson from writing the order. It is very possible that the timing is inappropriate for the sale to happen. Budget constraints or shared decision authority can create legitimate delays. It is imperative that the salesperson correctly perceive this reality which places the salesperson in a tenuous position.

Below is a summary of proactive strategies for dealing with rejection:

1. Divorce your ego from the sale—the prospect is not attacking you personally!

2. Remember that this "intimidating" individual you are facing may have a lot of problems that are creating this facade.

3. Do not automatically assume that the problem is on your end.

4. Plant a lot of seeds!

5. Admit to yourself that not buying could be a rational business decision at this time.

6. Positively anticipate rejection so you are not overwhelmed by it.

7. Watch out for distorted self-talk where your worth as a human being is associated with your success as a salesperson.

The results of handling rejection well are obvious. You are happier, feel better about yourself, and are more productive. Time is not wasted in self-indulged pity.

Perhaps the best way to remain on course is to take this advice I once read in an article written by a psychiatrist: Give your failure the minimal amount of attention it deserves, and keep on trying.

--------

http://www.sellingpower.com/content/article/index.php?a=8531/salespeople-develop-the-means-to-handle-rejection. Reprinted with permission from *Selling Power* magazine.

## CHAPTER SUMMARY

The process of obtaining commitment from the customer is simply the natural outcome of a well-orchestrated sales process. Once the seller has built value in the mind of the customer and recognized buying signals, all that remains is to ask for the sale. While there are several different methods for getting customers to agree to make a purchase, all salespeople need to learn to ethically interject scarcity into the conversation to spur a customer to action. Don't be afraid to be persistent and assertive during this phase of the sales call, assuming the seller has determined the right need and established value. It may take several attempts or approaches before coming to an agreement with the prospect. It is also important to maximize each sales opportunity through cross-selling, upselling, and acquiring referrals. When a sale is not made, leave the customer on a positive note and push forward to the next call with a positive mindset.

## INDUSTRY ADVICE
**Bill Guertin, *The 800-Pound Gorilla***

### RESOURCES AND REALITIES: NEGOTIATION IN SPORT SALES

In April of 1970, Apollo 13 was in trouble.

An internal explosion had badly damaged the NASA spacecraft, and it was discovered that the $CO_2$ level in the lunar module was rising quickly. If the roomful of scientists could not improvise a new $CO_2$ filter using only the materials that were aboard the undamaged part of the spacecraft, the astronauts would be dead in several hours.

A pile of the available items for the astronauts to use was gathered, and placed in a small room. "Gentlemen," their boss told the roomful of NASA experts, "we have to figure out a way to create a square filter like this, make it fit into a round hole like this, and have the astronauts build it using only the stuff we have here on the table."

In your negotiations with buyers in sport sales, there may be times when you feel a little like those NASA engineers. Your client will ask you to produce X results, and you can only get there using the resources you've been given—their budget, their requirements, and your inventory of available assets.

What will you do?

It starts with a thorough understanding of your "stuff"—the assets you have to work with. These might include:

- ▶ Your available seats (and the pros/cons of each location)
- ▶ Your inventory of giveaway items and special premiums
- ▶ Your on-field game experiences (i.e., meet-and-greets with players, photo ops, National Anthem, etc.)
- ▶ Your outfield signage inventory
- ▶ Your printed program ad spaces
- ▶ Your Jumbotron and the electronic ribbon board around the stadium
- ▶ Your broadcast inventory (# of commercials on radio/TV/Webcast)
- ▶ Your ability to do a mass e-mail blast to your newsletter subscribers
- ▶ The sponsorship of things like entry gates (the Coca-Cola Entrance), in-game features (the Verizon 'Call to the Bullpen'), or giveaways (i.e., Elvis bobbleheads sponsored by Cialis); and/or
- ▶ The naming rights to your team's mobile app.

You should also have a good understanding of what each of them is designed to do, what the benefits of each would be, and how they apply directly to the desired outcomes of the client. If a prospect wanted immediate foot traffic to their location after your games, for example, the assets you suggest—and the messaging you choose to apply to those assets—should be carefully considered. A coupon handed out to everyone that left your stadium promoting an after-game party or appetizer special would be an example of an asset that you might apply in that situation.

So let's say you're working with a prospect that gives you a list of criteria that they want to accomplish, but they don't give you a budget. "I want to see what you come up with," she says. "Get creative!"

You create an awesome proposal, showing justification for all the assets you've chosen to meet their specific objectives. As you're presenting the price, however, she balks and says, "$45,000? There's no way I could spend a penny more than $20,000!"

What can you do? Here are some guidelines I would suggest:

▶ **Do not cut your price.** Under no circumstances should you offer the same basket of items to your prospect for a lesser price. You will immediately undermine your brand, and give your prospect the impression that your product isn't worth what you're asking. Instead, begin to take items OUT of the proposal that would allow you to live with the budget, and still give the prospect what they're looking for. Here are the kinds of questions you'll want to ask:

— "What parts of this plan do you absolutely LOVE? If we're going to reconfigure this to meet your budget, which parts would you want to make sure to keep?"

— "Of all the elements we've suggested, which ones are you LEAST interested in? Which parts could we take out right away without much of a problem?"

▶ **Know what you can negotiate within your proposal, and what you can't.** Here are a few examples:

— Menu prices may be firm for food and beverage, but may have some wiggle room if there are larger quantities that can be negotiated;

— If a particular permanent sign location is one that hasn't moved well in the past few years, you may be able to bring the price down on THAT location vs. the one that you had suggested in your plan;

— You may have put an extra premium on a proposal to be the exclusive advertiser in their category (i.e., wireless carrier), and if you were to be able to remove the exclusivity clause (i.e., be able to offer similar assets to another carrier), you might be able to reduce the price of the sponsorship; or

— Extend payment terms to allow for a more balanced payment schedule vs. all upfront.

▶ **Create re-configured plans and prices based on their priorities.** Now, based on what you know, re-arrange the pieces to give them what they're looking for. What you'll find is most effective is that you leave something out that you know they want badly, but for a little bit more than their budget allows, you can include that piece. (i.e., *"We can't include that on-field game experience for your $20,000, but if you can get it to $25,000, we could bring your top 50 people onto the field for a photo, PLUS make sure everyone in your company gets to Opening Day to see your new sponsorship AND to watch the Top 50 being photographed, so they'll want to be in the photo NEXT year."*)

▶ **Never give a concession without getting something or removing value at the same time.** If you're going to concede on something they want in the negotiation, make sure there's something you get back in the exchange:

— "I could get you the extra premium item, but I would need to have 100% of your payment upfront vs. the six-month payment plan."

— "We could put in the 100 tickets for Opening Night, but we'd need to remove the towel sponsorship to do that. Does that work for you?"

> — "I know your President wants that naming rights sponsorship to our VIP Club, but in order to get that, I would need to remove the ribbon board ads AND the Jumbotron ads throughout the game to meet your budget. Are we OK to do that?"
>
> ▶ **Don't forget to close after a concession agreement!** Most sales reps stop short of asking for the sale after they've agreed to a mutual concession. It's as simple as saying, "So, with that change, can we say it's a done deal?"
>
> The NASA engineers in 1970 had never encountered anything like the issues resulting from the Apollo 13 explosion. Their training and knowledge of the entire picture, however, combined with their creativity and sense of urgency, kicked in when it was needed most.
>
> Your training on the team's assets, combined with your knowledge of the prospect's goals after a great fact-finding meeting, will guide you toward a negotiated solution that's a "win-win" for everyone.
>
> ─────────
> © Kendall Hunt Publishing Company

## CHAPTER ACTIVITIES

1. Explain why the sport industry is conducive to ethically applying the scarcity principle to create a sense of urgency.

2. Use the "You could, but" technique to create a sense of urgency in the following scenarios:

    a. I am really interested, but need to wait until my tax refund comes in.

    b. We probably want to renew, but will wait until before the season starts.

    c. I think we might want to do a large group outing on July 4, but I'll need to confirm that date with everyone in the group.

3. Assume you are ready to close the sale on a premium suite for a corporation. Create a sales dialogue between you and the decision-maker that results in a successful sale using the following closing methods:

    a. Direct request

    b. Benefit summary

    c. Legitimate alternative choice

4. Explain the difference between cross-selling and upselling.

5. Your prospect is having a hard time understanding how he could use tickets to 41 NBA home basketball games. Make up your own sales scenario, and then describe 10 ways the prospect could use the tickets.

6. Create a sales dialogue that demonstrates a salesperson successfully asking for a referral following the guidelines set forth in this chapter.

# CHAPTER COMPETENCY ASSESSMENT[8]

## COMPETENCY DOMAIN: CLOSING THE SALE

*Exemplary:* Consistently does all or almost all of the following:
- ► Effectively utilizes summary of the conversation to provide the customer the opportunity to agree on what has been discussed and then utilizes a question or statement to ask for the sale
- ► Recognizes buying signals and leverages those into asking for the sale
- ► Asks for the sale multiple times
- ► Uses urgency to spur the customer to action
- ► Confirms specific next steps that the customer and the seller will take prior to the next appointment if the sale is not finalized
- ► Closing ratio ranks in the top 20% of salespeople

*Skilled:* Does most of the following:
- ► Effectively utilizes summary of the conversation to provide the customer the opportunity to agree on what has been discussed and then utilizes a question or statement to ask for the sale
- ► Recognizes buying signals and leverages those into asking for the sale
- ► Asks for the sale at least once
- ► Uses urgency to spur the customer to action
- ► Confirms specific next steps that the customer and the seller will take prior to the next appointment if the sale is not finalized
- ► Closing ratio ranks in the top 40% of salespeople

*Adequate:* Does most of the following:
- ► Fails to recognize buying signals and misses opportunities to close the sale
- ► Fails to ask for the sale at some point during the call even when the right has been earned to ask
- ► Opts to send an e-mail with more information without asking for the sale when it would have been appropriate to ask for the sale
- ► Fails to create a sense of urgency
- ► Fails to establish appropriate next steps with the customer
- ► Closing ratio ranks in the bottom 40% of salespeople

*Novice:* Consistently does all or almost all of the following:
- ► Fails to recognize buying signals and misses opportunities to close the sale
- ► Gives up at the first sign of resistance from the customer, failing to ask for the sale
- ► Eager to send an e-mail to avoid asking for the sale
- ► Fails to establish appropriate next steps with the customer
- ► Closing ratio ranks in the bottom 20% of salespeople

---

8.  From "Competency Assessment for Entry-Level Sport Ticket Sales Professionals" by David Pierce and Richard Irwin, *Journal of Applied Sport Management*, Volume 8 (2), Summer 2016. Reprinted by permission of Sagamore Publishing. www.sagamorepub.com

## COMPETENCY DOMAIN: MAXIMIZING EACH SALE

*Exemplary*—Consistently does all or almost all of the following:

- ▶ Investigates referrals and upselling possibilities by asking cross-selling questions regarding where people work, what groups they are involved with, and who else is a fan of the team
- ▶ Successfully gets the customer to think creatively about who could use additional or better seats
- ▶ The dollars-to-total sales ratio ranks in the top 20% of salespeople

*Skilled*—Does most of the following:

- ▶ Investigates referrals and upselling possibilities by asking cross-selling questions regarding where people work, what groups they are involved with, and who else is a fan of the team
- ▶ Successfully gets the customer to think creatively about who could use additional or better seats
- ▶ The dollars-to-total sales ratio ranks in the top 40% of salespeople

*Adequate*—Does most of the following:

- ▶ Attempts to ask for referrals and investigates upselling opportunities, but misses key opportunities to utilize information gleaned in the needs analysis to ask the right question that may lead to a referral or upselling opportunity
- ▶ Misses the bigger picture of who is in a customer's network or the different ways in which the customer could use the tickets
- ▶ The dollars-to-total sales ratio ranks in the bottom 40% of salespeople

*Novice*—Consistently does all or almost all of the following:

- ▶ Takes the path of least resistance and rarely asks for referrals from clients and avoids investigating upselling opportunities with customers
- ▶ Fails to ask cross-selling questions that illuminate information on where customers work, what groups they are involved with, and who else they know are fans of the team
- ▶ The dollars-to-total sales ratio ranks in the bottom 20% of salespeople

# CHAPTER 11

# COMMUNICATION

**LEARNING OBJECTIVES**

After completing this chapter, you should be able to:

- ▶ Define the sales communication process.
- ▶ Explain the keys to sending effective verbal messages.
- ▶ Apply storytelling to paint a picture in the mind of the customer.
- ▶ Contrast positive and negative nonverbal cues.
- ▶ Explain the keys to sending effective nonverbal messages.
- ▶ Differentiate customer types in the social style matrix.
- ▶ Discuss strategies for actively listening to the customers.
- ▶ Identify the factors involved in building trust.

**KEY TERMS**

| | | |
|---|---|---|
| Active listening | Metaphor | Speaking rate |
| Analogy | Nonverbal | Story |
| Articulation | communication | Trust |
| Assertiveness | Physical appearance | Two-way communication |
| Body language | Proxemics | process |
| Body posture | Responsiveness | Verbal communication |
| Cliché | Sales communication | Verbal information |
| Empathy | Simile | Word picture |
| Inflection | Social style matrix | |

**COMPENTENCIES**

- ▶ Ability to empathize with the customer.
- ▶ Ability to listen.

- ▶ Ability to place the customer's interests ahead of personal own interests.
- ▶ Ability to develop a relationship with the customer.
- ▶ Ability to adapt to the personality and emotional style of the customer.
- ▶ Ability to relate to and build rapport with the customer.
- ▶ Ability to build trust with the customer.
- ▶ Demonstrate a sense of humor.
- ▶ Ability to appear assertive, but not pushy or aggressive.
- ▶ Ability to speak clearly.
- ▶ Possess strong verbal communication skills.
- ▶ Ability to speak intelligently.
- ▶ Ability to appear comfortable in conversation.
- ▶ Demonstrate sales-appropriate body language (posture, dress, facial expression).
- ▶ Ability to lead and be in control of the conversation.

## CHAPTER OVERVIEW

The communication process is at the heart of every sales interaction. The ability to demonstrate strong communication skills is a prerequisite to being successful in the sales profession. Poor communication skills can prevent sellers from being successful. This chapter focuses on explaining the communication process, sending effective verbal messages, sending positive nonverbal signals, interpreting the nonverbal messages sent by customers, adapting communication style to match key characteristics of the customer, actively listening to the customer, building trust and rapport, and avoiding breakdowns in communication. Demonstrating good communication skills forms the basis of building and maintaining mutually beneficial relationships with clients and fans.

Beyond applying these principles to the sales process, the fundamentals of good communication is beneficial in nearly any other endeavor in any profession. These principles can be especially useful in any type of job in the sport industry. Even if sales is not one's chosen profession, learning how to send positive verbal and nonverbal messages and in turn interpret the messages sent by others is a key success factor for upward mobility. In fact, a recent survey conducted by the National Association of Colleges and Employers found that the ability to verbally communicate with persons inside and outside the organization was the most sought after skill or quality of job applicants, followed closely by the ability to work in a team structure, which is built on being able to communicate.[1]

---

1. NACE. *The Skills and Qualities Employers Want in Their Class of 2013 Recruits.* Retrieved from http://www.naceweb.org/s10242012/skills-abilities-qualities-new-hires/

# COMMUNICATION PROCESS

**Sales communication** is the act of transmitting verbal and nonverbal information and understanding between seller and customer. Salespeople and customers send and receive messages through an exchange process with some type of response coming from each party. This process is illustrated through the **two-way communication process**, which begins when the sender translates thoughts into words (encoding) and the receiver decodes the message to understand what the sender intended to communicate (decoding). Two-way communication is required to make any type of sale. The prospect must understand the information contained in the seller's message to make an informed purchase decision. Two-way communication allows the seller to present a sales message, including benefits and value proposition, interpret the verbal and nonverbal reactions of the prospect, and answer questions or objections. Figure 11.1 summarizes the two-way flow of information within a sales interaction.

Unfortunately, problems with encoding and decoding messages result in breakdowns in communication. Senders may not say what they actually mean (encoding), and the receiver may not hear what was actually said (decoding). Sources of miscommunication include the physical environment, noises or other distractions, and making faulty assumptions.

- Physical environment—weather, room temperature, lighting
- Noises—sounds unrelated to messages being exchanged by the salesperson and customer (e.g., crowd noise, phones, traffic)
- Assumptions—making assumptions about what the customer believes is important

**SALES COMMUNICATION**
the act of transmitting verbal and nonverbal information and understanding between seller and customer

**TWO-WAY COMMUNICATION PROCESS**
when the sender translates thoughts into words (encoding) and the receiver decodes the message to understand what the sender intended to communicate (decoding)

## Figure 11.1

**Two-Way Flow of Information**

THE SENDER
Message encoded by Sender

THE RECEIVER
Message decoded by Receiver

THE RECEIVER
Receiver decodes the Senders' message

THE SENDER
Receiver encodes a message to Sender

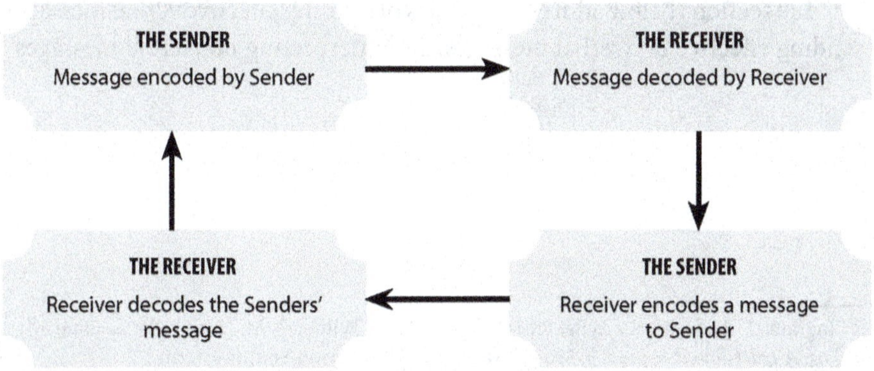

© Kendall Hunt Publishing

Below is an example of how communication can break down.

> *What the salesperson means to say*: Based on our success last season, our season ticket packages are really popular this year. Many of our top fans have already reserved a package.
>
> *What the salesperson says (encodes):* Tickets are going so fast this year our best seats are already taken.
>
> *What the customer hears*: I won't be able to get the seats I want.
>
> *What the customer thinks (decodes)*: I would have a better chance of getting the best seats on Stub Hub.
>
> *What the customer says*: I'm not interested in buying a package today.

**VERBAL COMMUNICATION**
the use of sounds and words to express a message

**NONVERBAL COMMUNICATION**
the process of sending and receiving messages without using spoken or written words

Communication is composed of verbal and non-verbal messages. **Verbal communication** is the use of sounds and words to express a message. Salespeople can manage their verbal communication through what they say and how they say it. **Nonverbal communication** is the process of sending and receiving messages without using spoken or written words. Salespeople manage and interpret nonverbal messages through appearance and body language. It is important for salespeople to send the right nonverbal messages and interpret the ones being sent by the prospect because nonverbal messages comprise 50% or more of the meaning conveyed within the communication process.[2] While scholars and communication experts disagree regarding the validity of the following statistic, it is often cited that total impact of communicated messages is 7% verbal (spoken), 38% tone of voice (how it was spoken), and 55% nonverbal (unspoken). Regardless of whether these exact percentages are correct, the point remains that at least half of the meaning delivered during a conversation stems from nonverbal cues. It is also important to recognize the interaction between verbal and nonverbal cues in communicating with customers. The importance of the interaction between verbal and nonverbal cues is found in studies showing that people remember 10% of what they read, 20% of what they see, 30% of what they hear, and 50% of what they hear and see.

The sections below address the basics of sending effective verbal messages, sending effective nonverbal messages, and interpreting nonverbal messages.

---

2. Ingram, T., LaForge, R., Avila, R., Schwepker, C., & Williams, M. (2006). *Professional selling: A trust-based approach,* 3rd ed. Mason, OH: Thomson Southwestern.

# SENDING EFFECTIVE VERBAL MESSAGES

## *Verbal Information*

American entrepreneur Jim Rohn once said, "Words do two major things. They provide food for the mind and create light for understanding and awareness." Salespeople provide customers with the food required to sustain the sales relationship until the customer understands how the product can fulfill their needs. **Verbal information** refers to statements of fact, opinion, and attitude that are encoded in the form of words, pictures, and numbers in such a way that they convey meaning to a receiver.[3] Research in cognitive psychology has found that pictures are more memorable than words.[4] Painting a picture through careful word selection and storytelling helps the prospect recall what was discussed in the conversation. This has important implications for sales professionals.

**VERBAL INFORMATION** to statements of fact, opinion, and attitude that are encoded in the form of words, pictures, and numbers in such a way that they convey meaning to a receiver

## CHOOSE WORDS THAT PAINT A VERBAL PICTURE

Nineteenth-century French poet Theophile Gautier once said, "Art is beauty, the perpetual invention of detail; the choice of words, the exquisite care of execution." Careful word selection is critical in aiding the prospect in understanding the message. Facts, details, and questions must be organized and connected in a logical order. Sales conversations that jump around from idea to idea risk being ineffective and the message not being received by the prospect. Effective utilization of a scripted outline can assist in keeping the seller organized throughout the call, but the seller also needs to adapt to where the customer takes the conversation.

In addition to maintaining a logical sequence within the conversation, careful selection of words can help paint a word picture for the prospect. It is commonly said that a picture is worth a thousand words. **A word picture** is a story designed to help the buyer visualize a point.[5] Salespeople can paint word pictures to help prospects understand their needs and the benefits of a product. Effective word pictures come in the form of similes, metaphors, analogies, and stories.

A **simile** is a figure of speech that makes a direct comparison, showing similarities between two different things. Similes typically use the worlds *like* or *as* to make the comparison. For example, in describing the benefit of having

**WORD PICTURE** a story designed to help the buyer visualize a point

**SIMILE** a figure of speech that makes a direct comparison, showing similarities between two different things

---

3. Ibid.

4. Mowen, J., & Minor, M. (1997). *Consumer behavior,* vol. 5. Upper Saddle River, NJ: Prentice Hall.

5. Weitz, B., Castleberry, S., & Tanner, J. (2007). *Selling: Building partnerships,* 7th ed. New York: McGraw-Hill Irwin.

a way to electronically transfer tickets to a friend as part of a season ticket package, the seller might say, *the ticketing transfer system is like an insurance policy against unused tickets*. In describing the playing ability of the seller's team's star player, he or she might say *Kevin Smith's game is smooth as silk*.

**METAPHOR**

a figure of speech which makes a comparison between two things that are different from each other but have some characteristics common between them

A **metaphor** is a figure of speech that makes a comparison between two things that are different from each other but have some characteristics common between them. When the seller portrays a person, place, thing, or action as being something else, even though it is not actually that "something else," he or she is speaking metaphorically.[6] When speaking with a customer about the features of a season ticket package, the seller might say, *Transferring tickets to coworkers through our mobile app is a breeze*. Or, when complimenting the prospect's abilities, the seller might say, *It sounds like you are the brains of this operation!*

**ANALOGY**

serves the same purpose as similes and metaphors, but analogies are more extensive and elaborate

An **analogy** serves the same purpose as similes and metaphors, but analogies are more extensive and elaborate. The example used in Chapter 7, where a doctor prescribing the right medicine was compared to a salesperson asking questions to recommend the right product or service, is an example of analogy. To illustrate, when talking to a prospect about the benefits of purchasing an annual membership to a pool or recreation center instead of paying each time they use the facility, the seller might say, *Having a membership for the year is like eating at an all-inclusive buffet instead of ordering a la carte. With the annual membership, you can use the facility when you want and do anything you want, instead of paying each time you want to do something.*

**STORY**

a brief account or example of people and events told to help "paint the picture in your prospect's mind why they need your product"

A **story** is a brief account or example of people and events told to help "paint the picture in your prospect's mind why they need your product."[7] Stories often include some combination of conflicts, trials, and problems that help the prospect consider different choices and the outcome of decisions that could be made. Stories are easy for prospects to grasp and create a way for the seller to connect the benefit of the product to the reality of their life. Stories help the seller move past data and facts toward the emotions of the prospect. "Data can persuade people, but it doesn't inspire them to act; to do that, you need to wrap your vision in a story that fires the imagination and stirs the soul."[8] The seller can introduce stories in a number of different ways, but phrases that can be particularly effective for weaving a story into the conversation include:

---

6. literarydevices.net

7. Delay, S. (2014, July 17). Let me give you an example…. *The Migala Report*. Retrieved from http://migalareport.com/storytellingworks

8. Monarth, H. (2014, March 11). The irresistible power of storytelling as a strategic business tool. *Harvard Business Review*. Retrieved from http://migalareport.com/storytellingworks https://hbr.org/2014/03/the-irresistible-power-of-storytelling-as-a-strategic-business-tool/?utm_medium=referral&utm_source=pulsenews.

- Let me give you an example . . .
- I want you to picture this . . .
- Imagine for a second that . . .
- Can I tell you a story?
- Mind if I share a story about . . .

Stories help the seller clarify words, symbols, and phrases that can mean different things to different people. These differences can be based on age, geographic location, business or industry, or other demographic characteristics. In Chapter 7, it was explained that the use of clarification questions is one way to nail down the meaning of words and phrases such as *we want to have a good time*. Similarly, stories can be used to create a visual picture that captures the customer's imagination and provides more exciting details behind ubiquitous phrases. For example, instead of simply agreeing with the customer that their family will have a good time at the game, the seller can tell a story the customer can emotionally connect with.

> Picture all of the unique memories you'll be able to create with your family by investing in a 15-game flexbook package. Your three-year-old will love heading out to the Kids Zone and playing in the Bounce Village, and your eight-year-old will be begging you to climb the rock wall with him. I know my five-year-old absolutely loves spinning the big wheel to win prizes. And then you can come back and enjoy the game at your seats and maybe even teach them a little bit about baseball.

Stories also help the seller illustrate why a prospect should buy tickets to the games instead of spending money on other entertainment options. The seller needs to be thinking, *Why should this person buy tickets to our games instead of spending money and time doing something else?* For example, when selling season tickets to a business, one of the key selling points is that the seller can bring a key client or prospect to a game. While bringing a client to a game is certainly one way in which the tickets can be used, it does not help explain why the customer would bring a client to the game instead of to a steakhouse or any other entertainment experience. This is where a story can be useful. For example,

> Let's picture your top prospect coming to a sold-out playoff game next year. The fans are going crazy, the atmosphere is electrical, and everyone in town wants a ticket to the game. And your client is going to be sitting on the 50-yard line in some of the best seats

in the house. We can even help you make reservations over at This Fancy and Popular Steakhouse for after the game. This is really going to make an impression.

In the article below, Steve DeLay introduces the importance of painting a visual picture for the prospect.

---

**Steve DeLay,** *The Migala Report*

### WHAT CHRIS FARLEY CAN TEACH YOU ABOUT TICKET SALES

"New Guy in The Corner Puking His Guts Out" Could Be One Of The Best Picture Painting Descriptions Ever. Are You Doing The Same?

To really get someone to want to buy your tickets, you have to paint a visual picture for your prospect of what buying your offer will mean to them.

I like to challenge salespeople to really paint a picture of what going to their games is like and what it would mean to a fan. Young salespeople will use words like "fun, exciting, interesting, fast-paced . . ." but in reality, those words mean different things to different people. They don't create much of a visual picture. What my friends consider fun most likely isn't the same thing I would consider fun. What parents with kids consider "interesting" is much different than what I would consider "interesting."

**Learn From a Master**

Chris Farley was one of the greatest SNL actors of all time. The movie *Tommy Boy* didn't do much at the box office but has some of the best salesperson scenes ever. Whenever I help teams with sales training and talk about painting a picture, here's the scene I use as an example. It's a tremendous example of how you can make brake pads seem interesting.

**Picture This**

To help create a mental image in your prospect's mind, you have to tell him that's what you're doing. You can start by simply saying, "Picture this . . ."

Now, get their imagination flowing. Use words and descriptions that create visual pictures.

Which descriptions are more visual?

"You'll love coming to the games with your family."

**OR**

"Imagine the memories you'll create with your family coming to the games. You can teach your son how to keep score. How much fun will you have giving your son and daughter a few bucks to buy themselves a souvenir in the team shop. If they buy themselves a tee-shirt, they'll probably want to wear it to school for the next week. You'll be high-fiving great plays, spilling popcorn cheering the game-winning touchdown . . ."

How about this example? Which one sounds more exciting?

"Our games are fast-paced and exciting."

**OR**

"You'll love the new offense our coaching staff is installing. They've promised we're going to run four or five wide receiver sets. We're going to be throwing deep bombs better than the old Oakland Raiders used to with Jim Plunkett in their Super Bowl years. Expect to see offensive series where we run the defense ragged with quick substitutions, no-huddle offenses, and touchdown drives that take :45 seconds. You won't be able to catch your breath cheering from one play to the next."

If you aren't excited by your description of why your prospect should buy your tickets, why would they be excited? It takes real, concentrated practice to get good at painting descriptive pictures. Take the lead from Chris Farley and make your sales pitch sizzle.

---

http://migalareport.com/chrisfarleycanhelp. Reprinted by permission of Steve DeLay.

Stories also help salespeople build rapport by revealing information about themselves. In addition to I/My stories, every salesperson should have the following three stories prepared to use at any time: Who I am, Who I represent, and Who I've helped (see Table 11.1).[9] These stories don't have to be overly complex and should communicate a clear message while not distracting from the overall flow of the conversation. The stories help the salesperson build a connection and trust with the customer.

## CAREFULLY SELECT VISUAL AIDS FOR SALES PRESENTATIONS

Visual aids that explain and reinforce the verbal message will aid the prospect's understanding and enhance recall of the message.[10] As discussed in Chapter 8, visual aids include presentation materials, samples, brochures, graphs, charts, and props. Images within a presentation (PowerPoint, written proposal, handout, etc.) can be incredibly powerful. For example, touting the ability of employees to bond outside the office during a group outing, then including pictures of employees at XYX Company having a great time at the game, supplemented by a testimonial from the group leader, creates a powerful image rooted in social proof. Props can also be an effective attention-

---

9.  Bosworth, M., & Zoldan, B. (2012). *What great salespeople do: The science of selling through emotional connection and the power of story.* New York: McGraw Hill.

10.  Ingram, T., LaForge, R., Avila, R., Schwepker, C., & Williams, M. (2006). *Professional selling: A trust-based approach*, 3rd ed. Mason, OH: Thomson Southwestern.

## Table 11.1

**Three Stories Every Seller Needs**

| Story | Purpose | Example |
|---|---|---|
| Who I Am | Describes your journey and how you ended up where you are today.<br><br>Demonstrates why you are doing what you're doing. | I sold advertising for a campus magazine when I was in college, and I fell in love with helping small business owners grow their business. I am passionate about helping companies find ways to use sports and entertainment to market their product and improve as a business. |
| Who I Represent | Describes the journey of the sport organization you represent.<br><br>Uses a specific, focused story to demonstrate something your organization does that illustrates your point. | Our team has been a staple on the west side of town for over 50 years. We have at least three generations of lifelong fans now that watch our games together. Our organization is committed to creating a family-oriented atmosphere that can create life-long memories for parents and children. |
| Who I've Helped | Describes the change that another customer experienced as a result of buying from you.<br><br>Demonstrates why the customer chose to buy from you. | We work with quite a few low teen handicappers here at the Golf Academy, and typically with six lessons and some practice time, they are able to drop their handicap below 10 by the end of the summer. In fact, Mike Johnson from last year's Academy was just out here this morning and told me that he is breaking 80 consistently. |

grabbing device. Even though the seller is selling an intangible experience, props like sports equipment (i.e., bat, glove, ball, helmet), trophies, autographed items, testimonials, and video highlights make an impression on the prospect. Any prop that can help the seller tell the team's story is appropriate. Most people like to talk sports, so props can be used to get the conversation started.

## LIMIT THE USE OF SLANG AND CLICHÉ PHRASES THAT CARRY LITTLE MEANING

**CLICHÉ**
overused phrases or sayings that show a lack of original thought

**Clichés** are overused phrases or sayings that show a lack of original thought. There are two types of clichés: general clichés and business clichés. General clichés are phrases that are used in general conversation that have become overused and therefore meaningless. Examples of general clichés include the following words or phrases:

- kind of
- definitely (or even worse, the dreaded "definitely, definitely")
- like
- yeah, no
- sort of
- you know
- pretty much
- basically
- essentially
- literally

Business clichés are words or phrases that have become so commonplace in business conversations to become almost meaningless.[11] These trite, hackneyed phrases don't make a real contribution to the conversation. Examples of business clichés include:

- Low-hanging fruit
- At the end of the day
- I'm not gonna lie
- Let's push the envelope
- Think outside the box
- Apples-to-apples comparison
- To tell you the truth
- These are actionable items
- Great deal
- No problem
- I can guarantee you

## AVOID USING OFF-COLOR LANGUAGE, JOKES, AND FOUL LANGUAGE

While this should go without saying, it is important to note that even with long-time customers, the seller should avoid using any off-color language, telling inappropriate jokes, and using language that could be perceived as foul by anyone.

---

11. Coombs, P. *Overused words and phrases to avoid in a sales call.* Retrieved from http://frontlinetraining.com/overused-words-and-phrases-to-avoid-in-a-sales-call/

## Voice Characteristics

A common saying is "It's not what you said, it's how you said it." This saying captures the importance of voice characteristics in the delivery of meaning through the spoken word. Poor voice and speech characteristics and habits will make it difficult for customers to grasp the message the seller is trying to deliver. Voice characteristics include speaking rates, loudness, inflection, and articulation.

**SPEAKING RATES**
the speed with which a
salesperson talks

**Speaking rates** refer to the speed with which a salesperson talks. While estimates slightly vary, people speak at a rate of 140 words per minute, with a range of 130 to 150. Within this range, faster speakers are perceived more favorably than slower speakers, particularly with respect to intelligence, credibility, and knowledge.[12] Outside of the range, speaking faster than this rate can cause problems with the customer receiving the complete message, while speaking slower than this can create a perception of incompetence. Salespeople can vary their speaking rates depending on the situation. For example, simple messages can be delivered at faster rates, while more difficult ideas should be delivered at slower rates. Varying speech rates can also assist with maintaining the interest of the customer.

Loudness should be varied within a sales presentation to add points of emphasis that indicate a certain point is more important, catch the customer's attention, and refocus the customer. Loudness should be adjusted to fit the situation and environment.

**INFLECTION**
the tone or pitch of
speech

**Inflection** refers to the tone or pitch of speech. Increasing and decreasing pitch ensures the seller does not sound monotonous. The seller's own personality and voice characteristics should shine through the call, but he or she can consciously think about using inflection to encourage the customer to pay attention or highlight certain elements of the message. For example, the seller's tone should decrease at the end of a sentence to indicate the completion of a thought and increase at the end of a sentence to indicate a question or uncertainty. Overall, high-pitched voices are perceived to be less truthful and empathetic, while lower-pitched voices are perceived to be more persuasive and truthful.[13] However, it is important to recognize the importance of developing personal style and not trying to imitate someone else, which can make a person seem uncomfortable.

**ARTICULATION**
the act of forming words
when speaking

**Articulation** is the act of forming words when speaking. To achieve good articulation, each word must be finished correctly to the last syllable and to

---

12. Peterson, R., Cannito, M., & Brown, S. (1995). An exploratory investigation of voice characteristics and selling effectiveness. *Journal of Personal Selling & Sales Management, 15*(1), 1–15.

13. Ingram, T., LaForge, R., Avila, R., Schwepker, C., & Williams, M. (2006). *Professional selling: A trust-based approach,* 3rd ed. Mason, OH: Thomson Southwestern.

## Figure 11.2

**Sending Effective Verbal Messages**

| Verbal Information | Voice Characteristics |
|---|---|
| ▶ Choose words that paint a verbal picture<br><br>▶ Carefully select visual aids for sales presentations<br><br>▶ Limit the use of slang and cliché phrases that carry little meaning<br><br>▶ Avoid using off-color language, jokes, and foul language | ▶ Speak at the right rate<br><br>▶ Use inflection to avoid sounding monotonous<br><br>▶ Articulate words correctly |

the final consonant. People in industries that rely on their voice for their livelihood (broadcasters, actors, musicians) often do voice exercises to improve articulation.[14] One of the most common articulation mistakes is to cut words short.[15] For example,

- **Secretary** is pronounced *secretry*, giving it three syllables instead of four
- **Every** is pronounced *evry*, giving it two syllables instead of three
- **Different** is pronounced *diffrent*, missing the middle syllable.
- **Athlete** is pronounced *athelete*, making the word three syllables long when it should only be two.

## SENDING EFFECTIVE NONVERBAL MESSAGES

Nonverbal communication can be difficult to manage. Hundreds of nonverbal signals are exchanged during a face-to-face sales interaction. This section introduces positive and negative nonverbal cues to help sellers use positive cues and avoid using negative cues. However, it is also important to recognize that the most effective gestures are natural and not forced.[16] It would be more harmful for the seller to use non-genuine positive nonverbal cues than to not use any at all. Ultimately, it is important to be cognizant of ways to enhance the message and avoid driving customers away with negative nonverbal cues.

14. Greenslade, S. F.V.C.M. (Hons), A.N.E.A. *Clear speaking.* Retrieved from http://www.afraid-of-speaking-a-speech.com/vocalexercises.html

15. Ibid.

16. Weitz, B., Castleberry, S., & Tanner, J. (2007). *Selling: Building partnerships,* 7th ed. New York: McGraw-Hill Irwin.

There are three primary cues that salespeople send customers in the delivery of their message: body language, physical appearance, and space.

---

**TYPES OF NONVERBAL COMMUNICATION**

▸ Handshake
▸ Body posture
▸ Gestures
▸ Nodding
▸ Shaking head
▸ Eye contact
▸ Eye roll
▸ Facial expressions
▸ Touch
▸ Space or proximity
▸ Dress
▸ Appearance
▸ Grooming habits
▸ Multitasking (using your phone while talking; wearing earphones while working)
▸ Space

---

## Body Language

**BODY LANGUAGE**
expresses thoughts, intentions, and feelings through physical behaviors such as facial expressions, eye movements, body movements, body posture, and handshakes

**Body language** expresses thoughts, intentions, and feelings through physical behaviors such as facial expressions, eye movements, body movements, body posture, and handshakes.

## FACIAL EXPRESSIONS

A natural, comfortable, and engaging smile is perhaps the most positive facial expression the seller can express to a customer because it signals agreement and interest. Uncertainty, disagreement, and skepticism are displayed through frowning, pursed lips, and squinted eyes. Suspicion and anger are accompanied by tightness along the jaw line. Uncertainty is signaled through the biting of one's lips.

## EYE MOVEMENTS

The seller can send positive nonverbal cues through eye contact. Eye contact implies honesty, confidence, interest, sincerity, trustworthiness, and concentration. However, avoid prolonged eye contact, or staring, since that is interpreted as a threat or a statement of power. Likewise, blank stares, looking away from the customer for a prolonged period of time, repeatedly looking at a watch, or checking messages or e-mails on the phone send the message that the seller is disinterested or bored.

## BODY MOVEMENTS

The movement of hands, arms, head, and legs can send positive and negative cues to the customer. Below is a summary of body movements and the messages they send.

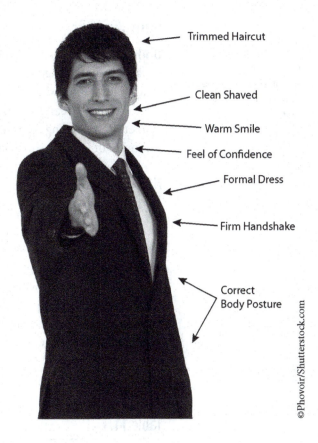

Trimmed Haircut

Clean Shaved

Warm Smile

Feel of Confidence

Formal Dress

Firm Handshake

Correct Body Posture

©Phovoir/Shutterstock.com

## Table 11.2

**Messages Sent Through Body Movements**

| Body Movement | Message |
|---|---|
| **Positive** | |
| Smooth, gradual movements | Calm, confident |
| Uncrossed arms and legs | Open, cooperative |
| Placement of hand on chin | Increased level of evaluation |
| Nodding of head | Agreement, understanding |
| Exposed palm | Receptive |
| **Negative** | |
| Pointing finger | Anger |
| Jerky and hurried movements | Nervous, stress |
| Crossed arms and legs | Disagreement, Defensive |
| Tight clasping of hands or fists | Increasing tension |
| Drumming of fingers or tapping of foot | Growing impatience |
| Fingering hair | Growing nervousness |
| Rubbing back of neck | Growing apprehension |

## BODY POSTURE

**BODY POSTURE**
the position or
orientation of the body
during a face-to-face
meeting

**Body posture** refers to the position or orientation of the body during a face-to-face meeting. In general, good body posture is better described by what it is not, rather than what it is. It is much easier to see what sends negative messages. However, leaning and sitting forward sends the message that the seller is interested and engaged in what the prospect is saying. In Table 11.3, see a summary of body postures and the messages they send.

## HANDSHAKES

The seller should not automatically extend his or her hand for a handshake in all situations. In a sales setting, particularly during the first meeting and when the customer is seated, shaking hands should be the prospect's choice. Follow the lead of the prospect. If a handshake is initiated, the seller should maintain eye contact with the customer and shake hands for approximately three seconds. The grip should be firm, but not overpowering. Avoid the limp handshake, where the hand has little or no grip, and avoid the bone-cruncher handshake, where the grip is too firm. In general, women should follow the

### Table 11.3

**Messages Sent Through Body Posture**

| Body Posture | Message |
|---|---|
| **Positive** | |
| Leaning forward in chair | Interested |
| Sitting forward on the edge of a chair | Engaged |
| Sitting on edge of table or arm of chair | Knowledgeable |
| **Negative** | |
| Shuffling feet | Lack of self-discipline |
| Slumping | Lack of self-confidence |
| Fidgeting | Nervous |
| Shifting from side to side | Apprehensive |
| Leaning away | Disinterested or bored |
| Overly erect posture | Rigid, inflexible |
| Sloppy posture | Unprofessional |
| Leaning back with hands placed behind head | Smug |

**Wet Fish Handshake**

**Appropriate Handshake**

same guidelines as men. Some communication experts believe that the type of handshake used by a person indicates something about their personality.[17]

## Physical Appearance

**Physical appearance** refers to attractiveness, grooming habits, and dress style. While researchers and sales leaders disagree about the extent to which physical attractiveness impacts success in sales, there is agreement that salespeople can control grooming habits and dress style. Physical appearance is important for four reasons:[18]

**PHYSICAL APPEARANCE**
refers to attractiveness, grooming habits, and dress style

1. Proper appearance gives the impression of professionalism and contributes to trustworthiness and respect.

2. Casual appearance indicates a casual approach to the prospect's needs.

3. Proper grooming instills confidence in salespeople.

4. Grooming can impact the attractiveness of a person and swing the odds in favor of a salesperson.

---

17. For more information on this topic, http://blog.meraevents.com/2014/08/05/7-types-handshakes-mean/

18. Burdett, E. (2013). Do Looks and Appearances Matter in Sales? *PeakSales Recruiting.* Retrieved from http://www.peaksalesrecruiting.com/how-important-are-looks-for-sales-professionals/.

## GROOMING HABITS

Grooming refers to general personal cleanliness and professional appearance related to things like hair, teeth, nails, breath, and personal hygiene. The seller must look the part of a competent salesperson to succeed, and those with poor grooming habits will not be successful in sales.[19] Unclean fingernails, disheveled hair, bad breath, clothes that smell like smoke, as well as visible tattoos and body piercings can negatively affect the impression formed by the customer.

## DRESS STYLE

The corporate culture and dress expectation within a sport organization will likely differ from the businesses the salesperson will visit. Not only will these businesses differ in corporate culture and expectation, but the seller will also work "game day" events with a specific dress expectation. This means that within the course of a single day the salesperson may need to wear two or three different types of outfits. Even as casual dress becomes more popular, in most cases it is still safe to overdress. Dress formally if it is believed the customer will be formally dressed. If the customer will be dressed casual, then properly pressed formal wear usually won't hurt, but under dressing will likely negatively impact the seller.[20]

Follow these four tips when determining what to wear:[21]

1.  If the client suggests dressing in business casual, do so.

2.  When in doubt, dress in business attire.

3.  When you call for an appointment, ask the prospect or gatekeeper about the dress code.

4.  Never dress down below the client's level of attire.

Other factors to consider include the temperature, the physical setting of the meeting, local cultural norms, professional aspirations (dress one level above your position), and personal style.[22]

---

19. Johnston, M., & Marshall, G. (2013). *Salesforce management,* 11th ed. New York: Routledge.

20. Burdett, E. (2013). Do looks and appearances matter in sales? *PeakSales Recruiting.* Retrieved from http://www.peaksalesrecruiting.com/how-important-are-looks-for-sales-professionals/.

21. Johnston, M., & Marshall, G. (2013). *Salesforce management,* 11th ed. New York: Routledge.

22. Weitz, B., Castleberry, S., & Tanner, J. (2007). *Selling: Building partnerships,* 7th ed. New York: McGraw-Hill. Irwin.

## Table 11.4

**The Role of Proxemics in Sales**

| Space | Distance in Feet | Who Belongs |
|---|---|---|
| Intimate | 0 to 2 | Closest relationships—Immediate family, loved ones |
| Personal | 2 to 4 | Close friends and associates |
| Social | 4 to 12 | Business client relationships, impersonal relationships |
| Public | Beyond 12 | General public, group settings like presentations |

## *Space*

**Proxemics** refers to the personal distance that people prefer to keep between themselves and other people. The distance between the seller and the client sends a powerful nonverbal message. Clients may perceive the seller to be intimidating and threatening if he or she is too close to them, but apprehensive and rigid if too far away. In North America, there are four main types of distances to consider, as outlined in Table 11.4.

Invading the customer's intimate or personal space may generate a negative reaction from the customer. If the seller sees a client moving back, folding their arms, or assuming any other defensive-type posture, then he or she should move back. The seller should typically begin interactions with a client in the social space and only move closer within that range of 4–12 feet if rapport has been established and the client indicates that a relationship has developed.

**PROXEMICS**
the personal distance that people prefer to keep between themselves and other people

## INTERPRETING NONVERBAL MESSAGES

In the same way the salesperson can send nonverbal messages to clients, clients send nonverbal messages to the salesperson. These nonverbal messages need to be interpreted correctly so the seller can gather an accurate picture of what the customer is thinking and feeling. Body language will tell the seller the most about the prospect's thoughts, feelings, and attitudes, particularly related to body angle, face, arms, hands, and legs. Body language signals can be grouped into three categories: acceptance signals, caution signals, and disagreement signals.[23]

---

23.  Futrell, C. (2006). *Fundamentals of selling*, 9th ed. New York: McGraw-Hill/Irwin.

Clients send acceptance signals to indicate a favorable disposition and willingness to listen. Acceptance signals include:

- ▶ Uncrossed arms and legs
- ▶ Leaning forward, toward you
- ▶ Smiling
- ▶ Nodding
- ▶ Chin held level
- ▶ Direct eye contact
- ▶ Open palms
- ▶ Excited reactions
- ▶ Positive voice tones
- ▶ Firm handshake
- ▶ Willingness to look at visual aids
- ▶ Relaxed body posture

**Positive Signals**

Clients send caution signals to indicate a neutral disposition that signals skepticism toward listening to the message. Common caution signals include:

- ▶ Leaning away from you
- ▶ Chin held down
- ▶ Scratching head
- ▶ Minimal facial expression
- ▶ Minimal eye contact
- ▶ Short, brief answers
- ▶ Arms crossed
- ▶ Hands on hips
- ▶ Yawning
- ▶ Hands fidgety or clasped
- ▶ Legs moving away from you
- ▶ Tapping or shaking feet with lots of movement

©HBRH/Shutterstock.com

©Kopytin Georgy/Shutterstock.com

©Kopytin Georgy/Shutterstock.com

**Negative Signals**

To respond effectively to clients sending caution signals, adjust the presentation on the fly, use open-ended questions to get the client talking, and project positive acceptance signals as discussed in the previous section.

Clients send disagreement signals to indicate a negative disposition that signals an unwillingness to continue the presentation or discussion. It may be best in this situation to stop the presentation or call. In other cases, the seller may be able to use open-ended questions to encourage dialogue and understand their attitude, demonstrate empathy, or take away any sales pressure that might exist. Common disagreement signals include:

▶ Retracted shoulders
▶ Leaning backward or turned away from you
▶ Wanting to move away from you
▶ Crossed arms or legs
▶ Furrowed eyebrow
▶ Frowning
▶ Pursed lips
▶ Wrinkled face
▶ Pointing fingers
▶ Almost no eye contact
▶ Negative voice tones
▶ Prolonged silence
▶ Minimal change in expression
▶ Hands indicate disapproval
▶ Clenched or clasped hands

## ADAPTING TO THE CUSTOMER

**SOCIAL STYLE MATRIX**
consists of four primary
types of communication
styles based on
two dimensions—
assertiveness and
responsiveness

Verbal and nonverbal messages also provide the seller with information about the customer's communication style. The ability to recognize and interpret customers' communication styles allows the seller to adapt behavior in a way that enhances rapport, relationship building, trust, and the content of the presentation. One popular training program used to help salespeople adapt their communication style is the **social style matrix**.[24] The matrix consists of four types of communication styles based on two dimensions—assertiveness and responsiveness.

---

24. Merrill, D., & Reid, R. (1981). *Personal styles and effective performance.* Radnor, PA: Chilton Book Company.

**Assertiveness** is the degree to which people have opinions about issues and attempt to persuade others to accept those opinions by dominating or controlling situations and conversations. Highly assertive people are not afraid to speak out about their opinions and have a take-charge attitude. Unassertive people hold back, let other people take charge, and are slow and deliberate in the communications. Table 11.5 summarizes the differences between assertive and unassertive behaviors.

**Responsiveness** is the degree to which people show emotion in social situations. Highly responsive people are openly emotional and show concern for others. They tend to be personable, friendly, and informal. Less responsive people are more conscious of controlling their emotions and can be described as impersonal, cautious, intellectual, formal, and businesslike. Table 11.6 summarizes the differences between low and high responsiveness.

**ASSERTIVENESS**
the degree to which people have opinions about issues and attempt to persuade others to accept those opinions by dominating or controlling situations and conversations

**RESPONSIVENESS**
the degree to which people show emotion in social situations. Highly responsive people are openly emotional and show concern for others

## Table 11.5

**Characteristics of Low and High Assertiveness**

| Low Assertiveness | High Assertiveness |
|---|---|
| Slow paced | Fast paced |
| Follower | Take charge |
| Avoids risks | Takes risks |
| Team player | Independent |
| Makes few statements | Makes many statements |
| Supportive | Directive |
| Moves deliberately | Moves rapidly |
| Easy going | Confrontational |

## Table 11.6

**Characteristics of Low and High Responsiveness**

| Low Responsiveness | High Responsiveness |
|---|---|
| Task oriented | Relationship oriented |
| Controls emotion | Show emotion |
| Rational | Emotional |
| Formal | Informal |
| Serious | Playful |
| Controlled facial expression | Animated facial expression |
| Organized | Unorganized |

## Figure 11.3

**Social Style Matrix**

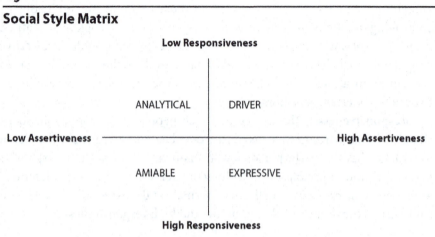

These two dimensions of social style form the social style matrix, shown in Figure 11.3. The four quadrants characterize people as having one of four different social styles based on demonstrated levels of assertiveness and responsiveness. "A salesperson's skill in properly classifying customers can provide valuable cues regarding customer attitudes and behaviors. In turn, these cues allow the salesperson to be more effective by adapting his or her communication and responses to better fit the customer's style."[25]

*Drivers* are high on assertiveness and low on responsiveness. Drivers are task-oriented and focused on bottom-line results. They don't want to be bothered with purely technical information and make decisions based on their own gut instinct. Drivers make quick decisions even if others are not on board with the decision. In their relationships, drivers are detached and competitive, only working with people because they have to. Drivers tend to be formal, businesslike, highly organized, and time efficient. Drivers are the most difficult of the four styles to build rapport with because they are typically all business all the time. The key to working with drivers is to match and mirror their behavior with a direct, businesslike, and organized presentation with immediate action items and follow-through. Proposals and presentation of benefits should focus on whatever the "bottom line" means to the customer.

*Expressives* are high on assertiveness and high on responsiveness. Highly animated and talkative, expressives possess warm personalities and value personal relationships, particularly with supporters or followers who can help them achieve goals. Their focus is typically on the big picture or future vision and they don't like to get bogged down with tactical details.

25. Ingram, T., LaForge, R., Avila, R., Schwepker, C., & Williams, M. (2006). *Professional selling: A trust-based approach,* 3rd ed. Mason, OH: Thomson Southwestern.

Expressives like to tell stories and be onstage. Decisions get made based on their personal opinion and the opinion of others. While they are quick to make decisions and take risk, they tend to be impatient and easily change their minds. The key to working with expressives is to let them talk, avoid specific details, talk about the big picture, use pictures and stories during presentations, and use testimonials or social proof that appeals to their need for status and recognition.

*Amiables* are low on assertiveness and high on responsiveness. Close relationships are highly valued by amiables, making them cooperative, friendly, easygoing, and nice people. Amiables avoid conflict and do not respond well to any type of sales pressure. Amiables rely on mutual respect and building consensus with other people rather than power and authority. As a result, they can be slow and timid decision-makers. Amiables are at risk to experience "buyer's remorse" because their unease in making a decision will cause them to change their mind shortly after the seller is done speaking or meeting with them. Amiables have a difficult time expressing their true feelings, and can mislead the seller for a long time during the sales cycle before unexpectedly saying *no* at the end. The key to working with amiables is to include time for chit-chat, take time to build personal relationships, proceed slowly, give them time to talk throughout the conversation, provide guarantees to make them feel comfortable, follow through on commitments, and talk about how the product can satisfy other people.

*Analyticals* are low on assertiveness and low on responsiveness. Analyticals tend to distrust making decisions based on authority, emotions, and personality relationships, instead favoring facts, principles, and logic. As a result, they tend to be slow decision-makers. Analyticals are typically meticulous, disciplined, quiet, reserved, and not too outgoing. The key to working with analyticals is to be accurate in the presentation of facts and details, support arguments with verifiable facts, move slowly through the presentation giving them time to think and ask questions, and avoid being direct or aggressive.

Interpreting a customer's social style is difficult and requires practice. The seller can gather information about the customer's social style through observation of behavior, active listening, and asking questions. Face-to-face interactions provide more information (verbal and nonverbal) from which to determine social style than selling that occurs only over the phone or through technology. Understanding a customer's social style will help the seller understand how they want to receive information, how they define value, what objections they are likely to raise, and on what basis they will make a commitment. Table 11.7 identifies recommended flexing behaviors for the four different social styles.

## Table 11.7

### Recommended Flexing Behaviors for Different Communication Styles

| Selling Task or Objective | Selling to the Analytical | Selling to the Driver | Selling to the Amiable | Selling to the Expressive |
|---|---|---|---|---|
| Setting an Appointment | ▲ Send a business letter specifying details about yourself and the company. <br> ▲ Follow the letter with a phone call to confirm expectations and set appointment. | ▲ Drivers may not take time to read your letter. <br> ▲ Contact them by phone first and follow up with a letter. <br> ▲ Keep call businesslike and to the point by identifying yourself, explain the business problem addressed by your product, and ask for appointment. <br> ▲ Letter should simply confirm time and date of appointment and include materials the driver might review prior to the meeting. | ▲ Send a letter with a personal touch stating who you are and why you are contacting the Amiable. <br> ▲ Letter should include your experience working with clients the prospect knows by reputation or experience, your reliability and follow-through, and the quality of your product/service. <br> ▲ Follow letter with a personal phone call. <br> ▲ Take time to be friendly, open, sincere, and to establish trust in the relationship. | ▲ Generally, a phone call is most appropriate. <br> ▲ Make your call open and friendly, stressing quick benefits, personal service, your experience, and your company's experience with its products and services. <br> ▲ If you send a letter, make it short and personal, stressing who you are, how you know of the Expressive, and what you are interested in talking about. |
| Opening the Call | ▲ Provide background information about you and the company. <br> ▲ Approach in an advisory capacity acknowledging buyer's expertise. <br> ▲ Show evidence that you have done your homework on buyer's situation. <br> ▲ Offer evidence of providing previous solutions. <br> ▲ Be conscious of how you are using buyer's time. | ▲ Listen and focus on driver's ideas and objectives. <br> ▲ Provide knowledge and insight relevant to driver's specific business problems. <br> ▲ Be personable but reserved and relatively formal. <br> ▲ Present factual evidence that establishes the business problem and resulting outcome. <br> ▲ Maintain a quick pace. Drivers value punctuality and efficient use of time. | ▲ Engage in informal conversation before getting down to business. <br> ▲ Demonstrate that you are personally interested in the Amiable's work and personal goals. <br> ▲ You will have to earn the right to learn more personally about the Amiable. <br> ▲ Demonstrate your product/ service knowledge by referencing a common acquaintance with whom you've done business. | ▲ Quickly describe the purpose of your call and establish credibility—you must earn the right to develop a business relationship with the Expressive. <br> ▲ Share stories about people you both know. <br> ▲ Share information the Expressive would perceive as exclusive. <br> ▲ Share your feelings and enthusiasm for the Expressive's ideas and goals. <br> ▲ Once the Expressive has confidence in your competence, take time to develop an open and trusting personal relationship. |

*(Continued)*

| Selling Task or Objective | Selling to the Analytical | Selling to the Driver | Selling to the Amiable | Selling to the Expressive |
|---|---|---|---|---|
| Gathering Information | ▲ Ask specific, fact-finding questions in a systematic manner.<br>▲ Establish comprehensive exchange of information.<br>▲ Encourage buyer to discuss ideas while focusing on factual information.<br>▲ Be thorough and unhurried—listen.<br>▲ Explain that you are in alignment with their thinking and can support their objectives. | ▲ Ask, don't tell. Ask fact-finding questions leading to what the driver values and rewards.<br>▲ Make line of questioning consistent with your call objective.<br>▲ Follow up on requests for information immediately.<br>▲ Support the buyer's beliefs; indicate how you can positively affect goals.<br>▲ Clarify the driver's expectations. | ▲ Create a cooperative atmosphere with an open exchange of information and feelings.<br>▲ Amiables tend to understate their objectives, so you may need to probe for details and specifics about their goals.<br>▲ Listen responsively. Give ample amounts of verbal and nonverbal feedback.<br>▲ Verify whether there are unresolved budget or cost justification issues.<br>▲ Find out who else will contribute to the buying decision.<br>▲ Summarize what you believe to be the Amiable's key ideas and feelings. | ▲ Begin by finding out the Expressive's perception of the situation and vision of the ideal outcome.<br>▲ Identify other people who should contribute to analysis and planning.<br>▲ Listen, then respond with plenty of verbal and non-verbal feedback that supports the Expressive's beliefs.<br>▲ Question carefully the critical data you'll need.<br>▲ Keep the discussion focused and moving toward a result.<br>▲ If the Expressive shows limited interest in specifics, summarize what has been discussed and begin to suggest ways to move the vision toward reality. |
| Reinforcing the Need to Change | ▲ Use their records to supply information.<br>▲ Use a logical approach.<br>▲ Illustrate with dollars and cents. | ▲ Be fast-paced and business-like. Be sure of your figures. Show the Driver the bottom line. Appeal to rational thinking and avoid appeal to emotions. | ▲ Address emotional needs in line with safety and comfort needs.<br>▲ Use the Amiable's own figures rather than your own.<br>▲ Do not push! | ▲ Support the Expressive's ideas and goals.<br>▲ Work toward his/her esteem needs.<br>▲ Supply data from people seen as leaders to the Expressive. |
| Providing the Sales Story | ▲ Provide detailed written proposal as part of presentation.<br>▲ Include strongest cost-benefit justifications.<br>▲ Support with third-party data.<br>▲ Be reserved and decisive but not aggressive.<br>▲ Limit emotional or testimonial appeals.<br>▲ Recommend specific course of action. | ▲ Present your recommendation so that the driver can compare alternative solutions and their probable outcomes.<br>▲ Provide documented options.<br>▲ Offer the best quality given the cost limitations.<br>▲ Be specific and factual without overwhelming the driver with details.<br>▲ Appeal to esteem and independence needs. | ▲ Define clearly in writing and make sure the Amiable understands:<br>▲ What you can do to support the Amiable's personal goals;<br>▲ What you will contribute and what the Amiable needs to contribute; and<br>▲ The support resources you intend to commit to the project. | ▲ Provide specific solutions to the Expressive's ideas—in writing.<br>▲ Build confidence that you have the necessary facts, but do not overwhelm the Expressive with details.<br>▲ Do not rush the discussion.<br>▲ Spend time developing ways to implement ideas.<br>▲ Appeal to personal esteem needs. |

*(Continued)*

| Selling Task or Objective | Selling to the Analytical | Selling to the Driver | Selling to the Amiable | Selling to the Expressive |
|---|---|---|---|---|
| Providing the Sales Story *(continued)* | ▲ Give buyer chance to review all documents related to purchase and delivery. | ▲ Reinforce the driver's preference for acting in a forthright manner.<br>▲ Summarize content quickly, then let Driver choose a course of action. | ▲ Provide a clear solution to the Amiable's problem with maximum assurances that this is the best solution and that there is no need to consider others.<br>▲ Ask the Amiable to involve other decision-makers.<br>▲ Satisfy needs by showing how your solution is best now and will be best in the future and support it with references and third-party evidence.<br>▲ Use testimonials from perceived experts and others close to the Amiable. | ▲ Try to get commitments to action in writing. |
| Asking for the Commitment | ▲ Ask for commitment in a low-key but direct manner.<br>▲ Expect to negotiate changes.<br>▲ Pay special attention to pricing issues.<br>▲ Work for commitment now to avoid Analytical's tendency to delay decisions.<br>▲ Cite data supporting company's service records.<br>▲ Respond to objections by emphasizing the Analytical's buying principles and objectivity. | ▲ Ask for the order directly.<br>▲ Put your offer in clear factual terms.<br>▲ Offer options and alternatives.<br>▲ Be prepared to negotiate changes and concessions.<br>▲ Drivers sometimes attach conditions to a sale.<br>▲ Offer the Driver time to consider the options.<br>▲ Anticipate objections in advance and come prepared with facts.<br>▲ Respond to objections based on Driver's values and priorities. | ▲ Ask for the order indirectly—do not push.<br>▲ Emphasize the guarantees that offer protection to the Amiable.<br>▲ Do not corner the Amiables, they want a way out if things go wrong.<br>▲ Guard against "buyer's remorse"—get a commitment even if you have to base it on a contingency.<br>▲ Stress your personal involvement after the sale.<br>▲ Encourage the Amiable to involve others in the final purchase decision.<br>▲ Welcome objections and be patient and thorough in responding to them. | ▲ When you have enough information to understand the need and have tested the appropriateness of the recommendation, assume the sale and ask for the order in a casual and informal way.<br>▲ When the opportunity presents itself, offer incentives to encourage the purchase.<br>▲ Do not confuse the issue by presenting too many options or choices.<br>▲ Get a definite commitment. Be sure the Expressive understands the decision to purchase.<br>▲ Save the details until after you have a firm buying decision. The Expressive believes it is the salesperson's job to handle details. |

*(Continued)*

| Selling Task or Objective | Selling to the Analytical | Selling to the Driver | Selling to the Amiable | Selling to the Expressive |
|---|---|---|---|---|
| Asking for the Commitment *(continued)* | | | ▲ When responding to objections:<br>  – Describe financial justification;<br>  – Refer to experts or others the Amiable respects; and<br>  – Keep in mind how the Amiable feels about and will be affected by the purchase decision. | ▲ In handling objections:<br>  – Describe what others have done to get over that hurdle;<br>  – Respond to the Expressive's enthusiasm for their goals;<br>  – Deal with how the recommendation meets with this buyer's options;<br>  – Restate benefits that focus on the satisfaction a buying decision will bring. |
| Providing Follow-up | ▲ Provide detailed implementation plan.<br>▲ Maintain regular contact.<br>▲ Check to confirm satisfactory and on-schedule delivery. | ▲ Set up communication process with the Driver that encourages quick exchange of information about check-points and milestones.<br>▲ Make sure you have a contingency plan to responsively implement corrections and incorporate changes.<br>▲ Make sure there are no surprises. | ▲ Immediately after the purchase decision is made, make a follow-up appointment.<br>▲ Initiate and maintain frequent contacts providing services such as:<br>  – Periodic progress reports on installation;<br>  – Arrangements for service and training;<br>  – Introduction of new products and services; and<br>  – Listening carefully to concerns, even those that seem trivial. | ▲ As soon as the order is signed, reaffirm the schedule for delivery and your personal relationship with the buyer, and introduce the implementation person or team.<br>▲ A social situation such as a lunch can be a very effective opportunity for following up on business with this buyer.<br>▲ Work toward becoming an ongoing member of the buyer's team.<br>▲ In case of any complaints, handle them yourself. Never refer them to another in your organization without the buyer's assent. |

## Other Factors

In addition to social style, the seller can also align actions to mirror the customer's language, tone, and business environment.

- ▶ Choose words that match the sophistication of your customer.
- ▶ Regulate the tone, volume, and pace of your voice to that of your customer.
- ▶ Maintain the same emotional level as the customer.
- ▶ Choose how formal you need to be based on the customer or the business environment.

## ACTIVE LISTENING

**ACTIVE LISTENING**
the cognitive process of actively sensing, interpreting, evaluating, and responding to the verbal and nonverbal messages of present or potential customers

To gather the information that is needed from the customer, the seller will need to be an expert listener. It is important that the seller excel in the ability to understand what the customer is and isn't communicating. Listening is an active process that takes intentional effort. **Active listening** is defined as the cognitive process of actively sensing, interpreting, evaluating, and responding to verbal and nonverbal messages. Active listening works hand-in-hand with the philosophy of asking questions outlined in Chapter 7. It won't do much good to spend 80% of the conversation letting the customer talk if the seller is not effectively listening to their verbal and nonverbal answers. Listening shows that the seller cares about what the prospect is trying to communicate, which helps build rapport. It communicates to the customer that *I really care about you.*

> After evaluating tens of thousands of sales calls at the MLS, National Sales Center, the importance of listening in a sales call has become very clear. It goes beyond listening to the clients' words. It's listening to their tone, background noises, change of pace, and pitch. Clients can be objection-hiding ninjas. If you don't have a laser focus and take in all elements of the call, you will miss important information that will be the difference between closing a deal or not.
>
> —Jeff Berryhill, *Major League Soccer*

Salespeople need to listen CAREfully—concentrate, acknowledge, restate, empathize, and fully grasp the main idea.[26]

## Concentrate

Because we can listen to five times more words per minute than we can speak, it is easy to become a lazy listener. However, good listening requires immense concentration. In fact, most people could benefit from improving their listening skills. Tips for concentrating include:

- ▶ Don't interrupt or cut the customer off.
- ▶ Focus on verbal and nonverbal cues.
- ▶ Visualize what the customer is trying to say.
- ▶ Take notes.
- ▶ Reduce or eliminate noise and distractions.

## Acknowledge

It is important to show customers they are being listened to. As discussed earlier in this chapter, body language can be used to show demonstrate listening—an occasional nod of the head, strong eye contact, alert head position, erect posture, etc. Use brief, softly spoken phrases like *yes*, *I see*, or *I understand* to acknowledge the customer while not impeding the flow of the conversation. These phrases encourage the customer to continue speaking. Tips to acknowledge include:

- ▶ Give subtle and encouraging feedback to facilitate flow of conversation.
- ▶ Utilize questions to keep the conversation on track.
- ▶ Use nonverbal cues to show that you understand the customer's message.

## Restate

Restating what the customer has just said shows the seller has been listening and confirms understanding of what the customer is thinking. It also helps to ensure that the customer is following along with the key points being

---

26. CARE taken from Cathcart, J. (1990). *Relationship selling: The key to getting and keeping customers.* New York: Berkley Publishing Group.

presented. Sellers should repeat, paraphrase, clarify, and summarize statements said by the prospect.

- ▶ **Repeat**—Repeat the customer's statement using their words to verify you understand the customer. This strategy should be used sparingly because customers don't want to feel like they are talking to a three-year-old who is repeating everything they are saying. It should be used to confirm very specific pieces of information.
- ▶ **Paraphrase**—Restate the customer's comment using your own words. Paraphrased statements are used with phrases like *Let me see if I understand you correctly . . .* and *what I'm hearing you say is . . .*
- ▶ **Clarify**—Ask a question to verify a customer's meaning. Use clarifying questions to check your conclusions, data, facts, or confirm an existing conclusion. Close-ended questions like *Is that correct?* and *Do I have that right?* are used to clarify.
- ▶ **Summarize**—At strategic points in the conversation, the seller can summarize a larger portion of the conversation to confirm understanding or re-state key points that have already been agreed upon. Summary statements work well with phrases like *Based on what you have told me* and *It sounds like what we've talked about today . . .*

## Empathize

**EMPATHY**
the ability to see things as others would see them

**Empathy** is the ability to see things as others would see them. It communicates to the customer that the seller understands how he or she feels. Empathy does not imply feeling sorry for someone (sympathy), but rather that the seller can see feelings, ideas, and situations from their perspective. Stated differently, it's the ability to put oneself in someone else's shoes. Practice empathy skills by seeing the world through the eyes of the customer. Empathy communicates *I'm here to help you* to the customer. By using phrases like *I see what you mean, I understand how you feel*, and *I can appreciate your point*, the seller sends a powerful message to the customer that he or she understands their feelings, ideas, and situation.

## Fully Grasp the Main Idea

It is commonly said "don't miss the forest for the trees." The trees in this case could be emotion-laden words, the way in which the message is delivered, and irrelevant facts. The ability to grasp main ideas, central themes, or big-picture concepts will help the seller avoid getting off-track during the conversation. Tips of grasping the main idea include:

- ▶ Judge the content of the message, not the customer's delivery style.
- ▶ Don't judge or evaluate the customers' message until their message is complete.

- ▶ Focus less on facts and more on central themes.
- ▶ Take notes, but limit note taking to key ideas discussed.
- ▶ Keep an open mind.
- ▶ Don't prejudge a prospect's situation.
- ▶ Read between the lines for what is not said.

## Silence

Novice salespeople assume that customers giving similar answers have the same problems, needs, and motivations. Customers find this frustrating because they are not being heard. A way to prevent this mistake is to utilize the *Golden Silence* sales technique, which employs a pause after asking a question and after the customer responds. It prevents the salesperson from forging ahead to the next question without listening to the customer's answer, thus reducing the likelihood the customer will feel interrogated. It also allows the customer to intently reflect on something that the seller has said. Don't be afraid to allow periods of silence during the conversation.

## Bad Listening Habits

In addition to all of the things the seller should do to be an effective listener, it also helps to think about the things he or she should do to avoid displaying irritating listening habits. Customers can become irritated by the following types of behaviors exhibited by the seller:[27]

- ▶ Doing all of the talking
- ▶ Interrupting the customer
- ▶ Not looking at the customer during the conversation
- ▶ Fidgeting with objects, looking at clock or watch
- ▶ Holding a poker face
- ▶ Putting words in the customer's mouth
- ▶ Asking a question about something the customer just answered
- ▶ Arguing with a customer
- ▶ Finishing sentences for the customer
- ▶ Sitting too close to the customer
- ▶ Acting like as if it is a favor to see the customer
- ▶ Acting like a know-it-all or always being the hero of the story
- ▶ Looking at the customer in a judgmental way

---

27. Cathcart, J. (1990). *Relationship selling: The key to getting and keeping customers.* New York: Berkley Publishing Group.

---

**LISTENING GUIDELINES**

▶ Listen attentively
▶ Pause (think) before replying
▶ Be comfortable with silence
▶ Paraphrase in your own words
▶ Interpret nonverbal signals and send positive signals
▶ Ask questions to clarify meaning
▶ Listen to the big picture
▶ Show the prospect you are listening by acknowledging what they are saying
▶ Restate the customer's position to clarify meaning
▶ Show empathy

---

## BUILDING TRUST

**TRUST**
an expectation by the customer that a salesperson will engage in actions supporting their interests

When is the last time you purchased something from someone you didn't trust? Would you make a repeat purchase from someone who didn't follow through on his or her promises? Would you recommend that a friend purchase from someone whom you don't trust? As you can see, building relationships is at the heart of consultative selling, and perhaps the most important way to build relationships is through trust. **Trust** is an expectation by the customer that a salesperson will engage in actions supporting their interests.

Customers trust salespeople who have the customer's best interest at heart instead of their own personal motivations. Building trust is important because the transition to relationship marketing in recent years is built on the personal connections that the organization can make with customers over the long-term. While organizations can leverage technology in many different ways, there is no better way to build a trust-based relationship with a prospect than through competent, dependable, and knowledge salespeople. Trust can be earned through dependability, honesty, customer orientation, and likability.[28]

Expertise refers to the salespersons' knowledge of the product, industry, competition, and the prospect. For ticket sales, product knowledge like seat locations, ticket prices, features, benefits, and payment options are foundational to demonstrating expertise with the customer. For sponsorship sales, it is important that the seller has expertise in the sport marketing industry. For golf memberships, it might be important that the seller has knowledge about

---

28. Ingram, T., LaForge, R., Avila, R., Schwepker, C., & Williams, M. (2006). *Professional selling: A trust-based approach,* 3rd ed. Mason, OH: Thomson Southwestern.

how other golf courses design their memberships. For all types of sales, it is important to know as much as possible about the prospect.

Dependability focuses on the predictability of the salesperson's actions. The extent to which salespeople do what they say they are going to do impacts the customer's trust level with the salesperson. It can be tempting to make a promise in order to close a sale, but salespeople should never promise something that cannot be delivered. Product knowledge is important so the seller doesn't overpromise or accidentally provide misinformation. Dependable salespeople are reliable and keep their promises.

Honesty refers to the truthfulness of the spoken word. It can be tempting to provide slightly misleading information to advance the sales process, but as in all areas of life "honesty is the best policy." It takes only one misleading statement to lose all credibility with a prospect. Demonstrating ethical behavior and honesty builds trust in any sales environment.

Customer orientation means placing as much emphasis on the customer's interests as the seller's own interests. This means making product recommendations that fit the customer's needs and the organization's needs. For example, the seller may earn a higher commission by selling a full season ticket package, but if the 14-game mini-plan is the best fit for the customer, the seller should avoid pushing the full season package just because there is more personal benefit than the 14-game plan. Having a customer orientation also means presenting any disadvantages or drawbacks to making a purchase. For example, letting customers know that the facility is closed on holidays is valuable information a customer needs to know before making a decision.

Likability is an emotional feeling experienced by the customer that refers to whether the customer enjoys doing business with the salesperson. People prefer to buy from people they like. Liking is based on physical attractiveness, first impressions, similarities, and compatibility. While physical attractiveness and first impressions are important at the beginning of a relationship, finding time to discuss issues and interests outside of business help increase likability as the relationship continues to progress. For example, likability is an important factor in a sponsor's decision to renew a sponsorship because the sponsor will have the length of the contract to know key sales and service personnel within an organization.

One simple tactic introduced in Chapter 5 that the seller can employ to facilitate trust is using the customer's name throughout the conversation. Some sales trainers and organizations recommend a certain number of times that a salesperson should use the customer's name during a sales call. For example:

- It's great to speak with you, *name*.
- *Name*, tell me more about . . .
- *Name*, I completely understand what you mean . . .

## BARRIERS TO COMMUNICATION

There are many obstacles that stand in the way of communicating effectively with clients. Communication between salesperson and customer could break down for any number of reasons, but eight factors stand out as communication barriers salespeople should be aware of.

1. **The sales message is not tailored to the customer**. The heart of consultative sales is conducting a needs analysis to tailor the sales pitch in a way that allows the client to uncover the need for the product. Failure to adapt the seller's presentation of the package to meet the needs of the client will shut down communications quickly. Remember, the seller's job is to make sure that customer knows *what's in it for me*.

2. **Disorganized sales presentation**. Disorganized presentations stem from lack of preparation, lack of product knowledge, incomplete needs analysis, and poor design of visual aids, leading to frustration and anger on the part of the client.

3. **Failure to listen**. Poor listening can stem from a client not listening to the seller, or the seller not listening to the client. Failure to listen leads to misunderstanding and confusion. Refer to the section above on active listening for how to improve listening skills.

4. **Noise**. Any sound unrelated to the sales conversation can distract the seller or the client. Selecting an environment that will limit distractions, avoiding behaviors that are distracting, and refocusing the client when a distraction occurs are important to communicate effectively.

5. **Sales message is too long**. Talking too much during a sales call, sending a lengthy voice mail or e-mail, or including too much content in an in-person presentation can overload the client with information and cause frustration or confusion that causes the customer to tune out the seller.

6. **Failure to adapt to the client's style**. It is important to adapt the presentation style to the personality and communication style of the customer when possible. Failure to do so will result in frustration for the client because he or she will want to receive information from the seller in a different way than he or she is providing.

7. **Poor management and interpretation of nonverbal cues**. Failure to interpret nonverbal cues and manage one's own nonverbal messages like body language, physical appearance, and proxemics can cause serious breakdowns in communication.

8. **Failure to build trust**. Missing one of the five key elements to building trust can result in the client not feeling comfortable with moving forward with the relationship.

## CHAPTER SUMMARY

This chapter provides an overview of how to utilize communication skills to build rapport with customers. These principles can be applied in nearly any type of business setting that sport salespeople might find themselves working in the future. While many people assume that communication skills come effortlessly to some people, good communication requires focused effort, practice, and reflection.

> The best way to improve verbal communication is to do it as often as possible and then assess those communications. At the MLS, National Sales Center, we are big believers on evaluating recorded calls. The most effective way to practice these skills is taking an honest assessment of your sales calls. Just like breaking down game-tape, this will be the most effective way to highlight areas of improvement.
>
> —Jeff Berryhill, *Major League Soccer*

**Jonathan Rossing, Department Chair, Communication Studies, Gonzaga University**

### IMPROVING SALES COMMUNICATION SKILLS THROUGH IMPROVISATION

*What is applied improvisation?*

Applied improvisation has quickly been spreading to Fortune 500 companies, MBA programs, and sales training programs in business and industry. This field is NOT trying to make CEOs into actors or managers into comedians. Instead, applied improvisation means taking the techniques, skills, and practices that the successful improvisers need onstage, but using those same skills to improve communication, teamwork, leadership, and performance in real-world situations like the workplace or sales.

### What are the key principles and skills of improvisation?

Improvisers start a show without props, costumes, characters, or lines. Performers don't know will be said or what will happen in the scene until it happens. With nothing more than a single suggestion from the audience, they create stories that delight the audience and make the audience think the actors had a script all along. Like any art, improvisation requires skill and regular practice. Vital improvisation skills include listening, being fully present in the moment, the ability to think quickly, and trusting yourself and others. Successful improvisers also follow a set of guidelines and principles such as:

- ▶ **"Yes, and":** Improvisers use the concept of "yes, and . . . " to move their scenes and stories forward. Saying "Yes" means that improvisers accept the reality or information that has been presented by their scene partner. Improvisers avoid *blocking* or *rejecting* ideas because these actions kill the momentum of the scene. The "and" reminds improvisers that they also have a responsibility to add information to the scene. They must contribute new ideas that give their fellow scene partners more information to respond to.

- ▶ **Recognize gifts/offers:** Improvisers have to create something from nothing. That means they need to learn how to see the value and opportunity in everything. Everything that a scene partner says and does represents an offer or "gift" to an improviser. The spoken words, the tone of voice, the gesture, the body language—all of these are offers that an improviser has to consider and potentially use in order to create an interesting scene. Improvisers also recognize mistakes as opportunities. A mispronounced word or a stumble could become the "gifts" that make the scene come together.

- ▶ **Make your scene partner look good:** Improv is an ensemble art. There is no single star of the show. Improvisers commit to the idea that their job is to make everyone else in the ensemble shine. No one tries to steal the scene or command the spotlight. Instead, they focus on setting each other up for success.

- ▶ **Tell interesting stories:** Audiences want engaging and interesting stories that give them a reason to keep watching. Therefore, improvisers have to practice the art of storytelling. They have to quickly create relationships between characters and establish conflict or needs that make the scene worth watching.

### What are the similarities between sales and improv?

Sales shares many similarities with the art of improvisation. Both require training, practice, and excellent communication. Just like improvisers, a sales professional never knows what situation she might walk into or what unexpected twists her customers and prospects might present. She has to respond spontaneously to whatever her client says and be flexible enough to change plans based on new information. Therefore, in sales, the principle of "Yes, and" is incredibly valuable. "Yes and" helps sales professionals practice their ability to roll with the unexpected and still listen to the client, connect with the client, and add meaningful information to the relationship. A salesperson who can discover the value in every new twist a client presents and who can accept and affirm even the most "off-script" encounters, is more capable of creating strong relationships with and solving problems for clients.

In addition, sales requires the skill to immediately size up a situation and recognize what is needed to move forward and progress. This ability requires the same sense of attention and presence in the moment that makes improvisers successful. In sales, learning to pick up on even the smallest cues from a client such as tone or body language, means you can respond more effectively to the client. In order to pick up on all the verbal and non-verbal "gifts" or offers in any situation, you have to develop your listening skills. Better listening leads to better questions for your client which leads to better information about your client that you can respond to with a "Yes and" framework. Strong listening can also help you determine more quickly when it is time to let go of a particular sale rather than continuing to spend energy pursuing something that won't be profitable.

The storytelling skills that make improvisers successful are also valuable in a sales context. A salesperson needs to know the story of his or her products, services, and brand, but more importantly, he or she needs to be able to tell an engaging story that relates to the client and helps the client *see him or herself* in the story. In a sales meeting, it is vital to discover what a client needs and learn more about the client in the moment. In other words, like improv, a sales pitch requires two people creating a story spontaneously. It's less effective to stick to a pre-set sales pitch. The skills that help improvisers also help sales professionals engage their clients and create a story about the product *with* the clients. Moreover, adopting the ensemble mindset ("make your scene partner look good") helps you shift the focus of your sales interactions. It's no longer about you and your sale, but it's about your prospects and their process of discovering how they fit into the story of the product.

### How to improve your improvisation skills

Sales professionals who learn and practice improv skills can become more adaptable amid constant change, more aware of and flexible with their clients' needs, and better prepared to adjust to unexpected twists. If you're thinking, "I can't do improv! I'm not funny" or "I can't act," *don't worry*. Applied improvisation isn't about entertainment, acting, or being funny. But you can benefit from practicing skills that make good improvisers. Many salespeople have reported benefits from taking an introductory improv class at a local theater. Companies have also been bringing applied improv professionals into the office to conduct training sessions in guidelines and skills of improvisation.

You can also learn more about these guidelines and skills from the following resources:

▶ *Yes And: How Improvisation Reverses "No, But" Thinking and Improves Creativity and Collaboration—Lessons from The Second City* by K. Leonard and T. Yorton.

▶ *Everything's an Offer: How To Do More with Less* by R. Poynton.

▶ *Ditch the Pitch: The Art of Improvised Persuasion* by S. Yastrow.

## CHAPTER ACTIVITIES

1. Think of a recent time when a face-to-face conversation resulted in a breakdown of communication. Discuss the factors that caused this miscommunication to occur. What was the result of the faulty encoding and decoding of the message?

2. Create a simile, metaphor, and analogy to describe the experience of attending a sporting event of your choosing.

3. Assume you are a group sales executive for a professional sports team of your choosing. Complete the following activities:

   a. Create a "Who am I" story.

   b. Create a "Who I represent" story.

   c. Create a "Who I've helped" story.

   d. Assume you cultivated a lead at a local high school with the athletic director. Knowing there are a variety of ways that the athletic department, coaches, athletes, and parents can use tickets to a college or professional sporting event, paint a picture through telling a story of why they should purchase tickets. Record a video where you tell a compelling story to the prospect.

4. Search online and find five images of people demonstrating positive non-verbal cues and negative non-verbal cues. For each image, describe the message the person is sending.

5. Identify and then describe a person you know that matches each personality type in the social style matrix. Explain how you would use the social style matrix to sell or persuade each person.

6. Explain how trust is formed between a salesperson and customer.

# CHAPTER COMPETENCY ASSESSMENT[29]

## COMPETENCY DOMAIN: RELATIONSHIP BUILDING

*Exemplary:* Consistently does all or almost all of the following:

- ► Develops a strong relationship with nearly all customers
- ► Shows empathy with customers
- ► Adapts personality and style to that of the customer
- ► Builds trust with customers
- ► Uses the customer's first name multiple times during the conversation
- ► Utilizes storytelling to connect with customers
- ► Demonstrates an appropriate sense of humor during calls and meetings
- ► Assumes assertive but not pushy demeanor
- ► Connects with the customer and has a natural conversation

*Skilled:* Does most of the following, but may need improvement in at least two areas:

- ► Develops a strong relationship with a majority of customers
- ► Shows empathy with customers
- ► Adapts personality and style to that of the customer
- ► Builds trust with customers
- ► Uses the customer's first name multiple times during the conversation
- ► Utilizes storytelling to connect with customers
- ► Demonstrates an appropriate sense of humor during calls and meetings
- ► Assumes assertive but not pushy demeanor
- ► Connects with the customer and has a natural conversation

*Adequate:* Does most of the following:

- ► Does not build rapport with the customer in majority of conversations
- ► Seems forced or unnatural in many conversations
- ► Fails to effectively empathize with most customers
- ► Builds trust with the customer in most cases
- ► Fails to recognize when the customer is uncomfortable with the conversation
- ► Neglects to regularly use the customer's first name and tell stories

*Novice:* Consistently does all or almost all of the following:

- ► Is unable to develop a relationship with customers
- ► Struggles to find common ground and enters into sales discussion without earning trust
- ► Fails to demonstrate empathy
- ► Charges ahead by presenting solutions or closing without connecting with the customer
- ► Fails to recognize lack of connection with the customer which leaves customer in discomfort
- ► Fails to get to know the customer and/or presents products that don't fit customer needs

---

29. From "Competency Assessment for Entry-Level Sport Ticket Sales Professionals" by David Pierce and Richard Irwin, *Journal of Applied Sport Management,* Volume 8 (2), Summer 2016. Reprinted by permission of Sagamore Publishing. www.sagamorepub.com

## COMPETENCY DOMAIN: COMMUNICATION SKILLS

*Exemplary*: Seller demonstrates strong verbal and non-verbal communication skills at all times, and consistently does all or almost all of the following:

- ▶ Speaks clearly and articulately while sounding comfortable in the conversation
- ▶ Avoids slang phrases and speaks in a professional manner at all times
- ▶ Uses warm posture and facial expressions in face-to-face meetings
- ▶ Regulates pitch, volume, tone, speed, and inflection of voice appropriately at all times

*Skilled*: Seller demonstrates strong verbal and non-verbal communication skills in most instances and does most of the following:

- ▶ Speaks clearly and articulately while sounding comfortable in the conversation
- ▶ Avoids slang phrases and speaks in a professional manner most of the time
- ▶ Uses warm posture and facial expressions in face-to-face meetings
- ▶ Regulates pitch, volume, tone, speed, and inflection of voice appropriately in most cases

*Adequate*: Seller demonstrates acceptable communication skills when interacting with customers, but needs assistance in at least two of the following areas:

- ▶ Clarity of speech
- ▶ Level of professionalism or intelligence in speech
- ▶ Regulation of pitch, volume, tone, speed, and inflection of voice
- ▶ Flow of conversation
- ▶ Body language
- ▶ Enthusiasm
- ▶ Managing non-verbal cues

*Novice*: Consistently does all or almost all of the following:

- ▶ Demonstrates poor verbal and non-verbal communication skills with customers
- ▶ Suffers from speech that is unclear, unintelligent, unprofessional, or uncomfortable
- ▶ Uses unprofessional or unapproachable body language in face-to-face settings
- ▶ Has difficulty regulating pitch, volume, tone, speed, and inflection of voice appropriately

# CHAPTER 12

---

# PROSPECTING

### LEARNING OBJECTIVES

After completing this chapter, you should be able to:

► Understand the importance of generating leads and prospects within the sales process.

► Articulate and define the various classifications of leads.

► Know the common sources of leads in sport sales settings.

► Understand how successful sales representatives and properties acquire leads.

► Know how sport organizations manage leads and utilize customer relationship management software.

### KEY TERMS

| | | |
|---|---|---|
| Cold lead | Hot lead | Prospects |
| Customer Relationship | Leads | Qualifying |
| Management (CRM) | Prospecting | Warm lead |

### COMPENTENCIES

► Ability to identify sources of leads and generate new prospects.

► Ability to conduct research and acquire relevant information about prospects.

► Ability to populate and utilize customer relationship software.

## CHAPTER OVERVIEW

Most major league sports teams ask their sales representatives to make between 75 and 125 sales calls a day. Making that many calls not only requires stamina and enthusiasm, but also leads and prospects. **Leads** are names and contact information for potential buyers. A **prospect**, meanwhile, is not simply any name and phone number, but rather someone who has a need, financial capacity, and authority to buy. Thus, **prospecting** is the continual process of identifying and contacting businesses and individuals in order to create a pool of qualified buyers. Prospecting is important for two reasons. First, the more qualified a list of leads, the better chance of success on sales calls. Second, prospecting helps replenish the appointments needed to sell, which helps avoid the up-and-down cycles in sales productivity. This chapter introduces classifications of leads, lead generation strategies, how to qualify leads, and how customer relationship management systems and technology can assist in the prospecting process.

**LEADS**
names and contact information for potential buyers

**PROSPECTS**
someone who has a need for or interest in the product, has the financial ability to purchase the product, and has the authority to buy the product

**PROSPECTING**
the continual process of identifying and contacting businesses and individuals in order to create a pool of qualified buyers

# PROSPECTS

To be a prospect, the lead must meet the following three criteria:

1. Has a need for or interest in the product;

2. Has the financial ability to purchase the product; and

3. Has the authority to buy the product.

Not every lead is a prospect. Sport organizations must qualify leads to determine which ones are viable prospects. The more qualified the lead list, the better chance of being successful on sales calls. Let's look a little more closely at the criteria for a prospect as listed above. The first item on the list is a need or interest in the product. A fan of the Pittsburgh Pirates would certainly meet these criteria for potentially buying Pirates tickets. However, others might also have a need or interest in tickets, even if they are not die-hard fans of the team. For example, a Pittsburgh-area business owner may not be a fan, but she probably has clients and employees who are, so she has a need for tickets. A father might not be a fan of the team but he wants to spend quality time doing a fun activity with his kids, so he has a need. College students from Pitt or Robert Morris might not necessarily be fans of the team, but they are excited about doing a social activity with their friends, and thus have a need for the product. (Recently, the Atlanta Hawks held a "Tinder" Night in which some attendees bought tickets in the hopes of making a romantic connection at Philips Arena in addition to, or perhaps instead of, rooting for the hometown team.) When discussing the needs or interests of a prospect, it is important to think beyond simple fandom.

Regarding the financial capability of purchasing the product, it may seem a safe assumption that a college student is unlikely to have the income to buy season tickets on the glass for an NHL team or a luxury suite at an NFL stadium. Those items are better suited for wealthy individuals or prominent businesses. Sellers can benefit greatly by having a rough idea of household income level or business marketing dollars available when pitching particular ticket packages to a person or corporation. However, it is important to note, financial ability may vary depending on level of fandom. For example, in his book *Winning the Customer*, former New England Patriots Chief Marketing Officer Lou Imbriano shared that when the NFL team first began selling club seats at Gillette Stadium, they incorrectly targeted current sponsors to see if they might be interested in purchasing additional seats. Those sponsors had far more financial ability to purchase seats than many of the Pats' individual season ticket holders. But what Imbriano discovered was the team's most passionate fans were far more willing to part with a greater percentage of their income compared to the team's sponsors, if it meant securing a better seat and greater team-related benefits that came with owning tickets in the club section. On a related note, many new ticket sellers who are often recent college graduates, could never fathom spending thousands or even tens of thousands of dollars on sports tickets. Yet for some individuals or businesses, spending $20,000 on a pair of lower bowl seats is a drop in the bucket. New ticket sellers need to overcome their fear of asking for a large sale because that same sale may not be intimidating at all for someone making $250,000 a year or for a business that has a six- or seven-figure marketing budget.

Finally, sellers should also consider whether the person they are planning to approach actually has the authority to approve the purchase of tickets. While many husbands may have the ability to use money from their bank account or credit card, they are hesitant to make a large purchase without first running it by their wife. A church youth leader may like the idea of buying tickets to a baseball game for his group, but might want to first make sure the group members feel the same way. In a business setting, a marketing manager may think buying season tickets to use for promoting her business might be a great idea but needs the company's CFO or accountant to actually approve a purchase order. Many sales managers suggest that when account executives set up sales meetings, they ask whether anyone else from the company needs to be involved for a decision to be made. If so, sales representatives need to make sure that person is present for the sales pitch.

## QUALIFYING LEADS

**QUALIFYING**
the process of trying to determine if a lead meets certain criteria

The process of trying to determine if a lead meets these criteria is sometimes referred to as **qualifying** a lead (the process of qualifying does not end when a seller calls a prospect, but rather continues during the initial and subsequent conversations). Years ago, many sport organizations divided up the phone book alphabetically and gave each sales representative a set of names. While this would be an easy way to generate thousands of leads, a phone book does not actually provide ticket buyer prospects. Without being able to differentiate which names in the phone book actually have an interest in attending a sporting event or the financial ability to buy season tickets, a sales representative would be very inefficient in selling. Ultimately that sales representative would likely become frustrated with the lack of results produced from cold-calling a phone book. That is why the process of developing good leads and prospects is important to sport organizations. While it is impossible to find out every detail about a prospect before initiating a conversation with them, effective teams and sellers spend some time researching or qualifying prospects, in order to more efficiently speak to the most promising prospective buyers.

Doing research on your prospects can help you build rapport. I recommend becoming an expert in the fields you are trying to sell. If you want to sell tickets to insurance agents, then study the insurance industry. The more you know about it, the easier it will be for you to make strong value propositions and to overcome objections. One of my areas of focus was coordinating group outings and experiences for Cub Scouts and Boy Scouts. To increase my odds of closing more groups, I made it my mission to learn as much about Scouting as I could. I got to the point where I could look at a uniform and know what part of the state the Scout was from, what rank he held, how active his Pack/Troop was and what accomplishments he had earned. Learning things like this gave me the confidence to walk into any meeting with a Scout leader and build instant rapport and credibility. The end result was taking the Scout category from less than 400 tickets in a season to more than 6,000 tickets . . . and that was for a minor league hockey team!

—Carl Manteau, *Milwaukee Bucks*

Today, most professional sports teams have become fairly sophisticated with how they develop and distribute leads to their sales team. Many minor league teams and college athletics departments are not quite as effective at developing leads and prospects, but progress is consistently being made. Procuring leads, however, is not the sole responsibility of a sales manager, director, or supervisor. Good sales representatives are always prospecting on their own. A recent study found that sport salespeople spend 5.5 hours per week engaged in prospecting activities.[1] In fact, later in this chapter, we will discuss some examples of how sales representatives have generated their own leads and prospect lists.

## CLASSIFYING LEADS

In the 1992 film *Glengarry Glen Ross*, Kevin Spacey plays a real estate sales manager who, with the help of Alec Baldwin's character, is responsible for motivating a sales team. One of their tactics in the film is to inform their sales representatives that Spacey's character possesses a stack of very promising and lucrative leads in his office. However, to get those leads—and earn the surefire commissions associated with them—the sales team members must first sell to several bottom-of-the-barrel prospects. Unfortunately, many sales organizations, including some sports teams, have subscribed to this tactic—asking entry level sales representatives to fight through old or poorly-procured leads in order to "prove" their sales abilities before ever having a chance to sell to more promising prospects. What more forward thinking sales organizations realize, however, is sales representatives can be far more successful if the best leads are prioritized and called first, leaving weaker leads until later or at a slower time in the sales cycle. So how does an organization classify its leads? A very simple classification system is to classify leads as hot, warm, and cold.

---

1. Pierce, D., Petersen, J., & Lee, D. (2013). Time allocation of sales activities in professional sport organizations. *The Journal of SPORT, 2*(1), 1–20.

## Hot Leads

**HOT LEAD**
prospects who have contacted the sport organization proactively seeking to buy tickets

**Hot leads** are often prospects who have contacted the sport organization proactively seeking to buy tickets. These leads may come in forms like a phone call inquiry, a response to a promotional offer, or an opt-in to an e-mail marketing campaign (perhaps a fan clicked on a "contact me if interested in tickets" button posted on an e-newsletter). Such leads clearly represent the best possibilities for a sale and should always be treated with high importance. When a team receives an inbound call from a prospect who is looking to buy, the call should always be transferred to a sales professional to complete the transaction. By speaking with a hot lead, a sales professional can gather more information and may realize the prospect is interested in multiple games or may provide links to future sales through referrals or groups. At minimum, sport teams should always collect as much basic information as possible from an inbound caller including the prospect's name and contact information. In addition, sales professionals should try to capture the reasons why the prospect is interested in attending a game, how they intend to use the tickets, the prospect's budget, and who might be attending the game with them. Throughout the interaction, the sales professional should be professional, upbeat, and enthusiastic about answering any of the prospect's questions or in responding to the prospect's reasons for attending. In some cases, a fan may choose an upper level seat because they believe it is the only one that fits their budget. In other cases, they may be able to afford lower seats, but prefer to sit up higher because it provides a better angle to watch the action of a football, soccer, or hockey game unfold. Learning more about the prospect allows the sales representative to make additional recommendations or inform the prospect of available promotional offers. Regardless, it is important the sport organization never disparage a prospect's buying intention by suggesting certain seats are not good or not providing prompt service.

It's almost scary how many basic elements of Sales 101 these guys are missing. Not asking for a caller's name, a total lack of needs assessment, no effort to build rapport, never asking for the sale or even contact information.

—Chris Denove, Senior Vice President of Research and Analytics, *Intellishop*

Handling hot leads may sound like common sense and observers might think all sport organizations would be effective at handling such calls. Unfortunately, that is not always the case. A recent study conducted by Intellishop used mystery shoppers to call Major League Baseball teams to inquire about buying tickets. In evaluating their experience, Intellishop's Senior Vice President of Research and Analytics, Chris Denove, suggested, "It's almost scary how many basic elements of Sales 101 these guys are missing. Not asking for a caller's name, a total lack of needs assessment, no effort to build rapport, never asking for the sale or even contact information."[2] The sales fundamentals presented

2. Eichelberger, C. (2011). *San Diego Padres have baseball's best sales staff, study finds.* Retrieved from http://www.bloomberg.com/news/articles/2011-06-06/padres-have-mlb-s-best-ticket-sales-staff-rockies-have-worst-study-finds

in earlier chapters still need to be utilized on inbound calls with hot leads. Unfortunately, many times sellers skip all of their sales training because they are so excited to get an easy sale, thus potentially leaving money on the table.

In addition, many sport organizations, particularly college athletics departments and minor league teams, staff their ticket box office with interns and student workers. These staff members are often the first point of contact for hot leads, but if those staff members are not well trained, they may communicate poorly or in an uniformed manner with a prospect. Veteran sales manager Jake Vernon, Vice President of Ticket Sales with the Minnesota Timberwolves, said that at his previous job, a box office staff member was approached by a customer who had recently attended his first game. The customer asked the ticket office worker if he could buy a season ticket for the remainder of the season. Since the team typically did not offer such a package, the worker dismissed the prospect by simply suggesting he just buy the few games he really wanted to attend, while not asking the prospect any questions regarding his motivation or even for his contact information. As a sales director, Vernon was dismayed at the missed opportunity to develop a relationship and sell the prospect some sort of ticket package.

## Warm Leads

Hot leads are typically prospects who have initiated contact with a team. **Warm leads**, on the other hand, are those in which some sort of contact or connection has already been made with the prospect prior to the seller making the sales call. Warm leads could also be those in which the prospect closely resembles other ticket buyers.

**WARM LEAD** prospects in which contact or connection has already been made with the prospect prior to the seller making the sales call

The most common warm leads among sport teams are those who have attended a game in the past. Past buyers have already shown an interest in the product and a willingness to buy. As such, they make the most likely target to buy again, preferably in larger quantities. Warm leads are attractive because a sales representative has an obvious connection with which to start the conversation. If a prospect attended a prior game, the seller will want to discuss the experience of that game—what the prospect liked or didn't like—which easily lends itself to a sales conversation. Some in the sales industry refer to such a connection point as a door opener.

Another outstanding generator of warm leads are current customers who can refer someone else. Sales conversations are easy to initiate with referrals because of the mutual connection. For instance, a sales representative might say, *Mike, I got your name from one of my other clients, Joe Smith, who said you enjoy coming to Tigers games and might be interested in learning more about the money you could save with one of our flex plan packages.* Sellers can also mention the proximity of seats to the person who offered the referral. For example, *Hi Mike, I got your number from Joe, who mentioned you had come with him to games in the past. I have a pair of seats only two rows back from Joe.*

As a good example of using referrals, a few years ago, the NBA's New Orleans Hornets (now Pelicans) ran a campaign called "I'm in are you?—100 Events in 100 Days." With this campaign, the team offered current season ticket holders the opportunity to host a Hornets-themed party in their home. The team would provide catering, prizes, and even appearances by team personnel. In exchange, season ticket holders were asked to invite their friends who might also be interested in buying tickets. At each event, the team's sales staff collected prospect data, then followed up with sales calls. That summer, the team sold 3,000 new season ticket packages, despite a looming NBA lockout.[3] The "I'm in are you?" campaign successfully generated many new leads because it was based on referrals from current season ticket holders. Surprisingly, many sales representatives do not ask for referrals. One study showed that 80% of current customers indicated they would be willing to offer a seller a referral, but only 20% of sellers bother to make the request.[4]

A third method of generating warm leads is to develop profiles of current ticket buyers, then try to find more people who are very similar to those buyers. A team that has done a good job of collecting data on their customers can produce profiles of those people most likely to buy; people who are in certain income brackets, live in certain zip codes, participate in certain activities, or have kids of certain ages. The challenge to the sport organization then becomes finding prospects who fit that profile and engaging them in meaningful communication. A few years ago, Full House Entertainment and Ohio University conducted a study demonstrating what industry sectors are most likely to purchase premium seating at sporting events. Topping their list were attorneys, insurance companies, and general contractors. Based upon this information, it would make sense that teams target every law firm, insurer, and home builder in a community first when prospecting to sell their premium tickets.

## Cold Leads

**COLD LEAD**
prospects who the seller does not know much about

**Cold leads** (and cold calling) refer to prospects whom the seller does not know much about. Cold leads might come from a list purchased by the team, a database filled with contacts made during a marketing event, or even a

---

3. Shapero, J. (2011). *New Orleans beats the lockout blues.* Retrieved from http://sports-forum.com/news/new_archive/index.html?article_id=421

4. Lorge, S. (2009). The Best Way to Prospect. *Sales & Marketing, Management 11* (80).

phone book. Cold leads are clearly the least preferred sales lead for any organization. Sport ticket sales expert Steve DeLay suggests teams who are struggling to generate significant leads can help warm cold leads up by sending targeted e-mails or snail mail to cold leads before they are actually contacted personally by a sales representative. Doing so not only positions the team a little more top of mind with the prospect, but also gives the seller one more item to use during the opening stage of the sales conversation (*Recently we sent out information about some of our teams' new ticket promotions this season. Did you receive your copy in the mail?*). Most teams and sellers, however, would prefer to not speak with cold leads if at all possible.

During his time as Vice President of Sales and Database Marketing with the Charlotte Hornets, Flavil Hampsten said the team used a six-step process to help prioritize hot, warm, and cold leads. The first step would be to create a specific ticket sales package. Second, the team would send out an e-mail to all their contacts to market the new product. Third, the team would categorize how respondents reacted to the e-mail. Those who immediately deleted the e-mail (the large majority) would be categorized as cold leads, while those who opened the e-mail would be categorized as warm leads. Recipients who opened the e-mail and actually clicked on one of the buttons embedded within the e-mail would automatically be moved to the hottest lead category. The fourth step would then be to send a snail mail post card offer to those who opened or clicked within the e-mail. Not until the fifth step would a sales representative actually contact the prospect, and at this stage, the seller would most likely invite the prospect to an in-arena event where the sixth step of a full-blown sales presentation would take place.

## GENERATING LEADS

### *Past Purchasers: Data Is King*

The most prominent source of leads are past ticket buyers. This might include lapsed season ticket holders or someone who has attended just a few games, whether as part of a group outing, with a family, or simply as a fan. However, if the organization does not possess any information about past purchasers, past purchasers are not a source of leads. Thus, the first step in generating this list of past ticket buyers is to always capture as much information about ticket buyers as possible. For most sport organizations, the first step in improving ticket sales involves collecting more and better data about fans. In Jon Spoelstra's seminal sport marketing book *Ice to the Eskimos*, he calls the collection of information about past ticket buyers the "Quick Fix Silver Bullet." Spoelstra, who spent time in the front office of several NBA franchises, explains that

©Lindsay Schoon/Shutterstock.com

getting past ticket buyers to purchase slightly more tickets and in slightly greater amounts (attending six games instead of four) is far more efficient and lucrative than constantly attempting to acquire new consumers. However, doing so requires active databases full of information on past attendees.

If someone buys a ticket as a walk-up sale five minutes prior to tip-off, with a long line of customers behind her, it may not always be easy or productive to collect many of the customer's details. However, even capturing a name and phone number or e-mail address is an important start. Those who buy tickets electronically are more likely to provide additional information such as a mailing address or the names of people with whom they are attending the game. Unfortunately, many team marketers know far too little about the people sitting in the stands watching their events. If someone attends a game as part of a group, uses tickets given as a gift, or buys tickets on a secondary market such as StubHub or eBay, the team may not capture the attendee's information. This is one reason many teams and athletic departments have established their own ticket exchange programs, so that attendees who buy tickets from resellers may go through the team's website to do so, allowing the team to capture valuable information.

When a group attends a sporting event, it is important for the team to collect information about all attendees, not just the group leader. Doing so allows the team to contact group members individually to follow up on their experience and invite them to attend again. In some cases, a group leader may provide detailed information on group attendees to the team. In other cases, the team can offer an incentive for group members to provide their contact information, perhaps though a group-specific raffle or prize giveaway. Some teams provide the attendees with a photo or some other small memento marking their attendance at a game (such as a "birth certificate" commemorating a young fan's first visit to a ball park). In order to receive these token items, fans must provide their e-mail address or other contact information.

Similarly, it is important to put a process in place to collect customer data on everyone who attends in a group, not just the person who purchased the ticket. The team collects information about the fan purchasing a group of tickets online, but it doesn't have any information about the other people attending in that group. Teams use business card drops, enter-to-win sweep-stakes, photo opportunities, and other tactics to collect information on those who are at the game but did not make the actual purchase.

Consider the following scenario to illustrate the importance of on-site prospecting. A casual golfer makes a tee time for himself and his three buddies at a local course for 9 a.m. on Thursday. On Thursday morning, the foursome show up, indicate that they have a reservation, pay their greens fees, and hit the links. Next month, the group tries another course and the process plays out again. However, what if the attendant at the pro shop had asked all four golfers for their contact information when they showed up to play? While the group was golfing, the attendant could quickly enter their information into a database and cross-reference to learn this was their first visit to the course. Two days later, the club's golf pro could follow up with a phone call, asking the golfers about their experience and learning that the group typically golfs together once a month. The golf pro could then send a customized e-mail to each member of the group, showcasing several of their entry-level memberships and specials, plus a coupon for swing lessons. Such efforts would clearly offer a positive ROI for the golf club, as there is relatively little expense in making these minor efforts. However, this kind of direct marketing is impossible if the only piece of information about the foursome the golf course has is the first and last name of the person making the tee time.

©Monkey Business Images/Shutterstock.com

## GROUP SALES

Group sales are an important source of ticket revenue for any sport organization. Courting groups can be a long process, as it can be difficult to identify the right group leader, create the right ticket package or experience, and give the group leader lead time to collect money and distribute tickets. However, if done well, group outings have a high ROI for teams, not just in the short-term sale, but also in the possibility of repeat group sales as well as the ability to create new fans. Many major league teams now hire full-time staff members focused specifically on group sales. In fact, ticket sales expert Steve DeLay recommends sport organizations hire one dedicated group sales representative for every 1,500 group sales leads in a team's database.

An effective group sales strategy begins with some homework. Sport managers should develop group sales categories. For instance, the company Full House Entertainment Database Marketing divides potential group sales into several major categories:

1. Businesses and company anniversaries (20 years in business, retirement parties, etc.);
2. Birthday parties (both kids parties and adult milestone parties); and
3. Other significant groups. This third category is further subdivided on their website into categories such as:
   (a) education (elementary schools, universities, etc.);
   (b) membership organizations (churches, civic groups, etc.);
   (c) social services (non-profits, youth sport/organizations, child care centers, etc.); and
   (d) others (park and recreation districts, military organizations, retirement homes, etc.)[1]

Once group lead categories are established, sales teams must then identify group leaders within those organizations and spend time assessing the specific needs of those groups by meeting with the group leaders. In some cases, teams may create inventory designed to be sold specifically to certain groups. For instance, an NHL team may develop a ticket package that includes an opportunity to play a game on the ice before team warmups, and would specifically target local youth teams. Or perhaps a team plans to sell an opportunity to perform the national anthem, targeted specifically to high school bands or church choirs. In other cases, inventory such as a high five tunnel, presentation of the game ball, or a picnic in the outfield bleachers, might be available to any interested group. In many cases, teams will establish a minimum ticket or revenue number that must be reached by the group to qualify for any value add-ons. Ticket sellers should keep in mind, effective needs assessment is just as important in group sales as it is with season ticket accounts. For instance, a college football team might help a Boy Scout troop earn badges through an activity on the field, or a church youth group might want to meet a player or coach with strong religious convictions after the game. After performing needs assessment, sales representatives may learn about a group's desire to fund-raise, have a unique meeting space, or network with other similar groups, all issues which can be addressed by a group outing to a sporting event. When the New York Mets first hosted Greek Heritage Day, the event was sparsely attended. After spending more time on needs assessment, they learned that many Greeks love to travel to Greece during the month of August. When the team moved the promotion up two months, they had much better results.[2] Some teams have begun holding special events for group leaders or inviting them to an early season game in an effort to show them the game experience. Other teams, such as the Tampa Bay Rays, have developed extensive incentivization programs targeted specifically at group leaders.

Teams need to collect information about all members of the group, not just the group leader. Ideally, group leaders will provide a list of contact information of all attendees prior to the game, but the reality is that most groups will change due to late additions, kids getting sick, or sudden changes in travel plans. The better method for collecting data from group attendees is to have group members provide the information in-game. To facilitate this, team personnel should have group attendees fill out raffle tickets to win a prize or offer to send an electronic photo of the group at the game to those who provide e-mail addresses (along with additional contact information).

1. *Full House*. (2015). Retrieved from http://www.fillthehouse.com/group-sales-leads.html
2. Dan Migala. "Ethnic Studies: How to Create Ethnic Promotional Nights That Grows Ticket Sales." Retrieved from http://migalareport.com/node/94

## *Customer Relationship Management*

Collecting as much information as possible about your customers is often the first step in improving team ticket sales. As such, consistent efforts should be made in capturing such data. Former New England Patriots Chief Marketing Officer Lou Imbriano suggests in his book *Winning the Customer* that collecting data from customers is just as important as collecting their money and that good sport organizations incentivize customers for providing information just as much as for purchases.[5] To use this data effectively, sport properties must have a mechanism to store and sort the information. Nearly all professional sport teams and major college athletics departments utilize a computer software program to help with **Customer Relationship Management (CRM)**. CRM systems allow employees to merge all information collected from any touchpoint with a customer into a single, easily accessible database, providing a 360-degree picture of that fan or prospect. Such software provides sales professionals with a powerful tool . . . as long as adequate data is entered and stored.

CRM systems allow organizations to keep track of the communication and contact fans have with a team. For instance, entry forms from ticket and suite giveaways, autograph requests, and newsletter sign-ups all provide a team with the contact information of people who have shown an interest in the product, which are then catalogued in the CRM system. To illustrate, the Washington Nationals teamed up with the Virginia Lottery to create a baseball-themed scratch-off ticket. Non-winning tickets could be sent to the team for the opportunity to be entered into a second chance drawing to win a suite for a game. This allowed the team to collect thousands of new leads from people who were at least interested in watching a Nationals game from a suite. College athletic departments have rich sources for lead generation from things like alumni databases, vendors who partner with the university, or families whose children attend summer sport camps. A robust CRM system with accurate data can provide important insights to sellers. For example, a seller could look at a client profile of a current customer and know that she has attended six games this season, is a subscriber of the team's newsletter, has a family of four, attended two concerts at the venue, and complained about

**CUSTOMER RELATIONSHIP MANAGEMENT (CRM)** allows employees to merge all information collected from any touchpoint with a customer into a single, easily accessible database, providing a 360-degree picture of that fan or prospect

©Trueffelpix/Shutterstock.com

5.  Imbriano, L. (2011). *Winning the customer: Turn consumers into fans and get them to spend more.* McGraw-Hill Education.

the fans sitting behind her the last time she attended a game. Knowing this information provides the seller valuable information prior to making a sales call to potentially sell a mini-plan in the team's family section next season.

---

### DATA COLLECTION WITH ONLINE SURVEYS

With the growth of digital technology, paper surveys are being replaced with online platforms for teams to gather information on fans that lead to increased sales. The Washington Capitals introduced an interactive survey tool called 'mywashcaps.com' to gather fan data. [insert footnote with the sports forum link). The Capitals created a simple and interactive online survey that started with uplifting rock music and incentivized fans to enter their personal information to win prizes. The questions asked in the survey were traditional questions like 'what type of fan are you,' but the way in which the survey was presented was unique. The user interface allowed the Capitals to generate leads and keep the fans engaged and entertained. The 'mywashcaps.com' initiative was heavily promoted by the Capitals on numerous media outlets and direct emails. The initiative resulted in thousands of entries. These leads helped make cold calls a little warmer.

---

http://www.sports-forum.com/news/archive/index.html?article_id=564

---

CRM systems are only as useful as the information entered into them. Many professional sport teams work hard to ensure they have entered as many data points as possible into the software. For instance, the Charlotte Hornets capture more than 50 data points from each buyer.[6] Data stored in CRM systems include:

- ► Gender
- ► Age/Birthdate
- ► Marital Status
- ► Number and Age of Children
- ► Employment Status
- ► Income
- ► Where media is consumed (print, television, web)
- ► Are tickets for business or personal use
- ► Attendance rate
- ► Number of years account has owned seats
- ► Renewal intent

---

6. Reese, J. (2013). *Ticket operations and sales management in sport.* Morgantown, WV: Fitness Information Technology.

This data might come from past conversations between a team seller and the consumer or it may come from external sources. SAS is a business analytics software company that produces CRM systems for many businesses. In the sport industry, they have partnered with organizations such as the Orlando Magic, New York Mets, Carolina Hurricanes, and Major League Soccer to develop effective CRM systems for marketing purposes. To populate those team and league databases, SAS suggests using several sources including internal data like ticket purchase information and newsletter subscriptions, external data like sweepstakes entries and promotions, and third party information from companies specializing in providing household income, occupation information, and education details from existing databases. Using all of this data helps a team paint a more complete picture of their customers from both a micro and macro perspective. Many teams and athletic departments today are utilizing pixel tag and "cookie" strategies to capture consumer profiles.[7] Pixel tags and "cookies" are computer codes that can be used on web browsers to monitor which web pages are being viewed. Although these tools do not extract personal identifiers, they can be used to develop profiles of the person using the web browser by comparing the sites and ads the user visits. These electronic profiles can then be used to electronically target specific ticket packages to end users. Other teams, such as the Washington Capitals, have utilized interactive surveys to collect customer data. To entice fans to complete the surveys, they create dynamic websites with opportunities to win prizes and learn more about the team.[8]

---

**Russell Scibetti, *The Business of Sports***

### BUILDING FAN PROFILES

In my most recent perusal of team marketing e-mails, I noticed one from the Minnesota Timberwolves with the subject line "Win a Suite for the Lakers Game by Completing Your Pack Profile." Being as data and CRM oriented as I am, I decided to take a closer look at how the team was using this e-mail and incentive to learn more about their fans, and I came away very impressed with the process.

To start, the email gave a brief, honest explanation as to why the team wants to know more about them.

---

7.  Migala, D. (2015). Keys to Revenue-Generating Digital Strategies: Grow. Engage. Transact. *The NACDA Report.* Retrieved from http://grfx.cstv.com/photos/schools/ nacda/sports/nacda/auto_pdf/2014-15/misc_non_event/NACDAReportJune2015.pdf

8.  National Sports Forum. Retrieved from http://www.sports-forum.com/news/archive/ index.html?article_id=564

Take two minutes to complete or update your Pack Profile, and you could win a Suite for your and 21 friends to see the Wolves vs. Lakers THIS SUNDAY. Help us get to know you a little better, and we can begin tailoring our communication to the information that will interest you the most.

I imagine that when the Timberwolves segmented their database, I was included because as a generic newsletter subscriber, they don't know enough about me to try and qualify me as a prospect. So, they can either attempt to call through their entire database, which will take an incredible amount of staff and time, or they can try to learn more about these semi-anonymous fans and target them with the appropriate products and messaging. Fans are typically quite willing to share information about their fandom to the team, and when you combine that with a valuable incentive such as the chance for a free suite night, the data you get back can have a huge impact on your sales and marketing efficiency

The Timberwolves did a really nice job with this particular data collection effort, breaking the process down into seven simple steps, focusing on key data points that align with their sales, marketing, and communications processes.

**Step 1: The Basics**—You always want to make sure you have the most accurate name, e-mail address, and phone number. Without this, you cannot connect with the fan or personalize the message in any way. Also, by splitting the process into steps, the entire process seems simpler for the user. If this was displayed as one large list, the fan might not even start, whereas even if the fan stops after step 1, the team is already better off.

**Step 2: Basic Demographics**—Age, gender, and relationship status are all data points that can point toward a prospect being likely to purchase. For example, I've seen general metrics where over 90% of season ticket buyers are male, but it can approach a 50/50 split for single game tickets. Additionally, having the date of birth gives the team an opportunity for a quality touchpoint every year. Finally, the birth year was not required ("It's a Secret . . . "). By splitting date of birth into three separate fields, you can get the date from everyone for your automated birthday message campaign, without pushing away fans that may not want to reveal their age. If this was a single date entry field, the fan would have to enter a year.

**Step 3: Fan Type**—Now we're starting to identify what type of buyer this fan represents but presenting it in a fun way that makes it easy for the fan to self-identify. This simple, one-click question can be used for targeting a wide range of future product offers.

- Fan selects from one of five options: casual fan, super fan, business, family, or night

**Step 4: Children**—If the fan clicks no, they go right to step 5. If they click yes, they see the additional section where they can enter their kids' names, genders, and birthdays. This section serves two purposes. Just having or not having children is often a significant variable when segmenting specific campaigns or building likelihood to purchase models for different products. Additionally, collecting the actual child information can help grow a team's kids club. As Scott O'Neil mentioned at the recent Ivy Sports Symposium, "research suggests the core time people become a fan is between five and nine years old."

**Step 5: Favorite Player**—This question is all about creating more effective messages through personalization. E-mail campaigns can contain images featuring a favorite player. The team can have multiple players record voice messages and each fan receives the automated call from their favorite player. Merchandise offers and even ticket packages can be branded based on the favorite player (e.g., Rubio's 9 Pack). This is another simple, one-click question that can have a large impact on fan engagement.

► Fan selects favorite player from a list of players pictured.

**Step 6: Favorite Opponents**—Besides the ability to target fans based on specific opponents, this question can also be used internally when creating new mini-plan packages, identifying common trends that could lead to well-received ticket packages.

► Fan selects favorite 3 opponents from teams listed.

**Step 7: Games Attended and Watched**—Another simple but effective question that can tell the team a lot about the fan's viability as a ticket buyer (game attendance) and general avidity (television viewership). For example, if someone does not attend games but watches a lot on television, exclude them from your season ticket e-mails and focus on smaller opportunities.

► How many games do you attend each year?

► How many games do you watch on television each year?

**Confirmation Page**—Always end with a thank you and an opportunity to continue engaging with the brand via the team website.

———

Link to entire article: http://www.thebusinessofsports.com/2014/12/11/building-fan-profiles/

Once these CRM systems are robustly populated, they are capable of a variety of functions. For one, a CRM system can be utilized to get current customers to spend more. Profiles might show that a current season ticket holder might be a great candidate to purchase club seats, or that a long-time ticket buyer might want to purchase a membership into a new team club or buy an exclusive retro jersey of their favorite player. CRM systems also allow sales professionals to observe past buying behavior. Buyers who regularly buy tickets in groups of four or more might be good candidates to buy family or small group mini-plans in the future. Buyers who have purchased only lower-priced inventory in the past might be good candidates to target with bargain offerings like Buy-One-Get-One free deals for a less popular Tuesday night game. Meanwhile, past buyers who attended games only against the best opponents can be targeted for ticket offers that feature higher priced marquee match-ups.

Besides giving sellers a snapshot of a prospect or current customer, CRM systems can also be used to develop models to help market more effectively to new customers. For instance, a CRM platform might help explain which fans are most likely to attend because of a bobblehead giveaway or a particular opponent. It might also show which fans are more affected by price or game time. CRM systems can assist in developing profiles of people most likely to buy certain ticket packages and can help predict likelihood of renewal. In fact, some CRM systems provide teams with rankings of prospects; a five-star prospect is very likely to buy, while a one-star prospect is not. They can also be utilized to send targeted communications to particular groups. For instance, a team may develop a family ticket promotion. Team marketers can then use their CRM system to generate an e-mail communication about the promotion and distribute it only to households with children.

Within the sport business landscape, several CRM systems currently exist, each capable of different functions. Some teams still rely on a basic spreadsheet produced by common database software like Microsoft Excel. In fact, not that long ago, some teams were relying on different colored notecards pinned to a wall. Newer CRM systems, however, provide so much more insight. They also come with a variety of price tags. According to a recent survey of North American sports and live entertainment companies, 60% spend at least $50,000 a year on their CRM system.[9] The most popular of these CRM systems are Microsoft Dynamics, Archtics, Salesforce, and Spectra (formerly Paciolan).[10] Other popular sport business systems include Turnkey Prospector, Veritix, SAS Sports Analytics, and Eloqua. While any of these software packages can provide terrific marketing data, it is incumbent on the end users of the software (marketers and sellers) to take full advantage of that data. In many cases, sport marketers and sellers do not take full advantage of the high-powered functions and analysis available with many of these CRM programs.

In their work with properties like Georgia Tech Athletics, the Aspire Group has developed four levels of sophistication in using CRM data. At the "crawl" level, CRM systems are only used to extract life cycle data such as buyer age or family stage. At the "walk" level, CRM systems are utilized to produce socio-economic demographic information about customers such as household income, geographic location, or past ticket purchase history. At the "run" level, more advanced features of the CRM system are used to produce marketing automation and lead scoring. This is done by analyzing behavioral and psychographic information about prospects such as knowing their spending history and hobbies. Finally, at the "sprint" level, teams use a fully-integrated "data warehouse" that allows marketers and sellers to create a complete picture of the fan and use the information to develop customized

9. Turnkey Sports and Entertainment. (2015). *2015 Data Systems Report.*
10. Ibid.

offers to meet the fans' needs. For example, by using a robust CRM system, a team might know a prospect's birthdate and favorite player. They can then tailor a ticket and jersey offer specifically for that fan's big day. The Aspire Group also suggests each of these CRM utilization levels come with increasing return on investment. For example, teams that are "crawling" with CRM might see a 3 to 1 ROI by investing in that sort of data, but a team that is "running" with their CRM would likely see a 10 to 1 ROI.

## Referrals

As discussed in Chapter 10, good sales representatives should always finish their conversations with prospects and clients by asking if they know of anyone else who might be interested in tickets. Many teams offer current ticket buyers an incentive to share referrals, often giving the current ticket buyer a discount on tickets when the referral buys tickets as well. Recently, many teams have begun utilizing social media to improve their lead generation. For example, the Oakland Raiders developed a refer-a-friend campaign aimed at members of the Raiders Facebook and Twitter accounts. The prize was two suite-level seats for a game, but fans increased their odds by opting in to receive sales information and sharing data about themselves and their friends. The contest resulted in 27,000 people leaving their information with the team. After "scrubbing" the data, the Raiders gained 4,600 new "hot" leads and 14,000 new newsletter subscribers.[11] The Boston Celtics, meanwhile, developed a particularly clever fantasy basketball game in which fans competed against one another via Facebook. The game was easy to learn and play, often taking

## Table 12.1

**New England Revolution Referral Program**

| Award Level | Tickets Referred | Prize Earned | Prize Options | |
|---|---|---|---|---|
| Trialist | 1 | Shirt | **1.** 2 field passes to watch warmups | **7.** 4 club tickets |
| Rookie | 2–4 | Choose one prize (#1–4) | **2.** 1 $50 stadium gift card | **8.** 1 game ball |
| Starter | 5–8 | Choose one additional (#1–8) | **3.** 1 player-autographed soccer ball | **9.** Visit team practice |
| Veteran | 9–14 | Choose one additional (#1–8) | **4.** 2 club tickets | **10.** 1 team autographed ball |
| All-Star | 15–19 | Choose one additional (#1–10) | **5.** 1 customized jersey | |
| MVP | 20+ | Trip for 2 to an away match | **6.** 1 $100 stadium gift card | |

11. National Sports Forum. Retrieved from http://www.sports-forum.com/news/archive/index.html?article_id=502

place in groups, but required players to submit their contact information to the team. The team could track game usage, and once fans became very active, the team could reach out to participants with sales opportunities. In 2012, the team generated over $200,000 in new revenue with the game.[12]

The New England Revolution in Major League Soccer offer 11 incentives for six different reward levels based on the number of season tickets referred by the customer.

## Social Media

The *SportsBusiness Journal* reported that the NBA has developed a partnership with LinkedIn. Many of its teams are now using the platform's Sales Navigator tool to help "sales executives to find the people in their networks who can introduce them to the people most likely to buy ticket plans or suites."[13] LinkedIn launched Sales Navigator as a stand-alone business-to-business social selling platform in 2014 to harness the power of the data housed on the site. Sales Navigator uses a combination of user-generated search criteria and algorithms to help sellers identify leads. In addition to identifying leads (as in the social listening activities described in Chapter 6), sellers can also identify leads using the search functionality in the Lead Builder. The Lead Builder allows the seller to identify leads using the following search criteria:

- ► Current company
- ► Current title
- ► Keywords
- ► Location
- ► Postal code
- ► Country
- ► Geographic radius
- ► Function (accounting, human resources, administrative, etc.)
- ► Seniority level (owner, vice president, partner, founder, etc.)
- ► Company size
- ► Industry

The leads generated through the initial search are then categorized on the basis of those who share experiences with the seller, those who have changed jobs in the past three months, and those who have been active on LinkedIn in the past month.

---

12. Finn, C. (2012, April 27). Celtics applying themselves with social media. *Boston Globe.* Retrieved from https://www.bostonglobe.com/sports/2012/04/26/celtics-applying-themselves-with-social-media/HeV8UxGw8GfjARvF3yaHcO/story.html

13. Ourand, J. (2015, April 20). How LinkedIn is helping the NBA sell. *SportsBusiness Journal.*

Searches in Sales Navigator can then be narrowed by the following criteria:

- ► Past company
- ► Years in current position
- ► Years in current company
- ► Years of experience
- ► LinkedIn group memberships
- ► School (university)
- ► Interests
- ► Leads that follow your company on LinkedIn

The technology behind LinkedIn also makes it easy for sellers to find prospects without searching in the Lead Builder in the following ways:

- ► Leads can be directly imported from the organization's Salesforce CRM
- ► LinkedIn makes recommendations it believes would be relevant to the seller based on previous searches and current connections
- ► Sellers can see how someone within their own organization can help them connect to one of the leads
- ► Sales Navigator home page provides updates on leads and companies

Once sellers have built their leads in Sales Navigator, they can progress with engaging prospects as described in Chapter 6.

## Online Research

Another source of leads is online research to acquire the name and contact information of organizations and decision-makers. Using basic search tools like Google, LinkedIn, and business databases like Hoovers, sellers can find important information on companies such as number of employees, annual sales, company mission, products and services offered, and contact information for the right decision-maker. This research can help identify corporations, nonprofit organizations, family owned business, and educational institutions. In addition to specific businesses and organizations, doing research will also help identify trade associations that align along geographic and vertical market needs. For example, local merchants in a community or region band together to lobby government, network, and serve the community. Organizations like the Chamber of Commerce or the Rotary Club are examples of trade associations that align along geographic lines. In the same way, businesses within the same industry band together to share best practices, network, and lobby government. Many of these associations, such as the National Restaurant Association or the National Association of Realtors, publish business membership directories online. Finally, affinity groups share a non-commercial interest or goal, to which people formally or informally belong. Affinity groups typically rally around a shared concern for a given issue or a common activity, role, interest, or skill. Examples of affinity groups include religious organizations, private social clubs, clubs focused on a specific hobby, and organizations that promote ethnic and cultural groups.

## Purchased Lists

Companies such as Info USA, Full House, and Turnkey will provide teams with lists and contact information of companies and individuals who may be interested in purchasing tickets. In 2012, professional sport organizations spent an average of $17,946 to purchase an average of 63,750 records per team.[14] The percentage of teams budgeting at least $1,000 on purchased lists has increased steadily from 51% in 2012, to 57% in 2013, and 68% in 2014.[15] Typically, these lists are purposively-generated based on particular demographic segments or characteristics a team is pursuing. For example, a team may want to buy lists of people who are of a certain age, income level, or live within a certain radius. While purchased lists can provide a significant number of new leads, these lists are typically viewed as the source producing the least efficient number of viable prospects. A recent study suggested only 38% of sport teams were satisfied with the lists of names of potential consumers they purchased, and only 45% were satisfied with the lists of businesses.[16]

## E-mail

Targeted e-mail communication is another tool sales representatives can use to grow and nurture their prospect database. Using e-mail communication in the sales process can be effective if used appropriately. Bombarding prospects with e-mails (spamming) is not appropriate. However, using electronic communication to follow up with a batch of new leads may provide positive results. For example, if members of a team were to conduct a kids' clinic at a local shopping center, team personnel might collect e-mail addresses as part of a prize giveaway. Following the promotion, the team might send out a follow-up e-mail, thanking recipients for their support and perhaps suggesting

14. https://intel.turnkeyse.com/2012/02/09/the-state-of-data-systems-in-sports-entertainment/
15. Turnkey Sports and Entertainment. (2014). *2014 Data Systems Study.*
16. Turnkey Sports and Entertainment. (2015). *2015 Data Systems Report.*

they sign up for the team newsletter. The e-mail may also contain an opt-in check box for
further ticket information. Such
an e-mail blast can help team
representatives sort through contacts to determine which might
be prospective leads. When using
e-mail communication in the
sales process, it is important to
not just think about the message
being sent, but also about how a
recipient will receive it and what
their next action in regard to the
message will be.

##  *Personal Networking: Always Be Prospecting*

Good sales representatives do not simply depend on the team to provide them
with all of their sales leads. Instead, sales representatives should always be
prospecting on their own, continually on the prowl for new potential ticket
buyers. In his book, *The 800-Pound Gorilla of Sales*, sport sales trainer Bill
Guertin tells the story of how former Minnesota Timberwolves ticket sales
executive Bryant Pfeiffer creatively and aggressively found new leads. Pfeiffer
once completed a large group sale to a pest control company after one of
the players on the T-Wolves called an opponent a cockroach. The resource-
ful sales rep also once sold season tickets to a Jeopardy contestant who lived
in Minneapolis, after the game show winner said he was a big sports fan in
an interview. Pfeiffer even sold season tickets to the father of a bride during
a wedding reception.[17] Sports Executive Jared Schoenfeld, meanwhile, said
while working for the Phoenix Suns, he was nearly run over one day by a
construction truck. He was able to copy down the construction company's
phone number from the truck and was set to fire off a complaint. After waiting awhile, however, he realized he held a promising lead, and eventually sold
the company a $45,000 premium ticket package.[18] Kyle Brant, Ticket Sales
Manager at the Orlando Magic, cultivated some great leads by joining Internet fan forums and chat boards to engage with Magic fans and discuss their
interest in attending future games.

17.  Guertin, B. (2010). *The 800-pound gorilla of sales.* Hoboken, NJ: John Wiley & Sons.

18.  Mullin, B., Hardy, S., & Sutton, W. (2014). *Sport marketing,* 4th ed. Champaign, IL:
Human Kinetics.

The sources of good sales leads are endless. In some cases, astute sales professionals can find new leads simply in their own personal contacts. In fact, teams such as the Dallas Stars and Portland Trailblazers have generated new leads simply by asking members of their own staff to send out a special or "exclusive" promotional offer to every person in their e-mail contact list. Because the promotional offer is sent by someone who works for the team, the recipient often thinks it is an exclusive opportunity and, because of human nature, is likely to forward the offer to their own friends. In fact, oftentimes these offers are intentionally crafted by the team to encourage the contact to forward the message, but only to those who might be interested in such a special offer. Such efforts have produced thousands of new leads for teams. Carrie Neville, Director of Ticketing and Fan Development with Cleveland State University, said she has had success finding group outing prospects through her fellow athletic department staff members simply by asking what activities they are involved in outside of work. Co-workers and friends who have kids involved in cheerleading, Boy Scouts, church youth groups, or little league teams are all great group sales leads. Sport tickets can provide all of these types of groups with a potential activity.

> Neville has had success finding group outing prospects through her fellow athletic department staff members simply by asking what activities they are involved in outside of work. Co-workers and friends who have kids involved in cheerleading, Boy Scouts, church youth groups, or little league teams are all great group sales leads. Sport tickets can provide all of these types of groups with a potential activity.
>
> —Carrie Neville,
> Director of Ticketing and Fan Development,
> *Cleveland State University*

Always prospecting also means networking on a regular basis. Certain times during the day are more promising for connecting with prospects. During down times, however, sales representatives should be seeking new leads. They may be working their current network and sifting through their social media connections. Good sales representatives are always attending events—whether they are team activities, business functions, or social occasions—and connecting with other individuals. This doesn't mean a sales representative is constantly putting a hard sell on every new person he or she meets. Instead, sales professionals should spend time getting to know new people and asking questions so that when the right opportunities do present themselves, the representative is ready to act. Sales executive Mark Washo suggests in his book *Break into Sports Through Ticket Sales* that effective representatives do not spend all their time at professional networking events talking to their co-workers or eating appetizers. Instead, he recommends working the room first and saving the final hour of the event to have fun.[19]

---

19. Washo, M. (2004). *Break into sports through ticket sales*. Kindle edition.

## CHAPTER SUMMARY

Generating leads is a key component in the ticket sales process. No matter what methods are utilized, teams and sport ticket sales professionals must develop a culture of prospecting throughout the entire organization. Far too often, sport teams spend the majority of their marketing efforts on attracting new fans to a game or event, and almost no effort in collecting contact information from attendees or potential consumers who visited a team website, watched a game on their tablet, or contemplated buying a ticket online but at the last minute chose not to purchase. If ticket sellers have information from these people, they have a far better opportunity to sell them tickets to future events. Think of the myriad ways someone can "touch" a sport team or organization: stadium tours, merchandise purchases, community outreach programs, sport clinics and camps, and school visits, just to name a few. At every one of these touchpoints, staff members from the sport organization are likely to be present, whether they are a community relations director, a marketing intern, a pro shop clerk, an assistant coach, or a volunteer tour guide. All of these team representatives should be thinking about lead generation whenever they interact with the public.

## CHAPTER ACTIVITIES

1. Imagine you are working for a new minor league baseball team. You need to develop prospect lists for your sales representatives but cannot rely on past season ticket buyers because this is a new franchise. Outline five different ways you could quickly develop prospect lists for your sellers.

2. There are numerous CRM platforms available to sport teams to help them collect and manage customer data. Conduct an Internet search to find at least three companies which offer CRM services to sport teams. What are some of the key differences between the platforms?

3. One challenge facing many ticket sales departments is their lack of insight into customers who attend through groups. For example, a business might buy 200 tickets for an employee outing, but the only contact information the team has is for the group leader. How could the team get information about all group attendees to add to their database?

4. In the age of "big data," what do companies and marketers know about you? Think of examples of how companies currently gather important data about your interests, buying habits, and demographic information. How could some of these data gathering techniques be utilized by sport organizations?

5. Assume your sport sales course is partnering with local professional franchises to sell group tickets and you are responsible for your own lead generation. How would you go about generating a list of qualified leads to contact?

# CHAPTER 13

## SALES FORCE MANAGEMENT

### LEARNING OBJECTIVES

After completing this chapter, you should be able to:

- ▶ Contrast the characteristics necessary for success as a salesperson and a sales manager.
- ▶ Describe the steps of the sales management process as they apply to sport organizations.
- ▶ Apply theories of motivation to improve performance of salespeople in sport organizations.
- ▶ Describe the characteristics of a positive sales culture within a sport organization.
- ▶ Discuss contemporary ways sport organizations are proactively identifying sales talent.

### KEY TERMS

| | |
|---|---|
| Assessment Centers | Motivation-Hygiene Theory |
| Behavioral Management | Psychometric Test |
| Commission | Sales Culture |
| Management | Scientific Management |
| Maslow's Hierarchy of Needs | Total Quality Management (TQM) |

## CHAPTER OVERVIEW

Identifying, recruiting, training, developing, and retaining sales talent is a key success factor for most sport organizations. While the majority of the book thus far has focused on the skills and knowledge needed to be a successful sport seller, this chapter introduces readers to the basic skills and knowledge needed to become an effective sport sales manager. Sales management is the attainment of sales goals through planning, staffing, training, directing, and evaluating organizational resources. Successful sales managers are critical as sport organizations constantly search for new talent, train current salespeople to improve their skills, and find new ways to keep their best salespeople motivated and productive. This is an important role in light of the high turnover rate in the sport sales industry.

## WHO MAKES A GOOD SALES MANAGER?

So who makes a good sales manager? In the sports world, do the best players always make the best coaches? The list of Hall of Fame athletes who struggled on the sideline (Isaiah Thomas, Ted Williams, Bart Starr, Wes Unseld, and Wayne Gretzky, to name a few) is lengthy. Why is this? Most people would probably agree that just because someone is good at a particular job, whether that job is playing professional football, developing computer software, or delivering pizza, it does not necessarily mean they are good at *managing* other people who do that same job. In the sales world, the job functions and skills required by sellers (calling prospects, overcoming objections, showing persistence) are often different than the job functions and skills associated with sales managers (hiring and training new employees, developing incentive plans, working with multiple personality types). Like the star athlete, a sport sales representative works within a team

©alarico/Shutterstock.com

**This statue memorializes the great feats of hockey legend Wayne Gretzky as a player, not as a coach**

framework, but is largely responsible only for individual performance. The manager, on the other hand, works in a similar fashion to the sports coach, working to achieve the best group performance from multiple individual contributors. This is an important distinction because the skill set necessary to be a great sales representative is different than the skill set needed to be an outstanding sales manager. In fact, in their book *Sport Promotion and Sales Management*, Irwin, Sutton, and McCarthy suggest the best sport salespeople are "very individualistic and concerned with personal success and accomplishment to a higher degree. Although that is what makes them successful as a top revenue producer, it does not translate as well in terms of developing and leading a sales team."[1]

## MANAGEMENT DEFINED

The art and science of managing others has been studied by researchers and executives for decades. Understanding how to help workers perform more effectively and efficiently for the betterment of an organization is valuable information, but it is also constantly evolving. Managers have varying opinions on what effective management looks like and there is disagreement among researchers as to how successful managers should manage. The following concepts represent some of the best practices incorporated by sales managers. It is important to note, however, that every sales staff, and every sales manager, is unique. This means some management styles may work better than others, depending on a variety of factors, including work environment, organizational culture, and personal attributes of both employees and managers.

So what is management? Most sport sales administrators would agree **management** is "the coordination and integration of resources to efficiently and effectively meet goals and objectives of an organization."[2] Well over 100 years ago, mining engineer Henri Fayol first introduced into the lexicon the functions of management, which he suggested were planning, organizing, commanding, coordinating, and controlling.[3] In his book, *Managing Organizations for Sport and Physical Activity*, Chelladurai suggests today's sport managers are still concerned with these primary functions, which he represents with the acronym POLE, standing for planning, organizing, leading,

**MANAGEMENT**
The coordination and integration of resources to effectively and efficiently meet the goals or objectives of an organization

---

1. Irwin, R., Sutton, W., & McCarthy, L. (2008). *Sport promotion and sales management.* Champaign, IL: Human Kinetics. p. 75.

2. Hurd, A., Barcelona, R., & Meldrum, J. (2008). *Leisure services management.* Champaign, IL: Human Kinetics.

3. Fayol, H. (1949). *General and industrial management.* London: Pitman.

and evaluating.[4] Good sales managers must be effective at all four of these functions.

In terms of planning, a sales manager must examine both internal conditions, like team resources or franchise culture, as well as external conditions, such as the economy or market size, to determine things like size of staff, proper sales goals for the year, strategies for training, and equipment needs. After a plan has been developed, sales managers must organize the work tasks and assign duties to their staff. For example, a manager might determine which staff members should attend sessions from an outside sales trainer or determine which staff members will focus on group sales for the year. The leadership component of management focuses on the relationship between the manager and the employee. Managers must figure out how to interact with workers in a manner that influences them to move toward organizational objectives. For instance, sales managers may lead through example by showing up to work early or handling difficult situations with calmness or a sense of humor. Good managers also understand what will motivate different staff members, whether it is a sales contest, a promotion, or an encouraging work environment. Lastly, effective managers must constantly and consistently evaluate the performance of their team to learn from mistakes and understand the collective thoughts from their team. Evaluation may be either formal, such as end-of-the-year evaluations, or informal, such as hallway conversations.

As the study of management has evolved, different theories and concepts have emerged. In the late 1800s and early 1900s, management thought-leaders like Henri Fayol, Fredrick Winslow Taylor, and Frank and Lillian Gilbreth espoused the concept of **scientific management**. Prior to their work, many managers spent little time rationally examining the way in which workers performed job functions. The pioneers of scientific management argued managers should carefully study job performance, develop a single most efficient manner in which to perform a task, teach that most efficient method to employees, and incentivize them to follow that method. For example, if an

**SCIENTIFIC MANAGEMENT**
managing a business according to principles of efficiency derived from experiments in methods of work and production

---

4. Chelladurai, P. (2014). *Managing organizations for sport and physical activity,* 4th ed. Scottsdale, AZ: Holcomb Hathaway.

employee's job was to build a house, proponents of scientific management might suggest that a manager determine which methods allow workers to most efficiently construct the wood frame, lay the brick work, and install plumbing or electrical work. In the sport sales world, sales managers employ the concept of scientific management when they have all new ticket representatives use the exact same sales script or employ a CRM scoring system which tells sellers precisely which prospects to call based on likelihood of purchase. In these cases, sales managers determine the most effective way to perform a job function from years of experience, observation, and analytics. From this research, the managers develop a method of performing a job which has shown to be effective. They then teach that method to new hires rather than allowing the employees to decide how to perform job functions.

While a scientific management approach can improve efficiency in the workplace, and is still a valuable concept to today's managers, research suggests other important elements to managing effectively. For instance, scientific management explores the best way to perform job functions, but places little emphasis on the relationship between the employee and manager. **Behavioral Management** researchers suggest people are not machines and must be seen as valuable assets or contributors to a firm's well-being if they are to be productive. As such, managers must be aware of the human dimension of the workplace and pay attention to things like employee-manager relationships, worker motivation, and group dynamics. Emerging from this movement in management studies was the notion that for employees to be most effective, managers cannot just focus on training and job function, but also must be aware of employees' needs. Employees that feel wanted, are in a secure job, do fulfilling work, and enjoy their office culture are going to perform better.

**BEHAVIORAL MANAGEMENT**
a theory of management examining how workplace productivity is impacted by employee motivation and the relationships among co-workers and managers

---

### COMPARING TWO APPROACHES

Look at two different sport sales departments. In the first, a cut-throat atmosphere is pervasive. The organization brings 20 interns aboard but makes it clear that only the top one or two performers will have any chance at a job. Representatives do not have access to the best leads and are more frequently disciplined for poor performance than rewarded for good performance. Managers are not receptive to employee feedback and employee needs are second to organizational needs. In the second organization, resources are invested to recruit and develop the best fits for the organization, rather than throwing poorly trained employees "to the wolves." Trainees or interns who do well are assisted in finding jobs with other teams if there are no positions available at the end of their internship. Managers get to know employees on a personal level and the office culture includes many sales contests and fun incentives geared toward both individual and team goals. Communication among staff and management is open and honest.

Among these two organizations, which is likely to have a more effective sales team? Management scholars of the Behavioral Era would certainly agree that the second team would be more productive.

While prior management research has focused both on scientific management and human behavior, a third school of management has also seen recent support. The Modern Era of Management stems primarily from the work of W. Edwards Deming and his concept of **Total Quality Management (TQM)**.[5] The focus of TQM is not on the worker (as it is with both scientific management and behavior management), but rather on outcomes and customer satisfaction. Managers who subscribe to the tenants of TQM use employee input, data analysis, and a strategic, systematic approach to develop an organization focused externally on consumers, rather than internally on employees or job function. TQM organizations are not all the same, as different firms employ unique approaches to meeting customer needs. However, to make such an approach work, managers need to have clearly defined values and vision, as well as recognize and encourage employee contributions. In the context of a sport sales team, a manager who subscribes to TQM would encourage representatives to be in constant communication with account holders and look for feedback on how to better meet account holders' needs. Such managers might develop new products (such as flexible mini-plans or shared premium spaces) that better accommodate the desires of ticket buyers. They are also likely to use surveys, focus groups, and other forms of customer feedback to guide strategy. A TQM sales manager is also likely to empower employees to make some autonomous decisions without management approval and would encourage employees to share their ideas with the rest of the team.

**TOTAL QUALITY MANAGEMENT (TQM)** a management theory suggesting all employees must be personally committed to maintaining high work standards and improving product or service quality, with a particular focus on customer satisfaction

---

### HAVE AN IDEA?

Former NBA executive Jon Spoelstra, in his book *Ice to the Eskimos*, writes that he went so far as to offer cash prizes to the employee who offered the worst idea in staff meetings.[6] Spoelstra was not actually seeking out the worst idea. Rather he believed his sales staff did not want to fail, but team members were afraid to offer ideas for improvement because if they did fail, the idea would be pinned on them. By rewarding outrageous or risky ideas, Spoelstra found his team actually produced better overall strategies, which improved their collective ability to sell.

---

The three approaches to management described above—scientific, behavioral, and modern—are not mutually exclusive. Elements of all three approaches are valuable to today's sales manager. All three approaches are described in very broad and general terms in this text. Future sales managers

---

5. Deming, W. (1986). *Out of the crisis*. Cambridge, MA: MIT Press.
6. Spoelstra, J. (1997). *Ice to the eskimos*. New York: HarperBusiness.

would be wise to learn more about each approach through additional course work and readings.

## RECRUITMENT

One of the primary challenges of any sport sales manager is assembling a strong sales staff. Doing so starts with recruiting and hiring excellent sales talent. Entry-level positions within the sport industry in general are rare and difficult to obtain. Most managers within the business of sports obtain more qualified employee applicants than they can hire. Sales positions in sport, however, seem to be an exception to this rule. While posted ticket sales job announcements for professional sport teams, college athletic departments, and other sport organizations will frequently attract hundreds of applicants, sport sales managers are often faced with a difficult challenge; few of those applicants will have any sales experience or even a good understanding of how the sales process works. In fact, a recent study suggested only 22% of sport management programs in the United States require a course in sport sales.[7] (This is particularly intriguing because the majority of entry-level jobs in the sport industry are sales positions.)

Because so few students aspiring to work in sports gain sales experience or complete a sales course, sport sales managers must spend far more of their time recruiting and developing talent than managers in other segments of the sport industry such as event management, public relations, or marketing. Most sales managers of professional sport teams or large third-party tickets sales companies such as The Aspire Group and IMG Learfield Ticket Solutions, will spend time every week reviewing resumes and networking with others in an effort to uncover sales talent, even when those managers are not looking to fill an immediate vacancy. The reality of sport sales is frequent staff turnover due to both promotion and burnout, meaning sales managers must always be on the lookout for new hires. In addition, many managers within professional sport teams and athletics departments who are looking to grow revenue, realize the best place to start is to hire more sales representatives, creating many more opportunities for job seekers.

> It is far more likely for a major league team to add sales positions than create new jobs in other areas such marketing, media relations, or event operations because of the direct revenue sellers are able to generate for the organization and because the ROI on new sales hires is easier to measure.

---

7. Eagleman, A., & McNary, E. (2010). What are we teaching our students? A descriptive examination of the current status of undergraduate sport management curricula in the United States. *Sport Management Education Journal, 4,* 1–17.

## WHAT'S THE RIGHT STAFF SIZE?

Ask any major league team ticket sales manager what is the fastest way to sell more tickets, and they are likely to tell you "win a championship" or sign the biggest superstar in the league to a long-term contract. The reality, however, is that only one hockey team can hoist the Stanley Cup and only one NBA team can announce LeBron James in their starting lineup. For all the other teams who won't win a championship (and even those that do) the most reliable, and least expensive, route to increasing ticket revenue is to hire more sales representatives. We have seen this play out many times in the sport industry. In the mid-2000's, the Arizona Diamondbacks hired president and CEO Derrick Hall to grow ticket sales. One of the first things he did was bump the number of ticket sellers from 15 to 50. Similarly, Vice President of Ticket Sales, Jim Van Stone, increased his sales team from 23 to 45 with the Washington Capitals.[1] The Philadelphia 76ers, in an effort to improve sales, have increased their sales team to over 100 sales team members.[2] Even the Professional Golf Association tour, in an effort to improve attendance and revenue at several of their tournaments, has recently added an inside sales team, hiring 12 account executives in the first year, the results of which were over one million dollars in new ticket revenue.[3] College athletics departments have also begun hiring more extensively in sales. For example, The Aspire Group has staffed clients such as Arizona State and Texas with over 30 individuals.[4]

So what is the right number of sales representatives for a team? The simple answer is to figure out how much new revenue the ticket sales team produces with each hire and continue to bring staff onboard until the return-on-investment diminishes to 1-to-1. As long as sales representatives are generating more revenue than they are costing the organization to employ, why wouldn't a sports team keep hiring new people? While this sounds great in theory, unfortunately many sport organizations do not hire based on this formula. Big-time NCAA Division I athletic departments in particular have other constraints when hiring, such as the need to get school approval on new hires, the inability to pay commissions, and tight departmental budgets, which slow down hiring efforts. Former NBA team president Jon Spoelstra suggests teams determine how many small businesses (10–50 employees) are located in their marketing area, then hire one sales representative for every 1,000 businesses.[5]

1. King, B. (2010, March 15). Always be closing. *SportsBusiness Journal.* Retrieved from
http://www.sportsbusinessdaily.com/Journal/Issues/2010/03/20100315/SBJ-In-Depth/Always-Be-Closing.aspx?
2. Sutton, B. (2014, July 14). For building, motivating sales staffs, one size does not fit all. *SportsBusiness Journal*, 15.
3. Smith, M. (2014, Nov. 17). PGA Tour call center celivers sales and staff promotions. *Street and Smith's Sports-Business Journal, 5.*
4. Carter, A. & Meitin, M. (2014). Filling the house. *Athletic Management,* 26.
5. Spoelstra, J. (2010, Dec. 6). A three-step strategy to sell out a stadium, absent a superstar. *Sports Business Daily.* Retrieved from http://www.sportsbusinessdaily.com/Journal/Issues/2010/12/20101206/From-The-Field-Of/Athree-Step-Strategy-To-Sell-Out-A-Stadium-Absent-A-Superstar.aspx?

In an effort to meet the demand of managing a ticket sales staff, sport sales managers have adopted several initiatives. Today, many professional sport teams are proactively recruiting at sport-related job fairs. Many major league teams have established a career fair event in which students interested in a job with the team can meet hiring managers and discuss openings. Often coupled with a home game, these team-sponsored career fairs allow prospective employees to meet with front office executives, exchange resumes, discuss the teams' work environment and hiring needs, and potentially interview for positions, typically in ticket sales. (For teams, these events also serve as a group sales opportunity, as registrants are often required to buy a game ticket to attend.)

---

### SALES COMBINES AND WORKSHOPS

Recently several organizations have met the challenge of finding future ticket sellers by participating in multi-team ticket sales training and recruitment events. The Sport Sales Combine, for example, brings together sales managers from numerous sport organizations to conduct a two-day workshop for those looking to break into sport sales. The combines are typically scheduled in conjunction with a major league game; past Combine partners include the Orlando Magic, New Jersey Devils, Tampa Bay Buccaneers, and Phoenix Suns.[8] Participants in the Combine gain a full day of sales training, then work the concourse of the arena or stadium during a game with the mission of collecting key information from single-game ticket buyers. Armed with the leads they collect at the game, attendees return to the workshop the next day and call their leads, while being coached by team sales managers. Other events, such as the annual Mount Union Sport Sales Workshop in Cleveland and the IMG Learfield Ticket Solutions Sales Showcase in Winston-Salem, North Carolina, provide attendees with the opportunity to receive instruction and interview with sales executives from major league, minor league, and NCAA Division I athletic departments.

---

Many major league teams are now producing their own specific sales recruitment collateral. Similar to university admissions offices, many sales managers, such as those at the NBA's Phoenix Suns, MLB's Pittsburgh Pirates, and the NHL's Columbus Blue Jackets, are creating booklets, videos, and online resources depicting the many perks and benefits of working for their organizations. These resources can be used as recruiting material by showing potential employees the highlights of a particular community, the work culture of the team's front office, salary, and benefits, or a listing of past recruits and sales representatives who have been promoted to higher ranking positions. Some teams even offer top prospective sellers incentives during the recruitment process such as game tickets, hotel accommodations, or even personalized game jerseys.

---

8. Retrieved from www.sportsalescombine.com

Another key for sport organizations wishing to develop sales talent pipelines is to develop relationships with universities that offer sales training courses. The business school at Baylor University has developed an entire curriculum focused on sport sales, with graduates of the program becoming some of the most highly sought after employees in major league sports.[9] Several other sport management programs have done an excellent job of cultivating sales talent, making it essential that any sport sales manager develop relationships with faculty at these, and similar, institutions. By developing relationships with faculty members, sales managers can begin to learn which students are best suited to sales and who shows the most promise as future sellers. This dramatically speeds up the arduous tasks of posting jobs, sifting through resumes, and interviewing candidates. In some cases, sport teams have found ways to embed themselves into the classroom, either as guest speakers, trainers, or even partners. When students are allowed to sell tickets for a team, this not only helps the team financially, but also allows the team to see how students perform; something difficult to replicate in an interview setting.

In addition, many teams are now utilizing their new hires as recruiters. If recent graduates are hired by major league teams and perform very well, sales managers might ask those successful hires if they have former classmates who would also be good prospective sellers. Managers also rely on their managerial network by knowing which teams are best at training sellers. If the sales manager for Team A is looking to hire a new sales representative and knows Team B has many good trainees, she may call a sales manager at Team B to see who might be looking for a job.

## HIRING

The outbound, proactive recruitment of sales talent is a growing trend within professional sports. Still, the primary method by which many teams and college athletics departments hire sales staff remains the more traditional "passive" approach of posting positions, reviewing applicants, interviewing the top candidates, conducting background checks, and offering positions to the best people. Recent college graduates applying for entry-level positions are often anxious about this hiring process and feel it moves too slowly. However, from a sales manager's perspective, the hiring process is arguably the most important thing managers do and should not be conducted haphazardly. Organizations are only as good as the people they hire. Because of this, it is crucial sales managers be willing to expend both the human and financial resources to hire the best employees possible.

9. Baylor Business. *Sports sponsorship and sales major.* Retrieved from http://www.baylor.edu/business/marketing/index.php?id=93587

What does it cost to hire a new sales representative? The answer is *it depends,* but any good manager will agree, the cost is not cheap. In fact, DePaul University annually conducts a Sales Effectiveness Survey, which examines trends in sales force management for many industry sectors. According to recent results from this survey, managers estimate the average cost of hiring a new sales account representative is in excess of $60,000![10]

Where does this expense come from? First, there are fixed costs associated with advertising a position and bringing individuals in for interviews (meals, accommodation, travel, etc.). Second, there is a financial cost from lost productivity during the hiring process. For example, when sales managers take time out of their schedules to review resumes (which can often number in the hundreds for entry-level positions within the sport industry), meet with candidates, and conduct reference checks, they are expending valuable hours, time which cannot be devoted to other components of their job like selling tickets, working with current staff members, and developing marketing initiatives. A third major expense in the hiring process is the time and resources necessary to train new employees. While the best sales teams are always devoting some time to coaching and development, training new employees requires the most time and energy. Some professional teams conduct as much as six weeks of training and orientation for new sales representatives before allowing them to start selling on their own. This time spent in training is resource intensive. In addition, new employees are typically less productive than experienced ones, hindering sales efficiency. Research in Major League Soccer has revealed that it takes approximately 45 days to fill vacant sales positions, and that first-year reps produce significantly less revenue than more experienced sales reps.

The cost of hiring new staff is steep. In the long run, it is more economical for sport organizations to do a thorough job hiring the right people and training them so they can be more productive employees than it is to hire hastily and train poorly. Doing the latter typically results in high employee turnover, which costs the organization. In the past, many sport organizations adopted a philosophy in sales of hiring several (sometimes dozens of) representatives at once, paying these new hires low wages, giving them minimal training, then having them hit the phones. What was the justification for this mentality? Sales managers knew the following:

▶ Entry-level positions within sport organizations typically attract hundreds of applicants.

▶ Sport sales positions are paid on commission, meaning those who are not successful early in their career do not last long and do not cost the organization a lot of money.

10.  Min, J. How much does it cost to replace a sales rep? $114,957. *Ideal.* Retrieved from http://www.idealcandidate.com/how-much-does-it-cost-to-replace-a-sales-rep-114957

▶ Many entry-level sales hires, because of their lack of sales experience, do not understand the challenges of working in sales and quickly decide the profession is not for them.

More recently, however, a shift has occurred in the profession. Sales managers are now seeing the high costs involved when they invest relatively little in the sales hiring process; high turnover means greater cost down the line. As a result, today many sport organizations are dedicating more resources on the front end of the hiring process (spending on proactive recruitment, training, and employee incentives) in order to cut down on the "back end" expense of high employee turnover. One result of this change is that many ticket sales managers are now engaged in year-round hiring and recruitment. Ten or 15 years ago, many sales managers posted job announcements only when they had a vacancy to fill. Today, successful sales managers are constantly looking for new employees and finding ways to bring promising sales talent into the fold, whether the team has a vacancy or not. This may mean prospective sales representatives are initially brought in as interns, hourly employees, or seasonal hires until a full-time position becomes available. In fact, some of the most successful sales programs now take on more trainees than they have room for, with the idea that if the team cannot hire them as full-time employees at the end of training, the team will help those same individuals find a position with another sport organization. While on the surface it may seem counter-intuitive for a team to train potential employees, then help them get hired elsewhere, this philosophy has many positive benefits for the team.

1. Trainees know the team is looking out for their best interests
2. Team always has a base of well-trained people who will be available to fill a vacancy, should one emerge
3. Team develops a reputation for developing talent, which helps in recruitment and in developing relationships with other organizations
4. Helping an entry-level employee find a job today will make that person more likely to return to the organization in the future

So what do effective sales managers look for in aspiring sales representatives? The most basic and logical answer is sales experience. Applicants with a track record of past sales success, whether in sports or another industry, should always make their way to the top of the resume stack. In fact, a recent study suggests hiring managers within sports value experience more than any other information typically found on a resume including type of degree obtained or college grade point average.[11] Dallas Mavericks owner Mark

---

11. Howell, S., McEvoy, C., & Sheppard, D. (2015). *An experimental assessment of hiring decision factors in Minor League Baseball.* Paper presented at the Sport Marketing Association Annual Conference.

Cuban suggested *If you can sell, you can find a job in sports. I will take a high school dropout who is caring, involved, and can sell over an MBA in sport management almost every time.*[12] While experience is often the first criteria sales managers desire in new employees, it should be noted some ticket sales managers prefer not to hire individuals with too much sales experience. In some cases, sport sales managers prefer to train their representatives in a very specific manner. Individuals who

have extensive sales experience, typically in an industry outside of sports, may have picked up poor sales habits or worked for an organization that teaches a very different sales philosophy. In such cases, a sport sales manager may prefer to hire someone with less experience so that the person can be coached in the sales approach taught by the team. From a financial perspective, novice sellers often can be hired for a lower salary than those long in experience.

As mentioned in Chapter 1, good sales managers are often looking for employees who are hard-working, enthusiastic, coachable, outgoing, creative, perseverant, and confident. In their training materials, the Boston Bruins suggest good sales representatives demonstrate empathy, are able to smile, are sincere, accept criticism, value other's opinions, have no hidden agendas, and are generally happy. Meanwhile, Mark McCormick, founder of sport marketing agency giant IMG, suggested good sport sales professionals believe in their product, believe in themselves, call on a high volume of prospects, listen, have a sense of humor, are willing to knock on old doors and follow up after the sale with the same aggressiveness as before the sale.[13] In his book *Break Into Sports Through Ticket Sales*, sport ticket sales expert Mark Warsho suggests good ticket sales representatives are competitive, self-starting, dedicated to their profession, are able to face rejection and deal with objections, and can maintain the composure when facing adversity.[14] Many of today's sport sales managers also want to see evidence candidates know what they are getting into with a job in sport sales. Candidates who suggest they are applying for a sales job simply because they love sports and want to work for their favorite team are quickly dismissed, as are those who suggest they are

12.  Cuban, M. (2013). *How to win at the sport of business.* Kindle edition.

13.  McCormack, M. (1996). *On selling.* Los Angeles: Dove Books.

14.  Washo, M. (2004). *Break into sports through ticket sales.* Kindle edition.

only interviewing for a sales position so they can find another position within the organization. Instead, managers look for candidates who understand the sales process and enjoy selling more than wanting simply to be employed by a popular sport team or organization.

So how do managers determine which sales applicants possess these traits? For starters, managers need to ask good interview questions. Simply asking candidates if they are hard-working or confident will almost certainly elicit an affirmative response (if it doesn't, red flags should immediately go up for the manager). Instead, managers should develop a series of questions requiring candidates to provide examples of a time they demonstrated enthusiasm during difficult circumstances or confidence while put in an unfamiliar situation. Effective sales managers will find ways to put candidates in situations where they need to physically exhibit the traits for which they are looking. In order to test perseverance, some sales managers have been known to establish a time for a phone interview with a candidate, then intentionally not answer the phone when the candidate calls. How the candidate responds to this difficult situation can tell the manager plenty about their potential as a sales professional; if the candidate gives up or leaves an annoyed voice mail, they are probably not getting hired. However, if the candidate leaves an enthusiastic message, then follows up with a second call the next day, the candidate has made a very favorable impression. Another technique is the group interview, popularized by Disney. In a group interview, several candidates (typically 5–10 individuals) are interviewed at the same time. Group interviews allow the hiring manager to observe which candidates emerge as leaders, which ones are good team players, and which candidates can stay composed in an uncomfortable situation. Teams such as the St. Louis Cardinals and New York Yankees have utilized this technique while interviewing sales candidates.

Another tool utilized by sales hiring managers are **psychometric tests** and **assessment centers**. Psychometric tests are standardized tests used by hiring managers to evaluate potential employees' mental abilities or personality. They do not focus on job functions, but rather innate or intrinsic qualities of an applicant. Perhaps the most notable psychometric test in sports is the Wonderlic exam taken by football players during the NFL draft combine. While the Wonderlic test does not assess a player's ability to physically block a pass rusher or run a route, it does reveal a player's ability to reason and think quickly under duress. Such tests are often used for hiring sales professionals in other industry segments, but have not been used as extensively in sport sales. The Philadelphia 76ers are one team that is moving toward the use of psychometric testing, asking all candidates to take a personality test prior to

**PSYCHOMETRIC TEST** standardized tests utilized to evaluate a person's mental abilities or personality

**ASSESSMENT CENTERS** process where candidates are evaluated for their suitability for employment by using simulation exercises interviewing.[15] More research is needed in this area to determine how well psychometric tests help predict sales success among sport teams.

Assessment centers employ the use of simulation exercises in the interview process to help managers evaluate candidates. One popular assessment center technique is the use of in-basket exercises. To use an in-basket exercise, a manager would give an interviewee a fictional stack of memos, e-mails, and voice mails that the candidate might see in the workplace (items that have been left in the candidate's "in-box"), particularly if that candidate had been out of the office for a few days. The interviewee will go through all the items and determine how and in what order to handle those demands. In explaining priorities, candidates reveal to the manager what sort of employees they would be and how they would go about the job. Another assessment center technique might include role-playing a sales call or producing some sort of sales collateral. While sales managers might not always refer to assessment centers by name, they are a very valuable tool in the interview process.

## TRAINING

Another critical function of sales management beyond hiring the right people is to provide training. The process of training begins with the initial orientation, which gets new salespeople up to speed on product knowledge (arena information, ticket plans, pricing), computer systems (e-mail, ticketing system, CRM), reporting (tracking tasks completed), game day responsibilities (visiting clients, interacting with prospects), and the sales process and philosophy of the organization. This process can last anywhere from a couple of hours to a couple of weeks or longer, depending on the sales leadership within the organization. The fundamentals established in the first few weeks of the onboarding process determine the slope of the learning curve for young sales reps.

©Graf Vishenka/Shutterstock.com

Many sport sales positions, particularly inside ticket sales positions, are filled by people just entering the workforce, with relatively little sales experience on their resume. Because of this, it is important for employers to provide extensive training and preparation for a sales career. Unfortunately, this does not always happen. Many minor league teams and college athletics departments,

15. Fischer, J. (2016, May 19). Despite tough on-court season, 76ers' sales staff finds success. *Sports Illustrated.* Retrieved from http://www.si.com/nba/2016/05/19/philadelphia-76ers-sales-tickets-nba-draft-lottery-sam-hinkie-brett-brown

within a day or two of hiring new sales team members, provide their employees with a list of names and a phone, then expect them to start calling. In fact, recent research suggests nearly a quarter of all outbound ticket sales representatives working for NCAA Division I college athletics departments receive fewer than two hours of training prior to making their first call, with nearly 7% reporting no training whatsoever.[16]

Not all sport organizations agree on the best practices for sales training. When it comes to training employees, every team or athletic department subscribes to a particular sales philosophy. For instance, some organizations rely heavily on scripts while other organizations prefer their sellers say whatever comes natural to them when engaging with prospects on the phone. Some organizations believe firmly in leaving voice mails, while other teams teach their sellers to only engage with a live person. Because of these differences, it is impossible to suggest a single most effective sales training model. There is no disagreement among sales managers, however, that both initial and ongoing training are critical to developing an effective sales staff. Essential training topics include scripting, needs analysis, handling objections, upselling, product knowledge, setting appointments, time management, prospecting, CRM training, presentation skills, and arena tours.

Sales managers may call on a host of methodologies when it comes to training. Role-playing is often the most popular and effective. Role-playing can be conducted privately between only the manager and the employee, or it can be used in large groups, allowing all sellers to observe, offer suggestions, and analyze the simulation. Other effective training tools include the use of audio and video recordings. Many professional sport teams use telecommunication software in order to record sales conversations for playback and analysis. Meanwhile, much like a football coach utilizes video to analyze player performance, sales managers often use video recording to analyze mock and actual sales presentations to help coach sales representatives through difficult situations or improve their selling techniques. Other training tools might include reading assignments, computer simulations, observations of other senior sellers, peer reviews, and self-evaluation. At the MLS National Sales Center, sales trainers Jeff Berryhill and Melanie Sieser work to make training fun and interactive. They develop training games such as "What's in the Box" to practice handling objections and include improvisational comedy lessons to help trainees understand how to deal with unexpected situations in sales.

Many professional teams also hire outside, or third-party, sales trainers to assist with teaching the nuances of sales on an ongoing basis. Third-party

16. Popp, N., Simmons, J., & McEvoy, C. (2015). *An examination of the impact of ticket sales training effectiveness with NCAA Division I athletics departments.* Paper presented at the Sport Marketing Association Annual Conference.

trainers can help with new ideas when training might become stale. They also allow trainees to hear a new voice and perspective. Some of the best third-party sales trainers on the market include professionals like Charlie Chislaghi, Steve DeLay, Bill Guertin, and Bernie Mullin. Sales managers should be cautioned that the use of outside sales trainers should never replace internal sales training; only enhance it. No matter who a team hires, the internal sales force managers are ultimately responsible for directing their team's efforts. Regardless of whether training is done in-house or outsourced, ongoing training programs should be completed on a regular basis with a diverse mix of training scenarios that offer trainees a high level of engagement and periodic control of the agenda, and allow for feedback on strengths and weaknesses.

# MOTIVATION

## *Overview of Motivation Theory*

Motivating a workforce has been a topic studied by management scholars for decades. Several prominent theories regarding motivation have emerged; some focused on what things specifically motivate employees (content theories) and others focused on how and why employees act the way they do to satisfy individual needs or desires (process theories).[17] Perhaps the most recognizable of these theories is **Maslow's Hierarchy of Needs**, which suggests all individuals have a hierarchy of needs layered in five levels: physiological, safety, love and social needs, esteem, and self-actualization. In terms of employee motivation, Maslow's theory suggests workers need to feel their needs are being met at the lowest level before they will be motivated by higher order needs. For example, if an employee's physiological needs are not being satisfied (such as not being paid a salary that allows them to afford adequate housing or meals), that employee will never be motivated by incentives addressing higher level needs such as an excellent office environment (social need) or a better job title (esteem).

**MASLOW'S HIERARCHY OF NEEDS**
psychological theory human behavior motivation based on five levels of "needs" that must be satisfied sequentially

In the late 1950s and early 1960s, a management scholar named Fredrick Herzberg suggested another approach to workforce motivation, the two-prong **Motivation-Hygiene Theory**. This theory postulates some attributes of a job do indeed motivate individuals; things such as public recognition of achievements, greater job responsibilities and oversight, and advancement opportunities. On the other hand, some of the elements employers traditionally have thought of as motivators, do not really incentivize employees to do better work. Instead, these "hygiene" factors represent expectations workers have of their employer, and if they are not present, will create dissatisfaction.

**MOTIVATION-HYGIENE THEORY**
management theory suggesting certain factors in the workplace cause employee job satisfaction while a separate set of factors cause dissatisfaction

17. Chelladurai, P. (2014). *Managing organizations for sport and physical activity.* Scottsdale, AZ: Holcomb Hathaway.

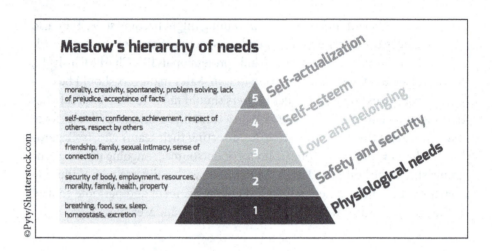

Examples of such factors include working conditions, workplace rules, and even salary. In other words, employees do not see things like a clean office environment or an acceptable pay check as motivation, but if these expectations are not adequately met, employees will be dissatisfied and will more likely give a less than optimal effort. The practical application for sales managers is that they must address both motivation and hygiene factors, but frequently only the "motivation" factors are effective at motivating staff members.

When examining how sales managers motivate their teams, it is also important to consider the concept of fairness or equality. A management researcher named J. Stacy Adams suggested workers will evaluate the outputs or rewards they receive both in the context of the effort (or inputs) workers expend to achieve the reward and how the reward compares to the rewards received by others. In order for a reward to be motivating, the worker should believe it is a fair outcome based on the effort expended and the results achieved. For example, a ticket seller who puts in many overtime hours to generate $100,000 in new business for a team will only be motivated by a commission bonus if it equals this effort. A $500 bonus may not seem fair compared to the amount of revenue generated, while a $5,000 bonus might seem more appropriate. However, the worker will also compare the bonus to what other coworkers or ticket sellers from other organizations earn. Some teams pay commissions to their ticket sellers based on sales team production rather than individual production. Adams would argue such a structure is much less motivating to the staff member who puts in a greater effort than coworkers; after all, the entire staff earns a similar bonus, which would appear to be unfair.

While these theories of motivation represent some of the more time-tested ideas, many other theories on employee motivation also exist. Other notable examples include Vroom's Expectancy Theory, Porter and Lawler's

Model, McClelland's Theory of Learned Needs, Alderfer's Existence, Relatedness, and Growth (ERG) Theory, and the concepts of Organizational Justice (Distributive, Procedural, and Interactional). The important lesson for would-be sales managers is the need to spend time understanding what makes sales employees tick and how to design an effective incentive plan for them.

---

**Jake Fisher, *Sports Illustrated***

### PHILADELPHIA 76'ERS SALES CULTURE

76ers head coach Brett Brown's barren roster fought tooth and nail only to muster 10 wins this season. General manager Sam Hinkie resigned as ownership swept the rug out from underneath him and his patient rebuild. Yet while near-chaos ensued in the franchise's basketball operations, the team's corporate faction experienced rousing success this season.

Even before the Sixers were granted the No. 1 overall pick on Tuesday, Philadelphia ranked third in the NBA in new season ticket sales for the 2016–17 campaign. Shortly after the calendar flipped to 2016, the Sixers saw the largest single sales day in organization history and they have renewed over 90% of its season ticket members each of the last three years.

"The culture of the Sixers' sales staff has been the main driver of their success," says Brendan Donohue, the NBA's Senior Vice President of Team Marketing and Business Operations. "It's vibrant, fun and contagious, with a terrific group of hard-working professionals who want to be a part of something bigger than themselves."

• • •

He emerges from the door at the center of the room on a hoverboard, materializing out of a thick haze from the nearby fog machine and entering a sea of screaming 20-somethings. This is not a Kanye West album debut. It's the 76ers' sales staff's pregame meeting, and the team's senior vice president of ticket sales and services, Jake Reynolds, is the moshpit's emcee. John Wall and the Washington Wizards are in town, the Wells Fargo Center a stone's throw from the 76ers' corporate offices in Philadelphia's Navy Yard. But before Reynolds can detail each associate's game duties for this February evening, he leads the entire staff in a raucous raffle.

The group is huddled at the center of the Sixers' sales floor, with two 7-foot baskets bookending the aisle in the middle of a maze of cubicles. A hands-slapping-knees drum roll ensues as Reynolds draws poker chips out of an enormous Tupperware box, each with staffers' names printed across the face. Nerlens Noel's signed jersey and a Jahlil Okafor-autographed poster are up for grabs among other prizes.

A chorus of cheers erupts with each winner, until today's stock of spoils has been awarded. Or so we thought. Reynolds announces one more give-away. The crowd shrieks in delight with the late addition of new Beats headphones. Only this time, Reynolds draws four names to compete in a rock-paper scissors tournament to claim the prize. The staff clad in designer suits instantaneously plays along, emphatically screaming, jumping, and sweating over the schoolyard gambit. "We do that before every game," Reynolds says. "We walk a very fine line between having fun and having too much fun." The 76ers now snap instead of clap inside their offices after the building warned their deafening festivities could be heard.

The corporate culture spawned from a brew of hope, zany energy, and innovation. At the heart is the Sixers' sales force, which has gone to greater lengths to incorporate youth than Hinkie did. The Sixers' 105-person sales team is the largest in the NBA and all of professional sports. Millennials comprise 99% of the department. "They want to run through walls, they want to change the world," CEO Scott O'Neil says.

The Sixers employ a strict criteria when hiring new sales associates. Management specifically looks for the "three C's" they deem congruent with their unique culture: Competitiveness, coachability, and curiosity. Philadelphia will soon introduce a 25–30 question personality test as part of its interview process, an attempt to compare candidates' results to those of the Sixers' elite ticket sales representatives. Additionally, the 76ers utilize a two-week onboarding process to immerse new employees within the office's controlled chaos, complete with a required reading and book report. Philadelphia swears by The Arbinger Institute's "Leadership and Self-Deception: Getting Out of the Box."

The 76ers then uncovered the stimulants for high-level, entry-salaried millennial performance, emphasizing a collective effort, providing daily free food, endless team memorabilia, and premium rewards. "We love to share our toys," says Chris Heck, the 76ers' Chief Revenue Officer. If the Sixers sold 700 new full-season tickets between Feb. 27 and April 15, the end of the regular season, the team would sponsor an Atlantic City trip for the entire staff. Upon reaching their "stretch goal" of 850 full-season tickets, the entire management team planned to shave their heads. Heck would move his desk from a private office overlooking the waterfront out to the middle of the sales floor. A buzzing clipper sent clumps of hair to the floor on April 27.

Red banners, printed with the team's Ballin' Ben Franklin secondary logo, hang from the sales room's ceiling, acknowledging all ticket representatives who have ever been promoted within the organization. Framed tie fragments adorn the back wall, having been snipped directly from associate's necks after completing their first sale over $10,000. The right wall displays a sales and service leaderboard with people's faces.

At a weekly meeting, the sales team MVP—voted by the reps themselves—is announced. A hard hat, signed by head coach Brett Brown, is awarded to a team member who "did the dirty work." A championship belt, golden boot, and bronze wolf statue also rotate around the office. "There's a lot of weekly awards," Reynolds laughs. The Sixers' five hoverboards are constantly fluttering around the room. Shots are perpetually flung at each basket. "You're always at risk of being dunked on," Reynolds warns.

**Long process finally pays off for 76ers during draft lottery**

"The root metaphor of sales often emphasizes competition and it seems like they've emphasized the community and the collective," says Jesica Speed Wiley, a professor and researcher of organizational communication at Northeastern University.

That interruption of traditional sales culture sparked an energy this season which reverberated through the phone as associates sold the team's message to their fan base. The 76ers wholeheartedly believe in the team's surplus of future assets, despite Hinkie's departure. "You're selling one of two things: You're either selling championships, or you're selling hope," Reynolds says. Ticket reps have pitched fans on the tantalizing prospect of healthy Joel Embiid, flashes of greatness from Nerlens Noel and Jahlil Okafor, unsung projects Jerami Grant and Robert Covington and overseas prospect Dario Saric. There's also the No. 1 pick in June's NBA draft. "This will soon become a harder seat than not," Heck says.

The hopeful intimation can only go so far with the on-court product so obviously lacking. To counteract the potential fragility of their message, the Sixers have created one of the most fan friendly arena experiences in sports. On opening night in 2012, the Sixers unveiled Big Bella, a 600-pound T-shirt gun capable of spitting out 100 T-shirts every 60 seconds. In August 2014, the Sixers purchased Quince Imaging's cutting-edge, projection-mapping technology to be beamed onto the Wells Fargo Center court.

Philadelphia is in a continuous search to reinvent the overall game experience. While Hinkie was scouting Melo Trimble and Diamond Stone at the University of Maryland this spring, he noticed an entertaining halftime hopscotch game and immediately phoned O'Neil. The 76ers regularly challenge one fan to a half-court shot during home games, with free season tickets on the line. There's been internal talks of installing a money-grab booth on the concourse, offering fans an opportunity to grab as many bills as they can toward a discount for future ticket purchases. The corporate brass considered distributing fly swatters to fans. The Sixers do rank third in the league in blocked shots after all.

"I want to create an atmosphere where a grandma, an 8-year-old kid, and a guy in a suit are all jumping for T-shirts, cheering, singing, dancing, and rooting for the Sixers," O'Neil says.

Perhaps the perfect confluence of it all lies in Brown's pregame ritual. Minutes before delivering his pre-tip locker room speech ahead of each home game, the spry 55-year-old coach meets with season ticket holders in the arena's press conference space. Brown pitched the idea himself during a weekly meeting. O'Neil asked if the New England native would be comfortable meeting with fans the following Tuesday. "And he shakes his head. 'No, every game,'" O'Neil recalls. "It is pretty amazing how candid, open, and engaging he is in telling our story and walking fans through the roller coaster ride we are on."

After raising Allen Iverson's No. 3 to the rafters during halftime against the Wizards on Mar. 1, 2014, the 76ers brought the banner back down to the floor following Philadelphia's loss to Washington. Season ticket holders lined the court to take pictures next to the iconic fabric. Wall bashfully emerged from the visiting locker room to ask the Sixers brass if he could pose next to Iverson's number, merrily taking part in the once-in-a-lifetime opportunity. Somehow, the 76ers bottled Wall's energy and shared it with a tuckered fan base. Whether that energy carries on—only time will tell.

## Motivating a Sport Sales Force

With sales representatives sometimes making 100+ calls a day, and frequently hearing "*no*" from prospects, it is critical sales managers create a positive and motivating work environment to keep employee morale high and, ultimately, to help sell more tickets. As a result, creating an environment where motivated people can give their best work and motivate others around them should be a high priority for sales managers. Keeping staff members motivated is paramount to reducing employee turnover and establishing an effective **sales culture**. Sales culture is the physical, emotional, and developmental environment where the act of selling takes place.[18]

**SALES CULTURE**
physical, emotional, and developmental environment where the act of selling takes place

Selling sports can be a fun and rewarding career. It is also a difficult one, particularly early on. New sales professionals often face a steep learning curve, must learn to think quickly on their feet in order to deal with difficult situations, and need to overcome rejection on a regular basis. In addition, during the early stages of a sport sales career, employees don't make a lot of money. Good sales managers understand all of these tough adjustments for their new hires (and even for their more veteran employees) and work to develop a good sales culture and work environment so that those hires stay motivated and dedicated to their profession.

Courtesy of David Pierce.

Leaderboard—the sales leaderboard shows who is hustling the most

Some professional teams, particularly those located in parts of the country that have higher costs of living, have begun providing their entry-level sales representatives with living assistance. For example, the Miami Dolphins and New York Mets, among other teams, now provide some of their new sales reps with living arrangements in the form of small furnished apartments, typically shared with another new hire. The Philadelphia 76ers, meanwhile, have begun providing lunches for their sales representatives in an effort to help keep the employees' living costs down and their enthusiasm up. Even the physical office environment has begun to change at many teams. Once relegated to the bowels of the stadium or even broom closets, sales rooms are now being moved to more prominent areas within team headquarters. Decorated with prominent team paraphernalia or

18. Irwin, R., Sutton, W., & McCarthy, L. (2008). *Sport promotion and sales management.* Champaign, IL: Human Kinetics.

Courtesy of David Pierce.

**Office—A typical sport sales work space**

organizational artifacts, many of these spaces at major league teams overlook the field, court, or ice. Teams are trying to balance the need to have individual spaces for employees with an open office structure that creates interaction among employees. Open sales rooms also allow managers to overhear sales conversations, creating more coaching and mentoring opportunities.

What are some of the more common incentivization programs ticket sales managers establish within their organization? For most teams, the plan starts with a **commission** scale. Financially incentivizing sellers to complete more sales certainly makes sense. Most professional sport teams offer sellers between 5 and 10% commission on all sales closed. Oftentimes these commission rates vary depending on the inventory sold; premium seats may earn a different commission compared to a group sale. From a managerial perspective, it is important to develop a commission plan that intentionally rewards sellers for making certain types of sales. For example, selling four new season tickets in the lower bowl should earn a higher commission rate than renewing four partial plans in the upper level. Some teams, such as the Golden State Warriors, have developed escalating commission structures so that when sellers reach certain sales goals, their commission percentage increases.[19] Commission plans should stay fairly consistent from year to year and not deviate within the season. It is important for sales managers to run a financial analysis prior to announcing commission rates to ensure that the organization or department can live with the results of a highly productive sales staff. Commission structures are particularly effective when dealing with inventory that has a longer

**COMMISSION**
a percentage of the total cost of a sale paid to the agent (employee) responsible for inducing the transaction

19. Sutton, B. (2014, July 14). For building, motivating sales staffs, one size does not fit all. *SportsBusiness Journal,* 15.

sales cycle such as premium seats and sponsorship. Some organizations pay commission on a weekly or bi-weekly basis, while other teams may distribute commission bonuses monthly, quarterly, or even yearly.

---

### COMMON COMMISSION STRUCTURE

- ▶ New seasons: 8%
- ▶ New mini-plans: 4%
- ▶ Groups: 5%
- ▶ New club seats: 8%
- ▶ Suites: 5%

---

While commission plans can provide effective motivation, they should not be the only source of encouragement. Effective sales managers realize new sales representatives take awhile to become more proficient at selling. As such, managers should find other ways to encourage those just starting in the profession, especially when trying to build good sales habits. Some teams, such as the NBA's Portland Trailblazers, develop a sales "hustle board," which is used to acknowledge good sales habits by employees, regardless of the number of sales closed. On the basketball court, "hustle" statistics might include rebounds, steals, or even passes deflected, aspects of the game that won't show up on *SportsCenter* but help a team win. In the sales room, "hustle" statistics could include number of calls made, amount of time spent on the phone, or the number of new leads generated. By recognizing sellers who are putting in the time and effort needed to succeed in sales, managers can build up sellers' confidence. Sales is a profession in which sometimes a lazy seller will occasionally get lucky with a big sale or a hard-working seller will hit a cold streak and can't seem to close anything. Over the long haul, the sellers who have the best habits and work the hardest have the best chance of long-term success. Sales managers need to realize this and incentivize not only short-term production (sales) but also the good habits which lead to long-term production.

Another powerful motivational tool is public recognition of accomplishments. In many sales rooms, managers install a bell or gong. When a big close is made, the sales representative can ring the bell or hit the gong, informing the rest of the office about the sale. While this may sound a little silly at first, public recognition

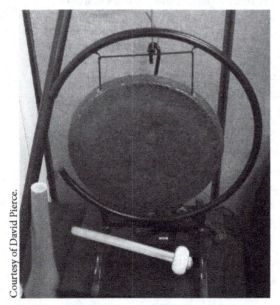

Courtesy of David Pierce.

**Gong—Salespeople ring the gong when they make a sale to keep the energy up in the sales room.**

of a success can serve as a reward, a culture-builder, and a motivator for other employees. Some teams have office celebrations for major sales or when team goals are met. The NBA's Minnesota Timberwolves recently installed a computer software platform called Hurrah! Leaderboards. This system interfaces with the team's CRM program and displays key sales statistics on video boards posted throughout the team's sales floor. For example, the video boards might list the five account representatives who

have made the most calls for the week, accompanied by headshots of those representatives. When a big sale is made, the system plays the seller's "walk-out" song so everyone in the office knows a teammate just had a big success. Many teams with great sales managers create "travelling trophies" that are awarded to top sellers for the week or month. These items could be things like a bobblehead, a heavyweight championship belt, or an actual trophy, which become proudly displayed in an employee's cubicle or office. Some organizations, such as MLB's Pittsburgh Pirates and the MLS National Sales Center, create Wall of Fame displays listing all-time sales records and recognizing entry-level sellers who have been promoted. In fact, when Pirates' sales trainees get promoted, they are asked to autograph a baseball, which is then displayed on a prominent wall. Sales managers at the NFL's Atlanta Falcons will hang a pennant from another team in their sales office when one of their trainees is hired by another franchise.

One of the benefits of managing a sport sales team is the abundance of unique non-cash incentives available. For example, when the NHL's Columbus Blue Jackets met a team sales goal, they took their sales team to watch an away game in another city. Playing a pick-up basketball game on the team court, meeting a star player, or earning autographed team memorabilia are all possible rewards a sport sales manager can dispense. When Michael Jordan became owner of the NBA's Charlotte Bobcats (now Hornets), he asked his management team what he could do to help improve sales. "They suggested that he periodically invite the top performers in ticket and sponsorship sales to his office for lunch, limiting the group to four so they could all feel connected with him."[20] How's that for motivation?

20.  King, B. (2010, Oct. 25). Jordan mingles with staff: Call me MJ. *SportsBusiness Journal*. Retrieved from http://www.sportsbusinessdaily.com/Journal/Issues/2010/10/20101025/ SBJ-In-Depth/Jordan-Mingles-With-Staff-Call-Me-MJ.aspx?

Creating motivating incentives is important in managing a sport sales team, but this is not the only skill needed by managers. Just as important is the ability to communicate effectively with staff members. Many of the biggest problems arising in sport organizations boil down to a lack of communication. Making sure dozens, or sometimes hundreds, of employees are on the same page in terms of organizational strategies, franchise or department vision, or even company policies and procedures is a very challenging task for managers, with no simple answers. Sales managers must work diligently to provide communication with their staff, often through multiple channels. The communication may take place in daily sales "huddles," weekly or monthly staff meetings, through annual performance reviews, or through more informal mentoring or coaching opportunities.

---

## COMMUNICATION IS KEY

The NHL's Chicago Blackhawks are one organization that has made very intentional efforts to improve communication throughout their staff. They produce a daily newsletter that is sent organization-wide, sharing everything from team accomplishments to new hires and from team practice times to any special guests that might be attending a game that evening. In addition, the Blackhawks take a very open and transparent approach to communication; they go so far as to inform their frontline ticket sellers of impending player transactions before that information is made public. Ticket sales representatives understand they cannot share such information with customers, but knowing about a big player trade can help shape their sales conversations. It also builds tremendous trust among the staff.[21]

---

It is also important for sales manager to understand employee needs. One challenge today's managers face is working with different generations of employees. Today's Generation Y or Millennial employee typically has different work expectations than previous generations; they tend to look for more flexibility in a job, desire more frequent feedback on work performance, and tend to value collaboration and connectivity to others. They also communicate more electronically and are more tech savvy. For sport sales managers, this can mean new approaches to the traditional sales supervisor role. In some cases, employees may be allowed to work remotely or in teams, rather than as individuals. It can also mean allowing sellers to communicate with prospects through means other than traditional telephone and face-to-face conversations. Sales managers who believe a good commission check is all the incentive or feedback an employee needs will likely see high turnover among Millennial employees. Many of today's sales managers cut their teeth in a

---

21. Botta, C. (2013, April 22). Biz and hockey sides aligning for Blackhawks. *SportsBusiness Journal.* Retrieved from www.sportsbusinessdaily.com/Journal/Issues/2013/04/22/Franchises/Blackhawks.aspx?

far different sales culture and are not always prepared to change managerial styles to adapt to today's entry-level employee. However, by not embracing, or at least acknowledging these differences, managers are setting themselves up for organizational conflict. Sales managers also must manage people at different stages of their career. While young and "hungry" sales reps may be willing to put in the long hours to develop a reputation and credentials, more seasoned sales reps may be able to rely on a pipeline of reliable customers and not have to work as hard to generate the same amount of revenue as younger sales reps. More experienced sellers may find the quality-of-life and family time factors more important than beginning sellers.

---

**Rocky Harris, Sr. Associate AD for Communications, Arizona State University**

## BECOMING A GREAT BOSS:
## THE SECRET OF MANAGING MILLENNIALS

### Does Gen Y get a bad rap?

The generation currently entering the workforce gets a bad rap. They are seen as entitled, spoiled, and difficult to manage. They don't follow rules. They expect to be rewarded without working for it. While some of this may be true (see chart below), the truth is each generation is misunderstood and treated unfairly by the older generations. I remember when it happened to me.

### Back to the future

The stereotype of my generation (Gen X) was we were underachievers known for cutting corners. Slackers.

| Millennial Generation Traits | |
|---|---|
| Special | Sense of entitlement; here to solve world's problems. |
| Sheltered | Parents advocated for and spared them from unpleasant experiences. |
| Confident | Motivated, goal-oriented, optimistic. |
| Team-oriented | Tight-knit, group-oriented rather than individualists. Egalitarian not hierarchical. |
| Pressured | Tightly scheduled as children; struggle with own time management. Pressure to succeed. |
| Conventional | Respectful, civic-minded, fear of non-conforming. Support social rules; connected to parents. |
| Source: Millennials Go to College (2003) by Neil Howe and William Strauss; www.lifecourse.com | |

In 2000, I was a recent college graduate interning at the San Francisco 49ers. One day I left early to attend a graduate sport management class at the University of San Francisco, about 90 minutes away. One of our seasoned executives said, *Typical youngster these days . . . sneaking out early. Has anyone in your generation ever worked a full day?*

Instead of letting him know I worked full-time for the 49ers with 12 hours of graduate courses and a part-time job on the weekends, I decided to leave without defending the truth or acknowledging his ignorance.

That day left a mark on me, making me dig deeper into why he would make a generalization without knowing me personally. That would be like me saying, "I'm surprised you're still awake this late in the day old man. Isn't it time for a nap?"

From that day forward, I realized like most stereotypes, creating generalizations about generations isn't productive.

"I employ the belief that every individual should be communicated to in a way that will yield results," said Kristen Gambetta Director of Client Services for the Houston Dynamo. "While there are generational qualities that come into play, it is important to get to know the individual to learn how to effectively motivate him or her to action. If you put your coworkers in a box based on their generation you may not be getting the most out of them."

**Forgetting to remember**

At one point in my career I forgot the lesson I learned.

When I first became a manager, I would complain about the generation below me: "They expect to be president of a team by the time they are 25 without doing any work to get there. They show up to work whenever they want rather than at 8 am when everyone else gets here." Sound familiar?

I was guilty of doing exactly what I complained about when I was younger. I stepped back and understood I painted everyone with the same broad brush. It wasn't fair.

**Managing differently**

In a survey conducted by Lee Hecht Harrison, more than 60% of employers experience tension between employees from different generations.

A good manager or leader manages each person differently. Why? Because they're different. Each employee is motivated by different factors. You have to know when to pull the right levers.

What do you do with the 22-year-old who thinks he can be team president at 25? Tap into ambition to get the most out of them. What about the one who gets to the office later than others? Look at productivity. As long as they stay late and get the work done, does it really matter when they arrive?

Even though this generation has a unique set of values, expectations, and approaches to work, so do people of ALL ages. The reason why people have a tough time understanding other generations is the same reason why managers have a challenging time managing employees: No two people are the same and they shouldn't be treated as such.

John Wooden said, "A coach is someone who can give correction without causing resentment." The only way to correct without causing resentment is to figure out what motivates and treat them accordingly.

"I find it unique to work with such a wide range in ages," said Houston Texans Senior Director of Communications, Kevin Cooper. "I find lots of knowledge can be exchanged between the generations. The ability to communicate and find common ground is where we need to be. There are modern problems that can use experienced solutions and older issues that require modern ingenuity. There in the middle—where respectful dialogue lies—is where business can move forward."

### A message to millennials

My guess is the young men and women entering the workforce deal with these generalizations throughout their young careers. My advice is to not make the same mistake I once did. Don't pass judgment on other generations. First, consider what motivates and drives those older than your generation. Second, as you progress in your career and start managing people, don't be quick to judge the next generation behind you. And, third, always remember what Mark Twain said, "All generalizations are false, including this one."

### A take from the front of the class

Michael Lysko, Director and Professor of Practice—*Southern Methodist University Sport Management Program*

As a Baby Boomer I've taught and coached Gen X and Gen Y. Here's my take on Millennials:

1. Don't underestimate their work ethic and desire to succeed.

2. When it comes to entitlement and career goals, I don't think that they are any different from Gen X'ers in that they want to be recognized and rewarded for effort and achievement.

3. They seem to have an inherent sense of fairness. They don't trust the mainstream media to give an unbiased view.

4. Media consumption patterns are much different than earlier generations—in that their interests are much more narrow and social media involves an exchange of ideas as opposed to an authoritative voice on the 6:00 news.

5. Most respect authority, but are more willing to question authority when they feel strongly about an issue.

6. Trust must be earned on an individual basis. It doesn't exist simply because of your title.

7. They may not expect to remain with a single employer for an extended period of time. They learned from their parents that circumstances can change quickly. They want to be in a position that allows the freedom to make choices that are in their own best interests.

## EVALUATION

There is no shortage of data on which to evaluate the performance of salespeople. As noted in other chapters, sales effort and performance are transparent, and it's difficult to hide when sales productivity numbers are readily available. Effectively leveraging the technology that powers CRM systems should provide sales managers with the following types of metrics:

- First touch calls—Calls to prospects for the first time
- Re-approach calls—Calls to those who have objected to the offer once before
- Opportunity calls—Calls to those who have received a specific product recommendation in the recent past and have been given time to decide
- Appointments set—Number of appointments that were set
- Break-up calls—Number of prospects with whom the salesperson has ended the sales cycle
- Total number of calls
- Length of calls—Time spent on each of the above types of calls
- Length of time between calls—Efficient, organized sellers are ready to make the next call soon after hanging up
- Closing ratio—Ratio of contacts reached that result in a close
- Revenue generated—Total revenue generated from packages sold

Beyond data that can be pulled from CRM technology, managers can evaluate sales calls from role-playing exercises, mock sales calls, and audio recordings. The sales competency rubrics presented in each of the sales process chapters in this textbook are good examples of ways in which managers evaluate their employees. These tools allow sales managers to examine performance beyond the final revenue generation figure and understand in which competency areas a salesperson may need additional training.

Employee evaluations can take two forms: informal and formal. Informal evaluations might include hallway conversations, casual words of encouragement or suggestions of how to do a better job, or even the occasional personal note written to an employee. These interactions can occur anytime or even daily. Formal evaluations, on the other hand, occur on a regularly scheduled basis (typically once a year, although some teams, such as the Columbus Blue Jackets, perform some sort of appraisal every few months) and usually take some standardized approach, such as a ratings form. These performance appraisals have two primary objectives. The first is to help the employee develop professionally by pointing out strengths and weaknesses or show areas for improvement. The second is administrative in nature, using the review to evaluate performance based on set criteria.[22] In sales, the evaluation appraisal might look at job performance compared to the sales goals established at the beginning of the year, the previous years' performance(s), or the performance of other sales reps. While the professional development appraisal is often the more helpful to the growth of the employee, the evaluation (or administration) appraisal is often the bigger concern for employees because it is typically used to determine promotions, pay raises, bonuses, or even job security. For example, during the performance appraisal, a sales manager may tell an employee she needs to improve at overcoming particular objections and needs to spend more time on the phone, which are things the employee can work on in the

"Your evaluation is based on the next 30 seconds. Go!"

©Cartoonresource/Shutterstock.com

future. However, the sales representative might only be concerned with the manager informing her that she meet her sales benchmarks and is in line for a promotion and pay raise.

Minor league baseball marketer Mike Veeck in his book *Fun is Good*, suggests annual performance reviews should serve as more than just an evaluation tool for the employee.[23] Instead, he argues annual performance appraisals should also serve as a feedback tool for the employee to share information with management. According to Veeck, good managers will use reviews to learn more about how employees think they can improve, what goals employees have for themselves and the organization, and the shortcomings of management or the organization. This approach allows the organization to learn and improve just as it helps the employee become better. Peer-, customer-, and self-reviews can also be utilized to paint a 360 degree portrait of appraisal

22. Chelladurai, P. (2014). *Managing organizations for sport and physical activity.* Scottsdale, AZ: Holcomb Hathaway.

23. Veeck, M. (2005). *Fun is good: How to create joy & passion in your workplace & career.* Emmaus, PA: Rodale.

and help an employee improve in areas that a manager might not always be able to observe.

## Discipline and Termination

No matter what sort of sales culture is developed within a sport organization, and no matter how strenuous the employee screening process is, sometimes employees end up being a poor fit. The field of sport sales has a high degree of turnover, some of which is due to managers dismissing employees who are not producing. The nature of sales allows for very clear performance indicators. Producers show up on the sales board and non-producers do not. Managers should work hard to develop the individuals they hire and they have an obligation to lay out a path toward success. The reality, though, is that sometimes employees do not stay on that path, forcing managers to take action.

Discipline should always be used as a corrective measure in an effort to improve performance. It should not be utilized simply as a punishment or retaliation. In order to be effective, discipline must be both meaningful and enforceable. Most managers will agree, a progressive form of discipline is effective in most cases. The first step is typically a verbal warning to the employee. When issuing a verbal warning, managers should carefully document the date and cause of the disciplinary measure. If the employee's inappropriate behavior continues, the next managerial action is typically a written warning. Written warnings should be issued in a private meeting between the employee and manager. It is good managerial practice to have employees agree in writing that they received and understood the nature of the warnings. If a written warning is also not effective at changing behavior, an intervention may take place in which the manager clearly explains both the problem and its impact on the organization. Then, in collaboration with the employee, the manager should develop a plan of action, including goals, step-by-step procedures, and consequences of not meeting expectations. If this intervention process is unsuccessful, then the only alternative is likely termination of the employee.

Good sales managers understand there is a right way and a wrong way to terminate an employee. First, managers should always have plenty of documentation justifying the termination. It is beneficial to talk to the sport organization's human resources or legal staff before firing an employee, to make sure the correct organizational procedures are followed. Second, when letting a difficult employee go, it is important to allow the person to leave with dignity. This means the termination meeting should be held in private, although some managers prefer to have a single witness present. Third, termination meetings should never be treated as negotiation sessions in which an employee argues for continued employment. When meeting with an employee who is about to be terminated, managers should already have a termination letter in hand, outlining the procedures and policies for the employee. Understandably, employees who have just been let go are often emotional or distraught. As such, they may not be thinking clearly or have a good recollection of the details discussed at a termination meeting—beyond knowing they are no longer employed. A termination letter might spell out for an employee items such as their legal rights, any compensation to which they might be entitled, and other unemployment benefits they may have.

In his book, *Ice to the Eskimos*, former NBA executive Jon Spoelstra suggests when managers must fire an employee, they should always bargain with upper administration for more termination pay. Spoelstra says there are three reasons for this:

- ▶ It is only fair to the employee. Terminated employees are rarely bad people; more often than not, they are just not a good fit for the organization.
- ▶ It helps the manager feel a little better about a very difficult situation.
- ▶ Most importantly, other employees of the organization will know about the action.

Spoelstra writes "employees will see and appreciate that if you're fair to the people that you fire, you'll really be fair to those that aren't fired."[24] Similarly, Veeck suggests sport managers allow terminated employees to "dictate the terms of the departure."[25] In a profession such as ticket sales, where productivity measures are often public (e.g., sales leaderboards), employees often know when things are not working out or no longer feel passionately about their job. In some cases, as Veeck points out, employees may actually be relieved to know it is time to move on.

Once an employee has been terminated, it is important managers follow up on several details. Dismissed employees should have an opportunity to clean out their office space or cubicle. Some sport organizations offer to have staff clean out the space. If doing so, managers should make sure at least two staff members are present so there is always an eyewitness present in case of theft claims by a disgruntled former employee. Once an employee is let go, managers should immediately cut off any password-protected computer access to team software or other materials and should immediately collect any team-issued keys, cards, or badges.

This brings up an interesting point. What if a ticket sales representative leaves one team and takes a position with another team in the same market? Should the representative be allowed to call on customers from relationships

24. Spoelstra, J. (1997). *Ice to the Eskimos*. New York: HarperBusiness. p. 187.

25. Veeck, M. (2005). *Fun is good: How to create joy & passion in your workplace & career.* Emmaus, PA: Rodale. p. 23.

built at the former team in an attempt to sell them inventory from the new team? Marketer Dan Migala posed this very question to several sales managers with professional sport teams. Here are some of their responses:[26]

▶ Some teams require employees to sign a non-compete clause when they are hired, so that if they do leave the team, they are not allowed to pursue their old clients for a certain period of time, perhaps 12 to 18 months.

▶ Other teams believe non-compete clauses are ineffective, and instead use other mechanisms such as discussing ethical behavior during an exit interview, withholding any commission pay due until it has been established that the employee is not trying to contact old customers, or reminding the employee it is still critical to maintain a relationship with the former employer because of things like reference checks.

▶ Some managers will go so far as to contact the new organization and discuss with them that their new employee should not be contacting former customers.

▶ Of course, all sport organizations should develop strong enough relationships with their customers that a change in employees will not greatly affect the customer's experience. Several managers suggested when a sales representative leaves an organization, the team should contact all of the former employee's past accounts and inform them of the situation while assuring them they will continue to receive outstanding service.

26. Migala, D. (2006, Sept. 4). Real life scenario: What would you do? *The Migala Report.* Retrieved from http://migalareport.com/node/197

# CHAPTER SUMMARY

While most of this book focuses on effective selling, this chapter outlines many basic tenets of effective sales force management. Managing sellers requires a different skill set than selling itself. Good sales managers understand the principles behind effective management such as recruitment, training, motivation, evaluation, and discipline. Within the field of sport sales, there is significant turnover, meaning managers must develop effective recruiting strategies to maintain adequate staffing levels. Once hired, new employees must receive ample and effective training before they are ready to sell, and should continue to receive regular training to keep their sales skills sharp. Effective managers also utilize various motivational techniques to keep employees engaged and productive. Performance evaluations, both formal and informal, should be a regular component of sales management. Finally, good managers recognize when employees are not performing well or are a poor organizational fit and take appropriate disciplinary actions, possibly ending with the properly executed termination of an employee.

# CHAPTER ACTIVITIES

1. Think of your past work experiences. What did your previous managers do well and what did they do poorly? What was the impact of your managers' actions on workplace productivity? Develop a personal management statement that contains at least five points of emphasis that you would enforce if you were managing a sales team for an arena league football franchise. Why did you select those specific points?

2. Imagine you have just been hired as the Director of Ticket Sales for Big State University. The athletics director has given you a budget to hire four ticket sales representatives. Explain three different ways you might effectively fill those positions and what will be the biggest challenges in doing so. Include things such as where you might advertise the positions, which events you might attend, with whom might you network, and how might you structure your interviews. What sorts of questions would you ask in your interviews?

3. Pretend you work for a minor league baseball team that has a relatively small budget. Develop a commission structure and incentive program that you believe would be fair and motivational for your ticket sellers, but will also help the club generate maximum revenue.

4. Find an example online of a formal evaluation or employee appraisal form. Would that form be an effective tool for evaluating a ticket sales employee? Why or why not? What would make it better?

5. Read *"Fun is Good"* by Mike Veeck and outline the 10 most important management principles you would take from the book. What is difficult about managing other people? Why do you think Veeck has been a successful front office manager of minor league baseball teams?

# CHAPTER 14

## CUSTOMER RETENTION FROM GAME TIME TO RENEWAL

### LIZ WANLESS

---

**LEARNING OBJECTIVES**

After completing this chapter, you should be able to:

► Explain the importance of establishing long-term customer relationships and understand the concept of customer lifetime value.

► Understand the significance of aftermarketing and service to customer retention and development.

► Recognize the difference between traditional and social customer relationship management (CRM).

► Identify how analytics and gaining customer feedback are central to customer retention strategy.

► Understand and apply steps to creating successful aftermarketing plans for various levels of sport organizations.

► Understand how to create an effective customer service plan.

► Recognize future technological trends in aftermarketing and customer service.

► Understand the importance of evaluation and steps to implementing successful evaluation strategy.

Contributed by Liz Wanless. © Kendall Hunt Publishing Company

## KEY TERMS

Aftermarketing

Analytical customer relationship
    management

Analytics

Behavioral customer relationship
    management

Big data

Customer behavior

Customer life cycle

Customer lifetime value

Customer loyalty

Customer retention

Customer sentiment

Customer service

Relationship marketing

Social customer relationship
    management

Sportscape

Touchpoints

Traditional customer relationship
    management

## CHAPTER OVERVIEW

The team will not always be winning, the economy will not always support discretionary income, and customers have many entertainment choices. Sport managers must face these obstacles head-on through cultivating strong relationships with customers. In losing streaks, in financial hardship, and regardless of other entertainment options, customers feeling a strong relationship with an organization will remain loyal to that organization; making purchases throughout their lifetime. Successful sales managers do not leave customer relationships to chance. Instead, they utilize systematic approaches to customer retention to ensure customers feel central to the organization. The competition in the marketplace for the customer's discretionary entertainment spending is intense, which means sport organizations must build long-term and sustainable relationships with their customers. Sport organizations that believe nothing can be done to influence a customer's renewal decision will find themselves in a constant battle to find new customers to replace those who have defected. Be the sport manager who cultivates loyal customers; commit to the key concepts and principles of customer retention strategy from game time to renewal.

# CUSTOMER RELATIONSHIPS: THE FOUNDATION OF RETENTION AND LOYALTY

Sport managers cultivate loyal customers through establishing relationships with their customers. A sport organization's strategy to develop relationships with customers varies by organization. The Ohio State University athletic program and a smaller mid-major athletic program won't have the same relationships with customers. Because Ohio State football season ticket sales are in high demand, ticket sales representatives prioritize season ticket availability and seat location according to donations made to the Ohio State Athletics Development Organization, the President's Club.[1] At Ball State University, a school in the Mid-America Conference, however, ticket sales professionals coordinate an outbound sales campaign to the surrounding community and actively recruit single game attendees in order to develop these customers into season ticket holders. Regardless of sport product demand, winning and losing seasons, or athletic department resources, successful sport managers will take deliberate action to create relationships with customers in order to transition a one-time customer into a loyal customer, a customer who continually feels that an organization's products or services are the best selection in comparison with other options. **Customer loyalty** fosters lifetime customers. Why are lifetime customers important?

Lifetime customers create lifetime value. Sport marketers utilize several ways to estimate **customer lifetime value**, the term used to describe the net profit associated with a long-term repeat customer. For instance, let's say you attend an Indiana Pacers game with a friend. The combined ticket value for this purchase is $96. If you both enjoy your experience and plan to attend again next year and the year after, you are now customers worth $288. This doesn't even include the amount of money you spend on concessions, merchandise, or parking. Maybe this becomes an annual tradition for you for the next 10 years. Now, your $96 purchase becomes a $960 purchase, again, not considering the extras or incremental price increases from year to year. If you enjoyed your experience so much that you purchased season tickets for the next ten years, your $96 purchase is now worth $59,586 in the club level corner at Banker's Life Fieldhouse. Smart sport managers know that recruiting and driving interest in new customers costs more and presents a greater challenge than encouraging returning customers to purchase or upgrade. The cost of acquiring new customers can be 5 to 10 times more expensive than satisfying and retaining current customers.

**CUSTOMER LOYALTY**
when a customer continually feels that an organization's products or services are the best selection

**CUSTOMER LIFETIME VALUE**
the net profit associated with a long-term repeat customer

---

1. *Public seat selection.* Retrieved from http://www.ohiostatebuckeyes.com/tickets/m-footbl-public-seat-selection.html

## CUSTOMERS ARE ASSETS WITH LIFETIME VALUE

Using the example of a fictional minor league baseball team, assume that the average per game price for season tickets is $10, there are 20 games in a season ticket plan, and that each account purchases 2.5 tickets. If each account spends $350 per season on ancillary items, the average annual expenditure for each account is $850. If the team has 1,000 season ticket holders, the total revenue generated from season ticket holders is $850,000. Assume the team has a retention rate of 80% and a defection rate of 20%. This means 800 season ticket holders renew for the next season while 200 do not renew. To calculate the average duration of being a season ticket holder, simply calculate the reciprocal of the defection rate (i.e., 1/20%). This means that season ticket holders stick around for an average of 5 years. The current lifetime value of each account is $4,250 (i.e., $850 * 5). Now, assume that the team creates a plan to improve season ticket holder retention, and that the retention rate increases to 90%. This results in season tickets holders remaining with the team for 10 years and the lifetime value of each account increasing to $8,500. In short, increasing renewals from 80% to 90% doubles the lifetime value of each account. It is important to note these calculations do not take the time value of money into account. These calculations are illustrated in Table 14.1.

## Table 14.1

**Customers Are Assets With Lifetime Value**

| Description | 80% Retention | 85% Retention | 90% Retention |
|---|---|---|---|
| Average price of season tickets | $10 | $10 | $10 |
| Games in Plan | 20 | 20 | 20 |
| Plans purchased per account | 2.5 | 2.5 | 2.5 |
| Ancillary spending per account | $350 | $350 | $350 |
| Average annual expenditure per account | $850 | $850 | $850 |
| Total number of accounts | 1,000 | 1,000 | 1,000 |
| Total Revenue Generated | $850,000 | $850,000 | $850,000 |
| Retention Rate | 80% | 85% | 90% |
| Average years per account | 5.0 | 6.7 | 10.0 |
| Current Lifetime Value of Account | $4,250 | $5,667 | $8,500 |
| Aggregate value of all accounts | $4,250,000 | $5,666,667 | $8,500,000 |

*Note: calculations do not account for time value of money

In the contemporary entertainment marketplace, customers have many entertainment options from which to choose. In the New York City area alone, sport fans can choose from seeing the Mets, Yankees, Nets, Knicks, Liberty, Giants, Jets, Devils, Islanders, and Rangers—and this just represents professional sport options. As team performance fluctuates, creating sales stability is of key importance. And as the economy changes and pocketbooks tighten, unless the customer feels a relationship to the team and organization, finding another and potentially less expensive entertainment option becomes all too easy. Why not just enjoy the game on the comfort of your own couch? Sport organizations creating successful and mutually beneficial customer relationships reduce the expense associated with driving new customers. Increased competition among entertainment providers means an increased importance placed on creating repeat customers with a lifetime value. So where do sport managers begin?

Creating a relationship with the customer base means incorporating the customer's needs and wants into the business model. Sport organizations at all levels, recreation to professional sport, with various levels of demand, from Ball State to Ohio State, must invest in their customers in order to retain customers for additional purchases. Fortunately, the sport manager can utilize strategies to encourage a lifetime relationship with customers. Unfortunately, however, some sport managers fall victim to ineffective attitudes and practices. Sport managers believing that winning or losing completely dictates renewal won't invest in strategies that will retain customers in losing streaks. Successful sport managers will instead harness strategies to create relationships with fans that keep customers coming back year after year regardless of economic hardship or win/loss records. Begin this process by working from a social CRM framework.

## WORKING FROM A SOCIAL CRM FRAMEWORK

Sport managers utilizing a social CRM framework strive to understand the customer, engage the customer, and personalize communication with the customer throughout the customer life cycle. With increased technology and growth of the use of analytics in sport, sport organizations can understand the customer by using one or a combination of philosophical approaches. **Analytical CRM** involves collecting customer data information and creating a model to increase customer revenues over the life cycle.[2] For example, if an organization collects season ticket holder demographic data, the organization can use trends in this data to predict those customers who will be most profitable and those who are most at-risk for non-renewal. Knowing this information can be critical to targeting the right message to the right type of consumer. **Behavioral CRM** utilizes focus groups or surveys to uncover the psychology of customer choice to inform a strategy to better retain customers.[3] For example, after conducting a focus group of rookie season ticket holders, a sport organization may find that rookie season ticket holders like to

**ANALYTICAL CUSTOMER RELATIONSHIP MANAGEMENT**
the collection of customer data information to create a model to increase customer revenues over the life cycle

**BEHAVIORAL CUSTOMER RELATIONSHIP MANAGEMENT**
the use of focus groups or surveys to uncover the psychology of customer choice to inform a strategy to better retain customers

2.  Kamakura, W., Mela, C., Ansari, A., Bodapati, A., Fader, P., Iyengar, R., et al. *Choice models and customer relationship*. Retrieved from http://www.anderson.ucla.edu/faculty/anand. bodapati/Choice-Models-and-CRM.pdf

3.  Ibid.

renew their tickets online instead of through an account executive. This may prompt the sport organization to include various methods for season ticket holders to renew. Business professionals may use a combination of analytical and behavioral CRM to inform business processes.

Regardless of the philosophical foundations informing CRM systems and which data managers decide to use, customer communication through modern media channels has greatly affected CRM. Sport fans can recognize contemporary CRM not only in the game experience, but also after the game experience is over. When fans live-tweet an event to appear on a video board or participate in an online fan forum to make comments about the game experience, they have participated in a sport organization's CRM system. If customers engaged with a team's social media site, participated in a contest to win free tickets, or purchased a ticket via a third-party vendor (e.g., Ticketmaster), these customers have also participated in a sport organization's CRM system. Even after the game, teams like the Florida Panthers eagerly gather data to create in-depth profiles of customers. When the Panthers initiated a partnership with Umbel, an analytics company specializing in uniting data from separate communication platforms to better inform marketing strategies, the team enjoyed a 7.5% return on advertisement spending, surpassing its goal.[4]

## The CRM Evolution

At one time, business controlled media and largely the public conversation with regard to products. Media had yet to be interactive, and websites, television commercials, and e-mail blasts served as examples of the one-way communication sport organizations typically exhibited with consumers. Now, the conversation has changed. Social media, in most cases, is public. With the advent and popularity of social media as well as public review sites, managers of any industry face pressure to cultivate strong relationships with customers to ensure customers review products favorably in public forums. Websites such as www.stadiumjourney.com not only include reviews of game experiences according to a range of variables from food and beverage to the surrounding stadium neighborhood, but they also include web forums for customers to comment. Word of mouth then becomes increasingly important.

In order to account for the media evolution, approaches to CRM have evolved. What used to be and in some cases still is in part one-way communication, a company targeting customers with messages to increase sales, now also includes customer-driven and customer-collaborative efforts. Like many other retail stores, Nike includes product feedback on their websites.

4. Umbel. *How data is helping sports teams increase ROI, even in off-season*. Retrieved from https://www.umbel.com/blog/sports/how-data-is-helping-sports-teams-increase-roi-even-in-off-season/

If customers purchase the Nike shoes in a store, they can fill out a survey regarding the purchase experience online with a code denoted on the receipt and redeem a $5 coupon. If the customer purchased online, Nike provides customers with forums to rate their product and buying experience from one to five stars with comments. This is Nike's way of collaborating with the customer and gaining feedback on the customer's terms. Nike uses this feedback to alter their product according to customer needs as well as to help other customers in the buying process. For example, if customers consistently rate that a shoe fits small, Nike will guide customers to purchase one size up.

A **traditional CRM** system can be described as a business's one-way communication method to increase sales throughout the **customer life cycle**: acquisition, retention, and development (customer development refers to the process of encouraging additional purchases across offered products). A minor league baseball team sending opening day promotional flyers to past customers represents a traditional CRM tactic. The business is the center of the communication directed at the customer on the receiving end.

A **social CRM** system, on the other hand, is an expansion of traditional CRM and can be described as a system involving customer engagement throughout the customer life cycle. A minor league baseball team may also send opening day promotional flyers to past customers, but may design the flyer and send date after using software to track social media comments about last year's opening day. They might also conduct a focus group to gauge customer sentiment with respect to upcoming opening day and the best timing to receive a flyer, if at all. While the traditional marketing mix is product, price, place, and promotion, social CRM makes a new P central to the traditional marketing mix: people. *Sport managers cannot move forward with a personalized approach to customer retention without firmly understanding how and why different types of customers consume their sport product.*

**TRADITIONAL CUSTOMER RELATIONSHIP MANAGEMENT** a business's one-way communication method to increase sales throughout the customer life cycle

**CUSTOMER LIFE CYCLE** the term used to describe the evolution of a customer's relationship with an organization from the decision to purchase a product, to using that product, to how the customer maintains loyalty with the organization and to ultimately, the relationship end

**SOCIAL CUSTOMER RELATIONSHIP MANAGEMENT** an expansion of traditional CRM; a CRM system involving customer engagement throughout the customer life cycle

## Table 14.2

**Traditional vs. Social CRM**

| Traditional CRM | Social CRM |
| --- | --- |
| One-way communication/direct advertising | Conversation and engagement |
| Customer service and support operating within business hours on the organization's preferred platform | Quick response on the customer preferred platform |
| Impersonal | Personalized |
| Customers share feedback by word of mouth in a small circle | Customers share feedback with millions online |
| Sales-driven | Conversation-driven, sales are a byproduct |

Adapted from http://oursocialtimes.com/traditional-crm-vs-social-crm-infographic/

## PRINCIPLE 1: GAINING, VALUING, AND UTILIZING CUSTOMER FEEDBACK

**CUSTOMER RETENTION**
the actionable steps a company takes to produce loyal and lifetime customers

The first principle in **customer retention** is knowing the importance of how to gain, value, and utilize customer feedback. Creating a relationship with customers means taking an interest in their opinions and preferences. Sport managers utilize information gathered from customer feedback in order to make better business decisions with the customer at the center of the decision-making process. Gaining feedback allows managers to identify the types of customers at-risk for failing to make a second purchase, to identify reoccurring issues customers may have with the product, and to assess customer satisfaction. Sport organizations choose various means to gain feedback from customers.

### Analytics for Customer Retention

**CUSTOMER SENTIMENT**
how a customer feels about a product or service

**CUSTOMER BEHAVIOR**
the study of the mechanisms by which a customer chooses to use or not use a product

**BIG DATA**
the collection and management of extremely large data sets from which managers can draw conclusions

**ANALYTICS**
the systematic analysis of data in order to provide information and/or insight

While technology has changed the way consumers and organizations communicate via social media platforms, technology has also changed the way sport organizatons approach understanding **customer sentiment** and predicting **customer behavior**. **Big data** refers to the collection and management of extremely large data sets from which managers can draw conclusions. Data **analytics** has been used to assess players and team play, most notably featured in the movie *Moneyball,* but the use of data analytics does not end there. Drawing conclusions from big data sets that capture information about consumers can aid managers in predicting consumer behavior and in identifying the types of consumers that might be high-risk; in other words, those consumers most likely to stop consuming the sport product. As analytics becomes increasingly popular in sport, sport managers can understand customer retention through collecting and analyzing data describing consumers.

©iQoncept/Shutterstock.com

The New York Red Bulls professional soccer team coordinates a partnership with Microsoft Dynamics. Microsoft Dynamics is a branch of Microsoft providing businesses with tailored approaches to collecting and analyzing data to potentially increase sales, improve marketing initiatives, and tailor social media platforms. For example, professional sport teams have utilized Microsoft Dynamics to assess consumer buying patterns. Microsoft Dynamics can then find purchasing patterns among consumer segments. Instead of e-mail blasting promotions to customers, professional sport teams can fit the promotion to the type of customer most likely to react to the promotion based on past customer purchases. The Orlando Magic use a specialized decision tree model to categorize customers. Customers are segmented into the following groups: most likely to renew, least likely to renew, and individuals who are most likely to show indecision. The Magic then choose to focus on the individuals who are most likely to show indecision, in order to sway their opinion. The New England Patriots use information

©Rawpixel.com/Shutterstock.com

such as game attendance records, merchandise purchase history, attendance at unique engagement events associated with the Patriots as well as with other events held at Gillette Stadium, preferred communication platforms, and website activity to better personalize target messages to consumers.[5] After adopting this analytical strategy in 2009, the Patriots achieved a 97% season ticket renewal.

---

### ANALYTICS IN COLLEGE SPORTS

The university environment has seen an increase in athletic director hires that can specifically handle analytics for customer retention and other business operations. In July of 2015, the University of Nebraska joined the list of universities hiring athletic directors with specialties in analytics. Tucker Zeleny assumed the role of Director of Sports Analytics and Data Analysis. Tucker not only evaluates individual as well as team performance, but also evaluates business operations of the athletics department. Several NCAA organizations—the NCAA College World Series, women's NCAA softball, the NCAA College Basketball Championships—utilize Major League Baseball Advanced Media (MLBAM) for a variety of analytical activities in customer retention and beyond. One such task involves strategically placing digital ads for consumers based on patterns in digital use and preferred communication platforms. When online shoppers purchase a product, advertisements for the item or related items show up on Facebook page or on web browsers the very next day following their purchase. This is an example of how an organization used analytics to strategically place a digital ad tailor-made for each consumer in an effort to retain that consumer.

---

Husker Mike. Nebraska Hires Director of Sports Analytics and Data Analysis. *cornnation.com*. Retrieved from http://www.cornnation.com/2015/7/8/8913787/nebraska-hires-director-of-sports-analytics-and-data-analysis

---

5.  Davenport, T. (2014, February). Analytics in sports: The new science of winning. *International Institute for Analytics.* Retrieved from http://www.sas.com/content/dam/SAS/en_us/doc/whitepaper2/iia-analytics-in-sports-106993.pdf

### Strategies to Gain Feedback

Not all sport organizations have the expertise or financial means to orchestrate sophisticated analytics plans; in fact, very few have implemented full-scale analytics marketing plans in an attempt to retain customers. Sometimes, the best way to understand the customer is to ask or seek out places/forums where customers are likely to express reactions to the sport product. Table 14.3 displays eight ways to gain feedback from customers during or following sport product consumption. Sport managers then use this feedback in order to change business processes to enhance the game experience.[6]

## Table 14.3

**Eight Ways to Gain Feedback From Customers**

| |
|---|
| **Focus Groups:** a small group of people (5 to 15) brought together under the guise of a moderator to discuss a topic. |
| **Online Surveys/Polls:** questionnaires provided to participants via the Internet, e-mail, etc. |
| **Analytical Software:** technology designed to gather and analyze data sets in order to enhance business objectives. |
| **Person-to-Person:** engaging an individual in a one-on-one conversation via the telephone or through in-person interview. |
| **Product Trials:** allowing customers to try or test the product prior to purchase or prior to bringing the product fully to market. |
| **Live Chat/Website Forums:** public online discussion sites. |
| **Monitor Social Media:** the act of tracking various social media sites in order to gain information. |
| **Offering Incentives:** designing "perks" to reward participants for sharing information. |

---

### CREATING NEW EXPERIENCES FROM CUSTOMER FEEDBACK

The Arizona Diamondbacks President Derrick Hall answered the call to create more opportunities for dog owners to bring their pets to the game.[6] After recognizing that customers repeatedly pleaded to bring pets on more occasions to Chase Field, the Diamondbacks partnered with PetSmart to create the PetSmart Patio, an indoor and outdoor play space for dogs and their humans behind the left-center field wall. Dog owners will have the opportunity to bring their pets to each of the 13 Sunday home games. Customers can also enjoy purchasing canine-safe treats and drinks for their pets. This Diamondback partnership with PetSmart resulted from managers addressing themes in customer feedback as well as understanding the importance of altering the game experience to customer preferences.

---

6.  Fisher, E. (2016, February 29). D-Backs give dogs their day at ballpark. *Sports Business Journal.* Retrieved from http://www.sportsbusinessdaily.com/Journal/Issues/2016/02/29/Marketing-and-Sponsorship/PetSmart-Diamondbacks.aspx?hl=customer%20feedback&sc=0

# PRINCIPLE 2: A COMPREHENSIVE CUSTOMER SERVICE PLAN

The second principle in customer retention is to incorporate a comprehensive customer service plan grounded in customer service excellence. Customer service refers to the interactions a business has with a customer before, during, and after a customer purchases a product. Think about the game experience. When customers pick up tickets at will-call did they spend a long time in line? When customers interacted with the ticket office personnel, did they walk away with a positive feeling or a negative feeling? Did the usher actively show customers to their seats, or did customers have to seek them out to ask? These game experience nuances affect perceptions of the overall game experience. Sport organizations can learn customer service excellence from the most magical place on earth.

## *The Disney Approach*

Many companies have harnessed customer service principles to advance their businesses; among the most notable is Disney. Disney's model of the customer as a guest has evolved over time but creating a culture of happy for guests remains at the center of their customer service operation. Disney calls this philosophy guestology: "the study of people for whom we provide service."[7] Through guestology, Disney works to make guests feel special, treats guests as individuals, treats all patrons with respect. Walt Disney took this approach from the very beginning of his business operations and created a world-renowned customer service standard.

> The first year [at Disneyland] I leased out the parking concession, brought in the usual security guards—things like that—but soon realized my mistake. I couldn't have outside help and still get over my idea of hospitality. So now we recruit and train every one of our employees. I tell the security police, for instance, that they are never to consider themselves cops. They are there to help people. The visitors are our Guests. It's like running a fine restaurant. Once you get the policy going, it grows.[8]
>
> —Walt Disney

---

7. Jones, B. Understand your customers using guestology. *Disney Institute.* Retrieved from https://disneyinstitute.com/blog/2012/08/understand-your-customers-using-guestology/90/
8. Ibid.

## Table 14.4

**Big Ideas From Little Guys**

| |
|---|
| Be Happy<br>—Make eye contact and smile |
| Be like Sneezy<br>—Greet and welcome each guest with the spirit of hospitality |
| Don't be Bashful<br>—Seek out contacts with Guests |
| Be like Doc<br>—Provide immediate service recovery |
| Don't be Grumpy<br>—Always display appropriate body language |
| Be like Sleepy<br>—Create dreams and preserve the magical Guest experience |
| Don't be Dopey<br>—Thank each customer |

As a result of the growing popularity of Disney principles in customer service, Disney formed the Disney Institute, a customer service consultation opportunity for businesses looking to improve their customer service. The Disney Institute offers professional development courses as well as customized business solutions in order to help businesses transform the customer experience one customer at a time. The Disney tradition infiltrated the sport industry. After Arizona State University lost 50% of its football season-ticket holders over the past five seasons, athletics personnel conducted an overhaul on how they approached customer service at games. A pervasive theme across the customer experience was consistent customer dissatisfaction. For example, customers purchased mini footballs outside the stadium only to have them turned away by ushers inside the stadium, a clear lack of communication between the sales staff and the event operations staff. Arizona State began the customer service transformation

© s_bukley/Shutterstock.com

through utilizing Disney principles. Staff flew to Disney for three days of meetings with the Disney Institute. The athletic department replaced employees and trained customer service representatives to help create a magical, memorable experience for game goers, a "service-first" mentality. The impact was immediate. E-mails poured in (9 out of 10) complementing Arizona State for making the change. Six weeks into the season, season-ticket renewals were 10% ahead of the previous year's benchmark.[9] The Orlando Magic, Arizona Cardinals, and University of Tennessee have all signed on to utilize the Disney approach. The Disney Institute operates under the premise that what seems like small, unimportant moments at first glance are just as important as star players.[10]

## *Sport Organization Approaches*

In order to create lifetime fans, sport organizations have adopted their own customer service plans unique to the vision organizations have for the customer experience. For the Spurs, customer service excellence is also the foundation of training their employees. The paragraph below is reprinted from the introduction of the Spurs employee training manual:

> Spurs Sports & Entertainment exists to provide the highest quality sports & entertainment experience our guests, supported by prompt, professional, courteous service, and to have a positive impact on our community. The continued growth and development of our values based, service centered culture is dependent upon each and every interaction you have with our guests and with each other. Acting in alignment with our mission, vision and values, and exhibiting our F.A.M.I.L.Y. service standards is the easiest roadmap to success and personal fulfillment in our organization. The more you do for others, the more you receive in return.

In order to achieve goals, the Spurs train each and every service position according to the F.A.M.I.L.Y. service standard outlined in Table 14.5. The San Antonio Spurs produce customer satisfaction through treating both employees and customers like family.

9.  Steinbach, P. (2013, January). Athletic departments apply disney principles to game day. *Athletic Business.* Retrieved from http://www.athleticbusiness.com/athletic-departments-apply-disney-principles-to-game-day.html#!/ccomment-comment=937

10.  Schoenfeldj, B. (2010, November 29). Customer-service magic. *Sports Business Journal.* Retrieved from http://www.sportsbusinessdaily.com/Journal/Issues/2010/11/20101129/This-Weeks-Issue.aspx

## Table 14.5

### FAMILY Standards for Promoting a Positive Fan Experience

| | Standard | Description | Examples |
|---|---|---|---|
| **Friendly Greeting & Fond Farewell** | Greet everyone with whom you come in contact<br><br>Thank guests for visiting our home. | Smile and verbally welcome each guest with your distinctive greeting.<br><br>Treat guests with an attitude of invitation as if they accepted your request to join them for the event. • Thank each patron for attending the event as they leave. • Acknowledge and show appreciation to our Season Ticket Holders who are wearing their Season Ticket Holder pins. | "We are so glad you are here!" • "Thanks for coming!" • "You chose a great event!" • "Enjoy the Game!" • "Have fun!" • "Was that a great game, or what?" • "Did you enjoy the show?" • "See you next time!" • "We appreciate your support!" • "Thanks for being a loyal Season Ticket Holder!" |
| **Arena Awareness** | Understand our offerings and know the building.<br><br>Give accurate directions. | Arm yourself with information about the AT&T Center, the building guidelines and the event. • Know where the ATM's, exits and restrooms are located relative to your work area. • Offer succinct directions to areas throughout the building and streets nearby. | Study the map and A to Z Guide to learn the AT&T Center. • Be familiar with general procedures, products sold and services offered throughout the venue. • Use the PRIDE Formula for giving directions using the Ruby Point. |
| **Make Memories** | Bring smiles, fun and excitement to every fan's experience. | Make our guests your number one priority. • Reinforce team pride by complimenting the fans on their attire. • Have fun and enjoy your role! • Make them smile, laugh, and feel good. • Make a personable relationship building comment. • Offer to take pictures of a group if you see them posing. | Focus on the fans. • Show your enthusiasm and team spirit. • Connect with each guest and create positive conversations. • Engage the fans by asking questions. • "Love your silver and black outfit!" • "Who is your favorite player?" • "Did you enjoy the game?" • "May I take the picture, so you can join the group shot?" |
| **Image Impact** | Maintain a neat and professional appearance wearing the proper uniform.<br><br>Be courteous and pleasant. | Wear a correct, complete and clean staff uniform. • Belt on pants is around the waist. • Grooming meets established guidelines. • No chewing gum, cell phones, headsets, iPods, OR reading materials should be visible. • Actively listen while maintaining good posture.<br><br>Be respectful and polite; say "Please" and "Thank You." | Use the SOFTEN Technique. • Use the correct words as outlined in the Building Bridges Word Choices. • Acknowledge the child first when they are walking with a parent. • Kneel down, make eye contact with the child at their level and welcome them individually. |
| **Look & Listen** | Anticipate our fan's needs.<br><br>Be proactive in assisting others and preventing problems. | Be aware of the Frequently Asked Questions in your area and be prepared with the correct answers. • Watch guests and be ready to help. • Address inappropriate behavior, profanity and inebriated fans. • Enforce the guidelines in a polite manner, explaining the reason for the guidelines. • Secure the area or clean up the mess when there is a spill. • Pick up trash and keep your area free of debris. | Observe the 10-5 Rule. • Offer to help a guest who is carrying a food tray or multiple beverages. • Offer directions to someone who looks in need of assistance by saying "May I help you find your seat?" • Abide by the 2 Second Rule. • Ask, "Is there anything I can do to make your game more enjoyable?" • Report repairs that need to be addressed. |
| **Your 100%** | Achieve a 100% score when Service Scouts are scouting for great service. | Support your colleagues and all AT&T Center partners. • No WAHmbulance Driving. • Treat each guest as if they are the scout who is observing your performance. | Project a positive attitude while you are representing Spurs Sports & Entertainment. • It will positively affect you, your colleagues and the patrons around you. |

Sport organizations should develop standards for customer service positions such as ticket scanners and ushers. Warm smiles and a friendly greeting are keys to initiating friendly contact with guests. Each of these positions are ambassadors for the team, arena, and even the community as a whole. Attitude and gratitude are key elements to creating a positive presence with guests.

The ticket scanner is one of the first individuals to greet the customer and will lay the groundwork for the customer's experience. Sport administrators should take steps to train these individuals to interact with customers according to the organization's vision for the customer service excellence. Guidelines for ticket scanners should include:

- distances at which the ticket scanner acknowledges the presence of the guest
- how to handle lost and counterfeit tickets
- re-entry procedures

The usher is a critical component to customer service excellence. If guests are feeling intimidated by the large arena setting, the ushers are central to ensuring guests feel comfortable. Ushers are tasked with greeting guests in a friendly and sincere way as well as with helping guests find seats and identifying safety issues. Guidelines for ushers include how to do the following:

- handle suspicious items
- greet the guest
- review tickets to ensure the guest is located in the seating area
- direct guests to the correct seating location
- answer commonly asked questions
- receive and respond to complaints
- keep the aisles clear
- identify prohibited items
- spot problems before they occur
- solve duplicate ticket issues
- know the location of key locations such as ATM, concessions, restrooms, escalators, and exits

## Creating a Customer Service Plan

Customer service plans are not one-size-fits-all. Planning effective customer service means sport managers consider the customer and the organizational vision prior to customer service plan design. Would the Boston Red Sox organization coordinate the same type of customer service plan as their triple A affiliate, the PawSox? Although closely related, the two teams have separate identities and different resources at their disposal. The following customer service rules will help guide the process of establishing customer service excellence for any organization.

## RULE 1: CUSTOMER SERVICE ON THEIR TERMS

**CUSTOMER SERVICE**
the interactions a business has with a customer before, during, and after a customer purchases a product

Understanding **customer service** means understanding customer preferences for the game experience, sport product use, and communication platforms. The most effective customer service places the customer at the forefront of the customer service plan. It might be more efficient and cost-effective to provide the same type of food and the same type of wait-in-line food service for customers attending sporting events. However, if food service were on the customer's terms, would season ticket holders be interested in the same food each game? Would customers choose just one option to obtain their food, and would that option be waiting in line? When sport managers make decisions to provide customer service on the customer's terms, trends such as communication options to place advanced food orders online, staff employed to bring customers food to their seats, and incorporating signature food items emerge. Realizing their customers also found interest in the craft beer scene, the Fort Wayne TinCaps, Class A minor league baseball team affiliate of the San Diego Padres, coordinated craft beer tasting nights at the ballpark. Customers enjoy unlimited tasting and buffet for $40 per person in groups larger than 20 during the game instead of prior to the game in the previous season. The result is a lucrative and trendy way for the TinCaps to continually retain customers according to customer preferences.

## RULE 2: DETERMINE VISION

Each organization should work to establish a customer service identity. Appropriate stakeholders should be involved. For the San Antonio Spurs, this identity surrounds the theme of treating customers and fellow coworkers like family, thereby creating a family-friendly environment. This identity involves the entire sport franchise from ticket sales professionals to customer service representatives. The Spurs train each usher, elevator guide, and ticket scanner according to the role they play in creating a family atmosphere. Sport professionals should consider the customer service vision that best represents the sport organization.

## RULE 3: FINDING COMPATIBILITY

Although the mission is to provide customer service on the customer's terms, this has to exist within the reality of the organization's resources and vision. Does providing customer service on the customer's terms find compatibility with the organization's vision for customer service? Where do the two find middle ground? Every customer may desire a personal wait staff, unlimited food with their service, and no waiting lines to enter the game. What sport organization can reasonably provide this opportunity for every customer? Sport managers, however, can reorganize staff to shorten lines, incorporate special entrances for high profile customers or season ticket holders, hire wait staff for luxury suite areas, and provide unlimited buffet deals for group sales. Customer service on the customer's terms must also exist within the organization's resources.

## RULE 4: DESIGN THE PLAN

Devoting attention to customer service means devoting the right number of individuals and organizational resources to work within the plan. Think about it. If one goal of a customer service plan is to ensure patrons feel comfortable finding their seat locations, it may be necessary to place an usher at every gate. If a second goal is to ensure season ticket holders enjoy benefits such as exclusive meet and greets with the coaches and players as the Columbus Blue Jackets offer to their season ticket holders, the proper personnel, planning, and training will need to be employed and implemented. This may involve creating a new Guest Relations position. As exemplified with the Spurs F.A.M.I.L.Y. approach to training employees, a specific and detailed approach will be necessary for program success.

## RULE 5: HIRE THE RIGHT PEOPLE: HIRE ATTITUDE, TRAIN SKILLS

When Murray Cohn, former VP of ticket sales for the NBA, and current President of Sports Sales Training and Consulting Inc., looks for individuals to hire, he seeks individuals with a positive and coachable attitude, strong work ethic, above average honesty and integrity and individuals that believe good is the enemy of great. From this attitude, he can train budding sales professionals, but he cannot train these traits. Performance Associates, Inc., authors of *Delivering Knock Your Socks Off Service*,[11] created a list of the ten deadly sins of customer service. These ten deadly sins describe how attitude can destroy customer relationships and customer retention (see Table 14.6). The basic concept is hire attitude and train skills.

11. Performance Associates, Inc. (2007). *Delivering knock your socks off service,* 4th ed. New York, NY: AMACOM.

## Table 14.6

### The Ten Deadly Sins of Customer Service Applied to Sport

| Concept | Definition | Sport Application Example |
|---|---|---|
| "I don't know" | Lack of knowledge with respect to the organization and product | Volunteer should know the answer to "where is the nearest bathroom" when asked by a fan. |
| "I don't care" | Apathetic employees | Ticket takers should greet each patron with enthusiastic body language. |
| "I can't be bothered" | Failing to make customers feel important | Account executives should take steps to thank season ticket holders, making them feel important. |
| "I don't like you" | Exuding rude behavior | Each in-game professional should maintain a professional standard regardless of customer complaints. |
| "I know it all" | Responding to customer concerns prior to fully understanding the concern | If a fan shows concern about parking options, a customer service representative should first aim to understand exactly why the customer is concerned prior to responding. |
| "You don't know anything" | Condescending employees | If a customer misunderstands something about ticket sales options, a ticket sales professional should help the customer understand instead of putting them down. |
| "We don't want your kind here" | Showing prejudice | In-game staff should treat each customer as equally important as the next. |
| "Don't come back" | Making customers feel unwelcome | Without customers, service professionals would not have a job. Even when lines get long and staff have been standing for long hours, it is important to be aware of making customers feel welcome. |
| "I'm right and you're wrong" | Proving to customers they are mistaken | When a customer does not display correct knowledge with respect to ticket seat locations, ushers should politely address the situation. |
| "Hurry up and wait" | Failing to respect time | Ticket takers should be aware that fans eagerly await entering the stadium. Efficient operations are important to a customer's time. |

## RULE 6: CUSTOMER SERVICE BEGINS WITHIN

An effective customer service plan starts within the organization. Employee behavior toward each other will eventually express itself outwardly in front of the customers or toward customers. Even though not all employees will interact directly with customers, all employees in the organization contribute to a positive—or worse, negative—customer service environment. When employees interact in a negative way, customers notice. At the Spurs organization, all new employees are trained on the F.A.M.I.L.Y. principles not only to ensure positive customer service becomes habitual, but also to create a positive and productive work environment.

## RULE 7: MANAGE THE SPORTSCAPE TO CREATE A POSITIVE EXPERIENCE

People are critical to the success of a customer service plan. However, it is also important to recognize that features in the facility can also impact customer retention. A critical component to any customer service plan in sports is to effectively manage the **sportscape**, the entire built and managed environment that the fan sees when attending a sporting event.[12] The physical environment of the stadium can significantly impact the extent to which fans desire to stay and return to the sport venue.[13] Managing the sportscape requires collaboration with the event and facility staff in the organization. Table 14.7 on the following page outlines the 11 key sportscape factors.

**SPORTSCAPE**
the entire built and managed environment that the fan sees when attending a sporting event

© Settawat Udom/Shutterstock.com

12. Wakefield, K. (2015). Team sports marketing. Retrieved from http://teamsportsmarketing.com

13. Wakefield, K., Blodgett, J., & Sloan, H. (1996). Measure and management of the sportscape. *Journal of Sport Management*, 10, 15–31.

## Table 14.7

**Sportscape Factors**

| Factor | Definition |
|---|---|
| Parking access | Ease of entry, ample parking, convenience of entry and exit |
| Architectural design | Attractive and interesting structural design, exterior appearance and landscaping |
| Interior décor | Color schemes, wall décor, lighting, and ambience |
| Facility layout | Visibility of layout and ease of going wherever you want to go |
| Wayfinding signage | Signage (including wayfinding markers) directing fans to seats, restrooms, services, and exits |
| Facility space | Enough space in restrooms, walkways, concessions, and seating areas to accommodate fans |
| Seat comfort | Knee room, elbow room, seat space, and comfort. Offers unobstructed view |
| Equipment quality | Functionality and aesthetically pleasing; in good order and repair |
| Scoreboards and sound systems | Quality of information: exciting, interesting, timely, and complete. Sound quality: music selection, volume, and clarity |
| Cleanliness | Restrooms, walkways, concessions, and seating areas |
| Perceived crowding | Feeling restricted, cramped, stuffy, and constrained due to facility layout; influenced by wayfinding signage and space. |

From *Team Sports* Marketing by Kirk L. Wakefield. Reprinted by permission of Kirk L. Wakefield.

## PRINCIPLE 3: RELATIONSHIP BUILDING THROUGH AFTERMARKETING

**AFTERMARKETING**
the approach to retaining or developing customers after the customer has purchased the product

**RELATIONSHIP MARKETING**
marketing strategy through which sport and non-sport managers pursue, retain, and develop customers throughout the customer life cycle in a co-collaborative approach

The third principle in customer retention to produce customers with lifetime value is creating and implementing an effective aftermarketing plan. After the customer leaves the game, what next? If the sport organization has provided a great game experience including customer service excellence, do sport organizations sit and wait for the customer to renew? Absolutely not. Sport managers looking to retain customers understand that the actions the company takes post-experience will affect the customer's decision to come to another game, deny attending, or to take advantage of additional products offered. **Aftermarketing** is the term used to describe how sport managers approach retaining or developing customers after the customer has purchased the product. It is important to utilize a social CRM framework to approach aftermarketing for customers. **Relationship marketing** is the term used to describe the marketing strategy through which sport and non-sport managers pursue, retain, and develop customers throughout the customer life cycle in a co-collaborative approach. Theodore Levitt was the first to introduce the concept that the buying experience, not just the product itself, influences customer satisfaction.[14] In essence, the relationship between the buyer and seller is a critical factor in how the consumer feels about the product. In 1983, Leonard Berry introduced the idea of relationship marketing and suggested involving customer preferences as central to business operations and decision-making.[15] When sport managers approach aftermarketing through relationship marketing, creative customer retention solutions take shape.

---

### STUDENT FAN LOYALTY PROGRAM AT OKLAHOMA UNIVERSITY

The University of Oklahoma athletic department routinely benefits from well-attended football games, but felt the need to create an aftermarketing strategy in order to maintain a consistent fan base for other sports, notably basketball.[16] Administrators partnered with Row27 and Paciolan to create a fan loyalty program that rewards fans with gear and invitations to unique events for repeat game attendance as well as for the duration the fan remains at the game. Scanning loyalty program tickets to basketball games works like a time stamp. Students are also rewarded with points for engaging on social media before, during, and after the game. The repeat contacts associated with the loyalty program replace direct advertising such as e-mail blasts. Instead, this contact creates a two-way approach to customer retention and development and incorporates fan engagement into the aftermarketing strategy.

---

When sport managers look to retain and develop customers who attended sport events or purchased sport products, where do they begin in devising an aftermarketing campaign? Consider aftermarketing strategies through relationship marketing, with the most important P, people, at the center of the campaign. Aftermarketing should be unique to the organization. Ohio State and Ball State will need to interact with their customers in a different way, and will also have vastly different resources to enact an aftermarketing plan. Follow the following six steps to incorporate aftermarketing through relationship marketing tailor-made for any sport organization.

---

14.  Levitt, T. (1969). *The marketing mode: Pathways to corporate growth.* New York, NY: McGraw-Hill.

15.  Berry, L. (1983). Relationship marketing. In L. L. Berry, G. L. Shostack, & G. D. Upah (Eds.), *Emerging perspectives on services marketing.* Chicago (p. 25–28). American Marketing Association.

16.  Smith, M. (2014, October 20). Fan activity integrated with loyalty programs. *Sports Business Journal.* Retrieved from http://www.sportsbusinessdaily.com/Journal/Issues/2013/10/14/Colleges/Paciolan.aspx?hl=customer%20retention&sc=1

## STEP 1: CLEAR DIRECTION

Prior to creating and enacting an aftermarketing plan, it is important for the organization's priorities and goals to be clear. Is the organization a minor league baseball team looking to increase retention among full-season ticket holders with an emphasis on renewing new season ticket holders? Or does the organization have several focuses such as retaining season ticket holders as well as creating a personalized promotion strategy for developing half-season ticket holders to purchase full season tickets? Without a clear direction, it is difficult to form a system that will aid in achieving the desired outcomes. Evaluate the current position and stay focused. Set SMART objectives to shape the direction (see Table 14.8).

## STEP 2: RELEVANT DATA AND FEEDBACK

Sport organizations should know their customers. Based on their goals, the next step is to understand the types of data needed in the decision-making process. A focused approach to data collection is necessary to making decisions based on this data. If the target group is understanding season ticket holders for renewal, for example, it would be necessary to gather information with respect to season ticket holders. Relevant information might include: (1) identifying the types of season ticket holders least likely to renew; (2) reasons why they might not renew; (3) understanding the types of season ticket holders most likely to renew; and (4) the type of communication season ticket

### Table 14.8

**Set SMART Objectives**

| S: SPECIFIC |
| --- |
| —Define the goal with clarity |
| —Answer who, what, where, and why |
| **M: MEASUREABLE** |
| —How will you know when your goal is accomplished? Track progress. |
| **A: ATTAINABLE** |
| —Set realistic goals for your organization. |
| **R: RELEVANT** |
| —Does this goal meet your organization's vision and needs? |
| **T: TIMELY** |
| —Establish a sense of urgency for your objective. Give it a time limit. |

holders prefer. Managers should strategically plan dates to gather and evaluate the data. Data collection may involve more than one type of data collection strategy and occur during several time periods that account for the fact that testing only one group of customers or testing that group at only one time period may not reveal a full understanding.

## STEP 3: RESOURCE EVALUATION

Of course, all of this data collection must happen within the boundaries of available resources. How much of the operating budget can be utilized for aftermarketing? Resource evaluation should involve a thorough examination of the budget and potential outsourced partnerships with analytics companies such as Microsoft dynamics or smaller firms such as Sports Analytics. These types of companies offer systems to gain insight into fans belonging to different segment groups, as well as operational analytics to streamline business processes. However, not all sport organizations will have the resources to outsource an analytics team or company or hire their own. Perhaps other means of data gathering will be a better use of resources for this type of organization. Regardless, data collection strategies should reflect the original goals.

## STEP 4: LOOK FOR PATTERNS AND THEMES

Upon collecting data about the consumers, it is important to look for patterns among consumers. In the same way that marketing professionals segment target markets, patterns and themes should be assessed based on the original targeted customers for the aftermarketing plan. For example, sport organizations have incorporated web-based purchasing modalities for the range of their products. If more than one customer comments that the web-based season ticket renewal process was complicated or difficult to use, this pattern in feedback should be applied when redeveloping the online format.

## STEP 5: AFTERMARKETING PLAN

The aftermarketing plan should be grounded in the original direction as well as patterns identified in customer data collection. The plan will be coordinated **touchpoints**, or points of contact from the organization to the buyer, throughout the customer life cycle. Communication with customers may change according to their stage in the life cycle and their market segment. It may also change according to new themes and patterns that develop throughout consistently gaining feedback from consumers. Sport organizations won't create relationships with twenty-year-old fans in the same way as relationships are created with sixty-year-old fans. Gaining feedback shows the sport manager how to best court customer relationships. The relationship

**TOUCHPOINTS**
points of contact from the organization to the buyer, throughout the customer life cycle

marketing plan may be a combination of fan loyalty programs, social media outlets, e-mail, face-to-face communication and additional modes for touchpoints. Important to the relationship marketing campaign, however, is the notion of two-way communication. The fan must feel central to the organization through providing feedback according to their wants and needs.

Ed Gagnon, President at Customer Service Solutions, Inc., offers the following advice for developing a 12-month touchpoint planning process with all account holders:

1. Because new customers are at greatest risk of defection, develop strategies that focus on building intelligence and relationship with first-year clients.

2. Conduct an at-risk profiling assessment by examining internal databases to determine the characteristics of the customer's lost in the past.

3. Conduct annual surveys that identify preferences, risk factors, and growth areas. Target clients who are less likely to renew with intense and customized efforts.

4. Identify the most profitable clients so more personalized and targeted retention efforts can be used for them.

5. Develop monthly touchpoint plans for all retention reps that ensure retention efforts are executed year-round.[17]

Aftermarketing through relationship marketing should be personal. Gaining feedback is critical to providing the personal approach. Communicate with the customer according to their preferences. Would they like to be contacted via e-mail, social media, or via face-to-face visiting? Take a personalized approach in gaining feedback from new season ticket holders to devise a consistent communication method. Technology has changed the way customers communicate to each other, but also how customers manage their time. Picking up on how technology has changed time management, Australian-based company ECal designed a

17. Gagnon, E. It's ticketing renewal season—use knowledge-based research to retain. *Ticketing Today*. Retrieved from http://ticketingtoday.com/its-ticketing-renewal-season-use-knowledge-based-research-to-retain/

system to maintain communication through a fan's digital calendar.[18] Fans choose notifications that are then downloaded to the calendar. Notifications include the regular game schedule, prioritized games, season ticket holder events, and other preferences. In this case, the customer chooses how the sport organization will communicate.

Taylor Deckard, Account Executive for the St. Louis Rams (now Los Angeles Rams) shared the organization's 365-Plan. Account executives manage over 1,000 accounts and coordinate touchpoints throughout the year, not just during the season. Account executives also share their contact information and make efforts to communicate on client preferred platforms. Refer to Table 14.9 for examples of organized contact throughout the year.

## Table 14.9

**St. Louis Rams (now Los Angeles Rams) 365 Aftermarketing Touchpoint Plan**

| |
|---|
| **Thank You Notes After Purchase:** Account executives send thank you notes and introduce themselves as the contact for the organization. |
| **Pre-Game E-mail:** Prior to the game, account executives will send e-mails with relevant game information such as parking and opponent statistics. |
| **Certificates for First Game Attendees:** When account executives learn that a member of the group is attending a game for the first time, he or she is recognized with a certificate. |
| **Face-to-Face Visits During the Game:** Account executives will also make contact with some of their season ticket holders during the game to introduce themselves and check on the customers' game experience. |
| **Game Experience Evaluation:** After the game, account executives contact season ticket holders personally to gain feedback about the game experience. |
| **First Renewal Reminder (late December):** Account executives call season ticket holders to remind them of the renewal deadlines and support the decision-making process. |
| **Second Renewal Reminder (February):** If the client has yet to renew, account executives make a second call to talk with clients and attempt to overcome objections to renewing. |
| **Final Deadline Renewal Notice (March/April):** Account executives send a final renewal notice and attempt to overcome any last objections. |
| **Birthday Notes:** Throughout the year, account executives will recognize season ticket holder and family birthdays. |
| **Newsworthy Notes:** Throughout the year, account executives will send team updates. |
| **Welcome Back Notes:** When it is almost time for the season to start, account executives send welcome back notes and ask clients if they have any questions. |

18. McClellan, P. (2015, April 19). Ecal taps into mobile-minded sports fans and digital calendar marketing. *Sporting News*. Retrieved from http://www.sportingnews.com/more-sports-news/4642033-digital-calendar-marketing-brands-athletes-teams-ecal

## STEP 6: INVOLVE STAKEHOLDERS AND FOLLOW THROUGH

Implementing aftermarketing plans as part of social CRM is often more than a one-person show. Depending on the size and scope of the sport organization, this may involve creating a new relationship manager position or several relationship management positions. Aside from assigning these positions with the task to communicate, listen, and help to create value for customers, sport managers must also involve sales teams and executives in following through with using the patterns in data and the designed aftermarketing plan. Incorporating stakeholders with the aftermarketing plan lays the groundwork for system support throughout its implementation. Following through necessitates persistence and attention to the original direction. For example, the Spurs involve the entire organization in the process and strategy to create lifetime relationships with customers from aftermarketing to customer service.

## PRINCIPLE 4: UTILIZE TECHNOLOGY

The fourth principle in customer retention to produce customers with lifetime value is utilizing technology in various stages of the customer experience from game time to the ticket renewal process. When customers make the decision to renew ticket purchases, sport organizations should include a variety of renewal options. Technology makes this possible. Third-party vendors such as Ticketmaster allow customers to create personal account profiles. Customers can log in and repurchase at the click of the mouse. These vendors also allow season ticket holders to e-mail tickets to friends, resell tickets online, and exchange tickets for other games later in the season. All of these technological features serve the customer and increase value for season ticket holders. In renewal, options matter. In some cases, customers will still want to renew via sending a check in the mail.

Successful sport managers anticipate trends. Technology will continue to change the way and the level that sport organizations gain feedback from consumers, implement aftermarketing plans, and offer customer service. When technology advances, consumer expectations evolve. Sport managers must evolve as well. This evolution has already sparked creativity in creating and managing the sportscape.[19] San Francisco facility design professionals identified that 30% of fans used their phones during the game. When San Francisco 49ers fans entered the new stadium that opened in 2014, fans engaged

19. Wakefield, K. (2015). *Team sports marketing.* Retrieved from http://teamsportsmarketing.com

with a new level of customer service.[20] Stadium designers incorporated full Wi-Fi capabilities and phone applications to track bathroom and concessions wait lines. The application also allows customers to order while seated. Fans enjoy the ability to stream replays at the touch of a finger. Stadium operators report fan satisfaction with this innovative move to increase technology capabilities for the in-game experience. In other stadiums, technology allows patrons to send videos of in-stands shenanigans

©Georgejmclittle/Shutterstock.com

to video board operators who pick and choose which videos to display on the big screen. Apps may also include exclusive content visible only to those in-game viewers. Technology is not without its downside, however. When the team performed poorly, customers used in-game forums to blast the team. Advances in technology improve the out-of-game experience as well. The same apps used to enhance live entertainment allow fans a more in-depth perspective when viewing the game in their own homes.

## PRINCIPLE 5: EVALUATION AND UPGRADE

Principle five in customer retention to produce customers with lifetime value is taking the time to evaluate customer retention strategies and making the effort to periodically improve strategies based on results of the evaluation process. Sport managers easily overlook this important step in establishing customer relationships to create customers for their lifetime. How do sport organizations know if what they are doing is working? How will professionals understand what to improve? Challenging and rigorous schedules should not preclude the sport manager from evaluating how the program or program initiatives have worked within the context of original objectives. After setting goals according to SMART principles, measuring outcomes shouldn't pose a conceptual challenge. Part of a successful evaluation process means having tracked activities. If the focus is to renew season ticket holders by 5%, an increased number of season ticket holders (hopefully 5%) have renewed

---

20. Stadium App. Retrieved from http://www.levisstadium.com/stadium-info/stadium-app/

based on the implemented program. If not, sport managers can look back on the implemented program and make decisions according to how the program fell short. This type of evaluation activity ensures sport managers upgrade their own practices to continually improve customer retention across the organization. Sport managers may choose several modes by which to evaluate customer retention efforts.

1. What is the return on investment? How much was invested in customer retention efforts versus the increase in renewal sales as a result?

2. How are customers reacting to customer retention efforts? Do they react favorably or negatively?

3. How do account executives or salespersons feel about the retention efforts? Do they feel this strategy is working or not working? Why or why not?

4. How many customers chose to renew their tickets or purchase other products with the organization? Did the percentage increase or decrease from the year prior?

5. How do customers feel about the product/benefits associated with game attendance or for purchasing season tickets?

6. How do our strategies to retain customers compare to other organizations' strategies?

Begin the evaluation process through charting goals in an evaluation matrix. Once goals are set, think about the metrics that will be involved with understanding whether or not goals have been achieved. What types of results will be important? Next, how will they be measured? Once these questions have been answered, it is important to take steps to plan critical times to measure. See Table 14.10 for an example of an evaluation matrix model.

To illustrate further, the Cleveland Cavaliers will evaluate the effectiveness of a new automatic renewal policy using these questions and framework. The Cavs were the first team in the NBA to implement an automatic renewal policy for season ticket holders in 2015. Traditionally, teams had to make contact with season ticket holders near the end of the season and obtain a commitment to renew for the next season. Under the automatic renewal policy, the terms of the membership are automatically renewed each year until the fan selects an opt-out option. If the opt-out option is chosen, the team can implement a strategy to retain the fan. According to Brad Sims, chief revenue officer for the Cavs, the new policy is now "like a gym or a country club, you are in until you want out. There is no chasing people down, and we can focus

## Table 14.10

**Evaluation Matrix Example**

| Goal | Metric | Measurement | Time |
|---|---|---|---|
| Increase rookie season ticket renewal by 5% | Number of rookie season ticket renewals | Report the number of season ticket holders choosing to renew in the past year.<br><br>Track the number of season ticket holders choosing to renew this year. | Measurements of the past year's renewals will be taken.<br><br>Measurements will be taken at the three periodic renewal deadlines after the season ends. |
| Educate 100% of rookie season ticket holders of special coach/player meet and greets to improve attendance | Number of rookie season ticket holders reached<br><br>Number of rookie season ticket holders at special coach/player meet and greets | Track calls/e-mails made to rookie season ticket holders with regard to special events.<br><br>Track rookie season ticket holder attendance at special events. | Updates every two weeks from rookie season ticket holder account executives.<br><br>Attendance recorded at each event. |

on engaging the fan."[21] This does not mean that the service staff doesn't have to do work to develop a relationship to encourage a renewal, but instead it simplifies the process for the customer and employees and allows the team to focus on engaging and serving the fan. At the start of the 2016 season and each year thereafter, the Cavs will incorporate a systematic evaluation process to track how the new system is or isn't working to achieve organizational objectives.

## CHAPTER SUMMARY

Future sport managers must accept the challenge of determining how the organization can best create lifetime relationships with the most important P and most important asset, **People**. Sport managers who fall victim to relying on the team's success or periods of economic growth miss the opportunity to create customers with lifetime value. Those sport managers who gain feedback from their customers from game time to renewal, work from a social CRM framework, and implement aftermarketing and customer service plans on the customers' terms enjoy customer retention, loyalty, and corresponding lifetime value regardless of the external circumstances.

21. Lombardo, J. (2015, March 2). Cavaliers first in NBA to require automatic renewal. *Sports Business Journal*.

## CHAPTER ACTIVITIES

1. You have just been hired as the Guest Relations Manager for a minor league baseball team. Fans posting on Trip Advisor Yelp have given the game day experience a significant number of negative reviews over the past two seasons. Additionally, retention rates have decreased from 80% to 70% in the past two seasons. Develop an action plan that stems the tide of defections and negative reviews.

2. Calculate the lifetime value of an account that spends $25 per ticket on a 30-game plan for 4 tickets and spends an average of $15 per game for the account on ancillary items. Assume the account stays active for 5 years.

3. Explain the difference between traditional CRM and social CRM and how sport organizations can leverage the power of social CRM.

4. Describe a time when you've experienced poor customer service from a sport organization. Discuss the factors that led to this poor service encounter and what the sport organization could do in the future to improve service.

5. Use the principles outlined in this chapter to conduct a customer service audit of a local sport venue or event. Consider the following questions:

   a. In what ways the does the sport organization integrate technology to serve the customer?

   b. Rate the venue using the sportscape factors.

   c. To what extent does it appear the sport organization utilizes traditional or social CRM?

   d. Describe the efforts made to get you to come back to another event.

   e. Describe interactions you observed between first touch personnel (ushers, ticket takers, box office, etc.) and fans.

   f. What could the sport organization do better with respect to its customer service and after-marketing initiatives?

# CHAPTER 15

## SPONSORSHIP SALES

### LEARNING OBJECTIVES

After completing this chapter, you should be able to:

- ▶ Understand how selling sponsorship differs from ticket sales.
- ▶ Demonstrate how sponsorship is a business decision made to achieve business objectives.
- ▶ See examples of the types of inventory sport properties sell.
- ▶ Identify various ways sponsorship sellers prospect for buyers.
- ▶ Know what prospective sponsorship buyers look for in a proposal and how to investigate a sponsorship prospect's needs.
- ▶ Articulate how effective sponsorship proposals are presented.
- ▶ Identify three specific ways in which pricing is developed for sponsorship packages.
- ▶ Understand the role and function of marketing agencies in the sponsorship sales process.

### KEY TERMS

Activation
Agency
A la carte pricing
Competitive market pricing
Cost-plus pricing
Inventory/Assets

Relative value pricing
Sponsorship
Sport property
Strategic fit
Value-in-Kind (VIK)

## CHAPTER OVERVIEW

The primary focus of this textbook is sport ticket sales. Tickets, however, represent just one of the assets sport organizations may sell. Others include things like merchandise, media rights, media (game programs, web content, media guides, newsletters) and subscriptions, concessions, and of course, sponsorships. **Sponsorships** are investments by corporations in a sport property to help support the firm's organizational, marketing, and promotional objectives or strategies.[1] Sponsorships are based on a mutual exchange between two entities, the sponsor and the sport organization, in which both parties provide and receive benefits concurrently.[2] Sponsorships have been a part of sports since the mid-nineteenth century,[3] and today represent a $15 billion segment of the industry in North America.[4] For many sport organizations, sponsorships are critical to their survival. Many professional sport stadiums may not have been built without the support of a corporate naming rights sponsor. Many sporting events, from the Olympic Games and the FIFA World Cup to the local 5K road race or beer-league softball tournament, rely extensively on sponsorship to fund their existence. Some sponsors are so embedded with a sport property that fans cannot help but think of one in conjunction with the other. English football fans cheer for teams in the Barclay's Premier League; Super Bowl 50 was held in San Francisco's Levi's Stadium, and just about any college football fan knows ESPN's College Game Day is powered by The Home Depot.

In some ways, selling sponsorship for a sport organization is similar to selling any other product. The steps of the sale, discussed in the context of ticket sales throughout most of this text, are essentially the same for selling sponsorship. However, a couple of key differences also exist as sponsorship is a relatively unique product. The purpose of this chapter is to examine the sponsorship sales process to see how sport sellers might take a different approach or focus on different aspects of selling compared to selling tickets or other products. It should be made clear, the point of this chapter is not to discuss the history of sport sponsorship, specific marketing and branding impacts of sponsorship, or even the intricate details of crafting effective sponsorship proposals. There are several excellent texts which discuss these specific elements, such as *Developing Successful Sport Sponsorship Plans* by David Stotlar, *Sponsorship for Sport Managers* by John Crompton, or *Sponsorship in Marketing* by T. Bettina Cornwell. Some sections of this chapter will

1. Shank, M. (2009). *Sports marketing: A strategic perspective,* 4th ed. Upper Saddle River, NJ: Pearson Prentice Hall.

2. Stotlar, D. (2005). *Developing successful sport sponsorship plans,* 2nd ed. Morgantown, WV: Fitness Information Technology.

3. Smart, B. (2015). Sport and the corporate world. In R. Giulianotti (Ed.), *Routledge handbook of the sociology of sport* (p. 417–427). New York: Routledge.

4. http://www.sponsorship.com/IEG/files/71/711f2f01-b6fa-46d3-9692-0cc1d563d9b7.pdf

examine the elements of a proposal and the objectives sponsors are trying to achieve through sponsorship, but readers should remember the focus is on the sales process itself, not necessarily the effectiveness and types of sport sponsorship.

# PURPOSE OF SPONSORSHIP

**SPONSORSHIPS**
investments by corporations in a sport property to help support the firm's organization, marketing, and promotional objectives or strategies

Perhaps the most important lesson for any sport organization or executive tasked with selling sponsorship is that sponsorships are marketing tools for companies. Sponsorship provides businesses a way to reach their key target markets in a cost-effective and meaningful way by tapping into the emotional connection and passion that fans have with their sport teams. Research has shown that passionate fans perceive the contributions of sponsors as valuable, which increases their feeling of allegiance to the sponsor.[5] As such, firms generally engage with sport properties because they want to achieve particular business objectives. Business owners and executives do NOT engage in sport sponsorships for the health and well-being of the sport organization. Many novice sport sponsorship sellers (and even some veteran ones) suggest firms become involved with a sport organization because a certain sponsorship is available at a particular price point or because the sponsor's support will help the sport organization meet its own financial goals. This is not an effective method of selling.

Consider this: many sport fans will buy tickets simply because they like a team and enjoy cheering on their team to victory. Firms, however, do not buy sponsorship simply because they enjoy being a sponsor and want the sport organization to do well. Firms want sport sponsorship to achieve a corporate objective that helps the sponsor improve some area of its business. In the early days of sport sponsorship, it was common for a sponsor to partner with a team simply because the CEO or president of the company liked having great seats and enjoyed seeing a company's sign or logo at the venue. Today, this is very rare. Sponsorship decisions are more strategic and need to produce a return on investment (ROI).

> Sponsorship sellers must put themselves in the shoes of the prospect and determine how a sponsorship delivers value to the prospect's business, regardless of what inventory the salesperson has to sell.

---

5. DeGaris, L. (2015). *Sports marketing: A practical approach.* New York: Routledge.

---

### FIND THE BEST SOLUTION FOR THE PROSPECT

In his book, *Winning the Customer*, former New England Patriots Chief Marketing Officer Lou Imbriano shares a story about a discussion he had with a television executive who was responsible for advertising during the local broadcasts of Patriots' pre-season games. The executive was concerned Imbriano had not sold all of the available ad slots for the broadcasts. Imbriano argued television advertising was not always the best solution for team sponsors and that he wouldn't sell the spots unless he thought it would help them meet their business objectives. When the television executive suggested he should just sell the spots, Imbriano explains, " . . . that rationale is exactly how most teams and leagues fail. They sell their inventory without thought or consideration of the sponsors' needs, regardless of the outcome. That's the old way of doing business, and anyone who is doing it that way will soon be looking for a new job. I really don't care what inventory we sell and whom we sell it to. What I am concerned with is that we are adding more partners each year and keeping the partners we have."[1]

---

1. Imbriano, L. (2011). *Winning the customer: Turn consumers into fans and get them to spend more.* Columbus, OH: McGraw-Hill. p. 96.

---

## LEVERAGING SPONSORSHIP ASSETS

Properties and sponsors must work together to convert the marketing potential of the properties into marketing results by identifying the exploitable assets that help the sponsor achieve its objectives. Sponsorship sellers must first identify the assets that possess marketing value for the sponsor. These assets form the basis of the **inventory** available to be sold. So what inventory do sport organizations have to sell? Many casual sport fans might believe the primary assets a sport team or event has to sell are signage and tickets/hospitality. Those two things certainly represent a healthy percentage of the inventory available within many sport organizations, but it is far from the only inventory. Other possibilities include media rights, in-game marketing and promotional activity, experiential opportunities, category exclusivity, and the ability to use the sport organization's unique assets such as logos, uniforms, venue, website, database, or even personnel.

Let's take a quick look at some of the categories a little more closely. Signage might include sponsor messages on the outfield wall at a minor league baseball field or the dasher boards at a National Hockey League game. It also might include backlit signs on a scoreboard, posters in the concourse, an advertisement in the game program or on the video board, or even virtual signage which only appears on a television broadcast. Tickets/Hospitality might

**INVENTORY/ASSETS** in terms of sponsorship sales, the attributes or elements a sport property owns and can sell to a firm. Examples of inventory or assets might include signage within the sport venue, tickets or hospitality, or trademarked logos.

include standard seating, but also may include seats in a suite or club area at an arena or access to a hospitality tent at a golf tournament or tailgating event.

Lynde outlines 10 common elements packaged in sport sponsorships.[6] They include:

| | Asset | Example |
|---|---|---|
| 1 | Intellectual Property | Use of team logos and other trademarked symbols |
| 2 | Category Exclusivity | Not allowing a sponsor's competitors to promote their business or products within the sport organization's events or facilities |
| 3 | Media | The opportunity to advertise during team-controlled media broadcasts, such as a pre-game coaches' show |
| 4 | Tickets/Hospitality | Sponsor receives tickets/access for guests to attend events |
| 5 | Venue Signage | Sponsor messaging is displayed within the sport venue |
| 6 | Sponsor Identification | Sport organization acknowledges sponsor as official partner in certain communications with the media and the public |
| 7 | Event Marketing/Special Events | Sponsor has a presence at sport organization's special events such as fan fests, press conferences, or team tailgate parties |
| 8 | In-Game Promotions | Sponsor recognized as provider of fan-centric activities during the event such as giveaways or contests |
| 9 | Pass-Through Rights | Benefits from sport organization that sponsor gives to its business partners. For example, if a soft drink company is a sponsor of a team, it might receive tickets, which it gives to grocery stores to use in promoting sales of the soft drink |
| 10 | Direct Marketing/Use of Property's Database | Sponsors gain access to the sport organization's member database (season ticket holders, marathon participants) allowing the sponsor to market directly to those potential consumers |

In addition to the inventory categories listed above, some organizations have gotten creative in the inventory they sell. For instance, sponsorship guru Dan Migala helped the Chicago White Sox use the start time for their games as a piece of inventory. First pitch for Chicago's home games is at 7:11, brought to White Sox fans by 7-Eleven convenience stores. Boxers and beach volleyball players have been known to sell space on their skin by displaying sponsor tattoos during competition. A couple of European clubs have chosen their team nickname based on a sponsor (such as Bayer Leverkusen or PSV Eindhoven), a practice replicated in North America by Major League Soccer's New York Red Bulls.

For a sport sponsorship seller, it is vital to know the types of assets available. However, as Imbriano illustrates, it is also critical sponsorship sellers do

6. Lynde, T. (2007). *Sponsorships 101: An insider's guide to sponsorships in corporate America.* Greensboro, NC: Lynde & Associates.

not simply take an approach of saying "I have five courtside signs, three pre-game radio reads, and four banner ads on the team webpage to sell. What do you want to buy?" Instead, sellers must recognize what inventory they possess in order to best package a sponsorship which matches the prospective buyer's needs. In some cases, this may even mean creating new inventory to help a sponsor achieve a certain objective. For instance, in the early 2000s, several sponsors and marketing agencies were looking to gain more television exposure within the very popular college football space. However, most traditional stadium signage opportunities in college football venues receive very little television camera exposure. That is until marketing firm Van Wagner Sports & Entertainment developed the idea of branded netting behind the goal posts, an idea snapped up quickly by insurance company Allstate.[7]

One area in which most sport organizations have specific inventory to pitch to prospects are in the product or service categories which have a prominent place within the sport organization's operations. For example, many sport organizations serve concessions during events. The ability for certain food and drink vendors to have exclusive or highly selective rights to sell their product at the event makes for a logical partnership. A sport organization may approach a soft drink manufacturer concerning a sponsorship which involves exclusive pouring rights at the venue or event. Coca-Cola may be very interested in paying a sport organization to be the only soft drink company to offer their products on-site. The same could be true of a bank, which might want exclusivity to ATM services available on-site, or a sporting goods manufacturer/retailer which would like the exclusive ability to sell their jerseys, hats, shoes, or sport equipment at the venue.

In addition to primary product and service suppliers, which offer categories of items typically found within sport events and venues, there are many

7. Lefton, T., & Smith, M. (2014, May 26). Allstate's net gain. *SportsBusiness Journal.* Retrieved from http://www.sportsbusinessdaily.com/Journal/Issues/2014/05/26/In-Depth/Allstate.aspx?

secondary product and service categories which also make sense as potential sponsors. These secondary categories include industry sectors closely aligned with a sport event, even though they do not necessarily sell their products at the competition venue. Instead, these secondary category sponsors provide products typically consumed by spectators before or after events. Grocery stores, for example, make logical partners for sport organizations because spectators might buy items for tailgating before a game or to eat at home when watching their favorite team play on television. Quick Service Restaurants (QSR's) are another common secondary sponsorship category, as are media outlets (television stations, newspapers, etc.) and gas stations. Again, each of these sponsor categories have a direct connection between what they offer and what sport spectators might consume directly before or after a game. Thus, it may make sense for a sport organization to position specific inventory to certain business. For example, a team may try to sell space on the back of a ticket stub to a pizza chain, with the idea spectators will redeem the coupon after a game. Selling that same inventory to an insurance company or a car dealership might not make sense, but for a secondary category such as a convenience store, it would be quite logical.

**ACTIVATION**
The strategic efforts designed to support and enhance the objectives of a sponsorship. Activation activities connect a sport property's consumers to the sponsor.

Sponsors can bring the sponsorship inventory assets to life by activating the sponsorship. **Activation** is the set of strategic efforts that are designed to support and enhance the sponsorship.[8] Industry convention holds that activation in the budget should at least equal the cost of the sponsorship rights fees.[9] Sellers are advised to understand the cost structure of activation strategies. Common activation strategies include public relations, advertising, sales promotions, direct marketing, and personal selling.[10] For example:

©Michaelpuche/Shutterstock.com

- ▶ Use theme-based advertising (general media)
- ▶ Advertise during the broadcast of the sponsored event
- ▶ Advertise in the event program
- ▶ Incorporate the sponsoree's logos on packaging and in promotional efforts

---

8.  Fullerton, S. (2010). *Sports marketing*, 2nd ed. New York: McGraw-Hill/Irwin.

9.  Ibid.

10.  DeGaris, L. (2015). *Sports marketing: A practical approach.* New York: Routledge.

- ▶ Distribute free products or premiums
- ▶ Provide prizes
- ▶ Place point-of-sale display
- ▶ Design push strategies directed at retailers
- ▶ Implement a consumer sales overlay
- ▶ Engage in cross-promotions with co-sponsors
- ▶ Institute an affinity marketing program
- ▶ Incorporate web tie-ins
- ▶ Provide hospitality

The goal of the above activation strategies is for the sponsor to develop a cohesive strategy between the brand message being sent through sponsorship and all of their other marketing initiatives.

## STEPS OF THE SALE

As covered extensively earlier in this text, the sales process includes at least six distinct steps. Effective sport sellers follow these steps whether they are selling tickets, sponsorship, or any other sport product. However, sponsorship sellers will also notice some subtle differences in most of these steps compared to those selling tickets. Some of these key subtleties are examined below. Recall, the primary steps of the sale include:

1. Prospecting/Research
2. Opening the Conversation/Build rapport
3. Needs Analysis
4. Sales Presentation
5. Handling Objections
6. Closing

### *Prospecting*

The first major difference in the sales process for sponsorship compared to tickets is the sheer volume of leads. In ticket sales, teams develop databases with thousands of leads, and it is common at the major league level for an inside sales representative to make over 100 calls a day. Within sponsorship sales, the lead database is not nearly as robust. For starters, only a finite number of companies will have a marketing budget large enough to afford a sport sponsorship. Second, in many cases, sport organizations will develop exclusive partnerships with sponsors, eliminating their competitors as prospects. For instance, if a team were to sign an exclusive agreement with Visa, they could not approach MasterCard or Discover with a sponsorship proposal. These two facts mean the pool of potential sponsorship buyers is not nearly as deep as it is for potential ticket buyers.

The good news for sponsorship sellers is that sport organizations need far more ticket buyers than sponsors to function financially. Most major league teams and major college athletics departments will have fewer than 150 corporate partners, but will have thousands of season ticket holders. For some sport organizations, a season ticket package may cost as little as $99. However, the lowest priced sponsorship inventory is likely in the thousands and can grow to as much as six, or even seven, figures. Therefore, sport organizations can see great return on investment among their sponsorship sellers, despite having far fewer leads upon which to call.

So where might a sponsorship seller begin looking for sponsor prospects? As mentioned earlier, sport organizations routinely fill primary and secondary sponsorship categories first. These are sponsors which might provide concessions in the venue or develop team merchandise. After these sponsor categories are filled, sellers may look internally for leads. In some cases, businesses might contact the sport organization looking to improve their marketing strategies. These "in-bound" contacts are always worth pursuing because the prospect has shown a great interest in partnering with the sport organization. Sport organizations may also consider their own needs for goods and services and could approach their vendors to develop a more extensive partnership. In these cases, the vendor may have the ability to improve its visibility and marketing initiatives through the high exposure provided by the sport organization, while the sport organization may either increase revenue or save on expenses. For example, all sport organizations have office supply needs, so they may develop a sponsorship proposal for Office Max or Staples in which marketing benefits are exchanged for both cash and products or supplies. The goods or services supplied by the organization in such an agreement are called **Value-in-Kind** or VIK. For example, a local restaurant may provide a sport organization with VIK in the form of catering for a team function or for media and event volunteers. Teams might develop VIK arrangements with a bus company, a tax preparation service provider, a computer manufacturer, or an athletic training supply business.

**VALUE-IN-KIND (VIK)**
The use of a sponsor's goods or services exchanged for a sport property's assets within a sponsorship agreement. The goods or services are traded in lieu of cash, often because it is less expensive for the sponsor, but also meets a need of a sport property which might otherwise have to buy the same goods or services (i.e., office computers).

---

### BE SMART WITH VALUE-IN-KIND

It is generally discouraged by sport organizations to sell sponsorships in exchange for VIK which is not essential to the organization. In the book *Turnaround*, former Salt Lake City Organizing Committee (SLCOC) President Mitt Romney discussed all the VIK his team procured for hosting the Olympic Games, much of which they could not use.[1] For example, he said Budweiser donated VIK beer, but they could not sell or serve it because it was not purchased through authorized Utah distributors. He also stated Sears donated thousands of dollars' worth of appliances, but SLCOC had no use for them and ultimately traded the product to a developer in order to receive lower costs on venue construction.

---

1. Romney, M. (2004). *Turnaround: Crisis, leadership and the Olympic games*. Washington DC: Regnery Publishing.

---

**STRATEGIC FIT**
the congruence between a sponsor's target market and the audience attracted by a sport property

When looking externally to find new sponsors, the general principle is to identify companies that are trying to reach the fans or participants that the sport property attracts. Properties deliver value to sponsors by providing access to their audience. In fact, sponsors will always want a projection of how many people they can reach and who they are reaching, which means it is important for properties to understand the demographic profile of their audience. The type and size of the audience is perhaps the greatest driver of value for the property. **Strategic fit** is the congruence between the sponsor's target market and the audience attracted by the sport property. Strategic fit can be achieved through the following:

▶ Demographics (age, gender, socioeconomic status, income)

▶ Geography (national, local, regional)

▶ Psychographics (values, attitudes, opinions, interests, and lifestyles)

▶ Brand image (is there a logical connection between the product and the team or sport?)

▶ Purchase behaviors (are the fans likely to buy the product?)

For example, 500 Festival, Inc. solicited a title sponsorship for its Mini Marathon event in Indianapolis that is held three weeks before the Indy 500. By analyzing data collected from its participants and from other running organizations, it developed a clear profile of its participants. The participants tend to be in their late 30s, travel, possess college degrees with high disposable income, and are interested in being active. This target market is concerned with building wealth through savings and retirement. As a result, the sponsorship sales team targeted financial services firms that focused on retirement, investments, and insurance, eventually selling the title sponsorship to One America.[11]

A second method used to prospect for potential sponsors is to find companies that are spending money on other sport sponsorships. If a firm is already engaged in sport sponsorship, the decision-makers within the firm most likely believe in the marketing benefits of a partnership. This will make it much easier for the sponsorship seller to start a conversation about the advantages of partnering with another sport organization. In order to learn what companies are already spending their marketing dollars on sponsorships, sellers simply investigate which organizations are currently sponsoring other teams. A look at other local team or athletic department websites, game programs, or even outfield wall signage would quickly reveal which area companies currently engage in sport sponsorship. In addition, sellers could consult sponsorship publications produced by organizations such as the *SportsBusiness Journal, IEG,* or the *Migala Report. IEG,* for example, produces an annual report of the biggest spenders in sponsorship for the previous year. This report might give a sales team an idea of which companies, or industry sectors, are most interested in marketing through sport sponsorships. If the top categories within the report include things like auto manufacturers, banks, and cell phone carriers, those would be obvious targets to approach. And while many large national companies might make major sponsorship decisions at the league level for only major league sports, they might also allocate marketing dollars to their local retailers and distributors who in turn can make investments in smaller local deals with minor league teams, college athletics departments, or area sport events. DeGaris outlined ten product categories that tend to be active sponsors in sport:[12]

- ▶ Mega-brands (Coke, Pepsi, McDonalds, Budwesier)
- ▶ Sports brands (Nike, Adidas, Under Armour)
- ▶ Fast-moving consumer goods (soft drinks, snack foods, personal care items)
- ▶ Financial services (banks, insurance)
- ▶ Auto (Toyota, Nissan)
- ▶ Telecommunications (Verizon, Sprint, Comcast)
- ▶ Travel (airlines, hotels)

11. http://files.ifea.com/Awards/2013Pinnacles/2013IFEA-HaasandWilkersonPinnacle-C43-B4-A2-500Festival.pdf

12. DeGaris, L. (2015). *Sports marketing: A practical approach.* New York: Routledge.

- ▶ Beer
- ▶ Gambling (casinos, lotteries)
- ▶ Retail

Savvy sponsorship sellers can also leverage other teams' sponsorships by approaching competitors of those brands. If McDonalds, UPS, or Verizon have exclusive deals with one team in a region, another sport organization might approach Wendy's, FedEx, or AT&T and suggest that to help them compete in the marketplace, those businesses may want to sign exclusive deals to limit their competitor's reach. For example, in Dayton, Ohio, the minor league baseball Dragons signed an exclusive partnership with RC Cola in an effort to gain market share from competitors Pepsi and Coca-Cola.[13] Because of home improvement company Lowe's long-standing relationship as an official sponsor of the NCAA, competitor The Home Depot struck a deal with ESPN to sponsor their pre-game college football show in an effort to get in front of rabid college football fans. See the article on the following page for a good example of how a company used a sport sponsorship to gain an advantage over a competitor.

## Table 15.1

**United States Companies Spending Greater Than $100 Million on Sport Sponsorship in 2014**

| Company | Amount |
|---|---|
| PepsiCo, Inc. | $360M |
| Anheuser-Busch InBev | $305M |
| The Coca-Cola Co. | $295M |
| Nike, Inc. | $265M |
| General Motors Co. | $195M |
| AT&T, Inc. | $190M |
| Toyota Motor Sales U.S.A., Inc. | $180M |
| Ford Motor Co. | $160M |
| Adidas North America, Inc. | $140M |
| Verizon Communications, Inc. | $125M |
| MillerCoors LLC | $120M |
| FedEx Corp. | $100M |

http://www.sponsorship.com/iegsr/2015/08/03/The-Deepest-Sponsorship-Pockets-of-2014--IEG-s-Top.aspx

---

13. Spoelstra, J. (2001). *Marketing outrageously.* Austin, TX: Bard Press.

**Gregory Karp,** *Chicago Tribune*

## AMERICAN AIRLINES SPONSORSHIP WITH CHICAGO CUBS

American Airlines has signed on as the official airline of the Chicago Cubs and Wrigley Field, stealing the designation from hometown carrier United Airlines and starting a major marketing push to boost its name at its Chicago hub.

United, based in Willis Tower in Chicago, signed a three-year deal in 2011 to be the exclusive airline of the Cubs and Wrigley Field and extended it through last year. It had been a sponsor since 2004.

But this season, American Airlines gets the start for the Cubs.

Even though it's based in Texas, American has eyes on the title of "Chicago's hometown airline," said Fernand Fernandez, American's vice president of global marketing.

"For us, it's really about putting a stake in the ground and saying, 'We're going to be No. 1 in Chicago,'" Fernandez said in an interview. "This is a big deal, a big relationship we have in Chicago."

At O'Hare International Airport, American and United go head-to-head—by far the two largest carriers at the airport, with United being slightly larger. Still, American has a huge presence, operating there for more than 30 years. It has about 500 flights a day and some 8,500 employees in Chicago.

American and Cubs officials declined to disclose terms of the deal, including money and the length of the sponsorship, except to say it's a "multiyear contract" and "long-term partnership" and that American would be the only airline sponsor.

The deal involves an American Airlines fixed sign on the brick wall by the Cubs' batting circle at Wrigley Field and video board features in the ballpark. Beginning with the 2017 season, American and the Cubs will add a new stadium club behind home plate for box seat ticket holders, the airline said. An existing stadium club previously sponsored by United will have a new non-airline sponsor, said Colin Faulkner, vice president of sales and partnerships with the Cubs.

### Why the change in airline sponsors?

Faulkner said the existing deal with United expired. "We really just shared a vision with the American folks for what we were doing here at Wrigley Field, with the path that we're on and the path that they're on," he said. "It really made a lot of sense."

In an agreement with a separate company also controlled by the Cubs' owner, the Ricketts family, American will sponsor a conference center in an office building to be developed in the new plaza next to Wrigley Field.

Exclusive sponsorship of the Cubs follows a pattern set by United to brand itself after its 2010 merger with Continental Airlines, when United became the exclusive airline at the ballpark. American's merger with US Airways is a little more than a year old, and it aims to market itself in highly competitive hubs in Chicago, Los Angeles, and New York, Fernandez said.

The Cubs sponsorship is only part of the branding strategy in Chicago, Fernandez said. "We plan to have a (marketing) presence there year-round," he said.

With its merger, American replaced United as the largest airline in the world.

The Cubs have embarked on a $375 million renovation of historic Wrigley Field, including installations of two large-scale video scoreboards and four advertising signs in the outfield.

With the expansion of advertising at the stadium, the team is on the hunt for new sponsors. The Cubs in December announced a deal with Wintrust Financial, making it the official bank of the team. It includes a Wintrust sign on top of the left field video board for this season and exclusive ATM provider rights, among other promotions.

Other so-called Legacy Partner sponsors are Anheuser-Busch, ATI Physical Therapy, Starwood Hotels and Resorts, Under Armour, and Sloan Valve.

Cubs Chairman Tom Ricketts said in a statement that the deal with American "will provide important resources to help us build a winning team on the field and save Wrigley Field for future generations."

The agreement also includes marketing opportunities for American Airlines at the Cubs' spring training facility, Sloan Park in Mesa, Arizona, American said.

But the deal doesn't necessarily mean that Cubs players fly American Airlines to away games. The deal is a marketing agreement, Faulkner said. "Of course, with American being our exclusive marketing partner in this category, we obviously want to do whatever we can to help support their business," Faulkner said.

It is also critical for sponsorship sellers to have their finger on the pulse of the local business community when prospecting. Large companies that are either headquartered or have a major presence in the vicinity of the sport organization are logical targets for several reasons, such as employee motivation, client entertainment, or community presence. However, those are not the only reasons for a team to approach a local company regarding a sponsorship. By tracking local business moves, sponsorship sellers can quickly recognize regional companies that may be trying to grow their presence in the community or need to hire more employees. Firms which advertise heavily may be looking to beat out competitors or grow brand awareness. Sport sponsorship can be an effective tool to assist with all of these objectives. The key for the seller at this stage of the game is to constantly be reading, whether it's the business section of the local newspaper, trade publications, or local business journals. Top sponsorship sellers truly understand the local business environment of the market in which they sell.

## *Building Rapport*

Another key difference between selling tickets and selling sponsorship is that sponsorship deals take far longer to complete. The process of learning about a prospective sponsor, understanding their needs, developing a proposal that makes sense, and getting buy-in from all parties may take months or even years, depending on the type of deal. As David Halberstam explains in his book, *The Fundamentals of Sports Media and Sponsorship Sales,* "Sports sellers fight to get audiences with decision-makers, then present them a conceptual framework and push hard to have the dollars approved. It takes time and the patience of a saint to shepherd the process through its lengthy gestation. The sales cycle seems punishingly unending."[14] As the previous quote attests, one challenge in selling sponsorship is timing. Many companies have budget cycles and cannot gain approval to spend marketing dollars at certain times of the fiscal or calendar year, no matter how well-aligned a sponsorship proposal meets their business objectives. Because of this extended timeline, sport organizations and potential sponsors often take a longer time to learn about one another's needs and strengths.

---

**Will Syring, Senior Manager of Business Development, Corporate Partnerships, Chicago Bulls**

### SPONSOR PARTNERSHIPS OFTEN TAKE TIME TO GROW

For my entire adult life, I've been in corporate partnership or sponsorship sales. Over the past seven years, I've begun to see patterns in client and prospect buying behavior. From my first sale to Michele's Sewing Basket for a couple thousand dollars (while working for the Kilsyth Basketball Club in Melbourne, Australia) to eight-figure, multi-year, highly integrated partnerships like we have here with the Bulls, the game remains the same; establish a common connection, eventually a common interest, and build an exceptional story.

There are times in this sales game that you will think the deal has no chance. It is at moments like this when it is imperative to remain professional and keep in touch. If they're negotiating with you, they want to buy. When I was working on the Chicago Bulls first global partnership with a company named Cinkciarz.pl, a foreign currency exchange partner based in Poland, there was a time when no e-mails or calls were returned for months. Out of the blue, after six months, negotiations started again. A deal quickly came together and after nearly a year of discussion, the Bulls had landed their first truly global partnership in team history.

---

14. Halberstam, D. (2016). *The fundamentals of sports media and sponsorship sales: Developing new accounts.* Urbana, IL: Sagamore Publishing. p. 63.

A majority of large partnerships take anywhere from two months to two years to come together and it takes polite persistency to continually engage prospects and current partners. What else does a good sponsorship seller do? Here are a few principles I've seen ring true when dealing with prospective sponsorship buyers:

- ▶ People like to do business with people they trust.
- ▶ No one has a budget for your particular program, it's your job to position the value so they find the budget. The idea finds the money.
- ▶ Use of humor is an effective way to humanize yourself.
- ▶ Most people have no idea what they want, help them find it and you'll win them over. Show them something of value and then build the relationship.
- ▶ Confidence comes from preparation and practice. Know your product and position yourself as the expert.
- ▶ Approach every person as a potential friend/ally.
- ▶ Make people look good for their bosses.
- ▶ Always ask for the business.
- ▶ Hold strong on an investment when you know you have something of value.
- ▶ Always respect the competition.
- ▶ Never underestimate the power of a handwritten note.
- ▶ Sell platforms not assets.
- ▶ Sponsorship is a research job. Not necessarily a "sales job."
- ▶ Know your prospects business inside and out but never anticipate to know someone's business better than they do. This is their life.
- ▶ People will remember and associate an experience with you, not necessarily you.
- ▶ Represent your clients with honor and defend them when presented with the opportunity. They help pay your bills.
- ▶ Get to a NO quickly and move on but always keep in touch.
- ▶ If not in a negotiation, abide by the rule of seven and send a note/e-mail/call no more or less than seven times in a year.
- ▶ Become an active listener and have a genuine interest in their business. Listen to understand, not to respond.
- ▶ People truly don't care what you know until they know how much you care.
- ▶ Most things in life and in sales come down to timing.

These are principles that I try to hold strong to every day. You will grow with each prospect meeting and pitch. Document the successes and, especially, the failures. You will find patterns. Adapt your style to fit your skill set.

Enjoy the ride.

---

## Needs Analysis

Of all the steps of the sale, perhaps the greatest difference between ticket sales and sponsorship sales shows up during the Needs Analysis stage. Needs analysis within sponsorship sales involves much more extensive research and probing before an appropriate proposal is presented. As suggested earlier in this chapter, most sponsors or potential sponsors have very specific business objectives they would like to achieve with sponsorship. It is up to the sales representative or sales team to understand those objectives, then create a sponsorship proposal to meet those needs. Unfortunately, many team sponsorship sellers try to sell pre-packaged inventory rather than truly understanding the sponsors' objectives and customizing an appropriate fit.

In order to uncover sponsors' objectives, sellers typically will establish a needs analysis meeting with key decision-makers and influencers. The sole purpose of this meeting is to learn specifically about the potential sponsor's business. Sponsorship sales presentations should never be made during this initial fact-finding meeting. Some large corporations receive so many sponsorship proposals that they are forced to develop mechanisms to screen the hundreds, or even thousands, of offers that come their way. Many of these businesses develop electronic portals allowing organizations to submit a sponsorship proposal, which may or may not be looked at by the company's marketing personnel. Often these submissions have little chance of being considered. Face-to-face appointments with decision-makers are far more effective, but it will take much more effort by the seller to gain the opportunity to sit across from the right decision-makers. In some cases, corporations may develop initial evaluation criteria which spell out the primary items they look for in a partnership and post it publicly for sport organizations to read. For example, Southwest Airlines suggests the four primary elements they seek in sponsorships include:[15]

- ▶ Broadcast rights during game telecasts
- ▶ Camera-visable signage within the venue
- ▶ Game-day communications and promotions
- ▶ The right to use league/team logos in their advertising

If a sport organization were seeking a partnership with Southwest, they would clearly need to develop a proposal that could meet these objectives. Anything else would be wasting both parties' time. At a recent National Sports Forum conference, several decision-makers from sport sponsors

15. Wakefield. K. (2007). *Team sports marketing.* Burlington, MA: Butterworth-Heinemann.

shared their thoughts on how sellers should approach them. Here are some of their suggestions:[16]

> ▶ **Dawn Turner, American Airlines:** "You must demonstrate in the first minute you talk to someone that you understand our business . . . Blind proposals just don't make sense. Don't send those; it doesn't work. We'd prefer that proposals come through our agencies that have the activation portion figured out."

> ▶ **Bill Moseley, AT&T:** "Don't sell me the first time you meet me. Listen first. If you don't know what my fundamental brand challenge is, you don't make an impression in the right way."

> ▶ **Chris Burton, SAP:** "We're investing heavily in the NBA All-Star Game, but not for the reason you think. We want to have a footprint in China, and the All-Star Game in China is a big deal." "Never underestimate the weight of the CEO on the decision, and his or her priorities! If our senior leaders want a deal done, that's huge."

> ▶ **Blaise D'Sylva, Anheuser Busch:** "You've got to know the activation plan in place, and know what that piece looks like . . . Every idea is great, but we have to prioritize everything based on a number of criteria. This wholesaler says that this particular sponsorship is important to me, and we have to listen to that. There's only so much money available, and that's the big challenge . . . If the idea is right, we're always receptive to that. If it's something we can squeeze in, something small, a few hundred thousand dollars or so, if it's a unique thing, we'll find the room . . . Beer brings people together. If the idea revolves around that—tailgating, retail branding, etc—we'll look at it."

Similar to B2B ticket sales, sponsorship sales appointments frequently start with a gatekeeper. To make a sale, the seller will need to get in front of the right audience, but gatekeepers may thwart future appointments or may send the seller to someone lower on the management hierarchy who does not have the authority to make decisions related to sponsorship. If sellers must go through a gatekeeper, many of the same lessons taught in Chapter 6 apply. In some cases, sponsorship sellers may write a letter or e-mail directly to the decision-maker, hoping to circumvent the gatekeeper. Halberstam[17] suggests sellers may first go to a firm's public relations department to gather contact information for the appropriate decision-makers if such data is not publicly

---

16.  Guertin, B. (2014, March 3). More notes and quotes from NSF 2014. *The Stadium Gorilla Report.*

17.  Halberstam, D. (2016). *The fundamentals of sports media and sponsorship sales: Developing new accounts.* Urbana, IL: Sagamore Publishing.

available online. Gaining an audience with the right decision-maker can be one of the most challenging aspects of selling sponsorship. In some cases, particularly when working with large organizations, it may take numerous meetings, phone calls, and letters, before the seller learns who the decision-maker is and how to schedule a meeting with that person.

If a sponsorship seller does gain time with a business decision-maker, what are the most common objectives the seller is likely to hear? Several sport management researchers and consulting firms have asked this very question, with multiple responses. Below are listed some of the most frequently cited sponsor objectives:

- Brand Awareness
- Targeting marketing messages to particular market segments
- Sales objectives
- Advantage over competitors
- Increase brand loyalty
- Showcase community and social responsibility
- Sampling and trial usage
- Showcase product
- Entertain clients
- Employee motivation and retention
- Demonstrate how the product performs

Sport sponsorships can be designed to effectively achieve each of these individual objectives, but no sponsorship can deliver everything to every sponsor. Consider this: In-venue signage is a common asset sold to companies, but which of the above objectives does in-venue signage effectively achieve? It is likely to help with brand awareness but does not assist a company with getting a sample of their product in to spectators' hands. Likewise, sponsorship packages which include premium tickets might assist in the objective of entertaining clients and motivating employees, but will do little to enable a business to showcase a new product to a large group of fans. Once a sponsorship seller understands key objectives, however, it becomes much easier for the seller to design a sponsorship proposal which meets those business needs. For example, if an electronics store wanted to drive more traffic to its retail outlet, the sponsorship seller might develop a package which includes a team autograph session on a Saturday morning at the store. Or if a cell phone company wanted to show off its latest line of smartphones, a sponsorship seller might suggest a marketing campaign in which a popular athlete uses the latest features of the device.

©photo.ua/Shutterstock.com

In some cases, a potential sponsor may have an idea for how the sport organization could help them achieve a particular objective, but the sport organization is unable to sell the inventory the sponsor desires. Sometimes the sport organization has already sold exclusive rights to a particular piece of inventory (such as naming rights to a building) and they are not able to also sell that inventory to another partner. In other cases, the sport organization may have negotiated exclusive rights for a particular sponsorship category (for example, only recognizing one car dealership as the official sponsor of the team), again limiting the number of prospective sponsors. In other circumstances, the sport organization may simply be unwilling to sell the desirable inventory for a variety of reasons. For example, the NFL has shunned selling jersey sponsorships of game uniforms despite the fact companies pay millions of dollars for that right in other leagues.[18] In another instance, the NCAA bans its member schools from selling any sort of sponsorship inventory to casinos because of the organization's strong anti-gambling stance. When the film *Spider-Man 2* was released in 2004, Columbia Pictures wanted to purchase the right to put spider web logos on the bases of certain MLB games, a deal that was nixed due to the sponsorship not fitting the traditions of baseball.[19]

## COME WITH AN OPEN MIND

When sponsorship sellers engage with potential sponsors for needs analysis, they should be well aware of the inventory and assets they have available to sell. However, they should also go into the meeting with an open mind so they can truly listen to the needs of the sponsor. While most sponsorship deals revolve around common assets such as signage, tickets, or hospitality options, today more and more businesses are seeking unique sponsorship opportunities and experiences tailored by the sport property to meet the business needs of the prospect. The ability to listen to sponsors and put

18. Perez, A., & Zillgitt, J. (2016, May 18). 76ers become first NBA team to announce jersey sponsor. *USA Today*. Retrieved from http://www.usatoday.com/story/sports/nba/sixers/2016/05/16/philadelphia-76ers-stubhub-jersey-sponsor/84434004/

19. Rovell, D. (2004, May 7). Baseball scales back movie promotion. *ESPN.com*. Retrieved from http://espn.go.com/espn/sportsbusiness/news/story?id=1796765

their needs above the property's own is critical to pitching sponsorship packages that are a fit for the sponsor. For example, by taking the time to listen to the needs of the University of Iowa Children's Hospital, the Cedar Rapids Kernals learned that the hospital wanted to celebrate the recovery of their patients at the games. So, instead of pitching traditional inventory, the team "established a pregame promotion that included their doctors introducing a specific child that rehabilitated in the facility. The doctor gives a quick overview of the treatment, introduces their family and medical staff, and the child ceremoniously jogs around the bases."[1]

1. http://migalareport.com/node/295

What sort of questions should the seller be asking during the needs assessment meeting? Sellers should ask questions about the salesperson, the company, other marketing efforts, and the industry in which the sponsor competes.[20] Useful questions might include items such as:

- ▶ What sport sponsorships have worked in the past?
- ▶ What objectives is the business looking to achieve through the sponsorship?
- ▶ What are the key challenges facing the business?
- ▶ What are the business' primary target markets or key demographics?
- ▶ Do the business' marketing objectives have certain time frames or seasonality?
- ▶ What is the organizational structure of the business (number of employees, department structure, decision-makers, etc.)?
- ▶ What might the approval process look like for marketing expenditures?
- ▶ How does the business measure success of marketing initiatives?

Each of these questions can provide a seller with valuable information to assist in the formulation of a sponsorship proposal. As Crompton points out,[21] sellers should not fear any negative perceptions toward sport sponsorship that may emerge from a needs analysis meeting. If a prospect is hesitant, fearful, or doubtful about how a sponsorship may help the organization, sellers should not argue or strongly disagree at this stage of the sales process. Instead, they should carefully note the prospect's concerns and be encouraged

20. DeGaris, L. (2015). *Sports marketing: A practical approach.* New York: Routledge.

21. Crompton, J. (2014). *Sponsorship for sport managers.* Morgantown, WV: FiT Publishing.

by valuable feedback. If the business shares concerns about the effectiveness of the sponsorship, it demonstrates consideration about a potential proposal and gives the selling team a specific target about what to address in a sales presentation. For example, perhaps a prospect has had a poor prior experience with sport sponsorship from a property that took money but did not deliver on results. In this case, the seller would be wise to develop a proposal in which benchmarking and follow-up are incorporated into the sponsorship package. Or perhaps the seller could develop a sponsorship agreement in which the sponsor only paid a percentage of the rights fee if certain objectives are met. In general, the worst needs assessment meeting is not one in which many objections and concerns are raised, but rather one in which the prospect is silent. If the seller knows the prospect's concerns, they are much easier to address.

In addition to conducting needs assessment with the prospect, sellers should also be conducting their own research on the prospective partner in order to better understand the company. For example, effective sponsorship sellers should be able to quickly uncover things such as the firm's number of employees, annual revenues, key clients and partners, business expansion plans, customer demographics, current marketing campaigns, and competitors through basic Internet searches. By understanding the prospect's current operating environment and challenges, the sponsorship seller can demonstrate a more nuanced appreciation of the company, can ask more informed questions during face-to-face needs assessment, and can better position sponsorship as a solution.

---

**J. W. Canon, Senior Project Lead, Sponsorships and Events, UPS**

### WHAT PROSPECTIVE SPONSORS (DON'T) WANT TO SEE FROM SELLERS

Sponsorship managers get a lot of proposals—literally in the hundreds, if not thousands, per week—so getting a potential sponsor's attention is really difficult. Here are some mistakes to avoid in order to help cut through the clutter.

**No Understanding of Prospect's Business**

Realize that you're not always going to have the benefit of talking to that potential customer ahead of time to get your shot, so **RESEARCH! RESEARCH! RESEARCH!** What is this sponsor currently doing and how are they leveraging it? Really make an effort to get to know your customer. If you don't, it shows.

### No Respect for Sponsor's Time

Your proposal MUST look good. Don't even think about sending a proposal that has poor spelling or is not formatted properly. Mistakes, misspells, grammatical errors and getting a name wrong show lack of forethought and respect for a sponsor's time. Do yourself a favor and get yourself an editor. You have to get every letter right, every word right and every paragraph right. You MUST labor over the details. And remember that spell-check is your best friend sometimes, but doesn't always catch everything.

### Large Digital Documents

Unless these materials have been requested, save your 100-page PowerPoint decks with lots of pictures for someone that asks for them. Sponsors get a TON of e-mail on a daily basis, and preventing them from receiving other important communications is an easy way to turn them off.

### Addressing Proposals to a Competitor or Another Company

A very smart man in our industry once said, "I may not be the only guy invited to the dance, but make me feel that way." The goal here is to make the sponsor feel special, like you're offering them a unique opportunity, and not just another [insert name here] proposal template that you just got done sending to 100 others.

### Unrealistic Fee Expectations

Make a proper valuation of your property and set realistic expectations. Sponsors compare proposals, so if you charge more, show how you are providing more value. And please understand that "in-kind" or "couponing" does not mean "FREE" to the sponsor. Somebody always has to pay.

### Not Distinguishing Between Sponsorships and Charitable Giving

Marketing budgets are reserved for business-building objectives, while donations come from philanthropic or foundation budgets. Know the difference and pick one.

### No Understanding of Measurement Metrics

The days of measuring only on "impressions" are gone and replaced with more complex "engagement" metrics. Millions of eyeballs don't mean anything if you don't have a mechanism for that sponsor to turn those eyeballs into sales.

### Not Offering to Share the Load

It's called a partnership for a reason. The more turnkey you can make it for the sponsor, the better. Don't make the sponsor work too hard. The words "opportunity to do 'X'" should never make it into a proposal. They already know that.

### Attempting to Involve Senior Management

Find out who is responsible, and target those individuals instead of the end-around to the CEO. Trying to leverage a relationship with senior management that simply doesn't exist will not get you far. Ultimately, you're going to end up working with that person if the company signs the deal, so why upset them from the get-go by going to their boss and forcing it through?

**Attempting to Skirt Agencies**

Treat them as you would a sponsor. They are an extension of the sponsor's staff. See the last point.

**Overly Aggressive Follow-Up**

Refrain from the repeated attempts to follow up after a proposal—e-mail, then phone, then fax, then e-mail again. Most sponsors are courteous enough to follow up, but realize they have priorities in their daily jobs just like you do. Silence is almost always a clear indicator of a sponsor's answer.

© Kendall Hunt Publishing Company

## Sales Presentation

Once a sport organization truly understands the needs of a potential partner, they can then begin tailoring the right package to present to the business. The sponsorship sales team should start by brainstorming ways in which the sport organization can help the prospect meet business objectives. Effective brainstorming allows many ideas to be heard and should encourage out-of-the-box thinking. In his book *Ice to the Eskimos*, former NBA executive Jon Spoelstra tells the story of think tank meetings with his sales staffs at the Portland Trailblazers and New Jersey Nets.[22] He would ask each staff members to jot down five ideas a day that could help improve the organization. The ideas could be big or small, but team members needed to update their list regularly. When the staff eventually met, they were armed with plenty of thoughts to get discussion moving. Spoelstra shares an example of an idea that came out of these meetings. The team transformed the media section behind the team benches to sponsor seating and signage, moving the media to a less prime perch—an idea that ultimately resulted in a $1 million a year sale for the team.

In some instances, it may be an effective sponsorship sales strategy to invite the prospect to experience or sample the product before seeing a sales presentation. Sutton, Lachowetz, and Clark[23] call this step an "intervention." Part of the seller's job might be to educate buyers (referred to as "eduselling") so they fully understand how the sponsorship might be effective. In some

---

22. Spoelstra, J. (1997). *Ice to the Eskimos*. New York: HarperBusiness.

23. Sutton, W., Lachowetz, T., & Clark, J. (2000). Eduselling: The role of customer education in selling to corporate clients in the sport industry. *Sport Marketing & Sponsorship*, 2, 145–158.

situations, it might be helpful for the prospect to attend a game in a suite or club seats before the proposal is made, not solely so the prospect can be "wined and dined," but also so the prospect can *feel* how the sponsorship may be effective. Seeing the intensity of a contest up close, witnessing the passion of the fan base, or understanding all the entertainment elements of game night can be powerful and enlightening. Maybe the sponsor has never been to a home game before, or if she has, perhaps she did not pay close attention to some of the team's assets. Since the sport sponsorship product can rarely be demonstrated in a board room, executing an intervention can be an important step in the sales process. The sales team should observe the prospect in this setting to see if there are certain elements that seem appealing or to answer questions.

After the sales team has brainstormed ideas and allowed the prospect to sample the product, they must then work to develop a proposal to pre-sent to the potential sponsor. Sales presentations can take many forms, from booklets and portfolios, to digital and electronic pieces, to even incorporating theatrical elements. No single presentation method is best, although there are plenty of presentation pitfalls to avoid.

---

### 10 THINGS TO DO BEFORE ANY SALES PRESENTATION[24]

**10.** Arrive early and bring extra charged batteries for electronic equipment.

**9.** Double check all spelling and grammar.

**8.** Try to walk around the room in which you will give your presentation to ensure your presentation will be visible to all audience members. If not, try to rearrange furniture.

**7.** Rehearse your presentation in front of critical coworkers to ensure you cover all your bases.

**6.** When receiving critiques during your rehearsal, listen. You don't have to make changes, but some sellers get so close to their ideas that they don't look at suggestions objectively.

**5.** Find out all you can about who will be in the room during the presentation. Do they have any biases?

**4.** Have a champion in the room who will advocate for your ideas.

**3.** Understand the vision of the company and the vision of your organization, as well as where they do, or can, mesh.

**2.** Understand what the company hopes to accomplish with your proposal.

**1.** Focus on your goal.

---

24. Schiffman, S. (2007). *Sales presentation techniques that really work!* Avon, MA: Adams Media.

Sponsorship sales presentations can take place at the prospect's business, at the sport organization's venue, or at a neutral site. Typically, the sport organization's home turf is the most effective place for a presentation, but it may be difficult to get all the relevant decision-makers in the facility. Who are the decision-makers? That is another challenge for the sales team. Decision-makers may include the president or CEO of a firm, but might also include senior level executives in marketing, sales, finance, or human resources. For some smaller organizations, a sponsorship decision might be made by just one individual, but for many sponsors, the decision is based on input from many individuals. Good sponsorship sales professionals must do their homework to learn who should have a seat at the table and which individuals will be advocates or adversaries. This research can be conducted by talking to gatekeepers and other contacts within the potential organization or through electronic searches via social media outlets and Internet search engines. The

©Chatchai Somwat/Shutterstock.com

seller should also have a good idea of how much time the sales team will be allotted so that all important points of the presentation can be made. It is important to know what audio/visual equipment will be available during the pitch.

During the presentation itself, the seller should begin by reiterating the prospect's objectives, then clearly demonstrating how the sport property intends to meet those objectives. For example, the seller might use team or event data to suggest how many fans might visit the prospect's car dealership or purchase gas from the prospect's service stations. Doing so demonstrates the property was actively listening during needs assessment and has customized a proposal which meets the sponsor's needs. Logistically, many sellers will avoid dimming lights during a presentation because it is important for the seller to clearly see the expressions and reactions of the decision-makers during the presentation. Also, in many cases it can be wise to hold off handing out materials until the end of the presentation. When people have a document in front of them, they will often peruse it during the presentation, which means they are not paying attention to the presenter. In some cases, it may be necessary to hand out materials before the presentation because the presenter plans to reference items during the presentation or because the decision-makers ask to see the materials. As a general rule, however, presenters should wait to distribute materials.

As Crompton suggests, the "most common complaint from company managers is that sponsorship proposals are too long, too descriptive, too generic, and bland, and not tailored to their needs."[25] Much like college professors, prospective sponsorship buyers are not easily impressed by lengthy documents. Rather it is the content that makes a strong sponsorship proposal, so authors should focus on hitting the key points while not wasting time with filler and fluff. The industry rule of thumb for sponsorship proposals is no more than three pages, consisting of:

> The most common complaint from company managers is that sponsorship proposals are too long, too descriptive, too generic, and bland, and not tailored to their needs.[25]
>
> —John Crompton

- ▸ an introductory paragraph;
- ▸ an overview of the property's fan demographics;
- ▸ highlights of how the inventory meets the prospect's needs;
- ▸ fee structure; and
- ▸ a call to action.[26]

And while just about every sport organization utilizes some sort of template for sponsorship proposals, it is critical to make sure each proposal is customized specifically for the prospect. While any typo looks sloppy, a proposal containing the wrong prospect's logo or name can be a deal-breaker. Some properties use the "find-replace" function on their word processor to ensure every past prospect name has been deleted from a proposal. For those wanting to learn more about how to deliver effective sponsorship proposals, veteran seller David Halberstam offers an excellent detailed chapter on the topic in his book *The Fundamentals of Sports Media and Sponsorship Sales*.

## Pricing

One of the major challenges for any sport property selling sponsorship is effective pricing. In many other types of sport sales, price is determined before the seller ever calls on a prospect. Sponsorship sales, on the other hand, can be unique as any particular bundle of sponsorship assets may be priced differently. As an extreme example, the cost of naming rights for a

25. Crompton, J. (2014). *Sponsorship for sport managers*. Morgantown, WV: FiT Publishing. p. 229.

26. Irwin, R., Sutton, W., & McCarthy, L. (2008). *Sport promotion and sales management*, 2nd ed. Champaign, IL: Human Kinetics.

facility may be flexible depending on the terms of the deal and other pieces of inventory included in the agreement. While determining sponsorship price is challenging, Irwin, Sutton, and McCarthy suggest sponsorship proposals should always contain some sort of price and that "proposals lacking a fee will generally not be given strong consideration".[27]

One goal of any aggressive sport organization is to derive as much revenue as possible from sponsorships. (It should be noted, however, that maximizing revenue is not always the objective. In some cases, sponsorship is only desired to cover particular expenses.) On the other hand, prospects have many ways to spend their marketing dollars, so a sponsorship proposal that offers little value and is not priced competitively in the marketplace will not be purchased. The critical ingredient for any sponsorship arrangement, then, is value. Sellers must remember sponsors are not concerned with the sport organization's financial needs. Thus, if a sport organization prices their sponsorship at $250,000 because the team needs $250,000 to meet payroll, it is of no concern to the buyer. Instead, the prospect wants to know if they will receive at least $250,000 worth of value from the sponsorship package. A good illustration of this point comes from the Women's United Soccer Association league, which formed, then quickly folded, in the early 2000s.[28] The league's business plan required the selling of four anchor sponsors at $10 million apiece for the fledgling league to meet budget. Businesses were interested in the league because of the growing support and popularity of women's soccer in the U.S. following the 1999 World Cup, but the WUSA failed to demonstrate to companies how a sponsor would receive $10 million worth of value, quickly torpedoing the venture.

Today's top sponsorship sellers know pricing inventory is critical. So how can they appropriately price their inventory? Three common techniques for pricing sponsorship are:

- ▶ Cost-plus
- ▶ Relative Value
- ▶ Competitive Market

**COST-PLUS PRICING**
a method of pricing sport sponsorship in which the costs of all elements of a sponsorship are added together, along with the sport property's desired profit margin, to develop a final cost

## COST PLUS

In simple terms, **cost-plus pricing** simply means a property adds together all costs associated with the sponsorship, then applies a markup percentage to derive a final cost. The markup percentage, or profit margin, is what the

---

27. Ibid. p. 186.

28. Stotlar, D. (2005). *Developing successful sport sponsorship plans,* 2nd ed. Morgantown, WV: Fitness Information Technology.

property makes on the sponsorship package. For example, if a minor league hockey team were to sell a sponsorship package consisting of dasher board signage and a suite to all home games, they might use cost-plus pricing to develop a sponsorship price. If the dasher board sign costs $200 to create, the face value of the suite tickets are $6,400 (8 tickets × $20 × 40 games), catering costs are $3,840 (8 people × $12 × 40 games), and parking costs are $800 (2 passes × $10 × 40 games), the total expenses are $11,240. The team might add roughly a 25% markup, bringing the total cost of the sponsorship to $14,000.

In some instances, cost-plus pricing can be a very appropriate method for determining sponsorship value. It is relatively easy to calculate, it is straightforward to both the seller and the buyer, and it is relatively easy to be applied consistently. However, cost-plus pricing can also be quite problematic in certain situations. Some sponsorship assets offer high value to a sponsor, but require a very low cost to produce. For example, a sponsored tweet by an athlete or a public address announcement during a game cost next to nothing to produce, but can have a very high value to sponsors wanting to share a brand message.

## RELATIVE VALUE

A second methodology for developing sponsorship pricing is **relative value**. Relative value pricing uses the prices of other marketing options to determine a value for the sponsorship assets. For example, if a college athletic department was trying to develop pricing for ribbon board signage in their football stadium, they might start by determining what it might cost a business to buy similar exposure through billboard, newspaper, television, or digital advertising. Most such mediums develop pricing rate cards which list what advertisers can expect to pay. These prices are often based on how many people will be exposed to the advertisement, often captured in metrics such as subscriber numbers, Nielsen ratings, or unique visitors. Once the number of people exposed to a message is calculated, media sellers typically develop a ratio of cost per exposure. In the advertising world, this is frequently called Cost Per Thousand or CPM. (The M in this acronym utilizes the Roman numeral for 1,000.) For example, if a newspaper has 300,000 subscribers, a one-column by 2-inch ad might cost $1,500, or a cost of $5 per thousand sets of eyeballs. By comparison, a billboard might have a CPM of $4, while an ad on television might have a CPM of $12. The CPM for recent Super Bowl ads are typically in the $40 range.[29]

**RELATIVE VALUE PRICING**
a method of pricing sport sponsorship in which the costs of other common marketing options (such as media or billboard advertising) are observed and used to derive a competitive sponsorship asset price

---

29. Smith, C. (2015, Jan. 16). Could a Super Bowl commercial really be worth $10 million? Surprisingly, yes. *Forbes*. Retrieved from http://www.forbes.com/sites/chrissmith/2015/01/16/could-a-super-bowl-commercial-really-be-worth-10-million/#2ab791537276

---

### CALCULATING EXPOSURE

For the **sport property**, calculating the number of exposures with a live attendance is fairly simple since just about every team tracks the number of tickets purchased. Thus for the athletic department mentioned at the beginning of this paragraph, total attendance for the season might be 308,000 fans (44,000 fans × 7 games). If costs for other advertising options might have a CPM of around $13, then a competitive price for in-venue signage might be around $4,000 (308,000 attendees / 1,000 × $13 CPM). This price would only be for the signage, not any other inventory such as tickets or hospitality. Also, the calculation only includes live attendance, but if the signage is placed in an area which gets plenty of air time during television broadcasts, the number of exposures would increase dramatically, and could be included in the price calculation. Also, properties will often suggest their viewers are more engaged and have a greater affinity for the product, compared to many other advertising mediums. As such, sport properties can charge a premium.

---

**SPORT PROPERTY**
any sport organization or entity, such as a team, league, event, venue, or athlete. In sponsorship terms, sport properties are the party which owns assets that can be sold to a firm for its marketing advantages

As with cost-plus, relative value pricing has its benefits and drawbacks. The good thing about relative value is that prospects can easily see how the value of the sponsorship compares to other marketing options. A potential sponsor might see that what the sport property is presenting offers much greater value than other current options. The downside to relative value pricing is that it is often limited to only certain types of inventory. Also some elements of the live sports experience do not have comparable alternatives. For example, if one of the benefits of a sponsorship package is category exclusivity, it can be difficult to compare this benefit to a similar option that the sponsor could get elsewhere.

## COMPETITIVE MARKET

**COMPETITIVE MARKET PRICING**
a method of pricing sport sponsorship in which the sport property examines sport sponsorships sold by other properties and determines the market value for comparable assets

The third method used in sponsorship pricing is the **competitive market approach**. A competitive market approach looks at what other sponsors have paid for similar sponsorship assets at other properties. Stadium naming rights provide a good example for this sort of pricing. If a Major League Baseball team is trying to sell corporate naming rights to their new stadium, they might look at what other recent stadium naming rights sold for, then adjust slightly for inflation, market size, and other variables.

Similar to the other pricing methods mentioned, the competitive market also works better in some situations compared to others. A positive aspect to this approach is that potential buyers will feel better about their purchase knowing other buyers have also purchased inventory at this price range. In this situation, both sides can rely on the marketplace to help determine the right pricing. It is also a simpler approach to pricing. For example, if a relative value approach was used for venue naming rights, it would be a very laborious process to determine the number of exposures the building produces based on not only in-venue attendance, but also how many times the facility is mentioned on television, on websites, or even the number of people who drive by the facility during their daily commute. The drawback to the competitive market approach is that it is not always easy to know what other sponsors have paid for sponsorships in the marketplace. While the price firms pay for sport facility naming rights are often made public, many other sponsorship deals are not publicly available and can be well-kept industry secrets. It can also be difficult to compare apples to apples because sponsors often purchase sponsorships that have been customized. In some cases, a sport property might develop inventory that is so unique, nothing in the marketplace is comparable.

One lesson for sponsorship sellers is that each pricing methodology is not mutually exclusive. In fact, effective pricing for sponsorships often rely on a combination of all three methodologies. Sellers may also consider pricing based on the return a sponsor might see. For example, if a property is selling a ticket stub coupon, they might consider redemption rate and what that would mean for the partner. If the coupon gave ticket holders half off their pizza order after the game, the property might calculate how much business that might generate for the sponsor and base pricing off the ROI.

If sponsorship pricing is performed strategically, it gives the seller great confidence in any negotiation session. Price integrity allows the seller to demonstrate to the buyer why it is priced the way it is and why that represents value. If pricing is determined based on a whim or the property's own fiscal needs, rather than the value the sponsorship offers to the prospect, it will be difficult for the seller to overcome any price objections the buyer might have. Sellers who price their sponsorship poorly are more likely to reduce pricing when the prospect objects during negotiations, which may lead to an immediate sale, but creates problems with other sponsors who have paid a higher price for similar inventory. Effective pricing allows the seller to stand firm during negotiations and can give them the confidence to walk away from a deal if the potential sponsor offers too low of a price. In many cases, this willingness to walk away from a deal ultimately gives the seller leverage. In some cases, a sponsorship proposal may include **a la carte pricing**, meaning each element or asset included in the proposal is priced separately. Thus, a seller may present a sponsorship proposal which includes signage, tickets and hospitality, concourse sampling, and radio advertisements during team broadcasts. In a la carte pricing, each of these items are priced separately, so the prospect might counter with an offer to buy three of the four elements at a lower price than the cost of all four assets.

**A LA CARTE PRICING** a method of pricing sport sponsorship so that each asset of a bundled sponsorship package is priced individually. This is done to allow assets to be added or removed from a sponsorship package and easily deriving a new price

## *Objections*

Objections are a natural part of sales. Rarely will a buyer purchase a product without first voicing concerns about the purchase. This is true for any "big ticket" purchase whether real estate, a vehicle, or a sponsorship package. In some cases, the objection will be too strong and cannot be overcome. However, in many other cases, effective sellers can counter objections with effective responses which may alleviate the prospect's concern or get the potential buyer to see things in a different light. So, what are some of the more common objections in sponsorship sales? Probably the most frequently mentioned objection is price or budget. Others might include:

- ► a lack of belief in sport marketing to meet business objectives;
- ► a down economy;
- ► engaged in too many other marketing efforts; and
- ► the sport property doesn't fit the right target demographics.

Effective sellers are prepared to respond to these objections in a number of ways. No single response will be universally effective to all objections, although responding empathetically, then presenting relevant testimonials are always a great option for countering objections (as discussed in Chapter 9). While objections are common in all sport sales, objections in sponsorship sales can be a little different than those frequently heard when selling tickets. First, many ticket buyers purchase because of their fandom for the team. Sponsorship, on the other hand, is much more frequently a business decision. As such, metrics such as ROI and the ability to lift sales are far more important to the purchase decision than whether a team just landed a good player in free agency or the team has made the playoffs the last three years. Second, timing is often more critical in the sponsorship buying realm than the ticket buying space. Because sponsorship packages cost so much more than ticket packages, the seller must understand that the best response to the "can't fit it in the budget this year" objection might be to ask when next year's budget cycle begins. Sponsorship sales take time to come together.

When sellers are preparing to make a sponsorship pitch, it is critical they are well-versed in what objections they may hear and how they might respond. Before making a sponsorship presentation to a prospect, many sellers give the same presentation to members of their sales team. Not only is this good practice for the presenter, but it also allows the other team members to poke holes in the proposal. This allows the seller to rehearse how to respond to certain criticisms and might help eliminate gaps in the proposal.

# USE OF AGENCIES

Another major difference between ticket sales and sponsorship sales is the potential use of agencies to help create a partnership. Marketing agencies such as IMG, Octagon, GMR, and Wasserman Media Group, are frequently hired by both brands and properties to help manage sport marketing decisions. Marketing agencies help with developing and soliciting sponsorships, negotiating contracts, and activating the sponsorship.[30] The real advantage in using marketing agencies is the industry knowledge and creativity they bring to partnerships. Agencies often have a strong handle on sport marketing trends, sponsorship pricing, and effective activation. These companies are hired to act on behalf of their client, whether it is a major bank or a tennis tournament, to develop a sponsorship that makes sense. When hired by brands, agencies can help ensure the brand engages with the property in effective ways to really meet business objectives and can provide a gauge as to whether the fee the property is asking represents market value. An **agency** may also make suggestions about the sponsorship proposal with ideas on how to improve activation or better develop messaging.

**AGENCY**
an establishment engaged in doing business for another entity. In terms of sport sponsorship, a marketing agency may act on behalf of a sponsor to negotiate terms, develop an activation plan, and ensure the partnership is executed effectively

For brands, hiring an agency gives them added expertise. An in-house marketing department for a corporation makes many decisions regarding campaigns, messaging, media buys, social media content, and other forms of advertising. These corporate marketing departments may lack a strong understanding of how sport marketing can be most effective because they have so many other responsibilities and may have limited human resources. Sport marketing agencies, on the other hand, work exclusively in the sport marketing space and have an excellent understanding of current trends and best practices. For example, a large appliance manufacturing company might receive hundreds of sponsorship proposals full of interesting ways to market through sports. An agency might be better equipped to sift through the proposals and understand which of them make the most sense to the company's primary objective of selling more product and which ones offer the greatest value.

Because many large brands use agencies to make sport sponsorship buying decisions, it is important for sellers to know the agencies and be willing to work with them as opposed to just the sponsor. The first step for the seller is to learn which agencies represent which brands. Second, it is important for sellers to develop relationships with the staff of various agencies even before pitching a proposal. Third, the seller needs to be willing to work with the agency to develop effective sponsorship and activation plans. While a

30. Crompton, J. (2014). *Sponsorship for sport managers*. Morgantown, WV: FiT Publishing.

property might pitch a traditional idea that has worked for other partners in the past, the agency may make suggestions or recommendations to alter the proposal, giving a client different assets that are more in line with business objectives. In most cases, during the sponsorship pitch, the seller will have representatives from both the prospect and the prospect's agency in the room. Finally, the agency will oversee the execution of the sponsorship on behalf of its client after an agreement is reached. Thus, it is important for the seller to maintain a strong relationship with the agency to handle any concerns during the life of the sponsorship.

## CHAPTER SUMMARY

The overall process for selling sponsorships is similar to selling any other product, including sports tickets. However, the way in which sellers approach each of the steps of the sale can be fairly different. The most critical difference is that sponsorships are business decisions in which the buyer wants to achieve a business objective. While some ticket buyers also use tickets to achieve business goals, many ticket buyers purchase because of their fandom. That is rarely true in the sponsorship world. In addition, sponsorship sales generally have fewer prospects available, take longer to complete, and are significantly more expensive. Effective sellers take considerable time conducting needs analysis and performing research before ever putting a potential proposal together. Sellers also must prepare to deliver sponsorship pitches in front of the right people and need to work hard at pricing proposals appropriately to both maximize revenue for the property but also represent value to the buyer. Finally, sponsorship sellers must be prepared to work with third-party marketing agencies who often work on behalf of buyers to develop more effective partnerships.

## CHAPTER ACTIVITIES

1.  How might a sponsorship seller develop a list of prospects to pursue?

2.  Find an old-fashion phone book and open to the yellow pages. Randomly select a business by closing your eyes and dropping your finger somewhere on the open page. Pretend you own or manage that business and develop three to five business objectives you believe that business might have. Once you have listed your business objectives, partner with another student and share your objectives so that your partner can try to develop solutions through sport sponsorship.

3.  Conduct an Internet search to try to find the criteria a business uses to evaluate sponsorship proposals. How does the website suggest sellers should initially present their sponsorship proposal? What elements is the sponsor looking for?

4. Go to a sporting event (or perhaps watch one on television). Observe how many sponsorship activations are being conducted. Write down five examples and list what objectives are likely being accomplished through the partnership. (Only one example should focus on signage.)

5. Explain how sponsorship sellers might develop pricing for their proposals.

6. A new hardware store chain is opening in a community of 200,000 people. The owner of the store wants to build brand awareness of his new business, wants to drive traffic to his store, and wants to be seen as offering higher quality service than his competitors. As the director of marketing and sales for the local minor league hockey team, develop a sponsorship proposal which addresses the business owner's objectives and present them to the owner in a customized presentation.

# GLOSSARY

**Account Executive (AE)**—TSRs who show promise and initial success as salespeople will have opportunities for promotion to account executives

**Activation**—The strategic efforts designed to support and enhance the objectives of a sponsorship. Activation activities connect a sport property's consumers to the sponsor

**Active listening**—the cognitive process of actively sensing, interpreting, evaluating, and responding to the verbal and nonverbal messages of present or potential customers

**Aftermarketing**—the approach to retaining or developing customers after the customer has purchased the product

**Agency**—An establishment engaged in doing business for another entity. In terms of sport sponsorship, a marketing agency may act on behalf of a sponsor to negotiate terms, develop an activation plan, and ensure the partnership is executed effectively

**Agenda**—customized game plan for the sales call or meeting

**A la carte pricing**—A method of pricing sport sponsorship so that each asset of a bundled sponsorship package is priced individually. This is done to allow assets to be added or removed from a sponsorship package and easily deriving a new price

**Analogy**—serves the same purpose as *similes* and *metaphors*, but analogies are more extensive and elaborate

**Analytical customer relationship management**—the collection of customer data information to create a model to increase customer revenues over the life cycle

**Analytics**—the systematic analysis of data in order to provide information and/or insight

**Anti-champion**—individual(s) who proactively speak out against the proposal because they prefer a proposal from a different organization or they prefer the status quo

**Articulation**—the act of forming words when speaking

**Assertiveness**—the degree to which people have opinions about issues and attempt to persuade others to accept those opinions by dominating or controlling situations and conversations

**Assessment Centers**—Process where candidates are evaluated for their suitability for employment by using simulation exercises

**Assumptive close**—phrased as a statement and is matched by nonverbal cues such as starting to complete an order form or setting up paperwork

**Authority**—rule stating that people tend to follow the lead of credible and knowledgeable experts

**Balance sheet close**—closing strategy using a visual to compare the advantages and disadvantages of buying

**Behavioral customer relationship management**—the use of focus groups or surveys to uncover the psychology of customer choice to inform a strategy to better retain customers

**Behavioral management**—A theory of management examining how workplace productivity is impacted by employee motivation and the relationships among co-workers and managers

**Benefit-in-waiting close**—unethical closing technique that offers the customer additional benefits or discounts after the initial offer has been presented.

**Benefit summary close**—closing strategy summarizing the most relevant features and benefits that the prospect has agreed to earlier in the conversation

**Benefit**—answers the question "what's in it for me" and is linked directly to their motivation for buying. It is important to remember that your prospect does not care what your product *is*, but only what your customer can do with the product

**Big data**—the collection and management of extremely large data sets from which managers can draw conclusions

**Body language**—expresses thoughts, intentions, and feelings through physical behaviors such as facial expressions, eye movements, body movements, body posture, and handshakes

**Body posture**—the position or orientation of the body during a face-to-face meeting

**Boiler room approach**—teams would hire a large number of entry-level sellers, provide them with minimal sales training, give them a short window to sell as much as they could, and then retain only the top few producers, while dismissing the remaining employees or interns

**Boomerang method**—turns the objection into the reason to buy

**Bottom-up approach**—begins the sales process by reaching out to lower-level executives and then work your way up the organization ladder as the sale progresses to a final decision

**Branding**—the process of creating a unique name and image for a product in the minds of consumers

**Bundle pricing**—packaging a group of separate products together into a single bundle at one price

**Business-to-business sales**—selling sport products to businesses for the primary purposes of entertaining clients and employees

**Business-to-consumer sales**—salesperson calls individuals who are probably interested in using the sport tickets for personal use

**Business side**—typically led by the team president, although these titles do vary from organization to organization

**Buying signals**—nonverbal and verbal indications that the customer is ready to buy

**Canned presentation**—is memorized presentation that exclusively focuses on the product

**Clarification question**—used to gather specific insight into a general word, phrase, or statement made by a prospect so as to eliminate confusion over its meaning

**Cliché**—overused phrases or sayings that show a lack of original thought

**Close-ended question**—questions that trigger a limited response, often yes or no answers

**Closing**—the process of asking for the customer's business

**Club seat**—more expensive seating that may include larger and more comfortable seats, wait staff service and higher end food and drink options

**Cold call**—a technique whereby a salesperson contacts individuals who have not previously expressed an interest in the product that is being sold. Door-to-door canvassing, calling names from a purchased lead list, or picking out names from a phone book or directory are common sources of unsolicited buyers

**Cold lead**—prospects who the seller does not know much about

**Commission**—A percentage of the total cost of a sale paid to the agent (employee) responsible for inducing the transaction

**Commitment question**—used to test agreement and pace the discussion toward a decision

**Comparison question**—use words like *compare, contrast, differ, whether,* and *versus* to yield more detailed information than the traditional open-ended question

**Compensation method**—acknowledges the validity of the customer's objection and then attempts to highlight a product feature that counterbalances the objection with an offsetting relevant benefit

**Competitive market pricing**—A method of pricing sport sponsorship in which the sport property examines sport sponsorships sold by other properties and determines the market value for comparable assets

**Confirmation question**—used to confirm the seller's understanding of something the customer has just stated

**Consistency**—focuses on the desire to be and to appear **consistent** with what you have already said or done

**Consultative selling**—a customer-focused sales method where the sales consultant asks questions in order to learn more about the customer before presenting a customized solution that will specifically address the needs or desires of the customer

**Consumer demand**—the quantity which consumers are willing to buy at a particular price, varies widely from product to product

**Continuous yes close**—the salesperson asks questions that are logically answered "yes" by the customer

**Corporate sales**—team focused on the sale and service of corporate sponsorships

**Cost-plus pricing**—A method of pricing sport sponsorship in which the costs of all elements of a sponsorship are added together, along with the sport property's desired profit margin, to develop a final cost

**Cross-selling**—involves offering additional products to support or complement the product or package the customer has already decided to purchase

**Customary pricing**—when a product is priced at a particular level for an extensive time period, perhaps even developing a known association with that certain price level

**Customer-focused selling**—the salesperson talks about the product or service in terms of what the customer wants, not in terms of what they are selling

**Customer behavior**—the study of the mechanisms by which a customer chooses to use or not use a product

**Customer life cycle**—the term used to describe the evolution of a customer's relationship with an organization from the decision to purchase a product, to using that product, to how the customer maintains loyalty with the organization and to ultimately, the relationship end

**Customer lifetime value**—the net profit associated with a long-term repeat customer

**Customer loyalty**—when a customer continually feels that an organization's products or services are the best selection.

**Customer relationship management**—a holistic process that includes identifying, attracting, differentiating, and retaining customers with the assistance of technology; allows employees to merge all information collected from any touchpoint with a customer into a single, easily accessible database, providing a 360-degree picture of that fan or prospect

**Customer retention**—the actionable steps a company takes to produce loyal and lifetime customers

**Customer sentiment**—how a customer feels about a product or service.

**Customer service**—the interactions a business has with a customer before, during, and after a customer purchases a product

**Decision-maker**—the person who has the final authority to accept or reject a proposal and is held accountable for that decision

**Desire**—stems from wanting to experience power, prestige, luxury, self-esteem, social status, instant gratification, significance, growth, and the like

**Direct denial**—relatively harsh responses that contain information and facts that indicate the prospect is incorrect

**Direct request close**—asking the customer for the sale in a straightforward manner

**Dominant buying motive**—buying motive that has the greatest influence on the customer's decision to buy

**Double-barreled question**—two questions at once

**Drive State**—exists when an individual is aroused to reduce or eliminate the unpleasant tension, thus restoring balance

**Dynamic pricing**—when organizations have the ability to change prices on a daily basis, or even more frequently, as demand changes

**Educational approach**—uses research and facts to support claims

**Eduselling**—the systematic and continuous dissemination of knowledge and assistance to the customer to enhance his or her knowledge about the product's benefits

**Elasticity**—small changes in price can cause larger changes in corresponding demand

**Empathy**—the ability to see things as others would see them

**Expansion question**—seek to acquire the same information as the open-ended questions identified above, but in a way that elicits more detailed information from the prospect

**Fans**—highly attached to the team, organization, coach, or players

**Fear close**—unethical closing technique emphasizing that something negative might occur if the customer does not purchase

**Feature**—an attribute, quality, or characteristics of a product or service

**Feel-felt-found**—three-step process including acknowledge the customer's feelings, extend the same feelings to a larger audience, and counter with a legitimate argument

**Flex-book plan**—buyers receive a specific number of tickets to use however they choose throughout the season.

**Forestalling**—addressing the objection before the prospect has a chance to

**Formula presentation**—highly structured presentations that follow a prepared outline that directs the overall structure of the presentation, but includes time for customer interaction and needs analysis

**Frequency escalator**—a framework for understanding how different types of consumers can be viewed based upon their level of using or purchasing the product

**Gatekeeper**—a person who keeps the decision-maker's work life organized by answering incoming calls, keeping his/her schedule, setting meetings, and generally protecting the decision-maker from time wasters

**Global question**—ask the customer to expand on a statement they just made in a way that invites them to *please continue*

**Group sales**—focused on selling tickets to groups of customers

**Group tickets**—focused on having a higher quantity of customers as a group attending a single game

**Halo effect**—how and what one does in one thing changes a person's perception about other things the person does

**Hidden objection**—an objection that has never been stated by the customer

**Hot lead**—prospects who have contacted the sport organization proactively seeking to buy tickets

**Humble disclaimer**—injects humility into an assertion that precedes a statement or question with the purpose of getting prospects to openly share their opinions and lower their defenses

**Hypothetical question**—asked out of interest when the answer has no real effect on the situation

**Implication question**—help the customer think about the potential consequences or impact of the problem and understand the urgency of satisfying the need or resolving the problem

**Impression management**—the process used by salespeople to manage the prospect's impression of them

**I/My Statement**—a story that describes a personal experience or the experience of someone else

**Inbound sales**—order-takers, waiting for the phone to ring from an inbound call, an order form and check to arrive in the mail, or for someone to show up at the ticket window

**Incentives**—items of perceived value added to an offer that encourage a purchase decision

**Indifferent**—individual(s) who don't care about the outcome of the sale

**Indirect denial**—used to correct a customer's misunderstanding, but in a gentle and tactful way that avoids directly telling the customer they are wrong

**Inflection**—the tone or pitch of speech

**Influencer**—the individual(s) who have access to the decision-maker and provides input that can sway the decision

**Informant**—individual(s) without a say in the final decision but who can provide critical information that will help the seller plan the next step in the sales process

**Inside sales**—sales personnel who utilize the telephone and/or online means to sell rather than traveling outside the organization's facility to sell face-to-face

**Internal champion**—Individual(s) supportive of ideas who will support a proposal within the organization to help secure a positive decision, essentially becoming a pseudo-salesperson within the organization

**Inventory/Assets**—in terms of sponsorship sales, the attributes or elements a sport property owns and can sell to a firm. Examples of inventory or assets might include signage within the sport venue, tickets or hospitality, or trademarked logos

**Issue-based question**—get prospects talking gaps between their present state and an ideal state

**Leads**—names and contact information for potential buyers

**Legitimate alternative choice close**—tests agreement by presenting the prospect with a choice between viable purchase options

**Lock-on question**—get the customer to elaborate on a feeling or emotion that the seller believes is important to confirming the needs he/she might have

**Logistics objection**—objection related to how the experience fits the customer's lifestyle

**Luxury suite**—private boxes that allow the customer to have a high-end living room of sorts within the stadium or arena

**Management**—The coordination and integration of resources to effectively and efficiently meet the goals or objectives of an organization

**Maslow's Hierarchy of Needs**—Psychological theory human behavior motivation based on five levels of "needs" that must be satisfied sequentially

**Membership club**—fans join a club as members rather than purchasing tickets as season ticket holders with the purpose of fostering a sense of belonging and connection

**Metaphor**—a figure of speech which makes a comparison between two things that are different from each other but have some characteristics common between them

**Mismatching**—the notion that people have an instinctive tendency to resist, push back, or respond to things you say in a contrarian manner

**Motivation-Hygiene Theory**—Management theory suggesting certain factors in the workplace cause employee job satisfaction while a separate set of factors cause dissatisfaction

**Motivation**—the driving force within individuals that impels them to action

**Need-payoff question**—focuses the customer's attention on the benefit derived from solving the problem or satisfying a need

**Needs analysis**—process of asking questions to identify customer needs, desires, motives, and problems

**Need**—is created when there is a gap between an individual's present state and an ideal state

**Negotiation close**—attempts to find a fair deal with which the customer and salesperson can be content

**No-Need objection**—objections stemming from a lack of need

**Nonverbal communication**—the process of sending and receiving messages without using spoken or written words

**Open-ended question**—allow customers to answer with varied responses and respond freely and spontaneously

**Operations side**—the sports aspects of the franchise, including the players, coaches, scouts, and oftentimes the medical staff

**Outbound call**—call initiated by a seller with a sport organization to a customer

**Outbound sales**—sales personnel who make outbound calls to prospects

**Outsourcing**—hiring third-party organizations to handle a portion of the business, such as selling tickets

**Pain**—stems from problems that evoke emotions like frustration, discontentment, confusion, boredom, embarrassment, anger, incompetence, stress, lack of knowledge, and the like

**Partial plan**—different types of ticket bundles below the size of the full season ticket but larger than just a game or two

**Penetration pricing**—prices are kept relatively low in order to sell a greater quantity with consumers finding the product to be a good value for the money

**Personal seat license**—a purchase that provides the PSL holder with the right to buy season tickets in a particular seat within a stadium or arena

**Physical appearance**—refers to attractiveness, grooming habits, and dress style

**Postponed objection**—addressing the objection at a later time

**Premium pricing**—also known as prestige pricing and involves charging high prices, those above other competitors, as it is consistent with a brand image of luxury and high quality

**Premium sales**—sales of the franchise's premium inventory

**Price objection**—when prospects claim that the price is too high, they can't afford the product, or that the product is not in their budget right now

**Primary ticket market**—when tickets are sold by the organization hosting the event

**Problem question**—bring a customer's implied needs, problems, and motives to the surface, or making them explicit

**Product-focused selling**—the salesperson exclusively focuses on the benefits, features, quality, and reputation of the product when trying to convince a customer to buy

**Product line pricing**—an organization not just setting prices for a single product, but rather establishing a systematic range of prices across a group of related products

**Product objection**—are related to the product, service, or experience and focused on a particular characteristic the customer does not like or need

**Prospecting**—the continual process of identifying and contacting businesses and individuals to create a pool of qualified buyers

**Prospects**—someone who has a need for or interest in the product, has the financial ability to purchase the product, and has the authority to buy the product

**Proxemics**—the personal distance that people prefer to keep between themselves and other people

**Psychometric Test**—Standardized tests utilized to evaluate a person's mental abilities or personality

**Purchase requirements**—conditions that have to be satisfied before a purchase can take place

**Qualifying**—the process of trying to determine if a lead meets certain criteria

**Redirect question**—channel the customer's thinking back to the agenda and the purpose of the conversation or meeting

**References**—can be geographic, industry, personal, or associative

**Referral**—a name of a person or company given to the salesperson as a lead by a customer

**Relationship marketing**—marketing strategy through which sport and non-sport managers pursue, retain, and develop customers throughout the customer life cycle in a co-collaborative approach

**Relative value pricing**—A method of pricing sport sponsorship in which the costs of other common marketing options (such as media or billboard advertising) are observed and used to derive a competitive sponsorship asset price

**Responsiveness**—the degree to which people show emotion in social situations. Highly responsive people are openly emotional and show concern for others

**Retention**—retaining existing customers

**Sales call anxiety**—fear of being negatively perceived or rejected by potential customers

**Sales collateral**—the collection of printed or electronic visual documents that are designed to generate sales, including items such as brochures, graphics, samples, photographs, illustrations, video, and testimonials

**Sales communication**—the act of transmitting verbal and nonverbal information and understanding between seller and customer

**Sales Culture**—Physical, emotional, and developmental environment where the act of selling takes place

**Sales event**—uniquely themed events typically hosted at a sport venue that leverage organizational assets to create excitement and attract a large quantity of qualified prospects

**Sales force management**—planning, staffing, training, directing, and evaluating salespeople

**Sales objection**—any concern or question raised by the customer at any point during the sales process

**Scarcity**—principle stating people want what they can't have

**Scientific Management**—Managing a business according to principles of efficiency derived from experiments in methods of work and production

**Scripted outline**—details the prescribed language used by sellers at certain points in the conversation, while providing a road map for other parts of the call.

**Season ticket sales**—focused on the sale of season tickets

**Season ticket**—provides access to every home game for the organization

**Secondary ticket market**—the subsequent reselling of tickets

**Selling point**—combination of relevant product features and their corresponding benefit

**Simile**—a figure of speech that makes a direct comparison, showing similarities between two different things

**Single game ticket**—individual tickets to games

**Site tour**—tour of the facility for the purpose of advancing the sale

**Situation question**—gather facts and background information about the prospect's existing situation

**Skim pricing**—keep prices high in order to generate higher revenues

**Small talk**—conversation centered on current events, hobbies, mutual friends, shared backgrounds, and sports that is used to break the ice prior to the actual sales presentation

**Social customer relationship management**—an expansion of traditional CRM; a CRM system involving customer engagement throughout the customer life cycle

**Social Proof**—states that people use information about how others have behaved to help determine their own proper conduct

**Social selling**—process of leveraging the seller's personal brand on social media to build relationships with clients that lead to appointments

**Social style matrix**—consists of four primary types of communication styles based on two dimensions—assertiveness and responsiveness

**Speaking rates**—the speed with which a salesperson talks

**Spectators**—typically do not have a strong social-psychological commitment to the team, organization, coach, or players

**SPIN questioning system**—sequences four types of questions designed to uncover a prospect's current situation and inherent problems, enhance the buyer's understanding of the consequences and implications of those problems, and lead to the proposed solution

**Sponsorships**—investments by corporations in a sport property to help support the firm's organization, marketing, and promotional objectives or strategies

**Sport hospitality**—food, beverage, and entertainment assets that accompany premium tickets in suites and club seating areas

**Sport organization objection**—objection related to team performance or quality

**Sport property**—Any sport organization or entity, such as a team, league, event, venue, or athlete. In sponsorship terms, sport properties are the party which owns assets that can be sold to a firm for its marketing advantages

**Sportscape**—the entire built and managed environment that the fan sees when attending a sporting event

**Stall objection**—used by customers to put off the buying decision until a later time

**Stalls**—delay to establishing an appointment

**Standing-room only close**—manipulative closing technique that uses urgency in an unethical manner by making false claims about product availability, prices, and deadlines

**Story**—a brief account or example of people and events told to help "paint the picture" in your prospect's mind why they need your product

**Strategic fit**—The congruence between a sponsor's target market and the audience attracted by a sport property

**Tension**—the unpleasant feeling when there is a need that remains unfulfilled

**Third-party approach**—salesperson uses the facts and opinions of others to justify a position

**Ticket operations**—sometimes called box office management, is a support function to the sales force of a professional sport franchise

**Ticket package**—a variety of different packages in order to meet the variety of different needs and wants possessed by consumers

**Ticket Sales Representative (TSR)**—also known as inside sales employees, these employees are tasked with selling tickets to customers

**Top-down approach**—based on the idea that a company's top officer has the greatest amount of decision-making power

**Total Quality Management (TQM)**—A management theory suggesting all employees must be personally committed to maintaining high work standards and improving product or service quality, with a particular focus on customer satisfaction

**Touchpoints**—points of contact from the organization to the buyer, throughout the customer life cycle

**Traditional customer relationship management**—a business's one-way communication method to increase sales throughout the customer life cycle

**Trust**—an expectation by the customer that a salesperson will engage in actions supporting their interests

**Two-way communication process**—when the sender translates thoughts into words (encoding) and the receiver decodes the message to understand what the sender intended to communicate (decoding)

**Upselling**—involves persuading a customer to purchase an upgraded version of the same type of product they are intending to buy

**Valid business reason**—a statement which justifies asking for the appointment with a decision-maker

**Value-in-Kind (VIK)**—The use of a sponsor's goods or services exchanged for a sport property's assets within a sponsorship agreement. The goods or services are traded in lieu of cash, often because it is less expensive for the sponsor, but also meets a need of a sport property which might otherwise have to buy the same goods or services (i.e., office computers)

**Value proposition**—benefits the customer has confirmed are relevant

**Value**—perceived benefits in relationship to the cost; total benefit provided to the customer.

**Variable ticket pricing**—prices vary based on anticipated demand

**Verbal communication**—the use of sounds and words to express a message

**Verbal information**—to statements of fact, opinion, and attitude that are encoded in the form of words, pictures, and numbers in such a way that they convey meaning to a receiver

**Want Pathway**—the pathway toward a specific consumption decision chosen by a person to reduce tension

**Warm call**—sales calls made to prospects who have had some sort of prior contact with the organization

**Warm lead**—prospects in which contact or connection has already been made with the prospect prior to the seller making the sales call

**Word picture**—a story designed to help the buyer visualize a point

# INDEX